T0373449

THE I TATTI
RENAISSANCE LIBRARY

James Hankins, General Editor

# GIOVIO

# PORTRAITS OF LEARNED MEN

ITRL 95

# PAOLO GIOVIO

✦ ✦ ✦

# PORTRAITS OF LEARNED MEN

EDITED AND TRANSLATED BY

## KENNETH GOUWENS

THE I TATTI RENAISSANCE LIBRARY

HARVARD UNIVERSITY PRESS

CAMBRIDGE, MASSACHUSETTS

LONDON, ENGLAND

2023

Series design by Dean Bornstein

First printing

*Library of Congress Cataloging-in-Publication Data*

Names: Giovio, Paolo, 1483–1552, author. | Giovio, Paolo, 1483–1552.
Elogia veris clarorum virorum imaginibus (Gouwens) |
Giovio, Paolo, 1483–1552. Elogia veris clarorum virorum imaginibus.
English (Gouwens) | Gouwens, Kenneth, editor, translator.
Title: Portraits of learned men / Paolo Giovio ;
edited and translated by Kenneth Gouwens.
Other titles: I Tatti Renaissance library ; 95.
Description: Cambridge, Massachusetts : Harvard University Press, 2023. |
Series: The I Tatti renaissance library ; 95 | Includes
bibliographical references and index.
Identifiers: LCCN 2022016639 | ISBN 9780674290150 (cloth)
Subjects: LCSH: Authors — Biography — Early works to 1800. | Scholars —
Italy — Biography — Early works to 1800. | Nobility — Italy — Biography — Early
works to 1800. | Renaissance — Italy — Biography — Early works to 1800. |
Italy — History — 1492–1559 — Biography — Early works to 1800.
Classification: LCC CT93 .G525 2023 | DDC 945/.070922 — dc23/eng/20220804
LC record available at https://lccn.loc.gov/2022016639

# Contents

ॐॐॐ

Introduction    ix

PORTRAITS OF LEARNED MEN

Liminal Poem by Onorato Fascitelli    2

Dedication to Ottavio Farnese    4

A Description of Giovio's Museum    10

The Arrangement of the Portraits    24

The Portraits

I. *Albertus Magnus* 28 · II. *St Thomas [Aquinas]* 30 · III. *John
[Duns] Scotus* 32 · IV. *Dante* 34 · V. *Francesco Petrarch* 38 ·
VI. *Boccaccio* 40 · VII. *Bartolus* 44 · VIII. *Baldus* 46 ·
IX. *Leonardo Bruni* 48 · X. *Poggio* 50 · XI. *Ambrogio [Traversari]
the Monk* 54 · XII. *Antonio Panormita* 56 · XIII. *Lorenzo
Valla* 60 · XIV. *Flavio Biondo* 62 · XV. *Pier Candido
Decembrio* 66 · XVI. *Donato Acciaiuoli* 68 · XVII. *Filelfo* 70 ·
XVIII. *Niccolò Perotti* 74 · XIX. *Platina* 78 · XX. *Cardinal Jacopo
[Ammannati] of Pavia* 80 · XXI. *Domizio Calderini* 84 ·
XXII. *Antonio Campano* 86 · XXIII. *Manuel Chrysoloras* 90 ·
XXIV. *Bessarion* 92 · XXV. *George of Trebizond* 98 ·
XXVI. *Theodore of Gaza* 100 · XXVII. *Argyropoulos* 104 ·
XXVIII. *Marullo Tarcaniota* 108 · XXIX. *Demetrius
Chalcondyles* 112 · XXX. *Marcus Musurus* 114 · XXXI. *Janus
Lascaris* 118 · XXXII. *Rudolf Agricola* 122 · XXXIII. *Leon Battista
Alberti* 124 · XXXIV. *Lorenzo de' Medici* 126 · XXXV. *Piero*

Leoni 130 · XXXVI. *Ermolao Barbaro* 134 · XXXVII. *Giorgio Merula* 136 · XXXVIII. *Poliziano* 140 · XXXIX. *[Pico della] Mirandola* 144 · XL. *Pomponio Leto* 146 ·
XLI. *Callimachus* 150 · XLII. *Girolamo Savonarola* 154 ·
XLIII. *Marsilio Ficino* 158 · XLIV. *Galeotto Marzio* 162 ·
XLV. *Elisio Calenzio* 166 · XLVI. *Pandolfo Collenuccio* 168 ·
XLVII. *Gioviano Pontano* 170 · XLVIII. *Marcantonio Coccio Sabellico* 174 · XLIX. *Lorenzo Lorenziani* 178 · L. *Antioco Tiberti* 180 · LI. *Filippo Beroaldo (the Elder)* 184 · LII. *Ercole Strozzi* 186 · LIII. *Bartolomeo Cocles* 190 · LIV. *Giovanni Cotta* 194 · LV. *Pietro Crinito* 196 · LVI. *Girolamo Donà* 200 ·
LVII. *Alessandro Achillini* 202 · LVIII. *Bernardino Corio* 204 ·
LIX. *Marcantonio della Torrre of Verona* 206 · LX. *Lancino Curti* 210 · LXI. *Baptista of Mantua, the Carmelite* 214 ·
LXII. *Francesco Mario Grapaldo* 216 · LXIII. *Thomas Linacre* 220 · LXIV. *Antonio the Nebrijan* 222 · LXV. *Bernardo Bibbiena* 226 · LXVI. *Giasone del Maino* 230 · LXVII. *Christophe de Longueil* 234 · LXVIII. *Aurelio Augurelli* 238 · LXIX. *Guido Postumo* 240 · LXX. *Niccolò Leoniceno* 242 · LXXI. *Pietro Pomponazzi* 246 · LXXII. *Andrea Marone* 248 · LXXIII. *Andrea Matteo Acquaviva* 252 · LXXIV. *Pietro Gravina* 256 ·
LXXV. *Pomponio Gaurico* 260 · LXXVI. *Marco Antonio Casanova* 264 · LXXVII. *Baldassare Castiglione* 266 ·
LXXVIII. *Andrea Navagero* 270 · LXXIX. *Giovanni Maria Cattaneo* 274 · LXXX. *Jacopo Sannazaro* 278 · LXXXI. *Giovanni Mainardi* 282 · LXXXII. *Camillo Querno the Archpoet* 284 ·
LXXXIII. *Alberto Pio of Carpi* 288 · LXXXIV. *Ludovico Ariosto* 294 · LXXXV. *Cardinal Egidio [of Viterbo]* 298 ·
LXXXVI. *Gianfrancesco Pico della Mirandola* 302 ·
LXXXVII. *Niccolò Machiavelli* 306 · LXXXVIII. *Filippo*

Decio 310 · LXXXIX. *Thomas More* 312 · XC. *The Cardinal of Rochester* 316 · XCI. *[Niccolò] Leonico Tomeo* 320 · XCII. *Agostino Nifo* 322 · XCIII. *Jean Ruel* 326 · XCIV. *Antonio Tebaldeo* 328 · XCV. *Erasmus of Rotterdam* 332 · XCVI. *Rutilio* 336 · XCVII. *Guillaume Budé* 338 · XCVIII. *Girolamo Aleandro* 340 · XCIX. *Lampridio* 344 · C. *Cardinal Gasparo Contarini* 348 · CI. *Heinrich Cornelius Agrippa* 352 · CII. *Battista Pio* 354 · CIII. *Francesco Arsilli* 358 · CIV. *[Mario] Molza* 362 · CV. *Albert Pigge* 366 · CVI. *Benedetto Giovio of Como* 368 · CVII. *Maffeo Vegio of Lodi* 374 · CVIII. *Giovanni Tortelli* 374 · CIX. *Bartolomeo Facio* 376 · CX. *Guarino of Verona* 378 · CXI. *Pierpaolo Vergerio* 378 · CXII. *Giacomo Bracelli the Ligurian* 380 · CXIII. *Giorgio Valla of Piacenza* 380 · CXIV. *Giovanni Simonetta* 382 · CXV. *Bernardo Giustinian of Venice* 382 · CXVI. *Cristoforo Persona of Rome* 384 · CXVII. *[Gregorio] Tifernate* 384 · CXVIII. *Raffaele [Maffei] of Volterra* 384 · CXIX. *Antonio Galateo* 386 · CXX. *Lodovico Celio of Rovigo* 388 · CXXI. *Jacques Lefèvre d'Etaples* 388 · CXXII. *Antonio Telesio of Cosenza* 390 · CXXIII. *Pietro Alcionio* 390 · CXXIV. *Peter Martyr d'Anghiera* 394 · CXXV. *Gabriele Altilio* 394 · CXXVI. *Marcello Virgilio of Florence* 396 · CXXVII. *Giano Parrasio* 398 · CXXVIII. *Georg Sauermann the German* 400 · CXXIX. *Celio Calcagnini of Ferrara* 400 · CXXX. *Agostino Giustiniani of Genoa* 402 · CXXXI. *Roberto Valturio* 402 · CXXXII. *Matteo Palmieri of Florence* 404 · CXXXIII. *Jacopo Angeli of Florence* 404 · CXXXIV. *Hector Boece* 406 · CXXXV. *Polydore Vergil* 406 · CXXXVI. *Gaguin the Frenchman* 408 · CXXXVII. *Marino [Barlezio] of Scutari* 408 · CXXXVIII. *Jakob Ziegler* 408 · CXXXIX. *Paolo Emili* 410 · CXL. *Germain de Brie* 410 ·

# · CONTENTS ·

CXLI. *Niccolò Tegrimi* 412 · CXLII. *Camillo Ghilini of Milan* 414 · CXLIII. *Johann Reuchlin the German* 416 · CXLIV. *Johannes Regiomontanus the German* 418 · CXLV. *Luis Vives of Valencia* 420 · CXLVI. *Cosimo de' Pazzi* 420

Peroration    424

Anonymous Liminal Poem    448


Note on the Text and Translation    453

Abbreviations    457

Notes to the Text    465

Notes to the Translation    471

Bibliography    621

Index    625

# Introduction

෨෨෨

The physician and humanist Paolo Giovio (1486–1552) was born and raised in Como, a city then in Milanese territory, and in 1511 he completed a doctorate in medicine and the arts at Pavia. Thereupon he moved to Rome, where, beyond practicing medicine and lecturing in moral philosophy at the university, he became active in the informal gatherings of Roman humanists led by Angelo Colocci and Johannes Goritz, which fostered scholarly exchange and literary composition.[1] Following the disgrace in 1517 of his initial patron, Cardinal Bendinello Sauli, Giovio moved to the protection of Cardinal Giulio de' Medici, cousin of Leo X (pope, 1513–21), in whose service he remained after Giulio's elevation as Clement VII (pope, 1523–34).[2] Later he became a cultural advisor of sorts to Cardinal Alessandro Farnese, grandson of Paul III (pope, 1534–49), in which capacity he obtained commissions for his protégé Giorgio Vasari, whom he also encouraged to write the *Lives of the Artists*. Finally, in 1550, after his hopes for more substantial patronage from the Farnese family had been disappointed, Giovio settled at the court of Cosimo I de' Medici in Florence, where he completed what he viewed as his masterpiece: the *Histories of His Own Time*.[3]

The works for which Giovio is best known today, however, are not the *Histories* but his two volumes of *Elogia*: one concerning notable literati (1546), the other surveying prominent military and political figures (1551).[4] The first of these, entitled *Portraits of Learned Men* (*Elogia veris clarorum virorum imaginibus*), is here newly edited and translated.

The two *Elogia* volumes look slim when set alongside the *Histories*, which provide a detailed narrative of politics and diplomacy from 1494 to 1547. Built substantially upon Giovio's collation of

eyewitness accounts, the *Histories* extend beyond Italy to encompass major events not only in Europe but also in Muscovy, the Ottoman Empire, and Mamluk Egypt. While Giovio also wrote dialogues, biographies, chorographies, and letters, it was as a historian that he wished to be remembered. Yet the *Elogia*, to which he devoted a small fraction of his time, have figured far larger in subsequent scholarship. The great Swiss historian of art Jacob Burckhardt drew vivid details from them for his *Civilization of the Renaissance in Italy* (1860), and they continue to be mined for lively anecdotes, many of which are unattested elsewhere.

Taken as a whole, *Portraits of Learned Men* provides an insightful synopsis of the contours, mentality, and trajectory of humanistic culture in Italy and Europe from the fourteenth to the mid-sixteenth century.[5] As he watched the foreign invasions of the Italian peninsula and the conquests that ensued, Giovio came to believe that the high culture of the Italian Renaissance — in which he had participated not only in Rome but also in Florence, Milan, Naples, and elsewhere — was in rapid decline, a perspective he had voiced nearly two decades before, in *Notable Men and Women*.[6] We may view the *Portraits* as a mature and more systematic effort than that dialogue to capture and commemorate a bygone period of efflorescence.[7] In this respect it resembles other catalogs of learned men written by Italian humanists of his time, notably Pierio Valeriano's *On the Ill Fortune of Learned Men*, which similarly sought to encapsulate their literary milieu and thus preserve it.[8]

Unlike others' catalogs, however, Giovio's *Portraits of Learned Men* was but an offshoot of a far more ambitious project of commemoration. At least since 1521, he had been collecting likenesses of learned men, and the following year he began procuring portraits of outstanding rulers and men of arms. Tireless in supplicating potential patrons, he rapidly expanded his collection, and in 1537 — with financial support from Alfonso del Vasto, one of the top captains in the army in Italy of Emperor Charles V — he began

construction on the southwest shore of Lake Como of a villa custom-made to display what he called his *musaeum* (literally, a "home of the Muses," but here carrying something resembling the modern sense of "museum").

To collect portraits of the illustrious was not in itself new: in the preceding century, for example, Duke Federico da Montefeltro had the likenesses of famous authors, including Dante and Petrarch, hung above the marquetry in the *studiolo* in Urbino. Nor was Giovio the only cultured Italian of his generation to collect portraits of famous contemporaries.[9] But his scheme was grander in conception, and to devote an entire villa to the display specifically of portraits was itself an innovation. It was also novel that, from the outset, he intended his museum to serve for public enjoyment.[10] A third innovation is that Giovio, who took pride in his commitment to historical accuracy, sought precise depictions rather than idealizations: preferably, the portraits should be painted from life, but where that was impossible they were to be copied from relatively reliable images, be they on coins or medallions or in the form of busts or paintings themselves done from life. Of course, the accuracy of such representations was far from guaranteed, but the gesture is clear: Giovio wished to display his subjects "warts and all." Taken together, the portraits would not only serve the traditional function of inspiring emulation but also provide a comprehensive, candid, and personal overview of the Republic of Letters as it had taken shape and flourished in Italy and Europe.

Initially, he had planned just to identify the subjects in brief; but in perhaps his most creative move, he decided to enlarge the inscriptions to the point that they became biographical sketches, many of them several hundred words in length. Written in Latin, they were to be inscribed on pieces of parchment and hung below the paintings of their subjects. Thus in each case there would be what Giovio's foremost biographer, Price Zimmermann, described

as "a nexus of features, moral character, and deeds," a scheme that "constituted the fullest expression of individuality reached during the Renaissance."[11] Unfortunately, the first editions of both volumes of *Elogia*, whose publication Giovio oversaw, lack the intended engravings of the portraits, which he had expressly stated were integral to the meaning.[12] They do, however, put on display for us his synoptic understanding of how integral a number of illustrious individuals were to major cultural and political transformations of his era.

The Latin word *elogium* has no satisfactory English equivalent. Few of the biographical sketches in *Portraits of Learned Men* are eulogies; many verge on character assassination. Most lie in between, mixing praise and blame in a way that resembles the oratorical genre of epideictic favored by humanists in their sermons before the popes. Giovio sought to impart an appreciation for each man as a flesh-and-blood human being whose foibles were integral to making him who he was, and who, each in his own distinct way, contributed to making the Republic of Letters what it was. Viewed collectively, these capsule biographies (as the Latin *elogia* may best be rendered) can be seen to trace the arc of the development of learned culture in the Renaissance.

That arc may look distorted to those who give pride of place to Florence, Venice, or even Rome. Although Giovio spent most of his career in the Eternal City, few of its humanists figure among the most highly praised. Moreover, while Italians predominate, *Portraits* included many scholars who were based elsewhere, in locales ranging from Spain and England to Illyria and Poland. Strikingly, the collection begins not with Dante or Petrarch, but instead with the thirteenth-century Bavarian polymath Albertus Magnus. That *elogium* is entirely positive, praising Albertus for his lofty intellect, influential teachings, and Christian humility. The portrayal of Aquinas is less glowing: Giovio notes his brilliance and "blameless life," but faults him for an extreme asceticism that ultimately

ruined his health. Then comes the scholastic theologian Duns Scotus: after acknowledging his subject's keen and subtle mind (albeit not the subjects to which he applied it), Giovio faults Scotus for contentiousness, murky writing, and even for corrupting the youth, in that he led his students into perplexity about matters of the faith.

The first Roman literati to appear are Lorenzo Valla and Flavio Biondo. Giovio especially lauds Giulio Pomponio Leto, a student of Valla who taught at the university for decades and hosted a thriving academy. Pomponio's early morning lectures were so popular that students would arrive at midnight to be sure of getting a seat. Praise of others in Rome, however, is usually qualified. For example, while Giovio lauds the erudition and oratorical skills of Egidio da Viterbo, head of the Augustinian order and confidant of several popes, he also casts aspersions on him: some people, we are told, "disparaged his splendid reputation, saying that he ingested cumin and inhaled the fumes from the smoldering of damp straw in order to give his face the pallor of an ascetic, and concealed with a reproachful severity an assortment of lusts." The final Roman to receive a portrait comes twenty-third from the last, Pietro Alcionio, an obstreperous malcontent who was almost universally reviled. That *elogium* can hardly reflect well on a culture that gave its subject a place of even modest honor.

The final capsule biography (no. 146) ostensibly treats a minor figure, Cosimo de' Pazzi of Florence (d. 1513), but mostly concerns Cosimo's brother Alessandro, whose awkward Tuscan renditions of Greek plays imitated to a fault the cadence of the originals. "All but monstrous in its utterly coarse meter and rhythm," Giovio writes, this mode of imitation "pleased nobody but those straining to be like the Greeks. Justly, therefore, the model of his new invention, having no imitators, remained its author's own and withered along with him." Thus the body of the *Elogia* of literati ends not with a bang but with a clunk. In the afterword Giovio describes

his intention to expand the collection of portraits in the museum to include the living. But there, he says, he must give more attention to foreigners, especially Germans, "since in a fateful migration not only Latin letters (to our shame!) but also Greek and Hebrew have crossed over into their lands." When he lists patrons both current and potential who may assist him in expanding his collection, he names Maecenases not in Italy but instead in Hungary, France, Spain, Portugal, and the Low Countries.

*Portraits of Learned Men* attests not only a perceived decline of Italian culture but also the incompleteness to which so grand a project was doomed. Initially, the volume on deceased literati was to end with Albert Pigge (d. 1542). But then in 1545 Giovio's beloved brother Benedetto died, and the author felt compelled to add him to the collection (no. 106). The forty *elogia* that follow it all concern individuals whose portraits he lacks, and the afterword reveals just how far Giovio's reach exceeded his grasp. In the six years that remained to him after the book's publication, he managed to bring to press a number of long-term projects, including his biography of Leo X (1548), the *Elogia* of illustrious men of arms (1551), and, in two installments, the *Histories* (1550, 1552), but he never wrote the planned volume of *elogia* of living literati.

The museum fell farther short of its ideal. It remains unclear how many of the portraits that Giovio had collected and initially stored in Rome ever made it to Como. Paintings of the villa done in the early 1600s attest the realization of something resembling what he had conceived, but the building soon fell into disrepair. In 1613 his heirs sold the property, and two years later the villa was razed to make way for a new one.[13] The portraits were dispersed. Many now are lost, and only a handful remain in Como, housed in its *pinacoteca*.

We may surmise that Giovio would have been distressed to see how quickly his villa deteriorated and its collection was dispersed. He would certainly have been disheartened at how small an im-

print his *Histories* have left upon the scholarly tradition. Perhaps he would derive at least some consolation were he to learn that *Portraits of Learned Men* is now available in a new edition and in fresh translations both in Italian and in English.[14]

Grants from the American Philosophical Society, the Renaissance Society of America, the University of Connecticut Research Foundation, and the Felberbaum Family Foundation enabled me to consult manuscripts in Como, where I benefited from the generosity of Sergio Lazzarini, Chiara Milani, and Magda Noseda. The archivists at the Centro Studi "Nicolò Rusca" — Anna Rossi, Elisabetta Canobbio, and Francesca Ferraris — were unfailingly welcoming, attentive, and helpful. A fellowship from the University of Connecticut's Humanities Institute provided a year's release time and a stimulating environment for work on the project.

Giovio's expansive survey of the *Respublica litterarum* has necessitated my ranging far beyond my expertise, and dozens of scholars kindly fielded questions related to their own. Our exchanges were a welcome reminder that even as departments of History in the United States focus increasingly on the twentieth and twenty-first centuries, there remains a vibrant Republic of Letters both here and abroad committed to studying what came before. I remain indebted to Price Zimmermann for his unrivaled mastery of all things Giovian and for his exceptional generosity. Finally, I thank three outstanding Latinists but for whose extensive interventions the translation would be far poorer: Gregory Guderian, Julia Haig Gaisser, and James Hankins. All errors that remain are, of course, my own.

## NOTES

1. For an introduction to Giovio's life and works, see *NMW*, xi–xiii, with references to earlier works; T. C. Price Zimmermann, "Giovio, Paolo," *DBI* 56 (2001); *ER*, 3:68; and Zimmermann (1995), the definitive biog-

raphy. Short references to works cited in this Introduction and in the Notes to the Translation are given in full in the Abbreviations or the Bibliography.

2. In 1517 Sauli was imprisoned and briefly expelled from the College of Cardinals because suspected of involvement in a conspiracy to murder Pope Leo X. How Giovio managed to migrate from Sauli's household to that of Giulio de' Medici remains a mystery.

3. *Historiarum sui temporis tomus primus* (*Histories of His Own Time*, vol. 1) (Florence: Torrentino, 1550); *Historiarum sui temporis tomus secundus* (*Histories of His Own Time*, vol. 2) (Florence: Torrentino, 1552).

4. Giovio (1546); Paolo Giovio, *Elogia virorum bellica virtute illustrium* (*Portraits of Men Illustrious in Military Prowess*) (Florence: Torrentino, 1551). For a close study of the *Elogia* (both volumes) as they relate to the museum, see Minonzio (2007). An important contribution came to my attention only after the copy-editing of this volume was completed: Claudia Tarallo, *Anatomie letterarie. Ritratti di intellettuali negli* Elogia di Paolo Giovio (Rome: Aracne editore, 2021).

5. Burckhardt also made extensive use of Giovio's *Life of Leo X* (1548).

6. *NMW*, which he began writing in late 1527.

7. Famously, in the *Life of Leo X* (1548), Giovio describes Leo's pontificate as a golden age that has since been followed by an age of iron.

8. See Valeriano, *DLI* (incomplete; begun in 1529). Other near-contemporary works that offer similar surveys of the learned include Arsilli's *De poetis Urbanis* (*On the Poets of Rome*), which appeared as an appendix to the *Coryciana* in 1524; a letter of 1529 from Jacopo Sadoleto to Angelo Colocci; Raffaele Maffei's *Commentaries* (1506); Francesco Berni's *Dialogue against Poets* (1526?); and Giraldi's *Modern Poets* (1551), published in this I Tatti Library (2011), edited by John N. Grant. Today, periodizations of the Italian Renaissance tend to be more expansive, often extending it well into the seventeenth century.

9. Aleci, "Images of Identity"; Cannata, "Giorgio Vasari." See also the discussion on possible classical influences (notably, both Pliny the Elder and Younger) on Giovio's conception of collecting portraits, in Klinger

(1991), 113–14; and above all the analysis of Giovio's museum and his description of it in Maffei, 129–70. The next volume scheduled to appear in the National Edition of Giovio's works, *IO* 10 (edited by Bruno Fasola et al.), will center on the iconography of the museum and its contents.

10. The phrase comes from an inscription on the façade, which is quoted in Anton Francesco Doni's letter to Agostino Landi ( July 20, 1543), printed in Alessandro Luzio, "Il Museo gioviano descritto da A. F. Doni," *Archivio storico lombardo*, series 2, vol. 16 (1901): 143–50, at 144: "Paulus Jovius Episcopus Nucerinus ob eruditi ingenii foecunditatem max[imam] Regum atque Pontificum gratiam liberalitatemque promeritus, cum in patria Como sibi vivens suorum temporum historiam conderet Museum cum perenni fonte amoenisque porticibus ad Larium *publicae hilaritati dedicavit*. MDXLIII." ("Paolo Giovio bishop of Nocera, who on account of the fecundity of his erudite brilliance merited the favor and liberality of the greatest kings and popes, while he was composing during his lifetimes in his native city of Como the history of his own times, *dedicated* this museum with its perennial fount and pleasant porticoes on Larius [Lake Como] *to public enjoyment*. 1543.") (emphasis added). Translation slightly altered from Zimmermann (1995), 188.

11. Zimmermann (1995), 160. The word "individualism" postdates the Renaissance and expresses a conception of the self foreign to premodernity: see John Jeffries Martin, *Myths of Renaissance Individualism* (New York: Palgrave Macmillan, 2004), especially 1–20. That said, Renaissance intellectuals were most definitely able to appreciate the particularity and special qualities of many of their peers. See, for example, *The Rhetorics of Life-writing in Early Modern Europe: Forms of Biography from Cassandra Fedele to Louis XIV*, ed. Thomas F. Mayer and Daniel R. Woolf (Ann Arbor: University of Michigan Press, 1995), especially the essay at 39–62 by T. C. Price Zimmermann, "Paolo Giovio and the Rhetoric of Individuality."

12. On Giovio's belief that a book of inscriptions written to accompany portraits needed to include engravings of the portraits, see his letter of December 5, 1544, to Daniele Barbaro (*IO*, 2:4) and the analysis of it in Minonzio (2007), 141. In this sense the closest surviving exemplar of what Giovio had envisioned for the *Elogia* of men of letters is the Perna edition of 1577: while problematic for its typographical errors and for

significant changes to the text that cast Protestant reformers in a more positive light, it is notable for the addition of beautiful engravings, by the Swiss artist Tobias Stimmer, of many of the subjects.

13. Thus the earliest painting of the villa (oil on canvas), in the *pinacoteca* in Como, postdates the building's destruction (its date is given in a cartouche at the center bottom as 1619).

14. See Franco Minonzio's heavily annotated Italian translation of the *Elogia* both of literati and of men of arms: *Elogi degli uomini illustri* (2006).

PAVLI IOVII
ELOGIA VERIS CLARORVM
VIRORVM
IMAGINIBVS APPOSITA
QVAE IN MVSAEO
IOVIANO COMI SPECTANTVR


PAOLO GIOVIO'S
PORTRAITS OF LEARNED MEN
ATTACHED TO THEIR IMAGES
WHICH ARE TO BE SEEN IN
GIOVIO'S MUSEUM AT COMO

*Honorati Fasitelii*

Nae debent Iovio viri elegantes
bonis artibus omnibus politi;
nae debent Iovio, elegantiarum
parenti artibus omnibus polito,
quantum vix animus capessat ullus.
Nec vivi modo, qui vident amantque
urbani senis et salem et lepores,
sed quos, lumine adempto, avarus Orcus
quis scit quo cohibet loco misellos.
Nam facit Iovius suis tabellis
excultis lepido suo labore
Lethi funera non timere vivos,
vitam vivere mortuos perennem.

# LIMINAL POEM

*By Onorato Fascitelli*

Truly,[1] men of taste who are refined in all cultural pursuits are indebted to Giovio. Truly, hardly any mind can grasp how greatly indebted they are to Giovio, the father of elegances, refined in all the arts. This is so not only for the living, who recognize and appreciate the wit and charm of this elderly sophisticate, but also for those wretches deprived of the light of life, whom greedy Orcus confines who-knows-where. For, now that Giovio has put the finishing touches on his painted panels, by his delightful work he makes it possible for the living not to fear the oblivion of Lethe,[2] and for the dead to have eternal life.

*Pauli Iovii Novocomensis episcopi Nucerini*
*Imagines clarorum virorvm*
*ad Octavium Farnesium urbis praefectum*

1 Perillustri quidem exemplo et vere more maiorum facis, Octavi Farnesi princeps iuventutis, qui socero Caesari singularis diligentiae invictaeque virtutis imperatori armatus comes, vel in tanto castrorum fremitu, incerta dubii ocii momenta Musis impertis: hac enim imitatione pernobili non modo C. Caesaris, qui unus summi iudicii summaeque virtutis fastigium tenuit, sed Antonii, Bruti, Catonis, Octavii memoria recolitur, quando hi, quod legimus, tui sanguinis vereque Romani Heroes, vel paludati et canente classico, nunquam literarum studia remiserint.

2 Quo fit ut hanc excelsi generosique ingenii indolem, quam non adulanter admirari licet, tibi magnopere gratulemur, quum e Belgis iucundiore quadam epistola, quae non in castris cum peracri Gallo hoste collatis sed in praepingui ocio perscripta videri possit, ultimam *Historiarum* mearum partem efflagites repetasque item vehementer, tanquam promissam et gerendo Bello Gallico valde opportunam, Argentoni viri gravissimi historiam, quam mihi nuper expetenti Nicolaus Rentius, vetus ac humanissimus amicus meus, e Gallica lingua in Italicam casta fide traduxit; ante omnia vero, tanquam eruditae iucunditatis munus, desideres clarorum virorum

4

# DEDICATION TO
# OTTAVIO FARNESE

Portraits of Famous Men
*by Paolo Giovio of Como, bishop of Nocera,*
*dedicated to Ottavio Farnese, Prefect of Rome*[1]

Certainly, Ottavio Farnese, Prince of Youth,[2] you follow the shin- 1
ing example and indeed the custom of our ancestors for, as a com-
rade in arms to your father-in-law, the emperor (a commander in
chief of the utmost assiduousness and unconquered valor), you
devote to the Muses fleeting moments of precarious respite, even
amid so deafening a clamor of war. This noblest kind of emulation
revives the memory not only of Julius Caesar, who alone reached
the peak of supreme good judgment and valor, but also of Antony,
Brutus, Cato, and Octavian, for these (as we read), your ancestors
and truly Roman heroes, never let go of their literary pursuits
even when they were dressed for battle and the trumpet was
sounding.

   And so it happens that I heartily congratulate you on that in- 2
nate quality of your lofty and noble mind which I may admire
without excessive flattery, since you urgently request the final portion of my *Histories* in a quite delightful letter from Flanders that
could have been written in the fullness of leisure instead of at the
front, in the teeth of a bitter French foe; since also you ask with
the same insistence for that history by Commynes, a highly distinguished man — it being promised and highly useful in conducting
the French War — which, at my request, my exquisitely refined old
friend Nicolas Raince recently translated from French into Italian
with the utmost fidelity;[3] but above all, because you crave, as a gift
of learned delight, the likenesses of famous men that are on

5

imagines quae in musaeo nostro ad Larium spectantur (et eas quidem per elogia, quod nisi longo difficilique labore parvis in tabellis
assimilanter expingi nequeant), scilicet ut tantorum ingeniorum
dotes, admirabili varietate stylo descriptae, elegantioris oblecta-
menti nomine ad animi iudicium transmittantur. Multo enim gravius pulchriusque videtur ingentium animorum virtutes propriis
annotatas elogiis ad admirationem intueri, quam ductas ex vero
diligenter effigies, inani quanquam iucunda oculis voluptate spectavisse.

3    Verum et obiter quoque requiris, quod nequaquam salvo pudore et integra fide praestari posse videtur, ut musaeum iucunde
graphiceque describam, postquam id tibi secus ac maxime cupie-
bas, properante Caesare, adire spectareque non licuit. Parebo itaque lubenter honesta petenti; sed egregia fide debitum professo,
aliquid mihi benigne condonandum existimo, scilicet ut per partes
huius aeris alieni grave onus commodissime dissolvatur. Tu vero
singulari humanitate iuvenis facile hoc dederis iam plane seni aegroque pedibus, ac his praesertim intempestivis caloribus circum-
vento, quos nobis longe maximos ab aestuoso Buxeto, dum Caesar,
belli quam pacis avidior, ad algidas Germaniae Alpes properaret,
in multo et pulverulento itinere subeundos reliquistis.

4    Mitto igitur ante omnia libellum, dulci brevitate periucundum
quo elogia tabulis pictis supposita continentur. E singulis enim
imaginibus singulae exemptiles tabellae dependent in membrana,
vitae atque operum summam praeferentes. Argentonus autem, qui

display in my museum on Lake Como, and these by means of the biographies, of course, as true copies can be painted on small panels only with long and tedious effort. These you request evidently so that the talents of such brilliant men, written down in a remarkable variety of styles, may, in the guise of cultured diversion, be submitted to the mind's judgment. Indeed, it is far more dignified and noble to contemplate to the point of wonder the virtues of lofty minds, all recorded in their own particular inscriptions, than to have gazed at pictures painstakingly drawn from real life: a pleasure that, while delightful to the eyes, rings hollow.

But in passing you also request something that I can't possibly 3 fulfill in complete good faith while keeping my modesty intact: that I might describe the museum delightfully and vividly since, as the emperor was in a rush, it wasn't possible for you to visit and see it, much as you had desired to do so. Accordingly, I shall gladly comply with your worthy requests. But now that in the best of faith I've openly acknowledged my indebtedness, I think that something must kindly be given to me, namely, that the heavy burden of this debt may be discharged as readily as possible, in installments. You, however, being a remarkably considerate young man, surely have already conceded this to one who is old and unsteady on his feet, especially as he has been beset by these unseasonable hot spells. While the emperor, keener for war than for peace, is hastening to the cold Alps in Germany, you have left me behind to endure the heat, which is at its worst by far on the long and dusty journey from sweltering Busseto.[4]

First and foremost, therefore, I'm sending a little book, delight- 4 ful in its endearing brevity, which contains the capsule biographies that have been placed below the painted panels. For, from each portrait hangs a detachable piece of parchment on which the essence of the subject's life and works is put into writing.[5] Commynes, however, who is being printed by a Venetian press, will

Veneto praelo excuditur, totius Italiae civitate donatus, ad te, ac ideo libenter quod ad Belgas suos redit, post paucos dies perveniet.

5     Quod vero ad *Historias* meas pertinet, eas nequaquam tuto tabellariis committi posse putaverim, ne interceptae quorundam animos offendant; nunquam enim vel aequissimus rerum gestarum scriptor victis pariter atque victoribus satisfecit, quo minus utrinque gratiam suam extenuet vel odium quaerat, quod eum facile sit factiosa superbaque iudicia subire qui, inter vivos libero ore locutus, tanquam posteris gratum facturus, non procul ab invidia Fortunae ludos perscribit. Vale.

reach you after a few days, happy to return to his people, the Flemings, now that he has been made a citizen of all Italy.[6]

But as for my *Histories*, I certainly wouldn't imagine that they could be entrusted safely to couriers lest, upon being intercepted, they give umbrage to some. Indeed, never has even the most impartial historian satisfied both the vanquished and the victors, and avoided losing both sides' favor or even incurring their hatred. For it easily happens that hostile and haughty judgments befall him who, having spoken freely among the living so as to make something for which posterity will be grateful, writes of the sport of Fortune with envy close at hand. Farewell.

# MVSAEI IOVIANI
# DESCRIPTIO

1   Publicatis ac in musaeo tanquam augusto virtutis templo dedicatis clarorum virorum tabulis, illae ipsae veluti spirantes imagines aequissimo iure deposcunt ut musaeum quoque, sua sacrata sedes, eodem conditoris stylo describatur; sed id vetat ingenuus pudor, qui tamen eruditis subrusticus videtur. Quis enim vanitate ingenii non praeclare stultus et ineptus est qui, quum sua miretur, ea demum pluris aestimet quam aliena? At is hercle multo stolidior evaserit qui, severe parceque narrando, consilii atque operis sui dignitatem elevet, ut modestiae laudem ferat; ille porro insanus poterit videri qui, dum sibi tenerius blandiendum existimat, certos veritatis fines ambitiosis excessibus perturbet.

2   Sed ego, si Musis hospitibus placet, aureae mediocritatis modum tenebo ut has suburbani literatique ocii delitias ita exprimam ut invidiam eorum iudicio, qui haec viderint, facile devitem indeque mihi securior ac uberior voluptas obveniat, quando et haec omnia Donius Etruscus vates, miscellaneo opere edito, ac ob id incolumi pudore meo disertissime decantarit. Neque enim, quum nihil maius et supra fortunam meam luculentius exprimi velim, vel adulantibus adeo verecunde subirascor ut dispudeat laeta fronte confiteri id esse musaeum, quod elegantes clarique hospites saepius

# A DESCRIPTION OF
GIOVIO'S MUSEUM

Now that the paintings of famous men have been put on public 1
display and enshrined in the museum as if in a venerable Temple
of Virtue,[1] the portraits themselves, as if drawing breath,[2] demand
with complete justification that the museum, their hallowed
abode,[3] likewise be described by its founder's same pen. But plain
modesty,[4] although it appears a bit boorish to the sophisticated,
counsels against this. For is not that man patently foolish and tact-
less in his inflated sense of his own brilliance who looks admiringly upon his own creations, judging them alone more valuable
than anyone else's? But Lord knows, he will come off as much
more of a dolt whose austere and spare account diminishes the
merit of his design and achievement in order to win praise for restraint. On the other hand, he can end up appearing a madman
who, supposing that he must flatter himself ever so gently, by an
excess of adulation confounds the well-defined bounds of the
truth.

But if it pleases my guests, the Muses, I will hew to the golden 2
mean to portray these charms of bucolic and cultured leisure in
such a way that I may easily avoid envy in the judgment of those
who have seen these things; and I will obtain a surer and more
abundant pleasure once the miscellany by the Tuscan poet Doni
has been published, in which he sings eloquently about them all,
and on that account with no harm done to my modesty.[5] Indeed,
while I wish nothing described as greater or more splendid than
befits my station, I do not get so blushingly annoyed, even at flat-
terers, that I am ashamed to admit with a cheerful countenance
that this is a museum which elegant and distinguished foreigners
often come to see, which is continually visited by my countrymen,

invisunt, perpetuo cives frequentant ipseque ante alios Alfonsus Davalus, utranque lauream meritus et praeclarus inchoati absolutique operis adiutor, omnibus aestivis secessibus anteponit.

3     Villa est in conspectu urbis, peninsulae modo in subiectum circumfusi Larii pelagus exporrecta; nam ad septentrionem quadrata fronte directisque lateribus in altum excurrit, arenoso puroque in littore, ob idque maxime salubri, in ipsis Plinianae villae vestigiis excitata. Hoc enim praeclaro religiosae vetustatis testimonio plurimum augetur aedificii decus, ac plena gloriae ac admirationis authoritas paratur. Iuvit hercle longo obrutam situ et penitus iacentem in patria clarissimi civis memoriam non ignobili studio et digna pietate suscitasse: manet adhuc stabili naturae munere laetissima loci facies, ac aeterna praecellentis structurae fundamenta extant, quanquam absolutis operibus et tempus edax et Larius ipse, vel subitis incrementis admirabilis potiusquam saevus dum perpetuo allidit et fluctibus pulsat, vehementer inviderint. Visuntur in profundo vado, quum lacus molli et vitreo aequore stratus et liquidus conquiescit, quadrata marmora, ingentes columnarum trunci devorataeque pyramides, quibus ante portum lunatae molis fauces ornabantur.

4     Ab Oriente enim totius aedificii obiectu et producta in cubitum lapidea mole adversus Aquilones, tranquillus portus efficitur, duplici quidem et decenti podio coronatus: alterum e cavedii porta effusos spectantesque marmoreis sedilibus excipit, quum applicantes ab urbe amicorum naviculae salutantur; alterum oblongam areae marginem quae portui imminet pectore tenus exornat. In

and which the foremost among them, Alfonso d'Avalos himself—
a man who has won both laurel crowns and has been a singular
supporter of the project from start to finish—prefers to all other
summer retreats.[6]

Within view of the city, the villa projects like a peninsula into   3
the adjacent expanse of Lake Como, which embraces it: for on the
north its rectangular façade and perpendicular sides extend into
deep water. It's built on a stretch of shore that is sandy and clean
(and on that account most salubrious), on the very ruins of Pliny's
villa.[7] Indeed, this distinguished evidence of venerable antiquity
exalts the splendor of the building most of all, and it is gaining a
glorious reputation as a marvel. Heaven knows it has been a pleasure to reawaken, with a not insignificant zeal and fitting patriotism, the memory of one's homeland's most celebrated citizen that
had been buried by long neglect and utterly ignored. Thanks to
Nature's unfailing favor, the spot is still delightful to behold, and
one sees the steadfast foundations of a superior construction, even
though both devouring time and Lake Como itself, more wonder-
ful than vicious in its sudden swells, constantly dashing against the
entire work with battering waves, have done tremendous harm to
it. When the lake is becalmed and crystal clear, one sees in its
depths the square blocks of marble, massive shafts of columns,
and engulfed pyramids that once adorned the crescent-shaped
jetty at the entrance to the harbor.

On its east, indeed, thanks to the shelter provided by the entire   4
building and to a breakwater of piled stones that protrude at an
angle, the harbor is made calm in the face of the northeastern
winds. It's also surrounded with an attractive twofold platform:[8]
one part, with marble benches, welcomes whoever comes through
the courtyard gate to watch and greet small boats as they arrive
conveying friends from the city; the other, which rises to chest
height, adorns the open area's oblong retaining wall which
overhangs the harbor. It's here that the spacious courtyard comes

hoc si quidem lata area desinit, binis inclusa viridariis murisque
pinnatis, quae hippodromi speciem praebet.

5     Ad dextram medio lacu insula exurgit, firmissimo pariete
circumsepta iucundaque eminentibus pomiferis arboribus: haec
austri flatus arcet, et portum obducto latere protegit; a continente
dirimitur euripo, quem Plinius viridem et gemmeum, nihil adulatione mentitus, appellabat. Hunc praealto ponte, ut navigia incli-
natis malis permeent, iungere cogitamus, si parta pace miseriarum
finis ostendatur ut, si lubet, vel invito Neptuno, ad institutam
piscinam transire liceat. Ibi enim ab alto lascive provecti pisces, ac
in insulam per oblata et coecis anfractibus insidiosa foramina pe-
netrantes, erepto reditu, tanquam latis carceribus asservantur, ut
duris tempestatibus exclusa piscatio nihil expetitum dubiis mensis
eripiat.

6     Ab ipso quoque insulae adverso latere, illa immortalis virgo abdita intus, quae Dorica vocatur Echo, excitantibus, quum laeto
clamore salutatur, celeri liberalique obsequio semper respondet,
nam duplicatas reddit voces, ac hisdem accentibus recantat. Et
tum quidem ex hoc inani sed dulci ioco blandissima capitur voluptas, quum circumvehimur cymbis natantesque pueros ad certamen
adhortamur argenteolosque nummos audaciae praemia urinanti-
bus in alto dispergimus.

7     Altera porro ad occasum area, minor quidem sed liberiore coeli
facie et multa oculis occurrentium montium varietate iucundior,
quam nominis vestri merito FARNESIAM vocamus; matutinis opaca
umbris, ita patescit ut sub podio tutam ab Euris stationem relinquat sinuososque Larii recessus ac oppida apricis promontoriis

to an end; enclosed by two gardens and by crenellated walls, it resembles a hippodrome.

On the right there rises up from the middle of the lake an is- 5 land, encircled with a very sturdy wall, and pleasant on account of its towering fruit trees.[9] It wards off the southern winds and protects the harbor, sheltering its flank. It is set apart from the mainland by a channel which Pliny, without the least exaggeration, called "green and sparkling."[10] Should my woes ever come to a settled end, I intend to span this with a bridge that's very high (so as to allow ships to pass through with masts lowered) so that even when Neptune is averse, one wishing to do so can cross over to the fish pond I've had built.[11] Fish freely travel there from deep water and make their way to the [inner part of the] island through the holes put in their path, treacherous on account of blind twists and turns. Their return blocked off, they're in custody (as it were) in spacious prisons, so that even when foul weather prevents fishing, nothing desired is lacking on account of a meal being planned in uncertainty.[12]

In addition, hiding on the far side of the island is that immortal 6 girl called "The Doric Echo."[13] Whenever greeted with a joyful shout, she always replies rapidly and with courteous compliance to those calling out: for she reproduces their voices twice, matching their intonation. And finally, in a trifling but diverting pastime, we find it most delightful to travel around in skiffs and incite the children who are swimming to a competition: we scatter silver coins on the lake floor as prizes for those diving.

Next, to the west there is the other courtyard, which I call 7 "Farnesian" in your honor. While admittedly smaller than the first, it offers a wider view of the sky and is more charming thanks to the great variety of mountains that greet the eye. Cool in the morning shade, it extends so that its overhang provides a mooring place protected from the southeast winds and a view in the distance of the lake's sinuous shoreline, the walled towns built on

imposita, innumerabiles item villas et veliferas commeantium classes longissime prospectet.

8     At hi a leva dextraque diversi portus, quod opportune decenterque evenit, toto interiacentis isthmi spacio coniunguntur, sic ut non absurda bimaris Corinthi similitudine, dum iocamur, hunc tanquam ab Aegeo Cenchraeum, illum ab Ionio Lechaeum vocitemus. Nam, qua terrestris aditus ad villam patet, isthmus, binis ingentibus munitus portis, oblongo tractu totius aedificii frontem aequate complet et exornat dignumque prorsus primaria ianua et perpicto atrio vestibulum praebet.

9     Hinc aliae atque aliae ex opposito aperiuntur valvae, quae, rectissimo transitu et valde grata intro spectantibus serie per concameratas topiario opere Iulianas vites ad hortos et ad sylvosos montes ducunt. Ab his per fictiles tubulos salientis aquae perennem et limpidissimum fontem duximus in Doricam porticum, magno quidem labore et reluctante saepe Nympha, quod ea, tanquam ex Oreadibus egregie sylvestris, opaci et silentis ocii cupida, haec tecta frequentia occursumque hominum timidissime devitaret, nunc, effecta blandior, sponte ascendit in statuam Deae Naturae erectam, et per papillas erumpit, ut in marmoreum labrum effundatur.

10     Hoc uno pulcherrimo fonte mire gaudet musaeum, inde enim ad summum apicem florentis elegantiae pervenit: nam interiora conclavia, porticus, diaetas, aestiva hibernaque cubicula instaurasse multo luculentius eximiisque picturis nobilius exornasse quivis alius, opibus ingenioque validior, facile potuit; nos autem loci genium secuti, ardenti quidem studio, sed dubia spe absolvendi

sunny promontories, the countless villas, and fleets of sailboats passing to and fro.

And these two harbors, conveniently and attractively situated 8 on the left and the right, have between them a wide isthmus, so that, drawing a sensible enough comparison to "Corinth on its two seas," we playfully call the one "Kenchreai" as if it were on the Aegean Sea, and the other "Lechaion" as if on the Ionian. For the isthmus provides land access to the villa by means of an oblong tract of land that harmoniously completes and adorns the entire front of the building and, by the two massive gates with which it's furnished, it opens onto the inner courtyard, which is fully worthy of the main doorway and the copiously painted reception hall.

From the gates at one end and the other, for those looking in- 9 side, sets of doors are opened that lead down straight and continuous passageways, through Julian vines trained into arbors, toward the gardens and wooded mountains. From the mountains I've brought to the Doric portico, via small clay pipes, the jetting water of a never-failing, crystal clear fountain. This took immense effort, since the Nymph often resisted.[14] Being from the Oreads and therefore fond of shaded and silent tranquility, especially that of woodlands, she's extremely shy of crowded groups of houses and of encounters with people. But now, having grown kinder, of her own accord she climbs into the statue of the goddess of Nature and streams forth from her breasts into a marble basin.

My museum glories remarkably in this one exceedingly beauti- 10 ful fountain. In fact, here it reaches the pinnacle of flourishing elegance: for anybody with more money and talent could easily have built much more splendid inner chambers, porticos, living rooms, and summer and winter bedrooms, and adorned them more richly with choice paintings. I, however, having sought harmony with the place's ambience[15] — certainly with ardent enthusiasm but with no sure expectation of bringing the work to completion — have built it

operis, ita per partes aedificavimus ut saepe sera poenitentia de Fortunae liberalitate desperasse videamur.

11    Sed qui villas a beatioribus et regulis, ac ideo supra civilis fortunae censum magnifice aedificatas non viderunt, aut benigniore iudicio non insulsi operis elegantiam parum eruditis sumptibus anteponunt, facile mirantur primam porticum ab hilari atrio statim occurrentem, quam a picturae argumento 'personatam' vocamus, quod prisco more hiantes comaedorum personas per intercolumnia volitantibus suspensas strophiis, dum oculos moratur et detinet, intrantibus ostendat, nam inauratae personae elegantioris vitae praecepta Laconicae brevitatis effundere videntur.

12    Hanc hyeme tepor eximius commendat, nam totam collectis radiis plurimus sol implet, quum ad meridiem pertendens aestivam (quam Doricam diximus) adeo celeriter relinquat ut prandere simul ac caenare propter fontem spumoso strepitu sonantem opacissimo loco possis, nisi te Apollo vates novemque sorores in illud spaciosum perillustreque conclave, a quo tota enim villa musaei nomen accepit, blandientes alliciant. Hoc enim, pluribus undique fenestris ac ianuis, circumvectum solem exortasque eodem cursu perennes auras aut admittit aut, quum lubet, obductis valvis excludit. In medio enim omnibus horis aequatae spirant aurae, adeo moderato et salubri spiritu ut Syrium in coelo ardere non sentias, ob idque damnatos menses, tanquam verna temperie mitigatos, nondum venisse, aut certe silenter effluxisse, quum nec aestues nec plane sitias, prorsus existimes. Tota enim villa ante meridiem, quum ex alto sol urget, obortis etesiis blandissime ventilatur.

in stages, so that it often looked as if I'd lost faith in Fortune's generosity, regretting the undertaking only too late.

But those who have not seen the magnificent villas built by 11 wealthier men and princes (and thus are beyond the means of a common citizen), or who, with more gracious judgment, prefer a work's understated elegance over unrefined extravagance, are quick to admire the first portico one encounters right after the cheerful atrium. From the theme of its decoration I call this portico "masked," because to those entering it displays comic actors' *personae*, mouths agape in the ancient manner, painted in the space between the columns so as to appear suspended by fluttering headbands. While the gilded masks catch and hold the eye, they seem to express with Laconic terseness maxims for a more elegant mode of living.[16]

In winter this portico's extraordinary warmth recommends it, 12 for the powerful sun floods the entirety with the intensity of its gathered rays when, pressing on toward the south, it so quickly leaves behind the summer portico (which I've called "Doric") that you could lunch as well as dine in dense shade next to the fountain as it resounds with its noisy foaming, were it not that the bard Apollo and the nine sisters, with their coaxing, lure you into the Museum, that spacious and resplendent room for which the entire villa is named. Its numerous windows and doors on all sides either let in the sun as he makes his rounds and the breezes that blow perennially in that same course, or, when desired, block them out when the shutters are closed. In fact, through its middle at all hours there circulate currents of air so temperate and healthful that you don't feel Sirius burning in the sky. For this reason you would be certain that the wretched months had not yet arrived, as if they had been mitigated by a spring temperature or at least had silently slipped away, since you feel neither hot nor thirsty. For until noon, when the sun beats down from on high, the entire villa is delightfully fanned by the etesian winds.[17]

13    In fronte quoque podium ab insigni proiectura clatris ferreis circumseptum in subiectas undas prominet, quo nihil ad prospectum iucundius excogitari potest. Inde enim ad proiectam escam allectos pisces hamata linea extrahere iuvat, et cum singulari voluptate innumeras natantium acies intueri; nam Larius ipse argenteo nitore translucidus, dum colores et species piscium ad oculos transmittit, spectantibus arridet.

14    Introrsus autem Apollo Citharaedus et Musae, suis instructae organis, coenantibus applaudunt. Invitat exinde loci mutatione gaudentes in proximum cubiculum suum Minerva, ubi priscorum civium simulachra visuntur utriusque ante alios Plinii antiquiorisque Caecilii et Rufi Caninii poetarum, Attilii item grammatici et Fabati, Neronis odio insignis.

15    Minervae autem iuncta est bibliotheca, parva quidem, sed lectissimis referta libris, a depicta imagine Mercurio dicata. Ab hoc demum itur ad Sirenas, id est cubiculum aliquanto retractius, tanquam honestae tributum voluptati; ac inde ad armamentarium, quod iuxta atrium, iure ipso, invicti Caesaris Caroli augusta insignia tuentur.

16    Caeterum maximo conclavi adiuncta est nobilis illa coenatio, tribus Gratiis merito consecrata, quae florido laqueari minoribusque septem Doricis columnis et facetissimo picturae genere mirabiliter adornatur, quum peritus optices pictor peristylii fugientis recessus ex obliquo, deceptis oculis, expresserit. Hinc quoque urbs ipsa pene tota conspicitur, et Larius peramoenis maeandris ad Germaniam reflexus, frequentique olea et lauro virentia littora, vitiferi colles, et nemorosa aut laeta pascuis nascentium Alpium

In the front there is also a balcony, enclosed by an iron railing,  13
that juts out from that glorious protrusion over the waters below.[18]
One can't imagine anything more pleasant than to look out from it
into the distance. Indeed, I enjoy angling from it with a hooked
line for fish attracted by scattered bait, and I take special pleasure
in looking out upon the countless schools of them swimming
about. For while Lake Como itself, clear and with a silvery sheen,
catches the eye with its variety of colors and species of fish, it
smiles upon those gazing at it.

Indoors, Apollo with his cithara and the Muses with their own  14
instruments serenade the diners. Then, Minerva invites anybody
wishing a change of scene into the adjoining room, which is hers,
where one sees statues of ancient citizens of Como: first and foremost, both of the Plinys; and, of the poets, Caninius Rufus, and
Caecilius before him; and also the grammarian Atilius; and Fabatus, noted for his hatred of Nero.[19]

Adjoining Minerva's room is a library dedicated to Mercury,  15
whose likeness is painted there. Granted, it's small, but it is filled
to capacity with exquisitely chosen books.[20] At length one moves
on from here to the Sirens: that is, to a little room that's somewhat recessed, as it is allotted to licit pleasures; and, from there,
into the armory, which adjoins the entry hall. Fittingly, the majestic insignia of the unconquered Emperor Charles watch over it.

Now, attached to the largest of the rooms is that noble one  16
where we dine.[21] Rightfully consecrated to the three Graces, it's
wonderfully adorned with a brightly colored coffered ceiling and
seven small Doric columns, and with a type of painting that is
exceedingly clever in that its creator, skilled in optics, has used
foreshortening to make the inner peristyle recede at an angle.
From this room, too, nearly the entire city is visible, as is Lake
Como, as in its delightful sinuousness it bends back up toward
Germany: its shores, verdant with olive trees and laurel; the vine-
covered hills; and the ridges of the Alps that rise up, either

iuga, nec plaustris quidem ardua, despectantur. Quocunque te
verteris, nova atque hilaris loci facies occurret, quae oculos reficiat,
nec unquam exsatiet.

17    Sed tum opima pleniorque voluptas ostenditur, quum ad pis-
cantes extremaque trahentes retia naviculis advolamus, ac incertae
sortis iactum mercari lubet, et capturae piscium intentis manibus
et oculis, interesse percupimus.

18    Quid dicam de superioribus caenaculis, in queis de nomine
virtutis ac honoris argumenta lepidissimis inscriptionibus ostend-
duntur? His hyeme nihil apricius luminosius atque tepidius expe-
riri videreque contigit, quum toto fere ambitu per varias fenestras
vitreis specularibus admittant soles et sine fece diem et Larius ipse,
ut pote qui nusquam gelascit, maritimi littoris naturam aemulatus,
mirum teporem praebet duriciemque hyemis suaviter frangit.

19    Interior autem villa, quod magnopere Musis expetitur, strepitu
vacua et alti plena silentii nitidaque munditiis ad secretiora studia,
vel festivis lusibus occupatum, comiter invitant; nam (ut diximus)
dirimente isthmo tanquam in aliam minorem domum, et equilia
hippodromo coniuncta et penuarias cellas et culinae totiusque familiae tumultum penitus excludit, aureae profecto quietis beata
sedes, ac exoptatae potiusquam concessae libertatis tranquillus et
salubris portus ita ut haec nobis Alexander frater tuus, idem maximus cardinalis et gratissimus Mecoenas, in aestuosa Roma publicis
muneribus occupatus, invidere possit.

wooded or luxuriant with pastures, and not too steep even for
carts. Wherever you look, there comes into view a novel and
cheering aspect of the place which refreshes the eyes without ever
cloying.

But then an abundant and more satisfying pleasure is offered    17
when we hasten in small boats toward fishermen hauling up their
nets. It's fun to bet on the uncertain yield of a net that has yet to
be drawn up. Eyes peeled and hands at the ready, we're eager to
attend the catch as onlookers.

What shall I say about the small rooms upstairs, where the    18
most delightful inscriptions address the themes of virtue and
honor? In wintertime, nothing sunnier, brighter, or warmer could
be experienced, since practically the whole way around, numerous
clear glass windows let in the sun's rays and unclouded daylight.[22]
And since Lake Como itself, in imitation of the seacoast, never
freezes over, it supplies surprising warmth and sweetly tempers the
harshness of winter.

The inside of the villa, however, offers what the Muses greatly    19
desire: spaces empty of noise, filled with a deep silence and glitter-
ingly clean, kindly invite even one engrossed in lively games to
more solitary pursuits; for the villa, set apart by an isthmus (as
I've said) as if to create another, smaller house, entirely shuts out
the stables that go with the racetrack, the larders and the commo-
tion of the kitchen, and the entire household. Certainly this is so
blessed an abode of golden calm, so quiet and salubrious a haven
of the freedom that is hoped for rather than granted, that it may
arouse the envy of your brother Alessandro, at once the most distinguished cardinal and the most beloved Maecenas, who is bogged
down in official responsibilities in sweltering Rome.

# ORDINES IMAGINVM

1    Imagines veros clarorum virorum vultus in tabulis pictis exprimentes, quas pertinaci multorum annorum studio sumptuosaque ac ob id prope insana curiositate toto fere terrarum orbe perquisitas in musaeo dedicavimus, quatuor omnino classibus distinguuntur.

2    Prima eorum est qui, fato functi, quum ingenii foecunditate floruerint, felicium operum monumenta posteris reliquerunt. Horum elogia primus hic liber, Octavi Farnesi, nomini tuo dicatus continet, eo quidem ordine diligenter servato ut ad exactam temporis rationem, qui primo vita excesserint, subsequentes antecedant. Nulla enim alia ordinis nobilitas quaeretur nisi quae fatali vitae exitu praescribetur. Hac enim saluberrima lege totam litem, quae de loco dignitateque ambitiose et turbulenter excitari possit, pacatis omnibus sustulimus.

3    Secunda classis horum erit qui hodie vivunt et, publicatis ingenii dotibus, illustri fama tanquam certissimo vigiliarum fructu perfruuntur. Sed horum elogia accuratiore demum studio proferremus, quum mollioris ocii locus parato et cupienti benigna saeculi sorte concedetur. Religiosa enim gravioris censurae trutina viventium laus expendenda videtur, ne amicitia, quae mihi cum literatis integerrima semper fuit, et hic ipse quo semper laetissime viximus perspicuae voluntatis candor recti iudicii elidat nervos, laudandique pariter et notandi libertatem eripiat. Quis enim

# THE ARRANGEMENT OF
THE PORTRAITS

To obtain the portraits I've enshrined in my museum, which ac-  1
curately depict on painted panels the countenances of famous
men, I had to search everywhere in practically the entire world
with many years of unflagging effort and with meticulous care
that's so costly as to be almost insane. They are divided into a total
of four groups.

The first of these comprises men who, having died when their  2
genius was in full flush, have bequeathed to posterity the monuments of their successful works. The first book, dedicated to you,
Ottavio Farnese, contains their inscriptions, arranged strictly according to chronology, so that those who first departed life precede
their successors: that is to say, no order of precedence will be
sought other than that which is prescribed by death. Indeed,
thanks to this exceedingly beneficial rule, all are satisfied: I've obvi-
ated any quarrel regarding placement and esteem which might
presumptuously and disruptively be stirred up.

The second group will include those still living who, since their  3
gifts of brilliance have been published, have as the most certain
fruit of their vigils the full enjoyment of an illustrious reputation.
But I should formulate the inscriptions for them later, with closer
attention, when the favorable condition of the times may grant me
the more peaceful leisure for which I am ready and eager. Indeed,
praise of the living is evidently to be weighed on the carefully cali-
brated scales of more severe judgment, lest my friendship with literati, which has always been absolutely unimpaired, and that very
candor of manifest goodwill with which I have always lived most
abundantly, should weaken the sinews of proper judgment and
take away my freedom to praise and, equally, to blame. For who

summae felicitatis ingenia satis laudaverit aut non insulse nota-
verit, quum iam provisa nominis aeternitate, omnem invidiam
superarint? Et quod non dispudeat, ad elimandum aequissimus
locus diligentiae relinquatur. In his recitandis ab aetatis honore
series ducetur, quum iuniores aequissimo iure natu maioribus
honestissimum locum concedant.

4      Tertia porro classis praecellentium operum artifices excipiet;
haec periucundo libello explicabitur, quum praeter picturae celatu-
raeque decus ex certis nobilium artificum monumentis demonstra-
tum, facetissimorum etiam hominum, qui dictis aut scriptis excitato risu aegrorum animorum curas allevarint, memoria renovetur.

5      Quarta erit maximorum pontificum regum et ducum qui, pace
et bello gloriam consecuti, praeclara ingentium facinorum exempla
imitanda aut vitanda posteris tradiderunt.

6      Harum imaginum populus stupenda varietate mirabilis tum
maxime incredibilem spectantibus afferet voluptatem, quum per
elogia sigillatim arguta brevitate describetur.

PRIMI LIBRI IMAGINES INCIPIVNT.

could ever sufficiently praise or fittingly censure the most successful geniuses when, their immortal fame already set in place, they
have risen beyond all envy? And one shouldn't blush to have ample
time remaining to polish one's work diligently.

The sequence in recording these will be governed by the distinction of age, since in the fairest judgment those born more recently
should cede the place of greatest honor to their elders.

The third grouping will single out the makers of preeminent    4
works of art. This will be explained in a little book that will be
most delightful, since beyond illustrating the splendor of painting
and engraving on the basis of authentic works of famous masters,
it will also revive the memory of the wittiest of men, who by their
speech and writing have lessened the anxieties of troubled minds
by stirring them to laughter.

The fourth will comprise the supreme pontiffs, kings, and com-    5
manders who, having sought after glory in peace and war, have
bequeathed to posterity splendid examples of outsized deeds to be
imitated or avoided.

The multitude of these portraits, extraordinary in its astonish-    6
ing variety, will give viewers the most amazing pleasure when each
in turn is described with eloquent concision in a capsule biography.

HERE BEGINS THE PORTRAITS OF
THE FIRST BOOK.

# I. Albertus Magnus

1 Sit hoc tibi, quanquam breve, elogiorum omnium merito luculentissimum Alberte Sveve Artobrigensium sanctissime antistes, postquam docendo scribendoque theologiae philosophiaeque totius locos omnes miris celsissimi ingenii tui luminibus illustrasti ut illud in literis nemini adhuc concessum et, quod vivo rara felicitate contigit, Magni cognomen assequerere.

2 Vixisti quippe caeteris aliquanto beatius, hoc est alterum et octogesimum aetatis annum, scilicet ut immortalitati tuae iusta gloria plenus interesses accumulatoque foecundissimi ingenii merito clarioris tituli munere dignus censerere. Deferebat enim Maximi cognomentum gymnasiorum omnium consensus nisi publico voto Christiana verecundia restitisses. Sed quid tibi maius Dii Immortales dare potuerunt quam ut diu in terris vivus et incolumis inusitatae nec unquam, nisi post fata, obvenientis gloriae fructum perciperes?

3 *Ferdinandi Balamii*

Magna parens altrixque virum Germania, alumni
    incedit merito laude superba sui.
Naturae ac rerum vires causasque latentes
    hoc nemo nobis doctius explicuit.
Magnus ob egregias foecundi pectoris artes
    dictus es, at Iovii nunc ope maior eris.

# THE PORTRAITS

## I. Albertus Magnus (ca. 1200–1280)

O Albertus—you, a Swabian from Lauingen[1] and the holiest of      1
bishops—please accept this *elogium* which, albeit brief, is deservedly the most splendid of all, since in your teachings and writings
you elucidated every argument in the entirety of theology and
philosophy with the exquisite brilliance of your exceedingly lofty
intellect. Thus you garnered the epithet "The Great"—a thing
never before conferred on a man of letters, and only by rare felicity
accorded to the living.

Certainly you lived somewhat more happily than others, to the      2
age of eighty-two, evidently so that, heavy-laden with earned glory,
you could behold your own undying fame, and so that once you'd
accumulated the accolades due a surpassingly fertile mind, you
might be judged worthy of the bestowal of a still more illustrious
title. For the universities were unanimous in desiring to confer
upon you the epithet "The Greatest." Out of Christian humility,
however, you stood firm against the collective will. But what
greater gift could the immortal gods have given you than that, living long and in good health, you might reap on earth the fruit of a
rare glory that has heretofore befallen only those who have died?

*By Ferdinando Balami*      3

Great Germany, mother and nurturer of men, rightly takes
pride in the praise of her son.[2] Nobody has explained to us
more learnedly than he the forces and secrets of Nature. For
the outstanding skills of your bountiful mind, you are called
"Great"; but now, thanks to Giovio's help, you will be greater.

4          *Iani Vitalis*

Natura has violas, Ratio haec tibi lilia passim
   ad tumulum spargunt, Theutone Magne, tuum.
Purpureis quarum tribulos avellis ab hortis
   et pulchris violis lilia mista seris
aviaque abstrusae pandis penetralia causae.
Vere igitur Magni nomine dignus eras.


## II. Sanctus Thomas

1   Divi Thomae Aquinatis haec erat facies quum imprimis studiorum honoribus decore iuventae hylaris versaretur. Nondum enim,
uti postea in flexu aetatis evenit, illa subtristis ac omni alia fere
durior parcissimae mensae disciplina iugesque demum lucubrationum vigiliae nobile ac ideo tenerum corpus afflixerant. Hic enim
plane adolescens, abdicata antiquae stirpis praeclara nobilitate (ad
quam hodie Alfonsus Davalus inter Caesaris duces longe clarissimus maternum genus refert) et spreto demum omni patrimonio,
neque familiae dignitati neque valetudini unquam pepercit ut, post
aedita divini ingenii monumenta, in coelum unde venerat vitae integer evolaret.

2   Idcirco defunctum in Volscis ad Amasenum amnem, quum supra naturae potestatem multa miracula operum ab eo aedita re-
nunciarentur, Ioannes Romanus pontifex ex senatusconsulto non
dubitavit quin eum solenni cerimonia inter divos referret. Obiit
non plane senex, quum eum humanae gloriae quae ei ex studiis

Everywhere around your tomb, Great German, Nature scatters these violets for you, and Reason, these lilies.[3] You pluck out the brambles from the purple gardens and weave together lilies mixed with beautiful violets. You blaze a trail into the trackless recesses of a recondite subject. Truly, you merited the epithet "The Great."

## II. St. Thomas [Aquinas] (1225–74)

This was how St. Thomas Aquinas looked when, in the splendor 1
of lighthearted youth, he was garnering the first laurels of his
studies. For not yet, as happens over time in life's changing course,
had that discipline of an exceedingly austere diet (a thing that's
rather sad, and more oppressive than just about anything else) and
indeed habitual studying late into the night ruined a body that was
noble and on that account delicate. For while he was still quite
young, he disowned the aristocratic rank of his ancient lineage (to
which Alfonso d'Avalos, by far the most famous among the emperor's commanders today, traces his descent on his mother's side[4])
and then rejected his entire inheritance. And he never showed
consideration either for the distinction of his family or for his
health, so that once he had produced monuments of divine genius,
blameless in life, he ascended to heaven, whence he had come.

On that account, after he had died by the Amaseno River in 2
Latium, since many supernatural miracles were reported to have
been performed by him, Pope John, in accordance with a recommendation from the college of cardinals, did not hesitate to canonize him in a solemn ceremony.[5] He died before growing old, at a
time when he'd had his fill[6] of the human glory that had befallen

maxima obvenerat, sacietas cepisset, scilicet ut alteram quam absoluta pietate promerebat, coelum suspiciens certiore voto sequeretur.

3                                   *Incerti*

Hic Thomae cineres positi; cui fata dedere
ingenium terris vivere, coelo animam.

## III. *Ioannes Scotus*

1   Nemo eorum qui non insano Christianae pietatis amore flagrantes
ultro sese coenobiis in servitutem addixerint, Ioanne Scoto in gravissimis studiis aut acrior aut subtilior fuit; quum admirandis
commentationum voluminibus aeditis, novam de nomine suo sec-
tam conderet, et in Aquinatis scripta non dissimulanter inveheretur.

2     Natus est in ultima Britannia, ad Calydoniam sylvam, ut minus
mirum sit Anacharsim summae sapientiae philosophum apud ve-
cordissimos Scythas crasso atque ingeniis excolendis importuno
coelo patriam habuisse. Verum hic protervo captiosoque disse-
rendi genere Christianis dogmatibus illusisse videtur quum, passim inducta quaestione dubitabundus, sacrarum rerum fidem nequaquam tenui figmentorum caligine confudisset. Sevit enim ideo
lites immortales, quando eius placita vel graviter ab adversae sectae
professoribus oppugnata, ex adverso ab eius discipulis acerrime

him to the utmost degree on account of his studies. By making a more reliable kind of vow — with an eye to heaven, if you will — he pursued that other glory, which he deserved on account of his perfect piety.

*Anonymous*                                                                    3

Here have been placed the ashes of Thomas, to whom the Fates granted that his genius live on earth, his soul in heaven.[7]


## III. John [Duns] Scotus (1265/66–1308)

Of those men who out of an ardent, yet not unhinged, love for   1
Christian piety have voluntarily sentenced themselves to the cloistered life, nobody has been either keener or subtler in the most ponderous studies than Duns Scotus. After having published admirable books of commentaries, he independently founded a new school of thought and openly inveighed against the writings of Aquinas.

He was born in the farthest reach of Britannia, near the Cale-   2
donian Forest[8] — which makes it less surprising that Anacharsis, a philosopher of consummate wisdom, lived among the barbarous Scythians under a murky sky that was adverse to the cultivation of intellectual gifts. But by his impudent and captious way of building an argument, he seems to have made sport of Christian doctrines: for, hesitating here and there on a question that had been raised, he obscured faith in religious matters with a dense fog of jargon. In this manner he sowed the seeds of interminable quarrels, because even when his tenets had been assailed by professors of an opposing school of thought, they were defended fiercely in

defendantur. Sed qui aliquot praeclara eius ordinis ingenia, ad optimam frugem nata, distorto scilicet ad veritatem itinere suspendisse perdidisseque videtur.

3   Manifesti aut certe occulti alicuius criminis apoplexia correptus, poenas persolvit ita quidem ut nimis festinato funere pro mortuo tumulatus, quum redeunte vita sero morbi impetum natura discuteret, frustra ad petendam opem miserabili mugitu aedito pulsatoque diu sepulchri lapide, eliso tandem capite perierit.

4   Et de alio quoque Ioanne Scoto quod ex Gallicis Annalibus Crinitus recitat, verum esse crediderim, eum a coniuratis discipulis, Divi Cassiani exemplo, graphiis confossum inulta morte concidisse.

5               *Iani Vitalis*

Quod nulli unquam hominum accidit, viator,
hic Scotus iaceo semel sepultus,
   et bis mortuus; omnibus sophistis argutus magis atque
      captiosus.


## IV. Danthes

1   Primus Italorum Danthes Aldigerius, non instituto vetustatis ordine tantum sed praecellenti gravis ingenii foecunditate, primum locum inter imagines meritus optimo iure conspicitur. Hunc Florentia, factiosa eo saeculo civitas, protulit; ab altaque mentis indole

turn by his students. But by having (shall we say) contorted the path to the truth, Scotus instilled doubt in several splendid geniuses of his order who had been bound for greatness, and brought them to ruin.

Seized by apoplexy from some open misdeed, or at least a hidden one, he suffered the consequences — indeed, in such a way that, his funeral having been too hurried, he was presumed dead and was buried. When nature dissipated the bout of disease and he regained consciousness, it was too late: as the poor fellow was shouting, vainly seeking help, and after he had long been beating his head against the sarcophagus, at last he bashed it in and died.[9]

I incline to believe, too, what Crinito mentioned, drawing upon *The Annals of France*, concerning another John Scotus: that, in imitation of the story of St. Cassian, his own students acting together pierced him through with their styluses — a death that went unavenged.[10]

*By Giano Vitale*      5

I, Scotus, lie here, once buried and twice dead: a thing, wayfarer, which has happened to no man ever. I'm more clever and captious than all the sophists.[11]


## IV. Dante (1265–1321)

With good reason, the first Italian to appear here is Dante Alighieri. He deserves first place among the portraits not only in the chronological order here followed, but also in the surpassing fecundity of his formidable genius. Florence, a city riven with factions in that era, produced him and, having recognized his

cognitum Octovirali supremae potestatis magistratu insignem fecit ut, mox fatali conversa turbine, et summum civem et Ethruscae linguae conditorem, tanquam saeva et ingrata patria, proscriberet.

2     Sed exilium vel toto Ethruriae principatu ei maius et gloriosius fuit, quum illam sub amara cogitatione excitatam occulti divinique ingenii vim exacuerit et inflammarit. Enata si quidem est in exilio *Comoedia* triplex Platonicae eruditionis lumine perillustris ut, abdicata patria, totius Italiae civitate donaretur.

3     Plenus ideo gloria perenni quum eam, quae piis mortalibus expetitur, coelestis aurae felicitatem tanto ore tantoque spiritu decantatam contemplaretur, nulla adhuc oborta canitie, Ravennae morbo interiit adeo mentis compos ut sex versus sepulchro incidendos componeret. Nec Ravennates in apparatu funeris publico totius Italiae civi defuerunt; quum enim sepulchrum e marmore condidissent, non obscure[1] exprobata Ethruscis acerbitate, novam sibi claritatem gloriosa pietate vendicarunt.

4                              *Ipsius Danthis*

Iura Monarchiae, superos, Phlegethonta lacusque
lustrando cecini, voluerunt Fata quousque.
Sed quia pars cessit melioribus hospita castris
auctoremque[2] suum petiit felicior astris.
Hic claudor Danthes patriis extorris ab oris
quem genuit parvi Florentia mater amoris.

superior mind, gave him the distinction of being in the most powerful magistracy, the Signoria.[12] After a fateful regime change, however, Florence, being a cruel and ungrateful fatherland, proscribed this man who was both an exceptional citizen and the founder of the Tuscan language.[13]

But exile for him was even greater and more glorious than total    2
dominion over Tuscany, since it sharpened and inflamed that force of a latent and divine genius that had been awakened amid bitter rumination. Accordingly, it was in exile that his threefold *Comedy*, shining brilliantly with the light of Platonic erudition, came into being, so that he who had renounced his native city was granted citizenship of all Italy.

Full, therefore, of everlasting glory when he contemplated that    3
blessedness of heavenly splendor which pious mortals seek, after having sung of it with such great eloquence and inspiration, he fell ill and died at Ravenna, his hair not yet grayed, and his intellect so undimmed that he composed six verses to be inscribed on his tomb. Nor did the Ravennans fail to perform elaborate public funeral rites for this citizen of all Italy: indeed, by erecting a marble tomb they conspicuously reproached the Florentines for their malice and, by this glorious act of devotion, laid claim to new celebrity for themselves.

### By Dante Himself[14]    4

So long as the Fates willed it, I surveyed and sang of the rights of monarchy, the gods in heaven, and Phlegethon and the waters of Hell.[15] But because the part of me that was a guest moved on toward a better encampment and sought its Maker more happily among the stars, I, Dante, am buried here: an exile from my native land, born of Florence, a mother of scant love.[16]

5 Sed tumulum vetustate collabentem, Bernardus Bembus Petri
Bembi Cardinalis pater, in ea urbe praetor, opere caelato et con-
camerato additoque hoc epigrammate luculenter exornavit:

> Exigua tumuli Danthes hic sorte iacebas
>   squallenti nulli cognite pene situ.
> At nunc marmoreo subnixus conderis arcu,
>   omnibus et cultu splendidiore nites.
> Nimirum Bembus Musis incensus Ethruscis
>   hoc tibi, quem imprimis hae coluere, dedit.

## V. Franciscus Petrarca

1 Franciscus Petrarca, eodem cive magistroque suo Danthe, Ethruscae linguae facultatem constitutam plane et certis adornatam numeris flagranter excepit, tanta ingenii solertia, duriora molliendo et
singulari suavitate variis modis flectendo numeros, ut enatam dudum et vix dum flores ostendentem eloquentiam, ingenti cultura,
ad absolutae maturitatis fructum summumque ideo exactae elegantiae fastigium perduxerit; eamque laudem sit consecutus ut in
eo poesis genere amatorioque praesertim castitate candore dulcedine nobilium poetarum et primus et ultimus sanis a scribendo
deterritis existimetur.

2 Sed tanti viri iudicium illudens Fortuna graviter fefellit: quum
haec aeternae felicitatis spiritum habitura tanquam temporaria
despiceret ut ex Latina *Africa*, unde ei in Capitolio insignis laurea
praemium fuit, certiorem et nobiliorem gloriam adsequeretur. Sed

But when the tomb was collapsing from age, Cardinal Pietro  5
Bembo's father, Bernardo, who was the *podestà* in that city, adorned
it lavishly with a carved vault and had this epigram added:[17]

> You used to lie here in the narrow confines of a tomb, Dante,
> unrecognized because of the squalid site. But now, you are
> interred under a marble arch and outshine all others in
> splendid elegance. Bembo, inflamed by the Tuscan Muses,
> provided this for you, whom they cherished above all others.

## V. *Francesco Petrarch (1304–74)*

Francesco Petrarch eagerly learned from Dante, his fellow citizen  1
and teacher, the command of the Tuscan language that his master
had standardized and endowed with set meters. He did this with
such great dexterity of mind—mitigating harshnesses and, with
remarkable sweetness, inflecting the cadences with varied meters—that by diligent cultivation he brought to mature fruition,
and therefore to the highest summit of exacting refinement, the
eloquence that had recently sprung forth and was just beginning to
flower. He also achieved the distinction that in the genre of poetry
and especially amatory poetry, he is considered both the first and
the last of the great poets in purity, beauty, and sweetness: so
much so that those of sound mind have been deterred from trying
their hand.

But Fortune, mocking the judgment of so great a man, deceived  2
him grievously when he spurned these works, which would enjoy
a life of everlasting favor, in order to pursue surer and nobler glory
from his Latin poem *Africa*, for which he was awarded a laurel
crown on the Capitoline.[18] But let us acknowledge that we are

debeamus plurimum, ingenuo sudore semper aestuanti, dum literas a multo aevo misere sepultas e Gothicis sepulchris excitaret;
modo eum tanquam Italicae linguae conditorem et principem ab
incomparabili divini ingenii virtute veneremur.

3    Concessit naturae plane senex ad Arquatum Patavini agri vicum
ubi tumulus carmine ab se composito nobilis conspicitur:

> Frigida Francisci lapis hic tegit ossa Petrarcae.
> Suscipe, Virgo parens, animam; sate virgine parce
> fessaque iam terris coeli requiescat in arce.

## VI. Boccacius

1    Boccacius, eodem felici saeculo quo renatae literae Latinae existimantur, Certaldo oppido editus, alteram in patria lingua pedestris
eloquentiae partem primus inchoavit et absolvit. Neglexerat eam
Danthes in altitudinem heroicae Comoediae divino furore carminum abreptus. Petrarca vero, Latina oratione delectatus, tanquam
ignobilem reliquerat ut discipulo, qui amore ei frater fuit, quota
sua pars, tanquam ex patrimonio, novae laudis legitimo nomine
haereditatis obveniret.

2    Non defuere tamen qui censerent neque Boccacium versu neque Petrarcam soluta oratione valuisse tantorum ingeniorum sortes
alternante Fortuna ideoque ambos acri iudicio in id munus inten-
disse nervos ad quod pronior atque liquidior styli vena perflueret.

most indebted to him for his indefatigable efforts at raising up from Gothic tombs literature that had so long lain miserably buried — provided that we also revere him for the incomparable excellence of his divine genius as the founder and master of the Italian language.

He died at quite an advanced age, at Arquà, a village in Paduan territory. There, one can see his tomb, notable for the poem that he himself composed for it:[19]

> This slab covers the cold bones of Francesco Petrarch. O Virgin Mother, take up his soul. O You who were of virgin born, have mercy and allow it, worn out now by earthly things, to find rest in the citadel of heaven.

## VI. Boccaccio (1313–75)

Born in the town of Certaldo in that same fortunate century when Latin literature is thought to have been reborn, Boccaccio was the first to have essayed and perfected writing in his native language in the other genre of eloquence, prose.[20] Dante, carried on high by the divine frenzy of the poetry of his heroic *Comedy*, had been indifferent to vernacular prose.[21] Petrarch, having in truth delighted in Latin eloquence, had left vernacular prose aside as insufficiently noble; that part, as if from a patrimony, accrued to his protégé, whom he loved like a brother, as a rightful inheritance of praiseworthy innovation.

Be that as it may, many were of the opinion that as for the vernacular, Boccaccio was weak in poetry and Petrarch in prose; but since Fortune gave each his share of great talent, both of them shrewdly directed their strength to the kind of work where the vein of their style flowed more readily and smoothly. But with a

Sed non dispari fato, et hic ipse in studiis opinione deceptus est, quum praecipuo ingentique labore ut certum sibi decus pararet; pene frustra desudarit. Obsolescunt enim et aegre quidem vitae spiritum retinent libri *De genealogia deorum*, *Varietateque fortunae* et *De fontibus* accurate potius quam feliciter elaborati, quando iam illae decem dierum fabulae, Milesiarum imitatione in gratiam oblectandi ocii, admirabili iucunditate compositae in omnium nationum linguas adoptentur et, sine ulla suspicione interitus, applaudente populo cunctorum operum gratiam antecedant.

3      Excessit e vita sexagesimo secundo aetatis anno. Sepulchrum eius cum marmorea effigie insculptis his carminibus in templo maximo Certaldi conspicitur:

Hac sub mole iacent cineres atque[3] ossa Ioannis.
Mens sedet ante Deum meritis ornata laborum.
Mortalis vitae genitor Boccacius illi,
patria Certaldum, studium fuit alma poesis.

4                                  *Myrtei*

Si quaeram cineres tuos Boccaci,
hic iacent; si animam, petivit astra.
Si qua gloria sit tuis libellis
maior, non ego Lydiusve linguae
cultor patriae et aemulus Latinae,
sed iudex erit aut iocis Cupido,
aut gaudens facili Venus loquela;
aut, quem dicere malo, totus orbis,
cui vivunt Veneres Cupidinesque
quibus cultior est tuus libellus
elegantior omnibus libellis.

fate not unlike Petrarch's, Boccaccio himself was deceived by his opinion of his literary efforts when, with special and intense effort, he set his sights upon a distinction for himself that he supposed certain. But this was mostly in vain, for the books on *The Genealogy of the Pagan Gods*, *On the Variability of Fortune*, and *On Springs*, rendered more meticulously than felicitously, are forgotten and indeed barely retain a breath of life. But already, the *Decameron*, composed with remarkable charm in imitation of Milesian tales for the sake of enjoyment in leisure, is being translated into the languages of all peoples.[22] Without any hint of dying away (since it meets with public applause), it surpasses the popularity of all his other works.

He departed from life in his sixty-second year. His tomb, along 3 with a marble statue, can be seen in the cathedral of Certaldo, with these poems inscribed upon it:[23]

Beneath this stone lie the ashes and bones of Giovanni. His mind, adorned with the merits of his labors, has a place in the presence of God. His earthly father was a Boccaccio;[24] his fatherland, Certaldo. Poetry, the source of nourishment, was his passion.

*By Mirteo*[25]    4

If I should search for your ashes, Boccaccio, here they lie; if for your spirit, it has made for the stars. Whether there should be some glorious achievement greater than your books, neither I nor the Tuscan, a cultivator of his native tongue and an imitator of Latin, will be the judge. Instead, it will be either Cupid, delighting in play, or Venus, rejoicing in lighthearted speech; or, as I prefer to say, the entire world, where live the amours and desires that make your book more elegant and refined than all others.

## VII. Bartholus

1   Bartholus Sentini in Umbria natus, magno acumine perspicacis ingenii ius civile professus, in omnibus Italiae gymnasiis exactae doctrinae documenta reliquit. Eum adversus studiorum labores indomitum extitisse ferunt consuevisseque uti in pertenui mensa certis cibi potusque mensuris ad tuendam valetudinem ut, quum saepe memoria laberetur, oblivionis incommoda assidua commentatione resarciret. Ob id voluptates omnes adeo severe reiecerat ut ne horula quidem extra naturae necessitatem studiis subtraheretur.

2   Sed eandem quoque severitatem supra aequum in torquendis necandisque noxiis exercuisse visus est, quum rerum capitalium iudiciis praeesset adeo ut reum furti nec rite confessum et insontem, praecipiti sententia supplicio affecerit. Ex ea acerbitate, quum invidiam populari voce conflatam subisset, conspectum hominum pudore vitabundus in arcanum ruris ocium evolvendis libris se abdidit, e qua demum studiorum intentione audacter egressus, aequales suos doctrinae firmitate et mira iudicii constantia superavit.

3   Donatus est, virtutis causa, a Carolo Quarto Imperatore gentilitiis Bohemiae regum insignibus, quibus purpurei leonis forma, aurato in campo, cum bicipiti cauda salientis exprimitur. Perusiae autem supremam in gymnasio claritatem consecutus, fortunas suas collocavit duxitque uxorem, sed irrita spe masculae prolis. Verum infinitos prope discipulos amore filii pares praecellentis doctrinae reliquit haeredes. Defuit ei Latinae eloquentiae facultas, ne summae gloriae fastigium teneret; et tamen est quod maxime

## VII. Bartolus (1314–57)

Born at Sassoferrato in Umbria, Bartolus[26] taught civil law with the great incisiveness of a penetrating intellect and has left proofs of his meticulous instruction in all the universities in Italy. They say he was dauntless in facing the hardships of studies. He was accustomed to eating carefully measured portions of food and drink in delicate meals to preserve his health in order that when his memory failed, as often it did, he compensated for the disadvantages of forgetfulness by relentless preparation. For this reason, he had shunned all pleasures with such stringency that he would not be drawn away from his studies for even the short space of an hour beyond what nature required.[27]

But he is seen also to have acted with the same excessive severity in torturing and executing criminals when he presided over capital trials: as a result, in a rush to judgment, he sentenced to death an accused thief who had not duly confessed and was innocent. When the hatred he incurred for this cruelty was inflamed in the court of public opinion, ashamed lest people should see him, he hid himself away, retiring to the country to pore over his books. When at last he emerged confidently from this immersion in study, he surpassed his contemporaries in the rigor of his teachings and the remarkable consistency of his judgment.

The emperor Charles IV decorated him for his excellence with the coat of arms of the kings of Bohemia, on which a purple lion rampant with a two-pointed tail is portrayed in a golden field. Then, after he had acquired the utmost distinction at the University of Perugia, he invested his wealth and took a wife, but his hope of having a son was vain. He did, however, leave behind as heirs of his exceptional teaching an almost infinite number of protégés, whom he loved like sons. He lacked eloquence in Latin, which kept him from gaining purchase on the pinnacle of glory.

miremur: illum in perpetuo docendi munere occupatum, tot et tanta volumina perscribere potuisse.

4    Quum quadragesimo sexto aetatis anno fato ereptus, iustum de inchoatis summa felicitate nec dum perfectis operibus desiderium posteris reliquerit. Sepultus est ad aram maximam in templo Divi Francisci.

5                              *[Myrtei]*

Hic est Bartholus ille, iuris ingens.
Lux et commodus explicator hic est
quem mors ante diem abstulit maligna.
Heu mors, invida et aevo iniqua nostro,
quae leges iterum iacere cogis!

## VIII. *Baldus*

1    Baldus, honesta Ubaldorum gente Perusiae natus, Bartholum praeceptorem subtilitate ingenii et varietate doctrinae superavit. Nam a patre medico celebri, priusquam ius civile attingeret, dialecticae atque philosophiae praeceptis haud mediocriter imbutus fuerat. Praecoci enim ingenio pene puer, non ad optimam modo frugem, sed rarissimo etiam naturae dono, ad longam senectutem pervenit. Verum praealto ingenio multa convolventi invertentique stabilis scientiae constantia deerat, quoniam subtilissime disputando atque enarrando, non humani modo sed divini quoque iuris intelligentia summus, refrigerato demum iudicio, post altercationes a Bartholo doctrinae robore vinceretur.

And yet, he had what we may most admire: while constantly employed in teaching, he was able to write so many voluminous books.

When he was snatched away by fate at the age of forty-six, he bequeathed to posterity a justified sense of loss regarding the works that he had sketched out most promisingly but had not yet brought to completion. He was interred near the high altar in the Church of San Francesco.[28]

4

### [By Mirteo][29]

5

Here is that mighty jurist, Bartolus, a luminary and an obliging expositor whom spiteful death snatched away before his time. Alas, Death, hateful and hostile to our era, who once again compel the laws to lie prostrate!

## VIII. Baldus (1320–1400)

Born into the respectable Ubaldi family of Perugia, Baldus[30] surpassed his teacher, Bartolus, in keenness of mind and range of erudition. For, before he entered upon the study of civil law, his father, a famous doctor, had abundantly instilled in him the basics of dialectics and philosophy. Indeed, not only did his precocious genius reach full maturity when he was little more than a boy; he also arrived at that rarest gift of nature, a ripe old age. But his brilliant intellect, which embraced and upended many subjects, lacked the constancy of stable learning: for although he was the greatest in understanding of both human and divine law, arguing and explicating with the utmost subtlety, once the intensity of the contests had cooled he was surpassed by Bartolus in solidity of erudition.

1

2 Eum eximia laude florentem, Ioannes Galeatius Vicecomes, potentia et gloria maximis regibus aequatus, quum Ticini gymnasium conderet, magnis praemiis evocavit. Ibi nunquam senescente nominis fama, nunquam in publico munere defessis viribus, ad septuagesimum sextum pervenit annum fatoque functus est paulo antequam ille princeps externarum gentium victor, properante fato moreretur. Ferunt Baldum Divi Francisci habitum, quum expiraret, induisse. Tumulus in eius divi aede cum hac rudi inscriptione conspicitur:

> Conditur hic Baldus, Francisci tegmine fultus,
> doctorum princeps, Perusina conditus arce.

## IX. Leonardus Aretinus

1 Primus in Italia Leonardus, Aretii natus, Graecarum literarum decus a multis saeculis barbarorum immani tyrannide proculcatum erexit atque restituit. Eius enim incomparabili beneficio morales Aristotelis libros optima fide traductos legimus. *Historiae* quoque ab eo eleganter conscriptae in manibus habentur.

2 Hac ingenii foecunditate florentem, Innocentius Septimus, quanquam plane iuvenem, gravissimo muneri parem epistolarum magistrum fecit. Ita demum erudite atque integre officio functus ut succedentibus quatuor pontificibus amplificata dignitate operam praestiterit. Senescenti opes creverunt cum aliena liberalitate tum sua tristi parsimonia cumulatae adeo ut Arlottus, mordaci sale perurbanus, in fabellis eius genium relicto corpore in fuga sitientem ridenter expresserit.

When Giangaleazzo Visconti, equal to the greatest kings in   2
power and glory, founded a university at Pavia, he lured the flourishing and extraordinarily famous Baldus with great rewards.
Here, the reputation of his name never weakening, his strength
never exhausted in public service, he reached the age of seventy-
six. He died shortly before that prince, the conqueror of foreign
nations, met his death, as fate was hastening. They say that Baldus
put on a Franciscan habit when he was dying. His tomb may be
seen in the church of that saint, with this unpolished inscription:[31]

> Here rests Baldus, fortified with the garb of a Franciscan;
> the prince of scholars, buried in the city of Perugia.

## IX. Leonardo Bruni (1369–1444)

Born in Arezzo, Leonardo[32] was the first in Italy to have revived   1
and restored the splendor of Greek literature that had been tram-
pled with monstrous tyranny by many centuries of barbarians.
Thanks to his unmatched service, we read the moral books of
Aristotle which he translated with the utmost fidelity.[33] We also
have in hand his elegantly written *Histories*.

Since despite his youth he was illustrious in this scholarly pro-   2
ductivity and worthy of a highly important post, Innocent VII
appointed him apostolic secretary.[34] He discharged this duty with
such erudition and integrity that, his reputation having grown, he
maintained that position under four subsequent pontiffs. As he
grew old, his wealth increased, amassed both by others' generosity
and by his own austere parsimony, which was so great that Arlotto, extremely clever in his biting wit, in his *Book of Jests* deri-
sively portrayed Bruni's guardian spirit as having fled from his
body stricken with thirst.[35]

3    Mortuus, quod ei nullo pudori fuit, furti damnatus est, quod
*Gothicam historiam* suppresso Procopii nomine publicasset, accusante Christophoro Persona, qui aliud exemplar nactus et Gothicam et Persicam simul atque Vandalicam Graeci authoris titulum
ingenue profitendo transtulerit. Novissime revocatus in Ethruriam
*Populi Florentini res gestas* perscripsit, nec multo post, senex divitiis
et gloria plenus, Florentiae vita functus est; dignus utique hoc
sepulchri titulo ac marmoris ornamento, quod in aede Sanctae
Crucis spectatur:

4    *Caroli Aretini*

Postquam Leonardus e vita migravit
historia luget, eloquentia muta est
ferturque Musas tum Graecas tum
Latinas, lachrymas tenere non potuisse.

## X. *Pogius*

1  Pogius e Terra Nova, Florentinae ditionis oppido, in hac luce Romani coeli optimis literis ingenium ita expolivit ut pontificiis scriniis sub Eugenio et Nicolao praeficeretur, aequatus scilicet honore
summis viris qui in eo munere fidelis eruditique ingenii operam
praestitissent. In his fuere Leonardus, Mapheus Vegius et Ioannes
Aurispa.

2    Erat consilio gravis et, quum luberet, facetiarum sale perurbanus ita ut mira et saepe subita varietate ad ciendum risum, modo

Death spared him the embarrassment of being found guilty of 3
literary theft for having published the *Gothic History* of Procopius
with the author's name suppressed. The accusation was made by
Cristoforo Persona who, having found another copy, had translated the Greek author's histories of the Goths, Persians, and
Vandals, honorably giving him due credit.[36] Recalled to Tuscany in
the last period of his life, Bruni finished writing the *History of the
Florentine People*.[37] Soon thereafter, he died in Florence an old man,
rich in wealth and in glory, and most worthy of the following inscription on his tomb, sculpted of marble, which can be seen in
the Church of Santa Croce:

### By Carlo of Arezzo[38]

4

Now that Leonardo has departed from this life, History is in
mourning, Eloquence is speechless, and it is said that the
Greek and Latin Muses alike have not been able to check
their tears.

## X. Poggio (1380–1459)

Poggio[39] was from Terranova, a town under Florentine rule. In the 1
favorable climate of Rome, he so refined his talents by studying
the classics that under Eugenius IV and Nicholas V he was put in
charge of papal correspondence.[40] Certainly he equaled in distinction the best men who had devoted their loyalty and scholarly
talents to that post, a group that includes Leonardo Bruni, Maffeo
Vegio, and Giovanni Aurispa.[41]

Although sober minded in offering counsel, when it suited him 2
he was exceptional at telling funny stories. With marvelous, often-
improvised ways of provoking laughter, sometimes he would use

praetextatis verbis uteretur, modo gravibus et malignis scommati-
bus alienae famae nomen perstringeret. Sed amarulento libello in
Vallam importune invectus, ab eodem pessime audiendo cumula-
tus maledicentiae suae poenas luit, quum Valla, suo felle turgidus,
et Facium et Panhormitam et Raudensem probrosis voluminibus
iugulasset. Erat quoque Pogius adeo intemperans obiurgator ut,
quum in theatro Pompei, loco et die celebri ubi bullatorum diplo-
matum censura habebatur, Georgio Trapezuntio malediceret, ab
eo acriter duplici colapho caederetur.

3      Transtulit demum e Graeco Diodorum Siculum; sed nobiles
aliquot libellos De infelicitate principum, Varietateque fortunae et De
avaritiae peste orationesque item plures composuit tanta ingenii
foecunditate ut Facetias etiam ad excitandum hylaritatem aegris
animis expetendas conscriberet. Sed, quod gratum et utile posteris
fuit, Ciceronis libros De finibus et De legibus a se in Germania de-
scriptos in Italiam primus attulit ita ut et ei quoque Quintilianum
in salsamentarii taberna repertum debere fateamur.

4      Novissime ex multa peregrinatione Romanaque aula exactae
aetatis senex Florentiam reversus, consumato oratore ac optimo
cive dignam patriae operam praestitit, conscripta Latine Historia
populi Florentini, quae a Iacobo demum filio in Ethruscum sermonem versa legitur. Hic, iam defuncto patre, ex Pactiano scelere
strangulatus, in praetorii fenestra cum caeteris pependit.

5                               Myrtei

Olim Pierides, olim Florentia mater,
    vivente risit Pogio.
Nunc tumulum hunc adit et donum pro carmine flores
    fert proque risu lachrymas

obscenities, and sometimes he would injure another's reputation with harsh and spiteful taunts. Having rudely inveighed against Valla in an acrimonious work,[42] which the latter took in the worst possible way, he got the comeuppance for his libel: for Valla, full of venom, had already ruined Facio, Panormita, and Antonio da Rho with his abusive writings.[43] Poggio also was so unbridled in invective that during the revision of papal briefs in the area of Pompey's theater — a conspicuous place and occasion — he insulted George of Trebizond, who in return landed two good punches.[44]

Later, he translated Diodorus Siculus from the Greek.[45] But he 3 also wrote several little books (*On the Ill Fortune of Princes*, *On the Variability of Fortune*, and *On Avarice*) and many orations. His intellectual creativity was evident, too, when he wrote the *Facetiae*, which are excellent for bringing cheer to those whose spirits are low.[46] But the thing most welcomed by posterity and useful to it is that he was the first to bring into Italy Cicero's books *On the Ends of Good and Evil* and *On Laws*, which he had transcribed while in Germany; and we should also admit that we are in his debt for the Quintilian he found in the shop of a dealer in salted fish.[47]

After having traveled widely, as an old man he at last returned 4 from the Roman Curia to Florence. There, he discharged a service to the fatherland that was worthy of a consummate orator and the finest citizen: he wrote in Latin the *History of the Florentine People*, which then was translated into Tuscan by his son Iacopo.[48] After the father's death, Iacopo was strangled for having taking part in the Pazzi Conspiracy, and he and the other culprits were hanged from a window of the Bargello.

*By Mirteo*[49]                                                        5

It used to be, while Poggio was living, that the Muses and Mother Florence laughed. Now, Mother Florence visits this tomb and brings as a gift flowers instead of poetry, and tears

quae nisi pro vera sat sint pietate, rogabit
Arnus ministret ut suas.


## XI. Ambrosius Monachus

1    Ambrosius monachus ex ordine Camaldulensium, qui supra Florentiam in opacis Apennini iugis dicatam coenobio vitam severe
ducunt, doctrinae gravitate ac ingenii praestantia aequales suos
antecessit. Graece enim atque Latine doctissimus, complectente
Cosmo et mox Eugenio et Nicolao admirantibus, summum eius
ordinis honorem, qui generalis praefecturae hodie dicitur, ita
adeptus est ut eum constanti iudicio patres purpurae destinarent.

2    Dionysium enim Areopagitam *De coelesti hierarchia* divino spiritu
proloquentem singulari eloquentiae puritate Latinis expresserat,
atque item Diogenem Laërtium, verum non eadem cura limaque
perpolitum. Sed et sacris operibus bibliothecam, quae ad Angelos
spectatur, cumulate refersit; quibus existimari potest nequaquam
ei vires et facultates sed animum omnino defuisse ut ad Romanae
facundiae fastigium perveniret: abstractus enim in altitudinem
Christianae contemplationis uti pium sacratumque virum decebat,
totius vitae ocium in divinis literis consumpsit.

3    Fuit hic vir, quod raro evenit, sine oris tristitia sanctus, semper
utique suavis atque serenus; ita procul a livore contentioneque
ut, quum Vallae Pogium reconciliare conaretur, eos neque plane
literatos neque item Christianos videri diceret, qui inducta simul-
tate sacrosanctum literarum decus probrosis libellis importune

instead of laughter. Should those tears not sufficiently satisfy
true devotion, Florence will ask the Arno to furnish its own.

## XI. Ambrogio [Traversari] the Monk (1386–1439)

The monk Ambrogio,[50] a member of the order of Camaldulen-  1
sians, who lead an austere and cloistered life in the shaded ridges
of the Apennines above Florence, surpassed his contemporaries
in profundity of erudition and excellence of mind.[51] Exceedingly
learned in Greek and Latin, with the support of Cosimo and then
the admiration of Eugenius and Nicholas, he obtained the highest
office of his order,[52] today called the Priorate General, doing so in
such a way that the cardinals unwaveringly aimed at his elevation
to the purple.[53]

He translated Dionysius the Areopagite's divinely inspired *On*  2
*the Celestial Hierarchy* with remarkable purity of Latin style, and
also rendered Diogenes Laertius, albeit not with the same polish
and care.[54] He also filled the library of the cloister of Santa Maria
degli Angeli with works on religious topics. From these things one
may infer that he lacked neither the vigor nor the skills to arrive at
the summit of Roman eloquence, but just the disposition to do so.
For, carried off to the height of Christian contemplation as was
befitting a pious and venerable man, over his entire life he devoted
his leisure time to religious texts.

This man was holy without having a sad countenance (a real  3
rarity), unfailingly cheerful and serene. He was so far removed
from envy and contentiousness that when he was trying to reconcile Poggio with Valla, he said that they were not showing themselves to be either literati or Christians, inasmuch as once they had
begun their feud, they had rudely defiled the hallowed dignity of
literature with their disgraceful screeds. He departed from life at

defoedarent. Excessit e vita plane senex tumulatusque est ad Angelos, ubi hoc carmen pius vates affixit.

4 *Spinelli*

Attica mella sapis, redoles quoque nectar ubique,
  tu qui divino numine nomen habes;
quod nisi dulce canis referens mysteria divum,
  dulcius hoc certe est nectare et ambrosia.

5 *Myrtei*

Viximus ambrosia, sed enim concessimus Orco;
  nunc iterum coelo redditur ambrosia.

## XII. *Antonius Panhormita*

1 Antonius Panhormita Siculus, Bononia equestri familia natus, qui
a Pontano alumno elegantiarum pater appellatur, elate genus suum
ab ultimis Britannis Becadellaque familia Bononia celebri repetebat, praeclaro genti insignium argumento, quod isdem militari in
scuto depictis alatis viperis uteretur. Sed maiorem profecto sibi ex
laude optimorum studiorum nobilitatem comparasse videri potest.

2 Moribus enim ac literis praestantibus exornatus, quum Philippo Mediolanensium Principi fertilis ingenii industriam obtulisset, tanta liberalitate susceptus est ut principem noscendae historiae cupidum familiariter doceret, et publice octingentis annuis
aureis elegantiores literas profiteretur. Hic est ille Philippus
qui summum clementiae fructum generosis exoptatum regibus

an advanced age and is entombed at Santa Maria degli Angeli, where a pious bard affixed this poem:

### By Spinelli[55]

4

You, who have a name with divine power, taste of Attic honey and emit the scent of nectar everywhere.[56] If, when you discuss divine mysteries, you do not sing anything melodious, it is nonetheless sweeter than nectar and ambrosia.

### By Mirteo[57]

5

We lived on ambrosia, but indeed we yielded to Death. Now, ambrosia is given back to heaven.

## XII. Antonio Panormita (1394–1471)

The Sicilian Antonio Panormita,[58] born into a knightly family of 1 Bolognese origin, was called the "Father of Elegance" by his student Pontano. He used to boast that he was descended from the remotest Britons[59] and from the distinguished Beccadelli family of Bologna, the coat of arms granted his family being a clear proof, because it bore the same depictions of winged vipers on its escutcheon. But without question we can see that he won greater distinction for himself from excellence in literary studies.

Endowed with outstanding character[60] and learning, when he 2 offered the assiduity of his fertile mind to Duke Filippo of Milan, he was welcomed with such great generosity that he privately tutored the prince, who was eager to study history, and gave public lectures on elegant literature for an annual salary of 800 gold ducats. This is that Filippo who had gloriously reaped the highest fruit of clemency that noble rulers longed for, when he not only

gloriosissime decerpsit quum Alfonsum Regem, navali praelio captum, non emiserit modo sed auctum copiis ac opibus in Regnum restituerit.

3     Verum, eo gravissimis bellis occupato, Panhormita Alfonso adhesit secretioris scrinii magister et studiorum expeditionumque omnium terra marique perpetuus comes. Scripsit epistolas, candidiore stylo sed maxime iucundo, victoris regis triumphum et de factis dictisque optimi eius regis aureum libellum quem Pius Pontifex, exemplis paribus intertextis, nobiliorem reddidisse videtur. Sed cum Valla demum ad exercendum maledicentiae dentem naturae acerbitate paratissimo simultatem concepit, eo quidem eventu ut mutuis veluti confixi telis foede admodum[4] inimicis risum excitarent.

4     Senex uxorem duxit Arcellam sibi magnopere dilectam liberosque suscepit, quorum honesta soboles Neapoli visitur. Postremo aeger vitaeque diffidens, in supremo morbo hoc carmen composuit, quod tumulo inscriberetur.

5                                        *Ipsius*

Quaerite Pierides alium qui ploret amores,
    quaerite qui regum fortia facta canat.
Me pater ille ingens hominum sator atque redemptor
    evocat, et sedes donat adire pias.

6                                  *Elisii Calentii*

Qui molles elegos et regum gesta canebat
    sacra Panhormitae contegit ossa lapis.

released King Alfonso, whom he had captured in a naval battle, but also restored him to his kingdom, furnished with money and troops.[61]

But when Filippo became involved in exceedingly arduous wars, Panormita attached himself to Alfonso as his chief private secretary and as constant companion in literary studies and on campaigns on both land and sea.[62] In a rather plain yet thoroughly delightful style, he wrote letters, a "triumph" of that victorious king, and a splendid little book on the deeds and sayings of that exceptional ruler, which Pope Pius seems to have made more excellent by insertion of parallel examples.[63] But in the end he quarreled with Valla, whose acerbic temperament made him only too ready to hurl vitriolic abuse. The upshot was that, pierced through with each other's darts, in a most sordid manner they provided amusement for their enemies.[64]

As an elderly man he took a wife, Arcella, whom he loved dearly, and had children, whose noble descendants one regularly sees in Naples.[65] In the end, sickly and despairing of life, in the midst of his final illness he composed this poem, which is inscribed on his tomb:

### By Panormita Himself[66]

Seek another, o Muses, to lament loves; seek another to sing of the brave deeds of kings. That Great Father, progenitor and redeemer of humans, summons me and grants me admittance to pious realms.

### By Elisio Calenzio[67]

A sacred stone covers the bones of Panormita, who sang tender elegiacs and sang of the deeds of kings.

7

*Iani Vitalis*

Has tibi dat violas, immortalesque amaranthos
ingeniorum altrix, et Martis alumna Panhormos,
non quia torpenti Musas excire veterno,
aut regum immensas potuisti assumere curas,
verum quod Crassos inter ditesque Lucullos,
integer Antoni voluisti vivere Codrus.


## XIII. *Laurentius Valla*

1 Laurentius Valla Romanus a Gothicis temporibus usque ad patrum nostrorum memoriam praealto sepultos somno cives suos ad
nobilium literarum studium excitavit. Indignatus enim tamdiu
corrumpi saeculum leguleorum et sophistarum immani conspiratione optimasque artes inculta sermonis barbarie defoedari, *Elegantiarum* libros edidit, traditis Romanae elocutionis praeceptis ex
accurata veterum scriptorum observatione, quibus iuventus aemu-
landi studio ad detergendas corruptarum literarum sordes accen-
deretur; eam quoque illustrati patrii sermonis laudem Graecae
literae cumularunt, quum Thucydides et Herodotus, historiae parentes, ipsius liberali labore e Graecia in Latium transierint.
2   Fuit Valla ingenio maxime libero, ob idque mordaci contentio-
soque ut pote qui aliena satyrico dente facile perstringeret et lites in
literis, quasi id opus esset, adversus ignorantes acerrimas sereret.
Extant enim invectivarum et recriminationum aliquot libri erudite
salseque perscripti quibus, dum laesi nominis famam tueretur,

Palermo, the nursemaid of geniuses and nursling of Mars, gives you these violets and everlasting amaranths: not because you were able to rouse the Muses from lethargic torpor or to shoulder the immense concerns of kings, but because you, Antonio, wanted to live like upright Codrus[69] among the Crassi and the rich Luculli.

## XIII. Lorenzo Valla (1406–57)

The Roman Lorenzo Valla[70] awakened to the study of the noblest  1
literature his fellow citizens, who had been immersed in deep sleep from the time of the Goths all the way down to the memory of our fathers. Indignant that the times were long corrupted by a monstrous conspiracy of pettifogging lawyers and sophists, and that the best arts were being defiled by uncouth barbarism of language, he published *The Elegances*, which imparted the precepts of Roman style, gleaned from meticulous attention to ancient writers, in order to inflame the youth in their zeal for imitation to clean away the filth from corrupted texts.[71] Knowledge of Greek added to the fame he had gained by clarifying the ancestral tongue; for, thanks to his generous labors, Thucydides and Herodotus, the fathers of history, crossed over from Greece to Latium.[72]

By nature Valla was exceptionally outspoken, and on that ac-  2
count biting and contentious inasmuch as he readily attacked others' works with satirical spite, and (as if this were necessary) in writings he fomented exceedingly virulent quarrels against the ignorant. We have, in fact, a number of books of learned and witty invectives and recriminations in which, while striking the pose of

Facium Lygurem, Panhormitam, Pogium et Raudensem iugulasse videri potest.

3    Flagellatis quoque regionum ludi magistris, uti multa bile redundans, quod nihil in aula pontificis sibi placeret, Neapolim ad Alphonsum Regem se contulit, apud quem de avitis bellis in Hispania atque Sicilia gestis historia perscripta est, sed eo styli charactere ut eius minime videri possit qui caeteris elegantiarum praecepta tradiderit. Edidit etiam opus *De falsa donatione Constantini*, pio et sacerdotis nomen professo criminosum atque nefarium, ut pontificii imperii authoritatem Graecorum scriptorum adstipulatione confirmatam convellere niteretur.

4    Sed mox eadem inconstantia regem deseruit, vel improbante Philelpho, ut nec plane senex in patria moreretur. Sepulchrum caelato ex marmore cum effigie ac elogio Catharina mater pientissimo filio posuit, quod in Laterano (eius enim templi flamen erat) introeuntibus ad dexteram spectatur. Obiit anno Christianae salutis MCCCCLVII Calendis Augusti.

5                          *Franchini Cosentini*

Laurens Valla iacet Romanae gloria linguae;
   primus enim docuit qua decet arte loqui.


## XIV. Flavius Blondus

1   E Foro Livii viae Aemiliae nota urbe Flavius Blondus prodiit, rudi adhuc veteris elegantiae saeculo. Is magno ausu singularique in-

the wounded party, he can be seen to have destroyed Facio the Ligurian, Panormita, Poggio, and Antonio da Rho.[73]

After he had scourged all the local Roman schoolteachers, when 3 he was overflowing with abundant gall, seemingly because nothing in the papal curia pleased him, he betook himself to King Alfonso in Naples, in whose court he penned a history of the dynastic wars waged in Spain and Sicily—but in a style of writing that might not in the least appear that of someone who had conveyed the precepts of elegance to others.[74] He also published *Concerning the False Donation of Constantine*, a work vituperative and abominable for a pious man who had entered the priesthood, since it strove to overthrow the authority of pontifical rule that had been sanctioned by the confirmation of Greek writers.[75]

But soon, with like fickleness, he deserted the king, to the dis- 4 approval even of Filelfo, and then died in his fatherland before he was yet old. His mother Catarina put up a tomb with a likeness carved from marble and a eulogy to her most dutiful son, which is visible on the right to those entering the Lateran (for he was a canon of that church). He died on the first of August in the 1,457th year of Christian salvation.

*By Franchino da Cosenza*[76] 5

[Here] lies Lorenzo Valla, glory of the Roman tongue. Indeed, he was the first to teach the art of speaking properly.

## XIV. Flavio Biondo (1392–1463)

Flavio Biondo[77] came from Forlì, a famous city on the Emilian 1 Road, in an era that until then was unsophisticated in the ancient elegance of language. With great daring and remarkable diligence,

dustria, nec infelici eventu, multorum annorum intermorientes res gestas e tenebris excitare orsus *Decadas* conscripsit, quibus ab inclinante Romano imperio, funesta tempora, ac ideo veritatis lumine orbata, in lucem proferuntur. De vetustate quoque collapsae Urbis ac eius demum resurgentis dignitate, erudito operosoque volumine publicato, quantam nec ambitiose quaesitam exoptarit in literis authoritatem adeptus est. Unde ei honestae opes favore pontificum accessere.

2     Liberis operam dare, quam sacris initiari maluit suscepitque Gasparem filium, quem uxor Margania Romani sanguinis nobilitasse visa est. Sed posteri, quanquam adauctis fortunis, conditori familiae minime responderunt.

3     Fato functus est septuagenarius tumulatusque in Capitolio extra limen templi Deiparae Virginis (id enim Iovis Tonantis olim fuisse putamus) quod non secus ac antiquitus, authore Tacito, centum gradibus adeatur.

4                           *Iani Vitalis*

Eruis e tenebris Romam dum, Blonde, sepultam,
    es novus ingenio Romulus atque Remus:
Illi Urbem struxere rudem, celeberrima surgit
    haec eadem studiis ingeniose tuis:
Barbarus illam hostis ruituram evertit, at isti
    nulla unquam poterunt tempora obesse tuae.
Iure triumphalis tibi facta est Roma sepulchrum,
    illi ut tu vivas, vivat ut illa tibi.

and an outcome by no means unsuccessful, he wrote the *Decades*, undertaken to bring out of the shadows the fading history of many years; by this work, the times since the decline of Roman authority—which were calamitous and for that reason deprived of the torch of truth—are brought forth into the light.[78] Once he had published a learned and painstaking book about Rome's ancient dignity, which had fallen and at last was rising up again, he acquired the literary standing he had longed for but not ambitiously pursued.[79] From this he gained honorable wealth from the favor of popes.

He preferred to have children rather than to take holy orders, 2 and he supported his son Gasparo, whom his wife Margania, of Roman blood, seems through that heritage to have ennobled. But his descendants, despite their increased fortunes, were not in the least worthy of the founder of the family.

He died at 70 and was entombed on the Campidoglio outside 3 the entrance to the Church of the Virgin Mother of God (we think, in fact, that it used to be the temple of Thundering Jupiter), which is approached by one hundred steps, just as it was in antiquity, according to Tacitus.[80]

*By Giano Vitale*[81]                                                              4

Since you bring long-buried Rome out of darkness, Biondo, your talent has made you a new Romulus and Remus. Those men built a primitive city, but by your literary pursuits, o gifted one, that same city emerges as spectacularly famous. A barbarian host destroyed that Rome, which was destined to fall, but no age could ever harm yours. Rightly, triumphant Rome has been made your tomb, so that you may live on thanks to it, just as it lives on thanks to you.

## XV. Petrus Candidus December

1 Candidus December e Viglebano urbe quae est inter Padum et
Ticinum, Laurentii Vallae testimonio exactissimae censurae grammaticus, Mediolani Graece Latineque docuit praestanti eruditionis
ac eloquentiae fama. Eius extat Appianus Alexandrinus e Graeco
in Latinum versus, id expetente Alphonso Rege, qui studiosissi-
mum quemque eius aetatis, ut ad locupletandam Latinam linguam
occultos Graeciae thesauros proferrent, liberaliter invitarat. Sed
manci passimque corrupti exemplaris Graeci vitio, vel laboriosus
interpres in eo opere sese candidum praestare non potuit, quum
alia multo felicius perscripserit.

2 In *Vita* enim Philippi Vicecomitis quae circumfertur, Sueto-
nium lepide admodum aemulatus, ita quod proposuerat, expressit
ut, aliquanto inverecundius quam scriptorem odio vacuum deceret,
stylum exercuisse iudicetur: quum vitia hominis occulta, nec ulli
magis quam ipsius pudori nocentia ob idque velanda prorsus, cupide nimis maligneque detexerit; in eo praesertim principe in quo
singularis illa divinaeque simillima clementiae laus, cum probro
multorum regum gloriose refulsit.

3 Fato functus est octogenarius senex Mediolani, non mediocribus[5] fortunis a Francisco Sfortia decenter honestatus meruitque
marmoreum sepulchrum cum effigie e suggestu iuventutem docen-
tis, quod in vestibulo Ambrosianae basilicae ad levam introeuntibus[6] occurrit; hoc rudi carmine inscripto, quod respondente
rhythmo non minus inepte quam ridicule clauditur.

## XV. *Pier Candido Decembrio (1399–1477)*

Candido Decembrio[82] of Vigevano, a city between the Po River   1
and Pavia, was in Lorenzo Valla's estimation a scholar of the most
exacting judgment. He taught Greek and Latin in Milan, where he
had a reputation for outstanding erudition and eloquence. We
have his Appian of Alexandria, translated from Greek into Latin
at the request of King Alfonso, who had invited to his court on
generous terms all the most learned men of his time that they
might publish the hidden treasures of Greece so as to enrich the
Latin language.[83] But since the Greek exemplar was defective and
corrupted here and there, even the industrious translator could not
achieve lucidity, although he was far more successful in other compositions.

In the *Life* of Filippo Visconti now in circulation, having wittily   2
imitated Suetonius, he expressed what he had in mind in such a
way that he is judged to have wielded his pen somewhat more
shamelessly than befits a writer without an ax to grind: for, with
excessive eagerness and spite, he exposed the man's hidden vices,
which were more harmful to his own honor than anything else,
and for that reason should have been concealed.[84] This is especially true for a prince whose reputation for a nearly divine clemency was singularly radiant when set alongside the ignominy of
many kings.

He died in Milan, an old man of eighty, fittingly having been   3
honored by Francesco Sforza with no small fortune; and he merited a marble tomb with a statue of him teaching the youth from a
dais. Those entering the vestibule of the Basilica of Sant'Ambrogio
can see it on the left, inscribed with this graceless poem, as inept
as it is ridiculous in its rhyming couplets:[85]

4    Scandere sydereas virtus si novit ad oras,
Candidus astra tenet in templo numen adorans:
pontifici summo, regi populoque ducique
hic Ligurum secreta dedit laudatus ubique:
miles eloquio clarus Graiisque camoenis
instructus, Latium studiis ornavit amoenis.
Mundanis fessus curis et in aethere pulchro
elatus gelido linquit sua membra sepulchro.

## XVI. Donatus Acciaiolus

1  Donatus Acciaiolus antiquae stirpis Florentinus, quum exortis
florentibus ingeniis de doctrinae laude certaretur, in utraque lingua generose admodum sese exercuit, ut ex *Moralibus* Aristotelis
luculenter apparet, quibus erudita et pereleganti commentatione
magnum lumen attulisse iudicatur, explosis scilicet sophistarum
interpretum ineptiis, quum, Eustratii Graeci placita secutus, certiore utique vestigio niteretur. Vertit etiam in Latinum e Plutarcho
clarorum heroum aliquot vitas longe omnium elegantissime.
Verum aliquanto nobilior evasit, quum Carolum cognomento
Magnum tanquam alterum Florentiae patriae conditorem Latino
libro celebrasset.

2    Sed vir consilio gravis, ac ob id obeundis Reipublicae muneribus occupatus, neque satis ocii ad studia literarum furari, neque
aetatem quod tenuissima valetudine uteretur longissime proferre,
potuit. Fato enim functus est Mediolani, quum legatus in Galliam
ulteriorem iter haberet ut inde implorata ope civitatem pontificiis
armis vexatam periculo liberaret. Nihil enim remisso odio Xystus,
post vindicatum Pactianae coniurationis facinus, Laurentium

If virtue knows how to ascend to the heavenly shores, Can-  4
dido possesses the stars, adoring God in the Church. Praised
everywhere, this man gave the secrets of the Ligurians to the
Supreme Pontiff, the king, the commander, and the popu-
lace. A soldier famous for eloquence and skilled in Greek
poetry, he adorned Latium with charming literary works.
Worn out by worldly cares and raised high in the beautiful
ether, he leaves his body to the icy tomb.

## XVI. Donato Acciaiuoli (1429–78)

When Donato Acciaiuoli,[86] a Florentine of an ancient lineage, was  1
competing for scholarly praise among the new generation of flourishing talents, he acquitted himself excellently in both Latin and
Greek, as is splendidly clear from Aristotle's *Ethics*: he is judged to
have shed much light on this work through his erudite and elegant
analysis, once he had cast out the infelicities of sophistical inter-
preters;[87] and, by following the tenets of the Greek commentator
Eustratius,[88] he moved ahead on a highly reliable path. He also
translated into Latin more eloquently than anyone else some lives
of famous heroes from Plutarch.[89] But he gained a greater reputation when, in a Latin book, he had celebrated Charlemagne as
another founder of his native Florence.[90]

Authoritative in counsel, and on that account preoccupied with  2
attending to affairs of state, he was able neither to steal enough
leisure time for the study of literature nor, because his health was
very feeble, to grow old. He died in Milan while on his way to
France as a legate tasked with seeking assistance in freeing from
danger a city under attack from papal armies.[91] For Sixtus, his
hatred undiminished after the crime of the Pazzi Conspiracy had
been avenged, was vehemently assailing Lorenzo de' Medici, who

Medicem, ex ea iniuria firmiore dominatu potitum, vehementissime persequebatur. Donati ossa ad vetustum gentis sepulchrum
Florentiam relata id Carthusiano in templo, hoc epigrammate inscripto legentibus indicatur.

3                              *[Politiani]*

Donatus nomen, patria est Florentia, gens mi
    Acciaiola domus, clarus eram eloquio.
Francorum ad regem, patriae dum orator abirem,
    in ducis anguigeri moenibus occubui,
sic vitam impendi patriae, quae me inde relatum
    inter maiorum nunc cineres sepelit.


## XVII. Philelphus

1  Tolentinates in publica decurionum domo Francisci Philelphi civis
effigiem cum equestris ordinis baltheo laureatam peregrinis hospitibus ostendunt adservantque etiam regii, diplomatis membranam
ad collatae dignitatis argumentum. Is Graecarum literarum amore
flagranter incensus, ut de Caballino fonte potaret, Parnasum
montem petivit in Athenarumque ruinis immortalium philosophorum vestigia pedibus calcavit. Porro inde Byzantium profectus
Emanuelis Chrysolorae filiam uxorem duxit, quae Graecae elocutionis magistra quotidiano usu Atticorum accentuum inepto sed
docili coniugis ori dulcedinem instillaret.

2      Reversum inde et Graece pariter ac Latine passim orantem Italiae principes admiranter exceperunt. Suscepto enim legationis

on account of that outrage had acquired firmer political control. Donato's remains were brought back to his family's ancient tomb in the Carthusian church in Florence.[92] With this engraved epigraph, the tomb proclaims:

[By Poliziano][93]    3

My name is Donato; my homeland, Florence; my lineage, the house of Acciaiuoli. I was famous for eloquence. While in transit as a legate to the king of France, I died in the castle of the duke of the serpent.[94] Thus I devoted my life to the fatherland which, in turn, has brought me back from that place and interred me among the ashes of my ancestors.

## XVII. Filelfo (1398–1481)

In their town hall the Tolentines display to foreign guests the    1
statue of a citizen, Francesco Filelfo,[95] crowned with a laurel and wearing the ornamental band of the equestrian order; and they even preserve a royal commendation on parchment as evidence of the bestowal of that dignity. Ardently inflamed with love of Greek literature, Filelfo headed for Mount Parnassus in order to drink from Hippocrene,[96] and among the ruins of Athens he trod in the footsteps of the immortal philosophers. Having next proceeded to Byzantium, he married Manuel Chrysoloras's daughter, a teacher of Greek rhetoric, who by daily practice poured the sweetness of Attic accents into the unprepared but receptive mouth of her husband.

Upon his return Italian princes admiringly received him, as he    2
was everywhere entreating them in Greek as well as in Latin: for, having taken on ambassadorial duties for the emperor Paleologus

munere Palaeologi Imperatoris Constantinopolitani Turcarum infesta arma aegre sustinentis, preces afferens, opem implorabat. Favere ei ante alios Eugenius Pontifex, Rex Alphonsus et, qui singularem iustitiae et bellicae virtutis coronam eo saeculo promeruit, Franciscus Sfortia, ab eo Heroico poemate celebratus.

3      Ingenio enim in studiis aestuante vario ambitioso, quum neminem sibi exaequari literaria laude pateretur, plura quam quisquam alius in omni dicendi genere volumina publicavit profitendoque singulis in urbibus eruditae iuventutis academias excitavit; nullam spem nobilioris gloriae Latinis aemulis de Romana facundia, nullam denique de Graeca, vel ipsis Graecis relicturus, nisi tantus eloquentiae fluvius, uti nullis moderati iudicii ripis castigatus, nimis late exundans et, mutato saepe alveo, turbulentus et incertus, dum sese diducit et abscedit in paludes, perspicui profluentis[7] dignitatem amisisset. Inter Graeca opera Latinitate donata, Xenophontis *Paedia Cyri* et ex Plutarcho aliquot heroum vitae et demum Hippocrates, non ita probantur a Graecis quam a Latinis perleguntur.

4      Vixit ad exactam aetatem nonagenario proximus periitque Bononiae adeo dissipatis rei domesticae copiis ut ad efferendum funus et cubiculi et coquinae instrumenta venierint. Et Marius filius egregie doctus paternae potius virtutis quam multae substantiae haeres relinqueretur. Sed in familia eruditae victoriae trophaeum permansit, nobili exceptum risu, quum Timotheo Graeculo, de vi syllabae contendenti victoque barbam ex pactione inexorabili superbia derasisset, uti lepide Myrteus his carminibus expressit.

at Constantinople, who was barely holding out against an attacking Turkish army, Filelfo, conveying his entreaties, implored their help. His foremost supporters were Pope Eugenius, King Alfonso, and Francesco Sforza, a man exceptional in that era for his justice and military prowess, whom he celebrated in an epic poem.[97]

As his multifaceted and ambitious mind was boiling over with zeal for learning, since he would not allow anyone to be viewed as his peer in literary reputation, he published more books in every genre of writing than did anyone else; and he inspired academies of learned youth in every single city where he lectured.[98] He would have left his Latin rivals no hope of surpassing him in Roman eloquence, nor even the Greeks themselves of outdoing him in Greek eloquence, had not so great a stream of eloquence, as it was confined by no banks of moderating judgment, overflowed too far, turbulent and unpredictable, its course often having shifted, so that while it ramified and ran off into swamps, it lost its distinction of flowing forth crystal clear. Among the Greek works he rendered in Latin were Xenophon's *Cyropaedia*, a number of Plutarch's *Lives* of heroes, and finally Hippocrates.[99] These were not so much commended by the Greeks as they were studied by Latin speakers.

He lived to be nearly ninety and died at Bologna, having so dissipated his wealth that the bedroom and kitchen furniture had to be sold to cover the funeral expenses.[100] Thus his outstandingly learned son Mario was heir to his father's prowess rather than to much of an estate. But there did remain in the family a trophy of a learned victory, won in a noble jest when, after beating the paltry Greek Timothy in a debate over the accent of a syllable, according to the terms of their agreement, he insisted upon shaving off Timothy's beard, as Mirteo wittily put it in these verses:

3

4

5 *Myrtei*

Nunquid sat tibi non fuit, Philelphe,
linguae gloria nobilis Latinae,
ni Graecas quoque pervagatus urbes
dignus coniuge nuptiisque Graecis
ferres Timothei novum triumphum?
Cui, dum una super ille dictione
tecum pignore certat atque barbam
abradi sibi ferre pollicetur
victus, aut positam pecuniam abs te
victor auferat. Abnegasti eadem
barbam posse pecunia obtinere
victor: atque novacula expedita
barbam illius habere maluisti:
Iam nunc non Italae Philelphe, sed sis
Graecae gloria nobilis palestrae.


## XVIII. *Nicolaus Perottus*

1 Sentinum Umbriae oppidum, cui hodie Saxoferrato nomen est,
Bartholo iureconsulto nobile, secundam a Nicolao Perotto claritatem accepit. Huic quum deessent opes, corporis vires, municipali
frugalitate atque duricia constitutae, perpetuis lucubrationum vigiliis minime defuerunt. Iuvenis in ludo pueros honestos docuit
tanto concursu ut mox Latinae linguae rudimenta utili compendio
ad normam digesta ob idque facile pueris perdiscenda publicarit.

2 Exinde Romae Graecas literas pertinaci studio consectatus fre-
tusque Bessarione generoso Mecoenate, adeo exacte feliciterque

Can it be that the noble glory of the Latin language was not enough for you, Filelfo, unless, having wandered through Greek cities and been worthy of taking a Greek bride, you should also win a new kind of triumph from Timothy? For he made a bet with you about one inflection and promised that, were he to be defeated, he would let his beard be shaved; or, as victor, he would collect from you the money you had staked. You, as the victor, would not allow him to keep the beard by paying the same amount and, with razor ready to hand, preferred to have his beard. Now indeed, Filelfo, you should be the noble glory not of the Italian rhetorical school, but of the Greek one.

## XVIII. Niccolò Perotti (1430–80)

The Umbrian town Sentinum, today called Sassoferrato, has acquired distinction first from the noble jurist Bartolus, and second, from Niccolò Perotti.[102] Although Perotti had lacked financial resources, the physical strength developed through provincial thrift and austerity did not fail him in his incessant studying late into the night. As a young man, he taught wellborn schoolboys and became so popular that soon he published a useful primer on the basics of Latin, set in systematic order and on that account easily memorized by the boys.[103]

Next, at Rome, having mastered Greek literature through assiduous study and relying upon a generous Maecenas, Bessarion,

profecit ut ab eo Polybius gravissimus historiarum scriptor Latinitati donaretur. Non defuere tamen ex aemulis qui eius auctoris traductionem antiquissimam fuisse furtoque surreptam existimarint, quod Thucydidem Diodorum Plutarchum et Appianum clarissimo ingeniorum certamine conversos, unus Polybius egregia fide Latinus aequabili et praedulci Romani sermonis puritate prorsus antecedat.

3      Composuit quoque volumen commentarii nomine in Martialem, *Cornucopiae* usurpato vetere Graeco lemmate nuncupatum, perutile quidem ac ob id fortasse sempiternum. Sed austero pudore suppressit editionem, quod humili et parum pudico opere quaesita laus dignitati minime responderet: partis enim opibus, archiepiscopatum Sipontinum adsecutus, seipso maior Perusiam Umbriamque regebat.

4      Excessit e vita senex apud Sentinum in villa viridariis et fontibus peramoena quam a pingui ocio Fugicuram appelavit.


5                                    *Myrtei*

In Villa Fugicura obit Perottus.
O villam nimis, et nimis beatam,
quae viventis heri levare curas
posset, nunc cineres tenet sepulti.
O villam domino beatiorem,
cui curas moriens reliquit omnes.

he advanced so far in precision and felicity of style that he could translate Polybius, a most eminent writer of histories, into Latin.[104] Among his rivals, however, there were those who supposed the translation of that author was an ancient one that he had made off with on the sly, since in its outstanding faithfulness and its uniform and sweet purity of Roman eloquence, the Latin Polybius alone had far surpassed the Thucydides, Diodorus, Plutarch, and Appian that had been translated in a celebrated contest of minds.

He also composed a volume of commentary on Martial called 3 *Cornucopiae* (evoking an old Greek title): a most useful work, and indeed on that account it may live on forever.[105] But with an austere bashfulness, he withheld it from publication, supposing that praise sought by a base and insufficiently chaste work did not in the least correspond to his dignity. And in fact, once he had grown wealthy and had obtained the archbishopric of Manfredonia, he outdid himself as governor of Perugia and Umbria.[106]

Having grown old, he exited this life at Sassoferato in a most 4 delightful villa with groves and fountains, which he called "Fugicura" after the ample leisure he enjoyed there.

*By Mirteo*[107]  5

Perotti died in the Villa Fugicura. O that too-fortunate, all-too-fortunate villa, which yesterday could have lightened the cares of a living master, but now holds the ashes of a dead one. O villa more fortunate than its owner, who in death left all his cares to you.

## XIX. Platina

1 Sacrati praesertim ordinis bonique mortales plurimum Platinae manibus debent, quando eius ingenuo labore ad exoptatam obscuri saeculi nec ideo perituram lucem pontificii principatus actionum incorrupta veritas nunciatur: quae procul eloquentiae illecebris, uti pura et incompta fidem praefert, et caeteris elaboratis operibus auget dignitatem. Neque enim vel dialogi *De vero bono*, *Veraque nobilitate*, et *De optimo cive* graviter conscripti, vel honestae voluptatis documenta scite tradita diu superessent, nisi vivacis historiae lateribus adfixa felici societate succederent et communi (quanquam impari) perennis vitae spiritu fruerentur.

2 Is plane egens et obscurus unoque tantum ingenio nobilis, Cremona Calixto Pontifice in Urbem venit. Cognitum Pius atque Bessarion erudito iudicio sacerdotiis minoribus exornarunt. Paulus vero Pontifex perinique maligneque delatum immaniter torsit. Xystus demum conditae ab se in Vaticano Bibliothecae praefecit, quum eo munere longe dignissimus haberetur.

3 In ea nobili custodia iam senex Fato functus est, Quirinalem domum cum laureto ad coronandos poetas Pomponio relinquens. Funus in Exquilias ad Mariae Maioris templum usque perductum est, flebili carmine celebrantibus poetis. Sepulchro autem, quod a leva ad tertiam columnam conspicitur, hoc epitaphium ab alumno Demetrio inscribi iussit, quum et haec quoque carmina amici lugentes affixissent:

## XIX. Platina (1421–81)

Men who are good, and especially those in religious orders, owe an 1
immense debt to the writings of Platina,[108] since by his noble labor the unvarnished truth about papal rule is brought to the light
that was longed for in a dark age, and on that account will live
on.[109] Free of any alluring rhetoric, this pure and unadorned truth
instead values credibility, and amplifies the dignity of his other,
more highly wrought works. Indeed, neither the earnestly written
dialogues *On the True Good*, *On True Nobility*, and *On the Best Citizen*, nor the cleverly related examples of honorable pleasure, would
have survived for long had it not been the case that, set alongside
the enduring history, they succeeded through a fortunate association with it, and benefited from the shared (if unequal) breath of
everlasting life.[110]

He came from Cremona to Rome utterly destitute and un- 2
known, noble only in his brilliance, during the pontificate of Ca-
lixtus.[111] Once acquainted with him, Pope Pius and Bessarion in
their learned judgment set him up in a minor clerical position.[112]
But then, after he'd been denounced utterly unjustly and spitefully,
Pope Paul savagely tortured him.[113] At last, Sixtus made him prefect of the library the pope had founded in the Vatican, since Platina was held to be the worthiest by far of that office.[114]

Already elderly, he died while holding that noble post, be- 3
queathing to Pomponio his house on the Quirinal along with the
laurel grove where poets were crowned. While poets commemorated him with elegies, the funeral procession arrived at the Basilica of Santa Maria Maggiore on the Esquiline.[115] On his tomb,
which one sees at the third column on the left, he instructed his
student Demetrio to inscribe this epitaph once his grieving friends,
too, had affixed their poems:[116]

Quisquis es (si pius), Platinam
et suos ne vexes; anguste
iacent et soli volunt esse.

4                    *Prosperi Spiritei*

Qui res pontificum sacras et gesta piorum
    quique ducum vitas nobile fecit opus,[8]
vivit adhuc Platina: et quanquam concesserit Orco,
    nil tamen in vatem Parca severa potest.

## XX. Iacobus Cardinalis Papiensis

1 Fuit hic vir inter sacrati ordinis senatores pari virtutis atque fortunae munere lectissimus. Erat enim cum optimarum literarum
studio et vigilantis ingenii fertilitate, tum animi iudicio styloque et
perspicuis moribus Pio Secundo persimilis, a quo adoptatus in
familiae nomen et ad purpurae decus evectus est.

2      Extant *Commentarii* gravissimarum actionum atque epistolae,
quibus senatoriae prudentiae potius et Christianae severitatis nomen quam perfectae orationis laudem petisse videri potest, quod
in cursu honorum maximis obeundis muneribus occupatus splen-
didum illud antea conceptum illustris eloquentiae lumen festinato
et pene praecipiti, uti necessitas ferebat, scribendi genere vehementer infuscarit.

3      Verum ea rudis adhuc saeculi ingenia facile summa ac admiranda censebantur, quae hodie, tanquam expergefactis censoribus,
vix in infimis literarii theatri gradibus sedem inveniunt. Sed

Whoever you are (if you are pious), may you not disturb
Platina and his kin. They lie in cramped quarters and want
to be alone.

By Prospero Spiriteo[117]                                                    4

Platina lives on, who made the sacred history of the popes,
the deeds of the pious, and the lives of commanders a noble
undertaking;[118] and although he yielded to death, nonetheless, stern Fate can do nothing against the bard.

## XX. Cardinal Jacopo [Ammannati] of Pavia[119] (1422–79)

Endowed equally with virtue and success, this man was the most    1
excellent of the senators of the sacred college.[120] Indeed, both in
zeal for the best literature and the fertility and quickness of an
alert mind as well as in inward resolve, writing style, and conspicuous good character, he was very like Pius II, by whom he was adopted into the Piccolomini family and exalted to the distinction of
the purple.

We have his *Commentaries*, concerning the most important pol-    2
icy decisions, and his letters. From these he may be seen to have
sought renown for senatorial prudence and Christian strictness,
rather than praise for perfect eloquence: for, busy assuming the
most demanding duties as he rose through the ranks, because of
the hurried and almost headlong manner of writing that was demanded, he cast a dark cloud over that splendid radiance of illustrious eloquence that he'd previously developed.

But in an era that was still unpolished, those talents were    3
judged easily the most lofty and admirable which today, now that
the critics have been awakened, hardly find a seat on the humblest
tiers of the literary stage. Perhaps satisfied with popular approval,

fortasse populari commendatione contentus, eam absolute scribendi gloriam uti levem et a doctissimis tantum ideoque paucissi-
mis intellectam sprevit ut ingenio ad sacrarum literarum studia
revocato, illam quam Dii superi dederant personae dignitatem religiose tueretur. His enim moribus sibi iter sternebat ad ipsum
rerum fastigium sed illudente Fortuna in summo fere deceptus
haesit, quum Fata potiorem ei viam ad coelum permunirent.

4    Periit enim non adhuc senex in secessu ad Cryptas Laurentia-
nas Vulsiniensis lacus, a circumforaneo medico miserabiliter ene-
catus, quum vir in omni negocio praeterquam in tuendae sanitatis
ratione prudentissimus ut quartanae febris tedium discuteret, im-
mite veratrum stulta propinatum manu, fato coactus ebibisset.

5    Scripserat antea ingenuae piaeque liberalitatis testamentum, sed
id Xystus Pontifex irritum fecit, quod pecunia satis grandis apud
mensarios occulte deposita tanquam frugi atque opes contemnentis censu amplior aestimatione publica videretur. Epigramma tamen ex eodem testamento in fiscum non venit, haeredibus utique
relictum, ut hoc modo marmoreae sepulchri tabulae inscriberetur.

6                              *Ipsius*

Luca ortu, Sena lege fuit mihi patria; nomen
    dum vixi Iacobus, mens bona pro genere.
Papa Pius sedem Papiensem detulit, idem
    cardineo ornavit munere, gente, domo;
quem colui vivens, non linquo mortuus; hic sum
    et prope sancta patris filius ossa cubo.
Vivite qui legitis, coelestia quaerite; nostra haec
    in cineres tandem gloria tota redit.

however, he despised the glory of finely wrought prose as inconsequential and as recognized only by the learned (and so, by just a few), so that once he had redirected his talents back to the studies of sacred texts, he reverently protected the dignity of a role that the gods above had given him. For by this practice he would smooth his way to the heights of worldly dignity. But, cheated by mocking Fortune, he was halted when almost at the top, since the Fates were laying down for him a better road to heaven.

He was not yet an old man when he died in seclusion, in San     4
Lorenzo alle Grotte on Lake Bolsena, wretchedly done in by an itinerant doctor.[121] For, in order to lessen exhaustion from a quartan fever, he who was highly skilled in all matters except in the ways to preserve health had by a foolish hand been given harsh hellebore to drink. As Fate willed, he downed it.

Earlier, he had written a will of noble and pious generosity, but     5
Pope Sixtus rendered it void because the substantial sum, secretly deposited with bankers, might appear to the public to exceed the means of a man who despised possessions and money. But the epitaph from that same will did not go to the exchequer: it, at least, was left to his heirs to be inscribed thus on the panel of his marble tomb:

*By the Man Himself*[122]     6

Lucca was my birthplace, but by law Siena was my fatherland. My name Jacopo while I lived, I had a good mind instead of a noble lineage. Pope Pius conferred upon me the bishopric of Pavia, and likewise adorned me with the rank of cardinal, and furnished me a place in his family and household. The man I cherished in life, I desert not in death. Here I am; and I, the son, rest near the holy bones of my father. Live well, you who read this; seek the heavens! In the end, this entire earthly glory of ours reverts to ashes.

## XXI. *Domitius Calderinus*

1 Calderia, Veronensis agri oppidum calidis aquis nobile, Domitium protulit; eum acri flagrantique ingenio ad gloriam anhelantem Bessarion Cardinalis excepit et extulit. Exinde, quum Romae profiteretur et obscura sensa duriorum poetarum admirabili reconditae lectionis testimonio dilucidasset, literarii splendoris assertor ac omnis obscuritatis illustrator acclamatus est.

2 Verum editis interpretationum commentariis, peracerbas, sed iuventuti maxime utiles, cum aemulis simultates exercuit ambitioso quidem et nimis aculeato dicendi genere, ex aliena inscitia (dum intemperanter perstringit atque remordet) nomen quaerens. Eo modo, aetate laudeque florentem sed imbecilli stomachi temperaturam nimiis lucubrationibus exterentem, quum digna multis saeculis opera conciperet, rapida febris eripuit.

3 Celebrante funus Academia, nobilis iuventus cum lachrymis vestem mutavit; mortem vero vel aemuli et principatum affectantis Politianus his carminibus prosecutus est:

*Politiani*

Hunc Domiti siccis tumulum qui transit ocellis
    vel Phoebi ignarus, vel male gratus homo est.
Intulit hic vatum coecis pia lumina chartis,
    obstrusum ad Musas hic patefecit iter.
Hunc Verona tulit, docti patria illa Catulli;
    huic letum[9] atque urnam Roma dedit iuveni.

## XXI. Domizio Calderini (1446–78)

Calderia, a town in Veronese territory noted for its hot springs, 1
brought forth Domizio.[123] As he was eagerly pursuing glory with a
keen and ardent mind, Cardinal Bessarion took him up and promoted him. Then, when he was lecturing at Rome and, in a remarkable demonstration of his recondite reading, had vividly
brought to light the hidden meanings of the more difficult poets,
he was hailed as the restorer of literary splendor and as the eluci-
dator of every obscurity.[124]

Once his expository treatises had been published, however, he 2
engaged in quarrels with rivals that were exceedingly bitter, albeit
highly useful to him at his youthful time of life, having, indeed,
an ostentatious and excessively barbed manner of speaking that
sought renown from others' ignorance while unrestrainedly slight-
ing and harrying them.[125] As in this way he enjoyed his youth and
honors but wore out the constitution of a weak stomach by excessive labor into the night, a fast-acting fever carried him off just as
he was undertaking works worthy to last many centuries.

When the Roman Academy was performing the funeral rites, 3
the noble youth in mourning attire wept, and Poliziano honored
the death and preeminence of even a rival with these touching
poems:

### By Poliziano[126]

Whoever passes by this tomb of Domizio with dry eyes is
either unacquainted with Apollo or an ingrate. This man
cast conscientious eyes on the recondite poems of bards; he
opened a previously hidden path to the Muses. Verona, that
fatherland of learned Catullus, gave him life; but when he
was a young man, Rome gave him death and a final resting
place.

4                              *Eiusdem scazon*

Asta, viator: pulverem vides sacrum,
quem verticosi turbat unda Benaci;
hoc mutat ipsum saepe Musa Libethron
fontemque Sisyphi ac vireta Permessi,
quippe hoc Domitius vagiit solo primum:
ille, ille doctus, ille quem probe nosti
dictata dantem Romulae iuventuti
mira eruentem sensa de penu vatum.
Abi, viator: sat oculis tuis debes.

## XXII. Antonius Campanus

1 Quis in praepinguis simiae rictu tantam excelsi atque habilis ingenii indolem? Quis in sordida stirpe tantam fortunam non miretur?
Antonium enim Campanum rustica mulier in agro fessa opere sub
lauro peperit et aluit; puerum argute loquacem aedituo sacerdoti
in famulatum et disciplinam tradidit. Ita feliciter perceptis literarum rudimentis, Neapoli mox paedagogus erudiendo nobili puero
mercede quaesitus est. Tantos autem in studiis Latinis quinquen-
nio processus fecit ut inde Perusiam transierit, scilicet ut in praeclara frequentis gymnasii luce profitendo illustri famae limen aperiret.

2 Nec multo post, a Perusinis civitate donatus, Pii Secundi Pontificis gratiam studiorum similitudine promeruit, a quo virtutis
honore Interamnatium praesul est creatus, et a Paulo successore
locupletatus. Sed postremo, eum Xystus immodice Tiphernatium

*A Scazon by the Same Poet*[127]     4

Pause for a moment, traveler: you look upon the sacred sand
that the waves of turbulent Lake Garda stir about. Often,
the Muse leaves Libethron, the fountain of Sisyphus, and
the verdant soils of Permessus for this place.[128] For on this
soil Domizio uttered his first cries: that learned Domizio
whom you know well, as he was giving lessons to the Roman
youth, unearthing wondrous thoughts from the storeroom of
the bards. Depart, traveler: you owe enough to your eyes.

## XXII. *Antonio Campano* (1429–77)

Who would not marvel at so great a natural endowment of lofty     1
and nimble genius in the gaping mouth of a fat monkey? Who
would not look in wonder upon so great a success in a base lineage? For a peasant woman, worn out by agricultural labor, bore
Antonio Campano[129] and nursed him under a laurel tree. She entrusted her talkative and clever son to the service and training of a
parish priest. So successfully had he learned the basics of literature
that he was soon sought out as a paid tutor for a noble boy in
Naples. And in fact, he made such great progress in Latin studies
over the following five years that he then moved to Perugia, evidently in order to open the door to illustrious fame by teaching in
the splendid daylight of a crowded university.[130]

Very soon, after he had been awarded Perugian citizenship, he     2
won the favor of Pope Pius II on account of the similarity of their
learned pursuits. The pope created him Bishop of Teramo thanks
to the esteem in which his virtue was held; and he was enriched by
Pius's successor, Paul.[131] But in the end, although his estimable

tyrannis faventem, quum multis urbibus integra nominis authoritate praefuisset, in exilium egit.

3    Fato functus est apud Senas a Pii memoria sibi gratissimas, invidente non plane seni longiorem vitam comitiali morbo. Inter multa orationum et multiplicis styli opera quae extant, avidissime Bracii incliti ducis vita perlegitur: digna posteritate, nisi rerum gestarum fidem adulatione poetica corrupisset.

4                          *Platinae*

Campanus iacet hic humili contectus in urna,
    qui vaga, dum vixit, sydera transiliit.
Historicus scripsit dixit cecinitque nec alter
    philosophus toto clarior in Latio.
Nil maius natura tulit: miracula coeli
    huius in ingenio cuncta stetere viri.
Deserto lugent Parnasi fonte sorores,
    et tumulus refugas lucis hic unus habet.
Vos quibus ingenium est: en quo contendimus omnes.
    Virtutis sola est gloria quae superest.

5                          *Politiani*

Ille ego laurigeros cui cinxit et infula crines,
    Campanus, Romae delitium, hic iaceo.
Mi ioca dictarunt Charites; nigro sale Momus,
    Mercurius niveo, tinxit utroque Venus.
Mi ioca, mi risus, placuit mihi uterque Cupido;
    si me fles, procul hinc, quaeso, viator, abi.

reputation had remained intact as ruler in many cities, Sixtus IV exiled him for having excessively supported the lords of Città di Castello.[132]

He died in Siena, which had welcomed him very warmly on account of the memory of Pius: an epileptic illness begrudging a longer life to one who was not all that old. Among the many orations and works in a variety of styles that survive, his *Life* of the illustrious commander Braccio is enthusiastically read. It would be worthy of posterity had he not spoiled the good faith of historical writing by extravagant fawning.[133]

### By Platina[134]

4

3

Here lies Campano, entombed in a humble urn, who while living vaulted over the wandering stars. He wrote history, delivered orations, and intoned poetry, and in all Latium no other philosopher was more famous. Nature has produced nothing greater: all the miracles of heaven were conspicuous in the genius of this man. The sisters have deserted the spring of Parnassus, and this solitary tomb holds them, refugees from light, as they mourn. O you who possess brilliance, observe where we're headed. The only glory that survives is that of virtue.

### By Poliziano[135]

5

Here I lie: Campano, the darling of Rome, upon whose laurel-crowned locks a miter rested. The Graces composed my witticisms. Momus imbued them with dark humor, Mercury with the light, and Venus with both. Jokes, laughter, and two-faced Cupid pleased me. If you weep for me, traveler, go far away from here.[136]

## XXIII. *Emanuel Chrysoloras*

1 Emanuelis Chrysolorae, qui primus Graecas literas variis barbarorum irruptionibus expulsas post septingentos annos in Italiam reportavit, tanta fuit in docendo liberalis ingenii humanitas ut eius praeclara facies prima inter Graecorum imagines illustri merito collocanda videatur, quanquam nulla extent, praeter artis grammaticae regulas, gravioris doctrinae monumenta. In docendo enim nunquam fessus, facile in scribendo desidiosus videri poterat, quum altera pars laudis exoptata nostris utili professione peteretur.

2 Is, Byzantio emissus a Ioanne Imperatore ut totius Europae reges adeundo pereunti Graeciae maturam opem imploraret, officium quidem laboriosa peregrinatione ita implevit ut in Italia subsisteret, Graecia scilicet praesenti metu liberata, quum Tamerlanes terror Orientis Baiazetem Othomannum, a terribili celeritate fulguris cognomen adeptum, ad Stellam Montem vivum cepisset.

3 Itaque Chrysoloras diro Graeciae hoste sublato laetus, Venetiis primum et mox Florentiae Romaeque ac demum Ticini, evocante ingentibus praemiis Ioanne Galeacio[10] principe, Graecarum literarum studium excitavit tanta felicitate uti ex eius schola summae nec ideo interiturae laudis ingenia prodierint. In queis fuere Leonardus Aretinus, Franciscus Barbarus, Philelphus, Guarinus et Pogius.

4 Postremo, quum ad tollendam pseudo pontificum controversiam indicta synodus tanti spectaculi cupidum excivisset, exauctorato Balthasare Cossa, Constantiae interiit, cuius tumulum Pogius his carminibus exornavit:

## XXIII. Manuel Chrysoloras (ca. 1349–1415)

This is Manuel Chrysoloras,[137] the first in 700 years to have car-  1
ried Greek literature back to Italy, whence it had been driven by
manifold barbarian invasions. He taught with such great humanity
and intellectual generosity that it is fitting for his illustrious countenance to appear in a place of honor, first among the portraits of
Greeks, even though there survives no written trace of his profound learning save for a primer on Greek grammar.[138] In fact,
though he never tired of teaching, he could easily appear indolent
when it came to writing, since that other half of his glory, so desirable among us, was sought by practical instruction.

The emperor John[139] sent him from Byzantium to beg the  2
timely help of all Europe's rulers in saving Greece from destruction. After arduous travels he fulfilled his charge in such a way
that he could stay on a while in Italy: for Greece had been freed
from immediate danger when Tamerlane, the terror of the east,
had captured alive at Mount Stella the Ottoman Bayezid (called
"Lightning" because of his terrible swiftness).[140]

Delighted by the destruction of Greece's dire enemy, he in-  3
spired the study of Greek literature first at Venice, then at Florence and Rome, and finally at Pavia, as Duke Giangaleazzo attracted him there with substantial inducements.[141] He was so
successful that from his schooling there came forth geniuses who
merited the very highest (and so, undying) praise. Among these
were Leonardo Bruni, Francesco Barbaro, Filelfo, Guarino, and
Poggio.[142]

Finally, when a church council had been convened to resolve the  4
papal schism, he went to Constance out of eagerness to see the
great spectacle, but died there soon after Baldassare Cossa had
been deposed.[143] Poggio adorned his tomb with these verses:[144]

Hic est Emanuel situs
sermonis decus Attici,
qui, dum quaerere opem patriae
affectae studet, huc iit.
Res belle cecidit tuis
votis, Italia, hic tibi
linguae restituit decus
Atticae ante reconditae.
Res belle cecidit tuis
votis, Emanuel: solo
consecutus in Italo
aeternum decus es tibi
quale Graecia non dedit,
bello perdita Graecia.

## XXIV. Bessarion

1 In celeberrimo gentium omnium concilio, quo Florentiae discep-
tantibus Graecis et Latinis praesidenteque Eugenio Christiani
dogmatis fides publici consensus authoritate firmata est, Bessario-
nis Niceni mirifica virtus senatorii ordinis ornamenta promeruit.
Datum est enim honori totius Graeciae ab antiqua pertinacia dis-
cedenti ut duo eius nominis Isidorus scilicet atque Bessarion in
sacra purpura conspicerentur.

2 Sed in Bessarione virtutes omnes usque adeo praecellenti tem-
peramento concentuque ad admirationem responderunt ut nemo
eo Christiana probitate spectatior, nemo admirabilior doctrina et
nemo denique generosis moribus ornatior atque splendidior, hoc
ipso a morte eius sexaginta annorum curriculo in senatu conspectus sit. Senatoriam enim gravitatem ore probo atque blandissimo

Here lies Manuel, the ornament of Attic speech who, when zealously seeking assistance for his afflicted fatherland, sailed here. When the business of war turned out well, Italy, by your prayers, this man restored to you the splendor of the Attic tongue that previously had been hidden away. Thanks to your prayers, Manuel, the war turned out favorably. On Italian soil you obtained the eternal glory that Greece did not give to you, since it had been destroyed by war.

## XXIV. Bessarion (1403/8–72)

In the celebrated council of all peoples in Florence, where Eugenius presided over debates between Greeks and Latins and the integrity of Christian dogma was unanimously affirmed, the singular virtue of Bessarion the Nicene earned the trappings of the cardinalate.[145] For it was determined that, to the honor of all Greece as it shed its longstanding obstinacy, two of its number, namely Isidore[146] and Bessarion, should be seen in holy purple.

But in Bessarion all the virtues marvelously corresponded to his surpassing moderation and cooperative temperament to such an extent that in the sixty years since his death, nobody in the college of cardinals has been more respected for Christian probity, more admirable in learning, nor more distinguished and eminent for noble character than he. Indeed, he seasoned a senatorial gravity with fine and exceedingly charming speech, and both in private

condiebat, ac ipsam viri optimi famam domi et foris nitida ac
hospitali disciplina et liberalis animi beneficentia tuebatur; quum
subactae Turcharum armis et ideo concidentis Graeciae ingenia,
diu iactata mari et terris, apud eum certissimum salutis portum
invenirent, et qui in Academia nomen darent eodem patrono atque
hospite uterentur.

3      Habitabat sub Quirinali ad Sanctos Apostolos; deducebatur
autem mane in Vaticanum, non exculto quidem et numeroso sed
uno virtutis nomine maxime decoro comitatu, quandoquidem
praeclara Graecae Latinaeque[11] linguae lumina peregrinorum re-
quisita oculis circa eum in triviis civium digito monstrarentur. In
his enim saepe conspecti sunt Trapezuntius, Gaza, Argyropylus,
Plethon, Philelphus, Blondus, Leonardus, Pogius, Valla, Siponti-
nus, Campanus, Platina, Domitius, nullo aevo perituri; quibus viris domi stipatus usque adeo extra invidiam gloriosa sui fama
fruebatur ut Eugenius, Nicolaus et Pius eum sibi successorem, si
fas esset, adoptare percuperent, neque optime de Republica merito
senatorum studia deerant.

4      Sed Paulo morte sublato, in comitiis, fatalis casus tantae spei
fortunam avertit. Ferunt enim tres summae authoritatis cardinales,
quum eo decreto, ut pontificem salutarent, abditum in cella con-
clavis adissent, nec admitterentur a Nicolao Perotto ianitore, quod
tum vir ineptus lucubranti parcendum diceret, usque adeo sto-
machatos ut sese indignanter avertentes responderent: 'Ergo nec
praensanti nec roganti quidem summa dignitas erit inculcanda
ut, quum a coelo suffragia expectet, superbis demum ac stolidis

and in public he upheld the very reputation of a man of honor by his cultivated and hospitable manner and by the kindness of his gentlemanly character. After the geniuses of Greece, which had been conquered by Turkish armies and for that reason brought to ruin, had long been cast about on land and sea, they found a steadfast safe haven in his household, and those who enrolled in his Academy benefited from having him as patron and host.[147]

He lived in the palace at the Church of Santi Apostoli, at the base of the Quirinal. In the mornings he was escorted to the Vatican by a retinue that was neither fashionable nor large, but highly distinguished solely on account of its reputation for talent, inasmuch as the most famous luminaries of the Greek and Latin languages, for whom pilgrims' eyes searched, were spotted around him by citizens in the public squares. Among these luminaries, indeed, were often seen Trebizond, Gaza, Argyropoulos, Pletho, Filelfo, Biondo, Bruni, Poggio, Valla, Manfredonia, Campano, Platina, and Domizio, men whose fame will never die, by whom he was surrounded at home; and he enjoyed so glorious a reputation, and without being hated, that Eugenius, Nicholas, and Pius were most eager to pick him as their successor, should it be God's will; nor, for good reason, was there a lack of concern in the college of cardinals to do what was best for the Church.[148] 3

But after [Pope] Paul's death, a fateful accident stole away the much hoped-for outcome of the election. For when three of the most powerful cardinals had approached him in his cell at the conclave in order that they might hail him as pope, they were not let in by the doorkeeper, Niccolò Perotti. Because the foolish man then said that Bessarion had to be left alone to his studies, the three cardinals are said to have been so enraged that, turning away resentfully, they responded: "So, should we have to force the highest dignity upon someone who is not striving for it, or even asking for it, and be compelled to yield to disdainful and stupid doormen while he awaits votes from heaven?" And immediately, they cast 4

ianitoribus pareamus?' statimque suffragia Xysto detulisse, quo
repente renunciato adoratoque, Bessarion dixisse fertur: 'Haec tua,
Nicolae, intempestiva sedulitas et tiaram mihi et tibi galerum eripuit.'

5      Nec multo post, cum honore legationis in Galliam est ablega-
tus, quod Xystus, nova licentia pontificatum nomine principatus
gerendum ratus, libere et graviter religioseque sententias dicentis
vultum non perferret. Sed Bessarion, dum e Gallia rediens concepto morbo Ravennae substitisset; septuagesimo septimo aetatis
anno moritur. Funus autem Romae celebratum in templo Aposto-
lorum, ubi marmoreum tumulum vivens sibi cum hac Graeca inscriptione extruxerat. Hanc sic vertit Maioranus Salentinus:

> Bessarion feci hunc tumulum, qui conderet ossa;
>     venerat unde olim spiritus astra petet.

6                               *Maiorani*

> Vivens adhuc feci hoc sepulchrum corpori
> Bessarion ad Deum remittens spiritum.
> Me docta genuit Graecia, at honores dedit
> Urbs Roma, quae mihi perpetuo est patria.

7                               *Iani Vitalis*

> Non tibi sit laudi sanctum celebrasse Platonem
>     castaque Socraticae frena pudicitiae,
> non quod virtutum exemplum, quod lumen honoris,
>     quod sol extinctae religionis eras,
> verum quod per te migravit Graecia Romam,
>     et didicit Latios Attica Musa sonos.
> Per te hinc Romanas miratur Tybris Athenas,
>     Argolicam et Romam Graecia, Bessarion.

their votes for Sixtus. It is reported that once the new pope had been announced and reverenced, Bessarion said: "This ill-timed assiduity of yours, Niccolò, has snatched away the tiara from me and the cardinal's hat from you."

Not long thereafter, he was sent off as a legate to France be- 5 cause Sixtus, with extraordinary presumption, had decided that the papacy must be run like a principate, and would not tolerate seeing the face of one expressing opinions freely and seriously and piously. But Bessarion died at the age of seventy-seven, while he was stopped at Ravenna, having become ill as he was returning from France.[149] His funeral rites, however, were celebrated in Rome at the Church of Santi Apostoli, where he had erected before his death a marble tomb for himself with a Greek inscription, which Maiorano of Salento translates thus:[150]

I, Bessarion, made this tomb so to bury my bones. My soul will make for the stars whence it once came.

### By Maiorano[151]     6

While still living, I, Bessarion, made this tomb for my body, sending my soul back to God. Learned Greece bore me, but the city of Rome, which is my everlasting home, gave me honors.

### By Giano Vitale[152]     7

May you be praised, not because you glorified venerable Plato and the chaste restraints of Socratic modesty, or because you were a paragon of the virtues or a luminary of dignity, the sun of an extinguished religion; but because through you Greece migrated to Rome and the Attic Muse acquired a Latin sound. Through you, Bessarion, the Tiber marvels at a Roman Athens, and Greece at an Argive Rome.

## XXV. *Georgius Trapezuntius*

1   Georgius Trapezuntius, in Creta natus, quod paternam originem e
Pontica celebri urbe duceret, vetustae patriae nomen asciscere
quam natale solum fateri maluit. Is Graecorum fere primus Romae
eo tum saeculo renascentibus literis, qui Graeca feliciore stylo in
Latinum verterit, existimatus est uti liquidissime constat ex Aristotelis sacrisque Eusebii Caesariensis operibus et ex rhetoricis
praeceptis Hermogenis.

2   Erat enim ingenio ad lucubrandum maxime valido vehementique sed, uti mox apparuit, tetrici livoris pleno: nam, quum se Peri-
pateticum profiteretur unumque Aristotelem extollendo celebraret,
usque adeo superba aure fuit ut nec divini quidem Platonis ingenium laudari pateretur, cuius etiam dogmata et mores peracerbe ac
insolenter edito famoso volumine laceraret.

3   Sed Bessarione, generosa eruditione illustrique facundia Platonem defendente, Georgius vim tanti fluminis sustinere non potuit,
quum publica invidia deflagraret, quod summae authoritatis philosophum magistrumque sanctioris vitae ac ideo Christianae disciplinae proximum, impio ac incesto ore proscidisset.

4   Habitavit iuxta Minervam, honesta domo sibi et posteris extructa, ad Divi Macuti[12] minores obeliscos, ducta uxore suscepto-
que filio, sed non eadem felicitate in literis educato. Is enim nomine Andreas, paternas lites excipiens Theodoro Gazae, tanquam
Georgii patris laudi decus maligne subtrahenti, rescripserat. Sed

## XXV. George of Trebizond (1396–ca. 1473)

George of Trebizond[153] was born on Crete, but because, he
claimed, his paternal line stemmed from a famous city on the
Black Sea, he preferred to appropriate the name of an ancestral
homeland rather than to acknowledge his native soil. At that time
when learning was being reborn, he was considered to be essentially the preeminent Greek in Rome, for he translated Greek into
Latin in a felicitous style, as is abundantly clear from his renditions of Aristotle, the religious writings of Eusebius of Caesarea,
and the rhetorical teachings of Hermogenes.[154]

He had an exceedingly powerful and vigorous mind suited for
studying late into the night but, as was soon evident, it was full of
vile spite: for, since he professed himself a Peripatetic and extolled
Aristotle alone, he was too haughty to tolerate hearing praise of
the brilliance even of the divine Plato, whose doctrines and character, too, he vehemently and insolently tore to shreds in a notorious
book that he published.[155]

But when Bessarion defended Plato with gentlemanly erudition
and lucid eloquence, George could not withstand the onrush of so
great a torrent when he was burned by the flames of public ani-
mosity, because he had castigated, with an impious and unholy
mouth, a philosopher of the highest authority and teacher of a
way of life that was holier, and therefore nearest to Christian
teaching.

He lived near the Minerva, having had a respectable house built
for him and his heirs near the small obelisks of San Macuto.[156] He
married and had a son, Andreas, whose education did not, however, produce the same favorable results.[157] Taking up his father's
quarrels, he wrote a reply to Theodore of Gaza, accusing him of
stealing glory from the praise owed his father, George.[158] But

1

2

3

4

Theodorus eam recriminandi libidinem rabiemque facile contempsit. Porro Georgius ad exactam senectutem pervenisse fertur ita ut
repuerascenti et propemodum deliro memoria tantarum rerum
elaberetur et circuiret Urbem solus, obtrito in pallio pileatus et
nodoso scipione vacillantis gradum sustinente.

5     Andreae filia haeres Fausto Madalenae Romano poetae lepido
collocata est. Hic multa de Georgii prosoceri doctrina et litium
acerbitate narrare solebat, quum Leoni ab amoenitate ingenii gratissimus in Academia floreret, sed is ante diem clade Urbis interiit.

6                       *Incerti*

Hac urna Trapezuntii quiescunt
Georgi ossa, parum deis amici,
quod acri et nimium procace lingua
Platonem superis parem petivit.

## XXVI. *Theodorus Gaza*

1     Theodorus Gaza, Thessalonicae honesto loco natus, Amurathe
Graeciam omnem victricibus armis quatiente in Italiam venit, acumine fertilitateque ingenii nemini secundus, quum Graecos omnes
linguae peritia eruditoque iudicio superaret.

2     Victorino autem Feltrense magistro usus usque adeo copiose et
diligenter Latinas literas didicit ut longe omnium Latinissime scriberet, nec plane dignosci posset an exactius et certius ab eo Latina

Theodore easily disregarded his fury and appetite for hurling accusations. In any case, George is said to have arrived at a ripe old age in such a way that, as he was in his second childhood and had pretty much lost his mind, the memory of important matters slipped away from him. He wandered about Rome alone, attired in a worn-out coat, and leaning on a knotty wooden cane to support him as he tottered.[159]

Andreas's daughter and heir married Fausto Maddaleni, the    5
delightful Roman poet.[160] When Fausto, beloved of Leo on account of his charming character, was flourishing in the Academy, he used to say many things about the erudition of his wife's grandfather George and the bitterness of his quarrels. But he died before his time, in the Sack of Rome.[161]

*Anonymous*[162]                                              6

In this urn rest the remains of George of Trebizond, too little a friend to the gods because, with a sharp and exceedingly insolent tongue, he attacked Plato, who was their equal.

## XXVI. Theodore of Gaza (ca. 1415–ca. 1476)

Born to a noble family in Thessalonica, Theodore of Gaza[163] came    1
to Italy just as Murad, his armies victorious, was shattering all of Greece.[164] Second to none in subtlety and fertility of mind, Gaza surpassed all the Greeks in linguistic skill and in the exercise of erudite good judgment.

Having studied under Vittorino da Feltre, he learned Latin literature so thoroughly and carefully that he wrote Latin by far the best of anyone. One could not easily determine whether he more

Graece, an ipsa Graeca Latine verterentur. Historias enim Aristotelis *De animalibus* et Theophrasti *De plantis* ita Latinas fecit ut Romanae linguae facultatem, quum nova vocabula solerter effingeret, audaci sed generosa translatione locupletarit. Tanta porro felicitate librum Marci Tullii *De senectute* Graecum reddiderit ut peritissimi praeter adaequatos sensus ipsam quoque Ciceronis eloquentiae maiestatem scite et graviter repraesentatam admirentur. Transtulit etiam *Problemata* Aristotelis et Hippocratis *Aphorismos* ut praestantissimis authoribus ad perspicuam fidem nec obscure ad salutem humani generis sua dignitas redderetur.

3    His vigiliis sacerdotium in Magna Graecia commendante Bessarione promeruit, quod certe satis esset moderato frugique homini et adversus omnis luxuriae voluptates invicto, nisi neglecta ratione totius redditus, rapacibus Graeculis et Brutiis rei familiaris curam demandasset. Novissime quum nobilissimas lucubrationes in membranis accurate perscriptas Xysto Pontifici detulisset, nec pecunia vel ipsius librarii premio digna redderetur, indignatus subagreste iudicium: 'Effugere hinc lubet,' inquit, 'postquam optimae segetes in olfactu praepinguibus asinis sordescunt.'

4    Atque ita in Brutios ad sacerdotii sacram sedem contendit. Nec multo post, plane senex, Fato functus est, nec iniqua quidem sorte, quum in Graecia natus et educatus in Italia, tanquam de utraque lingua benemeritus, in Magna Graecia tumularetur.

precisely and reliably translated Latin into Greek, or Greek itself into Latin. Indeed, he produced Latin versions of Aristotle's *On Animals* and Theophrastus's *On Plants* in such a way that by resourcefully contriving new words, with his bold and dignified translation he enriched the capacity of the Roman tongue.[165] Conversely, he rendered Marcus Tullius's book *On Old Age* into Greek with such great felicity that the most skilled men marvel that, beyond having captured the meaning, he ingeniously and authoritatively displayed the very majesty of Cicero's eloquence.[166] He also translated Aristotle's *Problems* and Hippocrates's *Aphorisms* in such a way that the dignity of those exceptional authors was rendered with evident faithfulness and clarity, for the benefit of humankind.[167]

By these products of his lucubrations, and upon Bessarion's 3 recommendation, he acquired a benefice in southern Italy,[168] a thing which surely would have been enough for a man who was temperate, frugal, and invincible against the enticements of every extravagance — were it not the case that, being careless about finances, he had entrusted the management of all his household possessions to rapacious Greeklings and Calabrians. Finally, once he had dedicated to Pope Sixtus the finest products of his labors, painstakingly written out on parchment, he did not get enough money in return even to pay the copyist. Offended by the pope's vulgarity, he said: "I'm happy to leave here, since the finest crops smell like filth to obese asses."[169]

And so, off he went to his priestly see in Calabria. Not long 4 afterward, full of years, he completed his destiny and was buried in Magna Graecia: most fittingly, since he was born in Greece and educated in Italy, and did laudable service in both languages.

5                                    *Pontani*

Sume Lyram, dic Musa modos, dum condimus umbram.
　　Et puer, et coluit numina vestra senex.
Indignus tellure, Deos Theodore petisti,
　　sera quidem, tamen est longa parata quies.
Virtute ingeniique bonis hoc ipse parasti,
　　ut coeli aspiceres aurea tecta senex.
Nos artus terra tegimus, tu caste sacerdos
　　da requiem aeternum; iam Theodore vale.


6                                    *Politiani*

Heu sacrum caput occubuit Theodorus, et hora
　　una obiere omnes reliquiae generis.
Nec tamen hoc querimur, nimis est potuisse videri,
　　non erat hic nostro tempore dignus honos.
Hoc dolet heu, quod neutra patri est nunc lingua superstes,
　　quae mittat iustas manibus inferias.


7                                    *Eiusdem*

Cum terram hinc nosset Theodorus, et aera et undas,
　　iam 'Restant,' inquit, 'sydera, terra vale.'


# XXVII. *Argyropylus*

1　Ioannes Argyropylus Byzantius, eodem Turcharum impetu Graecia eiectus, apud Cosmum Medicem gloriosa liberalitate literis

Take up the Lyre, Muse; set the rhythm, while we bury the dead. Both as a boy and as an old man he cultivated your approval. O Theodore, not having gotten what you deserved on earth, you've sought the gods; but indeed a long rest, late in coming, awaits you. By virtue and the goods of the mind, you yourself made preparations so that as an old man you might look upon the golden roofs of heaven. We cover the body with earth; may You, Pious Priest, grant eternal peace. Farewell, now, Theodore.

Alas, Theodore, our sacred head, has died, and in an hour all his remaining offspring have died. It is not this that we protest, however—this honor was not worthy of our age, and it is too much even that it could have seemed so. Alas, we grieve that now neither tongue survives its father to deliver suitable sacrifices to the spirits of the dead.

Once, from our side, Theodore had gotten to know the earth and the clouds and the waves. Now he says, "The stars are what remain. Farewell, earth."

## XXVII. Argyropoulos (1415–87)

John Argyropoulos,[173] a Byzantine expelled from Greece by that    1
same Turkish offensive, was esteemed by the house of Cosimo de'

faventem in honore fuit, tanta nominis existimatione ut, Petro filio nepotique Laurentio praeceptor datus, loco parentis haberetur; publice vero Florentinae iuventuti Graecos authores enarraret.

2    Grati idcirco animi erga Mediceae gentis proceres vigiliarum praeclara extant monumenta, consecrata in ea domo altrice verae virtutis. Aristotelis enim *Naturalia* atque *Moralia* generose transtulit ita applaudente Gaza vetere sodali, qui diversas Aristotelis partes vertendo desumpserat, ut quaedam ab se pariter translata combureret, ne amicissimi hominis crescenti famae efficerent, si ad aemulationem odiosa comparatione certaretur. Latina enim ubertate facundior et Graecorum modestissimus hoc facile dabat elate ambitioso et amplioris fortunae percupido, quod ipse omnis semper lucri et praesentis tanquam evanidae laudis contemptor extitisset: Argyropyli autem sermones cum fastidiosi tum graves eruditis auribus essent, et tum maxime quum Ciceronem Graecas ignorasse literas illoto ore praedicaret.

3    Pestilentia demum Ethruriam evastante, Romam venit profitendoque Graece Aristotelem ita opimis stipendiis vitam traduxit ut tota substantia quotidianis sumptibus aequaretur, et in extremo vitae actu iocatus ditiores amicos aeris alieni, condito testamento, haeredes relinqueret. Vini et cibi aeque avidus et capax, et multo abdomine ventricosus, immodico melopeponum aesu, autumnalem accersivit febrem, atque ita septuagesimo aetatis anno ereptus est. Ioannes autem Lascares eundem civem et magistrum hoc Graeco carmine laudavit, quod Maioranus Lascaris discipulus sic vertit:

Medici, who promoted literature with glorious generosity. Argyropoulos had such a distinguished reputation that, appointed tutor
to Cosimo's son Piero and grandson Lorenzo, he was thought of
as a father to them. Moreover, he gave public lectures interpreting
Greek authors for the youth of Florence.[174]

On account of his gratitude to the leaders of the Medici family,     2
we have splendid literary works from his late-night labors that
were dedicated in that household, the nourisher of true virtue.
Indeed, he nobly translated Aristotle's *Physics* and *Ethics* to such
approbation of his old colleague Gaza, who had chosen different
parts of Aristotle to translate, that he burned certain things that
he too had translated, lest they injure the growing reputation of a
close friend should they ever be pitted against each other in envious rivalry. Given that he was more eloquent in Latin style and
was the most unassuming of the Greeks, he readily did this favor
for one who was haughtily ambitious and intensely desirous of
greater fortune, whereas he himself had always stood out as a de-
spiser of wealth and the fleeting praise of the moment. The discourses of Argyropoulos, however, struck learned hearers as both
loathsome and disagreeable, and especially so when, with a foul
mouth, he proclaimed that Cicero had been ignorant of Greek
literature.

Finally he came to Rome, as plague was ravaging Tuscany, and     3
while teaching Aristotle in Greek, he led his life in such a way as
to spend every cent of his ample salary on day-to-day expenses.
And, in the last act of his life, when he made his will, as a joke he
made his richer friends heirs to his debt. As greedy for wine and
food as he was capable of putting it away, and having a massive
potbelly, by eating too much watermelon he brought on an autum-
nal fever, and thus died in his seventieth year. Janus Lascaris,
however, praised his fellow citizen and teacher with the following
Greek poem, which Lascaris's student Maiorano rendered thus:[175]

4    Hoc Argyropylus patria procul alta sophiae
       dogmata qui coluit, conditur in tumulo:
    Dat patria huic nomen, sacrum dat Roma sepulchrum,
       nescio quae potior huic fuerit patria:
    illa genus nomenque dedit, verum inclyta Roma
       nutrivit coluit perpetuoque tenet.

## XXVIII. *Marullus Tarchaniota*

1  Marullus Tarchaniota Graecus, inter alarios equites descriptus, Nicolao Ralla Spartano Duce in Italia militavit ita labore ac studio duri Martis cum tenerrimis Musis per intervalla feliciter adaequato ut non Graeco tantum sed Latino carmine admirandus evaderet. Nam Theodori ac Argyropyli decora vestigia subsecutus, nihil iam Graece doctum esse satis ad laudem putabat, nisi tota patrii sermonis facultas Romanae facundiae iungeretur; propterea Florentiae Alexandram eruditi ingenii puellam uxorem duxit, Bartholomaei Scalae vexilliferatus honore conspicui filiam. Hic est qui paulo ante Graecorum nomini favens cum Politiano, eius gentis ingeniis infesto maledicentissimis epistolis lites extenderat.

2  Verum Marullus, inquieto ingenio, nullibi sedem stabilem nactus, in cursu studiorum ac itinerum semper fuit, transferendique munus tanta contentione famaque ab aliis susceptum semper contempsit, quasi minime par aut certe nobilis gloria periculoso opere peteretur. Graviora idcirco meditantem; post editos

Here, far from his fatherland, is entombed Argyropoulos,    4
who cultivated the profound teachings of wisdom. The fatherland gave him his name; Rome gives him a holy sepulcher. I do not know which fatherland he preferred: the former bestowed family and name, but glorious Rome nourished
him, honored him, and holds him forever.

## XXVIII. *Marullo Tarcaniota* (1453–1500)

Marullo Tarcaniota,[176] a Greek assigned to the stradiots under the    1
command of the Spartan Nicola Rhallis, fought in Italy.[177] His toil
and zeal for harsh Mars were successfully equaled, when there
were breaks in the fighting, by his engagement with the tenderest
Muses, so that he turned out to be remarkable not only in Greek
verse but in Latin as well. For, having followed closely in the distinguished footsteps of Gaza and Argyropoulos, he now thought
it insufficiently praiseworthy to be learned in Greek unless complete mastery of his native speech were joined to Roman eloquence. For this reason, in Florence, he married a learned and
brilliant girl, Alessandra, the daughter of Bartolomeo Scala; the
latter had held the office of *gonfaloniere*.[178] Marullo is the man who
a little earlier, upholding the reputation of the Greeks, carried on
prolonged quarrels in the most hateful letters exchanged with Poliziano, who was hostile to the scholars of that people.[179]

But Marullo, restless in character, having found nowhere a    2
steady position, was always in motion both in his studies and
in his travels.[180] He always scorned the task of translating that
others undertook in so great a spirit of rivalry and hope of fame,
as though equal fame or a noble glory should be sought out
through [original] work that carried a higher risk. Thus he planned
weightier projects. After he'd published his books of epigrams,

epigrammatum libellos, quibus Apollo pereleganter arriserat, in Volaterrano, Cecina Amnis solito inflatior, fallente equum coeco vado, violenter abripuit, eo die quo Ludovicus Sfortia ab Helvetiis proditus ut,[13] ferrato in carcere miser expiraret, in ulteriorem Galliam est perductus. Luxere eum pari moestitia Graeci Latinique.

3                                  *Pontani*

Hoc vacuum tibi Pierides statuere sepulchrum,
    et Graia et Latia, clare Marulle, lyra;
ipse etenim Aonia in sylva atque Heliconis in antris
    laetus agens illic ocia grata teris;
illic formosae ludunt ad plectra puellae
    et tecum ad choreas carmina lecta canunt
et tibi responsant sylvae Peneiaque antra,
    plaudit et Ogygio roscida ripa lacu.
Nil praeter nomen tumulo: per opaca vagaris
    culta, per Elysium, docte Marulle, nemus;
hinc tibi se ad cantum adiungit formosa Corynna,
    cantat et ad calamos Delia culta tuos;
illic compositos exercet Cynthia saltus,
    exercet raros Lesbia blanda choros.
Nec Parca eripuit, Musae rapuere Marullum,
    Arnidi ne fieret grata rapina deae.
Sis felix igitur Musis comes et tua Musae
    ambrosio foveant membra adamata sinu.

4                                  *Tibaldei*

Hic[14] situs est celebris cithara gladioque Marullus,
    qui Thusco (heu facinus) liquit in amne animam.
Neptune immitis: meruit si mergier ille;
    Mergier Aonio flumine debuerat.

upon which Apollo had very rightly smiled, the Cecina River in Volterra, more swollen than usual, violently swept him away when a hidden shallow tripped his horse.[181] This happened on that day when Ludovico Sforza, who had been given up by the Swiss to die miserably in prison, was being led into northwestern Italy.[182] The Greeks and Latins mourned Marullo with equal grief.

### By Pontano[183]

3

The Muses have built this cenotaph for you, Marullo, renowned for both Greek and Latin poetry. Indeed, over there in the Aonian woods and in the grottoes of Helicon, you yourself joyfully while away welcome leisure time.[184] There, beautiful girls frolic to the sound of the lute, and along with you they sing poems chosen for the dances; and the woods and the Peneian caves echo you, and the riverbank, moist from the spring of Ogygius, applauds.[185] The tomb holds nothing but your name: learned Marullo, you wander through the shaded gardens, through the Elysian grove. Beautiful Corinna joins you in the song, and elegant Delia sings to your reedpipes. There, Cynthia executes graceful leaps; alluring Lesbia performs rare ones.[186] Fate did not take Marullo: the Muses carried him off, lest he become welcome prey for the goddess of the Arno.[187] Be you happy, therefore, as companion to the Muses, and may the Muses warm your beloved body at their ambrosial bosom.[188]

### By Tebaldeo[189]

4

Here lies Marullo, famed for the lute and the sword, who gave up the ghost in a Tuscan river (alas, what an outrage!). Merciless Neptune! If he deserved to be drowned, it ought to have happened in an Aonian river.

## XXIX. Demetrius Chalcondyles

1   Demetrius Chalcondyles, diligens grammaticus et supra Graecorum mores, quum nihil in eo fallaciarum aut fuci notaretur, vir
utique lenis et probus, scholam Florentiae instauravit, desertam ab
Argyropylo, et a Politiano deficientibus Graecis occupatam; sed
ambitioso peracrique aemulo multis bonis malisque artibus suggestus locum et nomen defendenti Demetrius cessit.

2   Latina praesertim facundia inferior, et ob id rarescente audito-
rio a iuventute destitutus, quandoquidem, vel apprime doctus facile ieiunus et hebes lascivis et delicatis auribus videri poterat:
quibus Politiani decantantis et varios spargentis flores iucunda ar-
gutaque vox et salsa comitas mira dulcedine placuisset. Sed mansit
Demetrio honestus gratiae locus apud Laurentium, vel infesto et
oblique semper incessente Politiano qui, quum neminem e Latinis
sibi parem pateretur, Graecis ipsis eruditior existimari volebat.
Divisit idcirco munera Laurentius ut aemulationis lites dirimeret
et filii praeceptorum contentione ad discendum accenderentur.

3   Sed eo principe virtutis eximiae morte sublato, Demetrius Mediolanum a Ludovico Sfortia accitus est, adducta secum uxore
Florentina, e qua iam liberos susceperat. Nec multo post, profitendo perscriptoque utili volumine rudimenta grammaticae publicavit, quod Theodori, quanquam insignis liber de arte eadem,
uti provectis et doctis scriptus durior videretur.

## *XXIX. Demetrius Chalcondyles (1423–1511)*

Demetrius Chalcondyles,[190] a diligent grammarian and a thoroughly kind and upright man, surpassed the morals of the Greeks, inasmuch as no deceit or artifice was observed in him. He restored the school in Florence from which Argyropoulos had departed and which, as no Greeks remained, had been taken over by Poliziano. But Demetrius gave way before his ambitious and exceedingly fierce rival, who was defending the lectern and the title by means fair and foul.

Demetrius's eloquence in Latin was distinctly inferior, and on that account he was deserted by the youth, the lecture hall crowd thinning out, because even an extremely learned man could readily seem lackluster and feeble to lascivious and pampered ears. The agreeable and melodious voice and witty elegance of Poliziano, as he was reciting and strewing flowers of different colors, pleased those ears with wondrous charm. But an honorable place of favor remained for Demetrius in Lorenzo's household, though he had to live with the hostility and constant indirect criticism of Poliziano who, even as he would not endure having any of the Latins as his equal, wanted to be thought more learned than the Greeks themselves. For this reason, Lorenzo gave them separate responsibilities so as to break up their quarrels, and in order that his sons be inflamed to learn by the tutors' rivalry.

But once that extraordinarily virtuous prince had succumbed to death, Demetrius was summoned to Milan by Ludovico Sforza. He brought with him from Florence his wife, who had already borne him children. Not long thereafter, by teaching and by a useful book he'd written, he disseminated the basics of grammar, because Theodore's book on the same subject, while distinguished, was considered too difficult, having been written for advanced students and for the learned.[191]

4    Uxor virili industria familiam regebat, ipso sene et literarum
studiis occupato; sed ea libertas in mire foecunda uxore dubiam
pudicitiae famam fecit, quanquam tres filii ipsam veri patris effigiem ore Graeco penitus referrent: Theophilus, natu maximus,
iuvenis turbulentus, quum Ticini Homerum profiteretur, nocturno
et petulanti certamine confossus interiit; et Basilius, mira ingenii
indole, evocante Leone ut in gymnasio Romano iuventutem doceret, paucis mensibus ex lenta febre contabuit. Seleucus vero, natu
minimus, ad pubertatem non accessit.

5    Caeterum Demetrius, octogenario maior, non plane miser,
quod nihil de obitu Theophili, occultante matre, didicisset, Mediolani Fato functus est, paulo ante quam Galli Iulii Pontificis et
Venetorum armis Italia pellerentur.


6                              *Incerti*

     Vivens corona nobilis iuventutis
     circumdabaris undequaque Demetri,
     dum ostenderes iter per Atticos campos.
     Certe beatus, si obtigisset morienti
     doctam videre tibi superstitem prolem:
     oculumque claudi languidum a tuis natis,
     aut hoc sepulchrum lachryma illorum spargi.


## XXX. *Marcus Musurus*

1   Marcus Musurus, genere Cretensis, exactae diligentiae grammati-
    cus et rarae felicitatis poeta, in gymnasio Patavino aliquandiu

His wife managed the family with manly diligence, since the old    4
man himself was caught up in literary pursuits. But that kind of
freedom, in a marvelously fertile wife, raised questions about her
chastity, even though three sons, in their Greek faces, perfectly
evoked the very likeness of their true father. Theophilus, the eldest, an unruly young man, died from a stab wound in a wanton
nocturnal fight when he was lecturing on Homer at Pavia; and
Basilius, gifted with extraordinary brilliance, even as Leo was in-
viting him to teach the youth in the Roman *Studium*, wasted away
over the course of a few months from a slow fever. But Seleucus,
the youngest, did not reach puberty.

Nevertheless, Demetrius, aged over eighty, was not completely    5
miserable, because he had learned nothing about the death of
Theophilus, whose mother kept that hidden from him. He died at
Milan shortly before the French were driven from Italy by the
armies of Pope Julius and of Venice.

*Anonymous*[192]    6

When living, Demetrius, you were surrounded by a circle of
the noble youth while you showed them a path through Attic fields. Surely you'd be blessed had it fallen to your lot as
you were dying to see your learned offspring live on, and to
have your children close your tired eyes or wet this tomb
with their tears.

## XXX. Marcus Musurus (ca. 1470–1517)

From a Cretan lineage, Marcus Musurus[193] was a meticulous phi-    1
lologist and an exceptionally talented poet. Having lectured on
Greek authors for some time at the University of Padua with a

Graecos authores interpraetatus, secunda perspicacis ingenii fama, ad integram doctrinae maturitatem pervenit. Sed saeva coniuratione externarum gentium, afflictis bello Venetis inde exturbatus, ita tranquillum ocium quaesivit ut Graeco carmine divi Platonis laudes decantaret; extat id poema et in limine operum Platonis legitur, commendatione publica cum antiquis elegantia comparandum.

2      Leone autem ingeniis illustribus praeclara praemia proponente, Romam venit. Nec multo post, Manilio Ralla, eruditi iudicii viro Graeco morte sublato, archiepiscopus Epidaurensis effectus est. Eam autem secundae fortunae celeritatem, quasi ab occultis fatis maiora praemia monstrarentur, immoderato animo tulit sic ut insana vehementique ambitione percitus, novum illud sacratae mitrae honorem nequaquam ingenii merito parem duceret nulloque pudore praeproperus ad purpuram aspiraret, quum saepe quereretur, Graeci generis neminem, quasi probro gentis, lectum fuisse, quando princeps in donanda purpura maxime liberalis, uno comitiali die, supra triginta nationum omnium delecta capita galero purpureo perornasset.

3      Ab hac intempestiva siti contabuit corpus adeo celeriter ut, obrepente morbo intercute, vix ostentatis mitrae insignibus expirarit. In templo pacis tumulatus est. Amiterninus autem Antonius sepulchro hoc distichon inscripsit:

Musure, mansure parum, properata tulisti
praemia: namque cito tradita, rapta cito.

favorable reputation for a penetrating intellect, he arrived at the full maturity of learning.[194] But after he was forced to leave, when Venice was afflicted with war by a fierce alliance of foreign nations, he sought out peaceful leisure in order to sing the praises of the divine Plato in a Greek poem, which survives bound in at the front of Plato's works.[195] The general opinion is that in elegance it merits comparison with the ancients.

When Leo was offering splendid remuneration to illustrious 2 talents, Musurus came to Rome.[196] Not long thereafter, when Manilio Rallo, a Greek of learned good judgment, had been carried off by death, Musurus was made archbishop of Monemvasia.[197] But he reacted to that rapidity of good fortune with boundless pride, as if greater prizes would be revealed by hidden fates, so that, propelled by insane and vehement ambition, he supposed that this new honor of the holy miter by no means matched up to the merit of his genius, and in too great a hurry he shamelessly aspired to the purple, although he often complained that in a single consistory, when the pope was especially generous in creating cardinals, elevating to the purple over thirty figures drawn from all nations, nobody of Greek origin had been chosen, as if to slight the Greeks.[198]

From this untimely craving, his body wasted away so quickly 3 that he died of a sudden attack of dropsy, just shortly after he had been invested with the trappings of his bishopric.[199] He was buried in the Church of Santa Maria della Pace, and Antonio d'Amiterno inscribed this distich on the tomb:[200]

O Musurus, destined to live too short a time, you won rushed prizes: for, quickly bestowed, they were quickly taken away.

## XXXI. Ioannes Lascares

1   Ioannes Lascares Graecorum fere omnium qui Othomanicis armis
patria pulsi in Italiam confugerint nobilissimus atque doctissimus
fuit. Stirpem enim sanguinis incorrupti ad imperatoris Constantinopolitani decus generosis moribus referebat ut pote qui ab ingenua educatione optimas literas imbibisset.

2   Naufragum excepit Laurentius Medices, cui nihil antiquius unquam fuit quam ingenia liberali beneficio devinxisse. Is tum ab-
solvendae bibliothecae studio tenebatur. Ob id Lascarem ad
conquirenda volumina Byzantium cum legatione ad Baiazetem bis
misit: nec defuit honesta petenti nusquam barbarus imperator,
quippe qui erat totius philosophiae studiosus Averroisque sectator
eximius; et de Laurentio privatim, tanquam de illustri cultore virtutis optime sentiret, quum paulo ante Bandinum percussorem
fratris, fuga in Asiam elapsum in cathenis ad supplicium tradidis-
set, singulari quidem religionis atque iustitiae exemplo, quod ille
immane scelus in templo ausus, merita poena plectendus censeretur. Itaque Lascares, tuto abdita Graeciae perscrutatus, quum patriae opes victoribus cessissent, nobiliora divitiis antiquae dignitatis volumina collegit ut in Italia servarentur.

3   Transivit demum in Galliam legatumque Ludovici Regis apud
Venetos egit; nec multo post, Leone veteris amicitiae nomine
liberaliter attollente, nobiles e Graecia pueros adduxit instituto

## XXXI. Janus Lascaris (1445–1534)

Janus Lascaris was the noblest and most learned of virtually all the   1
Greeks who took refuge in Italy when they had been driven from
their homeland by Ottoman arms.[201] Indeed, his lofty character
attested his legitimate descent from the glorious line of emperors
in Constantinople, as one might expect from a man who had as-
similated the best literature from his refined upbringing.[202]

Lorenzo de' Medici, to whom nothing ever was more important   2
than having brilliant men bound to him through generous support, took in Lascaris as one shipwrecked.[203] In those days, Lorenzo was intent upon the task of completing his library. On this
account he twice sent Lascaris to Byzantium, along with a legation
to Bayezid, to search for manuscripts.[204] Nor did that foreign ruler
ever fail to support his honorable requests, since he was an enthu-
siastic student of all philosophy and an exceptional adherent of
Averroes. (In addition, on a personal level, Bayezid esteemed Lorenzo highly as an illustrious cultivator of virtue, as was evident a
bit earlier when, in a remarkable instance of religious scruple and
justice, he had handed over in chains Bandini, the assassin of Lorenzo's brother, who had escaped by flight into Asia, in order that
he might be punished.[205] This he did because he thought that
someone who had dared to commit a savage crime in a church
must suffer his just deserts.) And so Lascaris scoured the remotest
corners of Greece in safety, and although the wealth of his fatherland had fallen to the victors, he obtained ancient books, things
nobler than riches, in order that they might be preserved in Italy.

Next, he passed over to France, and went to Venice on a mis-   3
sion from King Louis.[206] Soon thereafter, as Leo was generously
promoting him on account of their longstanding friendship, Lascaris brought noble boys from Greece to a school established on

ludo in Quirinali, ne Graeca lingua scite loquentium soboles interiret.

4    Valebat Latina facundia ita ut versus, qui extant perscriberet;
sed adeo contumaci sterilitate desidiosus erat ut in vertendo
Graeca vix Polybii *Castrametationem* efflagitantibus amicis expresserit, quod id studium (recto an maligno iudicio incertum) penitus
damnaret. Verum egregia cum laude praestitit ut Latini haberent
emendatiora, quae minore ipsorum labore verterentur.

5    Honestae facultates non certo nixae redditu, sed aliena liberalitate quaesitae, vel in rem negligenti, et sumptuose viventi nunquam defuerunt ut nonagenarius fere senex articulari morbo de-
formatus Romae moreretur. Sepultus est in aede Gothica Divae
Agathae supra Suburram fecitque sibi Graecum epitaphium quod
Maioranus sic vertit:

Lascaris in terra est aliena terra sepultus,
    nec nimis externam, quod quereretur,[15] erat.
Quam placidam, o hospes, reperit, sed deflet Achaeis
    libera quod nec adhuc patria fundat humum.


6                              *Tibaldei*

Lascaris hic Graium specimen: ne crede cadaver
    illius esse sub hoc marmore, sed statuam.
Altera quippe fuit Niobe: dolor impius illam
    natorum, hunc podagrae transtulit in lapidem.

the Quirinal lest the line of those speaking Greek expertly should die out.[207]

His Latin proficiency was so great that he wrote poetry, which  4
survives; but through a barren obstinacy he was so unproductive that in translating from Greek it was all he could do, at the entreaties of friends, to bring out the *Military Tactics* of Polybius, because whether on principle or out of spite, he was utterly dismissive of the craft of translation.[208] He does, however, deserve high praise for providing the Latins with more accurate Greek texts, which they could then translate with less labor.[209]

Respectable means that relied on no fixed compensation but  5
were gotten through others' generosity never failed him, even when he was careless with money and lived on a lavish scale. He died at Rome, disfigured by rheumatism, when he was nearly ninety. He was buried in the Church of Sant'Agata dei Goti in the Suburra district, and wrote a Greek epitaph for himself, which Maiorano translated thus:[210]

> The alien dust of Lascaris has been buried in the earth — but there was no cause for him to complain that it was too foreign. He found it a pleasant land, o visitor; but he weeps bitterly that his native land, not yet free, cannot pour earth over Greeks.

### By Tebaldeo[211] 6

This is a Greek representation of Lascaris:[212] you should believe that what is under this marble slab is not his body, but a statue. Certainly he was another Niobe: she was turned to stone by impious anguish for her children;[213] he, by the anguish of gout.

## XXXII. *Rodulphus Agricola*

1 Quis non te Rodulphe Agricola inusitato et plane portentoso conspirantium syderum concursu natum esse fateretur, si vim coelestis tam varie radiosi luminis non secus ac in astris cursum certior disciplina depraehenderet? Hausisti enim Hebraicas Graecasque literas usque adeo stupenda celeritate ut nequaquam Gruningiae in ultima Frixia,[16] sed Hierosolymis Athenisque natus ac educatus a doctissimis crederere. Latinas porro tanta felicitate didicisti docuistique ut exacta puritas ac illa nobilis ubertas Romanae eloquentiae nostro cum pudore in squallenti asperoque oceani littore quaerenda videatur. Vivent profecto in admirantium manibus tua illa, quae avide leguntur in dialecticis rhetoricisque praecepta, et divini ingenii carmina, quibus vel illustribus poetis numeros excussisti.

2 Nos vero, in magno vitae tuae desiderio, aut numinum aut certe syderum inconstantiam indignanter usquequaque mirabimur, quae tantis cumulatum muneribus terris tantum ostenderint, graviore quidem iniuria humani generis, quum ille, coelesti aura fortasse dignior in secundissimo foecunditatis cursu, raperetur. Defunctum Hingolstadio[17] Germaniae urbe gymnasio clara, decuriones sepulchri honore perornarunt. Hermolaus autem Barbarus, apud Caesarem legatus, inscripto epigrammate supremum amicitiae munus exolvit.

3 *Hermolai Barbari*

Invida clauserunt hoc marmore fata Rodulphum
Agricolam Frixi spemque decusque soli.

## XXXII. *Rudolf Agricola (ca. 1443–85)*

Were a more reliable science to comprehend the power of a light   1
of the celestial realm shining forth in variegated ways as well as it
does the course of the stars, who would not acknowledge that you,
Rudolf Agricola,[214] were born under an unusual and clearly por-
tentous conjunction of stars acting in harmony? For you devoured
Hebrew and Greek literature with such astonishing rapidity that
the most learned men might think it was not in Groningen,[215] in
remote Frisia, but in Jerusalem and Athens that you were born
and educated.[216] Moreover, you learned and taught Latin literature
with such success that, to our shame, it appears that the perfect
purity and noble copiousness of Roman eloquence must be sought
out on the desolate and rough coast of an ocean.[217] Certainly your
teachings on dialectic and rhetoric, which are read eagerly, and the
divinely inspired poems in which you hammered out the meters
even of famous poets, will live on in the hands of admirers.[218]

But we, missing you profoundly, will always marvel indignantly   2
at the inconstancy of the gods, or at least of the stars, because they
revealed to this earth just a glance of one endowed with such gifts.
But in fact the injury to the human race was more serious, in that
he who was perhaps better suited to heaven, was snatched away in
the midst of a most successful and productive career. When he
died at Ingolstadt,[219] a city of Germany famous for its university,
the town council honored him with a tomb. Ermolao Barbaro, an
ambassador to the emperor's court, discharged the ultimate task of
friendship by having this epigram inscribed:[220]

*By Ermolao Barbaro*   3

Within this marble the envious Fates sealed Rudolph Agricola, the hope and pride of the land of Frisia. Certainly in

Scilicet hoc uno meruit Germania, quicquid
laudis habet Latium, Graecia quicquid habet.


## XXXIII. *Leo Baptista Albertus*

1   Leoni Baptistae ex Albertorum familia Florentiae clara, Politianus,
audita eius morte, nobile encomium cecinit; nos autem eius ingenii
acumen et styli felicitatem in confragosa materia plurimum admiramur. Novum enim opus aedificatoriae facultatis, et propter linguae inopiam valde impeditum nec satis eloquentiae capax aggressus est, tanta facundia ut imperitos, obscuro rudique eius saeculo,
et certa disciplinae luce carentes architectos in semitam rectissimae
rationis deduxerit, quum Vitruvii praecepta densissimis obsessa
tenebris illustraret, ac inspectis antiquorum aedificiorum reliquiis
atque inde, accurata dimetiendi ratione, initiorum et finium ordinem depraehendisset ita ut inopem et, corruptis artibus, incultam
aetatem nostram admirabili abditarum rerum copia locupletasse
existimetur.

2      Scripsit etiam in pictura de recessibus et umbris lineisque ex
optices disciplina, quibus rerum imagines in eodem sitas plano
tanquam remotas et extantes, erudita manus exprimere consuevit.
Ex speculo quoque reflexis radiis suam ipsius effigiem arguto penicillo pereleganter est assecutus, quam apud Pallantem Oricella-
rium in hortis vidimus.

this one man Germany has earned whatever share of praise Latium and Greece possess.

## XXXIII. Leon Battista Alberti (1404–72)

Upon hearing of the death of Leon Battista[221] of the distinguished 1 Alberti family of Florence, Poliziano composed a noble encomium. For my part, I admire most his sharp mind and his felicitous style in dealing with difficult subject matter. For he undertook a work on architecture that was new, and on that account hindered greatly by the poverty of vocabulary and insufficiently suited to fluent expression.[222] This he did with such great fluency that he led onto the most correct and rational path architects who, in his dark and unpolished age, were inexpert and lacking the guiding light of learning. Indeed, he made clear the teachings of Vitruvius, which had been inaccessible, obscured by the densest shadows; and, once he had studied the ruins of ancient buildings and from that evidence made an exact reckoning of measurement, he grasped the principles of building from the initial to the final steps in such a way that he is thought to have enriched our age — which was poor and uncultivated, its arts having gone to ruin — with an admirable abundance of recondite knowledge.

He also wrote on the subject of painting: about backgrounds 2 and shadows, and lines drawn in accordance with the science of optics.[223] Using these, a skilled hand grew accustomed to portraying images that had been positioned on the same surface as if they were far away or projecting outward. In addition, from a mirror's reflection, with a skillful brush he tastefully succeeded in producing a likeness of himself, which I saw in Palla Rucellai's gardens.[224]

3    Extat etiam apologorum urbanae gravitatis libellus quo vel Eso-
pum inventionis amoenitate superasse iudicatur, et *Momus* summae gratiae dialogus, ac ideo cum antiquis operibus multorum
sententia comparandus.

4                             *Iani Vitalis*

Albertus iacet hic Leo, Leonem
quem Florentia iure nuncupavit,
quod princeps fuit eruditionum,
princeps ut Leo solus est ferarum.

## XXXIV. *Laurentius Medices*

1   Salve heros optime maxime, ingeniorum liberalis educator artiumque omnium et elegantiarum pater, ac unicus verae virtutis aestimator. Salve iterum immortale praeconium merite: quum, te vigilanter excubante, non Ethruria modo tua sed omnis quoque Italia
opulenta pace floruerit, scilicet ut mox, orbata te custode et vindice, intestina fatalique insania et externa immanitate vastata
concideret. Sed salve itidem, qui luculenter et fovisti Musas et feliciter exercuisti, praeclarus utique vatum hospes et aemulus, ideoque coelesti munere nomini tuo debita virenti laurea dignissime:
nisi haec fortuna tua putetur inferior, quando Cosmum avum,
eruditi saeculi decus, gloria superasse summe arduum videri poterit, nisi Leonem Decimum ad ornandam virtutem coelo datum
felici prole genuisses.

What is more, we have his elegant and refined little book of    3
*Apologues*, in which he is reckoned to have surpassed even Aesop in
pleasantness of invention; and the *Momus*, a dialogue so extraordinarily charming that many believe it merits comparison with ancient works.[225]

### By Giano Vitale[226]                                        4

Here lies Leon Alberti, whom Florence justifiably called "the
lion," because he was the foremost of the erudite, as the lion
alone is the foremost of the beasts.

## XXXIV. Lorenzo de' Medici[227] (1449–92)

Hail, best and greatest hero, generous foster father of geniuses,    1
father of all the arts and elegances, and unrivaled arbiter of true
excellence! Hail, again, you who have earned an undying proclamation of your fame, since under your vigilant watch not only
Tuscany but also all Italy flourished in sumptuous peace; whereas
it is clear that just after being deprived of you, its guardian and
defender, it collapsed, laid waste by fatal domestic folly and by
foreign savagery. But hail once more, you who both brilliantly fostered and profitably practiced the arts, distinguishing yourself as
both host and rival of poets; you so very deserving of the verdant
laurel due from heaven's bounty to your name — provided that this
crown not be thought beneath your state, since it could have
seemed supremely difficult to outshine the ornament of a learned
age, your grandfather Cosimo, had you not by a happy propaga-
tion produced Leo X, a gift to heaven for the embellishment of
virtue.

2                            *Iani Vitalis*

Nil mortale unquam vita tibi contigit omni
o patriae pater et decus immortale tuorum,
Laurenti, nisi cum te mors immitis ademit.
Illa quidem non te vitali lumine cassum
extinxit, verum quicquid sanctique bonique
orbis habet, tecum simul abstulit: aurea quando
saecula foedavit scabra rubigine ferri,
non tamen ulla unquam viderunt tempora dignum
te magis et titulis et maiestate decoro,
cui magnus Cosmus avus et cui filius altum
Maximus ille Leo princeps Romanus honorum
atque aeternarum laudum erexere theatrum.


3                             *Myrtei*

Occidit ut fato Medices Laurentius, ora
convertens in solicitas Florentia Musas,
dixit: Abite, aliud vobis nunc quaerite tectum.
Cui Musae: Nos hospitium sane perdimus usquam
quaerendum. Sed tu Medice Florentia rapto
amissum invenies nusquam. Quin desinis ipsa
esse illud decus et Latii, Florentia, lumen.
Nos erimus Musae: tum si quid nostra parente
ab Iove dat pietas sperare, videbimus ullo
tempore post heroa deorum in sede suprema
immortalem, alti nutu Iovis astra regentem.

*By Giano Vitale*[228]                                                    2

O Lorenzo, Father of your Country and immortal adornment of your people, nothing mortal ever touched you in all
your life except when cruel death carried you off. Certainly it
did not extinguish you as one lacking that light of life; but
whatever holiness and goodness the world possesses, death
snatched away along with you when it befouled the golden
age with the corroded rust of iron. Still, no eras ever have
seen one more worthy, both in distinction and majesty, than
you, whose grandfather, the great Cosimo, and whose son,
that greatest Roman prince Leo, built a lofty theater of honors and of eternal praise.

*By Mirteo*[229]                                                          3

When Lorenzo de' Medici met his fate, Florence turned toward the troubled Muses and said: "Depart; now seek another abode for yourselves." To her, the Muses responded:
"Truly, the hospitality we are losing can be found anywhere.
But now that Medici has been snatched away, you, Florence,
will find nowhere what you have lost. Yes, and you yourself,
Florence, will no longer be the famous adornment and light
of Latium. We Muses will remain. Then, if our piety gives
us anything to hope for from our father Jove, at some later
time we shall see the immortal hero on the highest throne of
the gods, ruling over the stars at the command of Jove on
high."

## XXXV. Petrus Leonius

1  Petrus Leonius Spoleti natus, multo acumine perspicacis ingenii
eruditaque facundia, inter medicos primus fere, prolato Galeno,
verum medicinae limen aperuit; quum in clarissimis Italiae gymnasiis profitendo exercendoque artem summa nominis authoritate,
non ex foeculentis Arabum lacunis sed ex purissimis Graecorum
fontibus haurienda praecepta artis atque remedia docuisset.

2  Is erat validis disciplinarum omnium praesidiis instructus ita ut
astrologiae et veteris item magiae peritissimus haberetur, quod de
eventu gravissimarum rerum divina praedictione iudicare consuevisset. Constat enim eum amicis saepe dixisse sibi subitae mortis
periculum in aqua portendi: unde flumina crebrasque navigationes
formidaret, quam ob causam, quum alia omnia ad quaestum et
decus secunda retinerent, e Patavio Venetiisque in Umbriam et
Spoletum emigrarit ut, mutata sede, navigationum occasiones effugeret.

3  Sed Fata ubique viam inveniunt. Inde enim Laurentio Medice
suprema valetudine tentato, Florentiam accitus, adeo inani aut
certe fatali spe concepta de salute decumbentis, occultans atrocis
morbi impetum contempsit, ut oblata ab aliis ex arte remedia
reiiceret et, insurgentis naturae viribus, nihil verendam morbi vim
facile cessuram polliceretur.

## XXXV. Piero Leoni (?–1492)

Piero Leoni, born in Spoleto, was endowed with the great keen-  1
ness of a penetrating mind and with accomplished eloquence.[230]
He was practically the first among doctors to open the true door
of medicine by making Galen widely known: for in holding forth
in the most famous universities of Italy and in practicing his craft
with the greatest distinction, he had taught that the precepts and
remedies of the art must be imbibed not from the filthy pools of
the Arabs but from the exceedingly pure springs of the Greeks.[231]

Stoutly fortified with every kind of learning provided by all  2
fields of knowledge, he was considered exceedingly skilled in astrology and in ancient magic, because he was accustomed to determining by means of divinely inspired prophecy the outcome of the
weightiest matters. In fact, it is well known that he often said to
friends that the danger of sudden death in water was foretold for
him, and so he was afraid of rivers and dreaded frequent voyages.
For this reason, although all the things that were promising wealth
and glory militated against his departure, he emigrated from Padua
and Venice to Umbria and Spoleto in order that, by changing his
residence, he might avoid sea travel.

But the Fates find a way everywhere.[232] For when Lorenzo de'  3
Medici was stricken with his final illness, Leoni, who had been
summoned to Florence, conceived a groundless or at least fatal
hope regarding the survival of the dying man.[233] And so, he concealed the onrush of the dreadful disease and made light of it to
such an extent that he rejected the remedies offered by other doctors and assured them that, since the strength of Lorenzo's constitution was rising up against it, they mustn't fear the onslaught of
an illness that soon would subside.

4    Verum non diu post ab ea cunctatione, detecta malignitate pituitae aegroque sensim deficienti, supervenit Lazarus Placentinus illustris medicus a Ludovico Sfortia Ticino missus, sera quidem afferens remedia, sed oblique Leonium iam toti familiae invisum perstringens, quod neglectis morbi initiis, facillimae curationis occasiones temere contemnentis imprudentia deperissent. Per hunc modum, expirante Laurentio, Leonius ex infamiae dolore, commota mente, exitialem insaniam lugentiumque familiarium laetale odium contraxit ita ut in proximae Caregio villae puteum sponte an illata vi incertum praeceps datus mergeretur.

5    Fuere qui Petri Medicis fervida ira mortem patris more barbaro vindicantis id scelus admissum crederent, uti Actius Syncerus Ethrusco carmine deploravit. Sed nullum omnino praeclarius patratae necis argumentum exortam inde suspicionem fovet quam ipsius authoris, par sceleri ad iustam poenam interitus, quum ille a clade Gallorum ad Lyrim aufugiens, in ostio[18] fluctibus nave obruta, foede perierit.

6                              *Iani Vitalis*

Dum timet astrologus sua Fata Leonius undas,
    et fugit e ripis, magne Timave, tuis,
illa eadem frustra fugientem adversa sequuntur,
    qua rapitur tacita nobilis Arnus aqua.
Hic tu florentem medicis, Florentia, curis
    praeruptum (o facinus!) corripis in puteum:
Astra repraesentant sic funera, dum fugit ille:
    tutius hunc poterant quam latuisse poli.

Not long after this delay, however, once the harmful nature of   4
his phlegm had been diagnosed and the sick man was in slow decline, there arrived the famous doctor Lazzaro of Piacenza,[234] sent
from Pavia by Ludovico Sforza. He administered cures that came
too late, but he indirectly blamed Leoni, whom the entire family
now hated in the belief that, since he had done nothing about the
initial stages of the disease, thanks to his imprudence in rashly
making light of it, the opportunity for an easy cure had been lost.
In this way, as Lorenzo was dying, Leoni, his mind in a frenzy,
incurred a deadly madness from the anguish of disgrace, and the
mortal hatred of the grieving members of Lorenzo's household, so
that he plunged headlong into a well of a villa near Careggi and
drowned.[235] It is unclear whether this act was voluntary or forced.

There were those who believed that Piero de' Medici, boiling   5
with rage, committed this crime, barbarously avenging the death
of his father, as Sannazaro lamented in a poem in Tuscan.[236] Certainly it's the case that no evidence has more clearly supported the
suspicion of premeditated murder than the violent death of the
instigator himself, a fitting and just penalty for the crime: Piero
was fleeing from the defeat of the French at the Garigliano River
when his ship foundered in the estuary, and he died wretchedly.[237]

*By Giano Vitale*[238]   6

While the astrologer Leoni, in dread of meeting his fate by
water, flees your shores, o great Timavo,[239] he flees in vain, as
that same hostile fate pursues him to where the noble Arno's[240] waters rush along in silence. Here you, Florence, dispatched him headlong into a well — what an outrage! — when
he was at the peak of his fame for cures. The stars painted a
death of this kind, while he himself fled from it: death was
able to escape his notice more securely than the heavens
could.

## XXXVI. Hermolaus Barbarus

1  Nulla hercle cuiusquam defuncti insignis effigies maiore merito quam tua in musaeo spectatur, Hermolae, eruditorum omnium omnibus numeris longe doctissime. Novocomensibus enim C. Plinium Secundum civem suum, ab imperitis invidiose surreptum, erudita praeclaraque sententia reddidisti; eumque eductum tenebris et multo squallentem situ, immenso radiantis ingenii tui lumine penitus illustrasti: scilicet ut, recepta antiqua dignitate, sibi persimilis in lucem prodiret, ac ea omnino quae in foro a Comensibus erecta est, dignus marmorea statua spectaretur.

2  Sed tibi publico nomine debemus omnes quod Themistium, tenebrosis Aristotelis operibus vivido splendore lucem afferentem, Latino sermone donaveris, ut quantus esses in physicis dialecticis atque rhetoricis, tot nobiles exuberantis ingenii foeturae testarentur; nec satis fuerit impeditissimam illam Geographiae sylvam, inaccessam multis nullique penitus exploratam, glorioso labore penetrasse, nisi ex ipso telluris et naturae germinantis gremio singulas salutares et noxias herbas traducto ac explorato Dioscoride aegris mortalibus demonstrasses; sed qui linguarum et disciplinarum omnium difficultates evasisse videris, longe maximo etiam invicti animi praeconio infestam virtuti tuae invidiam generose superasti, quum te speciosis honoribus perfunctum et tum supremam idcircoque gravissimam legationem Romae agentem Innocentius Octavus, admiratione virtutis, Aquileiensem patriarcham renuntiasset, vel non probante Senatu Veneto, qui nihil, vel

## XXXVI. Ermolao Barbaro (1453/54–93)

Lord knows, Ermolao,[241] that no portrait of any of the illustrious    1
deceased deserves to be on display in the museum more than that
of you, by far the most learned of all in every field. Indeed, with
erudite and splendid judgment, you restored to the people of
Como their fellow citizen, Pliny the Elder, whom envious incom-
petents had kidnapped. And, once you had brought him out from
the shadows and from the squalor of neglect, you thoroughly elucidated him with the boundless light of your brilliance.[242] Surely
you did this so that, once he had recovered his ancient dignity, he
would be viewed as entirely worthy of the marble statue which the
citizens of Como erected in the town square.

But we are all collectively in your debt because you made a    2
Latin translation of Themistius, who with his lively brilliance il-
luminated shadowy passages in Aristotle's works.[243] Thus the
many noble offspring of your fertile mind attest your eminence in
physics, dialectic, and rhetoric. Nor will it have been enough that,
laboring gloriously, you made inroads into that tangled forest of
geography[244] (a woods inaccessible to many and fully explored by
none), but for your having translated and interpreted Dioscorides,
and pointed out to suffering humankind which herbs from the
very bosom of the Earth and from budding nature are salutary,
and which are harmful.[245] But you, who appear to have gotten past
the difficulties of all languages and fields of knowledge, showed the
most praiseworthy quality of all — that of an indomitable spirit —
by nobly rising above the hostile envy directed against your prowess. This came about when you, who had held prominent posts,
were in Rome on your last and therefore most important embassy,
and Innocent VIII, impressed with your talent, named you Patriarch of Aquileia.[246] He did this despite the disapproval of the Venetian Senate, which maintained that even in cases of exceptional

inusitatae virtuti, extra leges tribuendum censuerat. Tulisti quippe
aequo animo suffragiorum severitatem quum ex eo tamen pari
merito tibi purpura pararetur.

3    Sed mors ante diem irrepsit, et pestilenti quidem morbo properata adeo ut quod a Pico Politianoque Florentia laboranti per dis-
positos equos mittebatur mirae potestatis antidotum veneni celeritate praeverterit, scilicet ut nimis severa patria optimi civis ossa
non haberet, quae sub colle hortorum ad Flumentanam portam
sepulchro condita e Campo Martio, ab erudita Romana iuventute
salutantur.

4    Barbariem Hermoleos[19] Latio qui depulit omnem
     Barbarus hic situs est; utraque lingua gemit.
     Urbs Venetum vitam, mortem dedit inclyta Roma,
     non potuit nasci nobiliusve mori.

## XXXVII. Georgius Merula

1    In Georgio Merula, ab Aquis Statiellis Alexandrino, ingenium
subagreste atque ideo ad lucubrationum labores maxime validum
nullisque obiter voluptatum illecebris lacessitum emicuit; passim
florentibus Graecarum literarum studiis, quarum felici societate
antiqui decoris ornamenta Latinae facultati tradebantur. Ob id
variae eruditionis laude celebratus, quadraginta amplius annos
cum Venetiis tum Mediolani iuventutem docuit, in alienos saepe
libros acerbius censuram exercens, quum saepe Calderini, Galeotti
et Politiani errata, vel certe praetermissa, notare contenderet,

merit no office should be granted without its legal sanction. You, for your part, bore with equanimity the stern inflexibility of those casting votes, even though the cardinalate, of which you were equally deserving, was intended for you.[247]

But death crept in before its time, and indeed was so hastened 3 by the plague that owing to the speed of the toxin, the end came before the arrival of an astonishingly potent antidote, which Pico and Poliziano had sent from Florence by a relay of horses. Surely this happened so that an exceedingly cruel fatherland might not possess the bones of its best citizen, which were taken from the Campo Marzio; entombed at the base of the Pincian Hill at the Flumentine Gate, they are visited by learned Roman youth.[248]

Here lies Ermolao Barbaro, who dislodged every barbarity 4 from Latium and is lamented jointly by the Latin and Greek languages. Venice gave him life; illustrious Rome gave him death. He could not have been born or died more nobly.

## XXXVII. Giorgio Merula (1430/31–94)

In Giorgio Merula,[249] an Alessandrian from Acqui, there shone 1 forth a brilliance that was somewhat unrefined, and therefore exceptionally suited to the hardships of burning the midnight oil, undistracted by any enticements to pleasure. With the study of Greek literature flourishing everywhere, the adornments of ancient splendor, by happy association, were bequeathed to Latin eloquence. Celebrated with praise on account of his wide-ranging erudition, Giorgio taught young men in both Venice and Milan for over forty years. Frequently he criticized others' books too harshly, since he often strove to record the errors (or at least omissions) of Calderini, Galeotto, and Poliziano, publishing pamphlets of

publicatis annotationum libellis, quibus late nomini fama apud stupentes grammaticos quaereretur.

2  Edidit etiam translationem Dionis *De Traiani gestis* sed, petenti Ludovico Sfortiae, historiam perscripsit Vicecomitum principum origines et bella continentem, sobrio quidem stylo ac ex omni parte Latino, sed in quo lectores minus austeri peramoena diverticula passim requirant. Caeterum postremi eius historiae libri meo iudicio iucundiores aeternum dormituri; denegata luce in abditis scriniis iacent, quum nemo e generosa stirpe Vicecomitum omnino prodeat, qui sepultum familiae patriaeque decus in lucem asserere velit; quandoquidem nemo fere sit ex ea gente qui non spreto verae virtutis nomine ab incondito luxu decoxisse videatur.

3  Periit exactae aetatis senex, tonsillis fauces occupantibus, Politiano obiter vehementi metu liberato, quum in *Miscellaneam* eius centuriam cohortes et alas, quae impetu obruerent, emissurus esse diceretur. Ludovicus princeps optime de literis merito, iustum funeris honorem persolvit elatusque est ad Aedem Eustorgianam, et hoc carmen sepulchro Lancinus inscripsit:

4  *Lancini Curtii*

Vixi aliis inter spinas mundique procellas,
nunc hospes coeli Merula, vivo mihi.

annotations by which he sought to spread his name among astonished philologists.[250]

He also published a translation of Dio's biography of Trajan, 2 while at the request of Ludovico Sforza he wrote a history comprising the origins and wars of the Visconti dukes.[251] Its style is dispassionate and the Latin consistently sound, though less somber readers will feel the absence here and there of delightful digressions. What is more, in my view, the greater charms of its final book will sleep the sleep eternal. Denied the light of day, they languish tucked away in boxes, since nobody comes forth from the noble line of the Visconti who might want to bring to light the buried honor of family and homeland: for, having scorned a reputation for true virtue, practically everyone in that lineage has gone bankrupt from undisciplined extravagance.[252]

He died at a ripe old age from a swelling of the tonsils that 3 obstructed his breathing. Thus Poliziano was relieved of dire fear, in that Merula was said to have been on the verge of dispatching troops and cavalry against his *Miscellanea* that would overwhelm it with their attack.[253] Duke Ludovico[254] gave him an honorable funeral, as befit someone exceedingly meritorious in letters. Merula was carried out for burial in the Basilica of Sant'Eustorgio, and Lancino inscribed this poem on the tomb:

*By Lancino Curti*[255]          4

Having lived for others among the thorns and tumults of the world, now I, Merula, live for myself, as a guest of heaven.

# *XXXVIII. Politianus*

1  Politianus a prima statim iuventa admirabilis ingenii nomen adeptus est, quum novo illustrique poemate Iuliani Medicis equestres ludos celebrasset, Luca Pulcio nobili poeta omnium confessione superato, qui Laurentii fratris ludicrum equestris pugnae spectaculum iisdem modis et numeris decantarat. In id enim e Graecis atque Latinis delectos flores populo stupendos contulisse censebatur. Nec multo post, Iuliano a Pactiis[20] in templo immaniter interfecto, eius vindicatae coniurationis historiam Latine ornatissimeque perscripsit. Professusque demum in gymnasio Graecas pariter Latinasque literas tantos de se excitavit clamores, favente iuventute, ut Demetrius Calchondyles vir Graecus praestantique doctrina, uti aridus atque ieiunus, a discipulis desereretur.

2  Exinde Herodianum Romane loquentem publicavit, cunctis haud dubie erepta laude, qui id generis munus ante susceperint; quanquam aemuli eam translationem, uti nos a Leone Pontifice accepimus, Gregorii Tiphernatis fuisse dicerent; quod passim inducto fuco et falsis nevorum coloribus interlita alieni styli habitum mentiretur. Sed eadem praecellenti studiorum omnium ubertate florentem, post editam *Miscellaneorum centuriam* publicataque Latina poemata, immatura mors oppressit.

3  Erat distortis saepe moribus, uti facie nequaquam ingenua et liberali, ab enormi praesertim naso subluscoque oculo perabsurda;

## XXXVIII. Poliziano (1454–94)

While still quite young, Poliziano[256] acquired a reputation for   1
wondrous brilliance from his celebrated original poem about Giuliano de' Medici's jousts.[257] Everyone acknowledged that he had far
surpassed the noble poet Luca Pulci, who, using the same rhythms
and meters, had sung of the performance in the tournament of
Giuliano's brother, Lorenzo.[258] Indeed, Poliziano, in his poem,
was judged to have gathered flowers plucked from Greek and
Latin authors, which astonished the public. Not long thereafter,
when Giuliano had been savagely killed in the Duomo by the
Pazzi, Poliziano wrote in Latin, and very elegantly, a finished history of the retribution for the conspiracy.[259] Finally, when he
taught Greek and Latin letters at the university, since the youth
favored him, he stirred up such great applause for himself that
Demetrius Chalcondyles, a surpassingly learned Greek, was abandoned by his students, who considered him dry and spiritless.[260]

Next, he published a Latin rendition of Herodian.[261] Without   2
a doubt he wrested away the renown of all who had earlier undertaken this task, although, as I learned from Pope Leo, his rivals
claimed the translation was actually that of Gregorio Tifernate,
but with the original style disguised by applying cosmetic changes
here and there and smearing on false colors and blemishes.[262] But
right when he was flourishing with exceptional productivity in all
his studies, after he had published the *Miscellaneorum centuria prima*
and some poems in Latin, he was overtaken by a premature and
sudden death.[263]

His behavior was often warped, as was his face, which wasn't   3
remotely candid or noble and was especially freakish because of
a disproportionately large nose and a lazy eye. And indeed, in

ingenio autem astuto aculeato occulteque livido, quum aliena semper irrideret, nec sua vel non iniquo iudicio expungi pateretur.

4    Ferunt eum ingenui adolescentis insano amore percitum facile
in laetalem morbum incidisse. Correpta enim cithara, quum eo
incendio et rapida febre torreretur, supremi furoris carmina decantavit ita ut mox delirantem, vox ipsa et digitorum nervi et vitalis
denique spiritus, inverecunda urgente morte, desererent, quum
maturando iudicio integrae stataeque aetatis anni, non sine gravi
Musarum iniuria doloreque saeculi festinante Fato eriperentur.
Vix enim quadragesimum quartum aetatis annum attigerat.

5    Sed eo praepropero vitae exitu profecto felix fuit, quod imminentem convulsae Medicae domus ruinam effugerit. Tumulo autem hoc carmen Crinitus discipulus affixit:


*Criniti*

Hic, hic, viator, paululum gradum siste.
Vatem potentis spiritus vides clarum
qui mente promptus acri et arduum spirans
ac summa quaeque et alta consequi suetus.
Is ille ego Angelus Politianus sum.
Fovit benigno me sinu Flora, et illic
in Fata cessi, Parthenopeos reges
cum Gallica arma irruerent minabunda.
Tu vale, et hoc sis meriti memor nostri.


6        *Politiani Tumulus a Bembo compositus*

Duceret extincto cum mors Laurente triumphum
  laetaque pullatis inveheretur equis

personality he was cunning, prickly, and furtively spiteful.[264] Always ridiculing others' works, he could not tolerate having his own skewered, even when it was being judged impartially.

They say that, smitten with insane love for a young nobleman, he fell readily into a fatal illness. For having seized his lute when he was scorched with fiery passion and with the rapid onset of a fever, he sang the most frenzied poems in such a way that soon he became delirious and, as a shameless death was coming upon him, his voice itself, the strength of his fingers and finally his vital spirit abandoned him. Thus the years that his judgment needed in order to mature were snatched away from him by the hastening of Fate — and not without serious injury to the Muses and the sorrow of his generation. He had just reached his forty-fourth year.

But in that precipitous exit from life he was surely fortunate in that he escaped the impending ruin of the tottering house of Medici. His student Crinito attached this poem to the tomb:

### By Crinito[265]

Here, traveler, here, halt for just a moment. You see a famous poet of powerful inspiration who, with a quick and keen mind and favoring the difficult, was accustomed to achieve the greatest and loftiest things. I am he, Angelo Poliziano. Florence took me to her kindly bosom; and there, I yielded to the Fates when the French army was invading, threatening the kings of Naples. Farewell, and by this remember my worth.

### The Tomb of Poliziano, Composed by Bembo[266]

When glad Death was leading the triumphal procession after Lorenzo had died, and was being drawn by horses in

respicit insano ferientem pollice chordas
   viscera singultu concutiente virum.
Mirata est tenuitque iugum; furit ipse pioque
   Laurentem cunctos flagitat ore Deos.
Miscebat precibus lachrymas, lachrymisque dolorem;
   verba ministrabat liberiora dolor.
Risit, et antiquae non immemor illa querelae
   Orphi Tartareae cum patuere viae,
'Hic etiam infernas tentat rescindere leges
   fertque suas' dixit 'in mea iura manus.'
Protinus et flentem percussit dura poetam;
   rupit et in medio pectora docta sono.
Heu, sic tu raptus, sic te mala Fata tulerunt,
   arbiter Ausoniae Politiane lyrae.

7                            *Incerti*

Politianus in hoc tumulo iacet Angelus, unum
   qui caput, et linguas, res nova, tres habuit.


## XXXIX. *Mirandula*

1   Ioannes Picus Mirandula merito cognomine Phoenix appellatus
est, quod in eum Dii superi supra familiae claritatem, omnis corporis ac animi vel rarissima dona contulerint. Mira enim altitudine
subtilis ingenii, decora facie lectissimisque moribus et incomparabili quum disputaret aut scriberet facundia, omnes eius saeculi sapientes in admirationem sui facile convertit.

2      Gravissimo autem opere, nec dum absoluto, tanta eruditione
atque vehementia astrologos totius divinationis vanitate confutata

mourning harness, She looked back and saw a man striking with frenzied thumb at the strings of his lyre, while sobbing shook him to his depths. She was amazed and reined in the chariot: the man himself is frantic and importunes all the gods for Lorenzo with devout lips. With his prayers he mingled tears and with tears his grief; grief supplied words all the more freely.[267] She laughed, and not at all unmindful of her ancient grievance, when the ways of the underworld opened up to Orpheus, She said: "This man is trying to abrogate the laws of the lower world, and raises his hands against my rights."[268] Straightaway harsh Death struck the weeping poet and broke his learned heart while yet in song. Alas, thus you have been snatched away, thus wicked fate has borne you off, Poliziano, great master of Ausonian song.

*Anonymous*[269]                                                          7

Angelo Poliziano lies in this tomb, who had something new: three tongues in one head.


## XXXIX. [Pico Della] Mirandola (1463–94)

Giovanni Pico della Mirandola[270] has deservedly been called the       1
Phoenix, because beyond the illustriousness of his family, the gods above bestowed upon him the most exquisite physical and mental endowments. Gifted with the marvelous loftiness of subtle brilliance, a handsome face, and the most excellent character, and incomparable eloquence whenever he was debating or writing, he readily attracted the admiration of all the savants of that era.[271]

In a weighty (albeit unfinished) work, once he had exposed the         2
foolishness of all divination, he attacked the astrologers so learnedly and vehemently that he might seem to have deterred the

persecutus est ut subtilium disciplinarum professores a scribendo
deterruisse videatur. In *Eptaplo* autem, dum sacrarum literarum
mysteria divino ore nobis recludit, et in *Apologetico* gravissimis disciplinarum omnium rationibus proposita ad disputandum ingenii
sui decreta defendit, se ipsum doctrinae atque memoriae felicitate
supergressus esse videtur.

3  Excessit e vita dignus coelo, trium et triginta annorum iuvenis,
eo die tam celebri quam postea Italiae maxime funesto, quo Carolus Galliae Rex Octavus Florentiam est ingressus; scilicet ut tanti
funeris luctus, quum sub signis ornatus in pompam externae gentis exercitus urbem intraret vel eo inusitato spectaculo et in tanta
receptae libertatis laetitia, minime vinceretur.

4            *Tibaldei*[21]

Ioannes iacet hic Mirandula, caetera norunt,
  et Tagus et Ganges, forsan et Antipodes.

## XL. *Pomponius Laetus*

1  Iulium Pomponium Laetum Sanseverina illustri familia in Picenti-
nis natum ferunt, adeoque insigni cura educatum ut ex adultera
matre alioqui pudica, illudente ei Salernitano principe, genitus
putaretur. Sed vigente demum bello et labante fortuna principalis
domus, animum ad literarum studia convertit, tanta antiqui moris
aemulatione et naturae temperantia optimas literas complexus, ut
Romae inter praeclara eius saeculi[22] ingenia conspicuus monstraretur. Nam Vallae praeceptoris aequata eruditionis opinione locum
exceperat.

professors of those abstruse disciplines from writing.[272] Both in the *Heptaplus* where, divinely inspired, he discloses to us the mysteries of Scripture, and in the *Apology*, where he deploys weighty arguments from all fields of scholarship in order to defend the ingenious theses that he had proposed for disputation, he appears to have surpassed himself in felicity of learning and memory.[273]

Worthy of heaven, he departed life as a young man of thirty-three, on the very day — later both famous and calamitous for Italy — when the French King Charles VIII entered Florence.[274] Surely the timing was thus in order that grief over so great a death would not in the least be overcome in the joy of recovered liberty or by the unusual spectacle when the army of an enemy people entered the city in procession with flags flying.[275]   3

*By Tebaldeo*[276]   4

Here lies Giovanni Mirandola; the Tagus, the Ganges, probably even the Antipodes know the rest.

## XL. *Pomponio Leto (1428–98)*

Giulio Pomponio Leto[277] is said to have been born of the distinguished house of Sanseverino in the Picentines,[278] and to have been brought up with such excellent care that he was believed to be the son of the prince of Salerno by an adulterous mother whose only lapse from virtue was her seduction by that nobleman.[279] But since this was a time of war and the fortunes of the prince's house were uncertain, he turned his mind to literary study, embracing fine literature with such emulation of the ancient manner and such natural self-control that at Rome he was noted as standing out among the foremost minds of that era. In fact, he had taken up the post of his teacher Valla, doing so with a learning that was judged equal to his.[280]   1

2    Sed eum mox Pauli Secundi iniuria percelebrem fecit, quum literatos quosdam, et in his Platinam atque Callimachum, tanquam impios atque maleficos tormentis excruciasset. Nam e Venetiis Romam pertractus ad dicendam causam, perpetua vitae innocentia tutus nihil terreri potuit, ut integro constantique animo indigna fateretur. Veterum enim ingeniorum illustria nomina sibi ipsis indiderant, quum in coetu sodalium laureati Musas colerent. Ea nominum novitate pontifex, elegantiae literarum imperitus suspiciosusque, vehementer offendebatur, quasi id esset occulta coniurantium tessera ad obeundum insigne facinus.

3    Xysto demum Innocentioque faventibus in gymnasio docuit incredibili nominis authoritate auditorumque frequentia adeo ut ante auroram profitentem Romana iuventus a media statim nocte praeoccupandis subselliis praeveniret. Descendebat e Quirinali saepe solus, Diogenis more praeferens lanternam,[23] quum opes contemneret, et iucunda frugalitate venerabilis haberetur. Simplici nanque et pene subagresti convictu usque adeo gaudebat ut quum frequenti semper limine coleretur, improvisi nobiles convivae, non sufficiente eius puero, per iocum admoniti coquinae manus admoverent. Unde perurbani sales multaeque facetiae sererentur.

4    Scripsit grammaticae compendium adultis pueris utile, et graviore demum stylo seriatim Romanos caesares gratissimoque libello in antiquae Urbis ruinis vera loca atque vocabula demonstravit. Sed in suggestu summam laudem promeruit, quod eo magis mirum videtur, quum in familiari sermone haesitante lingua

But soon he was made very famous by the injustice of Paul II, 2 who had afflicted with torture certain scholars, including Platina and Callimachus, on the grounds that they were irreligious and criminal.[281] When Pomponio was dragged back from Venice to Rome to plead his case, he was secure in the consistent innocence of his life and could not be frightened into confessing things unworthy of an irreproachable and steadfast soul.[282] When these scholars, wreathed with laurel, had gathered in the company of their fellows to pay court to the Muses, they bestowed upon themselves the names of great intellects of old. The pontiff, who was ignorant and suspicious of refined literature, was greatly offended by this novelty of names, as though that were some secret password among men conspiring to undertake an extraordinary crime.

Supported, at last, by Sixtus and Innocent, he taught at the 3 university, where his name was so incredibly authoritative and his audience so numerous that the young men of Rome would come as early as midnight to secure their seats, since he began his lectures before dawn.[283] Often he came down from the Quirinal alone, holding a lantern before him like Diogenes, because he despised wealth; and he was held in veneration for his pleasing thriftiness. He enjoyed dining in a manner so simple and almost crude that, since his threshold was always crowded with devotees and his servant had too much to do, distinguished people who unexpectedly came to dinner were reproved jokingly and would lend their hands to the cooking. Out of this came very cultured witticisms, and many pleasantries were exchanged.

He wrote a compendium of grammar, useful for older boys;[284] 4 and then, in a more serious style, a chronology of the Roman emperors;[285] and in a most delightful little book he attached the authentic place-names to specific sites in the ruins of the ancient City.[286] But on the platform he won the greatest acclaim, which seems all the more marvelous given that in private conversation he was accustomed to stutter with a stammering tongue; and yet, no

balbutire esset solitus, nec orantem demum aut clara voce lecti-
tantem ulla omnino oris titubantia deformaret.

5      Septuagenarius excessit e vita, quum gelidissimo vini potu
ventriculi calorem oppressisset. Elatus est auditorum insignium
piis humeris, honestante funus familia purpurata Alexandri Pontificis et laudante Marso oratore. Quum variis autem elegiis tumulus ornaretur, epigramma Pontani, consensu publico, locum obtinuit.

6                                  *Pontani*

Pomponi tibi pro tumulo sit laurea sylva;
      ossa maris rores myrteaque umbra tegant,
teque tegant artusque tuos violaeque rosaeque;
      ver habeat, Zephyros spiret et ipse cinis.
Stillet et ipse cinis quas et Parnasus et antra
      Thespia et ipsa suas Ascra ministrat aquas.


## XLI. *Callimachus*

1   Callimachus antiquo nomine, Philippus, Geminiano Ethruriae
oppido editus, ingenium lectissimis literis Romae excoluit. Nec
multo post, indignam insonte animo subiit calamitatem, quum
Paulus Secundus illustres academiae sodales, odio temere concepto,
tanquam maligne conspirantes persequeretur ita ut ipse ante alios
desumpti Graeci nominis reus tormentis et carcere poenas daret.

stumbling of speech disfigured him at all when he was delivering an oration or reciting aloud.[287]

In his seventies he departed from life as a result of having over-  5
powered the heat of his stomach with an icy draft of wine.[288] He was carried to his rest on the devoted shoulders of his outstanding pupils, and his funeral was graced by the cardinals of Pope Alexander's court and by a eulogy from the orator Marsi.[289] While his tomb was adorned with various elegies, by popular consensus an epigram of Pontano held pride of place:

*By Pontano*[290]  6

Pomponio, may a laurel grove serve as your tomb. May rosemary and the shade of myrtle cover your bones, and may violets and roses cloak you and your limbs. May your very ashes enjoy springtime and inhale zephyrs. May they drip with such waters as flow from Parnassus and the Thespian caves, and those that Ascra itself supplies.

## XLI. Callimachus (1437–97)

Known by the classical name of Callimachus, Filippo [Buonac-  1
corsi] was born in the Tuscan town of San Gimignano and cultivated his natural gifts in Rome by studying the choicest literature.[291] Soon, he suffered a misfortune unworthy of his guiltless character when Paul II, who had conceived an irrational hatred for distinguished members of the Academy, prosecuted them on the grounds that they were malevolent conspirators. For this reason Callimachus himself, guilty of being the first among them to assume a Greek name, was to be punished with torture and imprisonment.[292]

151

2     Ab ea autem iniuria indignabundus, in ultimas terras profectus, Cassimiro Sarmatiae Regi ingenii operam obtulit. Is, virtute fortunaque clarissimus sed pontificii nominis hostis, quattuor regum pater fuit. In honore tum erant optimae literae apud externos reges, uno prae caeteris[24] Matthia Corvino studiis ac artibus eximiis liberaliter favente. Itaque Callimachus Alberto filio praeceptor datur; a quo demum, post Cassimiri patris interitum ad summum familiaritatis atque potentiae locum evectus est, tanta Polonorum consternatione odioque ut eum tanquam impium, et Moldavicae cladis authorem tyrannidemque impotenti imperio exercendam regi suaderet, aula extruserint. Maligno enim iudicio nobilitatem, quod imperatae pecuniae et suscepto bello aversa esset, saevo hosti obiectandam esse censuerat ut nemo demum superesset qui libertatis per manum traditae iura tueretur.

3     Sed Callimachus, vel Alberto absentis desiderium vix ferente, quod invidiam minime sustineret, semi exul in villa Sarmatica apud veterem amicum occultatus, Fato cessit ita ut morte caelata sine funere, arefactus tepore clybani, in armario servaretur. Id rescivit Albertus et, pietatis ergo, Cracoviae in aede Trinitatis aereo sepulchro honestandum curavit.

4     Praecipuum eius ingenii monumentum extat *Historia* exactissime conscripta de rebus gestis Ladislai Sarmatiae atque Pannoniae Regis, qui ad Euxinum Varnensi acie ab Amurathe superatus interiit; adeo enim eleganter eius gravissimi muneris leges

Furious at this indignity, he set out for faraway lands and of-  2
fered his services to King Casimir of Poland.[293] That man, exceedingly famous for his virtue and his success, yet an enemy of the
papacy, was the father of four kings.[294] At that time the best literature was highly esteemed among foreign kings (of these, Matthias
Corvinus stood out in his generous support of the finest cultural
pursuits).[295] And so, Casimir appointed Callimachus tutor to his
son, Albert.[296] Following his father's death, Albert made Callimachus his closest confidante and elevated him to a position of immense power, thereby causing such great dismay and hatred among
the Poles that his erstwhile friends drove him out of the court for
being wicked, for instigating the disastrous Moldavian campaign,
and for persuading the king (so they supposed) to wield power as
a tyrant with unchecked authority.[297] Since the nobility had opposed undertaking the war and the levying of money for it, with
malice aforethought he had in fact recommended that they be sent
to the front lines against the savage foe, so that in the end nobody
would be left who might uphold the rights of liberty that they had
inherited.

But because Callimachus was unable to tolerate their spite, even  3
though Albert could hardly bear his absence, he became an exile of
sorts, hidden away in the Polish villa of an old friend. His death
there was kept secret and he lacked funeral obsequies; once his
body had been dried in an oven, it was stored in a chest.[298] When
Albert learned of this, out of a sense of pious obligation he saw to
it that Callimachus was honored with a bronze tomb in the
Church of the Holy Trinity in Cracow.[299]

There remains, as the chief monument to his brilliance, a highly  4
reliable history of the deeds of Ladislaus, King of Poland and
Hungary, who died when he was conquered by Murad in the
Battle of Varna, next to the Black Sea.[300] Indeed, Callimachus is
thought to have satisfied the requirements of this most weighty

implevisse existimatur, ut omnes qui a Cornelio Tacito per tot
saecula id scribendi genus attigerint, meo iudicio superarit.

*Iani Vitalis*

Aenea Callimachi quae circumplectitur ossa
    depositi meritis nobilis urna sui,
aenea sit quamvis, multo est pretiosior auro:
    Ethrusci felix hospita Callimachi.
Ipsi etiam Italia tantum decus auspice adepti
    ad sacra conveniunt busta Boristhenides
exultantque mero et choreis referuntque vicissim;
    dedicat haec Crispo Sarmatis ora suo.

## XLII. *Hieronymus Savonarola*

1 Mediceis Gallorum adventu Florentia pulsis, Hieronymus Savonarola Ferrariensis ex ordine Divi Dominici cucullatus usque adeo
austera vitae disciplina ac erudito subtilique ingenio et in sacris
concionibus admirabili facundia valuit ut populum, instaurandis
religionibus deditum, et tum novo receptae libertatis gaudio gesti-
entem, quo vellet, facile impelleret privatisque familiarum ac ipsis
quoque summi magistratus consiliis misceretur. Futura enim prae-
dicere, veluti divino adflatum numine credebant, quando nihil validius esset ad persuadendum specie ipsa pietatis in qua etiam
tuendae libertatis studium emineret.

task so eloquently that, in my opinion, he surpassed all who have attempted to write in that genre over all the centuries since Cornelius Tacitus.

By Giano Vitale[301]

5

The bronze urn which encloses the bones of Callimachus is ennobled by the merits of its contents: although bronze, it is far more precious than gold, as it is the fortunate host of Callimachus the Tuscan. And those along the Dnieper River themselves acquired the remains (so great the glory bestowed by Italy) and they assemble at the sacred tomb and exult with wine and dancing, swapping stories about him. The land of the Sarmatian consecrates this tomb to its Crispus.[302]

## XLII. Girolamo Savonarola (1452–98)

Once the Medici had been driven out of Florence at the coming of the French, Girolamo Savonarola of Ferrara, a cowled brother of the order of St. Dominic, became so powerful by means of his austere discipline, his learned and subtle intellect, and his remarkably eloquent sermons, that he easily impelled the people to go in whatever direction he might wish.[303] For they were committed to religious renewal, and just then were reveling in the newfound joy of their recovered liberty. He also became involved both in the private affairs of families and in the decisions of the highest magistracy.[304] They believed, in fact, that through divine inspiration he could predict the future; for nothing convinces more effectively than the very appearance of piety in which a zeal for safeguarding liberty is also manifest.

1

2    Sed nonnulli optimates astutis ingeniis adeundo consulendoque
eius authoritatem in immensum adaugebant, tanta quidem insania, quo illam sibi astruerent, ut ad Carolum Regem Pisas legatus
mitteretur, et integros quattuor annos Florentinorum animis ac
opibus imperaret.

3    Verum in eo Christianis hercle moribus ac optimis literis orna-
tissimo, ingenium ab occulta ambitione et nimio exitialique profe-
rendae veritatis studio inflammatum, adeo aestuanter efferbuit ut
capitale iudicium de suspectis nobilissimis septem civibus saeva
sententia praecipitarit; moresque Alexandri Summi Pontificis ve-
sana declamandi libertate quum acerbe sugillaret, sacrosanctam
potestatem in dubium devocarit; quamobrem reus maiestatis, de-
poscente pontifice concedenteque senatu et concrematis quidem
templi foribus, nec incruenta irruptione comprehenditur. Nam
inimicae factionis cives damnatorumque propinqui arma ceperant.
In eoque tumultu trucidatus est Franciscus Valorius partium
princeps, qui maturandae reorum necis author extiterat.

4    Caeterum de Savonarola tormentis excruciato confessoque latronum more, in medio foro miserabile supplicium est desumptum
ita ut strangulati corpus extemplo cremaretur, diverso quidem
animorum habitu, quum alii ardentes odio, iure execratum, atque
punitum succlamarent; alii vero lugentes, tanquam indigna morte
perempti e rogo cineres religiose colligerent.

5    Eius autem ingenii operum praecipua cum laude legitur glorio-
sus *Crucis triumphus* adversus eius saeculi sapientes garrulosque

But some among the elite increased his influence enormously 2
when, as a deliberate tactic, they approached him and sought his
advice, very foolishly supposing that by so doing they could themselves gain authority.[305] Thus it came about that he was sent as a
legate to King Charles at Pisa, and for four whole years he ruled
over the Florentines' minds and financial resources.

Lord knows, he was generously endowed with Christian morals 3
and with the finest literary education; but his temperament, inflamed by hidden ambition and by exceedingly destructive zeal for
making known the truth, became so feverishly overwrought that
with a savage denunciation he rushed through a capital sentence
against seven suspected offenders who were among the noblest
citizens.[306] In addition, when he was harshly castigating the morals of Pope Alexander in a frenzied and outspoken declamation,
he called into question the pontiff's sacred authority, on account
of which lèse-majesté the pope demanded his arrest, and the College
of Cardinals concurred.[307] He was in fact apprehended, not without bloodshed, at his church, after the doors had been set afire.[308]
For citizens in the opposing faction, as well as relatives of the men
sentenced to die, had taken up arms. And in that uprising Francesco Valori, the leader of the Savonarolan faction who had played
a pivotal role in hastening the execution of the accused men, was
savagely murdered.[309]

As for Savonarola, once he had been tortured like a common 4
criminal and had confessed, there was decreed for him a horrific
execution in the middle of the central piazza: he was to be strangled and his body immediately burned.[310] People were of different
minds about this: some, inflamed with hatred, were calling out
that his condemnation and punishment were just; but others,
mourning him as one whose death was undeserved, reverently
scooped up the ashes from the pyre.

Of the works his brilliant mind produced, the most praised is 5
his glorious *Triumph of the Cross*, written in Latin and directed at

sophistas Latine perscriptus. Utranque autem pii atque impii nominis famam cumulate promeruit, si duobus contrariis coenotaphiis credendum esse censeremus. Sed alterum quod lividus effudit honestus supprimet pudor ne supra miserabilis supplicii dolorem, insontis fortasse viri manes hac etiam aeterni carminis inurente nota crucientur.

6                                     *Marci Antonii Flaminii*

> Dum fera flamma tuos, Hieronyme, pascitur artus,
>     religio sanctas dilaniata comas
> flevit et 'O' dixit 'crudeles parcite flammae,
>     parcite, sunt isto viscera nostra rogo.'

## XLIII. *Marsilius Ficinus*

1   Quum clarissimi Graecorum Theodorus, Argyropylus et Trapezuntius, veluti ex condicto inter se distributis operibus, in traducendo Aristotele ad non obscuram aemulationem versarentur, unus Latinorum Marsilius Ficinus, divinae philosophiae amore incensus, transferendi Platonis negocium suscepit atque perfecit usque adeo festinata felicis ingenii foecunditate ut plerique in pusillo eius corpore, quod vix semihominem aequaret, tantam vim inusitati spiritus et tantas utriusque linguae facultates vigere mirarentur.

2       Nam eundem quoque insatiabilis studii tenorem secutus Plotinum, Iamblichum, Synesium et Psellum, Platonicae sectae nobiles

the world's "wise" men and the babbling sophists of his time.[311] He richly deserved his reputation both for piety and for impiety, if we can believe the conflicting evidence of two cenotaphs. But an honorable sense of decency will suppress the one that spite brought forth, lest, beyond the anguish of having faced a horrific execution, the shade of a man who was perhaps innocent should be tormented even further by being stigmatized in a poem that will live on.[312]

*By Marcantonio Flaminio*[313]    6

While the savage flame fed upon your body, Girolamo, religion tore out her sacred hair and wept and cried out, "Spare him, o cruel flames, spare him! My own flesh is on that pyre."

## XLIII. Marsilio Ficino (1433–99)

At a time when the most famous of the Greeks—Theodore, Argyropoulos, and Trebizond—were openly competing with one another in translating Aristotle, having distributed his works among them as if out of a common agreement, among the Latins only Marsilio Ficino, on fire with his love of divine philosophy, took up the task of translating Plato.[314] He brought this task to completion with such swift productivity of his fruitful mind that many marveled that in his tiny body, which was barely half normal stature, there flourished so great a force of unusual energy and such great skills in both Latin and Greek.    1

By following an equally intense course of insatiable study, he had also rendered into Latin Plotinus, Iamblichus, Synesius, and Psellos, outstanding writers of the Platonic sect. He did so at the    2

authores, Latinos effecerat, hortante quidem Cosmo Medice, et
mox tradita per manus summae virtutis haereditate, Petro filio et
Laurentio nepote suffragantibus. Ex ea si quidem ornatissimae
domus liberali disciplina Ficinus honestis aedibus, peramoena
villa, sacerdotio annuisque stipendiis atque muneribus sese adauc-
tum et cumulate perornatum sensit.

3      Contemnebat enim maiores opes vir minime ambitiosus et niti-
dae iucundaeque vitae ad bonam frugem percupidus, quum unam
studiorum laudem spectaret; nec ullis unquam contentionibus
misceretur, quod rerum omnium praeterquam vini subdulcis voluptates abdicasset; nulla quidem animi tristitia, quum esset omnino laetissimus, sed exactissima ratione ad tuendam valetudinem,
sicuti depraehendere licet ex libris *De triplici vita* editis. Adeo enim
morose sibi ad spem vitae blandiebatur ut saepe eadem die, quum
aër incalesceret aut aliquo spiritu moveretur, capitis tegumenta
permutaret.

4      Sed quum sodalium suorum acerba funera luxisset Laurentii,
Hermolai, Politiani, Mirandulae, qui uno anno perierunt, Landi-
nique item et Savonarolae, in Caregiana ipsius villa septuagenario
provectior febricula interiit: diro quidem omine, quum eodem die
punctoque temporis duo clarissima Italiae lumina, Ficinum ipsum
et Paulum Vitellium, summae invictaeque virtutis Florentinorum
imperatorem, aliquanto certiore inimicorum rabie quam noxa capi-
tali supplicio damnatum, vis ipsa fatalis extinxerit; et tum esset in
Alpibus Ludovicus Rex Gallorum, armatus irrumpens, ut singulas
illustres domos et ad unum fere omnes Italiae principatus everteret.

request of Cosimo de' Medici, and thereafter being handed down, as it were, as a most excellent inheritance, he enjoyed the patronage of Cosimo's son Piero and grandson Lorenzo. In accordance with the generous practice of that most distinguished of families, Ficino found himself enlarged in status and abundantly endowed with a respectable house, a delightful villa at Careggi, a priesthood, and an annual salary and perquisites.[315]

Not in the least ambitious, and desiring most the honorable 3 good of a cultivated and agreeable life, this man had no interest in increasing his wealth; for he aimed exclusively at the praiseworthy pursuit of studies. He never became embroiled in any controversies because he had renounced sensory pleasures of all kinds, except for semisweet wine. Nor, indeed, were his spirits low, since he was entirely happy, but he had the most precise regimen for protecting his health, as can be seen from the book he published on *The Triple Life.*[316] Indeed, he was so anxious in the deluded hope of extending his life that often on the same day, should the weather warm up or turn breezy, he would repeatedly change his head covering.

But after he mourned the bitter deaths of his companions Lo- 4 renzo, Ermolao, Poliziano, and Mirandola, who died in the space of one year, and then those of Landino and Savonarola, he died aged over seventy from a low-grade fever, at his own villa in Careggi.[317] This was indeed a dire omen, in that at the exact same moment of that day, a force ordained by fate extinguished the two brightest lights of Italy: Ficino himself, and Paolo Vitelli, a man of the most invincible prowess and captain of an army fighting on behalf of Florence, who was condemned to death by a certain frenzied anger of enemies rather than by wrongdoing.[318] This happened at that time when King Louis of France, having taken up arms, was in the Alps.[319] His invasion resulted in the ruin of every single illustrious ruling house and in the overthrow of practically all the governments of Italy.

5                             *Incerti*

Mores, ingenium Musae sophiaeque sepulta est
laus hic cum magni corpore Marsilii.

6                             *Incerti*

En hospes hic est Marsilius sophiae pater,
Platonicum qui dogma culpa temporum
situ obrutum, illustrans et Atticum decus
servans, Latio dedit. Fores primus sacras
divinae aperiens mentis actus numine,
vixit beatus ante Cosmi munere
Laurique Medicis, nunc revixit publico.

## XLIV. Galeottus Martius

1  Galeottum Martium Narnia genuit, robusto ingenio disciplinas omnes complectentem. Is Matthiae Corvino Pannoniae Regi praeceptor epistolarumque magister, et in castris miles et in palestra multarum palmarum athleta fortissimus, operam praestitit adeo feliciter ut omnium Horarum amicus et comes haberetur.

2  Scripsit librum *De homine* varia eruditione potiusquam eloquentia mirabilem, in quem non multo post invectus est Georgius Merula grammaticorum exactissimus. Sed ea vehementia Galeot-

Anonymous[320]

5

Here are interred, along with the body of the great Marsilio, an upright character,[321] the brilliance of poetic inspiration, and the glory of wisdom.

Anonymous[322]

6

Behold, traveler, this is Marsilio, the father of wisdom, who elucidated and preserved Attic splendor, and gave to Latium the teachings of Plato, which had languished in neglect through the fault of the times. Acted upon by the divine will, he was the first to open the sacred doors to the mind of God. Before, he lived blessed with the favor of Cosimo and Lorenzo de' Medici; now, he has come to life again blessed with the favor of the public.

## XLIV. Galeotto Marzio (ca. 1424–ca. 1494 or 1497)

Narni brought forth Galeotto Marzio,[323] a man whose powerful mind comprehended all fields of learning. Serving Matthias Corvinus, king of Hungary, as tutor and secretary he showed himself both an exceedingly brave soldier in the field and an uncommonly strong athlete with many wrestling victories. So successful was he at all this that he was held as a friend and confidant for all seasons.[324]

He wrote *On Humankind*, a book striking for wide-ranging erudition rather than for eloquence.[325] Soon thereafter, Giorgio Merula, the most exacting of grammarians, inveighed against it.[326] But Galeotto defended himself with like vehemence, so that the

1

2

tus se se defendit, uti apologeticus priore libro varietate eruditionis multo uberior censeri posset.

3   Scripsit etiam, et malo quidem infortunio quaedam in sacra moralique philosophia; nam ex ea lectione, quum omnibus gentibus integre et puriter, veluti ex iusta naturae lege, viventibus aeternos coelestis aurae fructus paratos diceret, a cucullatis sacerdotibus accusatus damnatusque est. Sed eum periculo celeriter exemit Xystus Pontifex, qui in minori fortuna eius fuerat auditor, non sine gravi tamen contumelia; nam in foro Veneto ad geminas columnas ad tribunal perductus est ut, impetrata venia, se falsa scripsisse fateretur.

4   Sed accidit ut id iudicium exortus in turba risus everteret salso ac repentino Galeotti dicterio excitatus: nam quum forte non ignobilis Venetus, e turba proximus strigosa proceritate et impudicae uxoris probro insignis, traductum ludibrio 'praepinguem porcum' appellasset, extemplo Galeottus renidentique ore 'pinguis' ait 'porcus, quam macer hircus esse malo.' Erat etiam Galeottus usque adeo tumenti abdomine ut quum sub vasto obesi corporis pondere, vel praegrandia iumenta fatiscerent, rheda curuli veheretur; ac demum senex ad Montem Annianum circa Ateste, arvina suffocatus interiret.

5           *Iani Vitalis*

Hanc galeam hunc posuit Galeottus Martius ensem
Mars tibi, et hanc citharam docto cum pectine Musis,
militia functus decantataque poesi.

refutation may be judged far richer in the variety of its erudition than was the initial book.[327]

He also wrote certain works on sacred and moral philosophy, 3 and to his own detriment;[328] for once they had been read—since he said that the eternal rewards of heaven had been prepared for all peoples living faultlessly and purely in accordance with the just law of nature—the friars accused and condemned him. But Pope Sixtus, who in less elevated days had been his pupil, quickly extricated him from danger.[329] He did not, however, escape serious contumely, for he was led out to the tribunal at the twin columns in the Venetian piazza[330] to beg for pardon and admit that he had written falsehoods.[331]

But it happened that the laughter of the crowd, incited by a 4 witty, off-the-cuff remark by Galeotto, broke up the proceedings; for when by chance the man next to him in the crowd, a Venetian noble noted both for his tall, scrawny physique and for the disgrace of his wife's immorality, had called him an "obese pig" as he was being paraded by, at once Galeotto said with a smile, "better to be a fat pig than a skinny goat."[332] In point of fact, Galeotto had such a great belly that he used to ride in a carriage, since even massive pack animals would break down under the tremendous weight of his obese body; and when he was an old man he finally died at Montagnana, near Este, smothered under his own lard.[333]

*By Giano Vitale*[334]                                                    5

Having engaged in military service and in singing poetry, Galeotto Marzio devoted to you, Mars, this helmet and sword, and to the Muses, this lute along with a skilled pick.

## XLV. Elisius Calentius

1   Huius ex Amphracta oppido semiappuli Musa, regnantibus Ara-
goniis Neapoli, insignis fuit, vel illustrium poetarum aemulatione
proposita. Tum enim Pontanus, Altilius, Gravina et Actius, immortali ingenio praediti vates, divina carmina factitabant. Sed Ca-
lentio, amatoriae vanitatis incendiis iuveniliter ustulato, aequo tor-
rentior vena, uti subitis impulsa casibus, nequaquam liquidissime
profluebat in varios alioqui carminum modos repentina largitate
mirabilis. Adamavit eum unice a puero contubernalem Pontanus,
suspexit Altilius, Actius vero Syncerus meritis laudibus exornavit.

2   Extant eius *Elegiae* teneris affectibus peramoenae et *Ranarum
cum muribus praelia* Homerico spiritu Latine decantata. Dicavit eas
vigilias Angelo Colotio, ab eruditi ingenii candore viro lectissimo,
quem hodie, vivido ingenio senem et sacrata infula clarum, salubris eloquentiae praecepta in hortis ingenue tradentem Romana
iuventus colit.

3   Moriens Calentius Lucium filium reliquit, ad quem legitur
epistola Pontani ad paternos mores studiaque eadem adolescentem
accendentis. Porro Calentius ipse, quum amore perditus oblitus-
que rei elegis inanibus diu haesisset, Fortunam sibi ad parandas
opes defuisse sero sensit ut hoc suo carmine fatetur:

> Talia post cineres de me toto orbe legantur
>     scriptaque sint tumulo carmina digna meo:
> ingenium Natura dedit, Fortuna poetae
>     defuit atque inopem vivere fecit amor.

## XLV. Elisio Calenzio[335] (1430–1502)

The literary talent of this half-Apulian, from the town of An- 1
fratta, was renowned when the Aragonese were ruling Naples; he
was even the rival of famous poets.[336] For at that time Pontano,
Altilio, Gravina, and Sannazaro, literati gifted with immortal brilliance, were wont to write divine poems. But in Calenzio, scorched
in his youth by the folly of young love, the vein poured forth in a
torrent more than was suitable, as if driven on by unexpected mis-
chances: hardly a limpid stream, but marvelous for the sudden
abundance and for the variety of poetic measures into which it
flowed. Pontano, his companion since boyhood, was especially
fond of him; Altilio admired him; and Sannazaro adorned him
with the praises he deserved.[337]

We have his *Elegies*, most pleasant in their tender emotions; and 2
the *Battle of the Frogs with the Mice*, in Homerically inspired Latin
verse.[338] He dedicated these labors to Angelo Colocci, a man
highly respected for the brilliance of his erudite genius, whom today's young Romans honor in his old age for his vigorous mind
and his holy miter,[339] as he freely teaches the principles of sound
eloquence in his gardens.

Calenzio died leaving a son, Lucio, to whom Pontano wrote a 3
well-known letter exhorting the young man to emulate his father's
character and path of learning. As for Elisio himself, lovestruck
and careless of money, he had persisted for a long time in his trifling elegies, realizing too late that Fortune had failed to endow
him with wealth, as he confesses in this poem of his:[340]

After my demise may things such as these be read about me
throughout the entire world (and may poems be written
worthy of my tomb): Nature bestowed genius, but Fortune
neglected the poet, and love made him live in destitution.

4 Moriens autem hoc carmen inscribendum Lucio filio mandavit.

*Ipsius*

Si tibi sit felix et faustum iter,
 qui sim discito paucis sodes.
Hic ego vates iaceo Calentius,
 somno sapiens gravi
 donec me tubicen aetheris excitet
vocans ad pias superum sedes.
Legistin? Amabo dic abiens; vale.


## XLVI. *Pandulphus Collenucius*

1 Pandulphus Collenucius Pisaurensis, ingenio peracri et studiorum rerumque omnium erudita notitia perornato, nobilissimarum Italiae urbium praeturas gessit functusque gravissimis legationum muneribus illustri facundia et gestu pernobili Latini oratoris nomen implevit. Caeterum tanto ingenio temperantia deerat ut nulla in arte summum laudis fastigium teneret. Insaciabili etenim cupiditate semper vagus in omnes disciplinas ferebatur, quum[25] esset ex professo iureconsultus, ut facile reliquarum facultatum principes disputatione scriptisque lacesseret, quod nihil nisi valde excellens probare esset solitus, et quaeque mediocria fastidiret.

2 Indignatione siquidem superba et ostentatione praecipiti Plinium adversus calumniatorem Leonicenum disertissime defendit, scripsit et libellum *De vipera* ac item facetissimum *Capitis et pilei dialogum,* postremo etiam Neapolitanorum regum res gestas

As he lay dying, he charged his son Lucio with having this  4
poem inscribed:

*By Calenzio Himself*

If your path is happy and propitious, please learn in just a
few words who I am. Here I lie, the poet Calenzio, in my
deep slumber, wisely waiting until the trumpeter of heaven
awakens me, beckoning me to the holy dwelling of heaven.
Have you finished reading? Please, repeat this as you leave.
Farewell.


## XLVI. Pandolfo Collenuccio (1444–1504)

Endowed with a keen intelligence and erudite knowledge of all  1
disciplines and subjects, Pandolfo Collenuccio of Pesaro served as
*podestà* in the most illustrious cities in Italy, and after fulfilling
critical diplomatic roles he used his conspicuous eloquence and
noble bearing to become the very model of a Latin orator.[341] But
his great genius so lacked moderation that in no discipline did he
gain a foothold on the peak of fame. Although by profession a
lawyer, because of his insatiable ambition he drifted unceasingly
from one field of learning to another, so that both in debate and in
his writings he unhesitatingly attacked the chief authorities in the
other disciplines, inclined to disapprove of anything not a masterpiece, and he despised whatever was merely average.[342]

With haughty scorn and impetuous display, at any rate, he elo-  2
quently defended Pliny against his detractor Leoniceno.[343] But he
also wrote a little book *On the Viper* and a very witty dialogue between *Head and Cap*, and lastly a history of the kings of Naples,

Ethrusco quidem sermone in gratiam Herculis Atestini, qui Latinas minime didicerat.

3    Multa autem lectu iucunda eleganter inchoata absolvere nequivit, quum apud Ioannem Sfortiam Pisaurensium tyrannum, quem depraehensis literis offenderat, supra veterum officiorum memoriam dissimulata recentis odii libido valuisset. Vir enim incaute tyranno fidens, ea nece indignus, in carcere strangulatus interiit.

4                    *Ferdinandi Balsamii Siculi*

Ignoscit Colenuccio tyrannus;
mox illum necat: o scelus nephandum,
vincens saevitiam Neronianam!

## *XLVII. Iovianus Pontanus*

1    Iovianus Pontanus, vir ad omne genus eloquentiae natus, Cereto Umbriae oppido metu profugiens quod ibi pater a factiosis civibus esset interfectus, Neapolim plane iuvenis et inops contendit. Ibi enim, liberali Alphonsi Regis studio condita celebri bibliotheca, literas in honore esse didicerat. Nec defuit honestus virtuti locus, Antonio Panhormita eruditi ingenii vim admirante; is tum erat excellentis doctrinae nomine regii scrinii magister.

2    Aspiravit demum his coeptis Fortuna usque adeo benigne ut, Ferdinandi Regis castra secutus, in demortui Panhormitae locum sufficeretur, unde illi mox honestae opes sed obsequii fide ac

composed in the Tuscan dialect as a favor to Ercole d'Este, whose Latin was negligible.[344]

He did not, however, live to complete many delightful works 3 elegantly begun, having in an intercepted letter offended Giovanni Sforza, the tyrant of Pesaro; the latter initially kept his anger hidden, but his passionate hatred prevailed over the memory of Collenuccio's former services.[345] Recklessly trusting a tyrant, he did not deserve to die as he did, strangled to death in prison.

*By Ferdinando Balsamo the Sicilian[346]* 4

The tyrant pardons Collenuccio, but soon he kills him. O unspeakable crime, outdoing the savagery of Nero!

## XLVII. Gioviano Pontano (1429–1503)

Gioviano Pontano, a man naturally suited for eloquence in every 1 genre, fled in terror from the Umbrian town of Cerreto because factious citizens there had murdered his father.[347] Quite young and poor, he headed to Naples where, he had learned, thanks to the generous support of King Alfonso a library had been founded and literature held a place of honor.[348] His abilities did not go unrecognized: on account of his learning and intelligence, he gained the admiration of Antonio Panormita, who then held the position of first secretary to the king on account of his exceptional scholarship.

At length, fortune favored these beginnings so generously that, 2 having followed King Ferdinando on a military campaign, he was named to succeed Panormita in the post vacated by the latter's death.[349] This provided a decent living but, as he wrote, his income

merito, uti scripsit, inferiores, nisi ad opimi muneris proventum
Ariadnae uxoris dotalis haereditas accessisset. Hac parta dignitate,
liberiore veluti studio Musas per omnes numeros exercuit tanta
habilis ingenii foecunditate ut neque poetis neque oratoribus, qui
tum maxime florerent, dignum secundae famae locum relinqueret.

3      Erat austero supercilio et toto oris habitu subagrestis, sed stylo
et sermone perurbanus quum saepissime vel in seriis multo cum
sale iocaretur. Habitus tamen est in omni censura, quanquam absolute pius, supra aequum mordax, vel eo quod non homines
modo sibi notos, sed gentium et urbium quoque omnium mores
acerba scribendi libertate perstringeret, sicuti ex variis dialogis,
*Charonte*que praesertim, intemperanter ostendit. Sed in pangendo
carmine quam texenda prosa cultior atque sublimior multis videtur, quandoquidem in historia non semper integra gravissimi in-
cessus dignitate ab eius muneris disciplina deflexisse existimari
possit, quum postea ab *Hesperidum hortis* citriorum suavissimis
odores spirans, atque inde divino carmine in altum evectus ad illa
ipsa excelso ore decantata sydera propius accesserit.

4      Vixit annos septuaginta septem, fato autem functus eodem
mense quo Alexander Sextus Pontifex vita excesserat. Tumulatus
est in sacello ab se sepulchri causa extructo e regione Davalorum
domus, ubi elogium ab se compositum in marmorea tabula spectatur.

> Vivus domum hanc mihi paravi
> in qua quiescerem mortuus.
> Noli, obsecro, iniuriam mortuo facere
> vivens quam fecerim nemini.
> Sum etenim Iovianus Pontanus,
> quem amaverunt bonae Musae,
> suspexerunt viri probi,
> honestaverunt reges domini.
> Scis iam qui sim, vel qui potius fuerim.

would have fallen short of his loyal and deserving service had it not been amply supplemented by the dowry of his wife, Ariadne.[350] Since this new status enabled him to undertake his studies as if with more unfettered enthusiasm, he cultivated the Muses in all meters with such fertile genius and skill that the most prominent poets and orators of that time were not remotely on his level.

His stern, haughty gaze and his whole countenance made him 3 seem rather provincial, but he was highly sophisticated in style and speech, since very often he bantered wittily, even on serious subjects. Though utterly honest, his criticisms were always thought scathing beyond what was fair; for indeed, writing with harsh candor, he reproved not only persons known to him but also the character of all nations and cities, as he demonstrated to a fault in various dialogues, especially the *Charon*.[351] But many see him as more refined and elevated when he composed poetry than when he wrote prose; for one might suppose that in writing history he strayed from the strictures of that task, not always maintaining the full dignity of its serious manner.[352] Thereafter, however, breathing the fragrances from the delightful orange *Gardens of the Hesperides* and rising from there by poetic inspiration, he approached the very stars about which he had often sung in a lofty style.[353]

He lived to the age of seventy-seven, dying in the same month 4 as Pope Alexander VI.[354] He was buried in the neighborhood of the house of the d'Avalos family, in a chapel that he himself had designed to be his tomb. There one sees a marble tablet with the epitaph that he composed:

> While living, I prepared for myself this dwelling in which to rest in death. Pray do no harm to me in death that in life I did to no one. Indeed, I am Gioviano Pontano, beloved by the virtuous Muses, admired by upright men, and rewarded by sovereign kings. Now you know who I am, or rather who

173

Ego vero te, hospes, in tenebris noscere nequeo,
sed te ipsum ut noscas rogo. Vale.

5                               *Myrtei*

Qui vos sydera clara citriosque
flores hesperidum hortulis virentes
versibus cecinit laboriosis,
Pontano date, sydera alma, lymphas;
vos, horti, date serta quae sepulchrum
ornent perpetuo cadente flore,
spargant perpetuo cadente rore.

6                        *Marci Antonii Flaminii*

Quae cecinit claro fulgentia lumina coelo
    Pontani doctis versibus Urania,
Phoebe tuis magnam lucem addidit ignibus, utque
    nunc melius niteant sydera cuncta facit.


## XLVIII. *Marcus Antonius Coccius Sabellicus*

1   Marcus Antonius Coccius Sabellicus ad vicum Varronis in via
Valeria iuxta Anienem fabro ferrario patre genitus ingentem et
prope ferream vim ingenii ad perdiscendas literas attulit, tanto
proventu ut plane imberbis apud Tyburtes ludum aperiret. Inde
vero collecta mercede et togula coerulea excultus nobilioris doctrinae cupiditate in Urbem ad Pomponium se contulit, a quo
uberrimi ingenii merito in collegium sodalium solenni cerimonia
cooptatus Sabellici cognomen tulit; mutabat enim nomen qui in

I was. Here in the darkness, stranger, I cannot know you, but I ask that you know yourself.[355] Farewell.

*By Mirteo*[356]  5

To Pontano who sang in well-wrought verses of bright stars and citrus flowers blooming in the Hesperides's gardens, give moisture, you nourishing stars; you gardens, adorn his tomb forever with wreaths of your drooping blossoms, sprinkling it forever with falling dew.

*By Marcantonio Flaminio*[357]  6

Urania, who has sung through Pontano's learned verses of the gleaming lights in the clear sky, has added great splendor to your radiance, Apollo, causing all the stars now to shine more brightly.

## XLVIII. *Marcantonio Coccio Sabellico (1436–1506)*

The son of an ironworker in Vicovaro, on the Valerian Way by the  1
banks of the Aniene, Marcantonio Coccio Sabellico brought to literary studies a mighty intellect, almost as strong as iron, with such success that when still a beardless youth he opened a school in Tivoli.[358] But having collected his salary there, and decked out in a little dark blue gown, he went off to Pomponio in Rome, eager for higher learning. For his abundance of talent Pomponio admitted him to his society of fellows. He took on the name "Sabellico," for everyone crowned with the laurel on the Quirinal hill changed

Quirinali sacra lauro coronabatur. In ea schola, quod censura literarum acerrimis iudicum ingeniis ageretur, multum sibi de incondita et subagresti Latinae orationis exuberantia detraxisse fertur.

2     Nec multo post, Roma excedens, Utino in oppido non procul ab Aquileia nobiles regionis adolescentes docuit. Parta demum insigni nominis fama quum regionem vetustatis authoritate percelebrem lepide descripsisset, decantato etiam versibus Carnico incendio et deplorata clade Sonciaca, idcirco eum Vicentini celebritate nominis exciti ambitiose duplicato stipendio conduxerunt. Nec ibi diu mansit, evocante Senatu Veneto ea conditione ut civitatis res gestas a fine Iustiniani conscriberet, et trecentis aureis in gymnasio profiteretur. In hoc munere perutilem iuventuti operam praestitit, quum in altero adulatione parum sobria rerum veritatem adumbrasse videretur.

3     Sed in *Enneadibus* omnium temporum ab orbe condito memoriam complexus, uti necesse fuit ingenti operis instituto festinanter indulgenti, res illustres praeclara cognitione dignissimas perobscura brevitate adeo vehementer offuscavit ut excitatam uberrimo titulo legentium cupiditatem passim eluserit, quum omnia in acervum angustissime coarctata, nequaquam certa effigie sed exiguis tantum punctis et lineis annotata designentur.

4     Id susceptum munus naviter secutus scribendo ad septuagesimum fere annum pervenit, Gallica tabe ex vaga Venere quaesita non obscure consumptus. De sepulchro autem vivens et incolumis tempestive sibi cavit, scilicet degeneri filio diffisus quem ex concubina susceperat, compositumque ab se carmen lapidi insculpsit — insigne quidem et meritum elogium, sed certe honestius si alieni ingenii pietas inscripsisset.

his name. It is said that he lost much of the unrefined and provincial effusiveness of his Latin oratory in that academy, where critics subjected literary compositions to the most severe of standards.

Departing from Rome soon after, he taught the sons of the local nobility in the town of Udine, not far from Aquileia. Eventually he acquired a distinguished reputation for his charming description of a region celebrated by virtue of its great antiquity and for his verses lamenting the fire in the Carnic Alps and the defeat at the Soča River.[359] On that account the Vicenzans, carried away by his fame, wooed him into their service by doubling his salary. He did not remain long there either, called away by the Venetian Senate to write the city's history from the death of Justinian and to teach at the university for a salary of three hundred gold ducats.[360] In the latter role he greatly benefited the city's youth, whereas in the former it seems he obscured the facts by too much flattery.[361]

But taking up in his *Enneads*[362] the history of all ages since the world began, as was inevitable for one who yielded hastily to an enormous project, he took achievements most deserving of clear explanation and so completely obfuscated them by his cryptic brevity that the readers' appetites, whetted by his exuberant title, were everywhere disappointed. For everything was compressed into a tight mass, not portrayed at all distinctly, but roughly sketched with just a few dots and lines.

He actively pursued this task, writing almost until the age of seventy but visibly wasting away from the French pox, which he had contracted through promiscuity.[363] While alive and healthy, however, he made timely provision for his tomb, evidently not trusting an illegitimate son he'd fathered by a mistress, and he had a stone carved with a verse of his own composition — a distinguished and worthy epitaph, to be sure, that would certainly have been more honorable if engraved as a tribute from somebody else:[364]

Quem non res hominum, non omnis ceperat aetas
scribentem, capit haec Coccion urna brevis.


## XLIX. *Laurentius Laurentianus*

1  Laurentius Laurentianus, aliquandiu Florentiae et Pisis philosophiam medicinamque professus, ingenium elegantibus literis deditum ad traducendum Hippocratem convertit, quod Theodorus
Gaza alioqui diligentissimus interpres circumscripti authoris laco-
nismis minime serio respondere videretur. Extant et eius eruditae
lucubrationes in Galenum medicinae principis arcana perobscure
interpretantem.

2      Sed in commentationum cursu plane miser atra bile correptus
est. Empturus enim domum ea pactione tertiam praetii partem
numerarat ut, nisi intra sextum mensem totius summae pecuniam
repraesentaret, arrabonis pecunia lucro venditoris amitteretur. Ad-
ventante vero die quum multa ei adversa spem fefellissent, diffisus
amicorum liberalitati et iacturae dolore perculsus, animum despon-
dit in profundumque puteum se coniecit sub id tempus quo Petrus
Soderinus, erecto populari dominatu, tanquam dictator perpetuus
summa cum moderatione Florentinae reipublicae praesidebat.


3                              *Myrtei*

Spe destitutus commodum sibi domum
parandi et anguste, magis quam patria
Florentia natum aedibus mirabili
decebat, infelicem agens vitam, miser
Laurentianus se puteo in praeceps dedit
angustiori, ne sepulchrum largius

When he was writing, no human limit, no age could contain
Coccio; now this little urn holds him inside.

## XLIX. *Lorenzo Lorenziani* (1459/60–1502)

After teaching philosophy and medicine for some time in Florence   1
and Pisa, Lorenzo Lorenziani turned his talent for literature to
rendering Hippocrates, believing that Theodore Gaza, an otherwise exacting translator, was wholly unsuited to the spare expressions of a concise author.[365] We also have his learned exposition of
Galen, who expounded the secrets of early medicine, though with
little clarity.[366]

But while writing his commentaries, the poor fellow fell into a   2
deep melancholy. He had made a down payment on a house,
fronting a third of the price with the agreement that, should he
not pay off the remainder within six months, he would forfeit the
deposit to the seller. But with the due date looming, many set-
backs thwarted his hopes. Lacking confidence in the generosity of
friends and grief-stricken at his loss, in despair he threw himself
headlong down a deep well. At the time, following a period of
popular sovereignty, Piero Soderini governed the Florentine Republic with moderation, as something of a dictator for life.[367]

### By Mirteo[368]   3

Robbed of the hope of getting himself a suitable home, and
living in poor circumstances — more cramped than was fitting for a native son of Florence, a city of palaces — the
wretched Lorenziani threw himself down a narrow well,
with the intention that in death he would not have a tomb

esset cadenti quam fuerat vivo domus:
Quae nunc parata literis illi patet
talis polo, qualem nequeat orbis dare.

## L. Antiochus Tibertus

1   Antiochus Tibertus Caesenas ingenuus puer a milite in ulteriorem Galliam perductus, amore literarum Lutetiae consedit, non abnuente hero, ut docilis ingenii adolescens optimis literis imbueretur. Post aliquot autem annos inde rediens in Italiam, profiteri coepit divinatorias artes magiae proximas. Eleganti enim libro *De chiromantia* edito tantum novae famae promeruit ut insigni concursu a curiosis et anxiis de toto vitae fortunaeque eventu consuleretur; nam ad corroborandam eius disciplinae authoritatem opportuna bonarum artium praesidia contulerat, usque adeo solerter atque feliciter ut viri doctissimi, plane conscii de vanitate incertae artis, id asseverarent quod vulgi testimonio crederetur.

2   Primus enim post Petrum Aponensem, magiae peritia celebrem, duobus saeculis iacentem et a cucullatis explosam artem excitarat. Tribus etiam libris *De physiognomia et pyromantia* compositis, ea tamen opinione ut nequaquam ex arcano artis avidissimo cuique futura praenoscendi rerum abditarum eventus praediceret, sed ex mirae prudentiae coniectura, tanquam illustri ratione demonstrare putaretur.

3   Praedixerat Guidoni Balneo, cui in togata Gallia propter inusitatum militaris animi vigorem Guerrae cognomentum fuit atque item Pandulpho Malatestae Ariminensium tyranno ex volae

more ample than the house he had in life. Now his writings have made him a dwelling in heaven such as the world could not give him.

## L. Antioco Tiberti (?–1499/1500)

Taken to France as a young boy by a soldier, with his master's consent the wellborn Antioco Tiberti[369] of Cesena settled in Paris for the love of literature, so that while a youth his receptive intellect was imbued with the best learning. Returning from there to Italy after several years, however, he began to profess arts of divination that verged on magic. Indeed, with the elegant book he published *On Palmistry*, he earned such newfound fame that the curious and the anxious flocked to him to learn how the whole of their lives and fortunes would turn out.[370] To validate the worth of his science, he had opportunely marshaled the support of the liberal arts, doing so with such skill and success that, although deeply learned men fully realized that this unreliable art was baseless, they affirmed what was commonly believed.

He was the first since the renowned magician Pietro d'Abano[371] to revive an art dormant for two centuries and condemned by the friars. He wrote three books *On Physiognomy and Pyromancy*, yet even so it was generally held that he wasn't really drawing on the secrets of his craft to foretell the outcomes of hidden things to anyone who wanted to foresee the future, but instead was demonstrating them through lucid reasoning based upon remarkably keen conjecture.[372]

He predicted to Guido da Bagno, called "Guerra" for the exceptional prowess he showed as a soldier in northern Italy, that he would be killed by an eminent friend on suspicion of treachery;[373] and from reading his palm, he told Pandolfo Malatesta, the tyrant

manus lineis futurum esse, ut hic pelleretur patria et dominatu exulque in extrema egestatis miseria periret, ille vero ab insigni amico perfidiae suspicione necaretur: memorabili hercle non omnino incertae artis argumento nisi Antiochus imminentem vitae suae exitum ignorasset, de quo tamen, sed fatali deceptus hora, minime dubitarat. Interfecit enim Pandulphus suo metu vel Bentivoli soceri iussu nimium saevus a suspecta virtute virum fortem quamvis amicum et partium ducem, ac ipsum Tibertum custodiae tradidit ut ex eventu supplicio servaretur.

4    Sed, quum occultam exitio fata viam aperirent, captivus et compedibus nexus custodis arcis filiam, mollis animi puellam, ita orando et blandiendo ad misericordiam amoremque pellexit ut ab ea restem impetraret et in fossam demitteretur. Sed compedum sonitu prodita fuga miser retractus et pari sorte cum puella securi percussus interiit. Nec in Pandulpho praedicentis fidem eadem fata fefellerunt, quando omnium egentissimus in hospitali diversorio desertus a liberis, saevitia infamis ac egestate, senex miser perierit.

5         *Floridi Sabini*

Exilium domino quod vaticinare potenti,
     dira morte insons perderis, Antioche.
O miseras arteis! quae non docuere salutis,
     cum tibi monstrarint hae quoque mortis iter.

of Rimini, that he would be driven from his city and dominion, dying an exile in the most miserable poverty.[374] The latter prediction would have provided memorable evidence, Lord knows, that his art was not in the least unreliable, had it not been for Antioco's failure to realize that his own death was imminent — a fact of which he had little doubt, though he was mistaken about the hour. For Pandolfo, rendered excessively cruel either out of his own terror or on the orders of his father-in-law Bentivoglio, did indeed execute a brave man [i.e., Guido] whose valor at arms he found suspect, even though the man was a friend and a commander in his faction.[375] He placed Tiberti in custody to await his punishment, depending on the outcome [of his predictions].[376]

But when the Fates revealed to him the way he would die, Tiberti, jailed and in irons, begged and flattered the castellan's daughter,[377] a girl of tender disposition. Coaxing her to mercy and love, he obtained from her a rope by which he could be let down into the moat. But the rattling of his shackles betrayed his flight, and the wretch was dragged back up and beheaded along with the girl.[378] Even so, Fate did not weaken the credibility of Tiberti's predictions in the case of Pandolfo, who would die a wretched old man, utterly destitute and abandoned by his children in a wayside boarding house, notorious for his cruelty as well as his poverty.[379]

4

*By Florido Sabini*[380]

5

Foretelling the exile of your powerful master, Antonio, though guiltless, you are done in by cruel death. O unhappy arts, which did not teach you the path of safety although they showed you the path of death!

## LI. *Philippus Beroaldus*

1 Beroaldum inter nobiles grammaticae professores summi nominis
celebritate et incredibili auditorum frequentia Bononiae docentem
externa praesertim iuventus effuse mirabatur, quum ex multa lectione felicique memoria abstrusae doctrinae opes venusto oris
gestu proferret et interpretando intacta ab aliis avide sectaretur.

2 Cupiebat enim obscuris authoribus lucem dare et rancidae vetustatis vocabula iam plane repudiata a sanis scriptoribus in usum
Romanae linguae revocare, uti apparuit ex commentariis in *Asinum
Aureum* Apulei, cuius familiaritate horridum eloquentiae genus
perversa quadam libidine induerat, ita ut honestae aures illud as-
perum impurae novitatis mirari primo et mox admittere cogeren-
tur. Sed ingenio maxime liberali et perhumano haec obsoleta et
ridenda doctioribus opportune condiebat ea fama ut qui omnia
didicisse et sedulo docuisse videri potuit, in delectu pinguis et su-
pinus evaserit.

3 Obiit non plane senex, paulo post id tempus quo Bononia terremotu concussa est et tyranni Bentivoli domum mirabili subsecu-
tae calamitatis praesagio dira fulmina percusserunt. Excepit doctrinae haereditatem eiusdem nominis fratris filius. Is nitidiore
ingenio, quum ad poeticam se contulisset, dignas aeternitate odas
conscripsit indeque a Leone Pontifice in intimam familiaritatem
est receptus, collata ei Vaticanae Bibliothecae praefectura; sed paratis honoribus immatura mors celeriter invidit.

## LI. Filippo Beroaldo (the Elder) (1453–1505)

Among noted teachers of philology Beroaldo[381] had the greatest    1
fame and a vast following; he lectured at Bologna to a worshipful
crowd of youths, especially foreigners, for by his charming oratory
he drew out a wealth of recondite learning from his extensive reading and fertile memory, and he eagerly ferreted out matters left
untouched in others' expositions.

He desired, in fact, to give visibility to obscure authors and to    2
reintroduce Latin words musty with age that sensible writers had
already thoroughly rejected. This was evident from his commentaries on the *Golden Ass* of Apuleius: drawing upon his intimate
understanding of this text, with a certain twisted pleasure he had
taken on a kind of uncouth eloquence.[382] The result was that respectable listeners were made initially to wonder at such disagreeable and distasteful strangeness, and presently to accept it. But his
very generous and kindly nature was so quick to season these
outmoded and laughable words with more learned ones that he,
who had the reputation of careful learning and teaching, turned
out a sloppy glutton in his lexical choices.

He died when not very old, right after Bologna was shaken by    3
an earthquake and violent lightning struck the palace of the tyrant
Bentivoglio: a remarkable foreboding of the disaster to follow.[383]
His intellectual heir was his nephew and namesake whose brilliance, once devoted to poetry, shone brighter: he wrote odes worthy of immortality for which Pope Leo welcomed him into his
inner circle and made him prefect of the Vatican Library.[384] But a
swift, untimely death denied him enjoyment of the honors he had
been given.

4 *Myrtei*

Saepe novos linguae mirata Bononia flores
non alios legit quam, Beroalde, tuos.
Te nunc amisso languent cum floribus horti,
et flet delitias ad tumulum illa suas.


## LII. *Hercules Strozza*

1 Hercules Strozza Ferrariensis, Tito poeta genitus, patrem longo
intervallo carminum nobilitate superavit. Illustri enim quodam lepore generosi et solertis ingenii in aula principis adeo clarus emine-
bat ut praeter gravioris consilii munera, in quibus egregie prudens
et paratus erat, theatralium etiam ludorum ac omnis elegantiae
arbiter censeretur. Nec quicquam de cultu corporis sumptuosisque
munditiis et splendore vitae Atestinis iuvenibus concederet.

2 Sed eum, hac civilis magnificentiae laude florentem amato-
riisque vanitatibus intemperanter deditum, ille impotens deorum
ac hominum dominator (ut Fabulae ferunt) Cupido saevus in
praecipitem locum arripuit, concepti siquidem amoris insaniam
adeo perditis sensibus alebat ut multa ac erudita largitione tenerri-
misque carminibus summi nominis matronam colere aliquanto
procacius quam liceret minime vereretur; qua improbitate, si non
molestus palam, gravis tamen quibusdam in arcano esse coeperat,
quum tot illecebrae una illa morum eleganti libertate male tegeren-
tur, ob idque ab odiosa obtrectatione timeri inciperet; quanquam
luxato olim poplite claudus nec alioqui plane formosus esset aut
iuvenis, praevalida scilicet apud zelotypos suspicione quum ille
inter iocos cum foeminis ad elevandam cruris deformitatem, lepido

*By Mirteo*[385]                    4

Bologna, often in wonder at new flowers of language, plucks
none other than yours, o Beroaldo. Now that you are gone
her gardens wilt along with their flowers, and she weeps for
her beloved at his tomb.

## LII. *Ercole Strozzi (ca. 1470–73 to 1508)*

Ercole Strozzi[386] of Ferrara, the poet Tito's son, far surpassed his   1
father in the excellence of his verse. Indeed, the brilliant charm of
his noble and clever mind shone forth in the princely court in such
a way that, beyond his more serious responsibilities as an advisor,
for which he was highly skilled and well equipped, he was also
considered a master of theatrical production and of every refinement;[387] nor did the youth of the House of d'Este outshine him
when it came to attire, costly luxuries, or magnificent living.

But just as his reputation for public grandeur blossomed and he   2
gave himself without restraint to philandering, cruel Cupid, who
according to myth reigns despotically over gods and men, brought
him to the brink of ruin, for he so senselessly nurtured a mad in-
fatuation that he had the presumption to court an eminent matron
somewhat more boldly than was permitted, lavishing upon her
gifts of learning and the tenderest poems.[388] Although they didn't
openly show their annoyance at this impropriety, certain individuals privately took umbrage, since the elegance of that one indulgence was poor cover for so many seductions, and for this reason
he went from being hated to being feared. For although he was
lame from having in the past dislocated his knee, and in any case
neither handsome nor young, suspicions prevailed among jealous
types when, jesting with women, he made light of his deformed

exemplo diceret non insulsam esse Venerem quae Vulcanum, probe virum quanquam loripedem, libenter admitteret.

3 Sed demum Taurellam illustrem forma et natalibus viduam usque adeo diris auspiciis adamavit ut quum rivalem haberet impotentem tyrannum cum ea fatales nuptias faceret, ut pudore coniugii repulsus rivalis arceretur. Sed id non tulit vir atrox et superbus brevique Hercules, dum a coena domum noctu mula reveheretur, interfectus est, neque caedis quisquam authorem silente praetore nominavit.


4 *Bembi*

Te ripa natum Eridani Permessus alebat,
    fecerat et vatem Marsque Venusque suum.
Iniecere manus iuveni et fatalia duris
    stamina pollicibus persecuere Deae.
Uxor honorata manes dum conderet urna,
    talia cum multis dicta[26] dedit lachrymis:
'Non potui tecum dulcem consumere vitam:
    at iam adero amplexans te cinerem ipsa cinis.'


5 *Tibaldei*

Herculis hic Strozzae tumulus quem condidit uxor
    Taurellae moerens Barbara gentis honos.
Plus dederit quamvis, non hac,[27] Mausole, meretur
    plus tua: fortuna haec, non pietate, minor.

leg using the witty example that Venus was no fool in freely accepting Vulcan since, though clubfooted, he was most definitely a man.

But in the end, out of an ill-starred passion for the beautiful 3 and highborn widow Torelli, he made a fateful marriage with her, thinking by the hindrance of holy wedlock to keep his rival, a crazed tyrant, at a distance.[389] But that violent and haughty man did not put up with this: shortly after, as Ercole rode a mule home after dinner one night, he was murdered. The *podestà* did not address the matter, and nobody named the assassin.

### By Bembo[390] 4

Born on the shores of the Po you were fed by Permessus;[391] Mars and Venus both had even made you their poet. The Fates took hold of you while still young, and their unyielding fingers cut the fateful thread. While your wife laid your spirit to rest in a suitable urn, amid a profusion of tears she spoke these words: "I could not end my life happily with you; but soon I will be here embracing you, ashes to ashes."

### By Tebaldeo[392] 5

Here is the tomb of Ercole Strozzi, built in her grief by his wife Barbara, the glory of the Torelli family. Although your wife gave more, Mausolus,[393] she is no more deserving than his: though of less means than yours, his wife felt no less devotion.

## LIII. Bartholomeus Cocles

1   Bartholomeus Cocles, humili genere Bononiae natus, ingenio nec mediocribus quidem literis imbuto sed a coelesti quodam munere divino ac admirabili, vaticinandi artes curiose atque feliciter excepit erectas nuper ac illustratas ab Antiocho: se enim metoposcopum et chiromantem profitebatur, magno hercle astrologorum pudore qui laboriosis geniturae supputationibus saepissime fallerentur.

2   Publicarat enim ingenti fama codicem cum effigie linearum characteres et notas artis continentem ut et hac quoque liberalitate, tanquam promulgato totius doctrinae mysterio, ignaras vitae eventus curiosorum mentes circumduceret, valido hercle accedente patrocinio Achillini summi philosophi, qui luculento prohemio adversus artis calumniatores, Coclitis scripta tanquam insigni galea muniverat usque adeo studiose ac apposite ut, intertextis passim ex physica ratione quibusdam nervis, probe constituta vallataque vel inanis facultas una iam nec ignobilis liberalium artium acclamatione publica censeretur, et eo quidem clariore authoris existimatione, quod ipsius Antiochi et Corvi Mirandulae placita gravibus argumentis tanquam incerta convellerentur, ita pronis ad credendum auribus ut multi, stabilis alioqui prudentiae, ab hoc adumbratae rationis praestigio circumducti penderent ab ore Coclitis et de privatis rebus statuerent, quandoquidem quotidianis praedictionibus, futura tanquam praesentia sentirentur.

3   Extat de his praeclarae ac admirabilis fidei catalogus ipsius Coclitis manu perscriptus, de iis quibus varia violentae mortis pericula denunciavit, exactissimo post eius interitum Fortunae

## LIII. Bartolomeo Cocles (1467–1504)

Bartolomeo Cocles[394] was born at Bologna of lowly origins. His   1
mind was untouched even by ordinary learning, but from some
sacred, marvelous endowment of heaven he diligently and successfully took up the art of prophecy recently revived and brought to
light by Antioco.[395] Indeed, he declared himself a physiognomist
and palm reader — to the mortification, Lord knows, of the astrologers, since they were very often mistaken in their elaborately
calculated horoscopes.

To immense acclaim, he had published a book of line drawings   2
containing the signs and symbols of his art, so as to draw in, by
this additional generosity as well, those ignorant minds eager to
know their destinies, as though he were making all his scientific
secrets known.[396] Indeed, he obtained the powerful reinforcement
of being endorsed by the great philosopher Achillini who, in his
splendid preface directed at the detractors of the craft, thoroughly
and fittingly defended the writings of Cocles as with a distinguished helmet, weaving a web of sorts of scientific proofs so that,
although prophecy was a skill of little substance, popular opinion
no longer considered it a lowly practice, but one of the liberal arts,
properly and securely founded.[397] The author, too, gained in prestige as by compelling arguments he demolished as unsound the
tenets of Corvo di Mirandola[398] and of Antioco himself. So gull-
ible were his hearers that many of sound judgment in other matters were led astray by the trickery of his counterfeited reasoning,
hanging on Cocles's every word and making decisions about private affairs, since in his daily predictions the future seemed as clear
as the present.

We have a list in Cocles's own hand of these wondrously accu-   3
rate predictions concerning those whom he declared at risk of
various violent deaths — which Fortune obligingly and precisely

obsequentis eventu comprobatus. Quo fit ut me quoque, invetera-
tae exercitationis in hac luce Romana non facile credulum senem,
in sententiam adducat ipse exactae aetatis et integri iudicii Lucas
Gauricus, quum ingenue fateatur se a Coclite severe amiceque ad-
monitum ut violenti cruciatus causas effugeret quum id ipse, sui
natalis negligentia patris ignarus, ex syderum scientia antevertisse
nequiverit. A Ioanne enim Bentivolo arreptus et ex praealta troclea
suspenso fune quinquies quassatus, ideo poenas dederat quod ex-
cessurum patria et dominatu in eius anni prognostico pronuncias-
set.

4      Sed aliquanto acerbiorem non irritae divinationis poenam
Cocles promeruit, quum invitus et plane coactus Hermeti Tyranni
filio dixerit futurum esse ut exul in acie caederetur. Non tulit san-
guinarius Hermes, fatali metu perculsus, vel provocatam oris libertatem iussitque Copono ut Cocles tanquam futuris inferiis suis
expiando dolori victima mactaretur.

5      Praeviderat necis discrimen Cocles ideoque secreta galea caput
munierat, ingenti gladio quem peritissime ambabus manibus regebat semper armatus. Sed fatales insidias vitare non potuit quum a
personato baiuli habitu Copono, dum serae ostii calculo iniecto
praepeditae clavem insereret, adacta in occipitium securi sterrere-
tur, non aliam quoque patrati facinoris causam afferente Copono
quam quod ipsi Cocles brevi et sceleste homicidam futurum
edixisset.

6              *Guidonis Posthumi (Coponus loquitur)*

       Quis melior vates, quis Coclite verior augur?
          Falsa canit, atque haec cogit habere fidem.

confirmed by the events following his own demise. It so happens that I too, who thanks to age and long experience under the Roman sun am not easily fooled, am persuaded to agree by Luca Gaurico, himself a man of maturity and sound judgment: for he admits candidly that Cocles sternly and affectionately warned him to avoid supplying any pretext for violent torture, something that, not knowing his birthdate on account of his father's indifference, he himself could not use astrological expertise to foresee. Indeed, Gaurico was seized by Giovanni II Bentivoglio and subjected to the strappado, being suspended and dropped five times as punishment for divulging in that year's prognostications that Bentivoglio would be exiled and deposed.

But Cocles earned rather a more severe punishment for the 4 truth of his predictions when, obviously under duress, he was forced to tell Ermete, the tyrant's son, that he would be banished and die in battle. In terror of death, the bloodthirsty Ermete could not tolerate this frank speech even though he had provoked it, and he commanded Coponi[399] to make of Cocles a sacrificial victim, as though to avert the anguish of his own impending funeral rites.

In anticipation of mortal danger Cocles wore a concealed hel- 5 met and was always armed with a massive sword which he wielded expertly using both hands. But he could not avoid the deadly trap set by Coponi who, disguised as a workman, dispatched him from behind with an ax blow to the head as he tried to unlock a door whose keyhole Coponi had jammed with a pebble. Coponi gave no excuse for committing this crime, other than Cocles's having made known to him that he was soon to become a foul murderer.

*By Guido Postumo (Coponi Speaks)*[400]     6

Who is a better prophet, a more reliable seer, than Cocles? His words are false, and yet they compel belief. He has just

Grande mihi nuper scelus ac grave crimen inussit
    quale vel ipsius pectus habere neges.
Puriter exegi tamen ac sine crimine vitam
    hactenus; ille autem dicere vera solet.
Quidnam hoc, Phoebe, igitur? Certe illum haud multa fefellit
    linea quam heu! nostras damnat habere manus.
Nanque ubi ob hoc nostra cecidit malus ille securi
    coepi ego, ne falsum diceret, esse nocens.

## LIV. Ioannes Cotta

1    Ioannes Cotta apud Alieniacum pontem, id est oppidum supra Athesim, humili genere ortus, praealtum in literis ingenium ostendit; in agresti enim ore generosi spiritus indoles ita latitabat ut in sermone scriptoque mira felicitas emineret. Hauserat enim pertinaci studio evolutis utriusque linguae optimis authoribus tantas eruditionis opes ut a stupenda memoria clarus haberetur et antiquae dignitatis carmina perscriberet.

2    Aperuerat ludum Laudi Pompeiae quod ibi nupta erat eius matertera. Sed demum inde Neapolim ad Pontanum se contulit secutusque aliquandiu Sanseverinum et Cabanilium proceres transivit ad Livianum Venetorum ducem, qui Musarum liberalis hospes academiam in agro Tarvisino ad Portum Naonem instituerat, evocatis in contubernium praecellentibus poetis, in queis longe demum clarissimi (praeter Cottam) Fracastorius,[28] Naugerius et Hieronymus Borgius evaserunt.

3    Ad Abduam autem ex ipsa Gallorum victoria Liviano fuso captoque Cotta insigni pietate se totius calamitatis et carceris

branded me with a great wickedness, a grave crime such as
one would deny even that one would contemplate. Although
I have lived blamelessly and had a spotless record until now,
he is known for speaking the truth. What, then, is this, o
Phoebus? Surely he is mistaken about the short line which
he condemns my hands — poor me! — for having. For this
reason, you see, I was innocent up until the moment when
that evil man fell beneath my ax, in order to validate his
prediction.

## LIV. Giovanni Cotta (1480 or 1482–1510)

Giovanni Cotta[401] came from humble origins near Legnago, a   1
town on the Adige River, and displayed great aptitude for learning.
Indeed, behind his rustic countenance lay hidden an inner nobility, so that from his speaking and writing sprang forth a surprising
eloquence, for he had absorbed from assiduous reading and study
of the best Greek and Roman authors such a wealth of learning
that he was famous for his astonishing memory, and he wrote poems fully worthy of the ancients.

He had opened a school in Lodi because his mother's sister   2
married there. But after a while, he went to join Pontano in Naples.[402] After some time in the retinues of noble families, the Sanseverino and the Cavaniglia, he moved on to the Venetian commander d'Alviano.[403] A generous host to the Muses, d'Alviano
had founded an academy in Trevisan territory, at Pordenone, calling up prominent poets to live together there, including some who
along with Cotta achieved lasting fame: Fracastoro, Navagero, and
Girolamo Borgia.[404]

But after the French victory at the Adda River[405] where   3
d'Alviano was conquered and captured, Cotta with remarkable

comitem obtulit, sed Galli inhumana acerbitate non misero tantum comitem, sed libros et calamum ac omnia denique tenebrosi
ocii solatia denegarunt. Implevit alterum officii munus Cotta sus-
ceptisque a Liviano mandatis, quum ad Iulium Pontificem Viter-
bium pervenisset, paucos post dies, oborta pestilenti febre, octo et
viginti annorum iuvenis interiit.

4      Epigrammata ac orationes eius extant sed *Chorographiae,* opus
nobile versibus inchoatum, et in Plinium erudita scholia perierunt.

5                          *Actii Synceri*

Sperabas tibi, docta, novum, Verona, Catullum:
    experta es duros bis viduata deos.
Nulla animum posthac res erigat, optima quando
    prima rapit celeri Parca inimica manu.
Quae tamen, ut vidit morientis frigida Cottae
    ora, suum fassa est crimen et erubuit.

6                    *Marci Antonii Flaminii*

Si fas cuique sui sensus expromere cordis,
    hoc equidem dicam pace, Catulle, tua.
Est tua Musa quidem dulcissima; Musa videtur
    ipsa tamen Cottae dulcior esse mihi.

## LV. Petrus Crinitus

1  Petrus Crinitus iucundo eruditoque ingenio iuvenis, quum a crispa
patris coma Ethrusco nomine Riccius vocaretur idque nomen

loyalty volunteered to share wholly in his calamity and imprisonment. In their heartless cruelty, however, the French refused the
miserable fellow not only a companion but the means to read or
write—or to do anything, in short, to brighten the gloom of his
idleness.[406] Cotta carried out another diplomatic task at d'Alviano's
behest, but once he reached Pope Julius in Viterbo a pestilential
fever suddenly came over him and after a few days he died, a
young man of twenty-eight.

His epigrams and orations survive but the *Chorographies*, an    4
unfinished noble work in verse, has been lost, along with his skillful annotations on Pliny.[407]

### By Sannazaro[408]    5

Learned Verona, you hoped to have a new Catullus. Twice
widowed, you have found that the gods are unkind. Hereafter let nothing cheer your spirit, since adverse Fate with a
quick hand snatches away the best first. Nonetheless, when
she looked upon the cold features of Cotta in death, she
confessed her crime and was ashamed.

### By Marcantonio Flaminio[409]    6

If one may be allowed to disclose the sentiments of the
heart, with all due respect, for my part, O Catullus, I will
say this: "Your Muse is very charming indeed, yet Cotta's is
more charming to me."

## LV. Pietro Crinito (1474–1507)

Pietro Crinito,[410] a charming and erudite young man, was called    1
"Riccio" in Tuscan on account of his father's curly hair, but he

fastidiret, Crinitus appellari maluit. Is non iniquo iudicio habitus est inter Politiani discipulos disertissimus. Extant enim, praeter non illepida poemata, libri De honesta disciplina supra viginti peramoena et copiosa varietate delectabiles, ac item quinque De poetis Latinis laboriose eruditeque perscripti.

2    Mortuo Politiano, patritiorum iuvenum qui ingenia literis excolebant vel genere et censu impar, promeruit ut apud eos et sodalis et magistri munus adimpleret. Nobiles enim adolescentes more Socratis adamandos pariter ac erudiendos corporis ac animi pulchritudine ductus praedicabat.

3    Sed tanta familiaritas nequaquam certis gravitatis atque modestiae finibus descripta, contumeliae ac item exitio locum aperuit. In Scandiciana enim Petri Martellii villa post hylarem coenam, quum petulantis convivae manu inter iocosam rixam frigidae cantharo perfusus obriguisset, insolentis iniuriae dolore saucius paucis diebus interiit, eo quidem sodalium graviore poenitentia acerbioreque iactura quod nondum quadragesimum aetatis annum attigisset.

4                          *Myrtei*

Priscos poetas vivere,
Crinite, dum doces, obis.
Ergo tibi superstites
debent poetae non minus:
ipse amplius nihil volens
debere, dono carmine
hoc te sepulchro conditum.

hated that name and preferred to go by "Crinito."[411] Not unjustly was he considered the most eloquent of Poliziano's students.[412] Aside from some graceful poems, we have his *On Honorable Learning*, which comprises over twenty books that please and delight by their rich variety; and also five books of laborious learning *On Latin Poets*.[413]

After the death of Poliziano, although Crinito was no match in breeding or wealth for the more aristocratic youths who were engaged in literary studies, he secured a place as both colleague and teacher among them. For, drawn by the beauty of body and soul, he would advocate that noble youths should be loved and educated in the Socratic manner.

But such great intimacy, with no clearly defined limits of decorum and restraint, opened the way to reproach and eventual ruin. For, after a lively dinner at Pietro Martelli's villa in Scandiano, in a brawl arising from a silly quarrel, he was drenched by an ill-mannered guest pouring a tankard of cold water over him, and the chill froze him. Wounded by so unaccustomed an insult, he died within a few days. His colleagues' remorse was all the more intense and their loss all the more bitter because he had not yet turned forty.

*By Mirteo*[414]

O Crinito, you met your end while teaching that the ancient poets live on. Accordingly, the poets outliving you owe you no less. Not wanting to be in your debt any longer, I offer this poem to you who are buried in this tomb.

## LVI. Hieronymus Donatus

1    Enituit in Hieronymo Donato patritio Veneto, supra oris atque staturae dignitatem, senatoria prudentia singularis, praecellenti doctrinae praesidio et multo rerum usu constituta. Attulisse si quidem videtur in omnem actionem mores longe lectissimos et praeclaris disciplinarum omnium luminibus illustres quibus postea Iulium Secundum Veneto nomini graviter iratum et, conspirantibus externis regibus, saevo bello maiestatis iniuriam vindicantem non lenierit modo sed impetrata pace ictoque foedere converterit. Quo felicis ingenii supremo opere iam pene convulsum radicitus eius reipublicae statum septennio restitutum vidimus.

2    Sed industriae suae fructum sentire non potuit, paulo ante Romae morbo extinctus quam Gallus gravis hostis Italia pelleretur. Verum ex ea legatione eximia laus, totius Italiae iudicio parta, perpetuis annalibus ad posteros transmittitur; nec erit ingrata patria quin meritum decus optimo civi instaurata nominis memoria persolvat.

3    Monumenta eius ingenii digna luce, quod publicis occupationibus absolvi nequiverant, filii suppresserunt, edito libro adversus Graecos vanissime de sacrorum principatu cum Romano pontifice contendentes. Legitur etiam libellus Alexandri Aphrodisei *De intellectu* e Graeco in Latinum puriter ac apposite traductus. Extant etiam aliquot epistolae multa styli gravitate conscriptae, ex his ea praesertim qua Gallici foederis compedes Maximiliano Caesari

## LVI. Girolamo Donà (before 1457–1511)

The Venetian patrician Girolamo Donà[415] was distinguished for   1
the dignity of his face and figure but even more so for a special
prudence becoming to a senator, a quality built upon an incomparable foundation of erudition and on extensive political experience.
He certainly seems to have brought to every activity a character by
far the worthiest and shining with brilliant radiance in all disciplines. Later, this caused Julius II not only to temper his actions
but to reverse them: from vengefully waging a savage war on the
Venetians in his fury at their affront to his sovereignty, even as
foreign kings plotted against him, he was persuaded to secure a
peace treaty.[416] By this crowning achievement of a salutary intellect, we saw Donà's republic restored in seven years' time to the
position from which it was nearly uprooted.

But Girolamo was not able to enjoy the fruit of his labor: he   2
died of an illness at Rome shortly before the oppressive French foe
was driven from Italy.[417] Nonetheless, the matchless fame that all
Italy in its judgment had bestowed on him for that mission is preserved for posterity in the annals of all time.[418] Nor will his fatherland be so ungrateful as to fail to pay the honor due an outstanding citizen by repeated remembrance of his name.

The literary monuments of his genius, which merited publica-   3
tion, were suppressed by his sons because in the midst of his official obligations he hadn't been able to bring them to completion.[419]
He did, however, publish a book against the Greeks who were
groundlessly disputing the Roman pontiff's primacy in sacred matters.[420] We also have his limpid and accurate Latin translation of a
brief book by Alexander of Aphrodisias, On the Intellect; and there
survive some letters written in an exceedingly solemn style, particularly one urging Emperor Maximilian to cast off the shackles of
his alliance with the French, and another in which he describes the

exuendas persuadet, altera qua concussae ingenti terremotu Cretae insulae, quum ipse praesideret, clades terroresque describit.

4                                              *Myrtei*

Donate, divôm munere
fudisti ut orbi nectaris
quantumque manat gratiae
divino ab ore coelitum,
servasti et exul patriam.
Diis restitutus denuo
orbi querenti deseris
nil praeter ossa et lachrymas.

## LVII. *Alexander Achillinus*

1   Alexander Achillinus Bononiensis accuratus Averrois interpres, quum Patavii philosophiam profiteretur, solidae constantisque doctrinae famam obtinuit, vel ipso Pomponatio acri aemulo insidiosa ambitione scholam eius depopulante. Erat enim a summa ingenii simplicitate ambiendi adulandique prorsus imperitus usque adeo ut salsae petulantique iuventuti, quanquam doctrinae nomine in honore esset, ridendus videretur; et tum maxime quum deambularet undulatis passibus, coccina in toga exoleti moris, astrictas scilicet habente manicas, et nullis a tergo defluentibus, rugis lutrina pelle fimbriatas renidentique semper fronte et sermone pingui vel inepti vel contemplantis ingenii vitia fateretur. Sed aemulum in corona veteratorie disputantem et risum salsa dicacitate saepius excitantem ipso invicto doctrinae robore superabat.

calamities and terrors of the island of Crete, which had been struck by a massive earthquake while he himself was governing it.[421]

*By Mirteo*[422]    4

By the gift of the gods, Donà, when you poured into the world all the nectar and grace that flows from the divine mouth of those on high, you preserved your fatherland even in exile. Once more restored to the heavens, you leave to the grieving world nothing but bones and tears.


## LVII. *Alessandro Achillini (1461 or 1463–1512)*

As a lecturer on philosophy at Padua, Alessandro Achillini of Bo-    1
logna, who was an exacting interpreter of Averroës, gained a reputation for sound and reliable scholarship even though Pomponazzi
himself, a bitter rival, was making off with his students by sneakily
currying their favor.[423] Being extremely naïve, Achillini was so utterly inexperienced at solicitation and flattery that petulant young
wags, although they esteemed his learning, thought him ridiculous. This was especially so when he walked about with a bouncy
gait, sporting an old-fashioned scarlet gown, with tight-fitting
sleeves trimmed with otter fur,[424] and no pleats in back; and his
constant smile and clumsy elocution betrayed a mind either foolish or distracted. But when his rival was holding forth amid a circle of listeners, arguing cleverly and too often eliciting laughter
with his witty sarcasm, Achillini would outdo him by the sheer
invincible strength of his learning.

2 Ediderat enim iampridem ex peripatetico dogmate singulos libros *De elementis, De intelligentiis* et *De orbibus,* secutus opiniones Averrois quibus totius ingenii sui fama nitebatur. Concidente autem Patavino gymnasio inter exorti belli strepitum, Bononiam reversus, excessit e vita quum nondum quinquagesimum explevisset annum. Tumulus eius cum hoc carmine in aede Divi Martini conspicitur:

3                                *Iani Vitalis*

Hospes, Achillinum tumulo qui quaeris in isto,
    falleris: ille suo iunctus Aristoteli
Elysium colit et, quas rerum hic discere causas
    vix potuit, plenis nunc videt ille oculis.
Tu modo, per campos dum nobilis umbra beatos
    errat, dic longum perpetuumque vale.


## LVIII. *Bernardinus Corius*

1 Non est cur Bernardinum Corium Mediolanensem quisquam eruditus contemnat et irrideat quod immensum rerum gestarum volumen incondito ac inepto sermone perscripserit. Honesto enim loco natus et gloriolae cupidus, quum pro ingenii captu vernacula idiotisque familiari lingua uteretur, optimam civibus suis attulit voluntatem idque unum scribendo respexit, quod curiosis aut nobiliore facundia scripturis maxime prodesset atque inde nominis ac industriae laus ad posteros proferretur. Nam si Caecilii Plinii testimonio historia quovismodo scripta delectat quod lux temporum, nuncia veritatis et magistra vitae censeatur, huic civi suo plurimum

Indeed, long before that, he had published books in the Aristo-  2
telian tradition following the teachings of Averroës: *On the elements*, *On intelligences*, and *On spheres*.[425] Upon these the reputation
of all his genius rested. When the University of Padua was in ruins amid the din of the war that had erupted, he returned to Bologna, where he died before turning fifty.[426] His tomb, in the
Church of San Martino, bears this poem:

*By Giano Vitale*[427]  3

Wayfarer, if you seek Achillini in this tomb, you are deceived. Joined with his Aristotle, he dwells in Elysium, and
now he sees clearly the causes of things which here he could
discern only dimly.[428] You now, while his noble shade wan-
ders through the fields of the blessed, bid him a long, never-
ending farewell.

## LVIII. *Bernardino Corio (1459–1519?)*

There is no reason any of the learned should despise and ridicule  1
Bernardino Corio[429] of Milan for having written a massive history
in an unrefined and indecorous style.[430] Wellborn and eager for a
bit of glory, when to the best of his ability he used the vernacular
tongue understood by the uneducated, he showed the greatest
goodwill toward his fellow citizens, his chief object in writing being to benefit most of all the inquisitive or those wishing to write
with more refined eloquence, and thus make his name and diligence known to future generations. For if, as Pliny the Younger
asserts, history written in whatever manner gives pleasure[431] on
the grounds that it is regarded as the illuminator of the times, the
herald of truth, and the instructor of life, Lombards will surely be

profecto Insubres debebunt, qui ingenuo labore intercisam et plane
sepultam gravissimarum rerum memoriam diligenter inquirendo
consuendoque ad singularem utilitatem posteris repraesentavit.

2      Fuit enim vir amantissimus patriae et nusquam factiosus, minu-
tiarum adeo diligens indagator ut, quum historiae studiosis perutilem et iucundam afferat voluptatem, nihil morosis et delicatis offi-
ciat. Nam in enarrandis rebus quibus ipse interfuit fide et diligentia
mirus agnoscitur, quando eum in aula splendide versantem et ex
secretioris archivii copia opportune adiutum nusquam arcana fefel-
lerint.

3      Periit Gallis Mediolano potitis ante sexagesimum aetatis annum, Ludovici Principis et Ascanii Cardinalis calamitate perturbatus. Publicavit historiae volumen vivus privato sumptu ac ob id
gravi rei familiaris damno, quoniam dum spectare gloriam videri
vellet, resarciendi sumptus novique lucri inanem spem astuta
chalcographorum persuasione concepisset. In sepulchro eius tale
inscriptum carmen legitur:

*Incerti*

Bernardine, tibi Insubres debere fatentur
non minus ac magno Roma superba Tito.

## LIX. *Marcus Antonius Turrianus Veronensis*

1      Quam vides Marci Antonii Turriani Veronensis effigiem nullis idcirco interlitam picturae coloribus sed carbone tantum atque unis

immensely indebted to this fellow citizen of theirs. Through his noble effort of diligently seeking out and stitching together a narrative of their momentous history, he made known to future generations, to their distinct advantage, a story that had been cut to pieces and completely buried.

A man deeply devoted to his country and in no way part of a  2
political faction, he was so industrious a researcher of details that even as he imparts great benefit and delight to those who study history, he does not put off the finicky and hypersensitive. For in relating events which he himself witnessed, he is acknowledged to be extraordinarily reliable and careful, since he was prominent at court and had the benefit of access to its rich private archive, and on no occasion did its secrets escape his notice.

He died before reaching sixty, upset by the misfortune of Duke  3
Ludovico and Cardinal Ascanio when the French took Milan.[432] A volume of his *History* was published within his lifetime and at his own expense, which severely damaged his finances: for while he wished to appear to aim at glory, thanks to the devious wheedling of the printers he had conceived a vain hope that he would make good the expense and turn a profit. On his tomb is inscribed a poem that reads thus:

*Anonymous*[433]

O Bernardino, the Lombards declare that they owe you no less than proud Rome does the great Livy.


## LIX. *Marcantonio della Torre of Verona (1479–1511)*

I have assigned to this space here the portrait you see of Marcan-  1
tonio della Torre of Verona:[434] not a painting daubed with colors,

umbrarum finibus deliniatam[29] hoc loco dicavimus, quod ille, divino praeditus ingenio, dum exactae aetatis inveterataeque authoritatis medicinae professores interpraetationum subtilitate superaret, prius immiti Fato gymnasiis est ereptus quam admirandae utilitatis exquisitaeque doctrinae inchoata opera absolverentur.

2    Elaborabat is profitendo simul atque secando damnatorum cadavera *Anatome*, volumen ex placitis Galeni, quo Mundinum rudis saeculi scriptorem et Zerbum in eodem negocio delyrantem iugularat. (Hic est Zerbus qui, ambitioso avaroque ingenio, quum accitus grandi pecunia penetrasset ad Triballos ut Schenderbassam, recenti et luctuosa in Euganeos irruptione clarissimum, intercute morbo liberaret, nec demum quod inflate promiserat morienti praestaret. A barbaris servis, ut domini manibus ea scilicet victima parentarent, trucidatus interiit, ita ut lepide Turrianus in eum iocaretur, quum libri eius errata dispungeret, quasi iure concisus esset, quod magna discentium iniuria perperam secando cadavera ipse vivus meritam talionis poenam subisset.)

3    Natus est Turrianus ex ea perillustri familia quae ante ducentos annos Insubribus imperarat, patre peracuto excellentique medicinae professore ita ut non mirum sit ab ineunte aetate in eadem educatum disciplina multo maturius quam quisque alius ad primos suggestus honores Patavii et Ticini pervenisse. Praeferebat os maxime venustum serena quadam comitate occurrentium animos alliciens; verum docendo et disputando mirus, prolatis Graecis authoribus pudendos errores et vitae quidem exitiales ostendebat in quos medici ex herbariae facultatis ac anatomes inscitia

but only a sketch with just a few lines of shading in charcoal, because just as he, gifted with divine genius, was surpassing the older, more established professors of medicine in the subtlety of his interpretations, he was snatched away from the universities by cruel Fate before he could complete the exceptionally useful and deeply learned works he had begun.

While simultaneously dissecting the cadavers of condemned 2 men and lecturing, he was formulating a book on anatomy based on the tenets of Galen, with which he had slaughtered Mondino, who wrote in a coarse century, and Zerbi, a nonsensical author on the same subject.[435] (This is the Zerbi who, being ambitious and greedy by nature, lured by a large sum, had traveled to Bosnia to cure from dropsy the pasha Skander Bey, famous for his recent, calamitous attack upon the Euganian Hills.[436] In the end, Zerbi did not make good on what he had extravagantly promised the dying man, and was butchered by Skander's barbarian servants in order that they might yield him up to the spirit of their lord as a sacrificial victim.[437] Accordingly, when della Torre enumerated the errors in Zerbi's book,[438] he remarked jokingly that it was fitting for Zerbi to have been cut to pieces: for his punishment while alive was just recompense for the massive injury done his pupils by flawed dissections of cadavers.)

Della Torre was descended from that very famous family which 3 had ruled over the Lombards 200 years earlier.[439] Given that his father was a keen-minded and prominent professor of medicine,[440] it does not surprise that Marcantonio, educated in the same discipline from an early age, obtained the foremost lectureships at Padua and Pavia much earlier than anybody else had. With an amiability full of calm assurance, he presented a most graceful countenance that elicited the affections of those he met. But at the same time he was a marvelous teacher and debater: by citing Greek authors he pointed out mistakes that were shameful and even fatal, into which doctors had fallen through ignorance of

cecidissent. Hoc eximio praeceptore in gymnasio Ticinensi studiorum nostrorum vigilias pro concione laudante, de liberalibus disciplinis atque arte medica lauream et annulum comprobatae dignitatis ornamenta accepimus.

4     Nec multos post menses, quum ad ripam Benaci Lacus secessisset, pestifera febre triginta trium annorum iuvenis ereptus est, quum Iulius Pontifex in pseudo-cardinales faventesque eis Gallos victricia arma in luctuosum utrisque Ravennatis pugnae eventum expediret. Luxere Turrianum cuncta gymnasia et diuturnis quidem lachrymis; nemo enim eo in literis absolutae virtutis illustrius specimen, nemo certiorem consumatae gloriae spem dederat. Ad meritos autem titulos Veronae nobili tumulo inscriptos Nicolaus Archius hoc lepidum carmen apposuit:

5                     *Nicolai Comitis Archii*

    Ante annos scivisse nocet, nam maxima virtus
      persuasit morti, ut crederet esse senem.

## LX. Lancinus Curtius

1 Lancinus Curtius, Mediolani honesta ortus familia, inter Merulae sectatores Graece et Latine doctissimus evasit; sed quadam volucri nec plane sana ingenii libertate per omnes scientias evagatus nusquam ad integrum decus constitisse videtur, ut pote qui passim utroque stylo et scaber et obscurus, dissipato variae doctrinae

herbal medicine and of anatomy. At the University of Pavia, this exceptional teacher praised my scholarly industry in an assembly when I received my degrees in liberal studies and in medicine, along with the laurel and ring as tokens of my achievement.[441]

Not many months later, after he had withdrawn to the shore of Lake Garda, he was snatched away by a pestilential fever, a young man of thirty-three. This was at the time when Pope Julius was readying conquering armies against the pseudo-cardinals and their French supporters, in advance of the Battle of Ravenna, whose outcome would be disastrous for both sides.[442] The entire university mourned della Torre with long-lasting tears. For indeed, nobody had set a more illustrious example than he of polished excellence in letters; nobody had given surer promise of reaching the pinnacle of distinction. To the well-deserved praises inscribed on his noble tomb at Verona, Nicolò d'Arco added on this charming poem:

*By Count Nicolò d'Arco*[443]                                    5

It is harmful to have knowledge beyond one's years; for his supreme worth made death believe he was old.

## LX. Lancino Curti (ca. 1450 or 1462–1512)

Born into a noble family in Milan, Lancino Curti[444] turned out to be the most accomplished Greek and Latin scholar of all Merula's students. But with a somewhat inconstant and not very sensible independence of mind, he seemingly wandered from one field of knowledge to another, stopping nowhere long enough to attain complete mastery. For, harsh and impenetrable here and there whether writing prose or poetry, he squandered the light of his

lumine, evoluisse cuncta volumina videri mallet quam puri et circumscripti poetae nomen appetisse.

2    Eius enim *Sylvae*, quae iampridem in publicum exiverunt, quanquam densa illa et peragresti arborum luxurie[30] uti maxime frondosae alteque surgentes quibusdam placere possint, praepedientibus tamen vepribus horridae inaccessaeque existimantur adeo ut urbanus lector, reformidata situs novitate, in limine haereat.

3    In libris porro epigrammatum videre est in multa duricie nonnunquam molles facetias quae risum salse permoveant. Sed hoc multo iucundius atque lepidius consecutus videtur quum praepingui Insubrum lingua scite numeros iocanter effunderet.

4    Anguineos etiam, quos vocant, versus miris modis et numeris conformabat ita ut recto et converso quoque ordine quadrati epigrammatis introrsus exempta verba aliud carmen efficerent quod priori sententiae per costas et diametros ex obliqua serie mirabiliter arrideret,[31] inani hercle et plane ridenda cum laude, quum tanto sudore delirantis ingenii ab inepta et rectis literarum studiis exitiali voluptate fama quaereretur.

5    Caeterum contentus parvo sibique soli (uti saepe dicebat) et genio suo vivens, et coelebs et liber sine labe nominis ad senectutem pervenit, nihil obiter immutato vetere cultu, quum caeteri cives non obscura confessione servitutis adventu Gallorum, peregrinam induti vestem et capillum ad aurem subtondentes, eum pristino more togatum prolixeque comatum petulanter irriderent.

6    Moriens de sepulchro sibi cavit, quod in templo Divi Marci extra Beatricem Portam cum vera effigie et hoc carmine spectatur:

variegated learning, preferring to give the impression that he had read all books rather than to have sought to be called a precise and disciplined poet.

We do have his *Woods*,[445] which appeared in print some time 2 ago. Although with their dense and utterly wild luxuriance of trees, the *Woods*, heavy with leaves and rising loftily, can please some, they are considered so thick and unapproachable that the urbane reader, dreading the strangeness of the place, stops at the edge.

Then in his *Epigrams*,[446] amid the overall austerity, one espies 3 occasional cleverness whose humor inspires hearty laughter. But he seems to have achieved that end with far more grace and charm when he jestingly poured forth verses with skillful use of the lush Insubrian tongue.[447]

There are also verses called "snakelike" which he molded in 4 strange shapes and meters, so that words that have been picked out from inside a square epigram that was legible backward and forward produce another poem which wondrously answers on its peripheries and diagonally the sentiment of the preceding one: a useless and ridiculous achievement, heaven knows, in that his deranged mind so exerted itself as to seek fame in a senseless pastime destructive to the cause of learning.[448]

At any rate, content with little and living for himself alone (as 5 he often used to say) and for his own pleasure, he arrived at old age unmarried and a slave to no one, with unblemished character. Nor did he change his external appearance in the slightest when the other citizens — who, donning foreign garb and cutting their locks up to their ears when the French arrived, thus openly acknowledging their servitude — rudely mocked him for his old-fashioned gown and long hair.

As he was dying, he attended to designing his tomb, which one 6 sees in the Church of San Marco that is outside the Beatrice Gate.[449] It bears a faithful likeness and this poem:

*Stephani Dulcini Cremonensis*

En virtutem mortis insciam!
vivet Lancinus Curtius
saecula per omnia;
tantum possunt Camoenae.


## LXI. Baptista Mantuanus Carmelita

1   Baptista, Carmelitani ordinis princeps, Mantuae ex Hispaniola gente honesta verum ex damnato coitu natus, naturam ad carmen attulit verum insatiabili Hebraicorum studiorum cupiditate ita occupatam ut, quum magnus et admirabilis in omnibus videri contenderet, in excolendis Musis curam ac diligentiam remittere cogeretur, quibus unis non dubius ad aeternitatem gradus parabatur, si certa laude contentus in reliquis inane nomen tempestive contempsisset.

2   Sed incidit in ea tempora quibus nullus mediocribus poetis locus erat; reperit tamen sibi aemulum incondito furore Consalvi Magni res gestas decantantem, cuius explosione claresceret. Is erat Cantalicius, pro bono poeta ab optimo duce mediocris etiam virtutis amantissimo liberaliter ditatus. Verum et hunc et ipsum quoque Carmelitam, desumpto eodem argumento, Gravina male[32] partae laudis loco strenue deturbavit, quum incohatum poema nobile Pontano atque Actio censoribus recitasset. Caeterum Carmelitae satis ad laudem fuit quod per quindecim saecula neglectos a civibus Andinos fontes salubriter ebiberit, scilicet ut fatali monitu

*By Stefano Dolcino of Cremona*

Behold, the virtue that knows not death! Lancino Curti will
live on for all time; such is the power of the Muses.

## LXI. *Baptista of Mantua, the Carmelite (1447–1516)*

Baptista, the head of the Carmelite order, was born into a noble    1
Spanish family in Mantua but from a forbidden union.[450] He applied his talents to poetry, but was so consumed by an insatiable
desire for Hebrew studies that, striving to appear great and worthy
of admiration in all disciplines, he was constrained to lessen his
engagement and diligence in cultivating the Muses. Only they
would have given him a reliable path to immortality, had he been
content with assured praise and known when to scorn empty fame
in other pursuits.

But in his age there was no place for average poets. Nonethe-    2
less, he found a rival singing the deeds of Gonsalvo the Great with
undisciplined frenzy whose expulsion from the stage made Baptista shine in comparison. This was Cantalicio,[451] whom that exceptional commander, who had a soft spot for even mediocre talent, generously rewarded as if he were actually a good poet. But
once Gravina had recited the beginnings of his excellent poem on
the same subject to the literary arbiters Pontano and Sannazaro,
he quickly toppled both Cantalicio and the Carmelite himself
from the pinnacle of fame on which they had undeservingly gained
purchase.[452] Still, the Carmelite got sufficient praise for having
drunk from Andes's salubrious springs, neglected by its citizens
for fifteen centuries, evidently so that at Fate's prompting the

limpidioris eius aquae siphones Laelio ac Hippolyto Capilupis fratribus monstrarentur.

3    Octogenario maior Mantuae decessit non plane felix, quum in extremo vitae actu defensionem contra criticos scribere cogeretur, qui eius poemata obeliscis non inanibus misere confodissent.[33] Sacrato poetae mortuo cucullati eius ordinis sacerdotes prolixe parentarunt. Federicus autem Princeps marmoream effigiem cum laurea posuit, quae in arcu lapideo iuxta Virgilii Maronis simulachrum pia hercle si non ridenda comparatione conspicitur.

4                                    *Myrtei*

    Alter hic iacet a Marone vates
    natus Mantuae, et is quidem poetae
    dignior titulo, nisi incidisset
    in fluctus varios scientiarum
    quo Musas coluit minore cura.
    Primus hic tamen a Marone natus
    Mantuae coluit poeta Musas
    Andinosque bibit sacro ore fontes.

## LXII. Franciscus Marius Grapaldus

1    Quum Parmenses post exactos Gallos ad Iulii Pontificis authoritatem se contulissent, Marius Grapaldus a praestanti facundia et insigni corporis proceritate legationis princeps, luculentam de laudibus invicti optimique pontificis habuit orationem ediditque item pari argumento carmina eximiae gravitatis. Quo demum officio apposite ac eleganter patriae praestito, honoris causa lauream a

spouts of that crystal clear water might be shown to the brothers
Lelio and Ippolito Capilupi.[453]

He died aged over eighty at Mantua, his happiness diminished 3
since he was compelled as his final act to write a defense against
critics who had thoroughly skewered his poems with the daggers
they in fact deserved.[454] The friars of his order performed lavish
funeral rites for their late sacred poet. Moreover, Prince Federico
set up a marble likeness of him crowned with laurel, which can be
seen in a stone arch alongside that of Vergil: a comparison that
would confer dignity, Lord knows, were it not so ridiculous.[455]

*By Mirteo*[456]                                                     4

Here lies the bard next after Maro to be born in Mantua.
Surely he would be worthier of the title of poet had he not
fallen into the various currents of the sciences and thus given
less attention to the Muses. Still, this man was the first poet
born at Mantua since Vergil to have cultivated the Muses,
and with holy mouth he drank from the Andean springs.


# LXII. *Francesco Mario Grapaldo (1460–1515)*

Once the French had been driven out and the people of Parma 1
submitted to the authority of Pope Julius, Mario Grapaldo,[457] appointed to head a delegation because of his surpassing eloquence
and imposing stature, delivered a splendid oration in praise of the
unconquered and most excellent pontiff, and he also recited poems
of extraordinary solemnity on the same subject.[458] After he'd fittingly and elegantly performed this service to his fatherland, his

pontifice de manu erudito capiti impositam solenni cerimonia in
Vaticano consecutus est. Exinde tanto honore alacer, Musas tanquam non obscure propitias vehementius lacessivit, ut ex publicatis poematibus ostenditur. Sed multo uberius et latius ingenii
famam propagavit edito libro *De partibus aedium*, quo per optimas
disciplinas perornatum diligenti cultura ingenium demonstravit.
Fato functus est in patria post quinquagesimum aetatis annum,
quum interiores meatus emittendo lotio globosior calculus ob-
struxisset.

2                            *Georgii Anselmi*

Emeritam[34] hic laurum Aonides, plectrumque lyramque
    grata tibi ex merito turba, Grapalde, dicat.
Ut tumuli misera erexit leve nomen inanis,
    soluit et ad vacuos ut sua iusta rogos.
Nam te nec fas est humili cohibere sepulchro
    tam rara insignem qui struis arte domum,
redditae ubi doctis voces vulgoque receptae
    haud dubiam faciunt non obiisse fidem.

3                            *Iani Vitalis*

Tu, Grapalde, tibi magna pro mole sepulchri
    erigis ingentem perpetuamque domum.
Occupat illa suis immensum finibus orbem
    altaque sublimis sydera tangit apex;
et merito, neque enim tumulo tua gloria claudi,
    cum volitet mundi claustra per ampla,[35] potest.

learned brow was graced with a laurel crown, given from the pope's own hand in a formal ceremony at the Vatican.[459] Emboldened by so great a distinction, as he supposed the Muses were openly showing their favor, he importuned them more energetically, as is evident from his published poems. But his intellect attained far greater and more widespread fame from a book he published *On the Parts of Houses*,[460] in which he demonstrated brilliance enhanced by diligent application to liberal studies. He died in his homeland aged over fifty, when a massive kidney stone blocked his urinary tract.

### By Giorgio Anselmi[461]                                                   2

Here, Grapaldo, the Muses dedicate to you the laurel, and the grateful crowd dedicates the plectrum and lyre that you deserved. How pitiable that it raised up the fleeting celebrity of a useless tomb and carried out its obsequies before an empty grave.[462] For it is not possible to confine in a humble sepulcher you who, by such rare art, build an outstanding home, where words bestowed by the learned and accepted by the crowd give clear assurance that you live on.

### By Giano Vitale[463]                                                      3

In place of a massive tomb, Grapaldo, you build a vast and everlasting home. Its bounds encompass the limitless world, and its lofty roof touches the stars on high; and rightly so, for your glory cannot be contained in a tomb, since it flies through the world's vast halls.

## LXIII. *Thomas Linacrus*

1 Thomas Linacrus, ex insula Britannia ad perdiscendas Graecas literas in Italiam profectus, Florentiae Demetrium et Politianum
audivit eaque enituit morum suavitate atque modestia ut a Magno
Laurentio liberis suis familiari studiorum consuetudine, quanquam aetate maior, socius adderetur. Inde vero multis variae doctrinae ornamentis adauctus, quum Romana quoque ingenia certius
agnoscenda ac opulentiores bibliothecas inspiciendas existimaret,
ad Urbem contendit.

2 In primo autem appulsu forte accidit ut Hermolao Barbaro
amicitia iungeretur. Nam ingresso Vaticanam Bibliothecam et
Graecos codices evolventi supervenit Hermolaus, ad pluteumque
humaniter accedens 'Non tu hercle,' inquit 'studiose hospes, uti ego
plane sum, Barbarus esse potes, quod lectissimum Platonis librum
(is erat *Phaedrus*) diligenter evolvas.' Ad id Linacrus laeto ore respondit: 'Nec tu, sacrate heros, alius esse iam potes quam ille fama
notus Patriarcha Italorum Latinissimus.'

3 Ab hac amicitia (uti casu evenit, feliciter conflata) egregiis demum voluminibus ditatus in Britanniam rediit datusque est praeceptor Arcturo regis filio, cui dicatam Procli *Sphaeram* legimus.
Transtulit demum ex felici vigilia Galeni librum *De tuenda valetudine*, quum in arte medica aeque doctus et fortunatus spectaretur.

4 Verum ab eo munere, veluti quaestuoso potiusquam ad pa-
randam perennem gloriam nobili, refugit ad antiqua optimarum
literarum studia, revocatus societate Latomeri atque Grocinii[36]
qui, constituto Triumviratu ad immortalem laudem, vertendum

## LXIII. Thomas Linacre (ca. 1460–1524)

Having gone from England to Italy to gain a mastery of Greek 1
literature, Thomas Linacre[464] studied in Florence with Demetrius
and Poliziano. He so stood out for his charm and modesty that
Lorenzo the Magnificent brought him into the household to study
alongside his own children, even though he was older than they.
After being enriched with the many adornments of wide-ranging
erudition, since he felt a need to become better acquainted as well
with Roman intellectuals and to explore richer libraries, he hastened from Florence to the Eternal City.

Immediately upon arriving, he happened to become friends 2
with Ermolao Barbaro.[465] For when he had entered the Vatican
Library and was leafing through Greek codices, Ermolao came
over and, approaching the desk in a genial manner, said: "My
goodness, studious visitor, you can't be a barbarian, as I [*Barbarus*]
clearly am, given that you're so diligently reading Plato's choicest
book" (it was the *Phaedrus*). To this Linacre responded smilingly,
"Nor can you, immortal hero, be other than the famous patriarch
who is the most Latin of the Italians."[466]

As a result of this friendship (as by chance it came about, so by 3
good fortune was it inflamed), Linacre returned to England with a
wealth of excellent volumes and was made tutor to the king's son,
Arthur, to whom (as I have read) he dedicated Proclus's *Sphere*.[467]
At length, since his learning in medicine seemed to match his success in practicing it, successfully working late into the night, he
translated Galen's book *On the Need to Preserve One's Health*.[468]

But since he viewed medicine as lucrative rather than as suffi- 4
ciently noble to secure everlasting fame, he went back to his old
studies of the best literature, drawn by the prospect of collaborat-
ing anew with Latimer and Grocyn. They had established a trium-
virate with a view to immortality, having undertaken jointly to

Aristotelem communicato labore susceperant. Sed Grocinius[37] ob[38] oblatum sibi sacerdotium a decreto fideque discessit et La-tomerus consilio excussus est, ita ut Linacro egregiae voluntatis decus maneret apud Henricum Octavum.

5    Sexagesimo autem et quarto aetatis anno ex dolore disruptae herniae vita excedens, honestam domum Londini medicorum collegio dedicavit.

6                    *Iani Vitalis*

Dum Linacrus adit Morinos patriosque Britannos
   artibus egregiis dives ab Italia,
ingentem molem saxorum in rupibus altis
   congerit ad fauces, alte Gebenna, tuas.
Floribus hinc viridique struem dum fronde coronat
   et sacer Assyrias pascitur ignis opes,
'Hoc tibi,' ait 'mater studiorum o sancta meorum,
   templum Linacrus dedicat, Italia;
tu modo cui docta assurgunt cum Pallade Athenae
   hoc de me pretium sedulitatis habe.'

## LXIV. *Antonius Nebrissensis*

1    Hispania, per mille amplius annos Vandalicis Punicisque armis occupantibus, Latinarum literarum splendore caruit, alioqui non obscura telluris coelique temperie maximorum ingeniorum ferax si Lucani, Senecarum, Silii Martialisque memoria recolatur, ut hic Averroem in Arabica lingua sapientiae lumine clarissimum omit-tamus. Hispaniae enim proceres totaque nobilitas perversam opinionem de literis induerant sic ut earum studia, quum pro

translate Aristotle. But Grocyn abandoned the plan and his promise, and went off to the benefice that had been bestowed upon him; and Latimer was removed from the project, so that the honor of exceptional favor at the court of Henry VIII befell Linacre.[469]

He died at age sixty-four from the anguish of a hernia. He bequeathed his fine home to the College of Physicians in London.[470]    5

*By Giano Vitale*[471]    6

On his journey from Italy to the Pas-de-Calais and to his native England, Linacre, rich in learned culture, piles up a massive heap of stones amid the high crags at the opening of your maw, lofty Gebenna.[472] Then, crowning the pile with flowers and verdant foliage, as a sacred fire consumes frankincense, he says: "O Italy, holy mother of my studies, to you, Linacre dedicates this temple. You, before whom Athens, with learned Pallas, rises to stand at attention, do accept this as payment from me, out of my diligence."

## LXIV. Antonio the Nebrijan (1441–1522)

For over a thousand years, while Vandal and Moorish armies occupied it, Spain lacked the splendor of Latin letters, whereas at other times its famously moderate soil and weather produced the greatest geniuses, if one should call to mind Lucan, the Senecas, Silius, and Martial, not to mention Averroës, the brightest light of Arabic wisdom. For the leaders of Spain and all its nobility had taken a skewed view of literature, so that when they fought for liberty from foreign peoples, literary pursuits were universally    1

libertate adversus externas gentes dimicarent, publica conspiratione damnarentur, quasi aliena importunaque virtuti bellicae qua
una salus et libertas omnium certiore laude pararetur. Sed post
Punicum nomen virtute Ferdinandi Regis Hispania pulsum, Antonii Nebrissensis ingenium emicuit; par antiquis grammaticis, si
par fortuna saeculi anhelanti ad veterem laudem opportune re-
spondisset.

2      Hic Nebrissae, quae olim Veneria fuit, ad Bethim natus; scribendo et docendo iuventutem, admonitis castigatisque natu maioribus, ad antiquum decus literarum vehementer erexit. Constat
enim eum literarum amore sponte exulantem fere totius Italiae
gymnasia collustrasse collegisseque dignos nobili voto Graecae Latinaeque linguae thesauros quibus terra patria ditaretur. Dicebat
enim proceribus ad arma natis sero exactae artis et disciplinae
exempla vel longo usu percepturos si literarum lumine carerent,
quo uno stolide sublato tota bellica laus celeriter evanescit et inter-
cidit. Paucis itaque annis effectum est ut nemo qui literarum studium reformidaret satis nobilis haberetur ipseque Antonius non
secus de restitutis postliminio literis quam Ferdinandus, Granata
capta Maurisque pulsis, gloriose triumpharet.

3      Scripsit ingenti cursu, orsus a grammaticae praeceptis, omnes
fere liberales disciplinas et sacras literas pervagatus, multa volumina quae extant. Expectatur autem summae utilitatis dictionarium quo Latine Graece ac Hebraice linguae documenta continentur, ab haerede filio hactenus impie suppressum, quum et ipsa
quoque pene ad exitum perducta Bethici Belli historia in lucem
non prodeat.

condemned on the grounds that they were unsuited and inimical to the martial prowess by which the collective safety and freedom would alone be secured with more assured glory. But after the Moors had been expelled from Spain by mighty King Ferdinand, the brilliance of Antonio de Nebrija[473] shone forth. He would have been the equal of those ancient scholars had he met with the equivalent fortune of living in an age that responded appropriately to one striving for excellence.

He was born near the Guadalquivir River in Nebrija, which 2 used to be known as Veneria.[474] By writing and teaching he vigorously elevated children to the ancient esteem for learning, admonishing and correcting the older ones. It's well-known that, willingly becoming an exile out of love of literature, he searched through the schools of nearly all Italy and collected Greek and Latin treasures with the noble aim of enriching his fatherland. Indeed, he used to say to the nobles, who by birth were destined to take up arms, that even after long experience they would grasp the lessons of the requisite skill and training only too late if they lacked the lamp of letters: for if this one thing is stupidly taken away, all martial glory quickly fades and perishes. And so in a few years it came about that nobody who recoiled from literary studies was thought sufficiently noble, and in restoring literature from exile Antonio himself triumphed no less gloriously than Ferdinand did in capturing Granada and driving out the Moors.

Beginning with grammatical texts, over the wide span of his 3 writing career Nebrija ranged through nearly all the liberal arts and sacred literature; many of his books are extant.[475] But we await the highly useful dictionary in which examples of the Latin, Greek, and Hebrew languages are contained: thus far it has been suppressed by his undutiful son and heir, while his history of the War of Granada, though nearly finished, likewise has not seen the light of day.[476]

4 Oppressit eum repentina paralysis quum ad septuagesimum
septimum aetatis annum pervenisset: tanto quidem corporis inge-
niiique vigore ut nihil de studiorum labore omnino remitteret et, ut
natura mulierosus, ad supremum usque diem venereis uteretur.
Obiit sub id tempus quo popularibus ulterioris Hispaniae, ad
arma consternatis adversus Belgas praesides tanquam avare impe-
rantes, graviter est tumultuatum.

5 *Myrtei*

Me putat aeternum saxo posuisse sub imo
    acerba mors, et fallitur:
non ingrata etenim mea gens volitare per ora
    dat, et per oras omnium.
Haec mihi pro reduci studio Latiisque Camoenis
    certe trophaeum non minus
quam tibi pro Mauris debet, Fernande, fugatis
    et pro recepta Baetica.

## LXV. Bernardus Bibienna

1 Homo valde mirus in utraque fortuna extitit Bernardus Divitius,
in oppido Bibienna, unde ei cognomen, ad summas Aretinorum
Alpes natus. Is a pueritia inter Mediceae familiae clientes primum
solertis industriae locum meritus, Leoni, patria pulso atque exuli,
singulari fide comes fuit et consiliorum quidem omnium particeps.
2 In multa enim et varia rerum commutatione diuturnoque usu
gravissimarum actionum peracutus, efficax et, quod unum in aula

When he was seventy-seven he was struck by a sudden paraly-  4
sis. At any rate, he had such great vigor of body and mind that he
hadn't in the least slackened from the work he put into his studies;
and as he was by nature fond of women, he was sexually active
until his final day. He died during that time when there was a violent uprising, the Castilians being driven to rebellion against the
greedy rule of their Flemish overlords.[477]

*By Mirteo*[478]  5

Bitter death thinks it has buried me eternally under the bot-
tommost stone, and it is deceived: for my countrymen, not
ungrateful, give me flight through the lips and through the
lands of all peoples.[479] On account of my having brought
back learning and Latin Muses, surely they owe me this as a
monument no less than they do to you, Ferdinand, for having put the Moors to flight and retaken Granada.

## LXV. Bernardo Bibbiena (1470–1520)

A man truly remarkable in both good fortune and bad, Bernardo  1
Dovizi[480] was born in Bibbiena (whence he got his sobriquet) in
the highest mountains in Arezzan territory. From boyhood he
earned a place of special prominence among clients of the Medici
family for his shrewdness and diligence. After Leo had been driven
out of his homeland and made an exile, Bibbiena was a particularly reliable companion and in fact took part in all decision-
making.[481]

Indeed, amid great and varied political upheavals and with  2
longstanding involvement in the most important business, he

maxime conducit, iucundus veterator evaserat, ita ut eum Leo rerum potitus inter propinquos maturato honore legerit in Senatum. Magno siquidem adiumento fuisse constabat in comitiis ad promerendas suffragatorum voluntates, quum antea nobilissimis cardinalium hero conciliatis ad petendum pontificatum expeditam viam astuta quadam urbanitate munivisset. Convivia enim in quibus erudito luxu certabatur, miris facetiis condire, seria iocis miscere, adulari resque arduas dissimulanter conficere solitus, ingenium nusquam absurdum aut ineptum in ocio pariter atque negocio feliciter afferebat.

3    Scripsit admirabili lepore comoediam *Calandram*, quae acta est in Vaticano ludis Lupercalibus per nobiles comoedos Romanae iuventutis in gratiam Isabellae Mantuani principis uxoris, usque adeo decenti apparatu ut nihil ad elegantiam theatralem ab eximio poeta comico doctius atque facetius compositum, aut magnificentius in scoena editum confiteri liceat, nisi tum caeteris patribus sacra purpura pudorem expressisset, quum tamen a minus severis dignitatem attulisse putaretur.

4    Abdicavit in ea numeros primus ut vernaculos sales dulcius atque liquidius foeminarum auribus infunderet, quo multi risus hilarior voluptas excitaretur. Id enim unum peti quaerique debere a non insulso poeta disserebat—quod in Terentiana scoena verecundi salis prudentiam admirari quidem non satis possint spectatores, ridere certe nequeant—quod nullam vel eruditae fabulae inesse gratiam putaret nisi ab excitato populo mixtus cachinno plausus redderetur.

emerged as an experienced hand who was exceedingly shrewd, effective, and—the one thing most advantageous at court—congenial, to such an extent that Leo, once in power, selected him, along with the pope's kinsmen, for the College of Cardinals, an honor that was expedited.[482] This he did because Bibbiena was of great help in gaining the goodwill of voters in his election, since with a certain cunning sophistication he had paved Leo's way to the papacy by winning over to his patron in advance the most eminent cardinals.[483] Indeed, Bibbiena was accustomed to enliven banquets where there was a competition for erudition and splendor, to mix serious matters with jests, to fawn, and to make arduous tasks look effortless. At leisure as well as work, he brought to bear a brilliance that was never awkward or indecorous.

He wrote the *Calandria*, a comedy of remarkable charm, which 3 was performed in the Vatican during Carnival—by renowned comedic actors drawn from the Roman youth, for the delectation of Isabella, wife of the Marquis of Mantua—with such fitting refinement that one can acknowledge that, with respect to theatrical taste, no outstanding comic playwright had composed anything more learned or clever, nor was anything grander produced on the stage. Although at the time some cardinals blushed for their holy purple, nonetheless those who were less straitlaced thought that he had added to its luster.[484]

He was the first in that genre to have done away with meters, 4 which he did in order to pour vernacular humor more sweetly and smoothly into women's ears, thereby inciting them to the more lighthearted pleasure of frequent laughter.[485] Indeed, he asserted that a writer with any sense about him must seek this as his sole aim, because—since an audience can't adequately appreciate, and certainly can't laugh at the good sense of chaste wit in a play by Terence—he thought that a play, however learned, finds no favor unless an engaged public responds with applause interspersed with laughter.

5     Periit non plane senex quum e legatione Gallica in Urbem re-
disset, intempestiva ambitione ad pontificatum aspirans si Leo, uti
in fatis erat, vita excederet, quod ei Rex Franciscus ex prolixa pol-
licitatione suffragaturus crederetur; id multo iunior habituque vi-
vacior Leo in imbecillo sene adeo indignanter tulisse fertur ut ipse
Bibienna tabifico veneno, ex frixis ovis de manu in mensa porrectis, se petitum suspiciosius quam decebat existimaret: inani certe
argumento quod insignium medicorum vel iterata exquisitaque
remedia minime profecissent.

6                          *Boccarini Aretini*

Trunca fides, lugent Charites, periere lepores,
    desipuere[39] sales, desipuere ioci.
Lurida nimirum Mors, quae Urbi invidit et orbi
    Divitium immiti funere corripuit.
Purpureos meruit titulos. Romae occidit, ortus
    est Bibiennae. Hoc te scire sat, hospes, erat.

## LXVI. *Iason Mainus*

1   Iasoni Maino Mediolanensi, uti ipse in gentilitiis insignibus prae-
scribere solebat, virtuti fortuna comes non defuit; natus enim ex
concubina, nequaquam eodem cultu quo aequales propinqui, sed
eodem pedagogo sibi tantum immiti atque aspero utebatur, ut ab
eo familiariter audivimus. Ex hac schola missus Ticinum ad ius
civile perdiscendum, primo anno ita ingenium ad vitia illamque

He died before he could grow old, after he had returned to 5
Rome from an embassy to France. He was aspiring to the papacy
with unseasonable ambition, if (as was fated) Leo were to pass
away, because it was thought that King Francis would come
through on a longstanding promise to support him. It's said that
Leo, who was much younger and more vigorous, bore this in the
feeble old man with such indignation that Bibbiena himself reckoned (with more suspicion than was seemly) that the pope had
tried to do him in with a slow-acting poison in the fried eggs that
he passed to him at table—basing his suspicion on the utterly useless evidence that even a course of complicated treatments by eminent doctors hadn't the least effect.[486]

*By Boccarino of Arezzo*[487]                                            6

The lyre has been silenced: the Graces are in mourning,
charms have passed away; witticisms have lost their savor, as
have jokes. No wonder ghastly Death, which envied Rome
and the world, has snatched Dovizi away by a pitiless demise. He earned the honor of the purple. He died in Rome;
he was born in Bibbiena. Knowing this, visitor, you know
enough.

## LXVI. Giasone del Maino (1435–1519)

For Giasone del Maino of Milan, as he himself used to write 1
above his family's coat of arms, virtue did not lack the companion-
ship of good fortune.[488] Born of a concubine, he did not enjoy the
same nurturing as relatives of the same age, but he had the same
preceptor who, as he intimated to me, was harsh and cruel only to
him. Sent from that school to Pavia to study civil law, in the first

supra caetera pestilentem aleam deflexit ut cum hospite decoqueret et iuris codicem in membranis scriptum, magno emptum pretio, foeneratori tradere cogeretur. Ipse vero demum sordida in toga, capite tonso quod id tinea deformis obsideret, ridiculus videbatur.

2  Sed mature et peracerbe castigatus, se ipsum collegit bonaeque frugis personam nequaquam mentitus, tanta contentione in studiis disputationibusque se se exercuit ut doctores ipsi aequalisque iuventus eum adeo celeriter atque feliciter profecisse mirarentur. Exinde suggestu dignus institutiones enarravit concessitque demum Patavium. Sed inde, quum secunda fama profiteretur, evocante Ludovico Sfortia Ticinum reversus est.

3  Ab eximia tum gravitate atque facundia summi oratoris laude fruebatur: nam optimis literis usque ad poeticum decus instructus, dicta scriptaque lepidissime condiebat; canoram vocem, valida latera, gestum oris excellentem ad suggestum afferens, explicati et perillustris solidique doctoris nomen tuebatur; consultoribus pretio gravis videri poterat nisi pecuniam acceptam, si causa decidissent, liberali pactione se continuo redditurum profiteretur.

4  Me audiente, interrogatus a Ludovico Gallorum Rege cur nunquam duxisset uxorem, 'Ut te commendante' inquit 'Iulius Pontifex ad purpureum galerum gestandum me habilem sciat.' Audiverat enim honoris causa eo die aurata in toga profitentem rex ipse, quinque cardinalibus et centum proceribus subsellia implentibus quum, Genua subacta, de Lyguribus triumphasset. Ea enim lectione dignitatem equestrem ob spectatum in acie facinus de manu regis traditam, accendendae virtutis ergo ad posteros manare diffinivit.

year his mind was diverted to vice, especially the one more disastrous than all others: gambling.[489] He lost so much that he was unable to pay his room and board, and was compelled to pawn the law textbook, written on parchment, for which he had paid an immense sum. In the end he looked ridiculous, clad in a filthy gown, his head shaved because it was ravaged by ringworm.

But after this harsh chastisement of youth he pulled himself together and, exhibiting a worthy character that was utterly unfeigned, he applied himself so diligently to his studies and to disputations that his young peers and even the professors marveled that he had progressed so far, so quickly. Now worthy of the professor's lectern, he expounded the *Institutiones* and at last departed for Padua.[490] While enjoying this good reputation, at the behest of Ludovico Sforza he returned from there to Pavia.[491]

Then, thanks to his extraordinary solemnity and eloquence, he enjoyed praise for being a perfect orator: for, expert in classical literature, including even poetry, he charmingly seasoned his speech and writings, bringing to the podium a harmonious voice, strong lungs, and graceful elocution. He sustained a reputation for being a clear, distinguished, genuine teacher. To his legal clients he might have appeared costly had he not, by a generous arrangement, stipulated that if he lost their case he would immediately return his fee.

When once, within my hearing, King Louis of France asked him why he had never married, he replied, "So that, upon your recommendation, Pope Julius may know that I am a suitable candidate for the purple hat." In fact, just that day, when the king himself, having defeated Genoa, had celebrated a triumph over the Ligurians, he had listened as Maino, in a golden gown, gave a speech of commendation with five cardinals and a hundred nobles in attendance. In that address he explained that a knighthood, conferred by a king for conspicuous accomplishment in battle, should be passed on to one's descendants as an incitement to valor.

5    Mortuus est Ticini[40] valde senex, extructa nobili domo emp-
tisque in Placentino latifundiis. Suburbano autem in templo Divi
Pauli sepulchrum cum his titulis ostenditur:

*Dardani Parmensis*

'Quis iacet hoc, hospes, tumulo?' 'Quis? Summus Iason.'
    'Ille'ne Frixeae vellere dives ovis?'
'Clarior hic illo longe est.' 'Quisnam? oro.' 'Maynus,
    excellens iuris gloria Caesarei.
Non fuit hoc quisquam iuris consultior alter
    qui extinctum posset reddere ius melius.
Sed tamen hoc summi vetuit mens dia parentis
    Caesaribus cupiens usque favere suis.'
Te audiit o! nimium felix qui iura legentem
    damnantemque acri plurima iudicio,
nec tamen infelix tua qui monimenta revolvit
    et memori condit lecta fovetque sinu.
Et quanquam obloqueris, plebs invida, solus Iason
    hic legum nodos difficiles soluit.
Amborum sic fama omnem vulgata per orbem:
    Ille nitens belli laude, sed iste togae.

## LXVII. *Christophorus Longolius*

1    Christophorus Longolius, Mechliniae[41] Belgicae sacerdote antistite
genitus et Lutetiae in scholis frugaliter educatus, partis disciplinarum omnium peramplis opibus aureo Leonis principatu Romam
venit, adeo dissimulata ingenii professione ut rubro pileo et astricta
penula Semigermani militis habitum mentiretur, quippe cui mens

He died at Pavia at quite an advanced age, having constructed a 5
noble home and bought large estates in Piacenza. His tomb, in the
Church of San Paolo Fuori le Mura,[492] bears these lines:

*By Dardano of Parma*[493]

"Stranger, who lies in this tomb?" "Who? The great Giasone." "The one that was rich with the fleece of Phrixus's
ram?"[494] "Far more famous than that one." "Pray, tell me
who?" "Maino, renowned for his eminence in Roman law.
There never was a legal mind more astute who could interpret defunct law better than he. But still, the divine mind of
the Father on High, ever desiring to show favor to His own
emperors, forbade this." O, too fortunate is he who heard
you, Giasone, expounding the law and adjudicating many
things with incisive judgment. Nor, moreover, is he unlucky
who reads your works, readily storing and cherishing them
in his heart. And although you, envious mob, rail at him,
this Giasone alone has loosed the tangled knots of the laws.
Thus the fame of both Jasons has spread over the entire
world — that one illustrious in war, but this one in peace.

## LXVII. *Christophe de Longueil (ca. 1488–1522)*

Born at Mechelen in Flanders, Christophe de Longueil was a 1
bishop's son.[495] Educated frugally in the schools of Paris, once he
had acquired abundant riches in all fields of learning he came to
Rome, in the golden age of Leo's rule.[496] He concealed any outward sign of his talent so that, with a red beret and a tight-fitting
coat, he assumed as a disguise the uniform of a Flemish soldier,

erat avide peregrinanti priscae felicitatis monumenta spectare, scrutari ingenia, bibliothecas excutere atque illud demum eruditae censurae iudicium quod frustra alibi quam sub Romano coelo quaeritur certius atque liquidius adipisci; sed intranti gymnasium et acute disputanti non insulsi literarum professores celeriter et comiter personam detraxerunt, ita ut mox honestissimi cives Romani Flaminius Tomarotius et Marius Castellanus alterna hospitii liberalitate intra penates receptum triennio aluerint, eique virtutis merito Romanae civitatis ius et nomen impetrarint.

2 Verum aliquanto post, emersit liber execrabilis maledicentiae veneno delibutus quem iuvenili declamatione perscripserat, Romani nominis antiquum decus barbaro livore proscindens. Infremuit Populus Romanus ea contumelia perturbatus, Celso Mellino adolescente clarissimo generosa oratione in Capitolio tanquam reum maiestatis accusante. Sed Longolius totius aulae clementia praemunitus, duabus orationibus publicatis se se eo nomine defendens iudicium populi subterfugit, quod nequaquam malignitate animi sed more sophistarum exercitationis studio materiae difficilis ac insolentis ideoque damnatae spei argumentum desumpsisset, scilicet ut sodales eius temere suscepti muneris vel infelicem audaciam mirarentur.

3 Transivit inde Patavium, his praesertim actionibus claritatem consecutus adhaesitque Petro Bembo et mox Reginaldo Polo Britanno, in quorum hodie sacra purpura summam pietatem atque doctrinam veneramur. In eius contubernio, quum ingentibus vigiliis libros adversus Lutherum diserte et graviter incohatos elaboraret, editis iam ad imitationem Ciceronis epistolis, febre consumptus est. Tumulum autem hoc carmine Bembus honestavit.

for he was eager to gaze in his travels upon the monuments of ancient splendor, to search out clever men, to explore libraries, and finally to acquire more precisely and purely that capacity for discriminating taste which is found under the Roman sky and sought in vain elsewhere. But when he went to the university and argued incisively, the professors of literature, who were no fools, quickly and courteously stripped off his disguise. Consequently, the most distinguished citizens of Rome, Flaminio Tomarozzi and Mario Castellani, soon took turns maintaining him as their household guest for three years and, on the strength of his virtuosity, obtained for him the title and standing of a Roman citizen.[497]

Soon thereafter, however, there came to light a book steeped in the venom of outrageous vituperation which he had written in his youth as a rhetorical exercise, shredding with barbarous malice Rome's claim to its ancient splendor.[498] Upset at this affront, the people of Rome were enraged, and the brilliant Roman youth Celso Mellini delivered a noble oration on the Capitoline charging him with *lèse majesté*.[499] But Longueil, protected by the favor of the entire court, slipped away to avoid the public trial.[500] In two published orations he defended himself on the grounds that he had selected his topic not out of spite but instead, in the manner of the sophists, as an exercise that would undoubtedly cause his colleagues to marvel at his boldness (even if unsuccessful) in taking on an assignment that was difficult and contrarian, and therefore doomed to fail.[501]

Having gained renown especially because of these speeches, he then went to Padua and joined first the household of Pietro Bembo and soon that of the Englishman Reginald Pole, both now cardinals whom we respect deeply for their surpassing piety and learning. While under Pole's roof, having already published letters written in imitation of Cicero, and laboring mightily on books against Luther that he had begun with skill and solemnity, he died from a fever.[502] Bembo adorned his tomb with this poem:

4

*Bembi*

Te iuvenem rapuere Deae fatalia nentes
stamina, cum scirent moriturum tempore nullo,
Longoli, tibi si canos seniumque dedissent.

## LXVIII. *Aurelius Augurellus*

1  Non est cur miremur in pusillo corpore vivacissimi hominis Aurelii Augurelli praealtum ingenium enituisse. Fit enim plerunque
natura ut innati spiritus vis ipsa collectior parvae compaginis
membra aptissime regat, et quod mentis est ad excogitandum plenius atque validius illustret.

2  Is Arimini natus vitam in literis perdiscendo docendoque ad
octogesimum tertium aetatis annum feliciter extendit Venetiisque
imprimis habitus est multo doctior et purior quam quisquam alius
qui Latinis Graecisque literis privato quodam officio ac ob id
quaestuosiore profiteretur. Extant eius *Odae* plures et paucae *Elegiae* Romana simplicitate decantatae, sed iambico versu a paucis
hactenus prospere tentato, visus est ad antiquae laudis metam
propius accessisse.

3  Novissime ridendus ille morbus, certae egestatis et cassi laboris
comes, curiosis ingeniis familiaris totum homunculum occupavit
metalla et succos in abditis fornacibus recoquentem ut ex argento
vivo concretum et ductile argentum ad cudendam monetam effice-
ret, et admirabilem abditarum naturae rerum massam conflando
purum inde aurum crearetur.

4  Sed ea cura inani voto suscepta nequaquam magno damno ei
cessit, quum ingenium ab irrita spe ad factitanda carmina vertere-

*By Bembo*[503]                                                      4

The goddesses who spin the threads of fate snatched you
away as a young man; for they knew, Longueil, that had they
given you gray hairs and old age, you would never die.

## LXVIII. *Aurelio Augurelli (ca. 1456–1524)*

We needn't marvel that the diminutive body of Aurelio Au-      1
gurelli,[504] the most vigorous of men, was distinguished by a lofty
intellect. For it happens frequently in nature that the more concentrated strength of the life force itself governs the parts of a
small frame most fittingly, and more brilliantly and powerfully il-
lumines the mind's capacity for thinking.

Born in Rimini, he lived happily as a scholar and teacher to his    2
eighty-third year, and in Venice in particular was considered much
more learned and refined than anyone else who taught Latin and
Greek on a private and therefore more lucrative basis.[505] We have
his many *Odes* and a few *Elegies*, composed in an unadorned Latin
style, but he seemed more nearly to have mastered the ancient
iambic verse, which few before him had attempted with any success.[506]

Eventually that risible affliction which is the companion of    3
chronic poverty and fruitless labor, and is no stranger to the inquisitive, completely overtook the little man. He reforged metals
and liquids in hidden furnaces to fashion from quicksilver a con-
densed and malleable silver for minting coins, and then, by melting down a remarkable mass of secret ingredients from nature, to
create pure gold.

But this pursuit, undertaken on the basis of wishful thinking,    4
did him no great harm, for his mind turned from vain hope to

tur ut fallacis et irrisae artis certitudinem carminum authoritate demonstraret, quum ipso conscientiae pudore inanis artifex proderetur. Scripsit enim *Chrysopoeiam* ad Leonem auri contemptorem ut prodige utenti ad alenda ingenia festosque et plane regios sumptus inexhaustae opes sine iniuria humani generis abunde suppeterent. Edidit etiam *Geruntica*, Petro Lipomano discipulo dicata, quem hodie Veronenses virtutis merito, antistitem venerantur.

5    Tarvisii, ubi flamen erat, quum ad forum in taberna libraria disputaret, apoplexia correptus subito interiit. Depicta est tumulo effigies, cui hoc ipse carmen subscripserat.

*Ipsius*

Aurelii Augurelli imago est quam vides,
uni vacantis literarum serio
studio et iocoso, dispari cura tamen:
hoc, ut vegetior sic fieret ad seria;
illo, ut iocosis uteretur firmior.

## LXIX. *Guido Posthumus*

1    Guido Posthumus Pisaurensis lepido et comi argutoque ingenio poeta quum *Elegias* et variis numeris carmina factitaret in aula Leonis conspicuus fuit. Patebat enim ea liberaliter, meridianis praesertim horis quum citharoedi[42] cessarent, his omnibus qui eruditae suavitatis oblectamenta ad ciendam hylaritatem intulissent.

2    Sed benigna principis manu saepe donatum et non insulse ad honores aspirantem regius invasit morbus, ex moribunda patriae

prolific verse, using the authority of poetry to attest the reliability of a false and ridiculous craft, even as the shame of his own conscience betrayed him as the charlatan he was. Indeed, he dedicated the *Chrysopoeia* to Leo, who was disdainful of gold, in order that without injury to humankind, limitless wealth might be available for him to spend lavishly on the support of clever men, on festivals, and obviously on the expenses of ruling.[507] He also published the *Geronticon*, dedicated to his student Pietro Lippomano, who today as bishop of Verona is honored for his virtue.[508]

As Augurelli was debating in a bookstore near the marketplace 5 of Treviso, where he was a canon, he had a stroke and died suddenly.[509] His tomb bears his likeness, beneath which he himself had had this poem inscribed:

## By Himself[510]

What you see is the likeness of Aurelio Augurelli, who dedicated his time entirely to the study of literature, both serious and playful, but with different motives: the playful, to face serious matters with some levity; the serious, to moderate humor with some gravity.

## LXIX. Guido Postumo (1479–1521)

Guido Postumo[511] of Pesaro, a poet with a charming, cultured, 1 and clever mind, distinguished himself at Leo's court by composing numerous *Elegies* and poems in various meters.[512] The court used to be freely accessible, especially during the midday hours when the musicians had finished their set, to all those who would bring in the pleasures of sweet learning to lift the spirit.

But as he was often receiving gifts from the prince's generous 2 hand and, not unreasonably, hoped for prestigious appointments,

sede procul dubio conceptus. Medici suaserunt ut Capranicum
secederet Sutrini agri vicum, aeris salubritate[43] percelebrem, atque
ita humanitate ac indulgentia Herculis Rangoni Cardinalis, cuius
opibus familiariter utebatur, eo devectus est. Verum non multo
post, exusto lenta febre toto viscere, vel adhuc iuvenis vim morbi
Fatique sustinere non potuit. In aede Divi Francisci tumulatum
poetae sodales his carminibus prosecuti sunt.

3                          *Tibaldei*

Posthumus hic situs est; ne dictum hoc nomine credas
    in lucem extincto quod patre prodierit.
Mortales neque enim talem genuere parentes
    Calliopea fuit mater, Apollo pater.

4                          *Iani Vitalis*

Quaerite nunc alium, Musae, quem semper ametis,
    qui vos semper amet. Posthumus occubuit.

## LXX. Nicolaus Leonicenus

1  Nemo profitentium medicorum Nicolao Leoniceno Vicentino vera
salutaris scientiae dogmata purius atque nitidius explicavit; nemo
errores sophistarum importuna garrulitate cuncta foedantium
eloquentius atque validius confutavit; nemo eo demum ad illustrem certioris peritiae fidem longius atque salubrius vitam pro-
duxit. Primus enim Graeca Galeni volumina Latine interpretando

he was stricken with jaundice, which he had undoubtedly contracted in his decaying homeland.[513] The doctors recommended that he withdraw to Capranica,[514] a village in the Sutri countryside famous for the salubriousness of its air, and so he was conveyed there thanks to the kindness and friendship of Cardinal Ercole Rangoni, who privately saw to his expenses. But not much later, when all his vitals had been consumed by a persistent fever, though still young he could not withstand the onslaught of the disease and of Fate. When he was entombed in the Church of San Francesco, his fellow poets honored him with these poems:

### By Tebaldeo[515]                                                          3

Here lies Postumo. Don't believe that he was called by this name because he came into the world after the death of his father. Indeed not: mortal parents did not give birth to one of his sort. Calliope was his mother, Apollo his father.

### By Giano Vitale[516]                                                      4

Now seek out another, Muses, whom you may always love and always be loved by. Postumo is dead.

## LXX. Niccolò Leoniceno (1428–1524)

No one among professors of medicine has set forth the true principles of the science of health more limpidly and splendidly than Niccolò Leoniceno of Vicenza.[517] No one has more eloquently and vigorously refuted the errors of sophists who besmirch everything with their vexatious blather. In evident confirmation of his superior knowledge, finally, no one has lived a longer or healthier life. For by translating the books of Galen from Greek into Latin, he

studiosis perdiscenda demonstravit; imperitorum latratibus publicatis summa eloquentia commentariis occurrerat ut pote qui, ab ineunte aetate optimis literis deditus, ingentes opes capacis et maxime constantis ingenii ad illustrandam medicinam contulisset.

2      Cibi enim et vini maxime abstinens somnique minimi, praesertim vero Veneris continentissimus usque adeo mollioris vitae voluptates abdicavit ut pecunias luxuriae⁴⁴ instrumenta nec agnita quidem monetae nota contemneret, oblatum et nulla delectum cura cibum caperet, nec unquam de fortuna quereretur quod unam vir acutus studiorum laudem respiceret, nec opportuna mediocris vitae subsidia benignitate Ferrariensium principum Herculis Alfonsique filii sibi defutura prospiceret. Eum hercle perfectum Stoicum putasses nisi honesto ori liberalis hylaritas affuisset.

3      Edidit eruditum et perelegantem librum qui *Romanus Medicus Antisophista* inscribitur, quum antea *De ordine trium doctrinarum* et *De virtute formativa* perutiles libellos publicasset. Dionis quoque *Historia* et Luciani *Dialogi*, vernacula loquentes lingua, Herculi Latinarum literarum imperito mire placuerunt.

4      Pervenit ad nonagesimum annum integerrimis sensibus vegetaque memoria nec incurva quidem cervice, quum esset staturae celsioris et sine scipione venerabilis. Quum ego aliquando comiter ab eo peterem ut ingenue proferret quonam arcano artis uteretur ut tanto corporis atque animi vigore vitia senectutis eluderet, 'Vividum' inquit 'ingenium perpetua, Iovi, vitae innocentia, salubre vero corpus hylari frugalitatis praesidio facile tuemur.' Tumulus eius in atrio aedis.

was the first to show that scholars needed to learn them thoroughly.[518] With the exceedingly eloquent commentaries he published, he countered the barking of the ignorant, being one who, given to scholarship from an early age, used the enormous strengths of his capacious and most steadfast mind to improve medical knowledge.

He ate sparingly, drank very little wine, and slept hardly at all,    2
but he was most restrained when it came to sex. He so renounced the delights of a softer life that he scorned money as the tool of extravagance, nor did he even recognize the denominations of coins. He took indiscriminately the food that was offered him. Nor did he ever complain about his fortune because, as a wise man, he concerned himself only with the praise that comes from studies. And he foresaw that, thanks to the generosity of the dukes of Ferrara, Ercole and his son Alfonso, he would not lack the support suitable for a modest style of life. Good Lord, you might have thought him a perfect Stoic, had not an abundant cheerfulness shown on his distinguished face.

He published a learned and tasteful book, *The Antisophist Ro-*    3
*man Doctor*, after he had turned out the highly useful treatises *On the Three Orders of Learning* and *On the Generative Force*.[519] In addition, the vernacular translations he made of Dio's *History* and of the *Dialogues* of Lucian gave extraordinary delight to Ercole, who did not know Latin.[520]

He reached his ninetieth year with his faculties fully intact and    4
with a vigorous memory, not stooped over even though he was quite tall, revered though he walked without a cane. When once I gently asked him to tell candidly by what secret art he was able with such great vigor of body and mind to avoid the debilities of old age, he said "I easily maintain a vigorous mind, Giovio, by a consistently pure life, but I keep my health of body with the help of cheerful frugality." His tomb is in the narthex of the Church of San Domenico in Ferrara.[521]

5 *Myrtei*

> Cui neque sat fuit et terras evolvere et undas
>   quaeque arcana tenent flumina terra mare,
> dum rerum caussas late vestigat et aegra
>   morborum revocat corpora colluvie,
> nunc Leonicenus tegitur parvo aggere terrae
>   cuius utramque volat fama per Hesperiam.

## LXXI. *Petrus Pomponatius*

1 Petrus Pomponatius Mantuanus in philosophia praeceptor meus inter peripateticos illustres primum suggestus locum obtinuit. Enarrabat enim Aristotelem simul ac Averroem suavi et praeclara voce, elocutione autem emendata et leni quum proponeret, volubili et concitata quum infringeret, porro quum diffiniret atque decerneret adeo gravi sedataque ut auditores in subselliis scriptitando explicatas sententias notis exciperent. At in coronis consessuque doctorum quum exercitatione perutili ad praetoriam porticum disputaretur, ita mirus evadebat ut saepe, ancipiti et cornuto Achillini enthymemate circumventus, superfuso facetiarum sale adversarii impetum ex illis gyris et maeandris explicatus eluderet.

2 Erat pusilla admodum sed quadrata corporis statura, capite nulla ex parte enormi vel insulso, ut pote oculis ad omnes animi habitus aptissime paratis et intentis.

3 Exorto bello Veneto post Achillini mortem, Bononiae professus est ubi cucullatos sacerdotes contra se in caput et nominis famam vehementissime concitavit; edito scilicet volumine quo animas post

It was not sufficient for him to reveal both the earth and the oceans, and what secrets the rivers, land, and sea hold, while he sought far and wide the causes of things and brought back the bodies of the sick from the decay of their illnesses. Now, Leoniceno lies beneath a small mound of earth, but his name travels through both the hemispheres.

## LXXI. *Pietro Pomponazzi (1462–1525)*

Pietro Pomponazzi[523] of Mantua, my philosophy teacher, was the   1
best lecturer of all the famous Peripatetics. For he expounded on Aristotle and Averroës together in a pleasant and crystal clear voice, with a delivery that was flawless and smooth in exposition, fluent and passionate in rebuttal, yet so deliberate and calm in summation and pronouncing judgment that his listeners on their benches used to take down his complete sentences in their notes. Yet in public gatherings and assemblies of the learned, when at the portico of the *podestà* they engaged most usefully in practice debates, he showed himself so remarkable that often, when beset by one of Achillini's sophistic syllogisms, by an effusion of humor he would escape its twists and turns and sidestep his adversary's attack.

His body was diminutive but stocky, his head being not in the   2
least disproportionate or awkward, in that his eyes were perfectly suited and attuned to express every state of mind.

At the outbreak of war in the Veneto, after Achillini had died,   3
Pomponazzi taught at Bologna, where he incurred the vehement rage of the cowled clergy against his person and good name, of course because he had published a book in which, in accordance

corporis mortem interituras ex sententia Aristotelis probare nitebatur, secutus Aphrodisei placita cuius dogmate ad corrumpen-
dam iuventutem dissolvendamque Christianae vitae disciplinam
nihil pestilentius induci potuit, quanquam in exemplo dudum
fuisset qui pariter scriptis assentiretur, vir sanctissimus atque doctissimus Thomas Caietanus Cardinalis.⁴⁵ Scripsit etiam *De fato* et
*De incantationum occulta potestate.*

4    Sexagesimo autem tertio aetatis anno stranguria oborta Bononiae fato functus est, relatusque inde Mantuam nobile sepulchrum
Herculis Gonzagae Cardinalis erga civem et magistrum liberali
pietate promeruit.


5                          *Iani Vitalis*

En animarum ingens globus, en legio omnivagantum
    quas tu perpetua luce carere negas.
Mortuus ut discas aeternam has vivere vitam,
    ad cineres ululant, Pomponiate, tuos.


## LXXII. *Andreas Maro*

1  Nullis omnino certioribus lineis nulloque exactiore penicillo
Andreae Maronis ingenium depinxerim quam si eisdem utar coloribus quibus illud, dum ille viveret, diligenter expressimus in dialogo nostro, quem in Aenaria insula dum Urbs Roma a Caesarianis capto pontifice vastaretur perscripsimus. Interrogante enim
Davalo his ferme verbis respondi, quum 'De viris et foeminis aetate nostra florentibus' iucundissimo censurae ordine disputaretur
et non temere in mentionem Andreae Maronis incidissemus. Is

with Aristotle, he sought to prove that once the body has died, the soul perishes.[524] Here he followed the tenets of Alexander of Aphrodisias, than whose doctrine nothing more destructive could have been introduced to corrupt the youth and loosen the discipline of the Christian life (although there was a recent precedent in Cardinal Tommaso Cajetan, an exceedingly holy and learned man who had likewise approved of these writings).[525] He also wrote *On Fate* and *On the Hidden Power of Incantations*.[526]

But in the sixty-third year of his life, he died at Bologna from a blocked urinary tract, and from there was conveyed to Mantua where he was awarded a noble tomb, thanks to the affectionate generosity of Cardinal Ercole Gonzaga toward a fellow citizen and a teacher.

4

*By Giano Vitale*[527]

5

Behold the massive crowd of souls; behold the legion of them wandering about, who you deny are missing out on eternal light. So that you may learn in death that they have eternal life, they howl, Pomponazzi, at your ashes.

## LXXII. Andrea Marone (1474/75–1528)

I couldn't at all paint the character of Andrea Marone[528] with more assured strokes or a more precise brush than with the same colors I used, carefully portraying it while he lived, in my dialogue composed on Ischia while the city of Rome was being devastated by Imperial troops and the pope held captive. For I used almost the same words answering [Alfonso] d'Avalos when, in our most pleasant discussion ranking the "notable men and women of our time," not incidentally Andrea Marone's name came up. (He was a

1

erat Brixianus, quanquam dimidiam patriam ab Euganeis Foroque Iulio repeteret. Cupiebat enim dux generosus cultorque Musarum poetam inusitata virtute praeditum e funesta clade Urbis eripere, quod ex me illum ter captum cruciatumque diu ac omnibus fortunis expoliatum miserabili ridendoque famescentis baiuli habitu in Urbe plena funeribus mendicare didicisset.

2 'Non est' inquam, 'Davale, cur tantopere Ethruscos vates ad expeditae facundiae laudem arguta cithara personantes admiremur; in eam enim peramoenae voluptatis consuetudinem mos patrius illos adduxit, quod faciles ad veniam aures dicere audentibus plurimum indulgeant, ita ut nec eos vel levi sibilo notandos putent qui haesitando, amissa celeritatis laude, vel in dissona vel in dispari syllaba peccaverint.

3 'Vere siquidem admirari et plaudentis clamorem attollere iuvat si novum Maronem audiamus. Is enim cum summa eruditorum admiratione[46] ex tempore ad quam iusseris quaestionem Latinos versus variis modis ac[47] numeris fundere consuevit—audax profecto negocium ac munus impudentiae vel temeritatis plenum, nisi id a natura impetu prope divino mira felicitas sequeretur. Fidibus et cantu Musas evocat et, quum semel coniectam in numeros mentem alacriore spiritu inflaverit, tanta vi in torrentis morem concitatus[48] fertur ut fortuita et subitariis tractibus ducta multum ante provisa et meditata carmina videantur. Canenti defixi exardent oculi, sudores manant, frontis venae contumescunt et, quod mirum est, eruditae aures tanquam alienae ac[49] intentae omnem impetum profluentium numerorum exactissima ratione moderantur.'[50]

Brescian, though one side of his family originated in the Euganean Hills and Friuli.) For that noble commander and patron of the Muses was eager to rescue a poet gifted with exceptional talent from the calamitous ruin of the Eternal City, having learned from me that Marone, who had been captured three times and tortured at length and robbed of all he had, was wandering about a city strewn with corpses, begging, in the pitiable and ridiculous garb of a starving pallbearer:[529]

"There's no reason to be surprised, d'Avalos, at the free-flowing 2 delivery of Tuscan poets when they sing to a tuneful lute. For an ancestral custom has led that exceedingly charming and pleasant practice to prevail among them, whereby an audience, ready to forgive poets, shows the greatest indulgence to those unafraid to speak, so that it thinks it shouldn't censure even with the slightest hiss those who by their hesitation break their pace and give offense with a syllable that is either dissonant or unmetrical.

"In fact, it truly does one good to admire and applaud loudly if 3 we are hearing this new Maro who, to the astonishment of the learned, has been accustomed to pour out Latin verses on the spot in a variety of meters and rhythms on whatever subject you name — a bold undertaking, to be sure, and an impudent and reckless performance if wondrous success did not follow naturally under a nearly divine impulse. He summons the Muses with lyre and song, and once he has turned his mind to verse and filled it with a heightened inspiration, like a torrent he is carried along with such force that his poems, though composed on the spur of the moment and without premeditation, seem the result of long advance planning and prior reflection. As he recites, his blazing eyes are motionless, he drips with sweat, the veins in his forehead swell, and — what is wondrous — as the verses flow forth, his trained ears, as though not his own, intently and precisely regulate every beat."

4    Exceptus est secundissimo plausu ac idcirco a Leone repraesentatae facultatis nomine sacerdotio donatus, quum post celebre convivium cui regum legati senatoresque aderant, de suscipiendo sacro bello dicere iussus, iucunda figurarum varietate decantavit, orsus hoc nobili carmine: 'Infelix Europa diu quassata tumultu / bellorum. . . .' Tum enim Selymus Turcarum Imperator, Campsone et Tomumbeio ultimis Aegypti regibus una atque altera acie devictis ac interfectis, magnum Europae intestino bello deflagranti terrorem intulerat.

5    Periit amissis poematibus infelix Maro, in vili caupona ad Scrofam lapideam Campi Martii ab omnibus desertus, quinquagesimo tertio aetatis anno, quum e Tybure quo perfugerat, vagantibus etiam ibi barbaris, in pestilentem Urbem urgente Fato rediisset.

6        *Myrtei*

Postquam secundum publica abstulit clades
Maronem et urna caruit infelix, campis
quaesitus Elysiis nec inventus Musis:
Phoebus furoris nam minister illius
quo carmen edere inclytum Maro suerat
inter Sybillas rapuit, aeternum ut vivat.

## LXXIII. *Andreas Matthaeus Aquavivius*

1    Nemo ex his qui illustribus orti familiis aetate nostra claruerunt, quum peculiari bellica laude ducerentur, Andrea Matthaeo Aquavivio ad Praecutinos Hadrianorum regulo se luculentius optimis

He was received with the most favorable acclaim, and on that   4
account was given a benefice by Leo in honor of the virtuosity
manifested when, at the end of a crowded banquet with royal ambassadors and cardinals in attendance, upon being asked to speak
about launching a crusade, he delivered a pleasantly varied composition that began with this noble line: "Unhappy Europe, long
battered by the tumult of wars. . . ." For at that time the emperor
of the Turks, Selim, who had defeated in successive battles and
killed the last two Egyptian sultans, Kansuh al-Ghuri and Tumanbey, had caused alarm throughout Europe, then ravaged by
internecine warfare.[530]

Having lost all his poems, the unfortunate Marone died in his   5
fifty-third year in a flophouse near the pig statue in the Campo
Marzio, abandoned by everyone.[531] Fate had driven him back to
plague-ravaged Rome from Tivoli, where he had taken refuge,
since the barbarians were roaming about even there.[532]

### By Mirteo[533]   6

After the collective disaster carried off the second Maro and
the unfortunate man lacked an urn, the Muses sought for
him in the Elysian Fields but didn't find him: for Phoebus,
who provides that frenzy by which Marone had become accustomed to pour out famous poetry, snatched him away to
eternal life among the Sibyls.

## LXXIII. Andrea Matteo Acquaviva (1458–1529)

None of the nobly born in our time, when they were pursuing   1
their own military glory, won greater honor in the most advanced
fields of study than Andrea Matteo Acquaviva,[534] the ruler of Atri

disciplinis exornavit, uti praeclare constat ex eo libro nobili pariter ac erudito qui *Encyclopaedia* inscribitur; et *De morali virtute* Plutarchi plenior liber subtili et copioso commentario persimilis ostendit.

2    Hic heros antiquae virtutis, uti casus tulit, bis bello praelioque adverso et vulneribus honestissime susceptis captus, forti animo tetri carceris calamitatem studiorum solatio ita lenivit ut ad eam exculti ingenii frugem, quae ab impotenti fortuna eripi non potest, generosa meditatione pervenerit. Sed quum eum victor Consalvus cum reliquis captivis in triumpho ducendum in Hispaniam mitteret, Rex Ferdinandus, prudentiae et lenitatis nomine maxime clarus, libertati pristinaeque fortunae restituit.

3    Tanto itaque usus beneficio per viginti quattuor annos egit iucundo in ocio vitam dicatam Musis, adeo splendide et vigilanter ut ad idem literarum honestissimum decus Belisarium fratrem Neretinorum regulum aemulanter invitaret, quem *De venatione* et *De singularis certaminis provocatione* scripsisse videmus. Caeterum vir tantus, quum Neapolitanos proceres candore, innocentia et liberalitate facile superaret, visus est parum accuratus et diligens in tuenda rei familiaris dignitate, quum in ultimo vitae actu praealtus animus contemptor opum institutae liberalitatis nervos inconditis sumptibus incidisset.

4    Fato functus est ad Conversanum Bario finitimum, septuagesimo secundo aetatis anno, quum Lotrechii Galli infelicibus armis Apulia quateretur.

5             *Marcelli Palonii Romani*

   Non minus aeternum ex Aquivivo[51] habet Hadria nomen
     nobilis immenso quam dedit ipsa Mari.

in Teramo, as is abundantly clear from that book both famous and scholarly called the *Encyclopedia*. Also demonstrating this is a denser book, very like a precise and exhaustive commentary, on Plutarch's *On Moral Virtue*.[535]

As chance would have it this hero, whose valor was like that of the ancients, twice a prisoner of war when the tide of battle had turned, and honorably wounded, bravely mitigated the misfortune of foul imprisonment by resorting to the solace of studies, so that through noble contemplation he gained the rewards of intellectual cultivation which uncontrollable fortune cannot strip away. But when his conqueror Gonsalvo sent him to Spain to be paraded in triumph along with the other prisoners, King Ferdinand, widely known for his wisdom and leniency, restored him to freedom and to his previous condition.

Thanks to this great favor, for twenty-four years he lived in happy retirement, dedicating his life to the Muses with such splendid concentration that he challenged his brother Belisario, the ruler of Nardò (who we see wrote *On Hunting* and *On Challenging to Single Combat*) to match his exalted literary glory.[536] But so great a man, although far superior to the Neapolitan barons in directness, integrity, and generosity, turned out to be somewhat careless and wasteful in safeguarding his patrimony: for, in the last stage of his life, this lofty spirit, contemptuous of wealth, through capricious spending had cut short his customary liberality.

He died in Conversano, on the border with Bari, in his seventy-second year, while Apulia was being battered by the ill-fated attacks of the Frenchman Lautrec.

*By Marcello Palonio the Roman*[537]

The fame given noble Atri by Acquaviva is no less lasting than the name it has itself given to the vast Adriatic.[538]

Adde freto suus est supero quod terminus: illi
nec limes, tellus ulla nec unda, datur.
Nam Musis ubi honos Martique togaeque manebit,
et lucebit ubi sol, Aquivivus[52] erit.

## LXXIV. Petrus Gravina

1 Natus est Petrus Gravina Catinae in Sicilia, sed ipse primam
domus originem a Capua repetebat. Natura ei admodum indul-
genter, praeter excellentis ingenii vim, summam etiam procero
corpori et venusto tribuit dignitatem firmitate imprimis et agilitate
quadam singulari quum in ludo pilae usque ad admirationem et
gladiatoria arte equestribusque armis ad militarem laudem exerce-
retur nataretque saepissime ad incredibilem urinandi patientiam,
quibus agitationibus ita firmavit corpus ut, nulla paulo saeviore
tentatus valetudine, ad extremam prope senectutem integro et
plane iuvenili vigore pervenerit.

2 Utebatur parciore mensa, sed ea semper nitida. Vinum a Vesevo
Surrentoque in honore erat, sed semper sobrie et moderate perpo-
tanti. Vitae genus adamavit quietum, cunctis solutum curis et liti-
bus, hilarique imprimis et tenera studiosorum adolescentium familiaritate gaudebat. Ingenio enim erat aperto liberali perblando,
cultu corporis nitido et sumptuoso, quum undulata toga uteretur
et serico latiore villoso pileo argenteam comam morose perornaret.

3 Quum in Aragonia aula versaretur emanarentque ab eo versiculi
ex nobili semper occasione argute lepideque perscripti, Pontano
carus esse coepit qui erat ingeniorum censor longe gravissimus,

Moreover, the sea we call Superum[539] has its boundary, whereas Matteo has none, neither earth nor sea. For wherever honor is given to cultural pursuits and to the arts of peace and war, and wherever the sun shines, there Acquaviva will be.

## LXXIV. *Pietro Gravina (ca. 1452–1528)*

Pietro Gravina[540] was born in Catania, in Sicily, but he himself 1 liked to say that his family had originated in Capua. In addition to giving him a powerful intellect, Nature most generously endowed him with fitness, consisting above all in a strength and agility remarkable even for a tall and handsome frame, for his ball-playing inspired amazement, his swordsmanship and skill at equestrian combat earned the praise of soldiers, and when he swam he very often stayed underwater for an astonishing length of time. With these exercises he so strengthened his body that, beset by no serious illness, he arrived almost at the extremity of old age with unimpaired and conspicuously youthful vigor.

He ate sparingly, but always elegantly. He loved the wines of 2 Vesuvius and Sorrento, but always drank with moderation and restraint. He adored a tranquil lifestyle, free from all worries and quarrels, and he enjoyed a lighthearted and tender intimacy with studious youths. Indeed, he had a candid, generous, and most amiable disposition. His attire was elegant and luxurious, for he wore a cascading gown and adorned his silver hair fussily with a broad cap of silken velvet.

While he was at the Aragonese court and, on every formal oc- 3 casion, let flow melodious and charming epigrams he'd written, he won the affection of Pontano, by far the most authoritative critic of the brilliant, who generously attested that affection in his divine

idque divinis operibus ad immortalem amici laudem benigne testatus est. Spectatae demum eius virtuti externus Mecoenas adfulsit Magnus Consalvus, qui ipsius victorias et trophaea Gallica heroico celebrantem in templo maximo Neapoli sacerdotii honore nobilitavit. Sed Consalvo in Hispaniam abducto quod regi in suspicionem affectati regni venisset, Prospero Columnae adhesit.

4    In pangendis elegis tenero quodam lepore sibi genium respondere fatebatur, sed in scribendo epigrammate uni ei haud dubie palmam tribuebat Actius Syncerus, qui et parcus et amarulentus in alieni operis censura laudator esse consuevisset.

5    Heroica poemata periisse tum ferunt, nisi iampridem a nobis lectitata compareant, quum Caesariani[53] a Gallis Neapoli obsessi, tanquam non in socia urbe, divina ac humana omnia conturbarent, ita ut non miretur quispiam tam paucis quae extant ingenii monumentis praeclari poetae famam constitisse: nam et multa ipse lugentibus amicis sponte delevit, veluti strepentibus armis saeculum indignatus, aut iratus Musis quod externi duces conceptae spei minus liberaliter arrisissent.

6    Sed dispari iudicii sorte id poema prope amissum querulus lugebat quo Surrentini ocii delitias elegantissime depinxerat. Sed Scipionis Capycii pietas dignum egregio nobilique poeta colligendi dispersa et publicandi officium praestitit, ut pene intercepta amico poetae vita redderetur. Non carebat quoque composti oratoris nomine, quanquam dum publice oraret una actionis laude contentus esse videretur.

works, to his friend's everlasting glory. At length, a foreign Maecenas smiled upon his conspicuous merit: Gonsalvo the Great, who
ennobled with a canonry in the cathedral chapter of Naples the
poet who celebrated in heroic verse the victories he himself had
won and the trophies he'd taken from the French.[541] But once
Gonsalvo was called to Spain because (it was said) the king had
come to suspect that he had royal ambitions, Gravina became attached to Prospero Colonna.[542]

He acknowledged that composing elegies with a certain tender    4
charm best suited his talent. But Jacopo Sannazaro, who tended in
his critiques of others' work to be sparing and caustic in his praise,
unhesitatingly gave first honors in the writing of epigrams to him
alone.

It's said that all his epic poems (unless those I read long ago    5
should surface) were destroyed when the Imperial troops, besieged
in Naples by the French, threw all things cultural and sacred into
disorder, as if they were not in an allied city, so that nobody
should be surprised that the reputation of so renowned a poet has
rested upon the few works of genius that survive. Moreover, to the
dismay of his friends, he himself willingly destroyed many of
them: perhaps amid the clash of arms he deemed his times unworthy of them, or was angry at the Muses because he thought foreign commanders were insufficiently favorable to the hopes he had
entertained.

He grieved bitterly and inordinately, however, for that poem,    6
nearly lost, in which he had described with consummate skill the
delights of leisure time in Sorrento.[543] But Scipione Capece devotedly set about the task, worthy of so outstanding and noble a poet,
of collecting and publishing his scattered works, restoring to his
friend the poet a life that was almost snatched away.[544] Nor did he
lack a reputation as a well-trained orator, although when he held
forth in public he seemed to be content with the praise of his delivery alone.

7 Decessit septuagesimo quarto aetatis anno, ad Concham oppidum Sidicini agri, quum ei in umbra meridianti castaneae echinus tibiae suram levissime pupugisset: temere enim scalpendo enatum est ulcus accersita laetali febricula. Adeo enim subtiles mortis causas fata inveniunt, quum ex decreto urgent.

8                                 *Iani Vitalis*

Hanc tibi pro tumuli Ianus Vitalis honore
ramosam laurum, magne Gravina, dicat,
hic ubi odorata manes requiescere in umbra
floribus in mediis et iuvet esse tuos.
Illa, Notis quoties rami quatientur et Euris,
perstrepet in laudes, sancte poeta, tuas.

## LXXV. *Pomponius Gauricus*

1 Argivae Iunonis Fanum, quod est Picentinorum nobile oppidum, geminos fratres Gauricos praestanti ingenio protulit: Lucam ipsum, quem astrologiae peritissimum felicique saepe eventu futura praedicentem in aula Pauli Tertii Pontificis admiramur; et Pomponium, non incelebrem poetam validaque in varias artes ardentis ingenii foecunditate mirabilem, nisi instabili genio abductus, dum fervide transcurrit et sectatur operum novitatem, in cunctis nusquam accuratus et diligens firmae prudentiae dignitatem amisisset.

2 Is Graecorum poetarum vitas Petri Criniti aemulatione qui de Latinis librum ediderat[54] Latine perscripsit, atque item geminos *De physiognomia* et *De architectura* libellos. Extat et eius volumen *De metallicis*, curiosorum insanae turbae gratissimum. Neque enim

He died in his seventy-fourth year at the town of Conca,[545] in 7
the territory of Teano, when a chestnut burr very lightly punctured his calf as he was taking a siesta in the shade: for by casually scratching it, he opened a sore, bringing upon himself a deadly infection.[546] Thus the Fates contrive subtle means of death when, at the appointed time, they draw near.

*By Giano Vitale*[547]     8

O mighty Gravina, Giano Vitale dedicates to you in place of a tomb the honor of this luxuriant laurel, where your spirit may be pleased to find rest in its fragrant shade, surrounded by flowers. As often as the branches are shaken by the East and South winds, o reverend poet, it will echo with your praises.

## LXXV. Pomponio Gaurico (1481/82–1529/30?)

Fano, a celebrated city in the Picentines that once belonged to the 1
Argive Juno, gave birth to two brothers of remarkable talent, the Gaurico twins:[548] that wunderkind Luca, the expert astronomer in the court of Pope Paul III, who often successfully predicts the future; and Pomponio, a poet who would have won praise and been admired for the great passion and strength of his intellect in varied disciplines, had not an unsound impulse led him to dash in hot pursuit of novelty, abandon all care and accuracy, and lose esteem for sound judgment.

He wrote in Latin lives of Greek poets to rival Pietro Crinito, 2
who had produced a book about Latin poets, and he also composed a pair of booklets, *On Physiognomy* and *On Architecture*.[549] In addition, we have his volume *On Metals*, exceedingly popular with

desunt qui aurum pariter et argentum ex ignobili materia inanibus
recoctionum artificiis procreari atque exprimi posse arbitrentur.

3    Exierunt etiam in publicum epigrammata aliquot et elegiae,
non dubia amatoriae vanitatis inditia; nam illustrem foeminam
arsisse constat enudasseque animi aegritudinem procaci Musarum
lenocinio adeo incaute et flagranter ut, quum Surrentina via Stabias peteret in eoque itinere ab obviis salutatus fuisset, nusquam
demum apparuerit—frustra eum Luca fratre per sexdecim annos
expectante quum, procul dubio ab ea suspicione trucidatus et cum
servis et iumentis, ne ullum caedis vestigium extaret, in subiectum
mare praecipitatus existimetur.

4                              *Myrtei*

Ibat Gauricus ad suos amores,
sed diu haud potuit suos amores
uti Gauricus: abstulere fata.
Verum nulla manet sepulchri imago.
Nanque (quod coluit pari labore
Musas et Venerem) vel a Camoenis
raptus creditur inter alta montis
qui iacet Stabias super vetustas,
vel pulchrae Veneri datus sacerdos
Tyrrheni Maris in Sinum profundum.

the crazy pseudo-scientific crowd, for we aren't free of those who suppose that by the pointless practice of melting a base substance, both gold and silver can be produced and extracted.[550]

There have also come to public attention some epigrams and elegies that document a foolish romance: for they make plain that he was burning with love for a noblewoman, and that with the Muses as shameless go-betweens, he so incautiously and ardently bared his suffering soul that, while traveling to Castellammare di Stabia by the road to Sorrento (and greeted by those he met en route), somewhere along the way he vanished. For sixteen years his brother Luca awaited him in vain; and no one doubted that he'd been butchered on account of rumors regarding his affair. It's thought that he, along with his servants and pack animals, was cast headlong into the sea below, so that no trace of the murder would remain.[551]

*By Mirteo*[552]  4

Gaurico was on the way to his love, but Gaurico could not long enjoy his love: the Fates snatched him away. But no sign of a tomb survives. In fact, because he was as devoted to the Muses as to Venus, it is believed he was either carried off by the Muses to the mountain heights overlooking ancient Stabiae or, as a priest to beautiful Venus, committed to the deep bosom of the Tyrrhenian Sea.

## LXXVI. *Marcus Antonius Casanova*

1 Marco Antonio Casanovae, Comense patre Romae genito, arguti epigrammatis palmam detulit illa ipsa Roma severae auris iudicio superba nec unquam inconfesso pudore poetis adulatrix, quod lepida et salsis finibus aculeata carmina factitaret. Elocutioni tamen casta puritas ac in numero saepe duro lenitas defuit, qualis in Catullo praetenero poeta conspicitur, quum ingeniose mordaci et impuro Martiali persimilis esse mallet et una praesertim peracutae circumductaeque sententiae gloria duceretur. Sed miscuisse utrumque genus tum iuvit quum paucorum versuum spectanda posteris elogia priscis Romanae virtutis heroibus, tanquam manentibus eorum statuis, inscripsisset.

2 Nemo autem eo simplicitate ac innocentia vitae melior, nemo urbana comitate iucundior existimari potuit, nisi Columnae familiae alumnus, in gratiam Pompeii Cardinalis, Clementis Pontificis famam intemperantissime lacerasset. Sed Clemens, se ipso et toto denique desumpto nomine maior et augustior, reo maiestatis captoque ad supplicium facile pepercit praeclara C. Caesaris imitatione, qui Catulliani dentis aeternum virus et lividam libertatem generosa dissimulatione contempserat.

3 Periit pestilenti correptus morbo quo cladem Urbis Fortuna nec innumeris saturata funeribus adcumularat quum, obsesso captoque pontifice, Pompeius ipse diverso ingenii habitu inimici calamitate laetaretur et ruentis patriae casum inani poenitentia deploraret.

## LXXVI. Marco Antonio Casanova (ca. 1477–1528)

Marco Antonio Casanova[553] was born at Rome of a father from    1
Como. Because he composed charming poems that culminated in
barbed witticisms, Rome itself, which takes pride in the judgment
of its unsparing ear and never stoops so low as to fawn upon poets, deemed him the best at composing ingenious epigrams.[554] His
delivery, however, was not pure, and his often-dissonant meter
lacked the kind of smoothness that is seen in Catullus, the tenderest of poets. Instead he preferred to be like the cleverly caustic and
shameless Martial, and coveted above all else the praise to be won
for sharp-witted and allusive aphorisms. But blending the two
styles pleased him when he inscribed short verse epigraphs dedicated to ancient heroes who exemplified Roman virtue, as if for
extant statues of them, for posterity to see.[555]

Nobody, meanwhile, could be thought to surpass him in hon-    2
esty or integrity, or to be more agreeable for gracious sophistication, were it not that as a client of the Colonna family he had
savagely torn apart Pope Clement's reputation in order to curry
the favor of Cardinal Pompeo. But Clement, rising in greatness
and dignity above not only himself but even the full meaning of
the name he had taken, indulgently absolved him from the charge
of lèse-majesté, freeing him from the prison where he was awaiting
execution.[556] This he did in splendid imitation of Julius Caesar,
who nobly pretended to ignore the perpetual venom and spiteful
brazenness of Catullus's malice.[557]

Casanova died from the plague that Fortune had inflicted in the    3
aftermath of the Sack of Rome, not satisfied with the countless
deaths it had caused.[558] The pope had been besieged and then
made a captive, while Pompeo's own mind was divided between
exulting over his enemy's misfortune and bewailing with vain re-
gret the ruined state of his homeland.[559]

4    Tumulatus est iuxta Naumachiam Campi Martii Laurentiano
in templo, quod olim Lucinae dicatum fuerat, et Blosius Palladius
sodalis, quod funeris honore caruisset, hoc pie inscripto carmine
tumulum spectantium oculis ad lachrymas indicavit:

5                            *Blosii Palladii*

Comensis Casanova, dum priores
et duces canit et canit poetas,
praecurtis epigrammatis perennem
ac longam sibi gloriam paravit.


## LXXVII. *Balthasar Castellio*

1   Hic est ille Balthasar Castellio Mantuae natus, ingenii laude Maroni civi suo plane secundus, qui ad exactam principalis aulae
normam militari civilique munere virum elegantem instituit; pa-
rique disciplina illustrem foeminam, descriptis lectissimorum morum finibus, effingit, quo opere iucundissimo Graecae Latinaeque
facultatis peramoenos flores decerpsisse videtur ut in unum volumen nobilioris vitae praecepta oblectamentaque honestissimi
ocii conferrentur; placere siquidem magnae fortunae viris, ut saepe
literarum expertibus ipsisque praesertim foeminis magnopere cupiebat, ob idque maluit vernacula quam Latina lingua stylum
Ethrusca molliorem exercuisse, scilicet ut imperiti ex antiquis
arguta manu surrepta translataque scitissime non agnoscentes,
ea omnia tanquam nova mirarentur. Scripsit et Latinas elegias

He was buried in the Church of San Lorenzo (once dedicated 4
to Lucina) in Campo Marzio near the *naumachia*.[560] Because he'd
had no funeral, with the following devoted verse inscription his
colleague Blosio Palladio drew viewers' attention to the tomb at
which they might shed tears:

*By Blosio Palladio*[561]                                          5

While Casanova of Como sang of the ancients, both commanders and poets, in epigrams of exceeding brevity he obtained for himself everlasting and far-reaching glory.

## LXXVII. Baldassare Castiglione (1478–1529)

Behold the famous Baldassare Castiglione,[562] born at Mantua, and 1
second only to his compatriot Vergil in renown for brilliance. He
teaches how the man of refinement undertakes his military and
civic duties according to the highest standards of a princely court,
and with equal erudition portrays the noble woman, setting out
the choicest rules of etiquette. In this delightful work he appears
to have plucked the loveliest flowers of Greek and Latin eloquence
so as to combine into one volume the precepts that lend greater
nobility to life and the delights of the most virtuous leisure. Since
he was quite eager to please high-ranking men (as they are often
ignorant of literature, and women even more so), he wielded a
gentler pen, choosing the Tuscan vernacular rather than Latin,
doubtless so that the inexperienced, not recognizing that he'd pilfered things from the ancients with a sneaky hand and expertly
translated them, might marvel at the seeming novelty of them all.
He also wrote Latin elegies and a long epic, *Cleopatra*, but he is

et grandi heroico *Cleopatram,* sed paucis admodum Ethruscis rhythmis, quum amatorii doloris finem superba comparatione desperaret, nobilis poetae famam tulisse iudicatur.

2    In sago autem togaque pariter habili ingenio et generoso quidem ore pacis bellique muneribus interfuit obivitque subitarias legationes ad reges atque pontifices, quum momenta gravissimarum rerum non modo praestantis animi fidem sed expediti corporis diligentiam celeritatemque requirerent. Novissime annis provectum sed medicamentis occultata canitie et multis cultus munditiis iuventae decus assectantem, quum eruditae artes in eo vigerent, Clemens ad Carolum Quintum in Hispaniam misit; ei non dubio honore purpurae destinato, nisi Fortuna Romanae urbi immane excidium struens utriusque vota fefellisset. Corruit enim mox Roma Caesarianorum ducum simulatis indutiis prodita viderique potuit Castellio in ea re non satis diligentem aut certe parum felicem operam praestitisse, quum delatum sibi in ea lugubri clade episcopatum Abulensem munere Caesaris accepisset.

3    Verum ea dignitate diu perfrui vel uberiorem expectare non licuit. Sublatus est enim occulta febre, quum vix quinquagesimum sextum attigisset annum, ad Mantuam in Carpetanis.[55] Funeri eius aulae proceres officium praestitere; nec eum chiromantis ariolus fefellit qui ex dextrae volae lineis eum dignitate auctum Mantuae, sed nequaquam in Hispania, moriturum praedixerat.

4                          *Iani Vitalis*

> Castalioneum ad tumulum dum Hispania tota
>    convenit et sancto iusta parat cineri,
> Scipiadum manes referunt dixisse: 'Secundum
>    hic docta amisit Mantua Virgilium.'

judged to have won fame as an outstanding poet for just a handful of Tuscan poems in which, arrogantly challenging his rivals, he despaired of his sufferings over love ever reaching an end.[563]

Astute and eloquent alike in military and civilian roles, he 2 shouldered responsibilities in both war and peace. And when crises required not only the loyalty of an exceptionally steadfast will but also the assiduity and alacrity of an agile body, he went on urgent legations to kings and popes. Finally, when he was well on in years (although he dyed his gray locks and sought the honor of youth by elegant primping), since his professional skills were still robust, Clement sent him to Charles V in Spain. Certainly he would have become a cardinal had not Fortune, devising monstrous destruction for the city of Rome, cheated the hopes of both the city and the humanist. For through the truce falsely declared by the emperor's commanders, Rome soon fell, and in that matter Castiglione appeared to have lent insufficient or certainly little-effective effort, since amid that grievous calamity he had accepted the emperor's offer of the bishopric of Ávila.[564]

But he was not permitted to enjoy that position long or to anticipate a richer one. For when he had barely reached fifty-six, while in Madrid he was carried off by an insidious attack of fever. The court dignitaries paid their respects at his funeral; nor did a palm-reading soothsayer deceive him, who from the lines of his right palm had predicted that after receiving a higher office he would die in "Mantua" — although he didn't say anything about Spain.[565]

*By Giano Vitale*[566]                                     4

While all Spain assembled at Castiglione's tomb and prepared the funeral rites for his holy ashes, the shades of the Scipios[567] were reported to say: "Here, learned Mantua has lost a second Vergil."

*Marci Antonii Flaminii*

Si truculenta ferox irrumpis in agmina, Marte
    diceris invicto, Castalione, satus;
at molli cithara si condis amabile carmen,
    Castalia natus diceris esse dea.


## 6

*Eiusdem*

Horrida terribilis cum tractas arma Maronis,
    Castalione, tui carmine digna facis;
idem cum molli vacuus requiescis in umbra
    Castaliae, aeterno digna Marone canis.


## LXXVIII. *Andreas Naugerius*

1  Andreas Naugerius patritii ordinis Sabellico Venetiis profitente Latinas literas, Graecas autem a Marco Musuro Cretense Patavii hausit; sed in Latinis delectu ac observatione praeceptore diligentior illum quem superior aetas insalubri[56] atque aspera styli novitate delectata contempserat candorem antiquae puritatis assecutus est, ut funebribus Liviani Ducis et Principis Lauredani laudationibus apparet. Proposito quidem Cicerone ad imitandum, quem Politianus et Hermolaus fastidisse videbantur ut pote qui, omnis eruditionis exundante copia instructi, aliquid in stylo proprium, quod peculiarem ex certa nota mentis effigiem referret, ex naturae genio effinxisse nobilius putarint quam servili imitatione enata ad novam frugem ingenia distorsisse. Magno tum quidem probro erat doctis ridendis pares simiis videri.

If, Castiglione, you launch a ferocious attack on savage armies, you are said to be sprung from invincible Mars. But if you compose a lovely poem with a tender lyre, you are called a son of the goddess Castalia.[569]

When, Castiglione, you treat of frightful war, you honor your fellow poet, awe-inspiring Maro. Likewise, when you repose at leisure in the gentle shade of Castalia, your songs are worthy of the everlasting Maro.[571]

## LXXVIII. Andrea Navagero (1483–1529)

The patrician Andrea Navagero[572] learned Latin from Sabellico   1 when he was lecturing in Venice, and Greek from a Cretan, Marcus Musurus, in Padua. More accurate in Latin diction and usage than his teacher, Navagero attained to that pure clarity of old, which the preceding age's attraction to useless and harsh stylistic innovation had caused it to scorn. One sees this in his funeral orations for the military leader d'Alviano and for Doge Loredan.[573] As his model for imitation he chose Cicero, whom Poliziano and Ermolao seemed to disdain: for, supplied with a superabundance of every kind of knowledge, they supposed it nobler to fashion from one's own inspiration something individual in style that reflected one's particular mindset, rather than to deform by servile imitation a mind born to bear new fruit.[574] Back then, indeed, scholars held that it was a great disgrace to seem like ridiculous apes.

2    Eodem quoque praestanti iudicio, quum epigrammata lepidissime scriberet, non salsis aculeatisque finibus sed tenera illa et praedulci prisca suavitate claudebat, adeo Martiali severus hostis ut quotannis stato die Musis dicato multa eius volumina tanquam impura cum execratione Vulcano dicarentur.

3    Nec minore felicitate Ethruscos numeros attigit, sed in Liviani contubernio castra secutus studiorum diligentiam remisit: et salubri quidem remedio, quum ingenium bilis atra veterum lucubrationum vigiliis accersita haud leviter afflixisset. Propterea scribendae Venetae historiae munus a senatu demandatum acceptoque liberali stipendio susceptum praestare non potuit, quanquam non desint qui eum in ipso statim limine feliciter exordientem religiosi operis gravitate deterritum existiment, quum infinita curiositate summoque labore et pertinaci memoria tantarum rerum notitia paranda videretur.

4    Verum in ea cogitatione, ut reipublicae operam praestaret a senatu ad Carolum Caesarem in Hispaniam missus, infaustam legationem suscepit, quum in id tempus incidisset quo Italiae principes, servitutis metu ad arma consternati, affectanti dominatum Italiae Caesari restitissent. Secunda autem suscepta legatione, quum exitiali festinatione, mutatis ad celeritatem iumentis, in Galliam percurrisset, vix dum salutato rege Blesio in oppido ad Ligerim febre correptus interiit quadragesimo septimo aetatis anno; omnique eum funeris honore rex, Musarum amicissimus, nec sine luctu prosecutus est.

He applied the same admirable discretion to his delightful epi-   2
grams, closing them not with witty barbs, but with the ancients'
sweet and tender charms. He was such a savage enemy to Martial
that every year, on an appointed day dedicated to the Muses, he
sacrificed many of Martial's books to Vulcan,[575] cursing them as
filth.

He was no less successful in writing Tuscan verse, but once hav-   3
ing joined d'Alviano's military camp he neglected his studies.[576]
This must have been a blessed relief, for the melancholy caused by
studying late into the night had wreaked havoc on his mind. For
this reason, although entrusted by the Senate with the task of
writing the history of Venice and awarded a generous stipend, he
was unable to make good on the undertaking.[577] There are some,
however, who think that, having made an auspicious beginning, he
was scared off at the very outset by the burden of such exacting
work: for he believed that the record of such great events required
infinite care, immense effort, and a tenacious memory.

But amid this rumination, when the Senate dispatched him in   4
the service of the republic to the court of the emperor Charles in
Spain, he undertook an embassy that could not succeed: for it
came at that time when Italian princes, fearing subjugation, had
mounted an armed resistance to the emperor, who aspired to
sovereignty over Italy. Having undertaken a second mission,
however, he hurried to France in deadly haste (with changes of
horses for speed); but soon after having met the king, he caught a
fever and died, in the town of Blois on the Loire. This was in the
forty-seventh year of his life. The king bestowed every funerary
honor on him and, being a great friend of the Muses, mourned his
passing.

5                   *Marci Antonii Flaminii*

Naugeri, ne quis tibi certet neve laboret
  in cassum laudes aequiparare tuas,
sive epigramma facis iuncto pede sive soluto
  defles magnanimum funera acerba virum.

## LXXIX. *Ioannes Marius Catanaeus*

1   Ioannes Marius Catanaeus Novariensis, Merulae Demetriique
discipulus, quum iustas ex utraque lingua facultates comparasset,
C. Plinii Caecilii Secundi epistolas erudito commentario interpre-
tatus est; collectaque inde non mediocris eruditionis fama, Romam se contulit in domoque Bendinelli Sauli Cardinalis cui ab
epistolis operam praestabat.

2   Tres Luciani dialogos diversi caracteris in Latinum vertit —
praetenero scilicet *Amores* vel parum pudicos, iucundo *Lapithas*,
gravi vero illum *De legibus conscribendae historiae*, tanquam in usum
suscepti a me eius muneris Iovio nomini dicatum — ex censura
quidem Scipionis Cartheromachi, quum ille in Academiam nomen
daret, magnopere laudatos. Descripsit demum carmine Genuam in
heri gratiam, atque inde poesis amore iam plane senex correptus
est, sera et parum ideo felici libidine, quum Musas nunquam ten-
tatis numeris in iuventa lacessisset.

3   Itaque Gotifredi Bolionis sacrum bellum sub titulo *Solymidos*,
quo potuit ore, decantatum est, in quo poemate non morosus et
aequus lector argumenti pietatem et quaedam schemata iucundae

May no one hope to vie with you, Navagero, nor labor in vain to measure up to your glory, whether writing epigrams in couplets or mourning in prose the bitter passing of great men.

## LXXIX. Giovanni Maria Cattaneo
### (2nd half of 15th cent.–1529/30)

Once Giovanni Maria Cattaneo[579] of Novara, a student of Merula  1
and of Demetrius, had acquired proper skills in both Latin and Greek, he published Pliny the Younger's letters along with a learned commentary.[580] Having won from this no small reputation for erudition, he went to Rome, where he served as a secretary in the household of Cardinal Bendinello Sauli.[581]

He translated three dialogues of Lucian in differing registers: he  2
rendered the *Loves* (which aren't all that chaste) in a very tender style; the *Lapithae*, lightheartedly; and, in a dignified manner, the well-known *Rules for Writing History*, which he dedicated "to Giovio" for use in the task I'd undertaken.[582] And when he put his name forward to join the Academy, in light of the opinion of Scipio Carteromachus,[583] these translations were highly praised. Finally, to please his patron, he wrote a poem describing Genoa.[584] Then, at quite an advanced age, he fell in love with poetry. Since he'd never bothered the Muses in his youth by attempting to write verse, the passion came too late and was not especially fruitful.

Therefore, as far as his eloquence allowed, he sang of the cru-  3
sade of Godfrey of Bouillon in a poem entitled *Suleiman*.[585] An unfussy and impartial reader will admire the devotion to its subject and certain rhetorical effects of pleasing novelty, even if he

novitatis admirabitur si carmina, tanquam salebrosa et distortis numeris luxata, probare noluerit. Id opus author, quum alieni ingenii iudicium subiturus ad Bembum me praesente detulisset, lecto statim titulo Bembus hylari comitate: 'Nunquam, Catanaee, putassem' inquit 'te, alioqui virum de utraque lingua optime meritum, hac ipsa qua nos gaudemus carminum facultate valuisse, quum nihil omnino ad quod Musae dulces arrideant in severo et militari vultu tuo prorsus emineat.'

4    Quo verbo ille perstrictus argute respondit: 'Ergo nec tu, Bembe, satis peritus phisiognomus videri potes, quum te Philomusi, poetae gratia tua florentis, a dedolatis ruditer maxillis et repando naso enormis vultus omnino deceperit.' Quo responso omnibus exortus est plenior cachinnus, quod Philomusus, poeta utique non insuavis et lyristes, Bembo sodalis e patria Pisauro, vespillonis senis buxeam faciem referret. Nondum autem perfecto poemate rediit ad pedestrem orationem, non obscure ipsa spe conceptae laudis destitutus, perscripsitque duos exactae eruditionis dialogos, *De potestate et cursu solis ac lunae* et *De ludis Romanis*, sed ingruente fatali morbo absolvi nequiverunt.

5    Periit in Urbe, quum abesset Clemens Carolo Caesari Romani Imperii insignia Bononiae traditurus, ideo caelata morte quod ita impetrandis sacerdotiis ex mora caveretur ut sepulchri et funeris honore caruerit, quum ab Academicis ad Vetulonias aquas secessisse crederetur.

doesn't care for the verses, which are lurching and broken up by distorted meters. When the author, seeking an expert's opinion, had submitted that work to Bembo in my presence, immediately upon reading the title Bembo said obligingly and in a friendly way, "I would never have supposed, Cattaneo, that you, a man of otherwise exemplary merit in both Latin and Greek, had skill in the very art of poetry that I enjoy, since there's absolutely nothing in your stern and soldierly countenance on which the sweet Muses might smile."

Offended by this comment, Cattaneo cleverly rejoined, "Then 4 you, Bembo, can't be considered a very good physiognomist, since you've been entirely deceived by the misshapen face of the poet Philomusus, with his crooked jawline and snub nose, who owes his success to you."[586] The laughter that this response aroused from everyone was the greater because Philomusus, who was at least a decent poet and lutenist, and a friend of Bembo's from his native Pesaro, had the sallow complexion of a geriatric undertaker. Evidently having lost hope, however, of the fame he'd anticipated, without finishing this poem Cattaneo returned to prose, and wrote two dialogues of impeccable erudition: *On the Influence and Course of the Sun and Moon* and *On the Festivals of the Romans*. But he was prevented from finishing them by the onset of a fatal illness.

He died in Rome while Clement was out of the city, having 5 gone off to bestow the regalia of Roman dominion upon the emperor Charles in Bologna.[587] His death was kept a secret in order that the many who had designs on his benefices might safeguard their interests during the delay.[588] As a result, he was deprived of the honor of a tomb and a funeral, inasmuch as his fellow academicians believed that he had gone off to the hot springs in Vetulonia.[589]

6                                    *Myrtei*

Vide, viator, quanta iactura occulti
esset sepulchri ni, ingeni sui claris
perennioribusque monimentis tectus,
adhuc ubique viveret Catanaeus.


## LXXX. *Iacobus Sanazarius*

1   Iacobus Sanazarius, equestris ordinis poeta Neapoli natus atque
educatus, quum praeclarum foecundi atque felicis ingenii specimen
daret, repudiato avito gentilitioque nomine 'Actius Syncerus' appellari voluit, adhortante Pontano qui Ioviani cognomen amicorum imitatione desumpserat. Sed origo vetustae stirpis e Sancto
Nazario, Laumellini agri oppido inter Padum et Ticinum non
ignobili unde maiores advenerant, non obscure petebatur.

2       Floruit amicitia Federici Regis, senescente Pontani gratia qui
Aragonum nomen vehementer offenderat, quum veluti personae
oblitus victorem Carolum invidiosa vel intempestiva oratione publice laudasset. Permansit in ea belli procella in officio Actius re-
deuntique Ferdinando Iuniori armatus inter fideles cives operam
praestitit, unde ei conspicuus in aula gratiae locus. Sed infestius
demum urgente Fortuna, quum Federicus regno pelleretur, constanti studio atque integra fide eum exulem in ulteriorem Galliam
secutus est, qua gratissimi animi testificatione singularem laudem
promeruisse vel eius inimici iudicabant.

*By Mirteo*[590]

See, wayfarer, how wasteful the seclusion of a tomb would be, did not Cattaneo live on everywhere, sheltered by the splendid and more enduring monuments of his brilliance.

## LXXX. Jacopo Sannazaro (1457–1530)

When Jacopo Sannazaro,[591] a poet and noble born and educated in Naples, was giving remarkable indications of his fertile and fruitful mind, having rejected his ancestral family name (at the urging of Pontano who, in imitation of his friends, had himself chosen the surname "Jovianus"), he chose to be called Actius Syncerus. The origins of his ancient lineage, however, clearly could be traced to San Nazzaro, a town of some importance in Lomellian territory, between the Po and Ticino Rivers, whence his ancestors had come.[592]

He prospered thanks to the friendship of King Frederick,[593] even as the favor that Pontano had enjoyed was waning: for Pontano had deeply offended the dignity of the House of Aragon when, as if forgetful of his official role, he had publicly praised the victor, Charles, in an odious or at least ill-timed oration.[594] Amid this tumult of war Jacopo remained in office and, having taken up arms, with other loyal citizens he gave assistance to the returning Ferdinando II. On this account he held a prominent place of favor at court. But in time, as Fortune attacked more savagely and Frederick was driven from power, with steadfast devotion and complete loyalty Sannazaro followed his patron into exile in France.[595] Even his enemies judged that he deserved singular praise for thus demonstrating his gratitude.

3 Scripsit, tanquam ambidexter, Ethrusca simul atque Latina carmina pari lepore saleque, arridentibus utrinque Musis, quum multo felle odii subamarus praepilata iacula iambis intorqueret aut amorum suorum dulcedine resolutus tenerrime lasciviret. Gravi autem et sacro poemate De partu Virginis, viginti annorum lima perpolito, summum decus frustra expectasse videri potuit, quum illae quae iuveni exciderant Piscatoriae eclogae, publico exceptae plausu, reliquorum operum famam oppresserint, ita ut eam publici tanquam iniqui iudicii querelam, aperto cum pudore nec tamen sine tacita voluptate, devoraret.

4 Vixit annos septuaginta duos, peramoeno virentique semper ingenio accuratoque et plane iuvenili cultu, inter amatorias oblectationes nunquam non festivus et hylaris. Ex dolore autem indignantis animi supremum concepit morbum, quod Philibertus Aurantius dux Caesaris Mergillinae villae suae delitias temere excisa turre deformasset: ea ad Pausilypi radices conspicitur.

5 Sed Aurantio demum acie interfecto, quum hora fatalis adveniret audito eius interitu se se in cubitum erigens 'Excedam' inquit 'e vita hoc meo non inani voto laetus, postquam barbarus Musarum hostis, ultore Marte, immanis iniuriae poenas persolvit.'

6 Sepultus est iuxta villam Mergillinam in templo Deiparae Virgini ab se dedicato. Marmoreo autem tumulo Bembus hoc carmen inscripsit:

He wrote poems as if ambidextrous, with equal charm and wit 3
in Tuscan and Latin, the Muses smiling upon both choices,
whether he was hurling somewhat bitter iambics like darts
drowned in hateful bile, or frolicking tenderly, without restraint,
amid the sweetness of his romances. But after he'd spent twenty
years perfecting his dignified and sacred poem *On the Birth of the
Virgin*, he might seem to have waited in vain for the highest honors: for those *Piscatorial Eclogues*, a product of his youth that received wide acclaim, so overshadowed his other works that he
swallowed his complaints of the injustice of public opinion with
an outward show of embarrassment, albeit not without some secret pleasure.[596]

He lived for seventy-two years, and until death his mind re- 4
mained delightful and fresh; he kept up a youthful appearance,
and in the midst of his romantic pleasures was always genial and
cheerful. But he was stricken by a fatal illness caused by grief and
anger at the injuries done to his beloved villa at Mergellina by the
emperor's commander Philibert of Orange, who needlessly destroyed its tower; its remains are visible at the base of Posillipo.[597]

On hearing that Orange had at last been killed in battle, San- 5
nazaro, nearing his own end, propped himself up on one elbow
and said, "I will depart from this life satisfied that my prayer has
not been in vain, now that Mars has taken vengeance and the bar-
baric enemy of the Muses has been punished for the monstrous
harm that he inflicted."

He was buried near his villa in Mergellina, in the church he had 6
dedicated to the Virgin Mother of God, and Bembo had this
poem inscribed on his marble tomb:[598]

*Bembi*

Da sacro cineri flores: hic ille Maroni
Syncerus, Musa proximus ut tumulo.

7          *Marci Antonii Flaminii*

Quantum Virgilio debebit sylva Maroni
et pastor, donec Musa Maronis erit,
tantum pene tibi debent piscator et acta,
Acti, divino proxime Virgilio.

## LXXXI. *Ioannes Manardus*

1 Ioannes Manardus Ferrariensis in Pannonia Vladislao Rege medendi artem exercuit, eandemque demum in gymnasio Ferrariae
professus epistolarum librum edidit quo magna medentibus et
pharmacopolis utilitas paratur, quum terrae frugibus Indicisque
praesertim in medicinae usum adoptatis, obsoleto antiquo nomine
et incerta virium potestate perobscuris, eruditam claritatem attu-
lerit.
2     Duxit autem uxorem, plane senex et articulorum dolore distor-
tus, ab aetate formaque florentis iuvenis toro dignam, adeo levi
iudicio et laetali quidem intemperantia ut maturando funeri suo
aliquanto prolis quam vitae cupidior ab amicis censeretur.

*By Bembo*

Lay your flowers upon these holy ashes: for here lies that Syncerus who was next to Vergil in poetry, as he is now in his tomb.

*By Marcantonio Flaminio*[599]     7

As much as the woods and the shepherd owe to Virgilius Maro, so long as his poetry shall endure, nearly so much do the fisherman and the seashore owe to you, Actius, who are next to the divine Vergil.


## LXXXI. *Giovanni Mainardi (1462–1536)*

Giovanni Mainardi[600] of Ferrara practiced the healing arts in Hun-    1
gary while Vladislav was King.[601] After going on to teach the same subject at the University of Ferrara, he published a book of *Letters* that is highly useful to physicians and pharmacists for having brought the light of learning to bear upon herbals and botani-cals — and especially those adopted from India, extremely obscure after their ancient names fell into disuse and their healing proper-ties were uncertain.[602]

When already quite elderly and arthritic, he took a wife whose    2
youth and beauty deserved the conjugal bed of a vigorous young man.[603] In so doing he displayed such poor judgment and, indeed, so lethal a lack of self-control that his friends thought he hastened his death by being more avid for offspring than for his own life.

3                      *Petri Cursii*

Dum, Manarde, vigil cum prole Coronidis esses,
    vidisti vitam perpetuam esse tuam.
At dum formosa cum Pallade coniuge dormis,
    sensisti mortem curvus adesse senex.
Hic nunc clare iaces et, quem Podalirion esse
    vidimus, annosum sustulit ipsa Venus.


## LXXXII. *Camillus Quernus Archipoeta*

1    Camillus Quernus e Monopoli Leonis fama excitus, quum non
dubiis unquam praemiis poetas in honore esse didicisset, in Urbem
venit lyram secum afferens ad quam suae *Alexiados* supra viginti
millia versuum decantaret. Arrisere ei statim Academiae sodales,
quod Apulo[57] praepingui vultu alacer et prolixe comatus omnino
dignus festa laurea videretur.

2    Itaque solenni exceptum epulo in insula Tyberis Aesculapio dicata potantemque saepe ingenti patera et totius ingenii opes pul-
sata lyra proferentem novo serti genere coronarunt, id erat ex
pampino, brassica et lauro eleganter intertextum, sic ut tam salse
quam lepide eius temulentia brassicae remedio cohibenda notaretur, et ipse publico consensu Archipoetae cognomen manantibus
prae gaudio lachrymis laetus acciperet salutareturque, itidem cum
plausu, hoc repetito saepe carmine:

Salve, brassicea virens corona
et lauro Archipoeta pampinoque,
dignus principis auribus Leonis!

*By Pietro Corsi*[604]  3

While keeping lively company with Coronis's son,[605] Mainardi, you supposed that you would live forever. But when, as a stooped-over old man, you slept beside beautiful Pallas, your wife, you felt death draw nigh. Now, plainly, here you lie; and Venus herself has stolen away the man heavy with age whom we looked upon as Podalirius.[606]

## LXXXII. *Camillo Querno the Archpoet (1470–1530)*

Lured from Monopoli by Leo's reputation and the discovery  1
that poets were being honored with unfailing rewards, Camillo Querno[607] arrived in Rome, lute in hand. To its accompaniment he intoned the verses — over twenty thousand of them — of his *Alexiad*. The members of the Academy at once smiled upon him, for this eager fellow, with a chubby Apulian face and long hair, looked to be thoroughly worthy of a festive laurel wreath.

And so, once they had welcomed him to a formal banquet on  2
the Tiber Island, which is sacred to Aesculapius,[608] as he quaffed from an enormous bowl and poured out all the riches of his genius to the strumming of his lute, they crowned him with a new kind of wreath: one elegantly interwoven from vine shoots, cabbage, and laurel, thus wittily and deftly prescribing cabbage as the cure for his inebriation.[609] And with tears of joy, he happily assumed the name "Archpoet," with which they unanimously acclaimed him. In the same way he was greeted with cheers and this anthem, repeated over and over:

Hail, Archpoet, verdant with a crown of cabbage, laurel, and vine leaves, worthy of Prince Leo's ears![610]

3    Nec multo post, tanto cognomine percelebris productus ad
Leonem infinita carmina in torrentis morem rotundo ore decantavit, fuitque diu inter instrumenta eruditae voluptatis longe gratissimus quum, coenante Leone, porrectis de manu semesis obsoniis
stans in fenestra vesceretur et de principis lagena perpotando sub-
itaria carmina factitaret, ea demum lege ut praescripto argumento
bina saltem carmina ad mensam tributi nomine solverentur, et in
poenam sterili vel inepto longe dilutissime foret perbibendum.

4    Ab hac autem opulenta hylarique sagina vehementem incidit in
podagram, sic ut bellissime ad risum evenerit, quum de se canere
iussus in hunc exametrum[58] erupisset — 'Archipoeta facit versus
pro mille poetis' — et demum haesitaret, inexpectatus princeps hoc
pentametro perargute responderit: 'Et pro mille aliis Archipoeta
bibit.' Tum vero astantibus obortus est risus et demum multo
maximus quum Quernus, stupens et interritus, hoc tertium non
inepte carmen induxisset — 'Porrige, quod faciat mihi carmina
docta, Falernum.' — idque Leo repente mutuatus a Virgilio subdi-
derit: 'Hoc etiam enervat debilitatque pedes.'

5    Mortuo autem Leone profligatisque poetis Neapolim rediit
ibique demum, quum Gallica arma perstreperent et, uti ipse in
miseriis perurbane dicebat, pro uno benigno Leone in multos feros
lupos incidisset, oppressus utraque praedurae egestatis et insanabilis morbi miseria in publica hospitali domo vitae finem invenit
quum, indignatus fortunae acerbitatem, prae dolore ventrem sibi
ac intima viscera forfice perfoderit.

Not long thereafter, famous for being possessed of such a sobri-  3
quet, he had an audience with Leo and elegantly poured out an
unending torrent of poetry.[611] For a long time he was the runaway
favorite among all means of erudite entertainment, for as Leo
dined, the Archpoet would stand at the window, feeding on the
scraps handed him and, while drinking deeply from the pope's
wine flask, would extemporize verses — but only on the condition
that at least two poems would be paid to the table as a tribute for
each theme assigned, and that he'd have to drink heavily diluted
wine as punishment for any that was insipid or inept.

From this sumptuous and carefree feasting, however, he got a  4
severe case of gout. And so, he occasioned the most delightful
laughter when, told to sing about himself, he broke into this hexameter: "The Archpoet writes enough verses for one thousand
poets"; and when he hesitated, suddenly the pope responded very
cleverly with this pentameter: "And drinks enough for a thousand
more."[612] Then indeed those present had a good laugh, which
reached a crescendo after Querno, stunned but undaunted, aptly
introduced this third verse: "Bring on the Falernian wine, which
will make my poems learned"; and Leo, borrowing from Vergil, at
once added: "And that, likewise, weakens and cripples the feet."[613]

But when Leo died and the poets were ruined, he returned at  5
last to Naples.[614] There, amid the clangor of French arms and
when, as he himself would quip in the midst of his misfortunes,
he had encountered many fierce wolves in place of one kindly
"Lion," he was crushed by the twin miseries of severe poverty and
incurable illness and, in a guesthouse, contrived to end his life:
indignant at Fortune's cruelty, in his grief he impaled himself,
driving a pair of scissors into his gut.

*Iani Vitalis*

Laurus brassica pampinus coronam
contextae simul hinc pares in unam
deflent interitum sui poetae,
quinimmo Archipoetae, et hinc lagenae
scyphique et cyathi, amphorae urceique
queruntur lepidum suum patronum
pro dulci modo Cretico et Phalerno
exhaurire acidas Stygis lacunas,
et sales periisse Quernianos
dum, vitae sibi prodigus molestae,
fodit viscera forfice. O severum
nostri temporis Apulum[59] Catonem!

## LXXXIII. *Albertus Pius Carpensis*

1  Lubet hoc loco, sub illustri scilicet imagine Alberti Pii, inter exempla Fortunae humanis consiliis maligne et petulanter illudentis, eius viri gravissimi genus opes ingenium mores studiaque referre ut vel hinc mortales inani rerum peritiae persuasione subnixi, Fortunam omni prudentia superiorem intelligant.

2  Is antiquissima stirpe ortus, a maioribus per manus traditum, quum ante ducentos annos Mutinae imperasset, in Campis Nacris Carpum nobile oppidum possedit optimisque literis generosisque moribus animum pariter et corpus excoluit. Erat enim a procera decentique statura ad arma nervis et spiritu validus ac habilis,

From now on, the laurel, cabbage, and vine shoot, woven together equally into one crown, weep over the death of their poet—indeed, of their Archpoet, and hence the flasks and goblets and carafes, the flagons and pitchers, lament that their charming patron instead of sweet Cretan and Falernian wine now drains the bitter pools of the Styx, and that the witticisms of Querno passed away when, casting off a life that had grown dismal to him, he stabbed his entrails with scissors. O stern Apulian, the Cato of our times!

## LXXXIII. *Alberto Pio of Carpi (1475–1531)*

Here, under the illustrious likeness of Alberto Pio,[616] amid exam-    1 ples of Fortune's spiteful and insolent mockery of human designs, I am pleased to recall the lineage, gifts, genius, character, and pursuits of this greatest of men, so that from his example even those mortals who rely on the vain conviction that they know all about how the world works may grasp that Fate is stronger than any practical wisdom.[617]

Of a most ancient lineage, he inherited from his forebears    2 Carpi, a famous town in the Nacrian Fields that two hundred years earlier had ruled over Modena.[618] He exercised his mind and body in equal measure, with the highest learning and noble comportment. Indeed, he was tall and graceful, his musculature and mettle made him formidable and adept in battle, and yet he'd

maximarum autem rerum negociis et literis praealtum et incomparabile ingenium attulerat.

3   Nihil enim vel praestantis doctrinae vel solertis industriae vel reconditae artis ardens eius ingenium semperque vividum et maxime efficax subterfugit. Erat enim celeri captu, expedita ratione tenacique memoria stupendus, eloquentia porro tanta ut in omni congressu et disputatione quum de arduis consuleretur, et odio amarus et amore praedulcis, tranquillitate lenis atque sedatus, et vehementia concitatus atque fulmineus, quo vellet principum animos impelleret; et summus bello et pace consultor et mirabilis occasionum inventor et artifex censeretur. Quattuor summis regibus et totidem maximis pontificibus in praeclaro semper honore legationum operam praestitit, vigilantia fide et providentia semper illustrem.

4   Sed uti occultae principum voluntates et erumpentia ex insperato eorum odia tulerunt, coactus est alterna partium studia profiteri, quod his omnino adhaerendum iudicaret, quibus Alphonsus Atestinus hostis esset, quocum[60] de possessione paterni agri disceptabat. Sed Atestini fortuna praeclare ipsa Pii prudentia virtuteque superior, privatam causam publicis cladibus involvit, atque ita capto Clemente Pontifice, quum urbs Roma foede periisset, ex arce emissus in Galliam enavigavit, ubi se paterna ditione Caesaris iudicio exutum audivit.

5   Inde ei diuturnus articularis morbus, quo misere convulsus cruciabatur, adauctus est; hunc diu aequo animo et Christiana patientia fortiter tulisse frustra fuit, quum saeva pestis fatalem horam adduceret. Obiit Lutetiae non plane senex sub id tempus quo Carolus Caesar et Solymanus irrito utrinque ausu ad Viennam Noricam certaturi credebantur.

applied his lofty and incomparable genius to literature and to managing the weightiest affairs of state.

In fact, not one whit of superior erudition or deft application or   3
arcane knowledge escaped his passionate intellect, ever lively and
supremely capable. His swift comprehension, agile reasoning, and
tenacious memory were astonishing. What's more, his eloquence
was so great that in every meeting or debate, when difficult matters were under discussion, with both bitter enmity and the sweet-
est amity, with soothing gentle serenity and passionate, thundering
ferocity, he moved the minds of princes to take the course that he
wished. He was judged to be the finest counselor in both war and
peace, and extraordinary at discovering and devising suitable opportunities. He went on missions for four eminent kings and as
many supreme pontiffs, always serving with exceptional distinction, always showing outstanding vigilance, loyalty, and foresight.

But under the compulsion of princes' secret designs and sud-   4
den, unexpected hatreds, he was forced to change allegiances, de-
ciding he had to cast his lot entirely with those opposed by Alfonso d'Este, with whom he struggled for control over his ancestral
land. But Alfonso's good fortune was conspicuously superior to
the prudence and prowess even of Pio, and their private legal dispute got caught up in public disasters. So when Pope Clement was
made a captive after the disgraceful fall of the city of Rome, Pio
was cast out from the fortress[619] and sailed away to France, where
he learned that at the emperor's behest, he'd been stripped of his
hereditary estates.

Then the wrenching agonies of the chronic rheumatism by   5
which he was tormented grew worse. He bore them bravely for a
long time, with equanimity and Christian patience, but to no avail,
since a devastating plague brought on his final hour. He died in
Paris, not really all that old, as the emperor Charles and Suleiman
were believed to be about to do battle over Vienna, a fruitless ven-
ture for both sides.

6    Rodulphus Pius fratris filius, quem aliquanto post Paulus
Pontifex eximiae virtutis merito legit in senatum, condito aeneo
sepulchro patrui memoriam prosecutus est. Sed Albertus ipse
multo perennius antea sibi struxerat, quum librum longe gravissimum adversus Lutherum perstricto etiam Erasmo Rhoterodamo[61]
publicasset.

7                    *Ferdinandi Balamii*

Insignes usu rerum studiisque Minervae
    perpaucos aetas prisca recensque dedit:
in solem assuetus doctos versare libellos
    quum prodit lucem non tulit insolitam.
Laudibus hunc omnes doctrinae et rebus agendis
    conspexere domi conspicuumque foris.
Hunc Arar, hunc Rhenus toties, hunc accola magni
    Eridani, hunc Tybris sensit et obstupuit.
Fortuna invidit, raperisque, Alberte, tuorum
    Italiaeque omnis cum gemitu et lachrymis.

8                    *Iulii Gonzagae*

Hoc decus Italiae tegitur, Pius ille, sepulchro,
    solerti ingenio consilioque potens.
Nulli hominum vis dicendi, facundia maior;
    ille sed et studiis auxit et arte magis.
Hunc reges, hunc pontifices sibi rebus agendis
    optarant socium consiliisque ducem.
Felix, spem senii natum nisi flesset ademptum
    et data in hostiles regna paterna manus.

His brother's son, Rodolfo Pio, whom some time later Pope    6
Paul created cardinal for his extraordinary virtue, honored his uncle's memory by having a bronze tomb constructed.[620] But Alberto
had already built himself a much more enduring monument when
he published by far the most authoritative book against Luther,
in which Erasmus of Rotterdam, too, received unfavorable mention.[621]

## By Ferdinando Balami[622]    7

Antiquity and modernity have produced precious few men
distinguished in both the conduct of public affairs and the
pursuits of Minerva. One used to examining learned treatises can't bear the unaccustomed light when he goes out
into the sun. But everyone, at home and abroad, saw both
from the glories of his erudition and from his deeds that this
man excelled. The Saône and the Rhine fell silent in his
presence, as often as did the dweller by the mighty Po and
the Tiber. Fortune has turned spiteful, Alberto, and you are
carried off amid the groaning and tears of your friends and
all Italy.

## By Giulio Gonzaga[623]    8

The gem of Italy, the famous Pio, nimble of mind and
mighty in counsel, is enclosed in this tomb. No mortal had
greater powers of speech and eloquence, yet he augmented
them further by his study and his skill. Kings and popes
chose him as an aide in affairs of state and as a guide to their
deliberations. He would have been happy had he not lamented the loss of his son,[624] the hope of his old age, and of
his ancestral domains, given over into hostile hands.

## LXXXIV. *Ludovicus Ariostus*

1 Ludovicus Ariostus nobili genere Ferrariae natus, quum paterna haereditas, inter numerosam fratrum sobolem diducta, ipsi pertenuis obvenisset, ingenium in literis vigilanter exercuit ut certo nobilique praesidio familiae nomen tueretur. Sed uti pari prope necessitatis et gloriae stimulo vehementer excitatus, feliciore certe iudicio inter primos Ethruscae linguae poetas celebrari quam inter Latinos in secundis gradibus consistere maluit, quod eius industriae labor, cum eruditis ac idiotis latissime dispensatus, uberiorem praesentis praemii et diffusae laudis fructum ostenderet.

2 Adhaesit comes Hippolyto Atestino Cardinali in Pannoniam profecto, quum ille erudito ac illustri comitatu apud reges Hungaros ambitiose gauderet. Sed iterum euntem quum sequi recusasset, usque adeo graviter offendit ut pene implacabilis odii discrimen adierit. Receptus inde est ab Alfonso Principe tanquam horarum omnium amicus et sodalis, cuius benigna manu urbanam domum extruxit, peramoena hortorum ubertate, frugi mensae quotidianos sumptus adaequantem.

3 In eo autem civili ocio extra aulae strepitum poemata factitavit, *Satyras* imprimis mordaci sale conspersas ac item comoedias plures theatrali voluptate saepe repetitas. Inter eas autem maxime *Suppositi* excellunt, inventionis atque successus amoenitate cum Plautinis facile contendentes, si utriusque saeculi mores non inepte comparentur.

4 Sed luculentissimum operum ob idque forsitan aeternum id volumen existimatur quo Orlandi fabulosi herois admiranda bello

## LXXXIV. Ludovico Ariosto (1474–1533)

Ludovico Ariosto was born into a noble family of Ferrara.[625] Since   1
the division of his father's estate among numerous siblings left little for him, he diligently applied his talents to literature so as to
maintain the family's dignity securely and honorably. But as he
was driven almost equally by necessity and by ambition, it was
surely a fortunate decision to seek renown among the foremost
Tuscan poets rather than settle for a place among Latin poets of
the second rank: for the fruits of his exertions, diffused among the
learned and the masses, could show a richer return in both immediate rewards and far-reaching reputation.

When Cardinal Ippolito d'Este set out for Hungary, Ludovico   2
accompanied him, since Ippolito ostentatiously took pleasure in
bringing a cohort of scholars and famous men to the Hungarian
kings. But when he was unwilling to follow him there a second
time, he so deeply offended Ippolito that he risked the almost im-
placable hatred of his patron.[626] Thereupon he was welcomed as
an inseparable friend and companion by Duke Alfonso, thanks to
whose generous patronage Ariosto had a house built within the
city with delightful and fruitful gardens, which were adequate to
the daily needs of his frugal table.

In this retirement from civil service, far from the clamor of the   3
court, he wrote many poems, most notably the *Satires*,[627] sprinkled
with biting wit; and not a few comedies, often reprised to the delight of audiences. Among these latter, *The Pretenders*[628] especially
stands out, easily rivaling the plays of Plautus in the charm of its
inventiveness and resolution, if the tastes of his times and ours
may meaningfully be compared.

But the work of his considered the most splendid, and so per-   4
haps everlasting, is that volume in which he sang in *ottava rima* of
the fabled hero Orlando's valor in combat.[629] With this, heaven

facinora octonario modulo decantavit, Boiardo hercle ipsoque Pulcio peregregie superatis, quandoquidem et hunc rerum et carminum accurata granditate devicerit ac illum, surrepto inventionis
titulo ac eo quidem variis elegantioris doctrinae luminibus illus-
trato, penitus extinxerit. Cuncta enim evolvisse volumina videtur
ut sibi undique collecta gratia ex iucundissimis floribus longe pul-
cherrimam ideoque perennem quo lepidum caput ornaretur coronam intexeret.

5      Interiit in patria scalari aetatis anno, quum diu pectoris angus-
tia ex pituitae stillicidio laborasset. Hoc autem carmen vivens
composuit ut sepulchro incideretur:

*Ipsius*

Ludovici Ariosti humantur ossa
sub hoc marmore, seu sub hac humo, seu
sub quicquid voluit benignus haeres,
sive haerede benignior comes, seu
opportunius incidens viator.
Nam scire haud potuit futura, sed nec
tanti erat vacuum sibi cadaver
ut urnam cuperet parare vivens.
Vivens ista tamen sibi paravit
quae scribi voluit suo sepulchro,
olim si quod haberet is sepulchrum,
ne cum spiritus, exili[62] peracto
praescripti spatio,[63] misellus artus
quos aegre ante reliquerat reposcet,
hac et hac cinerem hunc et hunc revellens
dum noscat proprium diu vagetur.[64]

knows, he distinctly surpassed Boiardo and Pulci himself: for he defeated the latter in the carefully wrought grandeur of the themes and cantos, and he obliterated Boiardo by robbing him of the title of his creation and embellishing it with various flourishes of greater learning.[630] For he appears to have leafed through every book to harvest from delightful passages everywhere and to weave, for his fine head, a crown of the utmost beauty, and therefore eternal.

He died in his native city in his climacteric year,[631] having long 5 suffered from bronchitis brought on by postnasal drip, but first he composed this poem to be carved on his tomb:

### By Ariosto Himself[632]

The bones of Ludovico Ariosto are interred under this marble, or under this soil, or under whatever was chosen by a well-disposed heir, or by a companion kinder than an heir, or by a wayfarer who quite opportunely chanced upon them. For the author could not know what was to be. But while alive, he was so little concerned for his lifeless corpse that he didn't bother to prepare an urn. Nonetheless, while living, he prepared for himself the words he wanted written on his tomb — should he one day have some kind of tomb — so that when his poor little spirit, the allotted span of its exile ended, claims the body it unwillingly left behind, it need not wander about for long digging up these ashes here and those there, until it should recognize its own.

## LXXXV. *Aegidius Cardinalis*

1 Non est cur te praeteream, Aegidi, humili quidem loco verum maxime illustri fato Viterbii nate, Christiani scilicet oratoris in sacra pergula primum atque ultimum decus merite, quanquam egregia illa ex arcanis Moseos deprompta sublimis ingenii monumenta tenebris adhuc impie supprimantur. Praestantissimum enim praeceptorem facile superasti Marianum, scilicet Genezanensem, Pontani et Politiani admiratione eruditoque praeconio inclytum: huius enim extat in *Epistolis* laudatio florentissima, illius vero nobile carmen quod in *Aegidio* dialogo tale legitur:

2      Qualis Alphei liquidos ad amnes
        sive Meandri viridante ripa
        concinit serum moriens in ipso
              funere cygnus
        talis ad plectrum ad thyasos deorum
        ludit in coelo Marianus ipsa
        morte victurus, Marianus ipso
              funere felix.
        Ipse sis felix faveasque nobis,
        ipse ades fessis, Mariane, rebus,
        tu preces audi miserorum et iras
              siste Tonantis.

3      Caeterum Marianus Aegidii comparatione ad optime gloriose-que dicendum nequaquam tanta ex Graecis novi et veteris instrumenti enarratoribus praesidia compararat, neque penetrarat ad Chaldaeos ut admiranda nostrae legis fundamenta revelaret, neque concionibus praedulce illud et nobile poeticum melos instillarat ut suspensos arrectis auribus animos suavitate carminum ad colendam pietatem revocaret.

## LXXXV. Cardinal Egidio [of Viterbo] (1469–1532)

Why should I pass over you, Egidio,[633] born at Viterbo to a    1
humble station but destined for exceptional glory: you who won
every last honor of a Christian orator in the pulpit (although those
masterpieces of sublime genius, drawn from the mysteries of Moses, are still impiously hidden from view).[634] Indeed, you easily
surpassed your very eminent teacher, Mariano of Genazzano, a
man made famous by the esteem and promotion of Poliziano and
Pontano: for the *Letters* of the former contain a most flowery panegyric, and the latter has a noble poem in his dialogue *Egidio* that
says:[635]

> Beside the crystal clear waters of the Alpheus or on the ver-    2
> dant bank of the Maeander, the swan, on the verge of dying,
> sings at its own funeral. So too in heaven, at the saints' rev-
> els, Mariano delights to play the lyre, finding triumph in
> death itself, happy at his own obsequies. Be well-disposed
> and protect us, Mariano; aid us in our infirmity. Hearken to
> the prayers of the unfortunate and stay the angry hand of
> the Thunderer.

But when compared with Egidio, Mariano had not acquired    3
from the Greek commentators on the Old and New Testaments
any great aids to noble and praiseworthy speech; nor had he
delved into Chaldean wisdom to reveal the remarkable roots of
our covenant or instilled into his sermons such gently uplifting
musicality as to bring back wavering spirits, by filling their ears
with the sweetness of song, to the practice of the faith.

4    Sed Aegidius, quum in suggestu vere admirabilis aequo iudicio
per omnes urbes oratoriae facultatis lauream mereretur, etiam
domi lepidissimis sermonibus novam laudem ferebat. Erat enim
eius ingenium exquisito literarum omnium delectu graviter in-
structum, sic ut in omnes exemplorum casus peramplas opes
alacris et expedita memoria suppeditaret; facundia porro tanta
dissimulatis illecebris audientes semper exhylarans atque demul-
cens ut ipso concionante vel maxima templa complerentur.

5    Ante autem id tempus quo totius eremitani ordinis praefectu-
ram a Iulio consecutus est, nonnunquam accidit ut Patavii optimis
literis operam navans factitata ab se lepida carmina ad lyram elegantissime decantaret. Ei demum Leo Pontifex virtutem omnem
liberaliter exornare solitus honorem purpurei galeri detulit quum,
Petruciana coniuratione et Umbrico bello circumventus, senatum
aut maligne aut segniter principis iniuriam ferentem supplere cogeretur.

6    Exinde functus est legatione in Hispaniam quum, Selymo post
debellatos Persas et duos Memphiticos reges interfectos nobis
arma comminante, Christianae gentes ad sacrum bellum excitan-
dae viderentur. Sexagesimo aetatis anno subita oppressus pituita
Romae interiit quum Clemens Carolum Caesarem Bononiae iterum excepisset, destinatus optatusque a multis ad pontificatum
tanquam par summo oneri.

7    Sed non deerant qui praeclari nominis famam verbis elevarent
quod pallorem oris sumpto cumino et suffitu udae paleae mentiretur, variasque libidines censoria severitate contegeret quas demum
malignus potius rumor quam ulla certi vestigii relicta proles de-
texit. Fit enim quadam naturae minime benigna sorte ut nulla

Although Egidio was truly remarkable on the dais, and by the     4
same verdict his eloquence triumphed in all cities, at the same
time he won fresh praise at home with his exquisite sermons. For
his mind had been fully equipped with a refined selection from all
branches of learning, so that his quick and agile memory furnished
him with an abundant stock of examples to meet every need.
What is more, through such eloquence and subtle means of per-
suasion, he always cheered and entranced listeners in such a way
that when he preached, even the largest churches were packed.

Before he obtained from Julius the headship of the entire order     5
of Augustinian hermits, it sometimes happened that, while he was
deeply immersed in his literary studies in Padua, he would tastefully sing to the lute delightful poems that he had composed.[636] At
last, Pope Leo, who was accustomed to rewarding every talent
generously, bestowed upon him the honor of the purple hat. This
he did on the occasion when, beset by the conspiracy of Petrucci
and the Umbrian war, he was compelled to pack the college of
cardinals, which either out of spite or indifference had allowed the
unjust attack upon the pope.[637]

Then as Selim, after vanquishing the Persians and having two     6
Egyptian rulers killed, threatened war against us, and it seemed
necessary to call Christian nations to a Crusade, Egidio went on a
legation to Spain.[638] After Clement had received the emperor
Charles at Bologna for the second time, Egidio, then aged sixty,
died in Rome of pulmonary edema.[639] Many had already decided
upon him as their candidate for the papacy, judging him capable of
shouldering that supreme responsibility.

Some, however, disparaged his splendid reputation, saying that     7
he ingested cumin and inhaled the fumes from the smoldering of
damp straw in order to give his face the pallor of an ascetic, and
concealed with a reproachful severity an assortment of lusts which
ultimately were brought to light more by malicious rumor than by
any surviving offspring known to be his. For it comes about by a

absolutae virtutis praeclara facies enitere possit, nisi aliquem vitii turpem naevum ad eludendam felicitatem ostendat.

8                              *Iani Vitalis*

Ante sacrosanctos cineres bona verba, viator,
   dicito. Divinus hic iacet Aegidius,
qui potuit lingua humanas inflectere mentes
   et trahere haerentes fervidus ad se animos.
Quicquid pandit Arabs divinum, quicquid Erembus
   dives Arameis occulit in tabulis
explicuit populis: et, si quid spiritus ultra
   sentit, adhuc sanctum quod meditetur habet.


## LXXXVI. *Ioannes Franciscus Picus Mirandula*

1   In Ioanne Francisco Pico Mirandulano, inter studiosos bonarum artium scribendique avidos, memoria verborum vehementer excelluit. Sed in ipso rerum delectu illud perillustre iudicium, quod summo viro Hippocrati maxime difficile existimatur, omnino non viguit. Frustra enim ad Ioannis patrui gloriam aspiranti ingressoque gravissimorum studiorum penetralia, quum insatiabili lectione duceretur, nusquam Minerva satis arriserat.

2   Extant eius sacra poemata, suis quoque commentariis illustrata ne legentibus minus clara viderentur, et libri de veritate fidei Christianae in quibus disciplinarum omnium acervus eminet. Sed acriter disputantem inter cucullatos magna etiam expeditae

certain sinister caprice of nature that no innocence can shine in all its splendor without bringing to light some base imperfection that mocks the very idea of blessedness.

*By Giano Vitale*[640]                                        8

As you stand before these consecrated ashes, wayfarer, say a prayer. Here lies the divine Egidio, who with his eloquence steered the course of people's thinking and zealously drew stubborn minds toward him. Whatever divine wisdom the Arabian revealed or wealthy Erembus concealed in Aramaic tablets,[641] Egidio made known to the nations; and if his soul still has the ability to perceive, he has as yet something holy on which to meditate.

## LXXXVI. Gianfrancesco Pico della Mirandola (1469–1533)

Among scholars passionately devoted to the liberal arts and to writing, Gianfrancesco Pico della Mirandola[642] prodigiously excelled in verbal memory. In his choice of subject matter, however, he completely lacked that prized sense of discernment which the great Hippocrates thought the most difficult of all things to acquire. Once he had probed the remotest recesses of the most profound studies in a vain effort to equal the glory of his uncle Giovanni, although he was driven by an unquenchable desire to study, Minerva did not smile.

We have his sacred poems, self-annotated lest readers find them insufficiently clear; and his books on the truth of the Christian faith, in which one finds a massive conglomeration of learning drawn from all fields.[643] But he also won praise for the erudition he had at his fingertips when he forcefully debated important

doctrinae laus sequebatur, quum scribentem vel mediocriter elo-
quentes minime probarent. Neque enim quid potissimum imitare-
tur constitutum habuisse videri potest ex duobus praesertim libellis *De optimo imitationis genere* ad Bembum perscriptis.

3      Sed quum in omnibus ingenii operibus sacras literas religiose
respiceret, contempsisse Latinae facundiae flores atque inde gloriam tanquam inanem existimari voluit, quanquam eius universa
literarum studia, tanquam illustri in homine et in domo sanctissimis moribus perornata, quum in minus severos iudices facile inci-
derent splendidiora viderentur. Et hercle vir antiqua simplicitate
potiusquam novo astu aequiora iudicia redimebat quum libros ip-
sos privato impressos sumptu liberali largitione publicaret.

4      Interfectus est cum Alberto filio — vir indignus adeo crudeli vitae exitu — a Galeotto fratris filio, quum nocturnis insidiis capta
arce Mirandulae dominatum ex paterno iure invadendum existi-
masset. Fuere qui crederent merita fortasse poena mulctatum,
quod cudendae monetae miserum artificem ipsius officinae prae-
positum, ex impuri auri et ad decumum subtiliter improbi detrimento[65] magnum sensim lucrum ipsi domino reddentem, crudeli
supplicio ad derivandam invidiam sustulisset, quum intellecta
fraus ipsius famae vehementer officeret palamque ea aurea moneta
ex eius effigie spectabilis vulgato vitii detrimento reiiceretur. Sed
iuvat audire quosdam virum alioqui integra fide optimum excu-
santes tanquam eius avarae fraudis penitus ignarum, quum in
uxorem, quod esset accurata et diligens materfamilias, tanquam
muliebris aviditatis probro notatam, eius flagitii nomen nullo cum
pudore referendum existiment.

matters with the cowled brothers. Yet even those of middling rhetorical ability did not think much of him as a writer. Nor indeed does it appear that he had decided upon what style in particular to imitate, especially from two tracts addressed to Bembo, *On the Best Kind of Imitation*.[644]

But since in all the products of his mind he showed scrupulous 3 respect for sacred writ, Gianfrancesco wished it to appear that he disdained the best of Latin eloquence and regarded as useless the glory to be gained from it. Yet all his literary efforts seemed to shine more brightly as, having a well-known man and a lineage famed for its great piety to recommend them, they easily met with charitable critics. And, heaven knows, a man who was simple and traditional rather than cunning and innovative procured more favorable judgments because he freely gave away copies of his books that he'd paid to have printed.

Gianfrancesco—a man unworthy of so cruel a death—was 4 murdered along with his son Alberto by his nephew Galeotto who, having taken the citadel by an assault at night, supposed himself justified in seizing the lordship of Mirandola as his paternal inheritance. Some thought that perhaps he deserved the punishment he got, because he had cruelly dispatched the unfortunate artisan in charge of his mint—who bit by bit had added greatly to his master's wealth by taking impure gold and producing coins a tenth too light—doing so in order to divert suspicion from himself: for the fraud, once discovered, severely damaged his reputation, and that gold coinage, recognizable from his portrait on it, was openly refused once word had gotten around that it was defective. But it's gratifying that some, excusing a noble man of otherwise untainted integrity as entirely unaware of this avaricious trickery, suppose that responsibility for that crime should shamelessly be attributed to his wife: as she was meticulous and hardworking in running the household, she was branded with the stigma of womanly greed.

5                              *Myrtei*

Hic Picus iaceo, atque me illa, quae iam
ante non potuere, nunc iniquo
me servant obitu arma literarum.
Aegre illud fero concidisse dextra
fratris filii; hoc elevor me adeptum
vitam pro studiis meis perennem.

## LXXXVII. Nicolaus Macchiavellus[66]

1 Quis non miretur in hoc Macchiavello[67] tantum valuisse naturam
ut in nulla vel certe mediocri Latinarum literarum cognitione ad
iustam recte scribendi facultatem pervenire potuerit? Habili siquidem ingenio ac, ubi solertiam intenderet, plane mirabili, cuncta
quae aggrederetur elegantissime perficiebat, sive seria sive iocosa
scriberentur.

2 In historia enim apprime gravis et astutus ita patriae favit ut,
dissimulatis factionum studiis impellente recondita libidine et lenis et asper incessisse iudicetur: egregia hercle cum laude nisi, uti
nos non imperiti rerum Ethruscarum praeclare conspicimus, praedulcis eloquentiae mella occulto veneno illita singulis operibus
infudisset—et tum etiam quum optimum principem formaret,
quum bellicis praeceptis ducem instrueret et denique, traditis
exactae prudentiae documentis, in deliberando et consulendo eximium senatorem effingeret.

3 Sed comiter aestimemus Ethruscos sales ad exemplar comoediae veteris Aristophanis in *Nicia* praesertim comoedia, in qua

Here I, Pico, lie, and those bastions of good literature which
before could not avail me, now save me from an unkind
death. It pains me to have died by the hand of my brother's
son, but I'm uplifted because in return for my studies I have
secured eternal life.

## LXXXVII. *Niccolò Machiavelli (1469–1527)*

Who wouldn't be amazed that the natural endowments of this   1
man, Machiavelli,[646] were so powerful that with no Latin, or at
best a mediocre knowledge of it, he could develop full-fledged
competence as a writer? For, with a mind that was nimble and
quite astonishing wherever he applied his skills, he elegantly finished everything he undertook, whether writing on serious subjects or playful ones.

Especially caustic and shrewd in writing history, he so favored   2
Florence that people think that, in concealing his zealous faction-
alism, he came out as either lenient or harsh, as his secret inclina-
tion impelled him: most honorably so, to be sure, had he not
mingled with the honey-sweet eloquence which he poured over his
every work a hidden venom, as we who are not unfamiliar with
Tuscan history recognize only too well—and this, even when he
was fashioning the perfect prince, when he instructed a commander in the art of war, or finally when, relating examples of
consummate judgment, he portrayed a senator who would be
outstanding in deliberation and counsel.[647]

But we should look with kindness upon his Tuscan wit, mod-   3
eled on the old comedy of Aristophanes: especially in the comedy

adeo iucunde vel in tristibus risum excitavit ut illi ipsi ex persona scite expressa in scenam inducti cives, quanquam praealte commorderentur, totam inustae notae iniuriam civili lenitate pertulerint. Actamque Florentiae, ex ea miri leporis fama Leo Pontifex, instaurato ludo, ut Urbi ea voluptas communicaretur cum toto scenae cultu ipsisque histrionibus Romam acciverit.

4      Constat eum, sicuti ipse nobis fatebatur, a Marcello Virgilio, cuius et notarius et assecla publici muneris fuit, Graecae atque Latinae linguae flores accepisse quos scriptis suis insereret. Ipse quoque, natura perargutus et docilis salsique iudicii plenus, pedestrem patrii sermonis facultatem a Boccacii conditoris vetustate diffluentem novis et plane Atticis vinculis astrinxerat[68] sic ut ille castigatior sed non purior aut gravior ociosis ingeniis existimetur.

5      Caeterum quod olim, eiecto Soderino a Mediceis, in quaestione tortus fuisset, ab his leniendo dolori annuam scribendae historiae mercedem promeruit, ita tamen ut aegre compresso odio, quum dicendo scribendoque Brutos et Cassios laudaret, eius coniurationis architectus fuisse putaretur in qua Aiacetus poeta et Alamanus, ex ipsa turma praetoria levissimus eques, concepti sceleris capite poenas dederunt.

6      Fuit exinde semper inops, uti irrisor et atheos. Fatoque functus est quum, accepto temere pharmaco quo se adversus morbos praemuniret, vitae suae iocabundus illusisset, paulo antequam Florentia, Caesarianis subacta armis, Mediceos veteres dominos recipere cogeretur.

*Nicia*, in which he inspired laughter so delightfully even from the serious-minded that those very citizens who were represented on the stage as shrewdly drawn characters, though they had been cut to the quick, bore with gentle courtesy all the indignity of the mark with which they had been branded. And after it was performed in Florence, Pope Leo, hearing reports of its extraordinary charm, arranged a revival of the festivity and had the play brought to Rome, along with the entire set and the very same actors, so that the city might share in that pleasure.[648]

It's a fact (as he himself used to tell me) that the Greek and    4 Latin he slipped into his writings had come from Marcello Virgilio, whom he served as secretary and assistant when he was working for the government. Being himself naturally shrewd, a quick study, and full of clever observations, Machiavelli had bound with new and conspicuously Attic chains the forcefulness of Tuscan prose, which had diverged from the archaism of its founder, Boccaccio. Thus his style is considered by leisured readers to be more orderly, but no plainer or more weighty.

Because Machiavelli was once examined under torture after the    5 Medici had expelled Soderini, to assuage his indignation they gave him an annual stipend to write history. But since he barely contained his enmity and praised men like Brutus and Cassius in both speech and writing, he was thought to have been the architect of that conspiracy in which the poet Diacceto and Alamanni, a paltry cavalryman in a provincial governor's regiment, paid with their heads for the crime they'd conceived.[649]

Thereafter, Machiavelli was always destitute, being viewed as a    6 mocker and an atheist.[650] Ever the comic, he made sport of his own life: he died from having rashly taken a medication as a prophylactic. This happened shortly before Florence, laid low by an Imperial army, was compelled to take back its old Medici rulers.[651]

7               *Antonii Vaccae Consilicensis*

Quisquis adis, sacro flores et serta sepulchro
    adde, puer, cineri debita dona ferens.
Nam veteres belli et pacis qui reddidit arteis
    iam pridem ignotas regibus et populis,
Ethruscae Macchiavellus[69] honos et gloria linguae,
    hic iacet. Hoc saxum non coluisse nefas.

## LXXXVIII. *Philippus Decius*

1   Pari fere gloria et dignitate Philippus Decius in professione humani divinique praesertim iuris floruit, Maini Iasonis et civis et
aemulus ac aetate simul aequalis, sed qui docendo et scribendo in
omnibus Italiae gymnasiis multo latius ingenii famam protulerit.
Enarrabat enim subtilissime et, uti saepe vidimus, longe omnium
acerrime disputabat.

2   Ab ipsis Pisis, ubi uxorem duxerat, Ticinum a Gallo praeside
opimis stipendiis evocatus, in id tempus incidit quo Ludovicus
Rex ad convellendam Iulii Pontificis authoritatem concilium Pisis
indixerat. Fugitivi ideoque rebelles aliquot cardinales in gratiam
regis synodum postulabant; ius vero indicendi[70] decernendique loci
pontifex ad se revocabat. Consultus propterea Decius super ea re
intemperanter contra maiestatem pontificis descripto[71] respondit,
secus ac Iason qui rogatus sententiam vel magno munere oblato
adduci non potuit ut non clementissime responderet.

3   Ob eam contumeliam Matthaeus Sedunensis Cardinalis, pulsis
Gallis, victore cum exercitu Ticinum urbem ingressus unam
omnium Decii domum militi diripiendam dedit. Tanto accepto

*By Antonio Vacca of Conselice*[652]    7

Lad, whoever you are who bring offerings due these ashes,
lay flowers and garlands on the holy tomb. For here lies one
who restored to kings and peoples the ancient arts of war
and peace that had long been unknown: Machiavelli, the
honor and glory of the Tuscan tongue. It's an impiety to
leave this stone untended.


## LXXXVIII. Filippo Decio (1454–1535/36)

Filippo Decio[653] was almost equally famous and respected as a    1
professor of civil and especially canon law. He was a compatriot
and rival of Giasone Maino and of the same age, but his writing
and teaching in all the universities of Italy made his talents far
more widely known. Indeed, he expounded with the utmost subtlety and, as I often witnessed, was by far the fiercest of debaters.

From Pisa, where he had taken a wife, Decio was lured to Pavia    2
by its French ruler who gave him a lavish salary.[654] This happened
just when King Louis had convened a council at Pisa intending to
overthrow Pope Julius's authority.[655] In order to oblige the king,
several cardinals, who were deserters and therefore insurgents,
were demanding the council. The pope, however, reasserted his
right to convene it and to designate the place where it would
meet.[656] When consulted on this matter, Decio responded rashly
with a brief against the pontiff's sovereignty — unlike Giasone
who, when asked his opinion, could not be induced even by a large
bribe to answer except with the utmost mildness.[657]

On account of this indignity, when the French had been routed    3
and Cardinal Matthaeus of Sion entered Pavia with the victorious
army, Decio's house was the only one he allowed the soldiers to

incommodo, in Galliam ex fuga profectus in civitate Biturigum ius divinum edocuit per duos ferme annos. Inde vero in Italiam reversum Senenses conduxerunt, qua in urbe, unica eius filia Senensi patritio collocata, octogenario maior interiit.

4    Delatusque est Pisas ad sepulchrum marmoreum magno sumptu ab se in maximi templi fronte constitutum, inscriptione adeo inepta ut si eam supponamus elegantibus ingeniis, non sine pudore boni mortui, ridenda videatur.

5                           *Iani Vitalis*

Dum curat Decius sibi sepulchrum
clarum marmore ponere eleganti,
inscripsit titulos ineruditos,
ut risum magis excitare possint
quam laudare hominem undecumque clarum.
Quod si non sibi cultius sepulchrum
quam doctos titulos et elegantes
curasset, modo mollius iaceret.

## LXXXIX. *Thomas Morus*

1    Fortuna impotens et suo more instabilis infestaque virtuti si unquam superbe et truculenter iocata est, sub hoc nuper Henrico Octavo in Britannia immanissime desaeviit, prostrato ante alios Thoma Moro quem rex, paulo ante praeclarus eximiae virtutis admirator, ad summos honores extulerat ut inde eum, fatali scilicet oborta insania mutatus in feram, crudeli mox impetu praecipitem

ransack.[658] Fleeing from such a misfortune, Decio made for France and taught canon law in the province of Berry for nearly two years. But when he returned to Italy, Siena hired him, and in that city, after he'd married off his only daughter to a Sienese nobleman, he died, aged over eighty.

His body was conveyed to Pisa, to a marble tomb which he had 4 installed for himself at great expense in front of the cathedral. The epitaph is so inept that if I were to append it here, it would seem risible to men of refinement and embarrassing to the dear departed.[659]

*By Giano Vitale*[660]    5

While Decio arranged to set up for himself a shining tomb
in elegant marble, the inscriptions carved for him were so
inept that they evoke more laughter than praise for a man in
all respects illustrious. If he'd had less concern for a fancy
tomb than for learned and polished inscriptions, he would
rest now more easily.

## LXXXIX. *Thomas More (1478–1535)*

If ever Fortune, by nature uncontrollable and fickle and hostile to 1 virtue, has made rude and savage sport, it's when recently she vented her rage most monstrously in England under the present Henry, the Eighth. Her foremost victim was Thomas More, whom the king, not long before a renowned admirer of uncommon virtue, had exalted to the highest position, only to turn thereafter into a monster with the onset of a deadly madness and, on a cruel

daret, quod ipsius furentis tyranni nefariae libidini vir omnibus
religionis atque iustitiae numeris longe optimus atque sanctissimus
adulari noluisset. Dum enim ille uxorem repudiare, pellicem indu-
cere filiamque magno probro abdicare properaret, Morus scrinii
magister pietatis ac innocentiae suae reus causam ad tribunal dicere coactus, impio iudicio nisi par metus ab irato et saevo mentes
excuteret, ita damnatus est uti latronum more teterrimo supplicii
genere necaretur; nec fas esset dilacerata membra propinquorum
pietate sepelire.

2    Sed Henricus, vel hoc uno facinore Phalaridis aemulus, eripere
non potuit quin ad sempiternam inusitati sceleris memoriam Mori
nomen in *Utopia* perenni constantiae laude frueretur. In ea enim
beatae gentis regione, optimis instituta legibus ac opulenta pace,
florentem rempublicam elegantissime descripsit, quum damnatos
corrupti saeculi mores fastidiret ut ad bene beateque vivendum
commento periucundo rectissima via monstraretur.


3                        *Iani Vitalis*

Dum Morus immeritae submittit colla securi
    et flent occasum pignora cara suum,
'Immo' ait 'infandi vitam deflete tyranni.
    Non moritur facinus qui grave morte fugit.'


4                   *Iacobi Exerichi Hispani*

Henricus Morum gladio iugulavit iniquo
    tam dignum vita quam fuit ipse nece.
Mortuus ille tamen vivet per saecula cuncta:
    post mortem virtus vivere sola facit.

and sudden impulse, to cast down that man who was by far the most authoritative on all points of religion and justice and was exceedingly holy—just because he had refused to express approval for the wicked lust of that raging tyrant. For while Henry rushed to repudiate his wife, replace her with his mistress, and shamelessly disinherit his daughter, More, his lord chancellor, after being forced to defend his loyalty and innocence in court, was condemned—by a decision that would have been impious were it not that a countervailing terror of the king's savage fury was shaking people out of their right minds—to die by the foulest form of execution, like a thief; nor was his dismembered body allowed burial according to the devoted wishes of his family.

But Henry, who by even this one deed rivaled Phalaris,[661] could 2 not keep More's steadfastness from enjoying lasting glory through his *Utopia*, keeping alive forever the memory of the king's uncommon wickedness.[662] For in that region of blessed people organized under the best laws and rich in peace, he most elegantly described a republic flourishing precisely because it scorned the wicked ways of his corrupt era. Thus by a most delightful fiction he pointed out the straightest path to living well and happily.

### By Giano Vitale[663]

3

When More bent his neck to the undeserved ax and his dear children bewailed his death, he said, "Weep rather for the life of an unspeakable tyrant. The one who by dying avoids a grave sin does not die."

### By Jaime Exerich the Spaniard[664]

4

With an unjust sword, Henry has butchered More, as worthy of life as Henry was of death. Having died, however, More will live on through all centuries. Virtue alone brings about life after death.

5                                    *Incerti*[72]

Hospes: Quis iacet in tumulo, cuius caput ense recisum est
    et natat in tetro sanguine canities?
Civis: Hic est ille Thomas Morus: sic fata rependunt
    tristia multa bonis et bona multa malis.
Hospes: Quae circumsistunt Divae lugubre cadaver?
    [Civis:] Diva tenax veri, sancta Fides, Nemesis;
harum prima odii causa, et fuit altera mortis,
    ultrix iniustae tertia caedis erit.


## XC. *Rossensis Cardinalis*

1   Pari quoque immanitatis portento ante paucos dies quam Morus
obtruncaretur, eadem sanguinarii regis rabies Britanniae lumen
extinxit Ioannem Ficerium antistitem Rossensem, animi pietate
candore constantia priscis illis atque sanctissimis Christiani ordinis patribus comparandum. Is, quum summa sacrae eruditionis et
probitatis authoritate clarissimus spectaretur, vel atrocissimi supplicii metu expugnari non potuit ut regi ex impudenti repudio
inauspicatas nuptias affectanti volens pareret.

2       Putabat enim regem, paulo ante admirabili virtutum omnium
concentu et rarissimis naturae atque fortunae muneribus praestantissimum, atrae bilis morbo correptum insanisse quod, iratus Romani pontificis sententiae qua fuerat ex divini iuris formula damnatus, pontificii imperii patrimonium invasisset. Non subscripsit

Visitor: Who lies in this tomb, whose head has been severed by a sword, and whose gray hair floats in foul blood?

Citizen: This is the great Thomas More. In this manner the Fates reward the good with many sorrows, and the evil with many blessings.

Visitor: What goddesses are gathered around the pitiful corpse?

[Citizen:] Truth-telling Fate,[666] Holy Faith, and Divine Justice. The first of these was the cause of the enmity, and the second the cause of his death. The third will be the avenger of his unjust murder.


## XC. *The Cardinal of Rochester (ca. 1469–1535)*

A few days before More was beheaded, with equally monstrous inhumanity the same king's bloodthirsty rage snuffed out the light of England, John Fisher,[667] bishop of Rochester, whose piety, candor, and constancy warrant comparison to the ancient and most holy Fathers of the Christian Church. When this man, whose sacred learning and moral probity gave him great influence, was put to the test, not even fear of the harshest torture could compel him to bend his will to the king who, fresh from a shameless divorce, was intent upon an inauspicious wedding.

In fact, Fisher thought that the king, who not long before had excelled in a remarkable blend of every virtue and in the rarest endowments of nature and fortune, had gone mad with melancholy: for, enraged at the Roman pontiff's decision that had condemned him on the basis of a provision of canon law, he had seized estates over which the papacy had dominion.[668]

ergo nefario rebellantis regis voto vir egregie pius integreque severus ac ideo in carcerem ductus est, ut vitae periculo et longo cruciatu imbecilli senis constantia frangeretur.

3     Id celebre factum ita Rossensi paravit laudem et Henrico invidiam cumulavit ut eum Paulus Tertius, ad exornandam virtutem natus, collato sacrae purpurae honore legerit in senatum. Sensit illico exprobrati odii vulnus rex superbus et impius sanctissimoque viro, modeste ea dignitatis fama permoto, caput in foro praecidit ne merita purpura ornaretur. Ferunt id caput, lanceae praefixum ut ludibrio terrorique caeteris foret, publicis lachrymis laudatum ac adoratum extitisse.

4     Reliquit ingenii monumenta eruditum volumen quo Lutheri opiniones gravissime confutarat, itemque alios utiles libros quibus sacri sacerdotii authoritatem defendit, et *De veritate corporis et sanguinis Christi in Eucharistia* libros quinque adversus Oecolampadium; sed is sibi admodum exitialis fuit quo Catharinae Reginae coniugium tuetur. Extat etiam religiosae meditationis explicatio in septem Davidicos Psalmos; reliqua in carcere purgatissime conscripta, quod damnatae causae nomen iugularent, tyrannus abolevit.

5                         *Incerti*

Tene viri tanti cervicem abscindere posse,
     tene cruore pio commaculare manus?
Si vita spolias Rossensem, barbare, quando
     ullum producet terra Britanna parem?

Accordingly, Rochester, a man of consummate faithfulness and
steadfast virtue, did not subscribe to the impious marriage of a
rebellious king and so was led off to prison, with the intention of
breaking the feeble old man's perseverance by the threat of death
and by protracted torture.

When this became widely known, it spurred such praise of 3
Rochester and heaped such obloquy upon Henry that Paul III,
whose nature it was to confer honor upon virtue, gave Rochester
the distinction of the sacred purple by appointment to the college
of cardinals. The proud and impious king immediately felt the injury of having his enmity reproached, and had that most holy man
(who in his humility had been deeply moved upon hearing of this
honor) beheaded in the public square lest he be adorned with the
purple he deserved. They say that his head, which had been
mounted on a pike to inspire mockery and terror in others, ended
up being praised and adored amid the general mourning.

He left behind as monuments of his brilliance a learned volume 4
in which he had forcefully confuted Luther's opinions; other useful
works, too, in which he defended the authority of the holy priesthood; and five books *On the Real Presence of the Body and Blood of
Christ in the Eucharist*, written against Oecolampadius.[669] But the
book in which he maintains the legitimacy of Henry's marriage to
Queen Catherine was surely fatal for him.[670] We also have his
meditative treatise on seven of David's Psalms.[671] His remaining
works, which he wrote and polished while in prison, were destroyed by the tyrant because he realized they obliterated the pretext of the legal action that had condemned the man.

*Anonymous*[672] 5

Do you think you can behead so great a man or pollute your
hands with his pious blood? If you, cruel one, deprive Rochester of life, when will British soil ever produce his equal?

Sed tu, sancte senex, aevo fruiture beato
laetus abi: in coelum te vocat ipse Deus.

## XCI. *Leonicus Tomaeus*

1 Leonicus Tomaeus, Epirota patre Venetiis genitus sed Patavio insi-
tus civis, quum Florentiae Graecas literas sub Demetrio didicisset,
primus Latinorum philosophorum Patavii Aristotelem Graece in-
terpretatus est. Philosophiam enim ex purissimis fontibus non ex
lutulentis rivulis salubriter hauriendam esse perdocebat, explosa
penitus sophistarum disciplina quae tum inter imperitos et barbaros principatum in scholis obtinebat, quum doctores excogitatis
barbara subtilitate dialecticorum figmentis physicas quaestiones
non ad veritatis lucem sed ad inanem disputandi garrulitatem re-
vocarent, et iuventus in gymnasio Arabum et barbarorum commentationes secuta a recto munitoque itinere in confragosas igno-
rantiae crepidines duceretur.

2 Scripsit erudite et luculenter commentarios in *Parva naturalia*
Aristotelis, ac item pereleganter aliquot quaestiones, et in his *De
intellectu, De alica* et *De astragalo,* tituli varietate iuventuti gratas et
utiles. Sed in libro *De varia historia,* quo ingens et peramoena reconditae lectionis copia exprimitur, omnes eius aetatis styli iucunditate superavit. Vita eius procul a contentione ambitioneque in
studioso mollique ocio versabatur ita ut, domi quam in schola
clarior, benevolis vera Peripateticorum et Academicorum dogmata
suavissima comitate pomeridianis horis explicaret.

3 Pervenit veneranda barbae canitie ad septuagesimum tertium
aetatis annum, mediocri substantia ipsaque civili frugalitate, et

But you, revered and holy man, go gladly to enjoy eternal happiness: God himself is calling you to heaven.

## XCI. [Niccolò] Leonico Tomeo (1456–1531)

Born in Venice to an Epirot father, Leonico Tomeo[673] was an adopted citizen of Padua. After studying Greek in Florence under Demetrius, he became the first of the Latin philosophers at Padua to expound Aristotle in the Greek.[674] Indeed, he taught that for philosophy to be of benefit, it must be imbibed from the purest springs, not from muddy runnels. He rejected completely the sophistical teaching which held pride of place in the schools among the ignorant and barbarous when, with figments of dialectic dreamed up with foreign subtlety, their professors reduced questions of natural philosophy not to the light of truth but to the empty babbling of dispute, and the youth in the university, following the commentaries of Arabs and barbarians, were led from the straight and reliable path onto craggy precipices of ignorance.[675]

With erudition and brilliance he penned commentaries on Aristotle's *Short Treatises on Nature*,[676] and also some felicitously written inquiries, among them *On the Intellect, On Groat Porridge*, and *On Jacks*,[677] a variety of titles pleasing and useful to the youth. But in the book *On Various Kinds of History*,[678] which exhibits an immense and enchanting store of obscure reading, he surpassed in stylistic charm all men of his era. He spent his life in studious and peaceful leisure, far from conflict and ambition, in such a way that in the afternoon, more brilliantly at home than at school, he expounded to friends with the most gracious generosity the true tenets of the Peripatetics and Academicians.[679]

He lived to his seventy-third year, his beard a venerable white. With middling wealth and the frugality befitting a private citizen,

coelebs et felix quod nemo vel innocentiae et doctrinae conscientia
vel munditia corporis vel animi nitore beatior aetate nostra fuerit.

4     Aluerat domi gruem de manu ipsius senili oblectamento cibaria
capientem per quadraginta annos. Is senio tabefactus quum periisset, ex eius desiderio triste omen concepit praedixitque nullo lacess-
situs morbo se non multo post adamati gruis fatum maturo vitae
exitu secuturum.

5     Patavini externaque gymnasii cultrix iuventus funus ornavere.
Sepulchrum autem Bembus faciundum curavit et carmine nobilitavit:

*Bembi*

Naturae si quid rerum te forte latebat,
  hoc legis in magno nunc, Leonice, Deo.

## XCII. *Augustinus Niphus*

1   Augustino Nipho, Suessae ad Auruncam nato sed ab urbe Trophea
in Brutiis oriundo, inter Aristotelicae sectae professores eximia
laus contigit quum in omnibus fere Italiae gymnasiis, Achillino et
Pomponatio florentibus, opima stipendia meruisset. Erat ingenio
fertili adaperto liberali, sermone autem Campanum pingue quoddam resonanti maxime libero et ad serendas fabulas in suggestu
coronaque ad voluptatem aurium periucundo, sed vel toto ore subagresti et penitus infaceto ita se ad urbanos iocos componebat, ut

he was both single and happy: for nobody in our time has been more blessed, whether for his sense of probity and erudition, his refined bearing, or his splendid intellect.

For forty years he kept in his home a pet crane which used to 4 amuse the old man by eating from his hand. Once it had withered away and died from old age, in his bereavement he came to believe this a grim omen and predicted that, although no illness assailed him, by an early death he would soon share the fate of his beloved pet.

The Paduans and the foreign students at the university paid 5 their respects at his funeral, but Bembo had his tomb erected and ennobled it with a poem:

*By Bembo*[680]

If perhaps anything of Nature lay hidden from you, o Leonico, now you behold it in the presence of Almighty God.

## XCII. Agostino Nifo (ca. 1470–1538)

Agostino Nifo[681] was born at Sessa Aurunca, but his family hailed 1 from the town of Tropea in Calabria.[682] He garnered extraordinary praise among professors of the Aristotelian school, as evidenced by the high salaries he earned in nearly all the universities of Italy at the time when Achillini and Pomponazzi were at the peak of their fame.[683] His mind was fertile, open, and generous, though his manner of speaking, completely frank, with something of a Campanian coarseness, was most pleasing to the ears when he wove stories on the dais or in a circle of listeners. And yet, for all his uncouth and unmannered mode of expression, he so composed himself to tell refined jests that he occasioned much wonder when,

valde mirarentur qui mox tacentis supercilium austeraque labra et lineamenta conspiceret.[73]

2 Scripsit in omnes Aristotelis libros perampla commentaria sed rudi et incondita quadam ubertate, ut tum mos erat, crassis et plane barbaris auribus accommodata, quod Latine recteque scribendi facultatem, tanquam inimicam optimis disciplinis, ab ipsa praesertim philosophia segregabant. Luculentius eius operum existimatur id quod pro Averroe adversus Algazellem disputante tum publicavit quum florente aetate a multo vigore ingenii nervosior haberetur. Quanquam ipse in opinione decretoque parum constans evariatoque saepe iudicio, commentationes in *Analytica priora* et in libros *De anima* tenerius adamasse videamus.

3 Parto demum ocio obrepenteque podagra, scripsit adversus astrologos moralesque libellos, et *De tyranno et rege* et *De auguriis*, varietate tituli vel parum curiosis expetendos et longiore quidem dignos vita, si plenior Latini sermonis spiritus accessisset.

4 Susceptis liberis et senescente uxore, septuagenarius senex puellae citra libidinem impotenti amore correptus est usque ad insaniam, ita ut plerique philosophum senem atque podagricum ad tibiae modos saltantem miserabili cum pudore conspexerint, unde illi maturatum vitae exitum constat.

5 Periit in patria nocturno itinere refrigeratus quum sero e Sinuessa rediisset, obortis scilicet tonsillis quae fauces obsederant, ea ipsa nocte Ethruriae admodum funesta qua Alexander Medices in lecto turpissime confossus interiit.

6 Galeacius Florimontius, quum praeceptori urnam poneret, hoc carmen incidi iussit:

once he fell silent, one observed his brow and stern lips and features.

He wrote extensive commentaries on all of Aristotle's books 2 but, as was then fashionable, with a certain unsophisticated and undisciplined volubility suited for dull and utterly barbarous ears: for they shunned the art of writing correct Latin as if it were opposed to the highest learning, especially philosophy itself. Of his works, the one arguing on behalf of Averroës against Al-Ghazali is considered quite brilliant.[684] He published it in his prime, when his vigorous intellect was thought to have made him more bold. Although he himself was inconstant in his opinions and convictions and often changed his mind, we may see how he more tenderly cherished his commentaries on the *Prior Analytics* and the books *On the Soul*.[685]

When at last he had retired and was suffering frequent attacks 3 of gout, he wrote against the astrologers, along with some pamphlets on morals, and *On the King and the Tyrant* and *On Divination*, a variety of titles to entice even the incurious, and surely worth preserving if only their Latin had been more inspired.[686]

As an old man of seventy with children and an aging wife, he 4 was brought to the point of insanity, powerless in his unavailing passion for a young girl, with the result that most looked on with embarrassment and pity at the old, gout-hobbled philosopher dancing to the strains of a flute, behavior that was thought to have hastened his end.

He died in Sessa Aurunca, whither he'd returned from Mon- 5 dragone very late, chilled from a night journey, his tonsils having swollen to the point that they obstructed the airway.[687] This happened on that very night that was utterly calamitous for Tuscany, when Alessandro de' Medici was most foully stabbed to death while in bed.[688]

When Galeazzo Florimonte[689] set up an urn for his teacher, he 6 ordered that this poem be inscribed on it:

*Incerti*

Dum lapidi titulum moerens Galeatius addit
   et tristi curat funera cum gemitu,
'Si quis honos tumuli, non hoc tibi, Nyphe, supremum
   sed patriae et misero stat mihi munus' ait.
Nae vivis meliore tui tu parte; levamen
   luctus non mediis quaerimus in lachrymis.

7                   *Marci Antonii Flaminii*

Qui docuit rerum Niphus cognoscere causas,
   non rerum oblitus hoc iacet in tumulo;
sed coelo meliore sui cum parte receptus
   nunc gaudet melius discere quam docuit.

## XCIII. Ioannes Ruellius

1 Ruellius in urbe Suessionum natus, quum susceptis liberis uxorem
extulisset, abdicata medendi arte sacerdotium in templo Deiparae
Virginis Lutetiae Parisiorum Poncherii antistitis liberalitate promeruit, totumque id ocium optimis literis, ut fortunis auctum decebat, impendit, non ignobili quidem gloriae proventu quum eruditionis authoritate Budaeo proximus esset et Latini sermonis
nitida puritate superior haberetur, ut praeclare indicat Dioscorides
in Latinum e Graeco emendate traductus.

2    Leguntur et libri aliquot probe fideliterque translati de mulomedicina et Actuarii medici volumen *De urinis*, sed proprio usus
ingenio libros tres *De natura stirpium* perscripsit, Theophrastum in
multis et Plinium eleganter aemulatus. Extant quoque singulari

*Anonymous*[690]

When the grieving Galeazzo added an inscription to the stone and attended to the funeral rites with a mournful sigh, he said: "If there's any honor in a tomb, this gift is the final one not for you, Nifo, but for your homeland and for us in our sorrow. Truly, the better part of you lives on, whereas we, with unceasing tears, seek to mitigate our grief."

*By Marcantonio Flaminio*[691]                                    7

Nifo, who taught how to recognize the causes of things and forgot them not, lies here in this tomb. But now his better part, welcomed into heaven, rejoices to learn better than he taught.

## XCIII. *Jean Ruel (1474–1537)*

A native of Soissons, Ruel[692] had a wife and children, but follow-    1
ing her death he gave up the practice of medicine and, through the generosity of the Parisian bishop Poncher, obtained a canonry in the Cathedral of the Virgin Mother in Paris.[693] As befitted a man of increased means, he devoted all his free time to literature, from which he obtained no mean glory: for in esteem as a scholar he was second only to Budé and was thought superior in the bright purity of his Latin style, as appears clearly from his flawless translation of Dioscorides into Latin.[694]

We also have several books *On Veterinary Medicine*[695] that he ac-    2
curately and faithfully rendered from Greek, and the doctor Actu-arius's volume *On Urine*.[696] Putting his own brilliance to work, however, he wrote three books of his own *On the Nature of Plants*, in which he elegantly imitated Pliny and Theophrastus in many

diligentia translati e Graeco quinque libri *De agricultura* ex viginti qui nomine Constantini circumferuntur; reliquos Coroneus Gallus vertisse dicitur, sed Cornarius Germanus expedita facundia celeber universos viginti Latinitate donatos nuper publicavit.

3     Erat Ruellius natura modestus et lenis, vultu multo rubore suffuso et resimis naribus, statura vero mediocri. Sexagesimo aetatis anno vita functus est, paulo ante quam Rex Franciscus nivosas Alpes traiiceret ut, copiis suis Caesarianorum impetu perculsis fortiter opem ferens, subalpina oppida summotis hostibus in fide confirmaret, ut inde in spem inauspicatae pacis induciae pararentur.

4                       *Dionysii Carronii*

Hic situs est in quo viguit medicina Ruellis,
   in quo naturae notitia atque poli,
in quo prima fuit dos Graium vertere scripta
   in Latium, ac Latio scribere digna Iove.
Olim erat affinis, nunc est conviva deorum,
   praemiaque illa sui grata laboris habet.

## XCIV. Antonius Tibaldeus

1     Hic primus fere post Petrarcam supra aemulantes Seraphinum atque Manutium plane extinctum Ethrusci carminis decus excitavit, usque adeo grata auribus alternantium numerorum suavitate ut, quum expetitis ubique eius iucundae facultatis illecebris in

respects.[697] We also have five books *On Agriculture*, translated from the Greek with great care from among the twenty that circulate under the name of Constantine.[698] (It's said that the Frenchman Corone rendered the remaining books; though Cornarius, a German famous for his flowing eloquence, recently published a Latin translation of all twenty.)[699]

Reserved and gentle in temperament, Ruel had a ruddy face    3
and a snub nose, and was of middling height. He passed away in his sixtieth year, shortly before King Francis crossed the snow-covered Alps, courageously bringing relief to his army which had been overpowered by an attack of Imperial troops. This he did to dislodge the enemy, shore up the allegiance of cities south of the Alps, and obtain a truce, hoping for the peace of which he had despaired.[700]

*By Denis Corone*[701]    4

Here lies Ruel, who acquired prowess in medicine, compre-hended earth and heaven, and had a talent of the first order for bringing Greek works into Latin, and in Latin for writing things worthy of Jove. Once my associate, now he's a table companion of the gods, enjoying the grateful rewards of his labors.

## XCIV. Antonio Tebaldeo[702] (1462–1537)

This man was virtually the first since Petrarch to revive the utterly    1
extinguished glory of Tuscan verse, in which he surpassed his rivals Serafino and Manuzio.[703] The charm of his alternating rhythms so pleased the ears that once he had made the rounds of princely courts (the pleasurable enticements of his work being

amatorios lusus principum aulas perambulasset, edita vel surrepta eius carmina a viris pariter et foeminis ad citharam cantarentur.

2 Sed tantam mox famam feliciore orti sydere Bembus et Syncerus aeternis carminibus oppresserunt. Agnovit ille tanto perstrictus fulgore ingenii sui fortunam atque ideo ad Latina carmina se convertit, quum in his ad genium non insulsa vena responderet. Sed factus grandaevus senex, ridente urbe Roma, carminum suorum Ethruscorum exequiis interfuit ita hercle ut evanescentis antiquae laudis magnam partem redimeret, quum epigrammata multo Latino sale leporeque conspersa inexpectatus edidisset.

3 Periit in Via Lata octogenarius senex, firmissimo corpore et celsa proceritate[74] semper erecto, stranguria cruciatus adeo graviter ut ex atra demum bile se ipso factus amarior saepe nec insulse delirare videretur, quum ianua fenestrisque penitus occlusis Carolum Caesarem, ex Africa relato insigni triumpho, ad eius limen transeuntem spectare noluerit quod eum minime iustum imperatorem putaret qui sub fide publica captae deletaeque Urbis scelus, quo maiestas eius vel extra culpam sugillari potuit, decumatis legionibus[75] minime vindicasset — quasi non satis fuerit in tantae cladis solatio Borbonium Dorbinium Moncatam et Aurantium, quattuor summos duces et patrati facinoris authores, singulis ictos fulminibus ultore magno numine spectavisse!

4 *Colae Bruni Messanensis*

Quae ripis te saepe suis stupuere canentem
Eridanus Tyberisque, parens ille, hic tuus hospes,

everywhere in demand for lovers' dalliances), his poems, whether published or pilfered, were sung to the lute by men and women alike.

But soon, Bembo and Sannazaro, born under a more auspicious star, overshadowed his great fame with their immortal verses. Dazzled by such brilliance, Tebaldeo recognized what it meant for his own talent, and so turned his attention to Latin verses, to which his gifts were well suited. But when he had grown very old, to the amusement of all Rome, he celebrated funeral rites for his own Tuscan poems, and would actually regain much of his old, fading reputation when, to everyone's surprise, he published epigrams sprinkled liberally with Latin wit and cleverness.

He died in his house on via Lata, an old man of eighty.[704] Always physically robust and standing tall, he suffered so intensely from kidney stones that in the end, embittered from an excess of ill humor, he seemed a bit deranged—albeit often not without reason. Thus, when he heard of the emperor Charles's celebration of his great African triumph, Tebaldeo shut his door and windows tightly, so as not to look upon him as he passed by his house: for he considered that emperor utterly unjust since, after having guaranteed Rome's safety, he had failed to punish his troops by decimation for capturing and sacking the city, a crime for which His Majesty could be castigated even if not directly responsible.[705] As if it weren't enough solace for so great a disaster to watch the four supreme commanders and perpetrators of the crime—Bourbon, Urbina, Moncada, and Orange—be struck down, each by a thunderbolt, through God's mighty vengeance![706]

### By Cola Bruno of Messina[707]

The songs, o bard Antonio, that often, to their astonishment, you sang along the shores of the Po that bore you and

credibile est, vates Antoni, nunc quoque campis
te canere Elysiis, turba admirante piorum.


## XCV. *Erasmus Rhoterodamus*[76]

1 Erasmus Rhoterodamus[77] ex insula Batavorum perpetuis eruditae
laudis honoribus extollendus videtur, postquam aetatis nostrae
scriptorum prope omnium decus ingenii fertilitate superarit. Is ab
adolescentia, pio religiosi animi decreto, ad cucullatos sacerdotes
se contulit tanquam humana despiceret sed, non multo post pertesus intempestivae servitutis votique temere suscepti, ea sacrati[78]
ordinis saepta transiliit ut ad excolendum ingenium plane liber per
omnia Europae gymnasia vagaretur. Contendebat enim cura ingenti ad summae gloriae fastigium, ad quod literarum omnium
cognitione perveniri posse intelligebat, quum iam ad arcana cuiusque doctrinae infinita lectione inusitataque memoria penetrasset.

2 Edidit *Moriam* atque inde primam nominis famam longissime
protulit, imitatione Luciani satyrae pungentis aculeos passim relinquens,[79] omnium scilicet sectarum actionibus ad insaniam revoca-
tis: opus quidem salsa aspergine periucundum vel gravibus et oc-
cupatis, sed sacrato viro prorsus indecorum quum divinis quoque
rebus illusisse videretur.

3 Sed mature demum, quod eius intemperantiae male audiendo
poenas daret, sanctiores literas complexus est tanta robustissimi
ingenii contentione ut vertendo Graeca et commentarios excu-
dendo plura quam quisquam alius volumina publicarit. Verum se

the Tiber that welcomed you, you're believed now also to sing in the fields of Elysium, admired by all the blessed souls.

## XCV. Erasmus of Rotterdam (1466–1536)

Erasmus of Rotterdam,[708] a city in Holland, seems to deserve the honor of everlasting praise for his erudition, after outshining nearly all other writers of our time with his prolific intellect. Upon reaching maturity, by a decision made in a spirit of devotion, he joined the cowled clergy, as he despised all things human. Soon thereafter, however, having grown disgusted with his inopportune slavery and of the vow he'd rashly made, he leaped over the walls of his religious community in order to range with complete freedom and cultivate his mind in all the universities of Europe.[709] Indeed, with immense zeal he strove toward the apex of supreme glory, realizing it could be reached through an encyclopedic knowledge of letters, since with his endless reading and prodigious memory he had already penetrated the mysteries of every branch of learning.

He published the *Praise of Folly* and thereby greatly enhanced his initial fame, leaving here and there, in imitation of Lucian, nettles of stinging satire, having effectively reduced to foolishness the claims of all the philosophical schools. Spiced with wit, this work delighted even the serious-minded and those caught up in business, but it was utterly indecorous for a consecrated man, since it seemed to make sport even of religion.

In time, however, since he was paying for these excesses with his reputation, he embraced more spiritual learning with such great exertion of his powerful mind that with his volumes of translations from Greek and his printed commentaries, he published more books than anybody else. But undoubtedly he would

ipso haud dubie cunctis admirabilior futurus, si Latinae linguae
conditores graviter imitari quam fervido properantique ingenio in-
dulgere maluisset. Quaerebat enim peculiarem laudem ex elocutionis atque structurae novitate quae nulla certa veterum aemulatione
pararetur, ut in *Ciceroniano* non occulti livoris plenus ostendit.

4      Tanta enim erat naturae foecunditas ut plena semper ac ideo
superfoetante alvo, varia et festinata luxuriantis ingenii prole delectatus, novum aliquid quod statim ederetur chalcographis tanquam
intentis obstetricibus parturiret.

5      Obiit apud Helvetios Friburgo in pago sive, ut aliqui afferunt,[80]
Basiliae, septuagesimum excedens aetatis annum, quum Carolus
Caesar in Provinciam irrumpens ad Aquas Sextias Francisco Gal-
liae Regi grave bellum intulisset.

6                                      *Iani Vitalis*

Lubrica si tibi mens fuit et spinosior aequo,
      ingenium certe nobile, Erasme, fuit.
Felix si mistas labruscas dulcibus uvis
      prodiga desisset vinea ferre tua.
Barbarie e media praeclarum sydus haberent
      et te Varronem tempora nostra suum.
Hanc tamen inscriptam his titulis posuere columnam:
      'Iactura hic laudum publica facta fuit.'

7                                      *Incerti*

Theutona terra suum quum miraretur Erasmum,
      'Hoc maius' potuit dicere 'nil genui.'

be more worthy of everyone's admiration had he chosen to imitate with dignity the founders of the Latin language rather than indulge his impetuous and impatient temperament, for he sought his own special distinction through the use of new expressions and arrangements contrived with no discernible effort to imitate the ancients, as he showed, brimming with undisguised spite, in *The Ciceronian*.[710]

So great was his natural fecundity that he delighted in a belly   4 that, while yet pregnant, was always conceiving anew, and in the motley and premature offspring of an overly fruitful mind. Whatever new thing he delivered was yielded up at once to the printers as though to overeager midwives.

Aged over seventy, he died in Switzerland in the canton of Fri-   5 bourg or, as some say, in Basel.[711] This was when the emperor Charles, by his attack on Provence at Aix, had begun an oppressive war against King Francis of France.[712]

#### By Giano Vitale[713]   6

If your character was slippery and more prickly than was fitting, Erasmus, certainly your genius was renowned. You would have been blessed, if only your overgrown vineyard had ceased to grow wild vines mingling with sweet grapes. Our times would consider you their brightest star, issuing from the midst of a barbarous land, and you would be their Varro. Still, they have erected this column, inscribed with these words: "Here, honors were paid at public expense."

#### Anonymous[714]   7

When a Teutonic land looked in wonder at its Erasmus, it was able to say, "I've produced nothing greater than this."

## XCVI. Rutilius

1 Rutilius, e Colonia oppido Vicentini agri, quum erudito diligentique eius ingenio Nicolaus Ridulphus Cardinalis familiariter uteretur, ex umbratili iureconsulto flamen evasit quod nunquam in forum prodiisset. Edidit enim volumen ab industria atque facundia commendatum de his qui, florente Romano Imperio, iuris intelligentia praestiterunt; quo laborioso elegantique opere Ciceronem obiter a multa mendorum labe repurgavit.

2 Maiora porro editurus videri potuit, nisi immatura mors lucubrantem Venetiis oppressisset. Amici autem poetae de eo, tanquam conspicui sepulchri honore ex humili fortuna facile carituro, haec carmina decantarunt:

#### Petri Cursii

Ut mors Rutilium sensit tot reddere vitae,
  'Styx, vale' ait, 'vitae iam patefacta via est.'

3 #### Croti

Exciri ut legum latores sensit ab Orco
  invida mors, fusis protulit haec lachrymis:
'Quam vere eiusdem est inferre auferreque leges,
  lege horum cum lex pene refixa mea est!'

4 #### Iani Vitalis

Vivitur in chartis, Rutili, felicius ipsis,
  cum videant mortem marmora et aera suam.

## XCVI. Rutilio (1504–38)

Rutilio[715] was from the town of Cologna Veneta, in Vicenzan ter- 1
ritory.[716] When Cardinal Niccolò Ridolfi added him to his household to put his erudition and diligence to use, given that he'd never
gone to court, he went from being a nonpracticing lawyer to being
a priest. With commendable assiduity and eloquence he published
a book about those at the height of the Roman Empire who stood
out for their exceptional understanding of the law.[717] While writing this painstaking and exacting work, along the way he cleansed
texts of Cicero from the stain of many errors.

It seemed he could have gone on to publish more important 2
works had not a premature death felled him as he was burning the
midnight oil in Venice. His poet friends recited the following
verses for him, supposing that, because of his humble circumstances, he might well lack the honor of a splendid tomb:

### By Pietro Corsi[718]

When Death realized that Rutilio was restoring so many to
life, she said, "Farewell, Styx! The path to life now lies open."

### By Crotti[719]                                                      3

When envious Death realized that legislators were being
brought back to life, she exclaimed tearfully: "How truly it is
the privilege of the same man both to introduce and repeal
laws, when he all but replaces my law with theirs!"

### By Giano Vitale[720]                                                4

Life is more apt to remain in the writings themselves, Rutilio, inasmuch as marbles and bronzes bear witness to their

Absumpsit priscos legum Libitina peritos;
   tu facis in scriptis vivere et esse tuis.
Quam merito illi igitur dicent, 'Aeternior aere
   est tua et aeternis pagina marmoribus.'

## XCVII. Gulielmus Budaeus

1    Nulli mortalium aetate nostra perpetuis lucubrationibus aspirante
Fortuna cum Graecae tum Latinae eruditionis maiores opes con-
tigerunt quam Gulielmo Budaeo, non Galliae modo sed totius
etiam Europae longe doctissimo. Natus Lutetiae praecellentium
disciplinarum celebri domicilio, dum perennem spectaret laudem
et rei familiaris fortunas honoresque ingenio suo et sperata gloria
viliores arbitraretur, sexaginta amplius aetatis annos in studiis
consumpsit, ita ut summae eruditionis libro *De asse* alteroque in
*Pandectas* edito, ac infinita demum lectione confectis *Commentariis*
quibus Graecae et Latinae facultatis ornamenta comparantur, nulli
communicata laude aequales omnes doctrinae authoritate superarit.

2    Sed qui in memoriae thesauris tantas divitias miro digestas ordine continebat, veluti occupatus in apparatu candidioris eloquentiae cultum neglexisse existimatur. Id enim in toto studiorum negocio longe gravissimum nemo nisi irrita spe senectuti unquam
reservavit.

3    Adaugebant nominis famam in perspicuo animo sanctissimi
mores, quibus aliquanto uberiora rei familiaris incrementa quam
pertinaci diligentia vel honoris ambitione educatis feliciter liberis
reliquit, quum Rex Franciscus, subita liberalitate inclytus, optimi

own death.[721] Libitina[722] carried away the ancient jurists, but you, in your works, bring them to life and being. How fitting it is, then, that they will say, "Your pages are more lasting than bronze or everlasting marble."

## XCVII. Guillaume Budé (1468–1540)

No one in our time, through extended, uninterrupted study and Fortune's favor, has amassed greater stores of both Latin and Greek erudition than Guillaume Budé,[723] by far the most learned man not only in France but in all Europe. He was born in Paris to a household renowned for superior learning. Since he looked to unending fame and valued his family's wealth and distinctions less than his own intelligence and hoped-for glory, he spent over sixty years of his life in study, producing a most learned book *On Coinage* and another on the *Pandects*, and at last, after boundless reading, completed the *Commentaries*, in which he compares the possibilities for rhetorical embellishment in Greek with those in Latin.[724] He surpassed all his contemporaries in the authority of his erudition, sharing the glory with no one.

But this man, who was storing up such great riches arranged in an ingenious system in the chambers of memory, being fixated on readying the content, is thought to have neglected to polish his style. This really is by far the most important thing in the entire scholarly enterprise, and in fact nobody has ever postponed it to late in life without disappointment.

His reputation was enhanced by his candor and utterly irreproachable character, thanks to which he bequeathed to his well-brought up children somewhat more of a patrimony than through unrelenting diligence or even ambition for honor: King Francis, renowned for spontaneous acts of generosity, supported the leisure

viri ocium foveret et ipse, supplicibus libellis praepositus, honestissimo proventu ditaretur.

4    Sed vir alioqui incorrupta mente compositus Erasmianae obtrectationis spicula ferre non potuit: quum facile indignabundus bile Gallica redundaret, ille autem contumaci odio incensus tela veneno Batavo delibuta iacularetur.

5    Septuagesimum tertium agentem annum oppressit febris longinquo et aestuoso ad Armoricum Oceanum itinere concepta. Pie autem tranquilleque vita excedens, condito testamento omnes honores funeris et tumuli penitus abdicavit ita ut, quum numerosa proles eum lugeret, noctu tumularetur. Fato functus est non multo post celebres illos hospitales triumphos quum Caesar, ab Hispania per mediam Galliam in Belgas profectus, gentem bello fessam festa passim hylaritate in spem pacis erexisset.

6                              *Iani Vitalis*

Qui sanctum simul et simul disertum
exquiris sapientiae magistrum,
    ultra quid petis? Hic iacet Budaeus.


7                              *Salmonii*

Budaeus voluit media de nocte sepulchro
    inferri, et nullas prorsus adesse faces.
Non factum ratione caret, clarissima quando
    ipse sibi lampas luxque corusca fuit.


## XCVIII. *Hieronymus Aleander*

1  Detur hoc incomparabili inusitatae memoriae felicitati, quae in Hieronymo Aleandro supra cuiusque vel antiqui saeculi captum

of this upstanding man; and Budé himself, put in charge of petitions, was enriched by a highly respectable income.[725]

Although otherwise calm and of sound mind, he could not endure the disparaging barbs of Erasmus. While Budé was quick to overflow with Gallic rage, Erasmus, inflamed with obstinate hatred, hurled darts steeped in Dutch venom.    4

In his seventy-third year he was done in by a fever contracted on a long, sweltering journey to the Brittany coast. Departing life piously and serenely, in his will he forbade any obsequies or tomb, so that although mourned by numerous offspring, he was buried at night. He died not long after those crowded triumphal processions held when the emperor, crossing through France on his way from Spain to Flanders, had with festive cheer inspired a people exhausted by war to hope for peace.[726]    5

### By Giano Vitale[727]    6

O you who search for a teacher of wisdom at once holy and eloquent, why look further? Here lies Budé.

### By Salmon[728]    7

Budé wished to be entombed in the middle of the night, and even forbade torchlight. There was good reason for this: for he himself was his own gleaming flambeau and brilliant light.

## XCVIII. Girolamo Aleandro (1480–1542)

It must be conceded to the exceptional good fortune of an uncommon memory in Girolamo Aleandro,[729] wonderfully surpassing the    1

admiranter excelluit, ut eius ex vero depicta facies, vel in pudenda ingenii sterilitate, inter foecundissimas imagines conspiciatur, quando nihil eum cuncta volumina cupide perlegentem vel rerum vel verborum omnino subterfugerit quin singula memoriter vel a multis annis longo sepulta silentio recitaret. Latinae enim Grae- caeque literae quum saepe alacriter iactabundo pro vernaculis ha- berentur, Hebraicas admirantibus Iudeis et suae stirpis eum facile credentibus solertissime didicit.

2      His ingenii dotibus insignis quum Lutetiae Parisiorum Graece docendo honorem praefecturae gymnasii concordi studiosae iuven- tutis acclamatione esset consecutus venissetque in Urbem, Leo Pontifex gravissimus ingeniorum aestimator eum extulit misitque legatum in Germaniam ut Lutheranae haeresis[81] initia disputa- tione tollerentur. Exinde Clemens Brundusinum casu potiusquam animi iudicio antistitem fecit. Paulus autem verae virtutis eruditus exornator legit in senatum. Laetatus est ea purpura per annos quinque, pervasurus haud dubie ad exactam aetatem nisi nimia tuendae valetudinis solicitudine intempestivis medicamentis sibi hercle insanus et infelix medicus viscera corrupisset.

3      In toto autem vitae cursu extemporanea facundia delectatus, sero ingenii labem sensit quum ad meditatam scriptionem purior eloquentiae vena, uti externo et praecipiti quodam luto perturbata, minime proflueret; ita spe melioris styli misere destitutus, quum vastum opus vasta illa memoria adversus singulos disciplinarum professores agitaret, Romae interiit fato suo vehementer indigna- tus, quum se praereptum anno uno ante climactericum inter anxia supremaque suspiria quereretur.

capacity of every age, even antiquity, that despite the shameful
sterility of his mind, his face, painted from life, should appear
among the portraits of the most productive intellects:[730] for not a
thing or word in all his eager and voluminous reading escaped
him, so that he could recall their details from memory, even those
consigned to oblivion for a great many years. Indeed, he was often
quick to boast that Latin and Greek were to him as native languages, and he became expert in Hebrew, to the astonishment of
the Jews, who readily believed he was one of their own.

Famed for these intellectual gifts, when teaching Greek in Paris    2
he was elected to the distinguished post of rector of the University
of Paris by unanimous vote of the students.[731] He then went on to
Rome, where Pope Leo, a most authoritative appraiser of brilliant
minds, promoted him, and sent him as a nuncio to Germany to
put down the beginnings of the Lutheran heresy by argument.[732]
Then, more by chance than by considered judgment, Clement
made him archbishop of Brindisi; but Paul, who knew how to reward true virtue, elevated him to the College of Cardinals.[733] He
enjoyed the purple for five years, and doubtless would have done
so to a ripe old age were it not that, too anxious about staying
healthy, he'd turned doctor (a foolish and unsuccessful one, Lord
knows), and ravaged his internal organs with ill-suited preventa-
tive medicines.

Having taken delight all his life in eloquent improvisation, he    3
was late to recognize the blemish on his talent when the vein of
eloquence, muddied by an inrush of turbid waters, did not flow
more pure to his carefully composed writings. Thus, while his vast
memory planned a vast work to attack particular professors in
various disciplines, in misery he despaired of attaining to a more
refined style. Vehemently resenting his fate, he met his end in
Rome, grumbling amid deep and troubled sighs that he was being
carried off a year before his climacteric.[734]

4  Tumulatus est in aede Transtyberina Divo Chrysogono dedicata, ea testamenti lege ut sepulchrum Graeco carmine ab se
composito cum reliquis titulis inscriberetur, quo novas clades im-
minere nobis ominatur in hanc sententiam:


5                              *Ipsius*

Excessi e vitae aerumnis facilisque lubensque,
    ne peiora ipsa morte dehinc videam.


6                          *Iani Vitalis*

Non tibi literulis ornare, Aleandre, sepulchrum
    fas erat, at vastam ponere pyramidem
Stesichorosque inter celebres sanctosque Platones
    ex auro solidam stare tibi statuam.
Vidimus in te uno divinae insignia mentis
    et plusquam humani par decus ingenii.
Nunc periit tecum quantum vix saecula mille,
    quantum vix praestent millia mille hominum.


## XCIX. *Lampridius*


1  Lampridius poeta Cremonensis, quum in colle Quirinali schola
Graecorum adolescentium instituente Lascare coalesceret, docendi
munus suscepit exercitatione perutili, quod argumenta proposita
utriusque linguae verbis et figuris ad mutuam ingeniorum aemulationem verterentur.
2  Sed erepto Leone et subinde eversis optimarum literarum studiis Patavium se contulit, ubi per aliquot annos domi ex collaticia

He was buried in Trastevere in the Church of San Crisogono,   4
his will stipulating that along with the other epitaphs, the tomb
should be inscribed with a Greek poem he had composed. In
the following sentence from it, he predicts that new calamities
await us:

By Himself[735]    5

I was ready and willing to escape life's troubles so as not to
see hereafter things worse than death itself.

By Giano Vitale[736]    6

It was fitting, Aleandro, not to adorn your tomb with brief
compositions, but instead to erect a vast pyramid, and to
have a solid gold statue of you standing amid the likes of the
famous Stesichorus[737] and revered Plato. In you alone we
saw the distinctions of a divine mind, and an equal endowment of superhuman brilliance. Now, there has died along
with you all that scarcely a thousand centuries, and scarcely
a thousand thousands of men, can offer.

## XCIX. Lampridio (1478–1539)

When the school for Greek youths headed by Lascaris was taking   1
shape on the Quirinal Hill, the Cremonese poet Lampridio accepted a post as instructor.[738] His pedagogical method proved
most effective, in that the themes he set had scholars competing
with one another to translate words and figures of speech of both
languages.

But after Leo died and, consequently, the studies of the best   2
literature came to an abrupt end, Lampridio moved to Padua,

mercede delectorum iuvenum Graecas et Latinas literas maiore quaestu quam gloria professus est. Nunquam enim, uti erat elato contumacique ingenio, adduci potuit ut publicum suggestum conscenderet, ne cum eloquentioribus vel minus eruditis ambiguae existimationis aleam subiret.

3    Novissime Federicus Gonzaga ut filio praeceptor esset Mantuam accivit. In eo munere, septenne discipulo et vix degustata principis liberalitate, minime senex lateris dolore surreptus est.

4    Scripsit *Odas* aemulatione Pindarica eruditas et graves, sed ob id plerisque minus iucundas quod, prisci imitationeque difficilis poetae cursum tanquam inflati et tortuosi fluminis sequutus, insolentior et durior Latinis auribus evaserit. Fit enim monente Flacco ut quae optima et excellenter Graece ornata intelliguntur, vel paribus numeris tractata, ad genium Latinae suavitatis minime respondeant.

5                                   *Myrtei*

Ergo ego, nobilium o genitrix atque hospita vatum
Mantua, quod nimium vicina Cremona Maroni
obfuerit solus poenas abs te ipse reposcor?
Ille soli tantum damnum tulit: ast ego de te,
Mantua, deque tuo meritus bene principe cara
pro patria et vitam et cineres tibi reddere cogor.

6                              *Aspasiae Amicae*

Sepulchro inscriptum in templo Sancti Andreae:
'Lampridium carum Musis hic Mantua servat.'

where for some years he taught Greek and Latin in his home, paid
by the shared contribution of a select group of young men.[739]
From this he got more profit than glory. For, as he was haughty
and stubborn, he could never be induced to ascend to the public
dais lest he risk his reputation alongside those who were more eloquent, even if less learned.[740]

Eventually Federico Gonzaga invited him to Mantua to serve as 3
his son's tutor.[741] In that position, when his student was seven and
Lampridio himself had barely tasted the marquis's generosity, he
was carried off by pleurisy, though still far from old.

He wrote learned and ponderous odes in emulation of Pindar, 4
which pleased few readers because, following in the channel of that
ancient, almost inimitable poet, like that of a swollen and twisting
river, he became too unfamiliar and difficult to Latin ears.[742] For it
often happens, as Horace cautioned, that things considered superior and finely rendered in Greek do not conform in the least to
Latin sensibility, even if they are fitted out in the same meters.[743]

### By Mirteo[744]   5

Am I then the only one you punish, o Mantua, who have
given life and shelter to famous poets, because Cremona, being too close, did injury to Maro?[745] He suffered only a loss
of land; whereas I, who have honored you, Mantua, and
your prince, am compelled to give both my life and my ashes
to you instead of to my beloved fatherland.

### By His Friend Aspasia[746]   6

An inscription for his tomb in the Church of Sant' Andrea:
"Here Mantua watches over Lampridio, beloved of the
Muses."

7          *Marci Antonii Flaminii*

Perdideras Varium, nostro sed tempore laudes
Lampridius renovat, docta Cremona, tuas.
Ille Sophocleo cantabat digna cothurno,
iste canit lyricos Pindarico ore modos.


## C. *Gaspar Contarenus Cardinalis*

1   Gaspar Contarenus patritii ordinis Venetus, ab insigni memoria
illustrique doctrina et corporis ac ingenii castitate mirabilis, ad
rempublicam ita accessit ut gravitate iudicii, consumatae prudentiae senatoribus aequaretur, atque inde maturata maximarum legationum munera capesseret, non aetatis quidem sed una virtutis
praerogativa commendatus.

2       Iuvenis enim, tanquam perfectus Peripateticus, Aristotelem a
calumnia defenderat, quanquam modestiae causa suppresso nomine, adversus Pomponatium praeceptorem quum ille, si non insano, impio tamen conatu, animas nostras interire cum corpore ex
Aristotelis sententia persuadere libro edito contendisset. Appulit
exinde ingenium ad sacras literas adeo diligenter ut ad normam
Christianae disciplinae librum de optimi antistitis officio publicaret. In ipso autem civilium honorum cursu honestum decorumque
sibi et patriae *De republica Venetorum* volumen edidit, ut institutae
leges ex antiquo more civitatis in mandandis honoribus ad memoriam posteritati traderentur.

3       Novissime Paulus Pontifex, augusta illa generosi iudicii maturi-
tate facile superiores principes antecedens, nihil tale expectantem

You had lost Varius,⁷⁴⁸ o learned Cremona, but in our time
Lampridio renews your praises. The former sang things worthy of Sophoclean tragedy; the latter sings lyric with the eloquence of Pindar.

## C. Cardinal Gasparo Contarini (1483–1542)

The Venetian patrician Gasparo Contarini⁷⁴⁹ was remarkable for    1
his outstanding memory, brilliant learning, and pure body and
mind. He entered the service of the republic in such a way that he
was held the equal of senators in judiciousness and consummate
prudence, and early on he undertook the most important diplomatic assignments, for which his qualification was not age, to be
sure, but excellence alone.⁷⁵⁰

While a young man, like a true Peripatetic he had defended    2
Aristotle from calumny (although he suppressed his own name
out of modesty), writing against his teacher Pomponazzi who, in
an attempt that was impious if not insane, had published a book
trying to argue on the basis of Aristotle's teachings that our souls
die along with the body.⁷⁵¹ Next, he applied his talents to religious
texts so diligently that he published a book on the ideal bishop's
responsibilities as defined according to the teachings of Christ.⁷⁵²
And, in the midst of his political career, he published a volume
that proved an honor and a tribute to both him and his fatherland,
*On the Venetian Republic*,⁷⁵³ to transmit to posterity the ancient,
customary laws of the city-state regarding the bestowal of honors.

Lastly, Pope Paul, who easily surpassed his predecessors in the    3
majestic strength of his noble good judgment, chose him for the
college of cardinals — something he wasn't at all expecting — and

in senatum legit purpuraque ornatum in Germaniam legatum misit, ut diris quorundam animis concepta Lutheri factio salubri adducto dogmate sanaretur.[82]

4    Sed post eam rem, casso labore semper actitatam, quum in Urbem rediisset, legatus Bononiae creatus est; in eoque munere paucos post menses, nondum sexagenarius, rapida febre interiit. Sepulchrum eius lateritii operis, in aede Divi Proculi ad levam, cum hoc carmine conspicitur:

5               *Marci Antonii Flaminii*

Contarene, tuo docuisti, magne, libello
    extinctis animas vivere corporibus.
Ergo iure tui vivunt monimenta libelli,
    et vivent saeclis innumerabilibus.

6                   *Eiusdem*

Descripsit ille maximus quondam Plato
longis suorum ambagibus voluminum
quis civitatis optimus foret status.
Sed hunc ab ipsa saeculorum origine
nec ulla vidit, nec videbit civitas.
At Contarenus optimam rempublicam
parvi libelli disputationibus
illam probavit esse quam millesima
iam cernit aestas Hadriatico in Mari
florere pace, literis, pecunia.

7                 *Iani Vitalis*

Contarene, tibi pietas dum dia parentat,
et queritur longo amissum res publica luctu,
'Ite' ait 'illustres animae, vitalia saecla

sent him in his purple robe as a legate to Germany, in order that
the Lutheran sect, conceived by the terrible minds of certain men,
might be healed through the application of sound doctrine.[754]

But after he had made his case time and again, always in vain, 4
he returned to Rome, where he was appointed legate to Bologna.[755] After a few months in that post he died of a fast-acting
fever, not yet sixty.[756] One sees his brick tomb on the left side of
the Church of San Procolo,[757] with this poem:

### By Marcantonio Flaminio[758]    5

O great Contarini, in your booklet you taught that souls live
on after bodies have been destroyed. Therefore, rightly, your
booklets live on as monuments to you, and will do so for
countless centuries.

### By the Same Author[759]    6

In ancient times, in the long, roundabout course of his writings, the great Plato described what the ideal form of a city-
state would be. But from the beginning of time, no polity
has seen this ideal form, nor will it do so. Yet Contarini,
with the arguments of his small pamphlet, has shown that
that best republic is the one that the thousandth summer
already sees flourishing on the Adriatic Sea in peace, learned
culture, and prosperity.

### By Giano Vitale[760]    7

O Contarini, while godlike Piety makes offerings to you and
the republic bewails its loss with prolonged grieving, it says,
"Go, o illustrious souls, you living generations of heroes:

heroum, et vestro athletae exornate sepulchrum
floribus: hic veris docuit rationibus esse
immortalem animam summa de mente creatam.'

## CI. *Henricus Cornelius Agrippa*

1 Quis in Henrici Cornelii Agrippae sedato vultu portentosum ingenium latuisse crediderit? Hic enim, immenso captu vastaque memoria scientiarum artiumque omnium rationes arcanaque intima
et summos apices complexus, disciplinas convellit, religiones in
dubium revocat studiorumque omnium labores festiva declamatione deridet, eoque vehementius atque validius quod tantae novitatis argumenta sacrarum literarum authoritate confirmentur,
quasi feliciore opere illudentis ingenii tantas opes ostentare nequiverit nisi vir, educatus in literis et a Caesare eruditionis ergo
equestris ordinis dignitate honestatus, importunos arietes inanis
eloquentiae aeternis optimarum literarum arcibus admovisset.

2 Sed ad hoc cum plausu a multis exceptum volumen *De vanitate
scientiarum*, alium addidit librum *De occulta philosophia* curiosis admodum pestilentem, quod opus, ex censura Christiana edicto vetitum, apud unos impios reperitur. Sed in utroque serio pariter et
ioco gravior atque lepidior ac ideo forsitan aeternus appareret, nisi
puriorem eloquentiam non secus ac reliquas facultates infelici vel
inepto iudicio contempsisset.

3 Excessit e vita nondum senex apud Lugdunum ignobili et tene-
broso in diversorio, multis eum tanquam necromantiae suspicione

adorn the sepulcher with flowers for your champion. This man taught with well-founded reasoning that the soul was created immortal out of the supreme mind."

## CI. *Heinrich Cornelius Agrippa* (1486–1535)

Who would have believed that an unnatural genius lurked behind the calm countenance of Heinrich Cornelius Agrippa?[761] Indeed, his boundless intellectual capacity and prodigious memory enabled him to grasp the principles, deepest mysteries, and finest points of all the arts and sciences. But he undermined the fields of learning, called religious beliefs into doubt and, with flippant rhetoric, scorned all learned labors — and all the more ardently and vigorously because, as he claimed, such novel arguments were confirmed by the authority of Scripture, as if a man well-schooled in literature and knighted by the emperor for his erudition couldn't vaunt his talent for mockery in more constructive work unless he had assailed the enduring citadels of the finest learning with monstrous battering rams of empty rhetoric.

But to this volume *On the Vanity of the Sciences*, which was received by many with approbation, is added another, *On Occult Philosophy*, a book exceedingly pernicious to the curious: prohibited by an edict resulting from Christian censorship, the work is found only in the possession of the impious.[762] Even so, he might have shown himself to be both more solemn in serious matters and more charming when jesting, and thereby perhaps have secured lasting fame, had he not through inauspicious or foolish judgment scorned refined eloquence every bit as much as he did other capacities.

He died before reaching old age, in an obscure and gloomy inn in Lyon. Many cursed him as a notorious necromancer, saying that

infamem execrantibus quod cacodaemonem nigri canis specie circumduceret ita ut, quum propinqua morte ad poenitentiam urge-
retur, cani collare loreum magicis per clavorum emblemata inscriptum notis exolverit in haec suprema verba irate prorumpens: 'Abi,
perdita bestia, quae me totum perdidisti!' Nec usquam familiaris
ille canis ac assiduus itinerum omnium comes et tum morientis
domini desertor postea conspectus est, quum praecipiti fugae saltu
in Ararim se immersisse nec enatasse ab his qui id vidisse assere-
bant existimetur.

4                    *Ioannis Baptistae Possevini*

Vivens quem cernis, ne te fortasse moretur
    os placidum, Stygii rex fuit iste lacus.
Quare etiam custodem habuit dum viveret Orci,
    cui nunc in tenebris praeda datus,[83] comitem.
Ast hic si ingenium moderari scisset, ad auras
    tantum isset quantum Tartara nigra subit.


## CII. Baptista Pius

1  Non erit ullo saeculo agrestibus praesertim grammaticis ingratum
   Pii nomen, urbanis autem et elegantibus viris unquam iniucun-
   dum. Robusto enim ingenio tenacique memoria praevalidus, doctissimi famam meruit quum obscuros authores interpretandos suscepisset, inepta quidem Beroaldi praeceptoris aemulatione, cuius
   in *Asinum* Apuleii commentationes exierant; in iis fuere Fulgentius, Sidonius et e poetis Plautus, Lucretius et Valerius Flaccus.

he led around an evil spirit in the shape of a black dog.[763] And so, when he was at death's door and was urged to repent, he removed the dog's leather collar, studded with magic incantations, and burst out angrily in these final words: "Away, damned beast, you've been my complete undoing!" Then the dog, who had been his familiar[764] and a constant companion in all his travels, deserted his dying master and was not seen anywhere thereafter: those who claimed to be eyewitnesses said it had leaped headlong into the Saône River and never swam to safety.[765]

By Giovan Battista Possevino[766]

4

Lest perhaps the friendly, animated face should give you pause: this wretch whom you see ruled over the Stygian lake. While he lived, he had as his sidekick hell's guardian, to whom now, among the shades, he is given as prey. But had he known how to keep his genius within bounds, he would have ascended as far into heaven as he now sinks low into black Tartarus.

## CII. Battista Pio (1460–1543)

In no age will the name of Pio[767] be unappreciated, especially among backwoods schoolteachers; but to sophisticated and elegant men it will always be distasteful. Endowed with a powerful intellect and a retentive memory, he earned the reputation of being exceedingly learned when, in an ill-conceived attempt to rival his teacher, Beroaldo (who'd published a commentary on Apuleius's *Golden Ass*), he undertook to interpret challenging writers such as Fulgentius, Sidonius, and the poets Plautus, Lucretius, and Valerius Flaccus.[768]

1

2      Exoleta enim rancidae vetustatis vocabula delectu insano sectabatur, admirante quidem discipulorum inscia turba, quum plane
a non insulsissimis rideretur. Si quidem eius sermo stylusque
Oscorum et Aboriginum linguam pingui atque aspera novitate re-
ferebant, quam nonnulli lascive ludentes discere percuperent nisi
contagiosi vitii periculo terrerentur, factum autem brevi est ut ea
obsoletae et ridendae passim elocutionis verba tanquam portenta
in scoenam transierint, confecta scilicet a lepidis ingeniis mirabili
fabula. Haec enim impressa extat qua suo habitu suoque idiomate
blaterantis[84] Pii persona inducitur, ab obiurgante reprehendente-
que Prisciano meritas flagello plagas, puerorum malediscentium
more, clunibus nudatis excipiens. Tum enim Phaedrus ad antiquae
pronunciationis decus Romanam iuventutem glorioso studio revocabat, quum ludis Capitolinis stupendo apparatu miraque felicitate
Plauti *Penulum* per ingenuos nobilesque comoedos repraesentata
florentis quondam Urbis fortuna edidisset, id expetente Leone
quod tum frater Iulianus a populo Romano civitate donaretur.

3      Caeterum Pius quadrato ingenio eos nasutorum rumores contempsit, sua conscientia profecto felix quod neminem se videre
diceret eruditi nomine dignum qui, de vi et tota facultate vel abstrusae lectionis interrogatus, praeclare et constanter prolato praesentis doctrinae thesauro minime responderet: id enim ipse vegeta
rerum omnium et in sene quidem admirabili recordatione tam
probe quam superbe praestare erat solitus. Sed vel sero ita explosi
styli vitium agnovit ut se totum ad Ciceronem reciperet et multa
in eo elucidando commentaretur.

4      Eum postremo, quum Bononiae, Mediolani et Lucae per quin-
quaginta annos docuisset, Paulus Pontifex tanquam veterem suum

He chased down obsolete words in a mad preference for the old    2
and musty, much to the admiration of the witless horde of his
students, but to the open ridicule of those who were not utter
fools. Strangely clumsy and coarse, his speech and writing recalled
the languages of the Oscans and Aborigines,[769] which some might
be eager to learn just for fun were they not afraid of contamina-
tion. Soon, however, these outmoded, often laughable expressions
found their way like freaks onto the stage, in a wondrous drama
composed by really clever talents. In fact, we have this in print: a
character based on Pio is introduced, dressed like him, blathering
in his idiom and, in the way of dimwitted schoolboys, receiving on
his bared buttocks a richly deserved whipping from a scolding and
reproving Priscian. This was in fact at the time when Fedra,[770]
with boastful zeal, was recalling the Roman youth to the glory of
ancient speech, since he had staged Plautus's *Poenulus* at a ceremony on the Capitoline with breathtaking display and wondrous
success, using well-known Roman actors, thus recalling the city's
vanished splendor. Leo commissioned the production because his
brother Giuliano was then being invested with citizenship by the
Roman people.[771]

But Pio in his self-assurance ignored the opinions of such sati-    3
rists, because, as he complacently said, he considered nobody worthy to be called "learned" who, upon being asked about the force
and full meaning of even an abstruse recitation, could not answer
very clearly and resolutely by quoting from the storehouse of erudition he had at his fingertips. For he himself, with a vivid, all-
embracing memory truly wondrous in an old man, was accustomed to do so both perfectly and pridefully. Only too late,
however, did he recognize the defects of his much-discredited style
and give himself over completely to Cicero, writing much on him
by way of commentary.

In the end, after fifty years spent teaching in Bologna, Milan,    4
and Lucca, Pope Paul invited him (as an old member of his

familiarem in Urbem accivit, publicoque in munere defunctus est octogenarius, summa temperaturae firmitate adversus morbos invictus. Contigit ei subitae ac inexpectatae mortis lenissimum genus quo divinus Plato felix fuisse iudicatur. Pransus enim hylariter et remota mensae mappa subinde lectitans Galeni librum in quo de signis propinquae mortis agitur, depraehendit fatales in unguibus maculas et dixit: 'Ergo saeva Parca instans vitae meae filum commordet.' Nec multo post, nullo acri clementis utique mortis impetu concussus, in complexu Probi Privernatis poetae leniter expiravit. Tumulatus est in templo Divi Eustachii his carminibus honestatus:

5

*Leonardi Marsi*

Ingenio tentasse Pius se se omnia cernens
   'Nunc repeto' dixit 'sydera; terra, vale.'

6

*Antonii Vaccae*

Felsina quem genuit, studiis consumptus et annis,
   ille poeta Pius, bibliotheca loquens,
hic situs est, quicum[85] priscae omnis gratia linguae
   et Plauti veteres interiere sales.


## CIII. *Franciscus Arsillus*

1  Franciscus Arsillus e Senogallia per triginta annos, alternante ingenii libidine, Aesculapio filio patrique Apollini sacra fecit, quum medicinam uti popularis et pedestris ordinis medicus ad alimenta vitae passim exerceret, et quotidiana fere carminum foetura

household) to Rome. While holding a public office there, he passed away in his eighties, his sturdy constitution having long been proof against all diseases.[772] There befell him the very gentle sort of sudden and unexpected death that the divine Plato is thought to have been so fortunate as to have undergone. After he had enjoyed lunch and the table had been cleared, as he was reading a book of Galen that details the signs of approaching death, he immediately recognized lethal stains on his fingernails, and said: "Thus Cruel Fate, drawing near, bites off the thread of my life." Not long thereafter, without any acute shock from a demise that was certainly kind, he gently breathed his last in the arms of the poet Probo da Piperno.[773] He was buried in the Church of Sant' Eustachio, honored with these verses:

*By Leonardo Marso*[774]                                          5

Pio, seeing that he had applied his mind to all things, said "Now, I return to the stars. Farewell, Earth!"

*By Antonio Vacca*[775]                                          6

Here lies the famous poet Pio, used up by studies and age, the walking dictionary whom Bologna brought forth. Along with him, there perished all the gracefulness of a bygone idiom and the ancient jests of Plautus.

## CIII. *Francesco Arsilli (ca. 1470–1540+)*

Francesco Arsilli[776] of Senigallia spent thirty years alternately propitiating Aesculapius and Apollo (son and father, respectively), making a living by serving the common people as a traveling physician, while delighting in producing poems almost daily. Being by          1

laetaretur. Natura enim frugi et aureae libertatis custos, Vaticanam
aulam et potentium limina contumaci quadam superbia devitabat.

2  Scripsit apposito carmine ad praescriptum proloquia Hippocratis, et lepidum item libellum *De poetis Urbanis*, mihi tanquam veteri
sodali dedicatum quum, Leone ingeniis liberaliter arridente multi
undique poetae illustres nequaquam ad inanes spes in Urbem
confluxissent et pulcherrimo quodam certamine a singulis in una
tantum statuae materia scriberetur; qua carminum farragine Cori-
tius homo Trevir humani iuris libellis praepositus uti perhumanus
poetarum hospes ac admirator inclaruit, ea scilicet statua insigni
marmorea Aureliano in templo dedicata invitatisque vatibus ut tria
numina, Christi Dei et Matris ac Aviae, uno in signo celebrarent.

3  Sed Arsillus, qui se se artis praesidio adversus morborum
contumeliam praemuniens vitam satis extenderat, intercute morbo
oppressus septuagesimum aetatis annum superare non potuit.

4  *Iani Vitalis*

Carminibus nostros celebrasti, Arsylle, poetas
    qualia dictarunt Phoebus et Aonides.
Nos memores grati officii tibi serta dicamus
    myrthea Pyrmillae munera grata tuae,
optamusque tibi sedes ubi sancta piorum
    Elysios inter dicitur esse cohors.

5  *Honorati Fasitelii*

Ergo videmus lumine hoc spirabili
    cassum iacere te quoque,
ut plebe quivis unus e vili iacet?
    Arsille, magno Apollini

nature temperate and protective of his treasured freedom, with a certain stubborn pride he kept clear of the Vatican court and the doorways of the powerful.[777]

He wrote on the principles of Hippocrates, with a poem added   2 to the introduction, and a charming little book *On Roman Poets*, dedicated to me as his old colleague in the academies.[778] At that time, when Leo was generously smiling upon the talented, many illustrious poets from everywhere had flocked to Rome, full of well-founded hopes. Then there was a splendid contest in which everyone wrote on the subject of just one statue. Having dedicated that distinguished marble in the Church of Sant' Agostino, Goritz, a man from Trier who managed the records of supplications[779] and who had gained renown as a most generous host and an admirer of poets, invited them to celebrate with a hodgepodge of verses the three divine presences in that one sculpture: those of Christ, his mother, and her mother.[780]

But Arsilli who, by fortifying himself through his art against   3 the assault of disease, had prolonged his life substantially, succumbed to dropsy before he could complete his seventieth year.

### By Giano Vitale[781]   4

Arsilli, you've honored our poets with verses of the kind that Apollo and the Muses frequently composed. Mindful of your much-appreciated service, we dedicate to your Pirmilla[782] garlands of myrtle leaves as offerings of thanks and pray that you have a place in the Elysian Fields, where the holy retinue of the pious is said to dwell.

### By Onorato Fascitelli[783]   5

So do we see that you too lie dead, cut off from the light of inspiration, lying here just like anybody from the lowly rabble? You, Arsilli, who were dear to great Apollo and the nine

novemque Musis care, sive poculis
    praesentibus morbi graves
essent levandi, sive dulci carmine
    dicenda mater aurea
cupidinum lususque furtorum leves?
    O vota nostra inania!
Quid dura Fati non potest necessitas?
    I, da[86] lyram mihi, puer,
manuque funde proniore Coecubum.
    Nunc sunt Lyaei munera,
nunc plectra cordi, nunc iuvat lectissimo
    cinxisse flore tempora:
Sicci, tenebris obsiti tristi in Styge,
    fortasse cras silebimus.

## CIV. Molsa

1  Marius Molsa Mutinensis, eximium atque habile ad poeticam
ingenium a natura consecutus, Latinis elegis et Ethruscis rhythmis
pari gratia ludendo Musas exercuit, tanta quidem omnium commendatione ut per triginta annos, qui Romae Mecoenatis nomen
tulere insigni liberalitate studioque adiutum adipiscendis honoribus efferre contenderint—praegravante semper eius genio quum,
redivivis toties amoribus occupatus, par ingenio studium subtrahe-
ret neque habitu vel incessu ullove nobili commertio carminum
famam tueretur. Foede prodigus honestique nescius pudoris, ne-
glectum rerum omnium ad innoxiae libertatis nomen revocabat,
usque adeo supine ut summae laudis et clarioris fortunae certissi-
mam spem facile corruperit.

Muses, whether dire illnesses needed treatment with effective potions or the golden mother of desires had to be sung in sweet verse along with the trifling games of furtive loves? Alas, prayers that we make for naught! Are there no limits to the harsh power of inevitable death? Come, boy, give me the lyre and pour the Caecuban wine with a more generous hand. Now, honors are due Dionysus; now, we wish to sing and play the lyre; now, it's pleasing to crown our heads with the choicest flowers. Perhaps tomorrow, when we're shriveled up, obscured by darkness in the gloomy Styx, we will be silent.

## CIV. [Mario] Molza (1489–1544)

Endowed by nature with an extraordinary mind well-suited for poetry, Mario Molza[784] of Modena cultivated the Muses, finding equal favor whether he dabbled in Latin elegies or Tuscan meters. In fact, so greatly was he esteemed by all that for thirty years those in Rome who were renowned Maecenases lavishly and zealously assisted him, competing to garner him honors. But his temperament always got in his way: obsessed so often by the renewal of so many love affairs, he shrank from putting in an effort equal to his brilliance, nor did he safeguard the reputation of his poems by either his attire, his bearing, or any honorable interactions. Obscenely lavish and having no regard for gentlemanly modesty, he dismissed his neglect of everything by calling it harmless liberty, doing so with such carelessness that he quickly ruined what had been certain prospects of the highest praise and a more illustrious career.

2    His moribus quum Venerem quam Minervam impensius coleret, ab illa meritum pudendo contactu miserabilis morbi quo periret venenum hausit. Ab hac vero sempiternam ingenii laudem retulit, non a iucundo tantum carmine quo lascivisse videtur, sed
pedestri etiam gravique facundia qua Laurentium Medicem, nefaria libidine antiquis statuis noctu illustria capita detrahentem,
apud Romanos ab ea iniuria dolore percitos accusavit.

3    Ea enim perscripta oratione, Laurentium usque adeo pudore et
metu perennis probri consternatum ferunt ut atroci animo, quo
inustam ignominiae notam novitate facinoris obscuraret, interfi-
ciendi principis amicique singularis immane consilium susceperit,
scilicet ut diis invitis patriae libertas pararetur, vel si cuncta humanae et fraternae simul amicitiae hospitalisque cubiculi sanctissima
iura tollerentur; nec regum omnium salutis interesset, quum eo
uno exemplo omnis vel in arcano vitae securitas expirarit dum ille
alte stertenti, tanquam tyranno, parum nobili si non scelesta manu
vitam eriperet.

4                    *Tryphonis*

Qui lepido veteres aequavit carmine Molsa
  hic iacet, aetatis maximus huius honos.

5                *Franchini Cossentini*

Molsa, iaces. Tua fama viget, tua scripta leguntur.
  Felix qui potuit vivere post obitum.

By this conduct he cultivated Venus more devotedly than he 2
did Minerva. Through sexual contact in service to the former, he
was infected with the miserable disease from which he would die.
Through cultivating Minerva, however, he won deathless glory for
talent expressed not only in the pleasant poetry in which he appears to have indulged, but also in the dignified and eloquent address in which he reprimanded Lorenzino de' Medici who, in the
dark of night and with criminal wantonness, decapitated some
statues of famous ancients. Molza delivered this speech to an audience of Romans who had been much distressed by that outrage.[785]

They say that once that speech was published, Lorenzino was 3
driven so frantic by shame and the fear of lasting disgrace that, in
order to obscure through a new crime the mark of dishonor with
which he'd been branded, with savage wrath he conceived the
monstrous plan of killing a prince who was also his friend.[786] Evidently he did this so that, contrary to God's will, the liberty of his
homeland might be restored, even if it meant violating all the most
sacrosanct laws of civil society, brotherly friendship, and hospitality. Nor had he cared about the safety of rulers in general, since by
this single act, all their impunity from mortal danger, even in private, perished when, with a hand ignoble if not criminal, he took
the life of a man sound asleep because he thought him a tyrant.

### By Trifone[787] 4

Here lies Molza, the adornment of this age, who in charming verse equaled the ancients.

### By Franchino of Cosenza[788] 5

You lie dead, Molza, but your reputation flourishes and your
writings are read. Happy is he who has been able to live on
after death.

*Marci Antonii Flaminii*

Postera dum numeros dulces mirabitur aetas
   sive, Tibulle, tuos sive, Petrarca, tuos,
tu quoque, Molsa, pari semper celebrabere fama,
   vel potius titulo duplice maior eris:
quicquid enim laudis dedit inclyta Musa duobus
   vatibus, hoc uni donat habere tibi.

## CV. Albertus Pighius

1   Magna hercle naturae illudentis inverecundia excellentem doctrinam cum illustri eloquentia coniunctam, si Christiani scriptoris decus spectetur, multa infaceti oris truculentia opertam in Alberto Pighio conspeximus. Is Campo Batavorum vico editus secutusque Adriani Pontificis fortunam, quae ex disciplinis peregre didicerat Latini sermonis elegantia feliciter exornavit, ita ut subtilissimarum scientiarum placita et si quid durum atque difficile ex sacris literis novitate rerum ac nominum scribentibus offertur prudenter ac molliter explicaret. Sed in disserendo vultus Scythico more contusus et enormis et aspero gutture vox educta et graviter resonantis nasi tumultus totam fere sapientiae gloriam deformabant.

2   Admirabili quoque cum ingenii tum manuum argutia excelluit ut pote qui aerea instrumenta deprehendendis syderum cursibus exactissime fabricaret, verum in libro *De hierarchia*, quo veluti acutissimo gladio Lutheri causam iugulavit, fere nemini concessam pietatis et doctrinae laudem adeptus est.

When a future age marvels at pleasant meters—be they yours, Tibullus, or yours, Petrarch—you too, Molza, will be celebrated with equal fame; or rather, you will be made even greater by your double distinction: for, all the praise the glorious Muse gave to those two bards, she bestows upon you alone.

## CV. Albert Pigge (ca. 1490–1542)

Heaven knows we saw in Albert Pigge[790] Nature's utterly shameless mockery: a union of extraordinary learning with lucid eloquence (provided we focus on his virtues as a Christian writer), but all of it concealed beneath a most ferocious, brutish countenance. Issuing from the Dutch town of Kampen and throwing his lot in with Pope Adrian, so successfully did he use Latin eloquence to refine subjects he had studied abroad that with good sense and ease he unraveled the principles of the most rarefied disciplines and whatever challenges and difficulties are presented to writers by unfamiliar things and names in the Scriptures. But when speaking publicly his face, flat like a Scythian's, his grotesquely harsh and throaty voice, and his resonant snorts pretty much disfigured the whole appeal of his wisdom.

He stood out as well for his remarkable nimbleness of both mind and hand, building exceedingly precise bronze instruments for tracking the movements of the stars, while with his book *On the Hierarchy*, with which he slit the throat of Luther's cause as with the sharpest sword, his piety and learning won honors such as almost no one had been granted.[791]

3     Quum id volumen commentaretur ut direptam ab impiis sacro-
sanctae potestatis haereditatem Romano Pontifici assereret, eum e
summo vitae periculo certissimum Dei maximi numen eripuit:
Bononiae enim in celeberrima pompa, quum transeunte coronato
Caesare Carolo Quinto pars lignei pontis iuxta Caesarem turbae
pondere corruisset, Albertus tignorum atque hominum ruina ita
oppressus est ut probitatis ac instituti operis merito servaretur.
Obiit nondum senex in patrio solo, sacerdotiis a Clemente et
Paulo liberaliter honestatus.

4                             *Myrtei*

Qui extrema Batavum profectus ora,
non bello ore, animo sed omniumque
praeclarus studio scientiarum,
pro republica et optima Quiritum
sede acer stetit hostis in Lutherum,
Albertus iacet hic. Sacrum sepulchro
da thus, maxime pontifex, et undam.

## CVI. *Benedictus Iovius Novocomensis*

1 Quo iusto nomine te appellem, Benedicte Iovi, qua satis digna
cum laude te prosequar vix scio. Amore si quidem naturaque germanus frater, summo charitatis officio pater optimus, moderatus
educator et diligens in literis magister extitisti, ut erga me, orba-
tum patre nec adhuc pubescentem, omne munus perfectae virtutis
adimpleres.

2     Sed haec alii fratribus fortasse plenius praestiterunt; tu certe,
quod ad spem immortalitatis pertinet, quum patriam historiam

While at work on that volume in defense of the Roman Pon- 3
tiff's hereditary claim to sacrosanct power, which the impious had
torn asunder, a crystal clear manifestation of the will of the Most-
High God rescued him from a most grave danger to his life. For, at
a thronged procession in Bologna, as the newly crowned Emperor
Charles V was crossing over a wooden bridge, a section of it next
to him collapsed under the weight of the crowd, and Albert was so
completely buried under fallen timbers and men that he could
only have been spared on account of his probity and the work he
had set about. He died on his native soil, not yet an old man, having been generously endowed with benefices by Clement and Paul.

### By Mirteo[792]     4

Having come all the way from farthest Holland, unattractive
in appearance but renowned for his intellect and expertise in
every discipline, here lies Albert, who as an advocate of the
state and of the holy Roman see fiercely took a stand against
Luther. O supreme pontiff, sprinkle holy incense and water
on his grave.

## CVI. Benedetto Giovio of Como (1471–1545)

I hardly know, Benedetto Giovio,[793] by what name I ought to ad- 1
dress you, with what praise I may adequately describe you. For
you proved to be my brother in affection as well as by birth; the
finest of fathers in that most important of duties, charity; and a
judicious guardian and an attentive literary tutor. Thus you fulfilled every obligation of perfect virtue toward me, who had been
rendered fatherless while still a child.

Others, perhaps, have more abundantly provided these things 2
for their brothers, but when it comes to the hope of eternal fame,

atque item res gestas et mores Helvetiorum eleganter perscriberes, ingenium meum veri gloriosique itineris monstrator aemulatione domestica succendisti, scilicet ut nostrorum temporum historiam cogniti orbis res gestas complectentem exordiri atque perficere posse, te demum admirante, feliciter auderemus.

3    Verum haec una erit tua peculiaris Christianae modestiae laus: quod frugi contentus vita ex nobili coniugio Ioviam familiam, vetustate quam fortunis clariorem, praeclara sobole amplificasti; supra id etiam felix, quod ambitiose patria nunquam pedem extuleris, nisi ut Mediolani Demetrium Graece profitentem pronunciationis causa audires qui eam linguam nullo praeeunte magistro didiceras, indeque perpetua vitae innocentia ac animi tranquillitate aequatus summis philosophis ad tertium et septuagesimum aetatis annum perveneris, nihil morbis corpore affecto vegetaque semper illa incredibili rerum et nominum memoria, et integro intentoque ardentis ingenii vigore quo dudum centum epistolas gravissimae eruditionis posteris dedicasti. Sed haec et Graecae traductionis non ignobilia opera cum lepidis poematibus eruditorum liberorum diligentia publicabit.

4    Ego vero te, quanquam ex merita pietate haud dubie coelesti felicitate beatum, frustra singulis horis cum fletu requiram, et eo quidem gravius atque molestius, quo instantis senectutis sperata solatia fato tuo mihi erepta satis dolere non possim, nisi tibi malorum finem et perennis boni vel sero partam possessionem impie aut impudenter invideam.

you showed the way of truth and glory with your elegantly written history of our homeland and your account of the deeds and customs of the Swiss, igniting in me the desire to emulate a kinsman.[794] Thus I was happily encouraged to begin, and with your admiration ultimately found the means to complete, a history of our times that encompasses what has happened in the known world.

But one glory of Christian propriety will be uniquely yours: that, satisfied with a temperate life, you enlarged the Giovio family, which is known for its ancient name more than for its fortunes, producing splendid children from a noble marriage. You were even more blessed in that you never were eager to set foot outside our homeland, except when for the sake of your pronunciation of Greek you traveled to hear Demetrius lecture in Milan, since you had learned that language without benefit of any tutoring. And having thus equaled the greatest philosophers in your consistently blameless life and tranquility of mind, you lived to your seventy-third year — your body not in the least impaired by disease, your memory for facts and names still vivid, and your incandescent mind's vigor intact and focused — lately dedicating to your progeny a hundred profoundly erudite letters. But it will be up to your learned children to publish these as well as your translations from Greek, which do not lack distinction, along with your charming poems.

Although you undoubtedly enjoy the blessings of heaven that your devotion has merited, yet every single hour I will tearfully look for you, in vain — and my sorrow and affliction are all the greater because I cannot adequately lament the hoped-for consolations of my imminent old age, taken from me by your death, without faithlessly and shamelessly begrudging you the end of your sufferings and your long-awaited attainment of the good that lasts forever.

5    Elatus est nobilium iuvenum humeris tumulatusque in templo
maximo, qui honos nemini adhuc nisi sacrato viro Comi contigit.


6              *Ioannis Baptistae Possevini Mantuani*

Claudere musaeum iam Paulus coeperat atque
    extremam chartis imposuisse manum
cum subito exclamat Benedictus: 'Muneris huius
    siccine me expertem, frater, abire sinis?'
'Non datur hoc' Iovius 'viventi' dixit; at ille,
    perpetuum sperans vivere, laetus obit.


7                      *Antonii Seronis*

Quod sis ultima pars Iovi libelli,
id fratris pietate et arte factum est,
ne vel charior aptiorve imago
olim quam tua iactet ulla se se
signasse hunc lepidissimum libellum.

                    * * *

8   Desiderantur autem a nobis multorum imagines qui praeclara,
quum iampridem obierint, scriptorum testificatione ingeniorum
suorum effigies famae consecrarunt. Frustra enim eas vel diligen-
tissima vestigatione perquisivimus, sic tamen ut minime despere-
mus viros elegantes huic honesto voto humaniter suffragaturos.
Alii enim aut statuas aut picturas publicis aut privatis in locis
ostendent, aut turpiter apud propinquos neglectas aut occultatas
indicabunt. Quid enim in toto nobilis officii genere honestius esse
poterit quam in musaeum, quo publicus virtutis honos ad exem-
plum et voluptatem continetur, exoptatas imagines liberali pietate
contulisse?

                    * * *

He was carried on the shoulders of noble youths and entombed    5
in the cathedral, an honor which until then had been accorded to
no layman in Como.

### By Giovanni Battista Possevino of Mantua[795]    6

Paolo was already completing the museum and had begun to
put the finishing touches on the inscriptions when suddenly
Benedetto exclaimed, "Brother, are you going to let me die
thus, without this tribute?" "This is not conceded to the living," said Giovio; whereupon that man rejoiced to die in the
hope of eternal life.

### By Antonio Serone[796]    7

Through your brother Giovio's faithfulness and craftsman-
ship, it's come about that you are the final chapter in his
book, allowing no other likeness one day to boast that, being
either dearer or more appropriate than yours, it has set the
seal on this most charming little text.

\* \* \*

Unfortunately, I don't have the likenesses of many who, though    8
long dead, have bequeathed to fame portraits of their talents by
the illustrious evidence of their writings. In fact, my assiduous
searching for them has been in vain; but I'm not about to give up
hope that men of refinement will generously rally to this worthy
cause. Some will draw my attention to statues or paintings in public or private locales, or will disclose ones that their kinsmen, to
their shame, have disregarded or hidden away. For of all the noble
obligations, what could be more honorable than with high-minded
liberality to have donated portraits that I so desire to a museum
where the public acknowledgment of excellence is contained for
instruction and for pleasure?

\* \* \*

## CVII. *Maphei Vegii Laudensis*

1 Qui, heroico spiritu Maronem feliciter aemulatus quum *Aeneidem* addito libro supplevisset, omnes fere a mille annis illustres poetas, nec excepto quidem Petrarca laureato, praeclara cum laude superavit. Sed gravioris quoque doctrinae et summae prudentiae opinione Martini Pontificis amicitiam consecutus, in conferendis sacerdotiis supplicium libellorum officio praefuit, ita ut mox Eugenio et Nicolao carissimus fuerit.

2 Extat et eius iucundus nobilisque dialogus de praestantia disceptantium terrae, solis et auri; et, ne quid ad cumulatam eruditionem vero Christiano deesset, quaedam etiam in sacris literis sincerae interpraetationis glossemata reliquit aureumque praesertim libellum de rebus antiquis memorabilibus Basilicae Sancti Petri, in quo donaria sepulchraque pontificum referuntur.

3                    *Iacobi Guidii Volaterrani*

Felix dum studet addito libello
Aeneam Vegius referre ad astra,
illustres alios it ante vates
asserta sibi gloria Maronis.

## CVIII. *Ioannis Tortelii*

1 Qui Aretii natus ingenium omnibus fere disciplinis excultum Romam attulit meruitque inde ut ab optimo pontifice Nicolao intra

## CVII. *Maffeo Vegio of Lodi (1406/7–58)*

Having written his supplement to the *Aeneid*, in its epic spirit a     1
fitting imitation of Vergil's, Vegio[797] outshone in praise the famous
poets of nearly a millennium, not to exclude even our poet-laureate
Petrarch. But his reputation for deep learning and exceeding discretion won him the affection of Pope Martin and superinten-
dency of petitions for the conferral of benefices, and he performed
in such a way that he was later invaluable to Eugenius and Nicholas.[798]

We have also his delightful and respected dialogue in which the     2
Earth, the sun, and gold dispute which among them is preeminent;[799] and, lest anything be lacking to complete the true Christian's learning, he also left a reliable glossary of unfamiliar terms
found in holy writ, and most importantly, a splendid little book
about notable antiquities in Saint Peter's Basilica, recording its al-
tars and papal tombs.

### By Jacopo Guidi of Volterra[800]     3

Since Vegio by adding a book succeeds in his aim of carrying
Aeneas to the stars, he surpasses other poets of renown, and
makes Vergil's glory his own.

## CVIII. *Giovanni Tortelli (ca. 1400–1466)*

Born in Arezzo, Giovanni Tortelli[801] brought to Rome a mind     1
trained in nearly all fields of knowledge, and on that basis he was
summoned by that best of popes, Nicholas, to take part in admin-

cubiculum curarum et consiliorum particeps et sacrorum studiorum adminiculator asciceretur. Suavitate enim sermonis hylarique
modestia aequales antecessit, inter quos pudenda simultas insanis
altercationibus excitata omnem literatae dignitatis existimationem
foedissime convellebat.

2    Sed Tortelius exacti grammatici laude contentus fuit, edito
nobili aeternoque volumine *De potestate literarum,* quo maximum
renascenti eloquentiae lumen adfulsisse videmus. Divi quoque
Athanasii vitam Eugenio expetenti Latinam fecit. Sed quid maius
Tortelio in toto genere laudum tribui non inepte potest, quando
eum Valla disertissimus omnium grammaticus tanquam summum
censorem sibi delegerit?

## CIX. Bartholomei Facii

1    Hunc Spedia, intimum Lunensi in portu Lyguriae oppidum, protulit utriusque linguae peritia insignem, sed certe clariorem si Ge-
nuensium victorias de Veneto hoste navalibus praeliis partas incor-
rupto iudicio perscripsisset. Nam Valla, quanquam suspectus
hostis et irrisor, nihil eum aequa prudentia, nihil ex lege conscribendae historiae dum illa conderet perpendisse testatur.

2    Sed Alfonsus Rex, verae gloriae cupidus, eum ideo liberali stipendio conduxerat ut res suae bello gestae, quae erant absoluto
scriptore dignissimae, posterorum memoriae mandarentur. Eo nomine, quanquam in diversa materia, Vallae aemulus factus, obtrectatione laudis peracrem virum ita pupugit ut talionis immortali
vulnere facile suscepto clarior evaserit — alioqui secundam famam

istration and deliberations, and to assist him in his sacred studies.[802] Indeed, in his sweet conversation and cheerful modesty
Tortelli surpassed his contemporaries, among whom shameful rivalry, fueled by violent altercations, disgracefully degraded the
dignity of all intellectual accomplishment.

But Tortelli was content with esteem as an exacting philologist, 2
publishing a respected and enduring book *On the Power of Letters* in
which we see him shine the brightest light on the rebirth of eloquence.[803] At the request of Eugenius he also translated into Latin
a life of St. Athanasius.[804] But what greater tribute could fittingly
be paid to Tortelli than that Valla, the most eloquent philologist of
all, chose him to be his most authoritative critic?[805]

## CIX. Bartolomeo Facio (no later than 1410–57)

Facio[806] came from La Spezia, the innermost town in the harbor 1
of Luni in Liguria. A noted expert in Latin and Greek, he would
surely have been more famous had his lengthy accounts of Genoa's
naval victories over its Venetian foe been impartial.[807] For Valla,
admittedly suspect as his enemy and maligner, attests that in composing this work Facio weighed nothing in an unbiased manner or
in accordance with the standards of writing history.

Now King Alfonso, in his eagerness for real glory, had hired 2
Facio with a generous stipend to document for future generations
his own military exploits, which richly merited treatment by an
impartial author for the benefit of future generations.[808] For this
reason he became Valla's rival, even though they were writing on
different subjects.[809] By disparaging his fame, Facio goaded the
short-tempered Valla to retaliate. The lasting wound that Valla
easily inflicted upon him actually enhanced Facio's reputation. He

meritus, quum Arrianum de rebus ab Alexandro Magno gestis e Graeco Latine loquentem edidisset.

3    Subsecutus est propere hostem Vallam, pari ac importuna Fatorum iniuria elegantioribus studiis ereptum, ita ut non infacete hoc carmen epitaphio subscribendum ederetur:

> Ne vel in Elysiis sine vindice Valla susurret,
> Facius haud multos post obit ipse dies.

## CX. *Guarini Veronensis*

Ab hoc insigni viro Graecae Latinaeque literae obscuris illis temporibus antiqui saeculi normam quadrataeque structurae ordinem et diu quaesitum decus receperunt. Huius quoque immortali beneficio Strabonem ferme totum legimus atque item aliquot Plutarchi *Vitas* in Latinum accurate conversas. Haec parta laus manavit ad filium qui, tali haereditate peculiariter honestatus, aemulatione patris quum iisdem studiis operam dedisset, rem utique et familiae nominis dignitatem diligenter adauxit.

## CXI. *Petri Pauli Vergerii*

Is Iustinopoli in Histria natus Chrysoloraeque discipulus Graecas literas ex purissimo fonte haustas illustribus discipulis humanissime refudit ut, inductis passim eius linguae rivulis, Italiam plane sitientem irrigaret. Latine autem scribendi singularis eo saeculo

did, however, merit the favorable notice he got for another work, his translation of Arrian's *Anabasis of Alexander* from Greek into Latin.[810]

He quickly went the way of his enemy Valla, torn from more learned pursuits by the same harsh blow of the Fates, so that these verses, composed to be added to his epitaph, are not without a certain humor:[811]

> Lest even in the Elysian Fields Valla should mutter something unchallenged, Facio himself died not many days after him.

## CX. *Guarino of Verona (1374–1460)*

From this illustrious man,[812] Greek and Latin letters in those dark ages recovered their ancient pattern, their well-ordered structure, and the splendor which had long been sought for them. Thanks, too, to his undying generosity we have nearly all of Strabo, and also several of Plutarch's *Lives* rendered meticulously into Latin.[813] The glory he had acquired descended to his son: singularly honored by such an inheritance, and having emulated his father by working in the same field, he industriously increased his family's livelihood as well as its dignity.

## CXI. *Pierpaolo Vergerio (ca. 1369–1444)*

A native of Capodistria and a pupil of Chrysoloras, this man[814] graciously poured out for his noble students drafts of Greek learning from the very purest spring, admitting here and there small streams of that language to water Italy, which plainly was thirsting for it. But his skill in writing Latin stood out as remarkable for

facultas enituit, uti apparet ex eo libello qui de educandis liberis ad exactam disciplinam peramoene atque prudenter scriptus, me puero, in scholis legebatur.

## CXII. Iacobi Bracellii Lyguris

Praeclaro huius exemplo liquidissime constat non esse usque adeo dura atque aspera Lygurum ingenia, quum a quibusdam damnatae eius terrae glabris cautibus assimilentur, ut non facile Musarum cultura molliantur. Scripsit enim Alfonsi Regis res bello gestas omnium scriptorum collatione qui nuper antecesserint longe gravissime, si eius saeculi nondum perpolitam eloquentiam cum ea conferamus quae demum inducta subtiliore antiquorum imitatione candidior evaserit.

## CXIII. Georgii Vallae Placentini

Qui disciplinas literasque omnes uno ingenti volumine complexus multa potius didicisse quam in eo celeri transcursu perdiscenda posteris reliquisse videtur, quandoquidem coacervantis omnia indefesseque scribentis requisitus ille Romanae elocutionis spiritus omnino defuerit quo uno voluminum vita praeclare alitur longissimeque producitur.

that era, as one may see from that little book on the education of children, very pleasingly and sensibly written for the purpose of accurate instruction, that was read in the schools when I was a boy.[815]

## CXII. Giacomo Bracelli the Ligurian (1390–1466+)

The distinguished example of this man[816] makes it abundantly clear that even though some have likened the nature of the Ligurians to the stark cliffs of that godforsaken land, it is not so coarse and harsh that the cultivation of the Muses cannot easily temper it.[817] In his history of King Alfonso's military exploits, Bracelli wrote far more magisterially than all the authors just before him — if, that is, we compare the unpolished style of his era with the eloquence that became purer, once a more sophisticated imitation of the ancients had at last been introduced.[818]

## CXIII. Giorgio Valla of Piacenza (1447–1500)

This man,[819] who embraced all fields of learning and letters in one massive tome, appears in that hurried, cursory treatment to have acquired knowledge about many things rather than to have bequeathed them to posterity to be mastered.[820] For he entirely lacked that spirit of Latin eloquence, a requirement of anyone who accumulates indiscriminately and writes tirelessly, for by this alone the life of books is splendidly nurtured and greatly prolonged.

## CXIV. Ioannis Simonetae

Hic Francisci Sfortiae res gestas, elocutione texturaque operis C. Caesarem alludendo imitatus, Latine perscripsit. Is demum liber, ut diffusius in castrisque praesertim a militibus legeretur, a Landino in Ethruscum sermonem conversus est. Erat Ioanni germanus frater Cichus, ille in Brutiis natus, qui Galeatio a coniuratis interfecto, quum pupilli incorrupta fide tutelam suscepisset, nefaria ambitione Ludovici patrui captus damnatusque fatalis constantiae suae abscissis cervicibus poenam subiit; mitiore aliquanto fortuna erga Ioannem quum in eadem quaestionis acerbitate diu tortus evaserit, valido scilicet apud tyrannum pudore, ne videretur ingrate sublatus, qui patrem summae virtutis principem, ne unquam interiret, beneficio literarum immortalem effecisset.

## CXV. Bernardi Iustiniani Veneti

Hic a prima patriae nascentis origine historiam scribere orsus, quod susceperat grave munus elegantissime perfecit ita ut eum nobili gloria dignum existimemus, quum patritius eruditoque patre genitus quod patriae debebat egregie cumulateque persolverit.

## CXIV. Giovanni Simonetta (ca. 1420–92)

This man[821] wrote a full account in Latin of Francesco Sforza's deeds in which, for his own diversion, he imitated Julius Caesar in the style and structure of his work.[822] In order that the book might be read widely, and especially by soldiers preparing strategies, Landino then translated it into the Tuscan dialect.[823] Giovanni was the brother of Cicco, who was born at the toe of the Italian peninsula.[824] After Galeazzo[825] had been killed in a conspiracy, Cicco, out of unshaken loyalty, became the guardian of his orphaned son.[826] The nefarious ambition of the boy's uncle, Ludovico, was such that Cicco, for his fatal constancy, was arrested, found guilty, and beheaded. Fortune was somewhat kinder to Giovanni. After being tortured at length in the same cruel interrogation, he was released, evidently because it would have shamed the tyrant to appear so ungrateful as to do away with him: for, to preserve the memory of Ludovico's father, a prince of consummate virtue, Giovanni had rendered him immortal through his writings.[827]

## CXV. Bernardo Giustinian of Venice (1408–89)

Having undertaken the history of his native land from its very beginnings, this man[828] went on to complete that burdensome task with consummate felicity.[829] In my estimation he deserves a glorious reputation since he, a patrician and a scholar's son, satisfied admirably and copiously the debt he owed his homeland.[830]

## CXVI. Christophori Personae Romani

Is, inter divae Balbinae flamines in Aventini montis coenobio prior appellatus, Procopium Latine loquentem fecit, non dubia in Leonardum Aretinum conflata invidia qui, suppresso Graeci authoris nomine, *Gothicam historiam* tanquam e variis scriptoribus decerptam pro sua Iuliano Caesarino Cardinali, qui ad Varnam ab Amurathe caesus periit, nullo pudore nuncuparat.

## CXVII. Gregorii[87] Tiphernatis

Huius doctissimi viri munere reliquam Strabonis partem, quam Guarinus non attigerat, in Latinum splendide traductam legimus. Fama quoque fertur Herodiani historias eius ingenio laboreque fuisse translatas, quasi eas morienti subtraxerit Politianus, vir in literario negocio saepe convictus furti. Sed vix credibile videtur ut vir in omni dicendi facultate opulentissimus, idem atque promptissimus, ex alieni ingenii labore famam probro et calumnia redundantem quaesisse voluerit.

## CXVIII. Raphaelis Volaterrani

Fuit hic vir infinitae prope lectionis, quippe qui disciplinas omnes in acervum coniecerit, utili potius in aliena desidia quam ad explicatae doctrinae decus nobili opere: non multo enim cum sale et

## CXVI. Cristoforo Persona of Rome (1416–85)

This man,[831] called upon to be prior of the monastery of Santa Balbina on the Aventine Hill, translated Procopius into Latin. By so doing, he brought unequivocal disgrace upon Leonardo Bruni: for, in the dedication of his *Gothic History* to that Cardinal Giuliano Cesarini who was killed by Murad at the Battle of Varna, Bruni had concealed the name of the Greek author, shamelessly passing the work off as his own gleanings from many writers.[832]

## CXVII. [Gregorio] Tifernate (1413/14–ca. 1464)

Thanks to the services of this exceedingly learned man, we read in a splendid Latin translation the remaining part of Strabo that Guarino had not touched.[833] Rumor has it that by his brilliance and hard work he also translated the *Histories* of Herodian, and that when he was at death's door, Poliziano, a man often proven guilty of literary theft, made off with them. Yet it scarcely seems credible that a man so well-endowed with every kind of eloquence and so quick-witted would have willingly sought from another's labors a notoriety that would bring disgrace and accusations upon him.

## CXVIII. Raffaele [Maffei] of Volterra (1451–1522)

That the reading of this man was virtually boundless is evidenced by his having tossed together all kinds of learning into a work more conducive to the idleness of others than ennobling to the adornment of scholarly exposition.[834] With little wit and no trap-

sine ornamento Latinae orationis cuncta astricto ordine ita digessit ut alibi quaerenda legentibus indicare videatur. Ea vero quae de principibus aetatis suae scripsit, tanquam timido ore carptim enarrata, rerum superiorum haud dubie fidem elevant ostenduntque ea omnino certa veritatis luce carere quae inter adulationem et metum nec praesentis nec futurae spe laudis intempestive publicantur. Sed multum hercle debemus ingenuo gratuitoque labori, quo hic integritate vitae vir optimus delicatis rerum noscendarum compendia demonstravit, et Procopium de Persico atque Vandalico bello sincere potius quam splendide convertit.

## CXIX. *Antonii Galathei*

Hic e Salentino extremo Italiae angulo perillustris medicus atque philosophus studia quae sectabatur optimis literis expolivit extenditque ingenium usque ad poeticam laudem, ob id a Pontano Hermolaoque gravissime celebratus. Eius extant,[88] praeter Ethrusca carmina et physicae quaestionis subtiles libellos, *Iapigia corographice*[89] *descripta* quae meo iudicio cum antiquis comparanda videtur. Sed tum cum lepore doctus et urbanus apparuit quum, in curatione podagrae leniendo dolori, eius insanabilis morbi encomium festivissime cecinisset.

pings of Latin style, he set out all things so compactly that he seemed to intend for his readers to investigate them elsewhere. The fact that he wrote selectively (as though from timidity) regarding the princes of his age certainly diminishes his credibility about prior matters and shows that things published unseasonably, in sycophancy or fear and not in the hope of either present or future praise, entirely lack the dependable clarity of truth.[835] Still and all, Lord knows, we are deeply indebted to this excellent, wholly virtuous man for the honorable and unremunerated labor by which he showed those dilettantes shortcuts to the acquisition of knowledge and translated (albeit with clarity rather than elegance) Procopius on the Persian and Vandal Wars.

## CXIX. *Antonio Galateo (1444 or 1448–1517)*[836]

By making use of his deep knowledge of the classics, this famous doctor and philosopher from Salento, in the remotest corner of Italy, added luster to the studies he pursued. He enlarged the scope of his talents to include excellence as a poet, for which he was very enthusiastically praised by Pontano and Ermolao.[837] Aside from his Tuscan poems and finely written books of natural science, his chorography of Iapygia stands out: in my estimation it merits comparison with ancient works in that genre.[838] But he displayed refinement and learning seasoned with wit at the time when, in order to alleviate the pain as he was being treated for gout, he lightheartedly delivered an encomium of that incurable disease.[839]

## CXX. *Ludovici Coelii Rodigini*

Huius multa volumina lectionum antiquarum, quum ingentes vigiliarum opes ostentent, plerique admirantur. Sed ea farrago, tanquam ex vetere horreo laboriose affectateque prolata, delicatis lectoribus quoddam subrancidum olere videtur: nullus enim compositi ac illustris styli nervus tanta in compage conspicitur. Sed eum tamen Patavii et Mediolani cum laude vel ob id quod egregiam totius habitus dignitatem attulisset e suggestu docentem audivimus.

## CXXI. *Iacobi Fabri Stapulensis*

1    Ab hoc homunculo genere staturaque perhumili sed ab ardenti ingenio cum optimatibus haud dubie conferendo, totius Galliae iuventus ad cultarum literarum studia alacriter excitata est. Faber enim ingeniorum appellari volebat quum in omni fere doctrinae genere ad docendum aptissimus haberetur. Defuit in eo, dum scriberet, illa Latini sermonis puritas quae diu aut neglecta apud externos aut parum accurate quaesita, non magnopere fervida ingenia delectabat. Scripsit commentarios in astronomicis iuventuti perutiles et scholia in moralem philosophiam perdiscentibus opportuna.

2    Aetate autem confectus quum sacras literas attigisset, a Lutheranae heresis veneno non procul affuit ita[90] ut in ea suspicione senex parum feliciter moreretur.

## CXX. Lodovico Celio[840] of Rovigo (1469–1525)

A good many people admire this man's numerous volumes of notes on ancient texts, supposing that they display vast riches gleaned from prolonged study.[841] To sensitive readers, however, that hodgepodge seems to have a certain foul odor to it, as though it had been brought out with elaborate toil from a musty storehouse.[842] Indeed, in so vast a compilation, one discerns no sinew of a well-ordered, lucid style. Nevertheless, when I heard him teaching from the podium at Padua and Milan, he actually did so commendably, owing to the exceptional dignity of his overall demeanor.[843]

## CXXI. Jacques Lefèvre d'Etaples (ca. 1450/60–1536)

This diminutive man, lowly in parentage and in stature, must undoubtedly be ranked among the best on account of his dazzling brilliance.[844] By him, the youth of all France were incited to embrace eagerly the study of fine literature.[845] He wished to be called a "maker of minds,"[846] inasmuch as he was thought the most skillful teacher of nearly every subject. His Latin writing lacked that stylistic purity that foreigners[847] had for a long time either neglected or attempted superficially, and in which their impetuous minds took little pleasure. He wrote commentaries on astronomy that were highly useful to youth, and scholia convenient for mastering moral philosophy.[848]

But when, enfeebled by age, he turned his attention to theology, he came close to accepting Luther's poisonous beliefs. Consequently, his death, as an old man under suspicion of heresy, was not a happy one.[849]

## CXXII. *Antonii Tilesii Cossentini*[91]

1    Hic, varia tenuique materia et minuto semper lemmate delectatus, non ignobilis poetae nomen tulit, quum in parvis singularis et plane conspicuus esse mallet quam in grandi charactere, veluti unus de populo, in turba tot vatum trita et centies repetita canentium mediocris et obscurus. Descripsit enim lepide et diligenter nonnulla curta poemata inexpectati ac ideo festivi semper argumenti, et in his zonarium *Reticulum* quo sacerdotum serica crumena suspenditur, fictilemque *Lucernam* tantum sibi olei dum Musas coleret exorbentem, et lucentem noctu volucrem *Cicindelam*[92] puerorum lusibus opportunam.

2    Reliquit et tragoediam in qua Danaem, sub *Aurei imbris* nomine, cum multo sententiarum verborumque splendore expressisse iudicatur: ac item breves libellos *De coronis* atque *coloribus* grammaticis, rei novitate gratissimos. At Romae in gymnasio Horatium comiter et tenere professus sacerdotium a Giberto promeruit effugitque cladem Urbis ut in patria non plane senex interiret.

## CXXIII. *Petri Alcyonii*

1    Is quum duarum urbium suppresso nomine se hybridam fateretur diuque in calchographorum officinis corrigendis erroribus menstrua mercede operam navasset, multa observatione ad praecellentem scribendi facultatem pervenit. Sed hic partus honos non

## CXXII. *Antonio Telesio of Cosenza (1482–1534)*

This man,[850] who always delighted in various inconsequential mat-  1
ters and trivial topics, had a reputation as a middling poet. He
chose to be unique and prominent in small things rather than, in
the grand style, to be a mediocre and obscure figure in the throng
of so many bards intoning banalities that have been a hundred
times repeated. With elegance and care he wrote some short poems on unexpected and therefore unfailingly amusing subjects,
such as the mesh bag in which a priest hangs a silken purse from
his waist; the earthenware lamp that consumed so much oil while
he was cultivating the Muses; and the firefly, glowing by night, so
well-suited to boys' games.[851]

He also left us a tragedy called *The Shower of Gold*, in which he  2
is considered to have portrayed Danaë brilliantly in both sentiment and diction; and two brief books, *On Crowns* and *On Grammatical Shadings*, which are much appreciated for the novelty of
their subjects.[852] After having taught Horace at the university in
Rome in a genial and sensitive manner, he gained a benefice from
Giberti.[853] He managed to escape from Rome during the Sack,
and would die in his homeland before having a chance to grow
old.[854]

## CXXIII. *Pietro Alcionio (ca. 1490–1528)*

Although he admitted to being of mixed parentage (without, how-  1
ever, divulging the names of the two cities),[855] and although he
had to work as a reader of proofs in printers' shops, living month
to month for a long time, thanks to his keen attentiveness he attained to outstanding literary skill.[856] Once acquired, however, this

erat in conspectu, quum nulla ex parte ingenuis sed plane plebeis et sordidis moribus foedaretur. Erat enim impudens gulae mancipium ita ut eodem saepe die bis et ter aliena tamen quadra coenitaret; nec in ea foeditate malus omnino medicus, quod domi demum in lecti limine per vomitum ipso crapulae onere levaretur.

2    Quum aliqua ex Aristotele perperam insolenterque vertisset, in eum Sepulveda, vir Hispanus egregie de literis meritus, edito volumine peracuta iacula contorsit non hercle indigna tanti philosophi vulneribus, si vindictae nomine merita poena mulctaretur, tanto quidem eruditorum applausu ut Alcyonius, ignominiae dolore misere consternatus, Hispani hostis libros in tabernis ut concremaret gravi pretio coemere cogeretur.

3    Sed luculento opere de toleranda exilii fortuna ita eruditionis ac eloquentiae famam sustentabat ut ex libro *De gloria* Ciceronis, quem nefaria malignitate aboleverat, multorum iudicio confectum crederetur. In eo enim tanquam vario centone, praeclara excellentis purpurae fila languentibus caeteris coloribus intertexta notabantur.[93]

4    Verum non multo post, confirmatae suspicionis invidiam duabus splendidissimis orationibus peregregie mitigavit, quum in clade Urbis vehementissime invectus in Caesarem populi Romani iniurias et barbarorum immanitatem summa perfecti oratoris eloquentia deplorasset.

worthy quality did not attract notice inasmuch as he was tainted by conduct not in the least gentlemanly, but utterly vulgar and coarse. He was such a shameless slave to gluttony that often, within the space of a day, he cadged meals at two or three different people's tables.[857] But in this disgraceful behavior, he was not entirely a bad doctor: for when at last he was home, he relieved himself of the burden of excessive drink by throwing up at the very edge of his bed.[858]

After he had translated some works of Aristotle incorrectly and 2 in an unconventional manner, Sepúlveda, a Spaniard who has rendered meritorious service to scholarship, published a book hurling needle-sharp darts at him.[859] These were not, Lord knows, unbefitting the injuries done to so great a philosopher, if in the name of vengeance a sufficient punishment could be exacted. Indeed, so great was the approbation of the learned that Alcionio, utterly overwhelmed with chagrin at the disgrace, was compelled to go to great expense to buy up his Spanish enemy's books in all the shops to burn them.[860]

But with a splendid work on enduring the misfortune of exile, 3 he so propped up a reputation for erudition and eloquence that many supposed it confected out of Cicero's book *On Glory*, which he had impiously and spitefully destroyed.[861] For it was discerned that in that motley patchwork, threads of choice purple outshone the other, fainter colors with which they were interwoven.

Soon, however, he distinctly lessened the ill will arising from 4 that well founded suspicion with two surpassingly splendid orations, when he inveighed passionately against the emperor about the Sack of Rome, and then lamented the unjust treatment of the Roman people and the savagery of the barbarians, showing the lofty eloquence of a perfect orator.[862]

## CXXIV. Petri Martyris Angleriae

1 Is est qui, apud Verbanum Cisalpinae Galliae Lacum natus, *Oceaneas decades rerum indicarum* conscripsit, quum in Hispania ascitus in regiam Ferdinando Regi ingenii ac industriae suae operam obtulisset. Nactus enim materiam luculento scriptore dignissimam, id ingenue fideliterque praestitit quod mediocris ingenii vires tulerunt sic ut ingentis et peramoenae occasionis argumentum[94] his praebuisse videatur quibus liberales Musae ad ornate copioseque scribendum facultates amplissimas contulerunt.

2 Extat etiam eius *Legatio* ad Campsonem Gaurum Memphiticum regem, suscepta viriliter integerrimeque descripta, quo vel brevi opere sublatae demum sultanorum tyrannidis et Mamaluchorum equitum, quorum nomen nobis erat obscurius, memoria relinquitur. Sed tum importune decessit quum Ferdinandi Cortesii in altero ad occidentem orbe invento subactoque inusitatae felicitatis victorias scripturus esse videretur.

## CXXV. Gabrielis Altilii

Gabriel Altilius, in Lucania natus, iunioris Ferdinandi Regis praeceptor, usque adeo molliter ac admirande in elegis et heroico carmine excelluit, sicuti ex epithalamio Isabellae Aragoniae perspici potest, ut Pontani atque Actii testimonio antiquis vatibus aequaretur. Is virtutis merito Policastri, ea urbs olim Buxentum fuit, antistes factus, a Musis per quas profecerat celeriter impudenterque discessit, magno hercle ingrati animi piaculo, nisi ad spem non

## CXXIV. Peter Martyr d'Anghiera (1457–1526)

This man[863] was born by Lake Maggiore in northern Italy. Summoned while in Spain to the royal court, and offering his talents and diligent service to King Ferdinand, he wrote the *Decades of the New World*.[864] Hitting upon a subject worthy of a writer of the first order, he applied to it faithfully and conscientiously all that the powers of an ordinary mind possessed, so that it seems he furnished a vast, alluring subject to those richly blessed by the Muses with the amplest resources of eloquent and ornate writing.

There is also his *Legation* to the Egyptian Sultan al-Ashraf Kansu al Ghuri, a mission he manfully undertook, which he described in meticulous detail.[865] This work, albeit brief, furnishes us with a written account of the tyrannical regime of the sultans and the Mamluk knights, at last overthrown, whose reputation was little known to us.[866] But he died at an unseasonable moment, just when he appeared on the verge of writing about the unprecedented successes of Hernán Cortés in that other world in the west that has been discovered and conquered.

## CXXV. Gabriele Altilio (ca. 1440–ca. 1501)

Born in Campania, Gabriele Altilio,[867] the tutor of King Ferdinand the Younger, excelled in smooth and admirable elegiacs and hexameters (as can be seen clearly from his epithalamium for Isabella d'Aragona) to the point that Pontano and Sannazaro ranked him alongside the poets of antiquity.[868] Having deservedly been made bishop of Policastro (once known as Buxentum), he quickly and shamefully abandoned the Muses who had made him successful. Lord knows he would have had to atone mightily for this

iniustae veniae ob id culpa tegeretur, quod ad sacras literas nequaquam ordinis oblitus tempestive confugisset. Mortuus est in sacrata sacerdotii sede sexaginta annis maior tulitque Pontani pietate supremi officii nobile carmen, quod pro titulo urnae marmoreae incideretur.

## CXXVI. Marcelli Virgilii Florentini

Eximia huius fuit in blando vultu cultoque sermone suavitas, et quum e suggestu iuventutem doceret aut in corona loqueretur doctrina multiplex ipsaque varietate mirabilis. Ex eo autem officii munere quod antea Aretini Pogiique fuerat ab epistolis reipublicae operam praestabat et, quum suppeteret ocium, tertio muneri vacare erat solitus. Susceperat enim Dioscoridem omnino traducendum, expetentibus Medicis; petebat enim ex eo labore non obscuram laudem, quod in perdificili herbario negocio ab ineunte aetate accuratissime desudasset. Sed edito opere statim in publicum exierunt duae omnino diversae interpretationes: altera Hermolai quae extincta putabatur, altera Ioannis Ruellii Galli a Latini styli mundiciis multo maxime laudata. Extat etiam nobilis oratio in contione habita quum Laurentio Medici Iuniori militaris imperii insignia traderentur.

ingratitude, were his guilt not concealed: for, mindful of his ecclesiastical office and in a not unjustified hope of forgiveness, he took timely refuge in religious writings. Aged over sixty, he died in his episcopal see, and Pontano honored his devotion in a noble poem of final tribute, to be inscribed as the epitaph on his marble urn.[869]

## CXXVI. Marcello Virgilio of Florence (1464/65–1521)

The charm of this man's engaging countenance and polished speech was extraordinary, and when he was teaching youth from the lectern or speaking to a circle of listeners, his learning was voluminous and remarkable for its very diversity.[870] In the post of chancellor, earlier held by Bruni and Poggio, he was also in charge of state correspondence. As time permitted, he would devote himself to a third task: for at the behest of the Medici he had undertaken to translate the complete works of Dioscorides.[871] He hoped to gain a great reputation from this effort, since from a tender age he had labored painstakingly on the exceedingly difficult science of herbals. But just as his work came out, two completely different translations were published: one, by Ermolao, considered a feeble production; and the other, by the Frenchman Jean Ruel, far and away the most highly praised of the three for its elegant Latinity.[872] We also have a famous oration that he delivered at the ceremony where the insignia of military command were conferred upon Lorenzo de' Medici the Younger.[873]

## CXXVII. Iani Parrhasii

1   Hic vir, honesta familia Cosentiae natus, quum e suggestu summa
facundiae maiestate Latinas literas Mediolani profiteretur, cunctos
nostri saeculi doctores erudito rerum omnium quae explicaret apparatu ac una praesertim rotundae pronunciationis gloria superavit. Duxerat uxorem Demetrii Chalcondylis filiam, qua felici
cognatione et socer et gener mutui suffragatores in scholis utriusque linguae imperium tenuerunt. Tanta Parrhasii fama ut Trivul-
tius, summae dignitatis sexagenarius imperator, inter iuvenes auditores conspiceretur.

2   Edidit commentarios in Claudianum et Nasonis *Ibim*, recondita
eruditione refertissimos. Novissime autem in manibus erat pene
absolutum volumen de rebus abstrusis per epistolam quaesitis.
Sed Mediolano excedere coactus est quum ludi magistri regionum,
saepe ab eo reprehensi redargutique ac ob id inscitiae pudore de-
coquentes, in eum conspirassent ita ut lasciva fabula Insubrum
auribus gravis excitaretur, tanquam auditores parum pudice dilec-
tos corrumperet.

3   Verum ab ea futili calumnia, tanquam literarum nomine clarissimus, conducente Leone cum Basilio uxoris fratre in Urbem venit. Sed tanti suggestus honore diu perfrui non potuit, articulare
morbo membra omnia saevissime deformante, unde ei maturatus
in patriam reditus cum vitae exitu contigit.

## CXXVII. *Giano Parrasio (1470–1522)*

When this man,[874] born in Cosenza to a noble family, lectured in   1
Milan on Latin literature with the utmost majesty of eloquence,
he surpassed all the other teachers of our age in the deep learning
he showed in all subjects that he treated, and above all in the per-
fection of his smooth elocution. He had married the daughter of
Demetrius Chalcondyles, thanks to which auspicious bond both
father- and son-in-law, supporting each other, were in charge of
the Greek and Latin classes.[875] Parrasio's fame was so great that
Trivulzio, a commander of the greatest reputation by then aged
sixty, could be spotted in the midst of his young pupils.[876]

He produced commentaries chock full of recondite erudition   2
on Claudian and on Ovid's *Ibis*. Ultimately, however, as he was
putting the finishing touches on a volume on abstruse matters,
written in the epistolary genre,[877] he was compelled to leave Milan
when the provincial schoolteachers, whom he had often criticized
and shown to be wrong—and who, through their shameful ignorance, were losing revenue—contrived a plot against him. They
circulated an obscene slander that weighed heavily on the ears of
the Insubrians: it was said that he seduced his students, whom he
loved in an impure way.

But he left that unfounded calumny behind him. Leo X hired   3
him on the basis of his distinguished literary reputation, and he
came to Rome along with his wife's brother, Basil.[878] He was not,
however, long able to enjoy so lofty an appointment, because gout
violently disfigured all his limbs, and he had to return precipi-
tously to his homeland, where he died.[879]

## CXXVIII. *Georgii Sauromani Germani*

Hic in Italia, quum iuris civilis studio operam dedisset eamque facultatem sine forensi agitatione parum nobilem nec fructuosam esse fateretur, ad humaniores literas ingenium traduxit adeo feliciter ut duabus orationibus in laudem Caroli Caesaris publicatis, totius academiae iudicio Longolio plenior atque torosior censeretur. Ob id civitate Romana donatus est egitque tenerum sodalem apud academicos, exuta quidem omni vocis moris atque habitus asperitate per aliquot annos, dum minuta caesaris negocia procuraret, Leoni Hadrianoque et demum Clementi eloquentiae nomine non ingratus. Sed in tumulto captae urbis ab Hispanis omnibus fortunis exutus, ne in tormentis expiraret a Germanis ita servatus est ut non multo post, crassante pestilentia, cum filio concubinaque perierit.

## CXXIX. *Coelii Calcagnini Ferrariensis*

1 Hic diu in patria iuventutem docuit honestissimo patre sed incerta matre genitus. Ab Atestino principe sacerdotio donatus est quum foecundum miteque ingenium et elegantes mores ad literas attulisset.

2 Pronior erat ad elegos quandoquidem in pedestri oratione ieiunus et scaber et sine dulcedine numerorum affectatus haberetur. Dum enim multa legisse videri vellet et plurima docere percuperet in *Epistolicis quaestionibus,* et titulo inepto et toties usurpata ab aliis materia nasutos offendit, et bilem movet nobilibus ingeniis quum

## CXXVIII. *Georg Sauermann the German (d. 1527)*

This man,[880] having applied himself to the study of Roman law and realizing that without courtroom practice his skills would not suffice for either fame or fortune, redirected his talents toward literary study in Italy. At this he was so successful that after the publication of two orations in praise of Emperor Charles V, the entire academy judged his style wider ranging and more muscular than that of Longueil.[881] On this account he was awarded Roman citizenship and for several years, while he managed minor business for the emperor, as a young member of the academy he cast aside all the roughness of his voice, manner, and demeanor. Because of his reputation for eloquence, he enjoyed the favor of Popes Leo, Adrian, and lastly Clement.[882] But in the Sack of Rome, the Spaniards deprived him of all his belongings. The Germans rescued him from death under torture, but shortly thereafter, as the plague was raging, he perished along with his mistress and son.[883]

## CXXIX. *Celio Calcagnini of Ferrara (1479–1541)*

For many years this man, born to a noble father but an unknown 1
mother, taught the youth in his native city.[884] Because he brought
to letters a fertile and gentle mind and refined taste, the Este duke
endowed him with a benefice.[885]

He inclined to elegiac verse, since in prose oratory he was held 2
to be dry, coarse, and affected, without the least sensitivity to cadence.[886] In fact, in his *Investigations into Letter-Writing*, while wishing to appear to have read many things and eager to teach still more, he piques highbrow critics both by the unsuitable title and by his frequent theft of material from others; and he arouses the

in libros Ciceronis *De officiis* inverecunde prorsus invehitur; qua in
re a festinante fato beneficium tulisse iudicari potest, quod luculentam Ciceronis defensionem a Maioragio in publicum pro-
deuntem et vivum proculdubio iugulaturam morte effugerit.

## CXXX. *Augustini Iustiniani Genuensis*

1   Hic, e secta Divi Dominici, linguarum varietate delectatus instrumenti veteris novique textus Hebraico Graeco et Chaldaeo sermone perscriptos curiosis repraesentavit; gravi quidem sumptu et
tenui cum laude, quum impressa domi praealta volumina emptores
rarissimos invenirent sic ut temere conceptam spem lucris inanes
initae rationes eluserint.

2   Sed factus inde Nebiensis antistes scribendae patriae historiae
negocium suscepit adeo ineptis ad id ingenii viribus ut praecipita-
tae editionis male audiendo poenas daret. Nec multo post, quum e
Genua in Corsicam incerta adhuc tempestate traiicere vellet, in
cursu fluctibus obrutus aut a Poenis praedonibus interceptus creditur, quum nullum usquam naufragii aut pyratarum praedae vestigium apparuerit.

## CXXXI. *Roberti Valturii*

Is Sigismondo Malatestae Ariminensium Principi militaris disciplinae praecepta e Graecorum et Latinorum historiis collecta perscripsit, eo luculentiore utilioreque volumine, quod explicatis

indignation of noble minds when he goes so far as to inveigh shamelessly against Cicero's *On Duties*.[887] With respect to this matter it can be judged a blessing of his premature fate that death saved him from witnessing the publication of Maioragio's brilliant defense of Cicero which, had he been alive, would surely have killed him.[888]

## CXXX. *Agostino Giustiniani of Genoa (1470–1536)*

This Dominican,[889] who delighted in studying a range of languages, set forth for inquiring minds the complete texts of the Old and New Testaments in Hebrew, Greek, and Chaldean.[890] From this he incurred great cost and gained but slight glory, inasmuch as the massive tomes which he had printed in-house found precious few buyers, and so his groundless calculations of profit frustrated his rashly conceived hopes.

Later, as the bishop of Nebbio, he undertook to write the history of his native city, though his powers were so unsuited to that task that he paid for the rushed publication with the abuse of it that ensued.[891] Soon thereafter, when he was trying to cross over from Genoa to Corsica while the weather was unsettled, he is thought to have either drowned or been captured en route by North African corsairs, although no trace of a shipwreck or of a pirate raid was ever found.

## CXXXI. *Roberto Valturio (1405–75)*

Valturio[892] copied out precepts of military science that he had culled from the histories of the Greeks and Romans, and dedicated the work to Sigismondo Malatesta, lord of Rimini.[893] The book was all the more splendid and useful because, after explain-

veterum machinarum artificiis totius bellici apparatus instrumenta secundum picturae imagines legentium oculis subiecerit.

## CXXXII. *Matthaei Palmerii Florentini*

Huius ingenio et industria Eusebii libro *De temporibus* addita est coronis. Scripsit etiam historiam Pisanam atque item poemata Latinis ac Ethruscis versibus, quodam etiam opere Danthis *Comoediam* aemulatus. Sed id nequaquam prospere successit, quum de divinis perperam incauteque locutus libro ex theologorum sententia damnato crematoque in haeresis Arrianae suspicionem inciderit.

## CXXXIII. *Iacobi Angeli Florentini*

Hic Ptolomaei *Cosmographiam* ex Graecis codicibus et tabulis diligentissime lineis ex picturae dimensione expressam Alexandro Quinto dedicavit, quo munere gentium omnium historiae ingentem requisitae lucis splendorem accepisse videntur, quum narratio maximarum rerum fere omnis tanquam lumine suo orbata et manca sordescat nisi, positis sub aspectum regionum tabulis, ex vero situ locorum totius rei gestae notitia, quod est mirae voluptatis, illustretur.

ing the technology of the ancient machines, he put before the readers' eyes illustrations of all the devices of war.[894]

## CXXXII. Matteo Palmieri of Florence (1406–75)

Through this man's brilliance and diligence, the final part was added on to Eusebius's *Chronicon*.[895] He also wrote a history of Pisa as well as poems both in Latin and in the Tuscan dialect, even imitating Dante's *Divine Comedy* in one work.[896] But that turned out spectacularly badly since he was suspected of Arianism for speaking inaccurately and rashly about divine matters, and his book was condemned by theologians and burned.[897]

## CXXXIII. Jacopo Angeli of Florence (ca. 1360–1410/11)

This man[898] dedicated to Pope Alexander V the *Geography* of Ptolemy, translated from the Greek codices and supplied with maps that had been copied with the utmost care, matching the dimensions of the originals.[899] By this contribution the histories of all peoples seem to have received a vast brilliance of necessary light, since nearly every account of the greatest matters would appear cheapened and impaired — deprived, as it were, of its illumination — were not the knowledge of all history elucidated by the presentation of accurate geographical maps of the sites, an extraordinarily delightful feature.[900]

## CXXXIV. *Hectoris Boethi*

Qui a prima origine Scotorum regum historiam Latine diligenter perscripsit, passim veteris chorographiae memor et moderatae libertatis nusquam oblitus, ita ut magnopere miremur extare de remotis ab orbe nostro Ebridum et Orcadum insulis mille amplius annorum memoriam, quum in Italia altrice ingeniorum tot saeculis post eiectos Gothos scriptores omnino defuerint, tanto quidem publicae dignitatis detrimento ut non dispudeat maioribus nostris indignari nisi satius fuerit amissae libertatis oblivisci quam, cum infami quodam pudore, calamitatis ac ignaviae nostrae vulnera refricasse.

## CXXXV. *Polidori Virgilii*

Hic Urbini natus, ubi adolevit optimis instructus literis, in Britanniam transivit. Quum antea lepido argumento proverbia excepta demum ab Erasmo et eruditissime amplificata publicasset, is ab hoc Henrico Rege fortunis adauctus flamenque Londinii creatus conscripsit *Historias rerum Britannicarum*, ea fide ut Scotis et Gallis saepe reclamantibus alieno potius arbitrio quam suo intexuisse multa in gratiam gentis existimetur, quod in recensendis minorum ducum nominibus tanquam gloriae avidis plurimum indulserit.

## CXXXIV. Hector Boece (ca. 1465–1536)

This man diligently wrote in Latin a history of the Scottish Kings from their earliest origins.[901] Mindful everywhere of ancient chorography, nowhere has he forgotten to maintain a tempered candor, so that we marvel greatly that there can be found a written tradition of over a thousand years concerning the islands of the Hebrides and Orkney, so remote from our region; whereas in Italy, that nursemaid of genius, writers were entirely lacking for so many centuries after the expulsion of the Goths. The damage done to our collective dignity was so great that it is no shame to be indignant at our ancestors — unless it were better to forget a freedom that has been lost than, with a certain disreputable bashfulness, to tear open the wounds of our calamity and cowardice.

## CXXXV. Polydore Vergil (ca. 1470–1555)

Born in Urbino, he grew up equipped with superior learning before moving to England.[902] Because he had previously published proverbs on charming themes, which were then taken up and expanded with great erudition by Erasmus, he obtained financial support from the Henry who was then king, and was given a benefice in London.[903] Thereupon he wrote his *English History*, doing so with such loyalty that it is thought he inserted many things chosen by persons other than himself (as the Scots and the French often loudly complain) so as to curry favor with the English nation, listing the names of minor dukes as if to pander most of all to those who were greedy for glory.[904]

## CXXXVI. *Guaghini Galli*

Huic Gallia plurimum debet, sed de fide illi viderint quorum interest incorruptam rerum memoriam ad posteros transmitti. Nam in his quae ad Italiam pertinent huius tempestatis usque adeo insolenter et pingui stylo caecutire solet ut qui nulla orationis ornamenta in eo conspiciunt passim eius imprudentiam stomachentur.

## CXXXVII. *Marini Becichemi Scodrensis*

Ab hoc Dalmata non insulse Latino Georgii Castrioti[95] Schenderbechi admirabiles res bello gestas quanquam inusitatis excessibus perscriptas legimus. Aequavit enim hic vir amore patriae et barbarorum odio a fide procul abductus, Epirotae reguli virtutem antiquis heroibus ita ut iustam egregie factorum gloriam, dum supra aequum in laudes prorumpit, suspicione mendacii elevasse censeatur.

## CXXXVIII. *Iacobi Ziegleri*

Quis eo Latinas literas quo Romana arma penetrare nequierint pervenisse non miretur? Hic enim in terra Gotica natus ac educatus adeo exacte, puriter et facunde Christierni Daniae[96] atque

## CXXXVI. Gaguin the Frenchman (ca. 1423–1501)

France is deeply indebted to this man, but those to whom it matters that an authentic record of history be transmitted to posterity should be on guard with respect to his reliability.[905] For, with regard to matters that concern Italy in these turbulent times, he generally errs so very arrogantly and in such clumsy prose that those who espy in the work no trace of stylistic elegance everywhere seethe with rage at his ignorance.[906]

## CXXXVII. Marino [Barlezio] of Scutari[907] (ca. 1450–ca. 1512)

We read that the remarkable military exploits of Giorgio Castriota Scanderbeg have been recorded by this Dalmatian Latinist, not inexpertly, if with unusual extravagance.[908] For, drawn away from reliability by his love of his homeland and hatred of barbarians, he ranked the valor of the Epirot prince alongside that of ancient heroes, so that when he bursts forth in praises beyond what is reasonable, through suspicion of dishonesty he is thought to have diminished the glory that Scanderbeg's illustrious deeds deserve.[909]

## CXXXVIII. Jakob Ziegler (before 1471–1549)

Who does not marvel that Latin letters have penetrated where the Roman army was unable to make inroads? For this man,[910] born and educated in a Gothic land, has recorded the savagery of

Norvegiae regis immanitatem neque ipsi sanguinario tyranno diu laetam neque demum diis ultoribus neglectam perscripsit ut eruditis gentibus pudori esse possit, quod Latinae facundiae fruges sub cimmerio coelo pene felicius ac uberius quam sub hac benigniore ac temperatiore plaga proveniant.

## CXXXIX. Pauli Aemilii

Hunc protulit Verona, Gallia aluit; Ludovicus Duodecimus sacerdotio in aede Deiparae Virginis Lutetiae Parisiorum exornavit quod orsus a primis Galliae regibus mille amplius annorum Gallicam historiam, laconica tamen brevitate, perscripsisset. Sed in sacri belli enarratione quum Gothifredi Bolionis virtute Hierosolimae caperentur, aliquanto luculentius ita se se diffudit ut medium iter non interitura cum laude tenuisse existimetur.

## CXL. Germani Brixii

1 Is ad Altisiodurum Galliae oppidum natus in poesi lauream meruit, Latino carmine edito de trium ingentium navium miserabili conflagratione, quum duae Britannicae Gallicam cognomento *Chordigeram* (haec erat inusitatae magnitudinis) harpagonibus comprehensam expugnare niterentur. Sed demum emendatiora

Christian, the king of Denmark and Norway[911]—which remained neither propitious for the bloodthirsty tyrant himself nor ignored for long by the avenging gods—and he has done so with such precision, purity, and eloquence that it can be a source of embarrassment to the learned nations that the harvests of Latin eloquence are coming forth almost more abundantly and fruitfully under a Cimmerian[912] sky than in this gentler and more temperate clime.

## CXXXIX. Paolo Emili (mid-15th cent.–1529)

Verona brought forth this man,[913] but France nourished him. Louis XII adorned him with a priesthood in the cathedral of Notre Dame at Paris because he had written, albeit with Spartan brevity, a history of France covering over a thousand years, beginning from its first kings.[914] But in his account of the crusade, at the point where Jerusalem was captured through the prowess of Godfrey of Bouillon, he extended himself a bit more eloquently, so that he is thought to have kept to the middle course, thereby winning undying fame.[915]

## CXL. Germain de Brie (ca. 1490–1538)

This man,[916] born in the town of Auxerre in France, won poetic 1 laurels after the publication of his Latin poem about the dreadful burning of three immense ships that occurred when two English vessels were striving to overcome a French one, the *Cordelière*, a ship of unusual size, which they had snagged with grappling hooks.[917] Later, however, he published more polished poems on a

poemata vario titulo publicavit. Inde vero pedestri orationi deditus transtulit e Graeco, uti Lascaris alumnum decebat, ex Chrysostomo Babylae vitam et libros septem *De sacerdotio* puritate sermonis minime contemnendos.

2 Senescentem sed adhuc plane robustum invasit atrae bilis morbus, ob id paulatim saevior atque lethalior effectus quum ex accumulato multo auro dimidiam fere partem furto sibi subtractam miser sensisset, ut credi par est, a domesticis, quibus nec vitam quidem postea credidit sic ut in itinere iuxta Ligerim apud Carnutes expirarit.

## CXLI. *Nicolai Tegrimi*

Is Lucae natus professione iurisconsultus post magistratus honestissimos in Italia gestos, patriam historiam egregia fide perscripsit; et in ea praecipue *Vitam Castruccii* qui Lucae, Pisarum et Pistorii dominatum tenuit et magnas Florentinis intulit clades. Cuius viri si tyrannidis invidiosum nomen facessat, inusitata bello virtus singulari laude celebranda iudicatur. Sed Macchiavellus Florentinus historicus, patrii veteris odii memor, petulanti malignitate non interituram memorabilis ducis famam fabulis involuit quum, vitam acerrimi hostis Ethrusco sermone scribere orsus, tam impudenti quam astuto illudendi genere sacrosanctam rerum gestarum fidem corruperit.

variety of subjects. Then, having turned to prose, he translated from the Greek (a task fitting for a student of Lascaris) Chrysostom's *Life of St. Babylas*, and seven books *On the Priesthood* commendable for their purity of style.[918]

When he was growing old yet still quite robust, he was afflicted 2 by melancholy, which gradually grew fiercer and more deadly after the poor fellow realized that almost half of his substantial wealth had been stolen from him — by members of his household, it is reasonably believed, and after that he did not even entrust his life to them. And so he died around Chartres, as he was journeying alongside the Loire River.

## CXLI. Niccolò Tegrimi (1448–1527)

After this man,[919] a jurist born in Lucca, had served with the greatest integrity in governments in Italy, he wrote with scrupulous honesty the history of his homeland, most notably a *Life* of Castruccio Castracane, who was lord of Lucca, Pisa, and Pistoia, and inflicted great casualties upon the Florentines.[920] Although Castruccio acquired the hateful reputation of being a tyrant, he deserves to be celebrated with singular praise for his exceptional skill in warfare. But with petulant malice, the Florentine historian Machiavelli, mindful of his homeland's longstanding hatred, clouded with falsehoods the undying reputation of that memorable commander when, having undertaken to write in the Tuscan dialect the life of the bitterest of Florence's enemies, he sullied the sacrosanct integrity of the historian's craft with mockery as shameless as it was clever.[921]

## CXLII. *Camilli Ghilini Mediolanensis*

1 Cuius extat liber exemplorum florida per omnes aetates varietate periucundus ac ipso pene Valerio Maximo argumenti hylaritate festivior. Ea rerum exempla diligenti gravique studio collegerat Baptista Fulgosius, gentilium suorum perfidia Genuae principatu deiectus; sed quoniam Latinae[97] orationis facultas minime suppeteret, ea materno sermone perscripserat ut aliquanto post ab hoc Ghilino Latine verteretur.

2 Fuere qui existimarent a Iacobo patre id opus longo vigiliarum labore compositum, in quotam haereditatis partem obvenisse filio adolescenti studiosoque liberali quidem indulgentia benevolentissimi patris, quum in eo eruditi ingenii certa indoles emineret qua vel alieni operis oborta suspicio praeclare discuti posse videretur. Erat enim Camillus in gravissimis legationum muneribus ob industriam cum summa fide prudentiaque coniunctam diu versatus, ita ut excitatae fabulae famam ridendo dilueret et perurbane se ab hoc furti genere non abhorrere fateretur, quando iure damnari non possit amore incensus adolescens si quid opulento patri arguta manu surripiat.

3 Periit in Sicilia apud Carolum Caesarem Francisci Sfortiae legatus quum, debellatis ad Tunetum barbaris, Augusus victor ad triumphum in Italiam reverteretur.

## CXLII. Camillo Ghilini[922] of Milan (1478–1535)

We have this man's book of *exempla*, delightful for its flowery vari-  1
ety extending over the course of all ages, and almost more charming in the wit of its material than Valerius Maximus himself. Battista Fregoso,[923] after being cast out from the dogeship of Genoa
by the treachery of his own kinsmen, had collected these instances
of exemplarity with diligence and focused energy. But since his
skill at Latin was not up to the task, he had written the work in
his mother tongue so that Ghilini rendered it later in Latin.[924]

There were those who reckoned that Camillo's father, Giacomo,  2
had worked tirelessly to compose it, but that it had fallen to the
lot of the young, studious son as an inheritance of sorts — indeed,
through the liberal indulgence of his doting father — since there
shone forth in him a definite natural disposition of refined brilliance which could clearly disperse the slightest hint of plagiarism.
Thanks to diligence combined with the utmost trustworthiness
and good judgment, Camillo had been engaged for a long time in
the weightiest diplomatic missions, so that he shrugged off with a
laugh the rumors that were stirred up, and he very nobly admitted
that he did not shrink from that kind of theft, inasmuch as one
could not rightly condemn a young man inflamed by love if, with
a skilled hand, he should make off with something that belonged
to a wealthy father.

He died in Sicily, as a legate of Francesco Sforza to the court of  3
Charles the Emperor when, having defeated the heathen at Tunis,
he was returning in triumph to Italy.[925]

## CXLIII. *Ioannis Reuclini Germani*

1 Hic est ille, Capnionis cognomento e patria lingua in Graecam verso ne Latine fumeus evaderet, Germanorum aetate nostra clarissimus qui, inusitato fretus ingenio, Graecas ac Hebraicas atque item Latinas literas in Germania pari felicitate propagavit, quum arcana Hebraeorum confirmandis Christianae legis praesidiis in lucem proferret effectricemque mirabilium operum Cabalae disciplinam apud valida atque expedita ad perdiscendum eius gentis ingenia profiteretur. Extat eius liber *De verbo mirifico* et de Cabalae scientiae placitis, eloquentia illustri ad Leonem Decimum perscriptus.

2 Circumferuntur etiam praeter graviores libros, quanquam suppresso nomine, ex eius officina *Obscurorum virorum epistolae*, admirabili facetiarum lepore conditae, quibus ad excitandum risum cucullatorum theologorum ineptissime atque ideo ridicule Latina lingua scribentium stylus exprimitur. Ulciscebatur enim infestam nomini suo turbam iucundissimo satyrae illudentis genere, quum maligna cucullatorum conspiratione tanquam Iudeis parum aequus hostis ac ex animo plane recutitus impietatis accusaretur. Hic liber avide coemptus et evulgatus adeo graviter calumniatores eius ordinis perculit ut coniurationis princeps Hostratus lethali dolore sauciatus interierit et reliqui aestuantes a Leone suppliciter impetrarint ut edicto divendi atque imprimi vetaretur.

3 Sed edicti maiestatem Reuclinus salso ingenio ludificatus secundum epistolarum volumen, tanquam ex titulo minime vetitum, altero quidem aculeatius impressoribus tradidit ita ut cucullati

## CXLIII. *Johann Reuchlin the German (1454/55–1522)*

This is the man who, having translated his surname from his na-  1
tive tongue into the Greek *Capnion* lest it be Latinized as *Fumeus*,
is the most distinguished German of our time.[926] Relying on his
exceptional brilliance, he disseminated Greek, Hebrew, and Latin
writings in Germany with equal success; for he brought forth into
the light the hidden secrets of the Jews so as to reinforce the bastions of the Christian faith, and he taught those of his fellow
Germans who were capable and quick-witted the science of the
Kabbalah as an effective agent of marvelous works. We have his
book *On the Marvelous Word* as well as *On the Tenets of Kabbalistic
Knowledge*, written with lucid eloquence and dedicated to Leo
X.[927]

Beyond these rather serious works, there also circulates a book  2
(from his circle, but without his name on it), the *Letters of Obscure
Men*, seasoned with wonderfully clever wit, in which the Latin
style of theologians in religious orders is held up to ridicule as utterly inept, and therefore ludicrous.[928] Indeed, he used the delightful genre of mocking satire to take vengeance on the mob vilifying
his reputation when a spiteful cabal of friars was accusing him of
impiety on the grounds that he was insufficiently hostile to the
Jews and obviously circumcised in spirit.[929] This book, eagerly
purchased and distributed, dismayed the false accusers among the
Dominicans so grievously that Hoogstraten, the instigator of the
conspiracy, was stricken with chagrin and died.[930] The others,
seething with rage, successfully petitioned Leo to issue an edict
preventing the printing or sale of the book.

But Reuchlin, having with razor wit made sport of the majesty  3
of the edict, delivered to the printers a second volume of letters
under the same title (as doing so was not prohibited) that was
even more barbed than the first; so that the friars, wretchedly

misere cum hydra luctantes animos in ea lite desponderint. Hostrati autem tumulo hoc nobile carmen Capnionis puer affixit:

Hic iacet Hostratus, viventem ferre patique
    quem potuere mali, non potuere boni.
Crescite ab hoc, taxi; crescant aconita sepulchro.
    Ausus erat, sub eo qui iacet, omne nefas.


## CXLIV. Ioannis De Monte Regio Germani

1 Hunc enim unum admirabili solertia divini ingenii astronomorum omnium qui hactenus floruerunt praestantissimum veneramur, quum decimam spheram totius coelestis globi supremam inclusasque diurna rotatione rapientem certissima supputatione sibi et posteris invenerit; hac ipsa aedepol gloriosa sapientiae palma Thalete, Eudoxo, Calippo Ptolomaeoque ipso, tantae scientiae conditore, ac Alfragano nobilior. Extant eius subtilissima commentaria in *Almagestum* Ptolomaei et mathematicae ratiocinationis exactus atque perutilis liber *De triangulis*.

2 Ab hac commendatione eruditi nominis creatus est a Xysto Quarto Ratisponensis episcopus accitusque Romam, ut annum ex vetusta intercalatione fastis minime respondentem ad statas ex cursu lunae pascales cerimonias revocaret: quod confici posse videbatur subductis semel aliquot diebus Martio mensi, qua una

wrestling with a hydra, gave up hope and quit the feud.[931] A student of Capnion had the following celebrated poem attached to Hoogstraten's tomb:[932]

Here lies Hoogstraten, whom the wicked but not the good were able to endure and tolerate while he lived. Spring forth from him, o yew trees! May wolf bane rise up from the tomb. He who lies beneath it dared every kind of wickedness.

## CXLIV. Johannes Regiomontanus the German (1436–76)

We stand in awe of the wondrous subtlety of the sublime genius 1 of this man,[933] who far surpassed all the other astronomers who have lived up to today. By an extremely accurate computation, he discovered for himself and posterity the tenth and highest sphere of the entire heavens, which in its daily rotation drags along with it the spheres it encloses. On the basis of just this glorious triumph of intellect, Lord knows, he is more famous than Thales, Eudoxus, Calippus, Ptolemy himself—the founder of such an important field of scholarship—and Alfraganus as well.[934] We have his exceedingly subtle commentaries on Ptolemy's *Almagest* and the rigorous and surpassingly useful book of mathematical reasoning, *On Triangles*.[935]

Because of the praise that his learned name had garnered, Sixtus IV created him bishop of Regensburg and summoned him to 2 Rome to bring the year (which, as a result of ancient intercalations, in no way conformed to the feast days) back in alignment with the Easter observances (based on the lunar cycle).[936] This seemed capable of accomplishment by subtracting just once several days from the month of March.[937] This single calculation would

ratione mille et quingentorum annorum excessus in cursu syderis non plane sensilis, toto demum cumulo depraehensus, emendatissime tolleretur. Sed crassante in urbe pestilentia fato surreptus, quod maxime cupiebat praestare non potuit.

## CXLV. Ludovici Vives Valentini

Hic quanquam ducta uxore apud Belgas liberis operam daret, sacrarum tamen literarum studia egregio digna sacerdote complexus, adeo profecit ut Divi Augustini librum De civitate Dei luculenta commentatione adiecta religiose admodum illustrarit, quum publice auctus stipendio liberales artes profiteretur legendaque posteris multa volumina perscriberet. Nondum senex fato functus est Brugis, quod est emporium Gessoriaci[98] littoris, prosequentibus magno luctu amissi praeceptoris memoriam Belgis omnibus sed maxime civibus Hispanis, quod eo doctiorem in Hispania superesse neminem faterentur.

## CXLVI. Cosmus Pactius

1 Cosmus Pactius, ex amita Leonis Decimi genitus, nobili vir ingenio elegantique doctrina praeditus, quum esset Florentinus archiepiscopus Maximum Tyrium Platonicae sectae philosophum e Graeco in Latinum scitissime vertit. Nec in eius ingenui muneris labore cessaturus videri poterat, tanquam virtutis et pietatis amore flagrantissimus, nisi importuna mors, vix dum Leone avunculo ad

have perfectly removed the accumulated deviation of 1,500 years, which is not perceptible to the senses in the sun's course, yet becomes noticeable when one considers the entire span of time. But with the plague raging in Rome, death took him before he could achieve what he most desired.

### CXLV. Luis Vives of Valencia (1492–1540)

Although this man,[938] who married in Flanders, was caring for his children, he nonetheless devoted himself to the studies of sacred writings suitable to an outstanding priest: he reverently elucidated St. Augustine's book *On the City of God* with a splendid commentary.[939] At the same time, endowed with a stipend, he was giving public lectures on the liberal arts and writing many volumes that should be read by posterity. He died at Bruges, a center of trade on the Gessoriac coast,[940] when not yet an old man. All the Flemings honored the memory of their lost teacher with great mourning, but the Spanish citizens especially so, since they recognized that in Spain there remained no one more learned than he.

### CXLVI. Cosimo de' Pazzi (1466–1513)

Cosimo de' Pazzi, born to Leo X's paternal aunt, was gifted with a noble intellect and elegant learning.[941] When he was archbishop of Florence, he made a most skillful Latin translation from the Greek of the Platonic philosopher Maximus of Tyre, and he was not likely to leave off the performance of that honorable service, inasmuch as he was burning with a passionate love of virtue and piety.[942] But shortly after his uncle[943] had been elevated to the pa-

1

pontificatum provecto, et optimorum consiliorum studia et para-
tae purpurae honorem intercepisset.

2    Haec subinde studia Alexander germanus frater diverso nec
utique multum felici itinere secutus est. Ad scribendas enim tra-
goedias ingenium appulit, eruditum hercle sed aliquanto quam
cothurnatum poetam deceret aridius, quod etiam et gracilitas ipsa
totius habitus et angustae vocis exilitas ex viventis fronte promitte-
rent. *Poeticam* autem Aristotelis non inepte uti difficilem in Latinum verterat. Ob id tanquam ex concepta artis ratione tragoediis
incumbebat, verum adeo intemperanter ut Graecas et ex his praesertim *Iphygeniam* in Latinum pariter et Ethruscum carmen vertendo propriaeque inventionis alias effundendo quae in theatris
agerentur intentae libidini vix modum imponeret, quanquam ab
Ethruscis histrionibus repudiarentur, qui exibilantis populi iudicium maximi instar periculi omnino fugiendum existimabant quod
ea poemata versibus constarent pede uno longioribus, ex nova scilicet ac ob id insolenti nostris auribus Graecorum imitatione, quae
numero et modo prorsus infaceto tanquam enormis nusquam nisi
graecissantibus arrideret.

3    Iure itaque novae inventionis exemplar, nemine imitante, apud
ipsum authorem stetit atque consenuit. Usque adeo difficile est
obsoletis nitorem et novis authoritatem feliciter attulisse.

pacy as Leo, an untimely death cut him off both from his lofty pursuits and from receiving the honor of the purple that had been intended for him.

His brother Alessandro[944] at once took up these studies, but on a different path that was certainly not very felicitous: he applied his mind to writing tragedies. That mind was learned, Lord knows, but considerably drier than became a tragic poet: a shortcoming that his appearance portended, for his build was scrawny and his voice thin and weak. Be that as it may, he had translated Aristotle's *Poetics* into Latin,[945] and not badly at that, given its difficulty. On this account he devoted himself to tragedies, believing that he had grasped the essence of the art, but with so little restraint that he set almost no bounds to his keen passion, rendering Greek plays, especially *Iphigenia*, into Latin as well as Tuscan verse, and bringing forth others of his own invention to be performed in theaters. But Tuscan actors, determined to avoid the worst of risks, that of being hissed off the stage by an audience, rejected his plays, whose verses were too long by a foot, in an imitation of the Greeks that was certainly new and on that account unfamiliar to our ears. All but monstrous in its utterly coarse meter and rhythm, it pleased nobody but those straining to be like the Greeks.

Justly, therefore, the model of his new invention, having no imitators, remained its author's own and withered along with him. How very difficult it is to succeed in conferring prestige upon old-fashioned ways and authority upon the new.

# [PERORATIO]

1     Lubet postremo desiderare quorundam externorum imagines Germanorumque praesertim, quum literae non Latinae modo cum pudore nostro sed Graecae et Hebraicae in eorum terras fatali commigratione transierint, ita ut eorum qui iam Fato functi caeteris clariores evaserunt, veras imagines a vivis et pari laude florentibus efflagitare non dubitem, quando id ab humanissimis, nisi violato Musarum sacramento, frustra expectari minime possit. Quis enim nisi plane barbarus et impius, vel exiguam laudem sine piaculo defunctis inviderit, quanquam ex peculiari sua ingenii foecunditate nullo aevo perituris? Pertinet, hercle, in quota parte exoptatae laudis ad producendam vitam, in albo atque ordine praecellentium hominum recenseri agnoscique item ex vera oris effigie ostendique posteris in perstricta nec inutili editorum operum censura, unde novam nobilitatem, veluti liberali nec sperata quadam adoptione, ad cumulatum decus induerint.

2     Emicuit dudum perillustris eruditio in Ioanne Oecolampadio, sed profecto clarius et luminosius illuxisset nisi eam dirae haereseos maculae defoedassent, dum enim Theophylactum maligna praevaricatione quaedam omittendo traducit et Christianae hostiae sacramentum repudiat, Rophense Britanno severa manu iugulante, redargutus concidit. Eadem fere novae sectae libido Zvvinglum, in sacris literis apud Helvetios clarum, cruento exito praecipitem dedit, facundia siquidem pestilenti ac impiis concionibus quum civitatem Helvetiorum, diductis in contraria studia simplicissimis et militaribus populis ad mutuas caedes concitasset, in

# PERORATION

In closing, I should express my desire for portraits of certain for- 1
eigners, especially Germans, since in a fateful migration not only
Latin letters (to our shame!) but also Greek and Hebrew have
crossed over into their lands. So, I do not hesitate to request, from
those still living who are equally famous, faithful likenesses of
those already deceased who were celebrated beyond the rest. Surely
men of the greatest refinement could not refuse this request, lest
they dishonor their allegiance to the Muses. For who, excepting
the completely barbarous and disrespectful, would not feel guilty
to begrudge the dead at least a modicum of glory, even though
they will never perish because of their own special fertility of intellect? Surely it is fitting, so as to prolong some part of the fame for
which they have yearned, that they be listed in a systematic regis-
ter of exceptional men, and likewise be recognized from accurate
portraits of their faces and brought to the attention of posterity by
a concise and edifying evaluation of their published works. From
these they might attain, as if by a generous and unexpected adop-
tion, new renown in addition to the distinction they already enjoy.

Not long ago, brilliant erudition shone forth in Johannes Oeco- 2
lampadius,[1] but it surely would have been clearer and brighter had
not dreadful stains of heresy defiled it: indeed, when in translating
Theophylact he maliciously prevaricated by omitting certain
things, and when he repudiated the Eucharist, being forcefully
confuted by the English Bishop of Rochester, he went down in
defeat.[2] Nearly the same zeal for a new sect sent the impetuous
Zwingli,[3] famous among the Swiss for his religious learning, headlong to a bloody death: for once he had split into opposing factions the utterly simpleminded yet belligerent peoples of Switzerland, he incited them to mutual slaughter in such a way that — God

acie trucidatus occubuit ita ut nefariae temeritatis poenas, Deo Maximo Vindice, dedisse credatur.

3    Contigit et honestissima laus ex studio nobilium literarum Bilibaldo Nurimbergensi, cuius extant nonnulla opera ex Gregorio Nazanzeno pie translata, et *Cosmographiae liber* ex Ptolomaeo accuratius quam antea traductus, et totius Germaniae urbium descriptiones, eruditam lucem obscuris regionibus afferentes.[1]

4    Quis Vadiano ex Sancto Gallo Helvetiorum insigni pago novae atque vetustae cosmographiae curiosus gratias non aget, quum libellum Pomponii Mellae perutili commentatione ex brevi et obscuro magnum illustremque reddiderit? Miramur quoque diligentiam laboremque viro regia in aula conspicuo longe honestissimum Cuspiniani Viennensis, a quo civili quadam facundia Germanorum et Bizantiorum caesarum imperia propinquitates, stemmata, mores atque exitus referuntur.

5    Viget apud nos eruditi nominis authoritate Coppus Basiliensis, ab exacta doctrina felicique artis industria medicus, Francisco Galliae Regi magnopere repetita saepe memoria desideratus. Suspicimus etiam ingenium Conradi Goclenii, vertendi Graeca docendique facultate apud Belgas magnopere celebratum. Venerantur iureconsulti nostri Zasium ex Harudum Constantia humani iuris intelligentia cum exactissimis scriptoribus conferendum.

6    Floret adhuc apud nos praedulcis et grata memoria Beati Rhaenani, ex eius enim ingenii liberalitate officinaque libraria, optimarum literarum magnas opes ad nos pervenisse conspicimus. Sunt etiam in celebri fama Camerarius, Graecae atque Latinae linguae ita peritus ut scribendo pernobilis Ciceronis imitator evaserit, et Copernicus absolutae subtilitatis mathematicus; atque item

being the greatest vindicator — he paid the penalty for abominable rashness.

Surpassing praise owing to his study of noble literature has also been accorded to Willibald of Nuremberg.[4] We have his faithful translations of some works of Gregory of Nazianzus, a version of Ptolemy's *Cosmography* translated with unprecedented accuracy, and descriptions of the cities of all Germany, casting the light of erudition upon little-known regions.[5]

Who among those interested in ancient and modern cosmography will not be grateful to Vadian,[6] from the famous canton of St. Gall in Switzerland, since he provided a highly useful commentary for Pomponio Mela's great and famous little book, which had previously had only a brief and obscure one?[7] We also marvel at Cuspinian[8] of Vienna's diligence and productivity, by far the most honorable accomplishment for an eminent man at a royal court. With eloquence befitting a civic orator, he wrote of the reigns, kin, family trees, character, and deaths of the German and Byzantine emperors.[9]

Cop[10] of Basel lives on among us, a physician of precise learning who practiced his art successfully. He is greatly missed by King Francis of France, who often mentions him. We also admire the brilliance of Conrad Goclenius,[11] highly celebrated among the Flemings for his prowess as a translator and teacher of Greek. Our jurists stand in awe of Zasius,[12] from Konstanz, in Germany.[13] In his understanding of civil law, he merits comparison with the most scrupulous writers.

There still lives on with us the very sweet and agreeable memory of Beatus Rhenanus,[14] for we observe that due to his magnanimity and that of his scribal workshop, a great wealth of the best literature has come down to us. Also widely renowned are Camerarius,[15] so expert at Greek and Latin that in writing he became an outstanding imitator of Cicero; and Copernicus,[16] a mathematician of the utmost exactitude; and also Albert Krantz,[17] who

Albertus Crantius, qui Danorum et Suecorum regna ad extremum Borealem Oceanum nostris obscura facundissime descripsit.

7     Sed qua demum veteri sodalitio digna pietate imaginem tuam, ut elogio nostro coronetur expectaverim, Ursine Gaspar Vindelice, paucis ante annis morte praepropera nobis erepte? Nobiles enim poetas laeto carmine, historicos vero styli gravitate, superabas. Sed in cumulo honestissimae laudis, uti integer vitae scelerisque purus, tranquilli animi probitate periculosi officii munus feliciter adimplebas, quum Maximilianum, summae indolis adolescentem Ferdinandi Caesaris designati filium patrui fortuna dignissimum, perfectis moribus ac literis erudires.

8     Sed cur reliquos enumerare non desino, postquam inanis spei votum infinitus eruditorum numerus interrumpit? Offertur enim latissima seges ab ipsa mirabili Germanici coeli foecunditate. Occulta hercle syderum commutatione evenisse arbitramur ut illud coelum, molestis Boreae flatibus, frigore geluque damnatum, horrida dudum torpentiaque ingenia mollierit ac excitarit. Neque enim contenti sua vetere militiae laude qua Martium decus Romanis gentium victoribus ereptum, stabili disciplinae severitate feliciter tuentur, ipsa etiam pacis ornamenta literas optimasque artes decoquenti Graeciae ac Italiae dormitanti (quod pudeat) abstulerunt.

9     Patrum siquidem nostrorum memoria architecti imprimis, ac exinde pictores, statuarii sculptores, mathematici et perargutae manus artifices, ac item aquileges septempedariique mensores e Germania petebantur. Nec mirum quum antea inusitatae et

most eloquently described kingdoms little-known to our writers, those of the Danes and the Swedes at the far end of the North Sea.[18]

And finally there's Caspar Ursinus of Silesia, taken from us by a precipitate death just a few years ago.[19] With what respectful affection befitting an old friendship might I await your likeness to crown it with my inscription? For you surpassed famous poets in luxuriant verse, yet also the historians in stylistic dignity. Having reached the pinnacle of honor and glory, blameless in mode of living and unblemished in character,[20] with the virtue of a calm mind you successfully fulfilled a demanding assignment when you instructed both in the finest morality and in literature Maximilian, a youth of surpassing natural endowments, son of the emperor-designate Ferdinand and most worthy of the good fortune of his paternal uncle.[21] 7

But I had better leave off listing the rest, since the infinite number of scholars makes it impossible to finish the task. Indeed, the exceedingly wide crop is bestowed by the marvelous fecundity of the German climate itself. I believe that, by some shift in the stars (a mysterious one, heaven knows), that climate consigned to vexing blasts of the north wind, cold, and ice has civilized and stimulated minds that not long ago were unrefined and lethargic. And, not content with their long-established excellence in war by which, with steadfast strictness of discipline, they successfully defend the martial distinction wrested from the Roman conquerors of the world, they have also carried off the very adornments of peace, learning, and the best arts — from Greece, as it was wasting away; and (for shame!) from Italy, as it was nodding off. 8

Accordingly, within the memory of our fathers, Germany first sought after our architects, then the painters, the sculptors of statues, the mathematicians and engravers, and likewise the hydraulics experts and land surveyors. Nor is this surprising, since earlier 9

portentosae inventionis, aereas formas excudendis libris et formi-
danda bello aenea tormenta nobis attulerint.

10   Sed haec infesti saeculi fortuna non usque adeo illis benigna
mater et nobis immitis extitit noverca ut nihil omnino ex pristina
haereditate reliquerit. Tenemus enim adhuc (si fas est vel modeste
gloriari tota pene libertatis possessione spoliatis) syncerae et constantis eloquentiae munitam arcem, qua (si castis Musis placet)
ingenuus Romani candoris pudor adversus externos inexpugnabilis
conservatur atque defenditur. In hac enim statione ad perenne decus optimo cuique civi intente vigilandum erit ut, Bembo Sadole-
toque signiferis, quod reliquum est e tanta maiorum substantia
generose tueamur, quanquam inani miseriarum nostrarum solatio,
postquam non iniquo iure apud nos convulsa libertas interiit, qua
una procul dubio altrice studiorum bonas artes excitari propaga-
rique conspicimus.

* * *

11   Quum iam confecto priore volumine quo Fato functorum imagines continentur, ad secundum non invita Minerva pervenerim
(id enim de vivis erit), censurae periculo gravius quidem sed ingeniorum illustrium religiosa commendatione iucundius, operae pretium[2] existimavi eorum nomina profiteri quorum tabulae pictae in
nostro conclavi immortalibus dicato spectantur.

12   Sit haec enim delectae sedis et instituti operis certa nuncupatio,
ut vel hinc viri elegantes, tanquam arridentis augurii laeto omine
accepto, suorum ingeniorum monumenta ad posteritatem aeterna
prospiciant, nec ideo gravate morem gerere velint, honesta mihi
pariter ac ipsis et denique grata omnibus expetenti.

they had brought us strange and marvelous inventions: bronze types for printing books, and dreadful bronze firearms for use in battle.[22]

But the fortune of this hostile century has proven to them not so kind a mother, or to us so cruel a stepmother, that she has left us nothing at all from our ancient heritage. Indeed, if we who have been deprived of nearly every vestige of liberty may boast even a little, we do still cling to the fortified citadel of pure and steadfast eloquence, by which (if it pleases the chaste Muses) the native honor of Roman purity is kept impregnable and defended against foreigners. For in this outpost, each and every one of the finest citizens must be keenly attentive to lasting glory so that, with Bembo and Sadoleto[23] as standard-bearers, we may nobly protect what remains of our ancient patrimony — though this is but hollow consolation for our miseries, since among us, and not without justice, liberty has been torn away and perished. We recognize beyond doubt that it is only when studies are nursed and fed by liberty that the liberal arts are inspired and disseminated.

* * *

Now that I have completed the first volume, which contains portraits of the deceased, and with Minerva's favor have arrived at the second (which indeed will treat of the living) — admittedly a more difficult task because of the risk of criticism, but more delightful for the conscientious praise of illustrious talents — I've judged it worthwhile to set out the names of those whose portraits are already on display in my hall dedicated to the immortals.

Let this, then, be the definitive announcement of the site chosen and the work being undertaken, so that from now on men of discriminating taste, as if recognizing an auspicious omen of a favorable future, may prepare in advance lasting monuments of their brilliance for future generations, and therefore ungrudgingly grant a favor which will bestow honor upon me and likewise upon themselves and, finally, will be gratifying to all.

13     Appello enim eos qui literarum amore voluptates abdicarunt et
bona spe diuturnae laudis aluntur, num laudari vel a mediocribus
poetis ineptum putent? Superbe quidem insaniunt si alienae liberalitatis munera fastidiant.

14     Idcirco mihi satis fuerit Italos blande ac humaniter admonuisse,
neque enim eos adeo austeros et illiberales fore crediderim quin
imagines scite pictas ad Musaeum minime transmittant. Quid
enim inverecundius, ne dicam agrestius, admitti poterit quam ab
exemplo tot insignium virorum omnino discessisse, qui hoc eruditae benignitatis officium laetissime praestiterunt? Quam ob rem
annotata nomina subdidimus ut qui absunt certam sedem benigne
sibi relictam intelligant, si, in hac florida ac immortali corona,
conspici decorum existimarint. His equidem ingenuis lusibus nostris, primos vigiliarum suarum fructus praedulci libatione degusta-
bunt. Quid enim viventi ac utique de ingenii virtute benemerito
beatius accidere potest, quam repraesentata alieni iudicii testificatione gloriam praesentire? Quid porro laetius atque iucundius
quam interesse posteritati suae, et denique Fatis invitis mortem
non timere, quam nemo, nisi anxius ante ipsum invidiae lacessen-
tis eventum, non timuit?

15     Nomina eorum qui adhuc vivunt et praeclara foecundi ingenii
gloria perfruuntur haec sunt. Imagines autem eo seriatim ordine
sedem obtinent ut dignitatem omnem vel fortunae vel generis ipse
unus aetatis honos antecedat.

Indeed, I call upon those who from love of literature have re-    13
nounced pleasures and are sustained by a reasonable hope of enduring glory: surely they would not suppose praise even from mediocre poets to be worthless! Surely they are insane in their
hauteur if they should scorn the gifts of another's generosity.

Therefore it will be enough for me to have brought this courte-    14
ously and kindly to the attention of Italians, for I should not think
them so rude and ill-bred that they would refuse to donate well-
painted portraits to the Museum. For what deed more shameful,
not to say churlish, could be committed than to fall away entirely
from the example of so many brilliant men who have most cheer-
fully fulfilled this obligation of scholarly courtesy? For this reason
I have supplied below the designated names in order that those
who are absent may recognize that a sure berth has kindly been
reserved for them, should they suppose it decorous to be seen in
this flowery and enduring garland. For truly, in these gentlemanly
diversions of mine, they will taste in a sweet libation the first fruits
of their vigils. For what greater happiness can befall anyone alive
and in any way meritorious for intellectual prowess than to have a
foretaste of glory through having the attestation of another's judgment put on display? Moreover, what could be more joyful and
pleasant than to be a living witness to one's legacy,[24] and finally,
despite the Fates, to be unafraid of death, which all have feared
unless they have prepared in advance for envy's assault?

These are the names of those who are alive and fully enjoy the    15
splendid glory of a fertile brilliance. Moreover, the portraits are
ordered in a series in such a way that the criterion of age itself
alone takes precedence over every other distinction, whether of
fortune or of lineage.

433

Petrus Bembus Cardinalis
Baptista Aegnatius
Iacobus Sadoletus Cardinalis
Georgius Trissinus
Hieronymus Fracastorius[3]
Hieronymus Vida Episcopus Albanus
Ioannes Pierius Valerianus
Romulus Amasaeus
Andreas Alciatus
Marcus Antonius Flaminius
Philippus Melancton
Ianus Vitalis
Reginaldus Polus Cardinalis
Daniel Barbarus
Antonius Mirandula
Philander Gallus
Honoratus Fasitellus
Basilius Zanchus.

17    Sed qua spe alienae benignitatis munus expectaverim, quum
haec nostra cupiditas ad externorum imagines extendatur, nisi viri
nobiles adiutent honestisque votis arrideant? Nulla enim res est
vel non plane ardua, quae illustri patrocinio non indigeat, ut recte
matureque perfici ac impetrari possit. Rogabo itaque veteres patro-
nos in provinciis dignitate atque opibus praecellentes sic ut eos
etiam pie obtester per communia Musarum sacra, ut hoc officium
expedite ac liberaliter praestare velint. Quid enim non praestabunt

*The Names of Those Whose Portraits I Possess* 16

Cardinal Pietro Bembo[25]
Battista Egnazio[26]
Cardinal Jacopo Sadoleto[27]
Giorgio Trissino[28]
Girolamo Fracastoro[29]
Girolamo Vida, bishop of Alba[30]
Giovanni Pierio Valeriano[31]
Romolo Amaseo[32]
Andrea Alciati[33]
Marcantonio Flaminio[34]
Philipp Melanchthon[35]
Giano Vitale[36]
Cardinal Reginald Pole[37]
Daniele Barbaro[38]
Antonio Mirandola[39]
Philandrier of France[40]
Onorato Fascitelli[41]
Basilio Zanchi.[42]

But with what hope might I await a gift of kindness from 17
abroad (inasmuch as this avidity of mine extends to portraits of
foreigners), unless noble men should help out and smile upon
honorable desires? Indeed, there's no cause, even if it is not conspicuously difficult, which does not require splendid patronage in
order that it may be completed and obtained properly and in a
timely manner. I will therefore query longstanding patrons abroad
who are men of preeminent dignity and wealth, beseeching them
reverently on the grounds of our shared devotion to the Muses, to
be willing to provide these things too, expeditiously and generously. For what will revered eminences not provide, who, having

sacrati proceres, qui se alumnos amatoresque Musarum professi nunquam verae gloriae nomen contempserunt?

18     Ita ut vel ab ultima Sarmatia, qua Latinae linguae septa Roxolanorum nivibus terminantur, mihi minime defuturum sperem Ioannem Dantiscum Varmiensem episcopum, qui multis legationum functus honoribus et poetica lauru coronatus, suae gentis nobilitatem ad eandem laudem accendit, ad quam praeclare aspirant Philippus Padnevius Martinusque Cromerius.

19     Nec in hoc aedepol erudito munere collocando suspense cunctabitur generosus ille Musarum hospes Otho Truchses Germaniae, decus et sacri senatus ornamentum, quum eius explorata liberalitas neque usu consenescat, neque praeterita existimatione satietur, nec aliud quicquam nisi extra invidiam positum perenneque respiciat. Nec id hercle mirum, postquam ille alioqui multis importunus maturatae purpurae splendor, nec perstrinxerit oculos, nec memoriae nervos eliserit, nec quicquam de syncero nobilique pudore vel leviter inumbrarit. Patefecit enim innatae virtutis studia in hoc dudum apud Vangiones conventu longe gravissimo, quum summa authoritate praeses ideoque reipublicae causa vehementer occupatus, omnes numeros perfectae virtutis expresserit ita ut ab eo iam non paucos quidem, sed ex feraci ingeniorum Germania integram per imagines lectissimorum virorum cohortem expectem, in qua, inter tantos Graecorum authorum interpretes divinarumque rerum scriptores, inclytum poetam Georgium Logum sodalem meum, si ita fas est, cum laurea signiferum exoptarim.

20     Nec Thomam quoque Nadastum, qui unus in Pannonia pari studio Martis et Palladis antiquum decus tuetur, quenquam omnino praetermissurum ex his, arbitror, quos intestini ac externi

declared themselves pupils and devotees of the Muses, have never disdained a reputation for true glory?

And so, even from the farthest reaches of Poland, where the 18 limits of the Latin language are bounded by Scythian snows, I should hope not to be missing Jan Dantyszek,[43] the bishop of Warmia, who, after having served on many embassies and being adorned with honors and the laurel crown for poetry, inspired the nobility of his people to the same glory toward which Filip Padniewski[44] and Marcin Kromer[45] are quite successfully aspiring.

Nor will that generous host of the Muses Otto Truchsess,[46] the 19 glory of Germany and jewel of the College of Cardinals, waffle or delay about fulfilling this task (an erudite one, heaven knows), since his demonstrated generosity neither wanes in application nor is satisfied with a reputation based on past deeds; nor does it have regard for anything whatsoever except what is placed beyond envy's reach and is everlasting. Nor is it unusual, Lord knows, since that splendor of early elevation to the purple, which in general has been problematic for many, neither dazzled his eyes nor broke down the sinews of memory, nor cast even the slightest shadow over anything pertaining to a sincere and lofty modesty. Indeed, he revealed the enthusiasms of a lofty nature a little while ago in that assembly at Worms, when, as a presider with the highest authority and therefore energetically engaged in affairs of state, he displayed the full measure of perfect virtue.[47] And so, I already await from him not just a few, but an entire cohort of portraits of the choicest men from Germany, so productive of geniuses. Among the many translators of Greek authors and writers of religious texts, I should greatly desire to see my friend (if I may call him so), the celebrated poet Georg von Logau,[48] as their laurel-crowned standard-bearer.

Nor, out of those whom the disasters of civil and foreign war 20 have left alive, do I think that anyone at all would fail to mention Thomas Nádasty:[49] he alone in Hungary upholds the ancient glory of Mars and Athena with equal dedication. Indeed, quite a

belli calamitas reliquos fecit. Iampridem enim amisimus sacrati ordinis antistites literarum atque virtutis studio praecellentes Ioannem Pannonium aeterno poemate edito stabili fama commendatum, et Philippum Moraeum Strigoniensem Mugaciana acie a barbaris interfectum; et, quos nuper non sera dies nobis eripuit, veteres amicos pietate ac altitudine animi Latinaque facundia illustres, dum tota Europa maximas legationes obirent, Stephanum inquam Brodericum Vacciensem Francapanem Agriensem et Statilium Albae Iuliae Dacorum sacerdotio insignem.

21    Sed florentissimi pauloante regni profecto miseret, tanquam subacti ac in foeda servitute plane morientis, quum in eo egregia illa ideoque non temere formidata barbaris veterum militum soboles interierit,[4] extincto nimirum Matthia Rege, cuius summae virtuti nusquam Fortuna defuit, pudore ingentis animi victa scilicet ut mox indignata imbelles firmissimi Regni dominos, uti suo more instabilis, non iniquo iure rebellaret.

22    Haec eadem pari incursu Dalmatas afflixit, apud quos valida ad capessendam ex literarum studiis laudem hac aetate ingenia floruerunt sed, ab assiduis barbarorum incursionibus exturbati vetere agro ac in extremas patrii littoris margines compulsi, tanquam de retinenda libertate desperantes, armis literas commutasse videri possunt, sic ut nemo dignus elogio compareat, nisi in lucem studiose producat cives suos Tranquillus Andronicus praeclarus Ciceronis aemulator, dum gravissimarum actionum ac Othomanicae legationis obscurorumque nobis itinerum commentaria perscribit.

23    Belgarum porro ingenia mihi hercle diligenter excudet et bona fide recensebit oraque delectorum, ni fallor, erudite picta benigne

while ago, we lost bishops of the holy order outstanding in their zeal for learning and for virtue: Janus Pannonius,[50] recognized with secure fame once his deathless poetry had been published; and Filip More[51] of Esztergom, killed by the barbarians in the Battle of Mohács. I also mention old friends illustrious in piety and high-mindedness and in Latin eloquence, whom recently death snatched away from us while they were going on the most important ambassadorial missions in all of Europe: István Brodarics,[52] Frangipane of Eger,[53] and Statilius,[54] the distinguished bishop of Alba Iulia in Transylvania.

But I do certainly pity a kingdom flourishing spectacularly not    21
long ago, conquered, and plainly withering away in disgraceful servitude now that a long dynasty of warriors, exceptional and so understandably dreadful to barbarians, has been extinguished. This of course came about by the death of King Matthias,[55] whose consummate prowess was nowhere forsaken by Fortune, won over by the purity of his lofty spirit — so that naturally, inconstant as she is, she soon took offense at the conciliatory rulers of a mighty kingdom, and not without justice took up arms against them.

In a similar attack, this same Fortune crushed the Dalmatians,    22
among whom in that age there flourished powerful minds capable of winning fame from literary studies. But now that they have been driven off their ancient terrain by unremitting attacks of barbarians and pushed to the far reaches of their ancestral coastline, as if despairing of preserving liberty, they may appear to have traded letters for arms, so that there is nobody meriting a portrait, unless the eminent Ciceronian stylist Tranquillus Andronicus[56] should assiduously bring public attention to his fellow citizens by writing commentaries on the most important deeds and about the embassy to the Turks and journeys unknown to our writers.

Of the great intellects of Flanders, furthermore, Antoine Perrenot,[57] bishop of Arras, is having portraits made for me (diligently, Lord knows) and will faithfully prepare a list, and unless    23

largietur Antonius Peronetus Atrebatensium antistes, modo ei
adeo graviter maximis officiis occupato haec ardens conficiendae
publicae pacis cura excolendis Musis ocium relinquat. Quod certe
necessario somno subtracturum crediderim, quum iam pondera
consiliorum ingentium ex sinu Caesaris, nimia plane vel importuna fatiscentis senis patris humeris pie subeundo naviter excipiat.
Sed valebit, opinor, Erasmi viri summi praeceptorisque memoria,
quum discipulorum eius insignis globus passim occurret, Petro
Nanio duce, quo optimarum literarum professore Lovaniensium
academia gloriatur. Qua in re se monitorem occupato Peroneto
facile praestabit Cornelius Cepaerus eruditi iudicii pondere, et in
tantis legationibus ac illustri totius Europae peregrinatione celebratus.

24    At non haec quoque speraverim ex opulenta Gallia quae, variae
et inconditae doctrinae acervos aliquandiu mirata, nunc primum
quid sit illud eximium in literis et perillustre decus intelligit repu-
diataque barbarie ita Latinae orationis puritate delectatur ut, si-
quid manes omnino sentiunt, Budaeum pariter ac Erasmum misere pudeat adeo agresti et senticosa via laudem vigiliis parem
omnino quaesivisse?

25    Aspirabit utique nobili voto luculenter Ioannes Bellaius praeclaro vetustae familiae ac insitae virtutis nomine Parisiorum antistes, et bis merita purpura senator amplissimus. Quid enim
amico veteri erudita praesertim ideoque minimi sumptus munera
cupienti non tribuet? qui perenni studio Graecis atque Latinis

I'm mistaken will generously give me the skillfully depicted likenesses of those selected — provided that this zeal for establishing
public peace allows him the leisure for cultivating the Muses when
he is so weighed down by the most important responsibilities. Of
course, I would expect him to steal that leisure from the sleep he
needs, given that already, out of filial piety, he is diligently taking
on weighty deliberations dear to the emperor's heart — burdens
plainly excessive and indeed unfit for the shoulders of his father,
who is elderly and in decline.[58] But I believe that the memory of
his teacher Erasmus, that greatest of men, will remain strong,
since the remarkable crowd of his students will be seen everywhere. Foremost among these is Pieter Nannick,[59] whom the
University of Leuven prides itself on having as a professor of the
choicest literature. In this matter, should Perrenot be too busy,
Cornelis de Schepper,[60] famous for the authority of his learned
judgment and for going on such great embassies and such important sojourns abroad in all of Europe, will readily offer himself as
an advisor.

But should I not also hope for these things from wealthy 24
France? For ages it has admired heaps of varied and unrefined
learning, but now for the first time discerns the special and exceedingly splendid glory in literature. And, having repudiated barbarism, it so delights in the purity of Latin eloquence that, if the
shades of the dead can feel, Budé and likewise Erasmus would
blush to have sought similar praise for studies by so rough and
thorny a path.

At any rate, the bishop of Paris, Jean du Bellay,[61] famous for the 25
reputation of his ancient lineage and of his innate virtue, and a
most distinguished cardinal who deserved the purple twice over,
will splendidly assist me in my noble commitment. For what will
he not bestow upon an old friend desiring gifts, especially those
that are refined and therefore inexpensive? He, who with contin-
ual devotion pays homage to the Greek and Latin Muses? He,

Musis sacra facit, qui ingenia fovet productaque in regiam, eruditi principis liberalitate protinus exornanda in luce constituit? Huic igitur non immerito viri doctissimi morem gerent benigneque docta ora pictoribus praebebunt ipseque ante alios Perionius vel religionis amore sacratis inclusus septis, qui Aristotelem Ciceronis ore loquentem fecit, dum Strebeum pari aemulatione conspicuum glorioso certamine superare contendit.

26      Quid non tribuet sodali Danesius, qui Budaei praeceptoris imaginem huc usque transmittit vir hercle summa eruditione Romanoque iudicio insignis, a quo propediem absolutae felicitatis partum expectamus? Nec puto Lazarum Baiphium libris de re vestiaria navalique percelebrem, et Guliermum Pellicerium, explicato totius rei herbariae negocio, publicae utilitati consulentem, quicquam vetere amicitia indignum admissuros.

27      Nec desiderio meo prorsus illudet ipse Castellanus, praecellentis doctrinae merito perpetuus comes ascitus regi ut inter mollissima coenae tempora rerum omnium origines et eventus infinitae regis memoriae recondenda repraesentet. Consequetur[5] et hos Tusanus in rei literariae substantia Budaei praeceptoris astutus haeres, quum id tantum adierit quod certum et salubre videbatur, totam autem parum comptae elocutionis intemperiem effugerit.

28      Nec ab his vestigiis longe aberunt poetae duo plane suaves et teneri, Salmonius Macrinus[6] Nicolausque Borbonius; et Regius, qui pedestri oratione poetarum honoribus adequatur. Postremo et ipse Vatablus: quanquam in celeberrimo gymnasio plenis subselliis

who fosters brilliant minds and, having brought them to the royal court, has put them on display to be honored at once with the largesse of a refined prince? Not undeservedly, therefore, the most learned men will oblige him and will courteously make their learned faces available to painters — and before the others, Périon[62] himself, even though from love of religion he is enclosed in a cloister. He made Aristotle speak with the eloquence of Cicero while, in a glorious contest, he strove to surpass Strébée,[63] notable for that very rivalry.

What won't Danès,[64] who even now is sending a portrait of his 26 teacher Budé, bestow upon a colleague? Lord knows he's a man outstanding in the loftiest erudition and in the judiciousness befitting a Roman, and I expect him soon to produce a completely successful work. Nor do I think that Lazare de Baïf,[65] exceedingly famous for his books on clothing and nautical matters,[66] and Guillaume Pellicier,[67] attending to the public good after having explained herbals of all kinds, would do anything unworthy of long-standing friendship.

Nor will my longing be entirely disappointed by Du Chastel[68] 27 himself, a constant companion to the king, taken on by him on account of his exceptional learning, in order that amid the calm dinner hours he might portray the origins and outcomes of all events, to be stored away in the king's boundless memory. And next will come Toussain,[69] a shrewd heir of his teacher Budé's literary assets, since he took possession only of what seemed reliable and beneficial, but eschewed all the immoderation of insufficiently polished expression.

And not lagging far behind will be two distinctly sweet and 28 tender poets, Salmon Macrin[70] and Nicolas Bourbon;[71] and there is Le Roy,[72] who in prose measures up to the reputations of poets. And lastly, there's Vatable[73] himself: although proud of the full benches in his very famous university, he will not refuse to provide

superbus, suam vel Hebraica duricie non plane faceti oris effigiem denegabit.

29    Sed ad quem modo confugiam qui in Hispania praecellentium ingeniorum delectum habeat ac eleganti viro dignum huius non indecorae liberalitatis officium praestet? Inter multos hercle qui severioribus divinarum rerum ac humanarum studiis dediti, tanquam reipublicae privataeque maxime utiles iudicantur, rari occurrunt elegantium literarum ornamentis insignes, quod hic omnis Latine scribendi lepor, a parum gravibus inani ambitione quaesitus, nulla omnino subsidia seriis facultatibus sed impedimenta nonnunquam afferre videatur.

30    Qua de causa, quum vigente adhuc seniorum opinione ipsi etiam totius Hispaniae proceres haec studia tanquam importuna militiae penitus abdicarent, hic excellens cultus quo disciplinae omnes exornantur, aliquanto serius quam alias in terras in Hispaniam pervenerit ita ut haec terra alioqui rerum omnium ferax acerrimorumque imprimis et sublimium ingeniorum altrix, quae tot nobiles aeternosque poetas ac oratores Romanae civitati quondam inseruit, hoc toto quod suspicimus, illustris eloquentiae honore penitus orbata censeri possit.

31    Agnovere tamen nonnulli maiorum incuriam, Nebrissa monitore ingeniaque sua ad hanc laudem feliciter extulerunt, in queis nuper emicuit Garcias Lassus, Horatiana suavitate odas scribere solitus; sed eum generose ad fastigium evadentem, dum alteram militiae laudem ardenter appetit, mors acerba elusit, et casu quidem ignobili, quum ad Aquas Sextias ex turricula ab agrestibus lapide caput ictus spectante Caesare concidisset.

32    Sed hodie procul dubio Ioannes Sepulveda Cordubensis ipsam eximiae laudis arcem obtinet, qui Graecae peritus linguae et scien-

a likeness of his face, which certainly isn't charming, with its perhaps Hebraic[74] austerity.

But in Spain, to whom now might I turn who has a muster of   29
exceptional talents and might perform this service, an honorable
act of generosity worthy of a man of refinement? Among the
many (Lord knows) dedicated to the more austere studies of
things human and divine, as these are adjudged especially useful to
the state and the private individual, men noted for the distinctions
of elegant literature are uncommon: for all this charm of writing
in Latin, pursued by dilettantes out of vain ambition, seems to offer no support at all, and often impediments, to serious skills.

For this reason — since the attitude of the older generation still   30
flourishes, even the foremost men of all Spain entirely forswear
these pursuits as unsuitable for the military — that lofty elegance
with which all the disciplines are adorned has arrived in Spain
somewhat later than in other countries. Consequently this country, in other respects productive of all things and above all the
nursemaid of the most acute and lofty geniuses, which once
brought so many noble and enduring poets and orators to the Roman state, can be considered entirely deprived of this whole thing
that we look up to, the honor of illustrious eloquence.

Nonetheless some, with Nebrija as their guide, have recognized   31
the neglectfulness of the elders and have successfully elevated their
minds to that glory. Among these, recently there came to light
Garcilaso,[75] accustomed to write odes with Horatian charm; but
while he was ardently striving after the other glory (that of the
military), bitter death cheated him just as he was nobly ascending
to the summit — and certainly by an ignoble accident, when at Aix,
as the emperor looked on, a stone thrown by peasants from a
small tower struck him in the head and he perished.[76]

But today, without doubt, Juan Sepúlveda[77] of Córdoba occu-   32
pies the very citadel of outstanding glory. Expert in Greek and
equipped with the robust defenses of nearly all fields of knowl-

tiarum prope omnium validis instructus praesidiis, dum assidue atque ideo feliciter stylum exercet, eloquentissimus evadit. Huic autem proximum accedere audimus Martinum Silicaeum Carthaginensem episcopum, qui lectissimis moribus ac literis virilique ingenio et casta facundia, dum Philippum Caesaris filium persancte et solerter edocet, optimum principem ad paternum decus et ad regni felicitatem instituit.

33    Reliqua porro ingenia quae foecunditatis egregiae aut maturae frugis specimen praebent, indicaturum scite atque fideliter crediderim Franciscum Mendocium Cardinalem, quem accipiendis de manu summi pontificis solennibus senatoriae dignitatis ornamentis propediem expectamus. Hic enim supra generis antiquum decus amplissimam ex optimis literis laudem spectat potiturque iam parta ex his studiis insigni gloria, quae nixa verae virtutis radicibus nunquam deflorescet.

34    Ea porro ingenia, quae ultima terrarum Lusitania ad oceanum nobis abscondit, a Michaele Sylvio Cardinale non diu quidem expectabimus; is enim, a varia doctrina poeta cultissimus ac omnis elegantiae iucundus arbiter, studia nostra vehementer amat et laudat, patriique decoris plane cupidus supra reliquos animosae gentis honores, hoc literatae laudis nomen, tanquam non postremae si non summae gloriae, minime contemnit.

35    At quid postremo ab ultima Britannia expectaverim nisi lugubres fortasse imagines, quum ibi optimi pauloante regis importuna crudelitas aeternae laudis proceres excisa plane virtute sustulerit?

FINIS

edge, while persistently and therefore successfully wielding a pen, he has become exceedingly eloquent. I've heard that next after him, moreover, comes Martínez Siliceo,[78] bishop of Cartagena, a man of refined character and learning, brilliance, and pure eloquence. As the resourceful and reverent teacher of the emperor's son Philip, he is training a most excellent prince to be the glory of his father and the good fortune of the realm.

Then there is Cardinal Francisco Mendoza,[79] who we expect 33 will receive any day now from the pope's hand the ceremonial trappings of the cardinalate. I'd like to think that he will knowingly and faithfully point out the remaining brilliant minds that give an indication of exceptional fertility or mature fruit. This man indeed looks beyond the venerable distinction of his lineage to the abundant glory of fine literature, and is already acquiring a conspicuous glory from his studies which, as it is nourished by the roots of true virtue, never withers.

Furthermore, we shall hope soon indeed to get from Cardinal 34 Miguel da Silva[80] those men of talent whom Portugal, the remotest of countries in the direction of the Atlantic, has hidden from us. For this man, whose wide-ranging erudition has made him an exceedingly refined poet and a delightful arbiter of every elegance, enthusiastically approves and praises my project. Conspicuously desiring the elegance of his fatherland over the other honors of a spirited nation, he does not in the least scorn this reputation for literary merit, for if it is not the supreme form of glory, it's not the least one, either.

But what, finally, ought I to await from distant Britain except 35 perhaps mournful portraits? For there, the relentless cruelty of the king, who until recently was the very best, has destroyed celebrated men of enduring fame, utterly demolishing excellence.

THE END

# [INCERTI]

Postquam relegit omnium
provinciarum Iovius intimos lares,
nec instituta substitit
via, vel alto territus montis iugo,
hinc dividentis Italos,
illinc Hiberos Bellicosa Gallia,
vel aestuosis Adriae
illinc procellis, hinc profundis fluctibus
turbatus inferi maris,
sed inter acreis evagatus milites
interque rauca cornua,
et fusa victorum hinc et hinc cadavera,
non otiosa indagine
tot inde retulit libros annalium.
Mox utriusque littoris
ora remensa, diligens felicibus
piscator inde retibus,
avara quicquid ante Neptunni[1] manus
celaverat nobis tulit.
Nunc inquietus patre deductus Iove
animusque terrestribus
non rebus explendus, velut celeri Noto
elatus, ubi coelestibus
explere se se latius rebus potest:
en aureo promit penu
quantum supremo Iuppiter magnus polo
pulchri recondit; et quia
nunquam moveri coelites queunt loco
ut sustulit Fati dies,

# ANONYMOUS LIMINAL POEM

Now that Giovio has traversed again the innermost dwell-
ings of all the provinces and hasn't halted the course he has
begun — neither frightened by the high mountain ranges that
on this side divide Italy and on that separate the Iberians
from warlike France, nor disturbed by the buffeting storms
of the Adriatic on the one side or the deep waves of the Tyrrhenian Sea on the other — but instead, having gone off
among the keen soldiers and the harshly resounding trum-
pets and the corpses of the vanquished strewn here and
there, with an expeditious striving after facts, he has written
so many books of histories. Now that he has retraced the
shores of both seas, a diligent fisherman with successful nets,
he brings forth whatever previously the stingy hand of Neptune had concealed from us. Now his restless mind, inherited from Father Jove, is unsated with earthly matters, as if
raised up by the swift south wind to where it can feast more
expansively on heavenly things. Behold! He brings forth
from the golden storeroom all the beauty great Jupiter keeps
hidden in the celestial vault on high. And since heavenly be-
ings can never be moved from that place once Death has
taken them, he has received individuals' faithful likenesses,

veras recepit singulorum imagines
quas dedicata Apollini,
Musisque Larium colentibus Lacum,
beata continet domus.
Has si videre longa te vetat via
aut morbus aut senium grave,
praesens libellus indicabit aureo
quovis monili carior.
Vos hinc remordet illa si cura, arduum
tentate coelum, posteri,
quod summa virtus sola dat recludier.

which are contained in a delightful abode dedicated to Apollo and to the Muses who inhabit Lake Como. If either a long journey or sickness or the impairments of old age prevent you from seeing them, this little book before you, dearer than any golden necklace, will make them known. Henceforth, o future generations, if that concern gnaws at you, reach for heaven on high, because it lies open only to the highest virtue.

# Note on the Text and Translation

## THE LATIN TEXT

We are fortunate to have an *editio princeps* that was prepared under Giovio's supervision: *Elogia veris clarorum virorum imaginibus apposita . . . Addita . . . Adriani pontificis vita* (Venice: Tramezzino, 1546). In addition, portions of drafts of most of the *elogia* of literati have survived in manuscript form and are housed in Como at the Centro Studi "Nicolò Rusca" in Fondo Aliati, cassetta 28, intorno 7. Checking the 1546 text against the drafts has on occasion facilitated comprehension. This move, however, is made with caution: many are in scribal hands, and those that are autograph are often quite rough, with numerous cancellations and addenda, not all of which appear in the printed version. Where variant readings from the manuscript are cited in the notes, they are identified as being either in scribal hand (*MSs*) or in Giovio's hand (*MSa*). The specific pages on which they appear (the *elogia* are not in order) are noted only when more than one manuscript version has survived.

Beyond consulting the *editio princeps* and the manuscripts, the editor systematically collated the 1546 edition with those printed in 1557, 1571, and 1577. Those of 1557 and 1571 are severely marred by errors, most but not all of them typographical. While that of 1577 marks some improvement over them, its precision falls far short of the 1546 edition. Its chief interest to scholars today, beyond the important addition of engraved portraits, is its doctoring of the text to make it congenial to Protestant readers. Its significant silent interventions are indicated in the notes below. The one modern Latin edition of the *Elogia*, edited by Renzo Meregazzi and published in 1972 as volume 8 of the National Edition of Giovio's works, is so riddled with errors that it is best disregarded entirely.

Orthography follows that of the 1546 edition, excepting capitalization, punctuation, and paragraph breaks. A number of Giovio's idiosyncrasies are maintained: e.g., *vix dum* (rather than *vixdum*); the drawing of a dis-

tinction between *quum* (a conjunction) and *cum* (a preposition), maintained except in epitaphs he did not compose; *authoritas* rather than *auc-
toritas*; *ocium* rather than *otium*; and *ut pote* rather than *utpote*. Banal
printing errors are silently corrected. In those cases where changes to the
text are conjectural, they are identified as such in the notes. While the
present text is by no means a critical edition, it will be the most reliable
option for anyone interested in reading the text as Giovio wished it to
appear.

## LATIN EDITIONS CONSULTED

*Elogia veris clarorum virorum imaginibus apposita quae in musaeo Ioviano Comi*
  *spectantur, addita in calce operis Adriani pontificis vita.* Venice: Michele
  Tramezzino, 1546. Abbreviated in the apparatus as *1546.*
*Elogia doctorum virorum ab avorum memoria publicatis ingenii monumentis il-*
  *lustrium.* Antwerp: Jean Bellère, 1557.
*Elogia doctorum virorum ab avorum memoria publicatis ingenii monumentis il-*
  *lustrium. Praeter nova Ioannis Latomi Bergani in singulos epigrammata adie-*
  *cimus ad priora Italicae editionis illustrium aliquot poetarum alia.* Basel:
  Pietro Perna, 1571.
*Elogia virorum literis illustrium quotquot vel nostra vel avorum memoria vixere,*
  *ex eiusdem Musaeo (cuius descriptionem una exhibemus) ad vivum expressis*
  *imaginibus exornata.* Basel: Pietro Perna, 1577. Abbreviated in the apparatus as *1577.*
*Elogia veris clarorum virorum imaginibus apposita quae in musaeo [Ioviano]*
  *Comi spectantur.* In *Gli elogi degli uomini illustri (Letterati – Artisti – Uo-*
  *mini d'arme)*, edited by Renzo Meregazzi, vol. 8 in *Pauli Iovii opera*,
  31–225. Rome: Istituto Poligrafico dello Stato, 1972.

## NOTE ON THE TRANSLATION

To date there has been only one English translation, that of Florence
Alden Gragg (1935). While eloquent and often faithful to Giovio's tone, it
has several major shortcomings. First, Gragg consulted only a distinctly
inferior edition of the *Elogia*, that of 1557. Second, the limitations on her
knowledge of the politics of Giovio's time are evident throughout. Third,

she omits most (albeit not quite all) of the epitaphs. Finally, she provides only 105 brief notes, most of which identify echoes of ancient works, whereas much in the text requires glossing for readers not intimately familiar with the Italian Renaissance.

The present editor admires Gragg's sensitivity to the Latin and has found some of her phrasings impossible to better, but seeks to provide a text that is at once accessible to the general reader and useful for specialists. Its glosses, while far from encyclopedic, provide a starting point for those wishing to explore in more detail the people, ideas, and events that appear in the text. To make the translation readable in twenty-first-century English, the editor has often reduced pleonasm of adjectives, changed passive constructions to active ones, eliminated inflationary uses of the comparative and superlative degrees, converted participial phrases to adjectives, regularized rhetorical schemes such as hendiadys, and so forth. It is hoped that the reader will appreciate the smoother prose that results from such interventions, which seek to move the text fully into English rather than leaving it suspended awkwardly in limbo between the two languages.

# Abbreviations

᠁

| | |
|---|---|
| Ariosto | Ludovico Ariosto, *Latin Poetry*, ed. and trans. Dennis Looney and D. Mark Possanza, ITRL 84 (Cambridge, MA: Harvard University Press, 2017). |
| Arsilli | Francesco Arsilli, "De Poetis Urbanis, ad Paulum Iovium Libellus," in *Coryciana*, 344–59. |
| BAV | Bibliotheca Apostolica Vaticana |
| Berni | Anne Reynolds, *Renaissance Humanism at the Court of Clement VII: Francesco Berni's Dialogue Against Poets in Context. Studies, with an edition and translation* (New York: Garland, 1997). |
| CE | Peter. G. Bietenholz and Thomas B. Deutscher, eds., *Contemporaries of Erasmus: A Biographical Register of the Renaissance and Reformation*, 3 vols. (Toronto: University of Toronto Press, 1985–87). |
| Cochrane | Eric Cochrane, *Historians and Historiography in the Italian Renaissance* (Chicago: University of Chicago Press, 1981). |
| *Coryciana* | *Coryciana*, ed. Jozef IJsewijn (Rome: Herder, 1997). |
| Croce | Benedetto Croce, *Poeti e scrittori del pieno e del tardo Rinascimento*, 3 vols. (Bari: Laterza, 1952–58). |
| CTC | *Catalogus Translationum et Commentariorum: Mediaeval and Renaissance Latin Translations and Commentaries; Annotated Lists and Guides*, ed. Paul Oskar Kristeller, F. Edward Cranz, |

|   | Virginia Brown, Greti Dinkova-Bruun, et al., 12 vols. to date (Washington, D.C.: Catholic University of America Press, 1960–). Online at http://catalogustranslationum.org/ |
|---|---|
| CV | *Condottieri di ventura*, maintained by dott. Roberto Damiani, www.condottieridiventura.it |
| D'Amico | John F. D'Amico, *Renaissance Humanism in Papal Rome: Humanists and Churchmen on the Eve of the Reformation* (Baltimore: Johns Hopkins University Press, 1983). |
| DBI | *Dizionario biografico degli italiani* (Rome: Istituto della Enciclopedia Italiana, 1960–). Online at https://www.treccani.it/biografie |
| DLI | Julia Haig Gaisser, *Pierio Valeriano on the Ill Fortune of Learned Men: A Renaissance Humanist and His World* (Ann Arbor: University of Michigan Press, 1999). |
| EB 11 | *Encyclopedia Brittanica*, 11th ed. (Project Gutenberg, 2010). |
| EH | Jean-François Maillard, J. Kecskeméti, and M. Portalier, *Europe des Humanistes: XIVe–XVIIe siècles*, 2nd ed. (Paris: CNRS; Turnhout: Brepols, 1998). |
| Elogi | Paolo Giovio, *Elogi degli uomini illustri*, ed. Franco Minonzio, trans. Andrea Guasparri and Franco Minonzio (Turin: Einaudi, 2006). |
| EMC | *The Encyclopedia of the Medieval Chronicle*, ed. Graeme Dunphy and Cristian Bratu, 2 vols. (Leiden: Brill, 2010). |
| ER | *Scribner's Encyclopedia of the Renaissance*, ed. Paul F. Grendler et al., 6 vols. (New York: Scribner's, 1999). |

| | |
|---|---|
| Erasmus, *Ciceronian* | Erasmus, *Ciceronianus*, trans. Betty I. Knott, vol. 28 (1986), in *Collected Works of Erasmus* (Toronto: University of Toronto Press, 1974–). |
| Erasmus, *Ciceronianus* | Erasmus, *Dialogus Ciceronianus*, ed. P. Mesnard, in *Opera Omnia* (Amsterdam: North-Holland Publishing Co., 1969–), vol. I-2 (1971). |
| Eubel | Konrad Eubel, *Hierarchia catholica medii aevi, sive Summorum pontificum, S. R. E. cardinalium, ecclesiarum antistitum series*, 3 vols. (Regensburg: Monasterium, 1913–23), vols. 2 (1914) and 3 (1923). |
| *FH* | Jean-François Maillard, Judith Kecskeméti, Catherine Magnien, and Monique Portalier, *La France des Humanistes: Hellénistes*, vol. 1 (Turnhout: Brepols, 1999). |
| Giovio (1546) | Paolo Giovio, *Elogia veris clarorum virorum imaginibus apposita . . . addita . . . Adriani pontificis vita* (Venice: Michele Tramezzino, 1546). |
| Giovio (1552) | Paolo Giovio, *Le iscrittioni poste sotto le vere imagini de gli huomini famosi: le quali à Como nel museo del Giovio si veggiono*, trans. Hippolito Orio (Florence: Lorenzo Torrentino, 1552). |
| Giovio (1557) | Paolo Giovio, *Elogia doctorum virorum ab avorum memoria publicatis ingenii monumentis illustrium.* (Antwerp: Jean Bellère, 1557). |
| Giovio (1558) | Paolo Giovio, *Le iscrittioni posto sotto le vere imagini de gli huomini famosi in lettere*, trans. Hippolito Orio (Venice: Francesco Bindoni, 1558). |
| Giovio (1571) | Paolo Giovio, *Elogia doctorum virorum ab avorum memoria publicatis ingenij monumentis illustrium. Praeter nova Ioannis Latomi Bergani in singulos* |

459

                         *epigrammata adiecimus ad priora Italicae editionis illustrium aliquot poetarum alia* (Basel: [Pietro Perna], 1571).

Giovio (1577)        Paolo Giovio, *Elogia virorum literis illustrium quotquot vel nostra vel avorum memoria vixere, ex eiusdem Musaeo (cuius descriptionem una exhibemus) ad vivum expressis imaginibus exornata* (Basel: Pietro Perna, 1577).

Giovio (1935)        Paolo Giovio, *An Italian Portrait Gallery; Being Brief Biographies of Scholars Illustrious within the memory of our grandfathers for the published monuments of their genius,* trans. Florence Alden Gragg (Boston: Chapman & Grimes, 1935).

Giovio (1999)        Paolo Giovio, *Ritratti degli uomini illustri,* ed. and trans. Carlo Caruso (Palermo: Sellerio editore, 1999).

Giraldi               Lilio Gregorio Giraldi, *Modern Poets,* ed. and trans. John N. Grant, ITRL 48 (Cambridge, MA: Harvard University Press, 2011).

GNC                 Heinz W. Cassirer, *God's New Covenant: A New Testament Translation* (Grand Rapids, MI: Eerdmans, 1989).

GSLI               *Giornale storico della letteratura italiana*

Gouwens          Kenneth Gouwens, *Remembering the Renaissance: Humanist Narratives of the Sack of Rome* (Leiden: E. J. Brill, 1998).

Grendler (2002)     Paul F. Grendler, *The Universities of the Italian Renaissance* (Baltimore: The Johns Hopkins University Press, 2002).

Guicciardini (1970)  Francesco Guicciardini, *The History of Florence,* trans. Mario Domandi (New York: Harper & Row, 1970).

| | |
|---|---|
| Guicciardini (1971) | Francesco Guicciardini, *Storia d'Italia*, ed. Silvana Seidel Menchi, 3 vols. (Turin: Einaudi, 1971). |
| *Humanism & Creativity* | *Humanism and Creativity in the Renaissance: Essays in Honor of Ronald G. Witt*, ed. Christopher S. Celenza and Kenneth Gouwens (Leiden: E. J. Brill, 2006). |
| IO | *Pauli Iovii opera*, 8 of 11 vols. to date [vols. 1–6 and 8–9] (Rome: Istituto Poligrafico dello Stato, [1957]–). |
| ITRL | I Tatti Renaissance Library |
| Jedin | Hubert Jedin, *A History of the Council of Trent*, trans. Ernest Graf, 2 vols. (London: Thomas Nelson and Sons, 1957). |
| Kidwell (1989) | Carol Kidwell, *Marullus: Soldier Poet of the Renaissance* (London: Duckworth, 1989). |
| Kidwell (1991) | Carol Kidwell, *Pontano: Poet and Prime Minister* (London: Duckworth, 1991). |
| Kidwell (1993) | Carol Kidwell, *Sannazaro and Arcadia* (London: Duckworth, 1993). |
| King | Margaret L. King, *Venetian Humanism in an Age of Patrician Dominance* (Princeton: Princeton University Press, 1986). |
| Klinger (1991) | Linda Susan Klinger, "The Portrait Collection of Paolo Giovio" 2 vols. (PhD diss., Princeton University, 1991). |
| L&S | Charlton T. Lewis and Charles Short, *A Latin Dictionary, founded on Andrews' Edition of Freund's Latin Dictionary* (Oxford: Clarendon, 1987). |
| LCL | Loeb Classical Library |
| Lee | Egmont Lee, *Sixtus IV and Men of Letters* (Rome: Edizioni di Storia e Letteratura, 1978). |

Maffei      Paolo Giovio, *Scritti d'arte: lessico ed ecfrasi*, ed. Sonia Maffei (Pisa: Scuola Normale Superiore, 1999).

Mallett (1974)      Michael E. Mallett, *Mercenaries and Their Masters: Warfare in Renaissance Italy* (Totowa, NJ: Rowman and Littlefield, 1974).

Mallett and Hale      Michael E. Mallett and John R. Hale, *The Military Organization of a Renaissance State: Venice c. 1400 to 1617* (Cambridge: Cambridge University Press, 1984).

Martines (2006)      Lauro Martines, *Fire in the City: Savonarola and the Struggle for the Soul of Renaissance Florence* (Oxford: Oxford University Press, 2006).

Minieri-Riccio      Camillo Minieri-Riccio, *Biografie degli accademici pontaniani* (Naples, 1881?).

Minonzio (2002)      Franco Minonzio, *Studi giovani: scienza, filosofia e letteratura nell'opera di Paolo Giovio*, 2 vols. (Como: Società Storica Comense, 2002) = *Raccolta storica della Società Storica Comense* 21 (2002) and 22 (2002).

Minonzio (2007)      Franco Minonzio, "Il Museo di Giovio e la galleria degli uomini illustri," in *Testi, immagini e filologia nel XVI secolo*, ed. Eliana Carrara and Silvia Ginzburg (Pisa: Edizioni della Normale, 2007), 77–146.

Minonzio (2012)      Franco Minonzio, *"Con l'appendice di molti eccellenti poeti." Gli epitaffi degli* Elogia *degli uomini d'arme di Paolo Giovio* (Cologno Monzese: Lampi di stampa, 2012).

MSa      Como. Centro Studi "Nicolò Rusca," Fondo Aliati, cassetta 28, intorno 7, autograph drafts of *elogia* of literati.

MSs      Como. Centro Studi "Nicolò Rusca," Fondo Aliati, cassetta 28, intorno 7, scribal drafts of *elogia* of literati.

| | |
|---|---|
| Najemy (2006) | John M. Najemy, *A History of Florence 1200–1575* (London: Blackwell, 2006). |
| *NMW* | Paolo Giovio, *Notable Men and Women of Our Time*, ed. and trans. Kenneth Gouwens, ITRL 56 (Cambridge, MA: Harvard University Press, 2013). |
| *OCD* | *The Oxford Classical Dictionary*, 4th ed., ed. Simon Hornblower, Antony Spawforth, and Esther Eidinow (Oxford: Oxford University Press, 2012). |
| *ODNB* | *Oxford Dictionary of National Biography*, Updating database (Oxford: Oxford University Press, 2004–). |
| *OLD* | *Oxford Latin Dictionary*, ed. P. G. W. Glare (Oxford: Clarendon, 1982). |
| *Orbis Latinus* | J. G. Th. Graesse, *Orbis Latinus: Lexicon lateinischer geographischer Namen des Mittelalters und der Neuzeit* (Berlin: Schmidt and Co., 1909), online at http://www.columbia.edu/acis/ets/Graesse/contents.html |
| Pastor | Ludwig von Pastor, *The History of the Popes from the Close of the Middle Ages*, 3rd ed., ed. F. I. Antrobus et al., 40 vols. (London: Kegan Paul, 1901–33). |
| *Poeti latini* | *Poeti latini del Quattrocento*, ed. Francesco Arnaldi, Lucia Gualdo Rosa, and Liliana Monti Sabia (Milan and Naples: Ricciardi, 1964). |
| *Pontificate of Clement* | *The Pontificate of Clement VII: History, Politics, Culture*, ed. Kenneth Gouwens and Sheryl E. Reiss (Aldershot: Ashgate, 2005). |
| Rabil | *Renaissance Humanism: Foundations, Forms, and Legacy*, ed. Albert Rabil, Jr., 3 vols. (Philadelphia: University of Pennsylvania Press, 1988). |

| | |
|---|---|
| *RLV* | Alessandro Perosa and John Sparrow, eds., *Renaissance Latin Verse: An Anthology* (London: Duckworth, 1979). |
| Sannazaro | Jacopo Sannazaro, *Latin poetry*, ed. and trans. Michael C. J. Putnam, ITRL 38 (Cambridge, MA: Harvard University Press, 2009). |
| Sanuto | Marino Sanuto, *I diarii di Marino Sanuto*, 58 vols. (Venice: Visentini, 1879–1902). |
| *SEP* | *Stanford Encyclopedia of Philosophy*, ed. Edward N. Zalta et al. (https://plato.stanford.edu). |
| Setton | Kenneth M. Setton, *The Papacy and the Levant (1204–1571)*, 4 vols. (Philadelphia: The American Philosophical Society, 1984). |
| Simonetta (2004) | Marcello Simonetta, *Rinascimento segreto: Il mondo del segretario da Petrarca a Machiavelli* (Milan: FrancoAngeli, 2004) |
| Spitz | Lewis W. Spitz, *The Religious Renaissance of the German Humanists* (Cambridge, MA: Harvard University Press, 1963). |
| Zimmermann (1995) | T. C. Price Zimmermann, *Paolo Giovio: The Historian and the Crisis of Sixteenth-Century Italy* (Princeton: Princeton University Press, 1995). |

# Notes to the Text

**ॐऽ२ॐ**

1. obscure] obscurae 1546

2. auctoremque *standard reading; see Manetti*] actoremque 1546, MSa

3. atque] ac 1546

4. admodum *MSa*] ad modum 1546

5. mediocribus *MSa*] mediocris 1546

6. introeuntibus *MSa*] intro euntibus 1546

7. profluentis *MSs*] pro fluentis 1546

8. *After* opus, *the MS adds four lines, which reappear in later editions, including that of 1577:* "Quique modum docuit, quo laudet honesta voluptas, / et quo ne iuvenes torqueat acer amor: // Pluraque quae longum est, properans censere, viator, / omnia sidereae pignora mentis erant."

9. letum] laetum 1546: loetum *MSs post corr.*

10. Galeacio *MSa*] Galeatio 1546

11. Latinaeque *MSa*] Latineque 1546

12. Macuti] Mauti 1546, MSa

13. Sfortia ab Helvetiis proditus ut 1546] Sfortia captus ut 1577

14. hic *MSs*] his 1546

15. quereretur] quaereretur 1546

16. Frixia 1546, *MSs*] Frisia *is the standard form*

17. Hingolstadio 1546, *MSs*] Heidelberga 1577 (*recte*)

18. in ostio] in Ostio 1546] ad ostio *MSs* (*sic; Giovio here changed* in *to read* ad *but evidently did not complete a revision*); *cf. the* elogium *of Piero de' Medici in the* editio princeps *of* Elogia virorum bellica virtute illustrium (*Florence: Torrentino, 1551*), 170: in ostio fluminis summersus interiit

19. *Sic*

20. Pactiis *(as in* elogium *146, title and text, both 1546 and MSa]* Pacciis 1546, MSs

21. *In 1577, this poem is attributed instead to Ercole Strozzi.*

22. saeculi MSs] saecula 1546

23. lanternam *edit. conjecture]* laternam 1546, MSs

24. prae caeteris] praecaeteris 1546, MSs

25. quum] cum 1546, MSs

26. dicta *sic in* Bembo, Lyric Poetry, ed. and trans. Mary P. Chatfield, ITRL 18 (Cambridge, MA: Harvard University Press, 2005), 98] verba 1546

27. hac MSs] haec 1546

28. Fracastorius] Fragastorius 1546

29. deliniatam MSa] diliniatam 1546

30. luxurie MSa *(p. 108)]* luxuriae 1546

31. arrideret MSa *(p. 104)]* arriderent 1546, MSa *(p. 108)*

32. male] malae 1546

33. confodissent] confodisset 1546

34. Emeritam] E meritam 1546

35. per ampla] perampla 1546

36. Grocinii] Gracinii 1546

37. Grocinius] Gracinius 1546

38. ob *(edit. conjecture)]* ad 1546

39. Desipuere] De sipuere 1546

40. Ticini] Ticinii 1546

41. Mechliniae] Macliniae 1546] Bruxellae MSs

42. citharoedi] citharedi 1546, MSa

43. *after* salubritate, *1577 ed. omits* percelebrem, atque ita humanitate

44. luxuriae] luxurie 1546] earum MSs

45. *1577 omits the passage* quanquam in exemplo dudum fuisset qui pariter scriptis assentiretur, vir sanctissimus atque doctissimus Thomas Caietanus Cardinalis, *which appears as an insertion in MSa (p. 64).*

46. *After* admiratione, *the text almost exactly follows the second Ischian dialogue, §16, for several lines. See NMW, 226.*

47. ac *MSs; NMW, 226 (= dial. II, §16)*] et *1546*

48. concitatus *MSs; NMW, 226 (= dial. II, §16)*] citatus *1546*

49. ac *MSs; NMW, 226 (= dial. II, §16)*] et *1546*

50. *Here ends the near-exact quotation from the second Ischian dialogue.*

51. *Sic*

52. *Sic*

53. Caesariani (*edit. conjecture*)] Caesariam *1546*

54. ediderat] aediderat *1546*] absolverat *MSa*

55. Carpetanis] Carpentanis *1546, MSs*

56. insalubri *MSs*] in salubri *1546*

57. Apulo *MSa*] Appulo *1546*

58. *Sic 1546, MSa*

59. Apulum] Appulum *1546*

60. quocum] quo cum *1546, MSa*

61. Rhoterodamo (*cf. elog. no. 95*)] Roterodamo *1546*

62. exili *MSs, Ariosto, no. LVIII*] hoc brevi *1546*

63. praescripti spatio *Ariosto, no. LVIII*] Praescripti spacio *MSs*] Praescripto spatio *1546*

64. diu vagetur *1546, MSs, Ariosto, no. LVIIIa*] vagus pererret *Ariosto, no. LVIII*

65. detrimento *supplevi ex MSa; it appears in two earlier versions of the sentence, both deleted*

66. Machiavellus (*cf. elog. no. 141, both 1546 and MSa; the standard form*] Macciavellus *1546*

67. Macchiavello] Macciavello *1546*] Maciavello *MSa*

68. astrinxerat *edit. conjecture*] astrixerat *1546*

69. Macchiavellus] Macciavellus *1546*

70. indicendi] in dicendi *1546*

71. descripto] de scripto *1546*

72. Incerti *1546*] Ioannis Secundi Hagiensis *1577*

73. conspiceret *sic in 1546, MSa*

74. proceritate *MSs*] prosperitate *1546*

75. decumatis legionibus *1546*] decumatis latronibus *MSs*

76. RHOTERODAMVS *1546*] RHOTEDAMVS *MSa*

77. Rhoterodamus *1546*] RHOTERDAMVS *MSa*

78. non multo post pertesus intempestivae servitutis votique temere suscepti, ea sacrati *edit. conjecture*] non multo post pertesus voti intempestivae servitutis votique temere suscepti, ea sacrati *1546*] non multo post pertesus voti onerosae servitutis eius sacrati *MSa*

79. relinquens *edit. conjecture*] reliquens *1546, MSa*

80. Friburgo in pago sive, ut aliqui afferunt *omitted in 1577 (presumably because Erasmus is known to have died in Basel)*

81. haeresis *1546, MSs*] doctrinae *1577*

82. quorundam animis concepta Lutheri factio salubri adducto dogmate sanaretur *1546*] quorundam animi concepta Lutheri sententia salubri adducto dogmate sanarentur *1577*

83. datus *edit. conjecture*] daret *1546*

84. blaterantis] blatterantis *1546*

85. quicum] qui cum *1546*

86. I, da] Ida *1546*

87. GREGORII] GEORGII *1546*

88. *Sic*

89. *Sic*

90. attigisset, a Lutheranae heresis veneno non procul affuit ita 1546] attigisset, a Lutheranae doctrina non procul abfuit ita 1577

91. *Sic; sc.* Telesius *or* Thylesius

92. Cicindelam] Cicindellam 1546

93. notabantur 1577] notabatur 1546

94. argumentum (*edit. conjecture*)] augumentum 1546

95. Castrioti *MSa*] Castreoti 1546

96. Daniae (*edit. conjecture*)] Daciae 1546] Datie *MSa*

97. Latinae (*edit. conjecture*)] Latine 1546

98. Gessoriaci *MSa*] Gossoriaci 1546

## PERORATION

1. *The section from the start of the preceding paragraph, beginning* Emicuit dudum, *until the phrase* literarum Bilibaldo Nurimbergensi, *varies significantly from 1546 to 1577, the latter edition reading (at 221):* Emicuit dudum perillustris eruditio in Ioanne Oecolampadio, sed profecto clarius et luminosius illuxisset, nisi Christianae hostiae sacramentum repudiasset. Eadem fere novae sectae libido Zvinglium in sacris literis apud Helvetios clarum incessit. Contigit et honestissima laus ex studio nobilium literarum Bilibaldo Nurimbergensi. . . .

2. operae pretium] operepretium 1546

3. Fracastorius] Fragastorius 1546

4. interierit (*edit. conjecture*)] interierint 1546

5. consequetur (*edit. conjecture*)] Consequentur 1546

6. Macrinus] Marinus 1546

## ANONYMOUS LIMINAL POEM

1. *Sic*

# Notes to the Translation

ॐॐ

## LIMINAL POEM

1. The poem is in phalaecean hendecasyllables. Onorato Fascitelli (1502–64), a protégé of Giovio, penned many epitaphs for the *elogia* both of literati and of men of arms. From Isernia in southern Italy, he studied under Pompeo Gaurico, and in 1519 he joined the Benedictine Order. He collaborated with Paolo Manuzio in editing the works of Ovid (1533–34) and of Lactantius (1535). His friends in Pauline Rome included not only Giovio but also many of the reformist religious thinkers historians identify as *spirituali* (e.g., Marcantonio Flaminio, Annibale Caro, Vittoria Colonna). See Minonzio (2012), 199–200, with further bibliography.

2. The river of forgetfulness in Hades. Thus, Fascitelli invokes both the passage into the underworld and the forgetting of the deceased from which Giovio has saved the subjects of his *elogia*.

## DEDICATION TO OTTAVIO FARNESE

1. Giampiero Brunelli, "Ottavio Farnese, duca di Parma," *DBI* 79 (2013). Giovio had spent nearly a decade in the service of Ottavio's brother, Cardinal Alessandro Farnese. Since Ottavio (1524–86) was married to Charles V's natural daughter, Margaret of Parma, Giovio hoped that the emperor might give Milan to the couple to rule, and he fantasized about their traveling from their new capital to visit his museum. See Zimmermann (1995), 203–4. Giovio errs in calling Ottavio "Prefect of Rome" (*Praefectum Urbis*), a position that his brother Orazio had received in 1545. See Donatella Rosselli, "Farnese, Orazio," *DBI* 45 (1995).

2. Here, the title *princeps iuventutis* (cf. *OCD,* 1247) seemingly alludes to Ottavio's position as designated successor to the duchy of Parma. In the Julio-Claudian principate, it referred to the emperor's heir; see Tacitus, *Annals* 1.3.

3. Philippe de Commynes, *La historia famosa di monsignor di Argenton delle guerre e costumi di Ludovico undecimo re di Francia*, trans. Nicolas Raince (Venice: Tramezzino, 1544). This translation comprises only the first six of the work's eight books. Raince, who dedicated the work to Giovio, served as secretary of the French ambassador to Rome. See Zimmermann (1995), 201; *Elogi*, 7–8n3. For an English translation, see Commynes, *The Memoirs of Philippe de Commynes*, ed. Samuel Kinser and trans. Isabelle Cazeaux, 2 vols. (Columbia: University of South Carolina Press, 1969). On Commynes (ca. 1447–1511) see *ER*, 2:58. Born into the Flemish nobility, he was raised at the Burgundian court. After years serving Charles the Bold, in 1472 he defected to the camp of King Louis XI of France.

4. Giovio had attended the meeting of Pope Paul III and Emperor Charles V in Busseto (June 22–24, 1543), after which he returned to Como. Writing to Cardinal Alessandro Farnese on July 24, 1543 (*IO*, 1:317), he described Busseto as "a stinking hole where sleep was banned."

5. In the dedicatory letter to Cosimo I de' Medici that opens the volume of *elogia* of men of arms, Giovio describes these capsule biographies as "lives written with laconic brevity."

6. That is, through Raince's Italian translation.

## A DESCRIPTION OF GIOVIO'S MUSEUM

1. By invoking the ancient Temple of Virtue, Giovio emphasizes his museum's celebratory and public purposes. See Livy 25.40.2–3; Maffei, 126n1; *OCD*, 704.

2. Vergil, *Aeneid* 6.847.

3. Vergil, *Aeneid* 1.681, 2.742.

4. On *ingenuus pudor*, see Pliny the Elder, *Natural History* Pref. 21.4.

5. On Doni (1513–74), see Giovanna Romei, "Doni, Anton Francesco," *DBI* 41 (1992); *ER*, 2:172–73; Paul F. Grendler, *Critics of the Italian World 1530–1560: Anton Francesco Doni, Nicolò Franco, and Ortensio Lando* (Madison: University of Wisconsin Press, 1969). Doni visited Giovio's museum

in the summer of 1543 and soon wrote two letters about it to friends. The first (July 17, 1543), a burlesque account formally addressed to Jacopo Tintoretto, was evidently intended for Lodovico Domenichi; see Klinger (1991), 1:69, 86n33. The second (July 20, 1543), addressed to Agostino Landi, provides a serious and more substantial description. It includes accounts of many *imprese* and inscriptions that were lost when the museum was destroyed in the seventeenth century, including Giovio's inscription for the façade: "Paolo Giovio bishop of Nocera, who on account of the fecundity of his erudite talent merited the favor and liberality of the greatest kings and popes, while he was composing during his lifetime in his native city of Como the history of his own times, dedicated this museum with its perennial fount and pleasant porticoes on Larius [Lake Como] to public enjoyment. 1543" (Zimmermann [1995], 187–88).

6. Alfonso d'Avalos, marchese del Vasto (1502–46), a longtime patron and friend of Giovio, who made him an interlocutor in *Notable Men and Women*. See *NMW*, xiii–xiv; Gaspare De Caro, "Avalos, Alfonso d', marchese del Vasto," *DBI* 4 (1962). Evidently the "two laurel crowns" are awarded d'Avalos for poetic and military prowess, as Orio explains in a silent addition to the text in Giovio (1552), 6.

7. Giovio knew better: it was in fact situated on the grounds of an ancient villa that Giovio's brother Benedetto had identified as having belonged to Caninius Rufus, a friend of Pliny the Younger. See Zimmermann (1995), 161; Minonzio (2007), 101.

8. For the rendering here of *podio* as "platform," see Minonzio's justification (with references to Vitruvius, Grapaldi, and especially Giovio's letter of 1504 to Giano Rasca) in *Elogi*, 16n7.

9. While the exact site of this long-disappeared island is elusive, it evidently was to the south of the villa.

10. Pliny the Younger, *Letters* 1.3.1: "euripus viridis et gemmeus."

11. A reference to his lacking at present the means to bring the project to completion. Cf. Giovio (1552), 7, where Orio's translation adds a gloss (here italicized) to clarify the meaning of Giovio's "si parta pace miseriarum finis ostendatur" ("should my woes ever come to a settled end"):

"se mai fatta la pace con le miserie, *il fine della povertà mia potrò vedere*" (emphasis added) ("if ever, indigence having been assuaged, I can see an end to my poverty").

12. Perhaps a reference to Terence, *Phormio* 342: "cena dubia apponitur."

13. Iris Lauterbach writes that "this 'surprise echo' feature of villa and garden architecture, typical of the mannerist concept of the *maraviglia*, recurs in the villa of Ferrante Gonzaga, which had been developed in close cooperation with his friend Giovio" (Lauterbach, "The Gardens of the Milanese 'Villeggiatura' in the Mid-Sixteenth Century," in *The Italian Garden: Art, Design and Culture*, ed. John Dixon Hunt [Cambridge: Cambridge University Press, 1996], 127–59, at 135).

14. *Nympha* here refers to the water itself.

15. For architectural design seeking harmony with its natural context, see Vitruvius 1.2, 7.

16. Cf. Gianoncelli, *L'antico museo*, 60–61.

17. The northwest winds that blow during the "dog days" of summer in the eastern Mediterranean.

18. That is, it opens out from the museum room.

19. Giovio draws upon one of Pliny the Younger's letters to Caninius Rufus (*Ep.* 1.3) for the description above of the channel on the island (*euripus viridis et gemmeus*). "Caecilius" is probably the comic poet Caecilius Statius (ca. 220–ca. 166 BCE), said to have been from Milan (*Mediolanum*), and so plausibly claimed for Como. "Atilius" is probably Pliny's friend Atilius Crescens (*Ep.* 6.8), who he says lived only a day's journey from him. On Calpurnius Fabatus, a correspondent of Pliny the Younger, see, e.g., Tacitus, *Annals* 16.8.3.

20. On the Renaissance revival of the classical ideal of a modest library whose books are carefully selected and arranged, see the discussion of Angelo Decembrio's *De politica litteraria* (1462) in Anthony Grafton, *Commerce with the Classics: Ancient Books and Renaissance Readers* (Ann Arbor: University of Michigan Press), 26–32.

21. The largest of the rooms is the "Museum."

22. Cf. Martial 8.14.4: "dies sine faece."

## THE PORTRAITS

1. Lauingen (*Artobriga*), a town in Bavaria on the Danube River.

2. The poem is in elegiac couplets. On its author see Paola Zambelli, "Balami, Ferdinando (Ferrante Siciliano)," *DBI* 5 (1963); *EH*, 49–50.

3. The author of this poem (in elegiac couplets), Giano Vitale (1485–1559), was from a noble family in Palermo and moved in 1510 to Rome, where he became active in its academies. His *Imperiae panaegyricus* (Rome: Beplin, ca. 1512) celebrated the courtesan Imperia. A protégé of Giovio, he contributed numerous poems to the *Elogia*. See Minonzio (2012), 214–15; *RLV*, 242–44; Giraldi, 97; *NMW*, 237.

4. Alfonso d'Avalos's mother was Laura Sanseverino.

5. Aquinas was canonized in 1323 by Pope John XXII, then in Avignon.

6. Cf. Tacitus, *Annals* 16.16.1.

7. The poem is an elegiac couplet.

8. The Caledonian Forest, mentioned by Pliny the Elder, is discussed by Giovio in *Scotia* (*Scotland*), where he describes its inhabitants as ferocious and unyielding (*IO*, 9:117).

9. On Giovio's juxtaposition of scholars' deaths with details of their lives and thought, see Minonzio's comments in *Elogi*, 28n4.

10. On this other "John Scotus," an Irish theologian (ca. 800–ca. 877), see Dermot Moran, "John Scottus Eriugena," *SEP* (revised October 17, 2004). Giovio draws the account of Eriugena's death, resembling that of St. Cassian of Imola (d. 363 CE), from Pietro Crinito, *De honesta disciplina*, bk. 24, chap. 11. Crinito (see Giovio's *elogium* of him below, no. 55) says that he read the story in Gaguin's *The Annals of the Gauls* (*Gallorum annalibus*). Moran, "John Scottus Eriugena," dismisses the story as "[a]n apocryphal tale, dating from the twelfth century."

11. The poem is in phalaecean hendecasyllables.

12. Giovio errs in describing the priorate (the Signoria) as an "eight-man magistracy": although it subsequently became so, at the time of Dante's selection the priors numbered only six.

13. On the legal proceedings against Dante and the sentence (January 27, 1302) that forced him to leave Florence, see Randolph Starn, *Contrary Commonwealth: The Theme of Exile in Medieval and Renaissance Italy* (Berkeley and Los Angeles: University of California Press, 1982), 60–85.

14. *Sic.* In fact, Bernardo Canaccio Scannabecchi, not Dante, composed this epitaph (in dactylic hexameter). See Ludovico Frati and Corrado Ricci, *Il sepolcro di Dante: Documenti raccolti* (Bologna: Commissione per i testi di lingua, 1969), viii–xii, 4; and Augusto Campana's article in *Enciclopedia dantesca* (Rome: Istituto della Enciclopedia Italiana, 1970), 2:710–13.

15. These lines appear to be modeled on a text in circulation in Dante's time, the *Appendix vergiliana*, in *Culex* 372–75: "Illi laude sua vigeant: ego Ditis opacos / cogor adire lacus viduatos lumine Phoebi / et vastum Phlegethonta pati, quo maxime Minos, / conscelerata pia discernis vincula sede."

16. Giannozzo Manetti cites this epitaph, albeit with minor variants, in both his *Life of Dante* and his tract *Against the Jews and the Gentiles*: Manetti, *Biographical Writings*, ed. and trans. Stefano U. Baldassarri and Rolf Bagemihl, ITRL 9 (Cambridge, MA: Harvard University Press, 2003), 60 and 138, respectively.

17. From 1481 to 1483 the Venetian patrician Bernardo Bembo (1433–1519) served as *podestà* (external judge) and captain of Ravenna. See King, 335–39, at 336. The epitaph, in elegiac couplets, was added to the tomb in 1483. Frati and Ricci, *Il sepolcro*, xiv–xv, 6.

18. Petrarch carefully orchestrated the invitation that led to his crowning as poet laureate, which took place in the Palace of the Senate on the Capitoline Hill on April 8, 1341. See *ER*, 4:453–54.

19. The poem is in dactylic hexameter.

20. According to Natalino Sapegno, "Boccaccio, Giovanni," *DBI* 10 (1968), he was probably born in Florence, not Certaldo.

21. Giovio's "carried on high" or "caught up into the heights" (*in altitudinem . . . abreptus*) may be a play on Paul's self-description in 2 Corinthians 12:2 as "caught up all the way to the third heaven" ("raptum . . . usque ad tertium caelum").

22. A reference to the *Milisiaka* of Aristides of Miletus, translated into Latin by Lucius Cornelius Sisenna under the title *Milesiae fabulae*. Notable writers in the tradition include Apuleius and Petronius. On the appropriation of their stories in the *Decameron*, see *Elogi*, 34n3.

23. The poem is in dactylic hexameter.

24. His father was Boccaccio (or, Boccaccino) of Chellino.

25. On the Udinese humanist Pietro Mirteo, see Gian Giuseppe Liruti di Vallafreda, *Notizie delle vite ed opere scritte da' letterati del Friuli*, 4 vols. (Venice: Modesto Fenzo, 1762), 2:127–31; Minonzio (2012), *ad indicem*; and Giraldi, 199. The poem is in phalaecean hendecasyllables.

26. Francesco Calasso, "Bartolo da Sassoferrato," *DBI* 6 (1964); *EH*, 56.

27. Cf. Cicero, *De senectute* 4.

28. The Chiesa di San Francesco al Prato in Perugia. His epitaph reads simply "Ossa Bartholi."

29. In the *editio princeps*, the poem (in phalaecean hendecasyllables) is unattributed.

30. "Ubaldi, Baldo degli," in *Enciclopedie on line*, at treccani.it; *EH*, 413; Joseph Canning, *The Political Thought of Baldus de Ubaldis* (Cambridge: Cambridge University Press, 1987); *NMW*, 53.

31. The poem is in dactylic hexameter.

32. See Cesare Vasoli, "Bruni, Leonardo, detto Leonardo Aretino," *DBI* 14 (1972); *ER*, 1:301–6; *EMC*, 1:218–19; James Hankins, "Humanism in the Vernacular: The Case of Leonardo Bruni," in *Humanism & Creativity*, 11–29.

33. In fact, his *ad sententiam* translation was highly controversial. In response to critics, including mendicants who compared it unfavorably to the thirteenth-century version by the scholastic Robert Grosseteste, he published *De recta interpretatione*, "the first theoretical discussion of translation in European history" (Hankins, in *ER*, 1:302). For detailed treatment of Bruni's rendition of the *Ethics* in its wider context, see David A. Lines, *Aristotle's Ethics in the Italian Renaissance (ca. 1300–1650): The Universities and the Problem of Moral Education* (Leiden: Brill, 2002), *ad indicem*, and James Hankins, "The Ethics Controversy," in his *Humanism and Platonism*

*in the Italian Renaissance*, 2 vols. (Rome: Storia e letteratura, 2003–4), 1:193–239.

34. Recommended to the pope by the Florentine chancellor Coluccio Salutati, Bruni obtained this post in 1405. When the Council of Constance deposed John XXIII (antipope) in 1414, Bruni returned to Florence.

35. A book of witticisms, attributed to Arlotto Mainardi (1396–1484), who was famed for cleverness and for devising practical jokes. See Giuseppe Crimi, "Mainardi, Arlotto," *DBI* 67 (2006). In was first printed as *Motti et facetie del Piovano Arlotto prete fiorentino piacevole molto*, ed. Bernardo Zucchetta (Florence: Bernardo Pacini, ca. 1512–16); for an English version see *Wit and Wisdom in the Italian Renaissance*, ed. Charles Speroni (Berkeley and Los Angeles: University of California Press, 1964), 79–128.

36. See the *elogium* of Cristoforo Persona (no. 116). Cochrane, 18, details how Bruni put the same material to different uses.

37. Bruni, *History of the Florentine People*, vol. 1: *Books I–IV*, ed. and trans. James Hankins, ITRL 3 (Cambridge, MA: Harvard University Press, 2001); ibid., *vol. 2: Books V–VIII*, ed. and trans. James Hankins, ITRL 16 (Cambridge, MA: Harvard University Press, 2004); ibid., *vol. 3: Books IX–XII. Memoirs*, ed. and trans. James Hankins, trans. D. J. W. Bradley, ITRL 27 (Cambridge, MA: Harvard University Press, 2007).

38. This is Carlo Marsuppini (1398?–1453), who succeeded Bruni as chancellor of Florence. See Paolo Viti, "Marsuppini, Carlo," *DBI* 71 (2008). Bruni's tomb was sculpted by Bernardo Rossellino.

39. See Emilio Bigi and Armando Petrucci, "Bracciolini, Poggio," *DBI* 13 (1971); *EH*, 80; *ER*, 1:274–76; *EMC*, 1:199. For editions of the works cited below, see Poggio Bracciolini, *Opera Omnia*, ed. Riccardo Fubini, 4 vols. (Turin: Bottega d'Erasmo, 1964).

40. Giovio errs; it was (anti)pope John XXIII who conferred this post upon Poggio, who held it, with the exception of the years 1415 to 1423, until 1453, when he accepted Florence's invitation to become the city's chancellor.

41. On Vegio see *elogium* 107. On Aurispa (1376–1459), who taught Greek in Florence and subsequently became tutor to a son of Niccolò III d'Este, see *DBI* 4 (1962); *EH*, 45; and Giraldi, 43–45.

42. Giovio refers to five orations that Poggio wrote against Valla, who responded with two *Antidotes* and an incomplete *Apology*. See *Elogi*, 42n3. Poggio's reputation for wit was based on the great popularity of his *Facetiae* (see note 46, below).

43. On Bartolomeo Facio, see *elogium* 109; on Antonio Beccadelli, called "Panormita," see *elogium* 12; and on Antonio da Rho (ca. 1398–ca. 1450/51), who succeeded to the chair of rhetoric in Milan upon Gasparino Barzizza's death in 1431, see Riccardo Fubini, "Antonio da Rho," *DBI* 3 (1961).

44. Giovio writes *in theatro Pompei loco* because by the late fifteenth century the papal chancery — the office where the fight took place — was located not on the Vatican hill, but in the environs of the site of the theater of Pompey. Usually the chancery was centered in the palace of vice-chancellor of the Church, which by the Cinquecento was the Palazzo della Cancelleria. This encounter between Poggio and George, however, took place on May 4, 1452, decades before that building's construction. The incident is reconstructed in John Monfasani, *George of Trebizond: A Biography and a Study of His Rhetoric and Logic* (Leiden: Brill, 1976), 109–111. George himself claimed to have fended off Poggio using just one hand. Writing to Poggio, he described his self-restraint (ibid., 110): "Rightly I could have bitten off the fingers you stuck in my mouth; I did not. Since I was seated and you were standing, I thought of squeezing your testicles with both hands and thus lay you out; I did not do it. I asked for a sword from the bystanders so that by fear of it I might drive you away. Nor was I mistaken. For like a Florentine woman, you took to flight."

45. Diodorus Siculus, *Historici clarissimi, bibliothecae, seu rerum antiquarum tum fabulosarum tum verarum historiae, priores libri sex*, trans. Poggio Bracciolini (Paris: Simon de Colines, 1531).

46. Within Poggio's lifetime the *Facetiae*, a collection of jokes and anecdotes written over the period 1438 to 1452, was his most popular work. It was printed twenty times before 1500.

47. In fact, Poggio found a complete manuscript of the *Institutio oratoria* in the Abbey of St. Gall. Previously, only part of the text had been known.

48. Written over the period 1453 to 1458, Poggio's *Historiae Florentini populi* did not appear in print in the original Latin until 1715. Cochrane, 29, offers a withering assessment: "[Poggio] followed Bruni almost page by page through his first three books, while backtracking from Bruni's critical accomplishments with one after another 'it-is-said' or *fertur*. . . . He attributed all political decisions to the 'Florentines' collectively, even after the rise of Cosimo de' Medici, whom he mentioned only once — and then only as ambassador to Venice! He buried all of Bruni's dramatic climaxes in a humdrum recitation of events. He broke off suddenly with the Peace of Naples in 1455 — which might have provided him with the most dramatic climax of all — as if it were just one more entry in the annals of a chronicler." The translation by Poggio's son Iacopo (1442–78) was published in 1476 and frequently reprinted. See Cesare Vasoli, "Bracciolini, Iacopo," *DBI* 13 (1971).

49. The poem is in dactylic hexameter, followed by iambic dimeter.

50. This is Ambrogio Traversari. See *EH*, 410; Charles L. Stinger, *Humanism and the Church Fathers: Ambrogio Traversari (1386–1439) and Christian Antiquity in the Italian Renaissance* (Albany: State University of New York Press, 1977); *EMC*, 2:1444.

51. The Camaldulensian order was founded by St. Romuald (952–1027), who established its first hermitage in Camaldoli, in eastern Tuscany.

52. On Traversari's friendship with Cosimo de' Medici, see Stinger, *Humanism*, 30–34; on Eugenius IV and Nicholas V's support of his patristic scholarship, ibid., 39, 154–56, 159–61, and *passim*. From 1401 until 1431, when he was elected general of his order, Traversari was cloistered in Santa Maria degli Angeli in Florence.

53. *Patres*, which could have the more general meaning of "leaders" (of the Church), is here rendered "cardinals" because humanists often addressed the College of Cardinals as *patres conscripti* (i.e., ancient Roman senators).

54. On Traversari's Latin translations of works of pseudo-Dionysius (including *De caelesti hierarchia*) and their favorable reception among the

learned, see Stinger, *Humanism*, 158–61. On the translation of Diogenes Laertius, presented to Cosimo de' Medici in 1433, see ibid., especially 70–77.

55. The poem is in elegiac couplets. This "Spinelli" remains to be identified.

56. Presumably a reference to St. Ambrose (ca. 339–397 CE). The poet plays on *Ambrogius/ambrosia* and on *nomen/numen*.

57. The poem is an elegiac couplet.

58. Panormita was the nickname of Antonio Beccadelli. Although his family originated in Bologna, he was born in Palermo. See Gianvito Resta, "Beccadelli, Antonio, detto il Panormita," *DBI* 7 (1970); *EMC*, 1:155–56; Giraldi, 43–45.

59. This refers to the people of the British Isles, not of Brittany. For the phrase *ultima Britannia*, see Catullus 29.

60. It is remarkable that Giovio does not mention Panormita's scandalous collection of epigrams, *The Hermaphrodite*, or contemporaries' assertions that he routinely violated sexual taboos. See Antonio Beccadelli, *The Hermaphrodite*, ed. Holt Parker, ITRL 42 (Cambridge, MA: Harvard University Press, 2010); and Antonio da Rho, "Philippic against Antonio Panormita," ed. and trans. in David Rutherford, *Early Renaissance Invective and the Controversies of Antonio da Rho* (Tempe: MRTS, 2005), 45–189. At the very least, *The Hermaphrodite* attests Beccadelli's interest in the range of rhetorical possibilities of sodomy, rape, and homoeroticism.

61. This is Filippo Maria Visconti, Duke of Milan (1412–47), whose forces captured King Alfonso V of Aragon in the Battle of Ponza (1435). Alfonso then managed to win over Visconti for an alliance against René of Anjou (the French claimant who ruled Naples from 1435 to 1442), and Visconti allowed him and his men to return to southern Italy, where in 1442 he would become King Alfonso I of Naples.

62. Panormita entered Alfonso's service in 1434. That year, a Milanese army led by the famous condottiere Niccolò Piccinino engaged Venetian troops in the Romagna. See Luigi Simeoni, *Le signorie*, 2 vols. (Milan: Casa Editrice Dottor Francesco Vallardi, 1950), 1:474–75.

63. Antonio Beccadelli, *Antonii Panormitae De dictis et factis Alphonsi regis Aragonum libri quatuor: Commentarium in eosdem Aeneae Sylvii quo capitatim cum Alphonsinis contendit* (Basel: Johann Herwagen and Johan Erasmus Froben, 1538).

64. For the two humanists' initially cordial relationship and how badly it soured, see for example letters 0B and 18 in Lorenzo Valla, *Correspondence*, ed. and trans. Brendan Cook, ITRL 60 (Cambridge, MA: Harvard University Press, 2013), 7–11 and 127–31, respectively; and Beccadelli, *Hermaphrodite*, 189–91 (= appendix, poems XIX and XX). As Valla writes in poem XIX, "You comb and touch the boy's long hair / but you always tear out your wife's. // Why do you do this, Beccadelli? Because he, not she is your wife. / A bugger does not like a woman's form."

65. The Neapolitan noblewoman Laura Arcella, whom he married in the mid-1450s (his previous wife, Filippa, had died).

66. The poem is in elegiac couplets.

67. The poem is an elegiac couplet. Giovio devotes *elogium* 45 to its author.

68. The poem is in dactylic hexameter.

69. Codrus, as described in Juvenal 3.203–11, is learned but destitute, and ultimately reduced to begging unsuccessfully for crusts of bread.

70. See Clementina Marsico, "Valla, Lorenzo," *DBI* 98 (2020); *EH*, 416; *ER*, 6:207–13; Maristella Lorch, "Lorenzo Valla," in Rabil, 1:332–49; *EMC*, 2:1467–68.

71. *De elegantiis linguae latinae* (Venice: Nicholas Jenson, 1471), which Valla completed in the 1440s (*Elegantiae* is often used in place of the full title).

72. On Valla's version of Thucydides, dedicated to Pope Nicholas V in 1452, see Grafton, *Commerce with the Classics*, 11–19, 49–52.

73. For Valla's attacks on Bartolomeo Facio, see *elogium* 109. Valla initially was on good terms with Antonio da Rho, who held the chair of rhetoric in Milan starting in 1431, but subsequently accused him of plagiarizing from the *Elegantiae* in his *De imitatione*.

74. *Historiarum Ferdinandi Regis Aragoniae libri* (1445–46).

75. Valla, *On the Donation of Constantine*, trans. G. W. Bowersock, ITRL 24 (Cambridge, MA: Harvard University Press, 2007). Although the tract is widely viewed as a masterpiece of applied philology, a century later the Vatican Librarian Agostino Steuco demonstrated its scholarly shortcomings in *Contra Laurentium Vallam De falsa Donatione Constantini libri duo* (Lyon: Sebastianus Gryphius, 1547). See Ronald K. Delph, "Valla *Grammaticus*, Agostino Steuco, and the Donation of Constantine," *Journal of the History of Ideas* 57 (1996): 55–77.

76. The poem is an elegiac couplet. On its author (1500–1559), see Franco Pignatti, "Franchino, Francesco," *DBI* 50 (1998). On his poetry and relationship with Giovio, see Minonzio (2012), 200–201 and *passim*.

77. Riccardo Fubini, "Biondo Flavio," *DBI* 10 (1968); *ER*, 1:231–32; *EMC*, 2:180–81.

78. Biondo, *Historiarum ab inclinatione romani imperii* (Books of History from the Fall of the Roman Empire, also known as the *Decades*), completed by 1453.

79. Flavio Biondo, *Roma instaurata [Rome Restored]* (Verona: Boninus de Boninis, 1481).

80. The Basilica of Santa Maria in Aracoeli, actually built on the site of the ancient Temple of Juno Moneta. The 124-step staircase known to Flavio and to Giovio dates from the mid-1300s.

81. The poem is in elegiac couplets.

82. Paolo Viti, "Decembrio, Pier Candido," *DBI* 33 (1987); *EH*, 145; *EMC*, 1:364.

83. According to Viti, it was in fact Nicholas V who in 1450 commissioned the translations of Appian (completed after the pope's death, and dedicated to Alfonso). To Giovio, the chief reason to study Greek was to benefit one's Latin.

84. Decembrio, *Vita Philippi Mariae Vicecomitis*, composed in 1447, in *Lives of the Milanese Tyrants*, ed. Massimo Zaggia, trans. Gary Ianziti, ITRL 88 (Cambridge, MA: Harvard University Press, 2019). Giovio repeats a common criticism, discussed by Ianziti in the ITRL edition.

85. The poem is in dactylic hexameter; ancient hexameters do not rhyme.

86. See Arnaldo D'Addario, "Acciaiuoli, Donato," *DBI* 1 (1960); *EH*, 20; Margery A. Ganz, "Donato Accciaiuoli and the Medici: A Strategy for Survival in '400 Florence," *Rinascimento*, ser. 2, vol. 22 (1982): 33–73.

87. Donato Acciaiuoli, *Expositio super libros ethicorum Aristotelis in novam traductionem Johannis Argyropyli* (Florence: San Jacopo di Ripoli, 1478).

88. Eustratius of Nicaea had written commentaries on Books 1 and 2 of the *Nicomachean Ethics*. See Katerina Ierodiakonou and Börje Bydén, "Byzantine Philosophy," in *SEP* (revised spring 2014).

89. Acciaiuoli's renderings of some of Plutarch's parallel lives (including that of Hannibal, which Giovio knew) appeared in print alongside translations of others by other humanists, e.g., in Plutarch, *Vitae parallelae*, translated into Latin by F. Filelfo, G. Tortelli, et al. (Rome: Ulrich Hans, 1470?).

90. Acciaiuoli, *Vita Caroli Magni*, ed. Wolfgang Strobl (Berlin: De Gruyter, 2013). According to Cochrane, 33, Acciaiuoli's "life of Charlemagne, notwithstanding its political significance at the moment of its composition (1461) and notwithstanding its subsequent diffusion as an appendix to most Italian editions of Plutarch, is essentially just a reworking of Einhard, with a few details added from Villani and the *Liber Pontificalis*." Giovio is silent about the the work's indebtedness to Bruni, on which see Donatella Bessi, "Donato Acciaiuoli e il volgarizzamento delle *Historiae*," *Interpres* 8 (1988): 41–102.

91. As described by D'Addario, "Acciaiuoli," the mission actually had the less ambitious goal of discerning the intentions of King Louis XI regarding the political situation in Italy. According to Ganz ("Donato," 65), "other than the document that attests to his selection and subsequent departure for France, no instructions for the mission seem to have survived."

92. This is the Certosa di Val d'Ema, founded in 1341 by Donato's kinsman Niccolò Acciaiuoli.

93. The poem is in elegiac couplets. It was included in Poliziano's *Book of Epigrams*, in *Greek and Latin Poetry*, no. XCIV, ed. and trans. Peter E. Knox, ITRL 86 (Cambridge, MA: Harvard University Press, 2018), III.

94. That is, the Sforza Castle (the coat of arms of the House of Sforza included a depiction of a serpent).

95. See Paolo Viti, "Filelfo, Francesco," *DBI* 47 (1997); *EH*, 185; *ER*, 2:363–64; *EMC*, 1:618; Giraldi, 51–53.

96. Hippocrene, literally "the horse's fountain," was a spring on Mount Helicon sacred to the Muses. It was said to have been formed by the hooves of Pegasus, and drinking of it was supposed to produce poetic inspiration.

97. For a critical edition of Book Three of the *Sforziad*, see Diana Robin, *Filelfo in Milan: Writings, 1451–1477* (Princeton: Princeton University Press, 1991), 177–96; and for interpretation of the poem as a whole, ibid., 56–81.

98. Among his numerous publications, see for example *Odes*, ed. and trans. Diana Robin, ITRL 41 (Cambridge, MA: Harvard University Press, 2009); and *On Exile*, ed. Jeroen De Keyser and trans. W. Scott Blanchard, ITRL 55 (Cambridge, MA: Harvard University Press, 2013).

99. Xenophon, *Cyropaedia*, ed. and trans. Filelfo (Rome or Milan, before February 18, 1477); versions of Plutarch's lives of Lycurgus and Numa Pompilius, dedicated to Cardinal Niccolò Albergati; and versions of Hippocrates, *De passionibus corporis* and *De flautibus*, dedicated to Filippo Maria Visconti.

100. Actually, he died not in Bologna but in Florence, where, thanks to Lorenzo de' Medici, he had just been appointed to teach Greek in the *Studio*. See Viti, "Filelfo"; *Elogi*, 61n7.

101. The poem is in phalaecean hendecasyllables.

102. See Paolo D'Alessandro, "Perotti, Niccolò," *DBI* 82 (2015); *EH*, 343; Giraldi, 47, 115.

103. The *Rudimenta grammatices*, first published in Rome in 1473.

104. Polybius, *Historiae*, trans. Niccolò Perotti (Rome: Sweynheym and Pannartz, 1473). On Cardinal Bessarion's mentorship of humanists, see *elogium* 24.

105. Niccolò Perotti, *Cornucopiae: sive commentariorum linguae latinae* (Venice: Paganino Paganini, 1489). The title invokes *The Horn of Amaltheia* by Sotion, mentioned by Aulus Gellius in *Atticae noctes* 1.8.1–2.

106. Pius II made Perotti archbishop of Manfredonia in October of 1458. Sixtus IV named him governor of Perugia in August of 1474.

107. The poem is in phalaecean hendecasyllables.

108. Stefan Bauer, "Sacchi, Bartolomeo, detto il Platina," *DBI* 89 (2017); *ER*, 5:52–53; *EMC*, 2:1222; Giraldi, 330.

109. *Liber de vita Christi et omnium pontificum* (1474; pub. Nuremberg: Anton Koburger, 1481), now being translated: *Lives of the Popes*, vol. 1, ed. and trans. Anthony F. D'Elia, ITRL 30 (Cambridge, MA: Harvard University Press, 2008). The book is no hagiography: Platina dispenses both praise and blame.

110. *De falso et vero bono; De vera nobilitate;* and *De optimo cive* (1474), ed. Felice Battaglia (Bologna: Zanichelli, 1944). The final work to which Giovio here refers is *De honesta voluptate et valetudine*, composed in 1465; see *On Right Pleasure and Good Health*, ed. and trans. Mary Ella Milham (Tempe: MRTS, 1998).

111. Actually, Platina had studied in Mantua, where he became tutor to Francesco Gonzaga (1444–83). After Gonzaga was created cardinal in 1461, Platina followed him to Rome and became active in the scholarly gatherings convened by Cardinal Bessarion and in the academy of Pomponio Leto.

112. It was in part through the agency of Cardinals Bessarion and Gonzaga that Platina was able to purchase a post in the College of Abbreviators, which prepared shortened versions of bulls and supervised their revision. Pius II had made the office of abbreviator venal in 1463.

113. Platina was outraged when Paul II (pope, 1464–71) dissolved the College of Abbreviators. After the humanist used a papal audience to demand the reversal of the decision, in the course of which he even questioned the validity of Paul's election, the pope had him imprisoned in Castel Sant'Angelo (September 1464). Through Cardinal Gonzaga's influence he was released the following January. He again fell afoul of Paul II in February 1468, when he and several other members of Leto's Academy were imprisoned on charges including sodomy, paganism, conspiracy, and heresy. Within a few months all charges were dropped. See *ER*, 5:53; and, on the conspiracy, the notes to *elogium* 40 (Pomponio Leto).

114. The appointment (1475) is commemorated in a famous fresco by Melozzo da Forlì. Platina's friendship with Sixtus's favorite nephew, Pietro Riario, surely helped his advancement.

115. Pomponio Leto delivered the eulogy.

116. On the author of the inscription, see Emilio Russo, "Guazzelli, Demetrio," *DBI* 60 (2003).

117. The poem is in elegiac couplets. Spiriteo remains obscure. But see Francesco Arisi, *Cremona literata*, 2 vols. (Parma: Pazzonus and Montius, 1702–5), 1:321, who mentions "*Prosper Spiriteus Viterbien.* Epigrammata."

118. The *editio princeps* of 1546 omits four lines of the Latin verses that appear in *MS*, fol. 10r, and again in the editions of 1557, 1571, and 1577.

119. This is Iacopo Ammannati-Piccolomini, on whom see Edith Pásztor, "Ammannati, Iacopo," *DBI* 2 (1960); and Giuseppe Calamari, *Il confidente di Pio II: Card. Iacopo Ammannati-Piccolomini (1422–1479)*, 2 vols. (Rome: Augustea, 1932).

120. "Senators" here is a classicizing term for "cardinals." Ammannati-Piccolomini had been named bishop of Pavia in July 1460 and was elevated to the cardinalate in December 1461.

121. San Lorenzo alle Grotte is on the Via Cassia, on the north side of the crater rim of Lake Bolsena.

122. The poem is in elegiac couplets.

123. Maurizio Campanelli, *Polemiche e filologia ai primordi della stampa: le Observationes di Domizio Calderini* (Rome: Edizioni di Storia e Letteratura, 2001), analyzes much of his work, including the commentary on Ovid's *Ibis* and the polemic against Giorgio Merula. Campanelli also provides a critical edition and Italian translation of Book Three of the *Observations*. See also Alessandro Perosa, "Calderini (Calderinus, Caldarinus, de Caldarinis), Domizio (Domitius, Domicius, Dominicus)," *DBI* 16 (1973); *EH*, 93, which identifies his birthplace as Torri del Benaco; and Giraldi, 47–49.

124. As Grafton and Jardine observed, choosing difficult works outside the central humanist curriculum "was an act of audacity, and might be enough to make a reputation. Domizio Calderini . . . repeatedly empha-

sised his boldness in lecturing on Statius' *Sylvae*, 'which nobody dared to do before me, and Ovid's *Ibis*, 'a work full of anger and obscurity.' He had his rewards: a chair in the university [the Studium Urbis, which subsequently became the University of Rome] by 1470, while he was still in his early thirties, a papal secretaryship by 1471 and a salary that quickly doubled": Anthony Grafton and Lisa Jardine, *From Humanism to the Humanities: Education and the Liberal Arts in Fifteenth- and Sixteenth-Century Europe* (Cambridge, MA: Harvard University Press, 1986), 83. See also Lee, 179–82.

125. On Calderini's polemical exchanges with rivals (including Valla and Poliziano), see Grafton and Jardine, *From Humanism*, 65–66, 81, 95–96; and William Parr Greswell, *Memoirs of Angelus Politianus*, 2nd ed. (Manchester: Cadell and Davies, 1805), 82–88.

126. The poem is in elegiac couplets; it was included in Poliziano's *Book of Epigrams*, no. XCIII, ed. Knox, p. 111.

127. The poem is in choliambic verse; it was included in Poliziano's *Book of Epigrams*, no. XCVII, ed. Knox, p. 117.

128. The fountain Libethros (or, Libethra) in Macedonia was sacred to the Muses (Pliny the Elder, *Natural History* 4.9.16), as were the Pernessus River in Boeotia (Vergil, *Eclogues* 6.64) and the Sisyphian font (Pyrene in Corinth, founded by Sisyphus; some identified Pyrene with Hippocrene).

129. Frank Rutger Hausmann, "Campano, Giovanni Antonio (Giannantonio)," *DBI* 17 (1974); *EH*, 95–96; Lee, 91–99; Riccardo Fubini, "Umanesimo curiale del Quattrocento: Nuovi studi su Giovanni'Antonio Campano," *Rivista Storica Italiana* 88 (1976): 745–55; and Giraldi, 45. For a selection from his Latin writings accompanied by Italian translations, ed. Lucia Gualdo Rosa, see *Poeti latini*, 787–837.

130. Campano was appointed public lecturer in rhetoric at Perugia in 1455.

131. Campano went to Rome in 1459 in the retinue of Cardinal Filippo Calandrini, thereafter establishing connections with two cardinals close to Pius II: Jacopo Ammannati (see *elogium* 20 above) and Francesco

Todeschini-Piccolomini. Pius made him bishop of Crotone in 1462 and of Teramo in 1463. In 1465, Paul II made him an archpresbyter at the Church of Sant' Eustachio. See Lee, 93–94.

132. In April 1472 Sixtus IV had named Campano governor of Todi, subsequently transferring him to Foligno and then to Città di Castello. He lost the pope's favor by assisting its unofficial ruler, Nicolò Vitelli, whom Sixtus was attempting to overthrow. See Lee, 97–99; *Elogi*, 72n4.

133. Campano, *Braccii Perusini vita et gesta*, ed. Roberto Valentini (Turin: Bottega d'Erasmo, 1966; orig. pub. 1929). Its subject is the famous *condottiere* Braccio Fortebracci da Montone (1368–1424). Cochrane, 52–53, offers a more positive assessment, highlighting Campano's commitment to the truth, "which the author went all the way to Aquila to ascertain; and [the work] qualified with a *fertur* ["it is reported"] whatever could not be documented by reliable oral testimony or by references in the Perugian chronicles." Cochrane does acknowledge, however, that Campano exalted Braccio and "quietly omitted any details that might have tarnished his hero's reputation."

134. The poem is in elegiac couplets.

135. The poem is in elegiac couplets; it was published in Poliziano's *Book of Epigrams*, no. XCV, ed. Knox, p. 113.

136. For Lucia Gualdo Rosa's Italian translation and notes on this poem, see *Poeti latini*, 1014–17. On Cupidus "Geminus," see ibid., 1016n5.

137. On Chrysoloras see *EH*, 117; *ER*, 1:448–50; Ian Thomson, "Manuel Chrysoloras and the Early Italian Renaissance," *Greek, Roman, and Byzantine Studies* 7 (1966): 63–82; Giraldi, 111; and the entry by Remigio Sabbadini on "Crisolora, Manuele" in the *Enciclopedia italiana* (1931), online at treccani.it.

138. This is the *Erotemata* (*Questions*), so-called because arranged in catechetical question-and-answer form. Other writings included some correspondence and a substantial euology of the despot Theodore I of Mistra (a brother of Manuel II Palaeologus).

139. *Sic.* In fact it was on behalf of Emperor Manuel II Palaeologus (r. 1391–1425), not John, that Chrysoloras first traveled to Italy in 1394–95.

140. Giovio's narrative here is misleading. At the start of 1400 Manuel II asked Chrysoloras (who was then teaching in Florence) to accompany him around Europe. The two met in Milan and traveled together to Pavia, but then the emperor went on to England and France without him. In Pavia Chrysoloras both represented the emperor (seeking financial support for the war against the Turks) and taught at the university. The forces of Tamerlane captured Bayezid II in their victory at the Battle of Ankara on July 28, 1402 (see Setton, 1:376 and note 35). Then in early 1403 Chrysoloras rejoined Manuel II for the voyage back to the Byzantine capital, but he would leave Constantinople permanently in November 1407. See Sabbadini, "Crisolora."

141. When Giangaleazzo Visconti became ruler of Lombardy in 1385, he "designated Pavia the sole university of the state": Grendler (2002), 126–27. After spending 1397 to 1400 in Florence, where his students included Pier Paolo Vergerio and Leonardo Bruni, Chrysoloras went to Pavia. His responsibilities in Lombardy, however, were not exclusively academic: see note 140 above.

142. On Guarino see *elogium* 110.

143. Chrysoloras had spent 1411 to 1413 in Rome in the court of (anti)pope John XXIII (Baldassare Cossa). In 1414 he followed John XXIII to the Council of Constance (1414–18), which proceeded to depose that papal claimant in May 1415, and another, Gregory XII, two months later.

144. The poem is in glyconics.

145. This is the general council of the Church, seeking to heal the East–West Schism of 1054, that convened in 1438–39, first in Ferrara and then in Florence. Originally from Trebizond, Bessarion was created Metropolitan in 1436 and bore the sobriquet *Nicenus* (the Nicene) for the rest of his life. In December 1439, as Bessarion was returning from the Council to Constantinople, Eugenius IV elevated him to the cardinalate so that he could serve as a mediator between the Greek and the Latin Churches. See Lotte Labowsky, "Bessarione," *DBI* 9 (1967); *EH*, 66; *ER*, 1:207–8; Giraldi, 111–15; and John Monfasani, *Byzantine Scholars in Renaissance Italy: Cardinal Bessarion and Other Emigrés* (Aldershot: Ashgate/Variorum, 1995).

146. Isidore of Kiev (ca. 1385–1463), patriarch of Russia.

147. On Bessarion's academy, see James Hankins, "Humanist Academies and the 'Platonic Academy of Florence,'" in *From the Roman Academy to the Danish Academy in Rome*, ed. Marianne Pade (Rome: Quasar, 2011), 31–46; and, from a different perspective, John Monfasani, "Two Fifteenth-Century 'Platonic Academies': Bessarion's and Ficino's," in ibid., 61–76, at 61–65.

148. The Platonist philosopher George Gemistus Pletho (1355–1452 or 1454), under whom Bessarion had earlier studied. "Manfredonia" is Niccolò Perotti, who was created archbishop of Manfredonia in 1458. "Domizio" is Domizio Calderini. Of those named, only Pletho lacks a portrait in Giovio's gallery. For the others, see *elogia* 9 (Bruni), 10 (Poggio), 13 (Valla), 14 (Flavio Biondo), 17 (Filelfo), 18 (Perotti), 19 (Platina), 21 (Calderini), 22 (Campano), 25 (George of Trebizond), 26 (Theodore of Gaza), and 27 (Argyropoulos).

149. Bessarion was younger than seventy-seven at the time of his death, given his birth at some point between 1403 and 1408.

150. The poem is an elegiac couplet. In *elogium* 27, Giovio identifies Maiorano as a student of Janus Lascaris.

151. The poem is in iambic trimeter.

152. The poem is in elegiac couplets.

153. Paolo Viti, "Giorgio da Trebisonda," *DBI* 55 (2001); *EH*, 203; *ER*, 3:38–39; Monfasani, *George of Trebizond*; Giraldi, 121–23.

154. Among George's translations from Aristotle are *On Rhetoric, On the Soul*, the *Physics, On Generation and Corruption*, zoological works, and the *Problems* (*Problemata*). For his rendering of the book by Eusebius of Caesarea, see Eusebius, *De preparatione evangelica* [*Preparation for the Gospel*] (Venice: Nicholas Jenson, 1470). The ancient Greek rhetorician Hermogenes of Tarsus (second century CE) was highly influential on George, whose first surviving treatise, which he sent to his teacher Vittorino da Feltre around 1420, was a synopsis of Hermogenes's *On Stylistic Forms* (*Peri ideon*). Hermogenes was a major influence on his *Five Books on Rhetoric* (*Rhetoricorum libri V*), published in 1434, which "innovatively combined Latin and Byzantine rhetoric in the analysis of Cicero and other Latin authors and remained a classic of Renaissance rhetoric into

the middle of the sixteenth century": *ER*, 3:38. Monfasani, *George of Trebizond*, 17–18, 248–55.

155. George's defense of Aristotelianism against Bessarion and his circle began in 1456 with his *Defense of Aristotle's "Problems"* and was fully articulated in his *Comparison of the Philosophers Plato and Aristotle* (completed by January 1458), to which Bessarion responded with *Against the Calumniator of Plato* (1469). Both works have now been critically edited by John Monfasani, *Vindicatio Aristotelis: Two Works of George Trebizond in the Plato-Aristotle Controversy of the Fifteenth Century* (Tempe, AZ: MRTS, 2021).

156. On the house in the Piazza San Macuto, near the Church of Santa Maria Sopra Minerva, see Monfasani, *George of Trebizond*, 34, 236. The *editio princeps* and the autograph draft of the *elogium* both omit the "c" (*sic*: Mauti). Orio's translation, at Giovio (1558), 60, reads "san Mauto"; Minonzio, at *Elogi*, 79, reads "San Mauro"; and Gragg, in Giovio (1935), reads "St. Maurus" (which follows *mauri* in the problematic 1557 edition upon which she relied). The Egyptian obelisk unearthed in 1373 in Piazza San Macuto and called "Macuteo" was one of a pair taken by the ancient Romans from the Temple of Ra in Heliopolis. In 1711, Pope Clement XI would order it moved to the center of Filippo Barigioni's fountain in the Piazza della Rotonda. See Brian A. Curran, Anthony Grafton, Pamela O. Long, and Benjamin Weiss, *Obelisk: A History* (Cambridge, MA: Burndy Library, 2009), 70–72, 180; illustration by van Aelst on 71.

157. Andreas did, however, have a successful career in the Curia, as attested for example in a bull of Sixtus IV in 1478 that refers to him as "secretarius secretus et domesticus." See Lee, 70–74.

158. Andreas wrote a letter to Gaza (1454) attacking him for redoing his father's translation of the *Problemata*. See *Collectanea Trapezuntiana: Texts, Documents, and Bibliographies*, ed. John Monfasani (Binghamton: MRTS, 1984), 778–79.

159. The story of George as senile and tottering about Rome aimlessly is owed to Raffaele Maffei, *Commentariorum libri octo et triginta* (Rome: Besicken, 1506). In his *Stromatum Libri X* (written 1518–21), however, Maffei

specifically retracted it. See Monfasani's "Addenda-Corrigenda to *George of Trebizond* and *Collectanea Trapezuntiana*," in *Vindicatio Aristotelis*, 1013–52.

160. Andreas willed much of his library to this daughter, Faustina, and her husband. See Lee, 74. On Fausto, see Gianni Ballistreri, "Capodiferro, Evangelista Maddaleni (Maddalena) de', detto Fausto," *DBI* 18 (1975).

161. Ballistreri, "Capodiferro," says he died "poco prima del sacco del 1527," but I incline to read "ante diem" as "before the time destined by fate," as in L&S, s.v. *ante*.

162. The poem is in hendecasyllables.

163. Concetta Bianca, "Gaza, Teodoro," *DBI* 52 (1999); *EH*, 403; *ER*, 3:21–22; *DLI*, 213, 292–93; Giraldi, 111–13.

164. The Ottoman sultan Murad II reigned from 1421 to 1451. In March 1430 Thessalonica, already under Ottoman attack for several years, fell to Murad. When Gaza departed for Italy in 1440, the sultan was laying siege (ultimately unsuccessfully) to Belgrade. See Colin Imber, *The Ottoman Empire, 1300–1650: The Structure of Power* (New York: Palgrave Macmillan, 2002), 22–25.

165. By the time of Nicholas V's death in 1555, Gaza "had completed a translation of much of Aristotle's massive zoological writings," and he finished the definitive version of them under Sixtus IV (*ER*, 3:22–23). See also Stefano Perfetti, "'Cultius atque integrius': Teodoro Gaza, traduttore umanistico del *De partibus animalium*," *Rinascimento*, ser. 2, vol. 35 (1995): 253–86. On his translation of *On the History of Plants* (*De historia plantarum*), which he dedicated to Nicholas V in 1451, see Charles B. Schmitt, "Theophrastus," in *CTC*, 2:266–68, 273–74.

166. Cicero, *Liber de senectute in Graecum translatus*, trans. Theodore of Gaza, ed. Ioannes Salanitro (Leipzig: Teubner, 1987).

167. He presented his translation of Aristotle's *Problemata* to Nicholas V in 1452. His translation of the *Aphorismata* of Hippocrates was printed in Venice in 1495.

168. In 1463, he went to live in the monastery of San Giovanni a Piro (on the Calabrian coast adjacent to Policastro Bussentino), of which Bessar-

ion had named him *procuratore*. He returned to Rome probably in 1467, then went back to San Giovanni a Piro in 1474.

169. In *DLI*, 213, Valeriano tells a similar story: "This man, whose learning had no peer for many years in any of the Greeks (or in the Latins either, I dare say), had dedicated to Pope Sixtus IV his nearly divine labors on Aristotle's *Historia Animalium*, which he had translated for reading in Latin, evidently hoping to win from the kindness of that prince the generous stipend he had earned through such great effort. But he brought back no more than fifty gold pieces (as if it were a great sum) from the man by whom he hoped to be covered completely with gold. Scorning his studies because he had been paid such a niggardly return for his long nights of toil, first he threw the coins into the Tiber, and then, inflamed by the injustice of the thing, he wasted away with inconsolable grief."

170. The poem is in elegiac couplets.

171. The poem is in elegiac couplets. It was published in Poliziano's *Book of Epigrams*, no. LXXXI, ed. Knox, p. 99.

172. The poem is in elegiac couplets, and was published in ibid., no. LXXXII, p. 99.

173. Emilio Bigi, "Argiropulo, Giovanni," *DBI* 4 (1962); *EH*, 42.

174. On Argyropoulos instructing Florentines in Aristotelian philosophy, see Arthur Field, *The Origins of the Platonic Academy of Florence* (Princeton: Princeton University Press, 1988), 107–26.

175. The poem is in elegiac couplets.

176. On Tarcaniota, see Donatella Coppini, "Marullo Tarcaniota, Michele," *DBI* 71 (2008); *EH*, 295; *CE*, 2:398–99; Kidwell (1989); Croce, 2:267–380 ("Appendice: Michele Marullo Tarcaniota"); *DLI*, 191–93, 306–7; Berni, 211, 324–27; Giraldi, 39–41; and Michael Marullus, *Poems*, trans. Charles Fantazzi, ITRL 54 (Cambridge, MA: Harvard University Press, 2012).

177. Stradiots were light cavalry drawn primarily from the region of Albania. Venice introduced them into Italian use in the 1460s and 1470s. See Mallett (1974), 119, 152–53. Marullo began his career as a mercenary

around age seventeen, serving initially in regions north of the Black Sea and along the Danube. The Nicola Rhallis mentioned here is probably the condottiere employed by Venice to fight the Turks in the Peloponnese starting in 1463 (he was killed in 1465). After returning from the East, Marullo continued his mercenary career in Italy, but its course has yet to be mapped with any certainty (most hypotheses depend on his epigrams as evidence). In mid-1476 he settled in Naples; he spent the late 1480s in Rome; then he went to Florence, where he was on good terms with the Medici, Pico, and, initially, Poliziano.

178. The marriage probably took place no earlier than 1496. On Alessandra's life and her deep erudition, see Kidwell (1989), 178–85. Bartolomeo Scala served a term as *gonfaloniere di giustizia* ("Standard-Bearer of Justice") in Florence in 1486; in that office he was the ceremonial head of state.

179. On this feud see Croce, 2:285–86; Kidwell (1989), 164–65.

180. In *DLI*, 191, Valeriano points to his lack of reliable patronage: "this man of such lofty intellect and great learning was forced to support himself by a soldier's pay as long as he lived and always dragged out his unhappy life in constant toil, never assisted enough by the liberality of any prince to devote himself to the leisured pursuit of letters."

181. According to Valeriano (*DLI*, 191), the river was then quite low: it was after his horse, mired in quicksand, rolled onto its side, pinning one of Marullo's legs, that "he perished by drowning in a tiny trickle of water." For Apollo smiling on light verse, and the use of *graviora* to refer to epic and war, see Ovid, *Amores* 1.1.

182. According to Kidwell (1989), 249, he in fact died on April 14, four days after the demise of Ludovico Sforza "il Moro."

183. The poem is in elegiac couplets.

184. On Mount Helicon (in Boeotia) and Aonia, sacred to the Muses and Apollo, see Statius, *Silvae* 4.4.90.

185. The Pena River in Thessaly, which feeds into the Vardar River, the most important in Macedonia; the spring of Ogyges: a reference to the spring of Dirce, in Thebes.

186. The four names refer to the poetic *dominae* of the Roman love elegists: Corinna (Ovid), Delia (Tibullus), Cynthia (Propertius), and Lesbia (Catullus).

187. Probably a reference to the fate of Hylas at the hands of the water nymphs in Propertius 1.20. Pontano evidently errs, in that Marullo drowned in the Cecina River, not the Arno.

188. For an authoritative Italian translation and detailed annotation of this poem, see the edition by Lucia Gualdo Rosa in *Poeti latini*, 538–39.

189. The poem is in elegiac couplets.

190. On Chalcondyles (Chalkondylas), see Armando Petrucci, "Calcondila, Demetrio," *DBI* 16 (1973); *EH*, 112; *CE*, 2:290–91; *NMW*, 385; *DLI*, 173, 281; Giraldi, 111. At some point in the years 1501 to 1506, Giovio had gone to Milan to study under Chalcondyles and Aulo Giano Parrasio.

191. On Chalcondyles's version of the *Erotemata*, see Wilson, *From Byzantium to Italy*, 110.

192. The poem is in choliambic verse.

193. Paolo Pellegrini, "Musuro, Marco," *DBI* 77 (2012); *EH*, 316–17; *CE*, 2:472–73; *DLI*, 95, 310–11.

194. Musurus taught Greek in Padua from 1503 to 1509.

195. Giovio refers here to the French incursions into Venetian territory in 1509, which included the devastating defeat of the Venetian troops under Bartolomeo d'Alviano in the Battle of Agnadello (May 14). Within three weeks, Padua fell to the French (the Venetians recovered it on July 17). See the description of the battle and its aftermath in *NMW*, 123; Mallett (1974), 252–54; Setton, 3:59–61; and Pastor, 6:313–17. The *Hapanta ta tou Platonos* [*Omnia Platonis opera*], ed. Musurus and Aldo Manuzio (Venice: Aldo Manuzio and Andrea Asolano, 1513), has been called Musurus's "most important philological work" (*CE*, 2:473). The long poem that precedes the text is a *Hymn to Plato* addressed to Leo X; for a text and translation, see Aldus Manutius, *The Greek Classics*, ed. N. G. Wilson, ITRL 70 (Cambridge, MA: Harvard University Press, 2016), 302–17.

196. The move to Rome occurred in 1516, after he had held the public lectureship in Greek in Venice for four years.

197. On Rallo (ca. 1447–ca. 1522), see Han Lamers, "Manilio Cabacio Rallo," at www.repertoriumpomponianum.it/pomponiani/rallo.htm (accessed April 22, 2019). He had come to Rome in the mid-1460s, when the Ottomans were conquering the Peloponnese. Active in the Academy of Pomponio Leto, he enjoyed the patronage of several cardinals, ultimately including Giulio de' Medici (the future Pope Clement VII). On June 19, 1516, Leo appointed Musurus archbishop of Monemvasia, in the Peloponnese. The previous year, that see had been combined with the bishoprics Hierapetra and Herronesou in Crete. He never visited any of them. See CE, 2:473; Eubel, 3:166, 248. Giovio inverts the order in which Rallo and Musurus held the see of Monemvasia: Leo had appointed Rallo to the position in 1517, following Musurus's death.

198. This is the "Great Promotion," Leo X's unprecedented creation of thirty-one cardinals (confirmed on July 31, 1517). See note 637 below.

199. Giraldi, 123, directly counters Giovio's perspective: "Although some individuals, unworthy of having such a great colleague, spread it around that he had died out of bitter disappointment that many had been elevated to the cardinalate over him, they did this because they had nothing else with which to insult this most learned and most modest of men." In DLI, 95, Valeriano portrays Musurus as actually having died because of his ecclesiastical distinctions and the loss of freedom they supposedly entailed.

200. Antonio Fabro (Antonius Faber Amiterninus, ca. 1449–1522) served as tutor to Giulio de' Medici and was appointed by Leo X to the chair of eloquence at the Roman Studium. See DLI, 117, 287–88; Coryciana, 112, 350, and 394. The poem is in elegiac couplets.

201. Massimo Ceresa, "Lascaris, Giano," DBI 63 (2004); EH, 260; CE, 2:292–94; DLI, 173–75, 299–300; Giraldi, 117–21.

202. His family, from Rhyndacus in Asia Minor, was a branch of the imperial house.

203. Before going to Florence, Lascaris had studied in Padua under Chalcondyles. By 1490 he was in the service of Lorenzo de' Medici.

204. This is Sultan Bayezid II (r. 1481–1512), on whose reign see Imber, *Ottoman Empire*, 37–44 and *passim*. Setton, 3:53, emphasizes the political dimension of these trips, which took place in 1490 to 1492: Lascaris "had used [the] two book–buying missions for Lorenzo de' Medici in order to inform himself of Turkish morale and resources as well as of the Ottoman military situation." On Lascaris and Lorenzo de' Medici, see *Elogi*, 96n2; Sebastiano Gentile, "Lorenzo e Giano Lascaris. Il fondo greco della biblioteca medicea privata," in *Lorenzo il Magnifico e il suo mondo*, ed. Gian Carlo Garfagnini (Florence: Olschki, 1994), 177–94.

205. Guido Pampaloni, "Bandini dei Baroncelli, Bernardo," *DBI* 5 (1963). For a rehabilitation of Bandini's character (sullied by Poliziano's tract on the Pazzi Conspiracy), see Lauro Martines, *April Blood: Florence and the Plot against the Medici* (Oxford: Oxford University Press, 2003), 169–71; and Marcello Simonetta, *The Montefeltro Conspiracy: A Renaissance Mystery Decoded* (New York: Doubleday, 2008), with mention of Bandini at 109–10, 128, 160–61. On December 29, 1479, Bandini was hanged from a window of the Bargello, attired in the Turkish garb he had been wearing when arrested in Constantinople: a scene drawn by the young Leonardo da Vinci. In this *elogium* Giovio elides two sultans: the one who had Bandini captured and extradited was Mehmed II (the Conqueror), who was succeeded in 1481 by his son, Bayezid II, whom Lascaris visited a decade later. The preceding description of the sultan's deep knowledge of philosophy and especially of Averroës would appear to fit Mehmed better than his successor.

206. Lascaris went over to the French in 1494, perhaps because he thought Charles VIII might lead a Crusade to liberate Byzantium from the Turks. According to Setton, 3:53, "Lascaris had probably advised Charles VIII concerning Turkish affairs during and after the French expedition when Charles was claiming that his conquest of Naples was the necessary prelude to the crusade." From 1504 to 1509 he would serve Charles's successor, Louis XII, as French ambassador in Venice. His continuing enthusiasm for a Crusade to liberate Byzantium is evident in

*Informatione ad impresa contro a Turchi,* a tract he wrote in 1508. See Setton, 3:53–54; *CE,* 2:293; Giraldi, 303.

207. Lascaris directed this school and supervised its editions of Greek texts (1513–18). See *DLI,* 299; Vittorio Fanelli, "Il ginnasio greco di Leone X a Roma," *Studi romani* 9 (1961): 379–93; and Stefano Pagliaroli, "Giano Lascari e il ginnasio greco," *Studi medievali e umanistici* 2 (2004): 215–93.

208. Polybius, *Liber ex Polibii historiis excerptus de militia Romanorum et castrorum metatione inventu rarissimus,* trans. Janus Lascaris (Venice: Giovanni Antonio Nicolini da Sabbio, 1529).

209. The *editiones principes* of Greek texts that he produced included the *Greek Anthology* and Callimachus (*Hymns*).

210. The poem is in elegiac couplets. For the original Greek epitaph and an English translation therefrom, see Marc D. Lautermann, "Janus Lascaris and the Greek Anthology," in *The Neo-Latin Epigram: A Learned and Witty Genre,* ed. Susanna de Beer, K. A. E. Enenkel, and David Rijser (Leuven: Leuven University Press, 2009), 40–65, at 42.

211. The poem is in elegiac couplets.

212. Seemingly a reference to an effigy of him on the tomb.

213. See Ovid, *Metamorphoses* 6.162–312, especially 280–85.

214. *Rudolph Agricola: Six Lives and Erasmus's Testimonies,* ed., trans., and annot. Fokke Akkerman; English trans. Rudy Bremer and Corrie Ooms Beck (Assen: Royal Van Gorcum, 2012), 3–7; *EH,* 24; *CE,* 1:15–17; Spitz, 20–40; *NMW,* 315; Giraldi, 143–45.

215. Agricola (né Roelof Huisman) was born in Baflo (around twelve miles north of Groningen), where his father, Hendrik Vries, was parish priest. The following year Vries became abbot of the Benedictine convent of Selward (Siloë), just outside the city walls of Groningen. *Rudolph Agricola,* ed. Akkerman et al., 3.

216. After earning his BA at the University of Erfurt (1458), Agricola spent time at the universities of Leuven (MA, 1465); Pavia, where he studied civil law (1468?–75); and Ferrara (1475–79), where he focused on Greek. Thereafter, he returned to Groningen to serve as the city's secretary.

217. One of Agricola's earlier biographers, his student Gerald Gelden-houwer of Nijmegen (1482–1542), similarly emphasizes his eloquence, erudition, and scholarly range: "The most Greek among Greeks, the most Latin among Latins, in poetry one might have called him another Virgil, in prose he reminded one of Poliziano by his charm, but surpassed him in grandeur. *Even his extempore speech was so pure, so natural, that you would swear that it was not some Frisian, but someone born and bred in the city of Rome that was speaking.* To such perfect eloquence he united an equally great erudition. He had fathomed all the mysteries of philosophy. There was no branch of music that he had not most scrupulously mastered. Toward the end of his life he had turned his whole mind to Hebrew literature, and to Holy Scripture" (*Rudolph Agricola*, ed. Akkerman et al., 103 [emphasis added]). On Giovio's invocations of climatic theories of culture, elaborated for example in his *Britannia*, see Minonzio's comments in *Elogi*, 99n3.

218. Agricola, *De inventione dialectica libri tres* = *Drei Bücher über die Inventio dialectica*, ed. and trans. Lothar Mundt (Tübingen: Niemeyer, 1992). According to Spitz, 28, Agricola "sought to demonstrate the true function of logic as an element basic to rhetoric which through straight thinking and effective style produces conviction." Ibid., 31: "Rhetoric provided the new key to his philosophy." Marc van der Poel concurs (*ER*, 1:19): "Despite its title, *De inventione* was a treatise on humanistic rhetoric." For more detailed analysis see Peter Mack, *Renaissance Argument: Valla and Agricola in the Traditions of Rhetoric and Dialectic* (Leiden: Brill, 1993). *Rudolph Agricola*, ed. Akkerman et al., 200, states that there are twenty-nine known Latin poems by Agricola. Editions of his poetry are detailed in Gerda C. Huisman, *Rudolph Agricola: A Bibliography of Printed Works and Translations* (Nieuwkoop: De Graaf Publishers, 1985), 129–32 (= entries 139–150).

219. *Sic.* Actually, he died in Heidelberg.

220. The poem, in elegiac couplets, also appears in Ermolao Barbaro, *Epistolae, orationes et carmina*, ed. Vittore Branca (Florence: Bibliopolis, 1943), 2:124.

221. Cecil Grayson and Giulio Carlo Argan, "Alberti, Leon Battista," *DBI* 1 (1960); *EH*, 27; *ER*, 1:27–32; Anthony Grafton, *Leon Battista Al-*

*berti: Master Builder of the Italian Renaissance* (New York: Hill and Wang, 2000).

222. Alberti, *De re aedificatoria* (completed 1452); *On the Art of Building in Ten Books*, trans. Joseph Rykwert, Neil Leach, and Robert Tavernor (Cambridge, MA: MIT Press, 1988).

223. That is, linear perspective. On the revival of the science of optics in the Middle Ages and Renaissance, see Samuel Y. Edgerton, *The Mirror, the Window, and the Telescope: How Renaissance Linear Perspective Changed Our Vision of the Universe* (Ithaca: Cornell University Press, 2009), 21–43. Alberti wrote *De pictura* in Latin in 1435, making an Italian translation the following year. See Alberti, *On Painting and On Sculpture: The Latin Texts of "De pictura" and "De statua,"* ed. and trans. Cecil Grayson (London: Phaidon, 1972).

224. Brunelleschi had used a mirror to facilitate painting in perspective: Edgerton, 44–51. For the ways that Alberti transcended that method, see ibid., 117–32. In his life of Alberti, Vasari, too, recalled this particular painting: "Also in Florence, in the house of Palla Rucellai, there is a self-portrait, done with the aid of a mirror"; quoted and translated by Grayson, in Alberti, *On Painting and on Sculpture*, 144.

225. See the edition and translation of the *Apologi*, or "One Hundred Apologues (1437)," in David Marsh, *Renaissance Fables: Aesopic Prose by Leon Battista Alberti, Bartolomeo Scala, Leonardo da Vinci, Bernardino Baldi* (Tempe: CMRS, 2004), 31–83. Alberti, *Momus*, trans. Sarah Knight; ed. Virginia Brown, ITRL 8 (Cambridge, MA: Harvard University Press, 2003). See Timothy Kircher, *Living Well in Renaissance Italy: The Virtues of Humanism and the Irony of Leon Battista Alberti* (Tempe: ACMRS, 2012), 225–56 (= chap. 7, "The Masks of Rhetoric and Alberti's *Momus*").

226. The poem is in hendecasyllables.

227. Ingebord Walter, "Medici, Lorenzo de'," *DBI* 73 (2009); *ER*, 4:93–97; Melissa Meriam Bullard, *Lorenzo il Magnifico: Image and Anxiety, Politics and Finance* (Florence: Olschki, 1994); and Ingebord Walter, *Lorenzo il Magnifico e il suo tempo* (Rome: Donzelli, 2005).

228. The poem is in dactylic hexameter.

229. The poem is in dactylic hexameter.

230. Franco Bacchelli, "Leoni (Lioni), Piero (Pier Leone, Pierleone da Spoleto)," *DBI* 64 (2005); Minonzio (2002), 2:408–17; Maike Rotzoll, *Pierleone da Spoleto: vita e opere di un medico del Rinascimento* (Florence: Olschki, 2000).

231. Although here Giovio is silent about earlier Renaissance scholarship on Galen and downplays Arabs' contributions to medicine, elsewhere he recognized the importance of the latter. See Minonzio (2002), 2:409–10; *Elogi*, 108n3.

232. Vergil, *Aeneid* 3.395: "fata viam invenient."

233. Actually, he was already Lorenzo's personal physician: *Elogi*, 108n4.

234. This is Lazzaro Tebaldi, who taught at the University of Pavia: see *Elogi*, 108n5.

235. According to Bacchelli, "Leoni," he was found in the well of the villa of Malcantone a San Gervasio (near Careggi), where he had been staying (the villa belonged to the Martelli).

236. Elsewhere, Giovio asserts Piero de' Medici's guilt as fact. See, for example, the portrayal of Piero in the *Elogia* of men of arms (bk. 4, no. 3), translated in *Elogi*, 690–94. For Sannazaro's poem, see his *Opere Volgari*, 2: *Sonetti e canzoni*, 216–20 (= no. 101), written ca. 1500; Rotzoll, *Pierleone*, 22n37. Demetrius Chalcondyles and the papal Master of Ceremonies Joannes Burchard concurred. In contrast, Pietro Crinito and, decades later, Pierio Valeriano described the death as a suicide. See, respectively, Crinito, *De honesta disciplina* 3.9; *DLI*, 145, with Gaisser's comparison of the two accounts at note 58. In his unfinished *Storie fiorentine* (1508–9), Francesco Guicciardini reported both versions: some took it as a portent of Lorenzo de' Medici's death, he writes, "that Lorenzo's physician, maestro Piero Leone da Spoleto, reputed to be the best in Italy, had in desperation thrown himself into a well and drowned; though some said he was thrown in" (Guicciardini [1970], 70). Rotzoll, *Pierleone*, 19–23, surveys a range of primary accounts without reaching a fixed conclusion as to the cause of the doctor's demise. His burial in a place of honor, in the Church of San Niccolò in Spoleto (April 29, 1492), suggests that the city's bishop did not believe the death a suicide. See Bacchelli, "Leoni."

237. Piero de' Medici died while fleeing the defeat of the French in the Battle of Garigliano (December 27–29, 1503), in which Imperial forces under Gonsalvo the Great and Bartolomeo d'Alviano soundly defeated a substantially larger French army under the command of Ludovico II del Vasto, marquis of Saluzzo. See Guicciardini (1971), 1:580–86.

238. The poem is in elegiac couplets.

239. The Timavo River is in the Friuli-Venezia Giulia region of Italy, now in the province of Trieste.

240. Vitale misidentifies the river.

241. Ermolao Barbaro (the Younger). See Emilio Bigi, "Barbaro, Ermolao (Almorò)," *DBI* 6 (1964); *EH*, 53; King, 322–23; Minonzio (2002), 2:417–23; *DLI*, 93, 265–66; *NMW*, 255, 283, 313.

242. A reference to Barbaro's most famous work, the *Castigationes Plinianae* (Rome: Silber, 1493).

243. Themistius, *Expositiones in Posteriora Aristotelis in physica. In libros de anima. In commentarios de memoria et reminiscentia. De somno et vigilia. De insomniis. De divinatione per somnum*, trans. Ermolao Barbaro (Venice: Bartolomeo Zani, 1499).

244. Barbaro's commentary on Pomponio Mela's *Cosmographia sive de situ orbis libri III*, the *Castigationes in P. Melam*, appeared in 1493 along with the *Castigationes Plinianae* (see note 242 above) and subsequently would be printed on its own.

245. For example, Ermolao Barbaro, *In Dioscoridem corollariorum libri quinque* (Cologne: Johann Soter, 1530); Dioscorides, *De medicinali materia*, trans. Ermolao Barbaro, in Giovanni Battista Egnazio, Ermolao Barbaro, et al., [Dioscorides and other medical texts] (Venice: Luigi Barbaro, Francesco Barbaro, et al., 1516).

246. In 1490 Barbaro went to Rome as Venice's ambassador. On March 6, 1491, Pope Innocent VIII made him Patriarch of Aquileia, in Istria, in Venetian territory (Eubel, 2:92).

247. According to Bigi, "Barbaro," Innocent bestowed the patriarchate upon Barbaro by a *motu proprio*, but the Venetians had a longstanding policy of not allowing ambassadors to accept gifts or appointments from

the sovereigns to whom they had been dispatched and objected to his elevation without their permission. The Senate replaced him as ambassador,
confiscated his property, and declared him an exile. Pope Innocent, for his
part, threatened to excommunicate Barbaro if he resigned the patriarchate.
He declined to take up residence, and so the see was effectively vacant until
he died (Niccolò Donati became its patriarch on September 13, 1497).

248. The poem that follows is in elegiac couplets.

249. This is Giorgio Merlani, who went by "Merula" because he traced
his origins (inaccurately) to an ancient Roman *gens* of that name. See
Alessandro Daneloni, "Merlani, Giorgio," *DBI* 73 (2009); *EH*, 303; *CE*,
2:437. He studied under Francesco Filelfo in Milan (ca. 1442–46) and
moved to Rome at least by the time of the jubilee in 1450. He is praised
in passing in *NMW*, 255, 313.

250. On Marzio (ca. 1424–92?), see Gabriella Miggiano, "Marzio, Galeotto," *DBI* 71 (2008). He met Merula in Rome in 1450, and both lived in
Padua in the early 1450s. A quarter-century later, Merula published a
direct attack on one of Marzio's compositions, Merula, *Georgii Alexandrini
in librum de homine Galeoti Narniensis opus* (Venice: Johann von Köln and
Johann Manthen, 1474/75), which elicited a response, Marzio, *Refutatio
obiectorum in librum De homine* (Bologna: Domenico de' Lapi; Venice:
Jacques Le Rouge; both 1476). See also *Adversus Domitii Calderini Commentarios in Martialem*, in *Enarrationes Satyrarum Juvenalis* (Venice: Gabriele
di Pietro, 1478), frequently reprinted; and *In Politianum* (1489/90), on
which see Laura Perotto Sali, "L'opuscolo inedito di Giorgio Merula contro i *Miscellanea* di Angelo Poliziano," *Interpres* 1 (1978): 146–83.

251. Dio Cassius, *Nervae et Trajani atque Adriani principum vitae*, trans.
Giorgio Merula, in *De Caesaribus libri III*, trans. Giovanni Battista Egnazio et al. (Venice: Aldo Manuzio and Andrea Torresani di Asolo, 1516);
Merula, *Historia Vicecomitum*, tracing the history of Milan from its origins
through the Battle of Parabiago and the death of Azzone Visconti in
1339. The latter work remained unfinished; extracts from Books 1 and 6
first appeared in print in Turin in 1527.

252. In *NMW*, 379–83, Giovio detailed how, during the French occupation of Milan, its citizens grew profligate and soft.

253. Merula charged that Poliziano in his *Miscellanea* had plagiarized and had launched underhanded attacks on him. *ER*, 5:116 (s.n. Poliziano); Daneloni, "Merlani."

254. That is, Ludovico "il Moro" Sforza.

255. The poem is an elegiac couplet.

256. Angelo Ambrogini of Montepulciano. See Emilio Bigi, "Ambrogini, Angelo, detto il Poliziano," *DBI* 2 (1960); *ER*, 5:114–16.

257. Poliziano began writing the *Stanze cominciate per la giostra del magnifico Giuliano di Piero de Medici* in 1475 but left off work on it by April 26, 1478, when Giuliano was murdered in the Pazzi Conspiracy. Angelo Poliziano, *The Stanze of Angelo Poliziano*, trans. David Quint (Amherst: University of Massachusetts Press, 1979). The joust had taken place in 1469.

258. It remains unclear whether the poem *La Giostra fatta in Fiorenza dal Magnifico Lorenzo de' Medici il vecchio* was written by Luca Pulci, by his brother Luigi, or begun by Luca and finished by Luigi. See *Elogi*, 117n3; and Alessio Decaria, "Pulci, Luca" and "Pulci, Luigi," both in *DBI* 85 (2016). In the latter entry, Decaria attributes the poem to Luigi. Both it and Poliziano's *Stanze* are vernacular poems in octaves.

259. *Politianae coniurationis commentarium* (1478); English ed., *The Pazzi Conspiracy*, trans. Elizabeth B. Welles, in *The Earthly Republic: Italian Humanists on Government and Society*, ed. Benjamin G. Kohl and Ronald G. Witt (Philadelphia: University of Pennsylvania Press, 1978), 305–22, with introduction at 293–303. Martines, *April Blood*, *passim*, emphasizes the liberties Poliziano took in sullying the character of the conspirators. See Welles, 298–300, on Sallust's *War with Catiline* as the humanist's model for this practice. The murder of Giuliano de' Medici took place in the cathedral of Florence on Sunday April 26, 1478.

260. He was hired as professor of rhetoric and poetry at the University of Florence in November 1480.

261. Herodian, *Historiae de imperio post Marcum vel de suis temporibus*, trans. Angelo Poliziano (Bologna: Bazaliero Bazalieri, 1493).

262. The charge of plagiarism is discredited by Revilo Pendleton Oliver, "Era plagiario Poliziano nelle sue traduzioni di Epitteto e di Erodiano?"

in *Il Poliziano e il suo tempo*, Atti del IV Convegno Internationale di studi sul Rinascimento, Florence, Palazzo Strozzi, 23–26 September 1954 (Florence: Sansoni, 1957), 253–71. On Tifernate, see *elogium* 117.

263. These include *De Ovidii exilio et morte* and *Ad iuventutem*. See Bigi, "Ambrogini."

264. In accordance with theories of physiognomy, Giovio here draws a parallel between Poliziano's distorted physical features and his character.

265. The poem is in choliambics.

266. The poem is in elegiac couplets. Its author, the Venetian patrician Pietro Bembo (1470–1547), excelled in writing both Ciceronian Latin and the Tuscan vernacular, for both of which he was a forceful advocate. Bembo served as domestic secretary to Pope Leo X (1513–21). In 1529 he was named librarian and historian of the Venetian Republic, in which capacity he continued the history of the city that Marcantonio Sabellico had begun. In 1539 Pope Paul III created him cardinal. See Carlo Dionisotti, "Bembo, Pietro," *DBI* 8 (1966); *EH*, 61; *CE*, 1:120–23; *ER*, 1:201–2; *NMW*, 217–19, 253, 261. The Latin text with the translation here reproduced may be found in Pietro Bembo, *Lyric Poetry — Etna*, trans. Mary P. Chatfield and Betty Radice, ITRL 18 (Cambridge, MA: Harvard University Press, 2005), 90–93.

267. The poem alludes to Poliziano's famous threnody on the death of Lorenzo, "Quis dabit capiti meo aquam," set to music by Heinrich Isaac.

268. The invocation recalls Poliziano's vernacular play, *The Tale of Orpheus* (*Fabula di Orfeo*), probably composed in 1480.

269. The poem is an elegiac couplet.

270. Franco Bacchelli, "Pico, Giovanni, conte della Mirandola e Concordia," *DBI* 83 (2015); *ER*, 5:16–20.

271. On Pico's facility at engaging in sophisticated scholarly debate in different styles and genres, see Francesco Bausi, *Nec rhetor neque philosophus: Fonti, lingua e stile nelle prime opere latine di Giovanni Pico della Mirandola (1484–87)* (Florence: Olschki, 1996).

272. Pico, *Disputationes adversus astrologiam divinatricem*, ed. Eugenio Garin, 2 vols. (Florence: Vallecchi, 1946–52). Giovio exaggerates the effect of

this work on the practice of astrology, which was still deemed a worthwhile subject of inquiry by the Royal Society in Isaac Newton's time (*ER*, 5:19). For Giovio's withering criticisms of the astrologer's craft and particular failed predictions, see *NMW*, 27–33, 41–47, and *passim*.

273. *Heptaplus, a Sevenfold Account of the Six Days of Genesis*, which Pico dedicated to Lorenzo de' Medici: *Heptaplus, de septiformi sex dierum geneseos enarratione* (Florence: Bartolomeo de' Libri, 1489). For an English rendition see Pico, *On the Dignity of Man, On Being and the One, Heptaplus*, trans. Charles Glenn Wallis, Paul J. W. Miller, and Douglas Carmichael (Indianapolis: Bobbs-Merrill, 1965). His exegesis here draws heavily on the Kabbalah. The second work is *Apologia conclusionum suarum* ([Naples], 1487). In late 1486 Pico had published his *Conclusiones*, a collection of nine hundred theses that were intended to be disputed at a philosophical summit in Rome. Pope Innocent VIII prevented the conference from taking place. He also "appointed a commission that first declared six of the theses suspect and condemned seven others, then rejected Pico's clarifications and repudiated all thirteen" (*ER*, 5:16). After Pico published his *Apology*, the pope denounced all nine hundred *conclusiones*.

274. Some contemporaries attributed Pico's death, on November 17, 1494, to poison.

275. Even as the French army asserted dominance over Florence, the citizens celebrated the recovery of a liberty that many believed had been lost in the later years of Medici hegemony (Piero de' Medici had been expelled from Florence in the course of the negotiations between the city and the French king).

276. The 1571 and 1577 editions of the *Elogia* attribute this elegiac couplet to Ercole Strozzi.

277. See Maria Accame, "Pomponio Leto, Giulio," *DBI* 84 (2015); *EH*, 270–71; www.repertoriumpomponianum.it; *ER*, 4:415–16; *DLI*, 219, 318–19.

278. The Picentines are the *Monti Picentini* in southern Italy. Italo Gallo, "Piceni e picentini: Paolo Giovio e la patria di Pomponio Leto," *Rassegna storica salernitana*, n.s. 5 (June 1986): 43–50, shows convincingly that Giovio does not mean the Marches in east-central Italy (location of the an-

cient region of *Picenum*), as many have taken it, but instead the Picentines in the province of Salerno. Cf. the use of *ager Picentinus* in Pliny the Elder, *Natural History* 3.70: "The 30 miles of Picentine territory between the district of Sorrento and the river Silaro belonged to the Etruscans; it was famous for the temple of Argive Juno founded by Jason. Further inland was Picentia, a town of Salerno" (LCL 352:55). Pomponio was in fact probably born in Diano (today, Teggiano) in Lucania, although some scholars trace his origins to Calabria.

279. In fact, he was the illegitimate son not of Roberto Sanseverino, prince of Salerno, but of Roberto's younger brother, Giovanni Sanseverino, count of Marsico (in Basilicata, in southern Italy). See Accame, "Pomponio Leto."

280. In the 1450s, after arriving in Rome, Pomponio studied Latin under Valla and then under Pietro Odi da Montopoli, whom he succeeded as professor of rhetoric at the Studium Urbis around 1465.

281. On the supposed conspiracy of 1468 to murder Pope Paul II, for which Pomponio was imprisoned along with several members of his academy (an informal gathering of scholars interested in antiquities, the classics, and more generally the revival of ancient Roman culture), see Accame, "Pomponio Leto"; Anthony F. D'Elia, *A Sudden Terror: The Plot to Murder the Pope in Renaissance Rome* (Cambridge, MA: Harvard University Press, 2009); and Kate Lowe, "The Political Crime of Conspiracy in Fifteenth- and Sixteenth-Century Rome," in *Crime, Society and the Law in Renaissance Italy*, ed. Trevor Dean and K. J. P. Lowe (Cambridge: Cambridge University Press, 1994), 184–203.

282. While in Venice as tutor to children in the Contarini and Michiel families in late 1467 and early 1468, Pomponio had already been accused of sodomy and arrested. In February 1468 he was extradited to Rome and imprisoned in Castel Sant'Angelo, charged again with sodomy, but now also with conspiracy against the pope and with heresy. Two trials ensued, in 1468 and 1469 (Paul II himself presided over the latter). Ultimately the charges were dropped, and in 1470 Pomponio was reinstated in his university post.

283. In the late 1470s, Pomponio refounded his academy, now prudently making it overtly a religious sodality.

284. See José Ruysschaert, "Les manuels de grammaire latine composés par Pomponio Leto," *Scriptorium* 8 (1954): 98–107.

285. *Romanae historiae compendium ab interitu Gordiani Iunioris usque ad Iustinum III* (Venice: Bernardino dei Vitali, 1499).

286. Probably the *Excerpta a Pomponio dum inter ambulandum cuidam domino ultramontano reliquias ac ruinas urbis ostenderet*, first published under the title *De Romanae urbis vetustate* (Rome: Giacomo Mazzocchi, 1510), but perhaps instead the *Notitia regionum urbis Romae*, also known as the *Regionarium*.

287. On Pomponio's eloquence and his speech impediment, see also Giovio's remarks in *NMW*, 283–85.

288. Most experts date his death to 1498 (others, to 1497).

289. Evidently, Pietro Marsi (Petrus Marsus Cesensis). The more famous humanist Paolo Marsi da Pescina (also an associate of Pomponio) had died in 1484.

290. This poem, in elegiac couplets, is Pontano, *Tumulus* 1.16.

291. This is Filippo Buonaccorsi, who assumed the Latin name Callimachus Experiens. See Michael T. Tworek, "Filippo Buonaccorsi," at http://repertoriumpomponianum.it/pomponiani/buonaccorsi_filippo.htm (accessed February 12, 2018). For further detail see Harold B. Segel, *Renaissance Culture in Poland: The Rise of Humanism, 1470–1543* (Ithaca: Cornell University Press, 1989), 36–82 and *passim*; Domenico Caccamo, "Buonaccorsi, Filippo," *DBI* 15 (1972); D'Elia, *Sudden Terror*, 94–103 and *passim*. Callimachus went to Rome in 1461.

292. Giovio's reference to Callimachus as "guilty of having been the first" among the academicians "to assume a Greek name" may be an oblique reference to accusations of sodomy leveled at Callimachus by Pomponio Leto and others. When writing in his own defense, Pomponio referred to Callimachus as a man of *perversos mores*: see Richard J. Palermino, "The Roman Academy, The Catacombs and the Conspiracy of 1468," *Archivum*

*historiae pontificiae* 18 (1980): 117–55, at 126, 126–27n36. For a nuanced reading of the political context and especially of an epigram that Pomponio, while imprisoned in Castel Sant'Angelo, wrote about Callimachus, see Paola Medioli Masotti, "L'Accademia romana e la congiura del 1468," *Italia medioevale e umanistica* 25 (1982): 189–204. Acting on the advice of Cardinal Bessarion, Callimachus (then in the service of Bartolomeo Roverella, Cardinal of Ravenna) managed to flee, thereby avoiding the imprisonment and torture that some of his fellow academicians would suffer. See Palermino, "Roman Academy," 125–26.

293. Casimir IV Jagiellon (1427–92), made grand duke of Lithuania in 1440, had become king of Poland in 1447. Before Callimachus found lasting safety there, his flight from papal authorities had taken him to Cyprus, Chios, and Constantinople. His protectors and patrons in Poland included members of the Tebaldi family of Florence, to whom he was related, and powerful bishops including Gregory of Sanok and Zbigniew Oleśnicki. See Tworek, "Filippo Buonaccorsi."

294. Casimir IV's sons included Ladislaus II, king of Bohemia and Hungary, 1490–1516; John I Albert (Jan Olbracht), king of Poland, 1492–1501; Alexander I, king of Poland, 1501–6; and Sigismund I the Old, king of Poland, 1506–48.

295. Matthias Corvinus (Mátyás Hunyadi; 1443–90), king of Hungary, 1458–90. See *CE*, 2:408–9; *ER*, 2:91–93; Marcus Tanner, *The Raven King: Matthias Corvinus and the Fate of his Lost Library* (New Haven: Yale University Press, 2008).

296. This is John I Albert (Jan Olbracht).

297. Following Casimir IV's death (June 7, 1492), Callimachus left the country for Vienna to await resolution of the succession controversy. On September 23, John Albert was elevated to the Polish throne. Ladislaus, Casimir's eldest son, was now king of both Bohemia and Hungary. Their brother Alexander became grand duke of Lithuania. See Segel, *Renaissance Culture*, 61. A dispatch of Jan Pot to the Venetian Senate in May 1495 attests Callimachus's profound influence over the new king. Segel summarizes thus (ibid., 62): "To set the doge's [Agostino Barbarigo's] mind at ease that in Poland Callimachus's authority was as be-

fore, Pot drew up the report. . . . The document makes the important point that not only was Callimachus's position at the Polish court virtually unassailable, but the king himself was obedient to him." The well-documented hostility of the nobles toward Callimachus was owed to his advocacy of centralizing power under the king at the expense of their authority. In late 1495/early 1496, King John Albert and his brother Alexander, Grand Duke of Lithuania, formulated plans for a joint military campaign to free from Ottoman control two port cities on the Black Sea — Kilia (Chilia, Kilya) and Bilhorod (Akkerman) — that Sultan Bayezid II had taken in 1484. In these negotiations, Callimachus had acted as John Albert's ambassador to Alexander. The campaign itself, which took place in 1497, resulted in disaster when Stephen III (the Great) of Moldavia surprised and decimated the Polish cavalry. Callimachus, who had already died in 1496, became the scapegoat. See Segel, *Renaissance Culture*, 65.

298. According to Cacciamo, "Buonaccorsi," however, he died in Cracow on November 1, 1496, while he was preparing the campaign against the Turks in Moldavia. Giovio's reconstruction of the circumstances of Callimachus's demise was dismissed by the Polish historian, diplomat, and prince-bishop Marcin Kromer (1512–89), in his *De origine et rebus gestis Polonorum libri XXX* (Basel: Oporinus, 1568). On Kromer, see Peroration, note 45, below. See Minonzio's comments in *Elogi*, 126n3. Palermino, "Roman Academy," 126n34, comments that "the intrigues which have been associated with his [Callimachus's] last years in Poland appear to be more fabrications of Paolo Giovio than fact."

299. On the bronze funeral slab and its inscriptions, see Segel, *Renaissance Culture*, 64–65; and Marcin Szyma, "Where is the Burial Place of Filippo Buonaccorsi, called Callimachus? From the Research on the Topography of the Dominican Church in Cracow," in *Epigraphica & Sepulcralia* 7, ed. Jiří Roháček (Prague, 2016), 59–78, with a photograph of the sepulchral slab at 73.

300. Callimachus wrote *Historia de rege Vladislao seu de clade Varnensi* sometime between 1484 and 1490 and dedicated it to Casimir IV. Its subject is Ladislaus (Władysław) III, who became king of Poland in 1434 and then king of Hungary in 1440. He died in the Battle of Varna (No-

vember 10, 1444), in which his troops were defeated by Sultan Murad II. Ladislaus was succeeded by his younger brother, Casimir (i.e., Casimir IV, Callimachus's patron). The text of the *Historia* was first printed in Augsburg in 1518. For a modern critical edition and Polish translation see Buonaccorsi, *Historia de rege Vladislao,* ed. Irmina Lichońska, trans. Anna Komornicka, with historical commentaries by Thaddaeus Kowalewski (Warsaw: Państwowe Wydawnictwo Naukowe, 1961). Cochrane, 349, writes that this text "remained the standard history of the period, in the Augsburg (1518) and Cracow (1582) editions, well after the publication of the geographical-political survey of Poland by Marcin Kromer . . . in 1578."

301. The poem is in elegiac couplets.

302. That is, to the historian Sallust (Gaius Sallustius Crispus).

303. See Stefano Dall'Aglio, "Savonarola, Girolamo," *DBI* 91 (2018); Donald Weinstein, *Savonarola: The Rise and Fall of a Renaissance Prophet* (New Haven: Yale University Press, 2011); *ER,* 5:406–10; Martines (2006); Roberto Ridolfi, *The Life of Girolamo Savonarola,* trans. Cecil Grayson (New York: Knopf, 1959); Girolamo Savonarola, *Selected Writings of Girolamo Savonarola: Religion and Politics, 1490–1498,* ed. and trans. Anne Borelli and Maria Pastore Passaro (New Haven: Yale University Press, 2006); and idem, *Apologetic Writings,* ed. and trans. M. Michèle Mulchahey, ITRL 68 (Cambridge, MA: Harvard University Press, 2015).

304. That is, the Florentine *Signoria.*

305. "Elite": the *ottimati,* or "best men," as Florence's elite families were collectively called, in imitation of Cicero's *optimates.*

306. A reference to the execution in 1497 of five conspirators (Giovio errs in writing seven) who had sought to return Piero de' Medici to power: Bernardo del Nero, Niccolò Ridolfi, Lorenzo Tornabuoni, Giannozzo Pucci, and Giovanni Cambi. Although in 1494 Savonarola had supported a new law guaranteeing the right of appeal to the Great Council, he did not intervene when his allies denied that right to the conspirators. See Najemy (2006), 398; Mark Jurdjevic, *Guardians of Republicanism: The Valori Family in the Florentine Renaissance* (Oxford: Oxford University Press, 2008), 12, 88–94. Whereas Giovio blames Savonarola for the

rushed execution of the conspirators, modern scholarship casts serious doubt on the rumors that he had actively intervened. See Weinstein, *Savonarola*, 241–44; Martines (2006), 197–200.

307. For Savonarola's criticisms of Alexander VI's morals, see Martines (2006), 121–39. His challenge to the legitimacy of the pontiff's authority was expressed, for example, in a sermon he delivered on March 14, 1498: "He is not to be called Pope, and he is not to be obeyed, when he commands against the will of God." Quoted by Ridolfi, *Life*, 230. Alexander VI issued the brief of excommunication on May 12, 1497, which threatened the same punishment to anyone who thereafter attended Savonarola's sermons or had other contact with him. The order of excommunication arrived in Florence on June 18 and was read aloud in five of the city's churches (Weinstein, *Savonarola*, 228–29). According to a dispatch of March 18, 1498, to the Florentine *Signoria* from Domenico Bonsi, the city's ambassador in Rome, Alexander had consulted the cardinals, who had encouraged him to insist upon Savonarola's arrest: Martines (2006), 217.

308. On the afternoon of Palm Sunday (April 8, 1498), the day after the planned ordeal by fire between a Dominican and a Franciscan had been rained out, a mob laid siege to the Dominican convent of San Marco and set fire to its main and side gates: Martines (2006), 239. For an account of Savonarola's surrender to representatives of the Florentine government, see ibid., 242.

309. On the evening of April 8, while San Marco was under siege, Francesco Valori was murdered by a mob in the streets not far from his house. See Martines (2006), 239; Najemy (2006), 399; Jurdjevic, *Guardians, passim*. On Valori's crucial role in denying the right of the conspirators to appeal to the Great Council, see Martines (2006), 195–96. Among Valori's killers were Vincenzio Ridolfi and Simone Tornabuoni, each related to a conspirator who had been executed: Ridolfi, *Life*, 247.

310. On the conditions and expectations of judicial torture, which differed based upon one's finances and reputation, see Thomas V. Cohen, "A Long Day in Monte Rotondo: The Politics of Jeopardy in a Village Uprising (1558)," *Contemporary Studies in Society and History* 33 (1991): 639–68.

311. Savonarola, *Triumphus Crucis*, ed. and trans. Mario Ferrara (Rome: Belardetti, 1961). Weinstein, *Savonarola*, 349n31, describes its fourth book as "a refutation of the rivals of the true faith, namely, philosophy, astrology, Judaism, Islam, and heretical Christian sects." Savonarola was not, however, opposed to philosophy per se. In this fourth book (chap. 2), while he criticizes the shortcomings of philosophy (above all, that it cannot lead one to eternal beatitude), he concedes that philosophers got many things right and that a judicious use of their work can be beneficial to Christians.

312. This final sentence does not appear in the manuscript of the *elogium* of Savonarola (Centro Nicolò Rusca, Fondo Aliati, Cassetta 28, intorno 7, fols. 72r–v [= 135–36]). Instead, immediately following the favorable epitaph by Flaminio is a prose epitaph (in scribal hand), with two cancellations and an addendum in Giovio's hand (here shown in italics): "Incerti avthoris. / Frater Hieronymvs Savonarola Divi Dominici non flamen pius, sed flamma impia, inauspicatae garrulitatis concionator, postquam prestigijs sanctimoniae, Florentiam diu delusit, strangulatus, combustus ~~nequissime~~, nequissimis umbris, victima corruit. Viator quisquis es, tanquam canis aegiptius, legens fugito; Namque sub nocentissimo cinere, praesentissimum ~~virus~~ latitat *venenum*." ("Fra Girolamo Savonarola, not a pious cleric of the order of St. Dominic but instead an impious torch, a demagogue of ill-omened loquacity, long duped Florence with pretenses of sanctity. Once strangled and consumed by fire, he came to grief, a sacrificial victim offered to the most-wretched shades. Wayfarer, whoever you are that's reading this: run like an Egyptian dog! For in fact, under the exceedingly criminal ash there lurks the most egregious poison." (On Egyptian dogs lapping up water from the Nile on the run so as not to be caught by crocodiles, see Pliny, *Natural History* 8.149.) This prose epitaph also appears in scribal hand, without the alterations, at fol. 13r of the same manuscript, and in at least two earlier sources, where it is followed by an even more devastating epitaph, in elegiac couplets (unattributed, but evidently by Panfilo Sasso): Hieronymus Brilinger, "Die Aufzeichnungen des Kaplans Hieronymus Brilinger 1474 bis 1525," *Basler Chroniken* (Leipzig) 7 (1915): 191–231, at 203; and a letter

from Michael Hummelberg of Ravensburg to Josse Bade, dated January 11, 1512, in Adalbert Horawitz, *Michael Hummelberger. Eine biographische Skizze* (Berlin: S. Calvary and Co., 1875), 37–38.

313. The poem is in elegiac couplets.

314. Christopher S. Celenza, "Marsilio Ficino," revised September 2, 2017, in *SEP*; Cesare Vasoli, "Ficino, Marsilio," *DBI* 47 (1997); *EH*, 184; *ER*, 2:353–57; and James Hankins, *Plato in the Italian Renaissance*, 2 vols. (Leiden: Brill, 1990), 1:267–359, 2:454–85, and *passim*. Ficino published *The Complete Works of Plato* (*Platonis Opera Omnia*) in 1484 (he had completed all his drafts of the translations by 1468–69). It comprises "all those works contained in the nine tetralogies (some now considered spurious), an arrangement attributed by Diogenes Laertius (*Lives of the Philosophers* 3.59) to Thrasyllus (possibly the otherwise unknown court astrologer to Tiberius); included were thirty-five dialogues and the Platonic *Letters*": Celenza, "Marsilio Ficino."

315. In 1462 Cosimo de' Medici gave Ficino a house within Florence, the rental of which provided him with a regular income. The following year, Cosimo gave him the property at Careggi. He was ordained in 1473 and went on to become a canon of the cathedral in Florence.

316. Giovio errs badly in describing Ficino as "entirely happy": he was known for being melancholic. The *De triplici vita* (1489) became a bestseller, appearing in close to thirty editions over the following century and a half. For a modern English version, see Ficino, *Three Books on Life*, trans. Carol V. Kaske and John R. Clark (Tempe, AZ: MRTS, 1998).

317. Lorenzo de' Medici, Ermolao Barbaro the Younger, Angelo Poliziano, and Pico della Mirandola all died in 1492. Cristoforo Landino and Girolamo Savonarola both died in 1498. Ficino's ultimate judgment on Savonarola, however, was far from sympathetic: in a letter he wrote to the College of Cardinals in the aftermath of the friar's execution, he apologized on behalf of himself and the many other Florentines who had been deceived by "the Antichrist Hieronymus of Ferrara, the greatest of hypocrites." As Weinstein summarizes, "According to Ficino, Savonarola had simulated virtue and concealed his vices, he had a 'Lucife-

rean pride,' and he had mixed prophecies with lies in order to deceive the people" (Donald Weinstein, *Savonarola and Florence: Prophecy and Patriotism in the Renaissance* [Princeton: Princeton University Press, 1970], 186).

318. In 1499 the Florentine government accused its *condottiere* Paolo Vitelli (1461–99) of having collaborated with the city's enemies and of having sabotaged that summer's campaign against Pisa. On his military career see the entry "Paolo Vitelli Signore di Montone," in Roberto Damiani, *Il dizionario anagrafico dei condottieri di ventura*, online at www.condottieridiventura.it. Interrogated and tortured, Vitelli never confessed but was nonetheless executed. Najemy (2006), 402, notes the widespread suspicion in Florence that Vitelli had conspired with certain members of the elite (*ottimati*) "to prolong the war and prevent a Florentine victory in order to impoverish the *popolo* with taxes and provoke a political crisis that would bring down the council and reinstate the Medici." Guicciardini (1970), 166–73, discusses Vitelli's siege of Pisa, assesses his strengths and weaknesses, and asserts (at 171) that "so far as the princip[al] cause of his execution is concerned, it is almost certain that he was innocent."

319. Ficino died on October 1, 1499. Five days later, Louis XII would enter Milan in triumph (it had fallen to French control on September 6).

320. The poem is an elegiac couplet.

321. Ficino believed that to combine literary learning with good moral character was "Platonic." See Celenza, "Marsilio Ficino."

322. The poem is in iambic trimeter. It is incised beneath Ficino's portrait bust in the south wall of the Florentine Duomo.

323. Gabriella Miggiano, "Marzio, Galeotto," DBI 71 (2008); Minonzio (2002), 2:429–45; Minonzio's notes in *Elogi*, 134; DLI, 307–8; CE, 2:404–5.

324. In 1460 Corvinus had arranged the appointment of Marzio as bishop of Pécs, and late the following year Marzio's friend Janus Pannonius (János Csezmicze), whom he had met when both were studying in Ferrara in 1447 at the school of Guarino Guarini of Verona, invited him to Hungary. Pannonius's kinsman, the Hungarian bishop János Vi-

téz, a patron of a humanist sodality, introduced Marzio to Corvinus. See Miggiano, "Marzio."

325. Galeotto Marzio, *De homine et eius partibus* (Venice: N. Jenson, ca. 1471).

326. On Merula's book attacking Marzio's work, see *elogium* 37 (Merula) and note 250 above.

327. Marzio, *Refutatio obiectorum in librum De homine* (Bologna: Domenico de' Lapi; Venice: Jacques Le Rouge; both 1476).

328. After returning from Bologna to Montagnana in 1477, he dedicated to Corvinus his *De incognitis vulgo*, cited and summarized in Miggiano, "Marzio."

329. Giovio's claim that Sixtus IV had once been Marzio's pupil cannot be sustained chronologically: Miggiano, "Marzio."

330. That is, the Piazzetta San Marco.

331. Marzio was arrested in Montagnana in late 1477 or early 1478 and taken to Venice, where his goods were confiscated and he was imprisoned and tortured. Following two retractions, he was sent to the pope in Rome, who reduced the penalty to public abjuration and the condemnation of the book. Miggiano, "Marzio."

332. "Hircus," here rendered "goat," may be a Latinization of the Italian *becco*, which can mean not only "billy goat" but also "cuckold."

333. The translation of this sentence is adapted from Gaisser in *DLI*, 307.

334. The poem is in dactylic hexameter.

335. Simona Foà, "Gallucci, Luigi (Elisio Calenzio)," *DBI* 51 (1998); *EH*, 196; Maria Grazia De Ruggiero, *Il poetico narrare di Elisio Calenzio, umanista del Quattrocento napoletano* (Salerno: Edizioni Palazzo Vargas, 2004).

336. Evidently he was born not in Anfratta (near Bari) but in Fratte (renamed "Ausonia" in the nineteenth century), in the province of Frosinone. See Foà, "Gallucci." In *Elogi*, 136n2, Minonzio suggests the reading "Anfratta" may be owed to its appearance in the title of his elegies in BAV MS Vat. Lat. 2833, fols. 67–103: *Elisii Calentii Amphratensis Elegiae Aurimpiae ad Angelum Colotium Aesinatem.*

337. At Giovio (1935), 178n49, Gragg cites Sannazaro, *Elegies* 1.21: "Elysiusque hedera comptus florente capillos / rara sed Aoniis concinat apta choris."

338. Perhaps the elegies are those in MS Vat. Lat. 2833, cited above. Calenzio, *Opuscula Elisii Calentii poetae clarissimi* (Rome: Johann Besicken, 1503). According to Minonzio (*Elogi*, 136n2), Colocci edited the volume at the urging of Calenzio's son Lucio. In *Croacus Elisii Calentii Amphratensis de bello ranarum, in quo adolescens locatus est* (Strasbourg: Matthias Schürer, [1512]), Calenzio imitates the *Batrachomyomachia*, or *Battle of the Frogs and Mice*, which had been attributed to Homer.

339. Colocci was made bishop of Nocera Umbra in 1537.

340. The poem is in elegiac couplets.

341. Eduardo Melfi, "Collenuccio (Coldonese, da Coldenose), Pandolfo," *DBI* 27 (1982), is fundamental but ridden with errors; *EH*, 122–23; *DLI*, 207–9, 282–83; Giraldi, 161–63, 279. On Collenuccio's wedding orations, see Anthony F. D'Elia, *The Renaissance of Marriage in Fifteenth-Century Italy* (Cambridge, MA: Harvard University Press, 2004), *ad indicem*.

342. *A lawyer*: In 1465 Collenuccio earned a doctorate in jurisprudence at the University of Padua, where he studied under Bartolomeo Cipolla.

343. Niccolò Leoniceno, *De Plinii et aliorum in medicina erroribus* (Ferrara: Lorenzo Rossi and Andrea Grassi, 1492). In response, Collenuccio published *Defensio Pliniana adversus Nicolai Leoniceni accusationem* (Ferrara: André Belfort, 1493).

344. Collenuccio, *De vipera libellus*, ed. Annibale Collenuccio (Venice: Giovanni Pietro Quarengi, 1506); *Beretta et testa, descritte et intitulate Philotimo* (Rome: Francesco Minizio Calvo, 1524); and *Compendio de le istorie del Regno di Napoli* (1498), translated for Ercole I d'Este (1431–1505), duke of Ferrara, Modena, and Reggio. Hailed as the Neapolitan equivalent of Sabellico's history of Venice, "it was translated into French, Latin, and Spanish; and it went through fifteen partial or complete editions in the Italian original between 1539 and 1613" (Cochrane, 155–57, at 155).

345. Upon the death of Costanzo Sforza of Pesaro in 1483, Collenuccio helped establish Costanzo's widow, Camilla, and his illegitimate son,

Giovanni, in power. After Giovanni definitively took full control, the humanist, who had supported Camilla, became suspect, was imprisoned for sixteen months, and then pursued opportunities elsewhere. As an ambassador of Ercole I d'Este, duke of Ferrara, Collenuccio returned to Pesaro in October 1500 immediately after Cesare Borgia had taken the city. Following Alexander VI's death, in August 1503, Giovanni Sforza retook Pesaro. The following May, with the support of Isabella d'Este, Collenuccio wrote to Giovanni in hopes of returning. Giovanni feigned forgiveness but, following Collenuccio's return, promptly reneged and had him executed. See Melfi, "Collenuccio."

346. The poem is in phalaecean hendecasyllables.

347. Bruno Figliuolo, "Pontano, Giovanni," *DBI* 84 (2015); *EH*, 354; *CE*, 3:113–14; *ER*, 5:118–20; Kidwell (1993); Jerry H. Bentley, *Politics and Culture in Renaissance Naples* (Princeton: Princeton University Press, 1987), 127–37, 176–94, and *passim*; Cochrane, 151–52 and *passim*.

348. Pontano had first gone to Perugia. Probably in 1447, he joined the military camp in Tuscany of King Alfonso I (the Magnanimous), entering Naples in the king's retinue the following year. On Alfonso's systematization of the royal library and its importance as a locus of literary education and learned discussions, see Bentley, *Politics and Culture*, 56–59; *Elogi*, 141n2.

349. Ferdinando I (Ferrante I), king of Naples, 1458–94. See Alan Ryder, "Ferdinando I d'Aragona, re di Napoli," *DBI* 46 (1996). Pontano had already received prestigious appointments in the years before Panormita's death (1471): for example, in 1462, he became *consigliere regio* and *luogotenente del gran camerario*. He was appointed first secretary to Ferrante only in 1487.

350. In a marriage arranged by Ferdinando I, in 1461 Pontano wed Adriana (Ariana) Sassone, from a Neapolitan noble family, whom he called Ariadne. See Kidwell (1991), 77.

351. See Giovanni Pontano, *Dialogues*, ed. and trans. Julia H. Gaisser, ITRL 53, 91, 92 (Cambridge, MA: Harvard University Press, 2012–20). The *Charon* is in volume 1.

352. He wrote a history of the first War of the Barons, which ended in 1464. Pontano, *De bello Neapolitano et De sermone* (Naples: Mayr, 1509). On his view of the genre of historical writing, see the long discussion of historiography in the *Actius*: Pontano, *Dialogues*, vol. 2.

353. Evidently a reference to the *Urania*, which celebrates in verse the Muse of Astronomy. *The Gardens of the Hesperides* appears in ITRL volume 94, ed. and trans. Luke Roman (Cambridge, MA: Harvard University Press, 2022).

354. *Sic.* Alexander VI died on August 18, 1503; Pontano, on September 17.

355. The phrase *te ipsum ut noscas rogo* invokes *te ipsum nosce*, the standard Latin translation of one of the two sayings on the Oracle at Delphi.

356. The poem is in phalaecean hendecasyllables.

357. The poem is in elegiac couplets.

358. Francesco Tateo, "Coccio, Marcantonio, detto Marcantonio Sabellico," *DBI* 26 (1982); *CE*, 3:181–82; King, 425–27 and *passim*; *DLI*, 125, 279–80.

359. Sabellico, *De vetustate Aquileiae et Fori Iulii libri VI* (Venice: Antonio d'Avignon, ca. 1480). The conflagration and the defeat to which Giovio here refers were due to Turkish raids in Istria and Friuli in 1477. As Setton writes (2:327), "the fires of burning woods, farmhouses, and villages were visible in Venice from atop the campanile in the Piazza San Marco."

360. According to King, 426, starting in 1485 Sabellico taught in the Scuola di San Marco as second lecturer (following the demise of Giorgio Valla in 1500, he became first lecturer). Upon dedicating the first thirty-two books of his history of Venice to the doge and the Senate, in 1486 he was rewarded with an annual salary of two hundred (not three hundred) ducats.

361. See Cochrane, 83–86 and *passim*, who writes (at 84) that "Sabellico managed to combine the principal defects both of Quattrocento humanist historiography and of the Venetian chronicle tradition."

362. Sabellico, *Enneades . . . ab orbe condito ad inclinationem Romani imperii* (Venice: Bernardino and Matteo Vitali, 1498).

363. That is, syphilis, called *la maladie italienne* by the French, and *la maladia francese* by the Italians.

364. The poem is an elegiac couplet.

365. Margherita Palumbo, "Lorenzi, Lorenzo," *DBI* 66 (2006); *EH*, 276 (s.n. Lorenzano, Lorenzo); Minonzio (2002), 2:445–51.

366. According to Palumbo, "Lorenzi," he had aimed to translate all the works of Hippocrates and Galen. Printed Latin versions include Galen's *Ars medica* (Pavia, 1506), *De crisibus* (Bologna: Berengario da Carpi, 1522), and *De differentiis febrium libri duo* (Venice: Bernardino dei Vitali, 1538); Hippocrates, *Praedictiones sive Prognostica* (Paris: Henri Estienne, 1516), and *Aphorismi* (Paris: Claude Chevallon, 1526).

367. That is, as *Gonfaloniere per Vita*, a position established in 1502 and held by Soderini for the following decade. Upon their return to Florence in 1512, the Medici abolished the office. See Humfrey C. Butters, *Governors and Government in Early Sixteenth Century Florence, 1502–1519* (Oxford: Clarendon Press, 1985).

368. The poem is in iambic trimeter.

369. On Tiberti see Minonzio (2002), 2:451–53. On the tense relationship between members of the Tiberti and other noble families in Cesena in the late 1490s, see Pier Giovanni Fabbri, "Cesare Borgia a Cesena. Istituzioni, vita politica e società nella cronaca di Giuliano Fantaguzzi dal 1486 al 1500," *Archivio storico italiano* 148, no. 1 (543) (January–March 1990): 69–102, at 93–94.

370. Tiberti, *De Chiromantia* (Bologna: Benedetto Ettore, 1494). For details on this edition, see Minonzio (2002), 2:451–52n560.

371. On d'Abano (ca. 1250–1315/16), see Iolanda Ventura, "Pietro d'Abano," *DBI* 83 (2015).

372. While no evidence of this composition has come to light, contemporary evidence indicates that such a work was at least planned. See Minonzio's comments in *Elogi*, 148–49n3.

373. On the military career of Guido Guerra da Bagno (1467–95), see the entry "Guido da Bagno" in Damiani, *Dizionario anagrafico*. It is, in fact, Pandolfo (or, "Pandolfaccio") Malatesta (see below) who had Guido

Guerra decapitated in November 1495. For a contemporary account see Andrea Bernardi, who describes Pandolfo as having invited Guido to dinner, thereupon ordering his beheading: *Cronache forlivesi di Andrea Bernardi (Novacula) dal 1476 al 1517*, ed. Giuseppe Mazzatinti (Bologna: R. Deputazione di Storia Patria, 1895), 1:114–15. Carlo Tonini, *Compendio della Storia di Rimini. 1: Dalle origini all'anno 1500, ultimo della signoria malatestiana* (Bologna: Forni Editore, 1969), 624–25, portrays Guido Guerra as guilty of conspiracy against Malatesta (and therefore deserving of his end), but that charge is refuted in Anna Falcioni, "Malatesta, Pandolfo," *DBI* 68 (2007). Ernst Breisach, *Caterina Sforza: A Renaissance Virago* (Chicago: University of Chicago Press, 1967), 168, surmises that Guido was decapitated "not so much for his numerous misdeeds as for siding with the Milanese and French in 1494 and for profiting from it at the cost of Rimini and Venice."

374. Pandolfo (or, "Pandolfaccio") Malatesta (1475–1538/39), illegitimate son of Roberto "the Magnificent" Malatesta, lord of Rimini. See Falcioni, "Malatesta." In 1485, aged ten, Pandolfo married Violante Bentivoglio, daughter of Giovanni II. On Pandolfo's military career see Damiani, *Dizionario anagrafico*, s.n. "Pandolfo Malatesta (Pandolfaccio Malatesta) Di Verucchio."

375. That is, Giovanni II Bentivoglio (1443–1508), unofficial *signore* of Bologna since 1463. Falcioni, "Malatesta," thinks it likely that Bentivoglio influenced the decision.

376. In October 1498, in the town of Coriano, Pandolfo had Antioco and six of his men imprisoned under suspicion of conspiracy (Antioco had already given over another of his men, Zoanno Batista da Monte Colombo). Following their transfer to Rimini, the six soldiers were hanged, but for the moment Pandolfo was sufficiently interested in Antioco's abilities at divining that he left him alive. When Antioco predicted that Pandolfo would soon lose his state, he was put in chains pending the outcome of the prophecy: Gian Ludovico Masetti Zannini, "La signoria di Pandolfo IV," in *La signoria di Pandolfo IV Malatesti (1482–1528)*, ed. Zannini and Anna Falcioni (Rimini: Bruno Ghigi Editore, 2003), 19–189, at 73–74. See especially the account in a chronicle written in 1520–21, now in a modern critical edition: Giuliano Fantaguzzi, *Caos*, ed. Michele

Andrea Pistocchi, 2 vols. (Rome: Istituto storico italiano per il Medio Evo, 2012), 1:166; and that in Cesare Clementini, *Raccolto istorico della fondatione di Rimino e dell'origine, e vita de' Malatesti*, 2 vols. (Bologna: Forni Editore, 1969; orig. pub. Rimini, 1617–27), 2:582–83 (vol. 2 published posthumously, edited by Cesare's son Clementino Clementini). See also the mentions of Antioco in two letters of Zorzi (Giorgio) Franco, dated, respectively, October 11 and 13, 1498, in Sanuto, 2: cols. 34, 40–41.

377. Evidently Giovio errs: both Fantaguzzi and Clementini specify that she was the castellan's niece, not his daughter.

378. According to Fantaguzzi, *Caos*, 1:166, Antioco had been the fifteen-year-old girl's tutor, and the two had contrived to flee together, but her paternal uncle (the castellan) caught them and thereupon killed her, perhaps doing so in order to keep the four hundred ducats that her father had entrusted to him for her dowry. Clementini, *Raccolto istorico*, 2:382–83, suggests that she came under Antioco's sway because of either his attractiveness, his kindness, his efforts to persuade her, some blood connection between them or, "as one could well believe," the use of black magic. Clementini specifies that Antioco was apprehended because of his inability to get the chains off his feet. Neither Fantaguzzi nor Clementini supports Giovio's claim that Tiberti was beheaded. Fantaguzzi, *Caos*, 1:166, says that following the incident Antioco was placed in a far-tighter cell, and after an unspecified time "fo morto" (meaning either "he died" or "he was killed"). In an entry for the year 1500, Fantaguzzi notes the discovery of Antioco's body, buried nude, in the fortress of Rimini (ibid., 1:233). Clementini, *Raccolto istorico*, 2:383, corroborates these details, and unlike Fantaguzzi he specifies that Pandolfo had ordered Antioco killed.

379. Although Pandolfo and his son Sigismondo Malatesta used the opportunity provided by the Sack of Rome to retake Rimini on June 14, 1527, they were expelled on June 17, 1528. Thereafter, Pandolfo did indeed live in poverty, but according to Falcioni, "Malatesta," he went on to marry a second time (his first wife having died), to Ippolita di Sebastiano Tebaldi, with whom he had two children. He died in Rome.

380. The poem is in elegiac couplets.

381. Myron Gilmore, "Beroaldo, Filippo, senior," *DBI* 9 (1967); *EH*, 64–65; *CE*, 1:135.

382. Beroaldo, *Commentarii a Philippo Beroaldo conditi in* Asinum aureum Lucii Apulei (Bologna: Benedictus Hector, 1500). For extensive analysis of this work, see Julia Haig Gaisser, *The Fortunes of Apuleius and the Golden Ass: A Study in Transmission and Reception* (Princeton: Princeton University Press, 2008), 197–243.

383. Giovanni II Bentivoglio was driven from power by troops of Pope Julius II in autumn 1506. See Gaspare De Caro, "Bentivoglio, Giovanni," *DBI* 8 (1966); Pastor, 6:276–79.

384. On Filippo Beroaldo the Younger (1472–1518), see Ettore Paratore, "Beroaldo, Filippo, iunior," *DBI* 9 (1967); *EH*, 64; *CE*, 1:135; *DLI*, 121, 267–68, and *passim*. Beroaldo the Younger succeeded Tommaso Fedra Inghirami as Vatican librarian in 1516. Just over a decade earlier, he had become secretary of Cardinal Giovanni de' Medici (the future Leo X). At least in 1514, he was teaching at the University of Rome. Antonio Lelio would collect and publish his poems posthumously: *Phillippi Beroaldi Bononiensis iunioris carminum ad Augustum Trivultium Cardinalem libri III* (Rome: Antonio Blado, 1530).

385. The poem is in elegiac couplets.

386. Giada Guassardo, "Strozzi, Ercole," *DBI* 94 (2019); *DLI*, 113, 322–23; Giraldi, 59–61. His father was Tito Vespasiano Strozzi (1424–1505).

387. The phrase *omnis elegantiae arbiter* seemingly alludes to Tacitus's description of Petronius as *elegantiae arbiter*.

388. This matron may in fact be Lucrezia Borgia. For analysis of the poem on hunting, which he dedicated to her, see Alberto Pavan, "Ercole Strozzi's 'Venatio': Classical Inheritance and Contemporary Models of a Neo-Latin hunting poem," *Humanistica Lovaniensia: Journal of Neo-Latin Studies* 59 (2010): 29–54; and Pavan, "Scene di caccia per Lucrezia Borgia. Introduzione alla *Venatio* di Ercole Strozzi," *Schifanoia* 36/37 (2009): 115–42. Ferdinand Gregorovius, *Lucretia Borgia: According to Original Documents and Correspondence of Her Day*, trans. John Leslie Garner (New York: Blom, 1968), 324–25, describes Strozzi's funeral ode for Cesare Borgia as having celebrated his victories in "pompous verse" and then having pro-

ceeded to console Lucrezia with "philosophic platitudes." See also Claudio Cazzola, "Per una lettura degli epigrammi latini di Tito ed Ercole Strozzi per Lucrezia Borgia," *Schifanoia* 26/27 (2004): 7–37.

389. Barbara Torelli, whose father Marsilio was count of Montechiarugolo, was the widow of Ercole Bentivoglio (whose father, Sante Bentivoglio, had been *signore* of Bologna). See Gaspare De Caro, "Bentivoglio, Ercole," *DBI* 8 (1966). She and Strozzi wed in May 1508. Although Alfonso I d'Este has often been blamed for the murder, it was probably instigated by a member of the circle of Ercole Bentivoglio (perhaps Galeazzo Sforza, *signore* of Pesaro) and had to do with a dispute over the dowry given for her first marriage. See Guassardo, "Strozzi," with further bibliography.

390. The poem is in elegiac couplets.

391. A river on Mount Helicon.

392. The poem is in elegiac couplets.

393. Mausolus ruled Caria from 377 to 353 BCE in conjunction with Artemisia, who was both his full sister and his wife.

394. Raffaella Zaccaria, "Della Rocca, Bartolomeo, detto Cocles," *DBI* 37 (1989).

395. That is, Antioco Tiberti; see *elogium* 50.

396. Bartolomeo Cocles, *Chyromantie ac physionomie Anastasis* (Bologna: Giovanni Antonio de Benedetti, 1504). Eleven years later it was republished, bound in with works on physiognomy by Aristotle, Michael Scot, and Achillini, in *Infinita nature secreta quibuslibet hominibus contingentia previdenda, cavenda ac prosequenda declarant in hoc libro contenta* [Pavia: per B. de Garaldis, 1515].

397. Alessandro Achillini, a teacher of Cocles, had published his *Questio de subiecto physionomiae et chyromantiae* in 1503. See the *elogium* (no. 57) of Achillini.

398. Andrea Corvo, born in Carpi in the mid-Quattrocento, took up residence in Mirandola probably in 1470. Augusto De Ferrari, "Corvo, Andrea," *DBI* 29 (1983). His *Chiromantia*, initially published in the late

fifteenth century, was frequently reprinted (e.g., *Picta chyromantia*, Venice, 1513), and soon thereafter appeared in Italian and French translations.

399. Zaccaria, "Della Rocca," identifies the assassin only as "one Antonio Caponi."

400. The poem is in elegiac couplets.

401. Roberto Ricciardi, "Cotta, Giovanni," *DBI* 30 (1984); *EH*, 133; *CE*, 1:349; *RLV*, 218–20; G. Battista Pighi, *Giovanni Cotta: Poeta e diplomatico legnaghese del Rinascimento* (Verona: Palazzo Giuliari, 1967); V. Mistruzzi, "Giovanni Cotta," *GSLI*, Supp. 22–23 (1924): 1–131; *DLI*, 137, 283–84; Giraldi, 73, 282. Cotta was born at Vangadizza, in the environs of Legnago (a town on the Adige River in Veronese territory), where he attended a school run by Enrico Merlo (d. 1491).

402. Evidently he moved to Naples before Pontano's death in September 1503. There he gained a reputation as an imitator both of Pontano and of Catullus.

403. Bartolomeo d'Alviano (1455–1515). See Piero Pieri, "Alviano, Bartolomeo d'," *DBI* 2 (1960); *CE*, 1:38–39. Regarding his military career, see *NMW*, 91, 123, 125, 129, 147, 175, 201–3, and 279. In *NMW*, Giovio praises d'Alviano as a fierce warrior and effective trainer of leaders but faults him for temerity, for example, at *NMW*, 175: "All men recognize the extent of the unfortunate audacity and fatal rashness of the exceedingly aggressive Venetian commander, d'Alviano. Twice in the space of one hour, when hopes had increased and the situation was already on a sure footing, he disgracefully lost his troops and brought the republic into the greatest jeopardy." Cotta served Bartolomeo d'Alviano both as a secretary and as a diplomat. He had met Bartolomeo's brother, Bernardino, in 1506 and entered Bartolomeo's service the following year.

404. Following his conquest of Pordenone for Venice, on July 15, 1508, d'Alviano was invested with it as his fief. See Mallett and Hale, 64, 188. On d'Alviano's "Livian Academy" in Pordenone, see the sources cited in *Elogi*, 160n3. On Borgia see Elena Valeri, *Italia dilacerata: Girolamo Borgia nella cultura storica del Rinascimento* (Milan: FrancoAngeli, 2007).

405. This is the Battle of Agnadello (1509), in which the French king Louis XII led his troops to victory. Afterward, most of Venice's possessions on the Italian mainland rebelled against it.

406. According to Ricciardi, "Cotta," he accompanied d'Alviano to prison but from there was sent to Venice to explain the defeat to the Senate. Upon returing to Milan, he was not allowed to rejoin d'Alviano in his captivity.

407. Giovanni Cotta and Andrea Navagero, *Carmina* (Turin: RES, 1991). I have been unable to consult *The Latin Poems of Giovanni Cotta: Together with an English translation, Notes, and a Full Concordance*, ed. Allan M. Wilson (Cheadle Hulme: A. M. Wilson, 1998).

408. This poem, in elegiac couplets, is Sannazaro, Epigram 2.39. See Jacopo Sannazaro, *Latin Poetry*, trans. Michael C. J. Putnam, ITRL 38 (Cambridge, MA: Harvard University Press, 2009).

409. The poem is in elegiac couplets.

410. Roberto Ricciardi, "Del Riccio Baldi, Pietro (Crinitus Petrus)," *DBI* 38 (1990); *EH*, 146; *CE*, 1:358–59.

411. In the vernacular, *riccio* means "curly," and *crinito* refers to having a full head of hair. Presumably, he disliked being called *riccio* because it can also mean "hedgehog" and serve as a euphemism for the female pudenda: see Valter Boggione and Giovanni Casalegno, *Dizionario letterario del lessico amoroso: metafore, eufemismi, trivialismi* (Turin: UTET, 2000), 475, citing the *Canti carnascialeschi*.

412. Giraldi, 65, offers a cooler evaluation: "The Florentine Pietro Crinito left behind poems of different genres. These are quite attractive but certainly much like the prose works that he left. In all his work he seems to promise much, but he doesn't fulfill that promise, and all his writings appeal more to the ear than the mind. I would almost call them 'tuneful trifles'" (*nugae canorae*).

413. Crinito, *De honesta disciplina*, ed. Carlo Angeleri (Rome: Fratelli Bocca, 1955); idem, *De poetis latinis* (Florence: Filippo Giunta, 1505).

414. The poem is in iambic dimeter.

415. Paola Rigo, "Donà (Donati, Donato), Girolamo," *DBI* 40 (1991); *EH*, 156; *DLI*, 139, 286–87; King, 234–36, 366–68, and *passim*.

416. On Donà's service as Venetian envoy to Julius II, see Setton, 3:64–68, 80–82, and *passim*; Pastor, 6:258, 316, 318–19; Guicciardini (1971), 2:822, 883, 970. On July 8, 1509, of the six Venetian envoys sent to Julius II, the pope absolved from excommunication only Donà, whom he granted an audience. On an earlier embassy to Pope Julius (May 5, 1505), Donà had delivered a flowery oration, which (according to the Florentine ambassador Giovanni Acciaiuoli) elicited only a perfunctory reaction ("La risposta della Santità del Papa fu breve et in sul tirato et *pro forma*"): cited by Paola Rigo, "Catalogo e tradizione degli scritti di Girolamo Donato," *Rendiconti dell'Accademia Nazionale dei Lincei. Classe di scienze morali, storiche e filologiche*, ser. 8, 31 (1976): 49–80, at 61–62. Being Venetian ambassador to Pope Julius II was not an enviable assignment. Writing to Giulio de' Medici a month after Donà's demise, Cardinal Bibbiena recalled that as Donà lay terminally ill he quipped that death would be sweet to him because it would get him out of having to negotiate further with Julius: Bernardo Dovizi da Bibbiena, *Epistolario*, ed. G. L. Moncallero, 2 vols. (Florence: Olschki, 1955), 1:348 (November 20, 1511, from Civitavecchia).

417. Donà died on October 20, 1511, just two weeks after the conclusion of the new Holy League against the French: Setton, 3:81.

418. Guicciardini ends a chapter of the *Storia d'Italia* (bk. 10, chap. 5) with mention of Donà's death and praise of his diplomatic talents: Guicciardini (1971), 2:970.

419. As often, Giovio calls attention to scholars' need for release time to devote to their work (something of which he perennially felt he deserved more).

420. Donà, *Apologeticus ad Graecos de principatu Romanae Ecclesiae* (Rome: Calvo, 1525). According to Minonzio, at *Elogi*, 165n6, this work was originally written in Greek in collaboration with Arsenio Apostoli.

421. The *De intellectu* to which Giovio refers is the commentary of Alexander of Aphrodisias on Aristotle's *On the Soul: Enarratio de anima ex Aristotelis institutione* ([Brescia: Misinti, 1495]). Donà delivered the *Ad Caesa-*

*rem pro re Christiana oratio* as Venetian ambassador to Maximilian in 1501. See King, 367. He went to Crete in mid-1506. His account of the earthquake (which struck on the night of May 29, 1508) appears in a letter of July 15, 1508, addressed to Pietro Contarini di Valsanzibio ("Eusebianus"). Ibid.

422. The poem is in iambic dimeter.

423. Bruno Nardi, "Achillini, Alessandro," *DBI* 1 (1960); *EH*, 21. On this *elogium* see Minonzio (2002), 2:466–97. After earning his degree at the University of Bologna in 1484, Achillini remained there to teach logic (1484–87), natural philosophy (1487–94), and theoretical medicine (1494–97), and then held the lectureships in both natural philosophy and theoretical medicine (1497–1506). An adherent of the Bentivoglio, he left Bologna only days before Pope Julius II's troops entered the city on November 11, 1506. Thereupon, he moved to Padua, where he taught natural philosophy alongside Pomponazzi. While Giovio was studying natural philosophy at Padua from autumn 1506 to spring 1507, he witnessed the disputations between Achillini and Pomponazzi, which took place in the portico of the *podestà*: Zimmermann (1995), 7.

424. Otter was a tawdry substitute for more expensive furs, such as lynx or sable. In Achillini's time, gowns not only had fur trim around the cuffs, neck, and hem, but also had a complete lining of fur that could be replaced in the summer with silk taffeta or linen.

425. *De elementis* (1505); *Quodlibeta de intelligentiis* (1494); *De orbibus* (1498).

426. Following the Venetian defeat at the Battle of Agnadello (May 14, 1509) during the War of the League of Cambrai, Padua threw off Venetian rule to align with Emperor Maximilian, but the Venetians retook the city in mid-July. The university suffered badly, losing students as well as professors, including Pomponazzi, who went to the University of Bologna. The Venetians began rebuilding the University of Padua in 1517. See Grendler (2002), 31–32. Cf. Nardi, "Achillini," who dates Achillini's return to Bologna to September 14, 1508, well before Padua's revolt against Venice.

427. The poem is in elegiac couplets.

428. Cf. Vergil, *Georgics* 2.490: "Felix, qui potuit rerum cognoscere causas"; perhaps also a reference to I Corinthians 13:12: "At present our sight

of things is one through a mirror which throws them into bewildering confusion, but there will be a time when we shall see them face to face. At present my knowledge is one yielding but partial glimpses, but there will be a time when I shall know completely" (*GNC*, 318).

429. Franca Petrucci, "Corio, Bernardino," *DBI* 29 (1983); Cochrane, 117–18 and *passim*.

430. Corio, *Patria historia* ([Milan: Alessandro Minuziano, 1503]). Corio is one of only three authors in Giovio's *Elogia* who wrote exclusively in the vernacular (*Elogi*, 170n1). Petrucci, "Corio," attends in detail to Corio's scholarly shortcomings. The *Historia* was nonetheless highly influential, according to Cochrane, 118: "Corio retreated from history into chronicle through most of the second half of his work. And it was largely because he succeeded at least in this form in bringing his account down to his own day, rather than because of the quality either of his language or of his narration, that his work, rather than those of Merula or Calco, was recognized as the Milanese equivalent of Sabellico's 'definitive' history of Venice well into the sixteenth century." Among the historians offering searing criticisms of Corio's scholarship was Scipione Ammirato (1531–1601), who referred at one point to his "singular negligence" (ibid., 286).

431. Pliny the Younger, *Letters*, 5.8.4: "Orationi enim et carmini parva gratia, nisi eloquentia est summa: historia quoquo modo scripta delectat."

432. Ludovico "Il Moro" Sforza (1452–1508) and Ascanio Sforza (1455–1505; created cardinal in 1484). In fact, Ludovico had been handed over to the French in 1500, and both he and Ascanio died probably over a decade before Corio did.

433. The poem is an elegiac couplet.

434. Augusto De Ferrari, "Dalla [*sic*] Torre, Marco Antonio," *DBI* 32 (1986); *EH*, 148; *Elogi*, 172–74n3; *DLI*, 135–37, 284–85. For a close reading of this *elogium*, see Minonzio (2002), 2:497–502.

435. On the anatomist Mondino (d. 1326), see Franco Bacchelli, "Liuzzi, Mondino de'," *DBI* 65 (2005). On Gabriele Zerbi (1455–1504/5), see the brief biography by Gaisser (*DLI*, 330); and L. R. Lind, *Studies in Pre-Vesalian Anatomy: Biography, Translations, Documents* (Philadelphia: American Philosophical Society, 1975), 141–56.

436. Giovio's "ad Triballos" refers to the Triballi, a people of Lower Moetia in antiquity. See Pliny the Elder, *Natural History* 3.149, 4.3, 4.33; cf. OLD. According to Lind, *Pre-Vesalian Anatomy*, 145, Zerbi was paid three hundred ducats a month to attend to the pasha Skander Bey (Iskender Pasha, Sanjakbey of Bosnia) at the Turkish court in Bossina (Bosnia). On Skander Bey, see *DLI*, 141n55; Valeriano's account of his demise in ibid., 141–43; and Sydney Nettleton Fisher, *The Foreign Relations of Turkey, 1481–1512* (Urbana: University of Illinois Press, 1948), 30–31, 70–71, and *passim*. The Euganean Hills are south of Padua; this was an attack on Venetian territory. According to Fisher, 70–71, in the summer of 1499 Skander Bey led troops from Sarajevo into Friuli and Carinthia and subsequently "ravaged the country around the Isonzo River in September and sent a cavalry force across the Tagliamenta. The Venetians were frightened and imagined that Venice would be attacked or that the Turks were planning to join forces with Milan, but with the approach of winter, Iskender Pasha withdrew his men and returned to Bosnia." On Skander Bey's military exploits, see also Joseph J. Hammer, *L'Histoire de l'empire ottoman depuis son origine jusqu'à nos jours*, trans. J. J. Hellert, 18 vols. (Paris, 1835–43), 4:59–61.

437. In a letter of January 13, 1505, the Venetian proveditor Girolamo Contarini, writing from Ragusa, noted that Skander had died on November 26 and that Zerbi, along with his son, had been "chopped to pieces" (*tajato a pezi*) by the Turks (Sanuto, 6: col. 122).

438. The book is probably Zerbi's *Liber anathomie corporis humani et singulorum membrorum illius* (Venice: Boneto Locatello, 1502). For a synopsis and analysis, see Lind, *Pre-Vesalian Anatomy*, 154–56, who writes (at 156): "The abundant detail, the numerous authorities quoted, and the attempt to cover the subject of anatomy with encyclopedic thoroughness but with chief reliance upon Galen make the *Anathomia* the superior work it is for its time."

439. Members of the della Torre family held a variety of positions of leadership in Milan and environs in the thirteenth century, reaching the peak of their power under Napoleone (Napo) della Torre, who in 1265 succeeded his cousin Filippo as *Anziano del Popolo*. The family's power was eclipsed, although it did not entirely disappear, after Ottone Visconti

defeated Napo in battle in 1277, beginning a dynasty that would last until 1447. See Anna Caso, "Della Torre, Napoleone, detto Napo," *DBI* 37 (1989).

440. On Marco Antonio's father, Girolamo (1444–1506), who taught medicine to great acclaim at the University of Padua, see Raffaella Zaccaria, "Della Torre, Girolamo," *DBI* 37 (1989); *EH*, 148.

441. According to Grendler (2002), 177–78, the successful candidate "received books in his subject, first closed to symbolize the knowledge within the book, then opened to signify that the doctor would teach these books. Next came a gold ring which represented the marriage between the doctor and his subject. Finally came the doctor's biretta (the three-cornered hat of the scholar), which he was entitled to wear." The *laurea* that Giovio mentions in this passage appears to be metaphorical: neither a crown of laurels nor a written certificate formed parts of the standard ceremony.

442. Giovio's "pseudo-cardinals" are those who participated in the schismatic *Conciliabulum* of Pisa, which began in autumn 1511 and was supported and encouraged by Louis XII of France. See Christine Shaw, *Julius II: The Warrior Pope* (Oxford: Blackwell, 1993), 281–86. In the Battle of Ravenna (April 11, 1512), France and Ferrara won a Pyrrhic victory over the Holy League (Spanish and papal armies), after which much of Louis XII's army returned to France.

443. The poem is an elegiac couplet.

444. Eduardo Melfi, "Curti, Lancino," *DBI* 31 (1985); Giraldi, 101–3, 241nn76–77, 283.

445. Curti, *Sylvarum libri decem* (Milan: Rocco and Ambrogio da Valle, 1521).

446. Curti, *Epigrammaton libri decem* (Milan: Rocco and Ambrogio da Valle, 1521).

447. That is, Milanese dialect.

448. In *Modern Poets*, Giraldi drew upon the present *elogium* for his description of Curti's poetry: "He also wrote, in marvelous meter and rhymes, verses that are called 'snakelike,' named after the turning and

twisting of a snake's coils, in imitation of Rhabanus, so it seems. . . . For in the case of the two poets 'in an epigram written in the form of a square grid, words extracted when the poem is read in the normal order and then in the reverse order make a second poem that seems to relate in a marvelous way to the first poem, when the vertical borders and oblique diagonals are read.'" According to John Grant, "Giraldi's use of the word 'snakelike' [*anguineos*] has nothing to do with the modern definition of serpentine verse." He suggests that the "pattern-poems" to which Giraldi refers "could be poems, like some of Rhabanus Maurus' that were written in a square grid, where each cell housed one letter. Then letters in a diagonal, horizontal, or vertical line could be marked out in some way, creating words and sentences. Curti also composed poems where the lines, being of different lengths, turned the poem into a representation of some object or figure." Giraldi, 103, 241nn76–77.

449. That is, the Pusterla Beatrice, which Lodovico il Moro named after his wife, Beatrice d'Este.

450. On Baptista of Mantua, see Andrea Severi, "Spagnoli, Battista, detto Battista Mantovano, Battista Carmelita," *DBI* 93 (2018); *EH*, 393; *CE*, 2:375; *RLV*, 99–106; Giraldi, 57–59, 259; William Ernest Painter, "Baptista Mantuanus, Carmelite Humanist" (PhD thesis, University of Missouri, 1961); Daniela Marrone, "*L'Apologeticon*' di Battista Spagnoli," *Atti e Memorie*, Accademia Nazionale Virgiliana di Scienze Lettere e Arti, Mantua 68 (2000): 18–155. In Mantua he studied under Gregorio Tifernate and Giorgio Merula. Elected prior-general of the Carmelite Order in 1513, he was beatified by Pope Leo XIII in 1885. Spitz, 12, identifies Baptista, Valla, Ficino, and Pico as the "most popular Italian humanists among their German counterparts." Jakob Wimpfeling went so far as to praise Baptista above all other Italians, writing that his "clean and pure poems could be taught to the youth by a mature teacher without poison and because love for poesy did not extinguish in him zeal for the Sacred Book and of philosophy" (ibid., 45–46). See also Morimichi Watanabe, "Martin Luther's Relations with Italian Humanists: With Special Reference to Ioannes Baptista Mantuanus," *Lutherjahrbuch* 54 (1987): 23–47. For his poetry see *The Eclogues of Baptista Mantuanus*, ed. Wilfred P. Mustard (Baltimore: Johns Hopkins University Press, 1911); and now, in

hypertext, *Adulescentia: The Eclogues of Baptista Mantuanus (1498)*, ed. Lee Piepho, 2nd ed., http://www.philological.bham.ac.uk/mantuanus (accessed September 8, 2018); Gwenda Echard, "The 'Eclogues' of Baptista Mantuanus: A Mediaeval and Humanist Synthesis," *Latomus* 45 (1986): 837–47, who notes (at 837) that the work became "a standard text in humanist schools." In *Love's Labor's Lost* (IV.ii.89–90), Shakespeare's character Holophernes misquotes the first line of Baptista's opening eclogue, saying "Facile precor gelida quando pecas omnia sub umbra ruminat, and so forth," and comments (at lines 94–95): "Old Mantuan, old Mantuan! Who understandeth thee not, loves thee not." The actual opening line of the eclogue, entitled "Faustus, de honesto amore et felici eius exitu," is "*Fauste*, precor, gelida quando *pecus omne* sub umbra ruminat" (emphasis added). See Mantuanus, *Eclogues*, ed. Mustard, 63. Erasmus compared Baptista to Vergil (1496) and, in a letter to Wimpfeling (1517), expressed a strong preference for his poetry over that of Marullo Tarcaniota (on whom see *elogium* 28): Painter, "Baptista Mantuanus," 229. *Ex coitu damnato* (of a forbidden union) is a legal term for a category comprising children born as a result of incest or adultery. Baptista's father, Pietro Spagnolo, was married to Costanza de Magii of Brescia. It has been suggested that Pietro had some children by a mistress, Paola de Mazè (also a Brescian), Baptista and his older brother Tolomeo most commonly being named among them (ibid., 7). Stefano Davari, *Della famiglia Spagnolo, quale risulta dai documenti dell'Archivio storico Gonzaga* (Mantua: Stab. Tip. Eredi Segna, 1873), 6–9, argues that Baptista probably was illegitimate. But Painter, "Baptista Mantuanus," 6–16, cautions that such assertions remain conjectural. For a sixteenth-century law regarding *ex coitu damnato*, see Miriam J. Levy, "The Rights of the Individual in Habsburg Civil Law: Joseph II and the Illegitimate," *Man and Nature/L'homme et la nature* 10 (1991): 105–12, at 106.

451. This is Giovanni Battista Valentini (ca. 1450–1510), called "il Cantalicio" after his home town, Cantalice, in Latium. The long poem he dedicated to Gonsalvo "the Great" is *De his recepta Parthenope, Gonsalvia* (Naples: Mair, 1506), mentioned in passing by Giraldi, 65. Giovio's assessment of Cantalicio's muse was already withering in 1527–28: see *NMW*, 217.

452. This is Pietro Gravina, the subject of *elogium* 74. Probably in 1494, he moved to Naples, where he was active in the Accademia Pontaniana and became close friends with Pontano, Sannazaro, and Girolamo Carbone. Gonsalvo arranged for Gravina to become canon of the cathedral in Naples. His epic poem *Consalvia* remained unfinished.

453. The villa of Andes was the legendary birthplace of Vergil. On the Capilupi brothers, Lelio (1497–1560) and Ippolito (1511–80), see, respectively, Claudio Mutini, "Capilupi, Lelio," *DBI* 18 (1975); and Gaspare De Caro, "Capilupi, Ippolito," *DBI* 18 (1975); Giraldi, 207–9, 272. In Giraldi's view (207–9), "Their poetry, both Latin and Tuscan, is bedecked with many gems of genius, even if it has not been subject to the final polishing tools of a Petrarch or a Vergil, and demonstrates that they are worthy of being included among the poets of our age." Their poems, along with those of their brother Camillo, were published in 1570 in a collection entitled *Capiluporum carmina*.

454. Cf. Pliny the Younger, *Letters*, 9.26.13: "Exspecto, ut quaedam ex hac epistula ut illud 'gubernacula gemunt' et 'diis maris proximus' isdem notis quibus ea, de quibus scribo, confodias" ("I am waiting for you to strike out certain expressions in this letter [such as 'the rudder groans' and 'equal to the gods of the sea'] by the same rule as you attack the passages I am quoting" [LCL 59:136]). Thus critics have "stabbed" the text with use of obelisks, or daggers (††), to indicate flawed passages. In *Elogi*, 180n7, Minonzio takes this as referring to the *Apologeticon*, which had first appeared in print decades earlier (Bologna, 1488). For a critical edition with Italian translation and commentary, see Daniela Marrone, "L'*Apologeticon*," who lists twenty-nine editions of the work (ibid., 46–49), which was intended to counter charges that his three-book poem dedicated to the Virgin, *Parthenices Marianae*, was pagan in its classicizing.

455. This was one of three busts commissioned in 1514 by the humanist Battista Fiera (not by Federico Gonzaga; Giovio errs), in honor of Francesco II Gonzaga, to adorn the Porta Nuova arch that linked his house with the Convent of San Francesco. Between the busts of Vergil and Baptista was a larger one of Francesco II. Accompanying them was an inscription by Fiera: ARGVMENTVM VTRIQUE INGENS SI SECLA COISSENT ("Had the centuries coincided, there'd be a strong argument for each of

the two"; but cf. J. B. Trapp's reading, "How splendid for each of these had they lived at the same time"). Trapp says that Baptista's bust "was probably originally taken from a life-mask": see *Splendours of the Gonzaga*, exh. cat., ed. David Chambers and Jane Martineau (London: Victoria and Albert Museum, 1981), 155–56 (cat. no. 100), at 156. See the entry by Rodolfo Signorini in *La Prima Donna del Mondo: Isabella d'Este, Fürstin und Mäzenatin der Renaissance*, exh. cat., ed. Sylvia Ferino-Pagden (Vienna: Kunsthistorisches Museum, 1994), 121–26, cat nos. 54–56. The surviving busts of all three, in terracotta, are probably copies after others; they are housed in the Museo della Città at Palazzo San Sebastiano, Mantua. See Molly Bourne, *Francesco II Gonzaga: The Soldier-Prince as Patron* (Rome: Bulzoni, 2008), 288n8. Evidently Giovio was not alone in disrespecting the monument. Within months after its completion in 1514, a notice bearing the marquis of Gonzaga's official seal was posted on it forbidding its defacement — and soon thereafter, someone hurled feces at the notice itself: see Rodolfo Signorini, "Epigrafi di Battista Fiera," in Daniela Ferrari and Sergio Marinelli, *Scritti per Chiara Tellini Perina* (Mantua: Gianluigi Arcari Editore, 2011), 57–76, at 61–62.

456. The poem is in phalaecean hendecasyllables.

457. Anna Siekiera, "Grapaldo, Francesco Mario," *DBI* 58 (2002); Giraldi, 99, 298; Ireneo Affò, *Memorie degli scrittori e letterati parmigiani* (Bologna: Forni Editore, 1969–), 125–50. He is also known, less accurately, as Francesco Maria Gripaldi.

458. On October 8, 1512, Julius II had absorbed Parma (along with Piacenza) into the Papal States. The embassy, including Grapaldo as its secretary, left Parma on October 27. At a ceremony held in the gardens of the Belvedere of the Vatican on November 11, he delivered an oration and then intoned poems on the subject of the liberation of Italy from the French.

459. Following the presentations by Vicenzo Pimpinella and Grapaldo at the ceremony on November 11, Julius II and Mattias Lang (bishop of Gurk, and envoy of Holy Roman Emperor Maximilian to the papacy) jointly crowned both of them poets laureate. See Affò, *Memorie*, 3:137–41, who notes that Grapaldo had himself requested the honor of the laurel.

Giraldi, 99, mentions Grapaldo's coronation but writes dismissively of his poetic abilities.

460. *De partibus aedium* (Parma: Angelus Ugoletus, [1494]).

461. On Anselmi (before 1459–1528), see Mario Quattrucci, "Anselmi, Giorgio," *DBI* 3 (1961); Giraldi, 75, 256. The poem is in elegiac couplets.

462. According to Siekiera, "Grapaldo," at his son's request, he was buried in the monastery of San Giovanni Evangelista in Parma.

463. The poem is in elegiac couplets.

464. Vivian Nutton, "Linacre, Thomas," 2008 version, in *ODNB*; *EH*, 272; *CE*, 2:331–32; *Linacre Studies: Essays on the Life and Work of Thomas Linacre, c. 1460–1524*, ed. Francis Romeril Maddison, Margaret Pelling, and Charles Webster (Oxford: Clarendon Press, 1977); and, specifically on this *elogium*, Minonzio (2002), 2:503–7. Linacre left England for Italy in 1487. He had already begun the study of Greek at Oxford. Nutton dates his time in Florence to "two years around 1489." In *NMW*, 333, Giovio had written of him briefly but glowingly: "In England Thomas Linacre surpasses all others in his erudition and sophisticated style; he translated some books of Galen and the *Sphere* of Proclus into very elegant Latin." Demetrius: Demetrius Chalcondyles; see *elogium* 29.

465. Ermolao Barbaro the Younger: see *elogium* 36.

466. Innocent VIII elevated Barbaro to the patriarchate of Aquileia only in 1491. Linacre was already in Rome, however, at least by November 1490. According to Charles B. Schmitt, "There is no evidence for the connection of Linacre with Barbaro other than Giovio's statement": Schmitt, "Thomas Linacre and Italy," in *Linacre Studies*, 36–75, at 41n1.

467. This is the Latin translation of the pseudo-Proclan *Sphaera* published by the Aldine Press in 1499. Its dedicatee was Henry VII's son Arthur, Prince of Wales (1486–1502). Linacre had returned to London no later than August 1499. The *Sphaera* was in fact an excerpt of four chapters from an elementary survey of astronomy by the Greek author Geminus (fl. first century BCE). Linacre's was the first complete Latin translation. See Robert B. Todd, "Geminus and the Ps.-Proclan *Sphaera*," in *CTC* 8 (2003), 7–48.

468. *De sanitate tuenda* (Paris, 1517). He subsequently published Latin translations of Galen's *Methodus medendi* (Paris, 1519); *De temperamentis* and *De inaequali intemperie* (Cambridge, 1521); *De naturalibus facultatibus* (London, 1523); *De usu pulsuum* (London, 1523–24); and *De Symptomatum differentiis* and *De symptomatum causis* (London, 1524). Of these works, only the *Methodus medendi* was available in print in Greek before 1525. Thus, as Nutton notes, Linacre "worked from Greek manuscripts, probably in his own library, and he appears to have used a manuscript of the *Methodus medendi* as well as the printed text (Venice, 1500)."

469. In his *Descriptio Britanniae*, completed in 1546 and first published two years later, Giovio also mentioned Linacre's proposed collaboration with Latimer and Grocyn: *Descriptio Britanniae, Scotiae, Hyberniae et Orchadum* (Venice: Tramezzino, 1548), 13r–v; *IO*, 9:100. Included in the 1548 volume, beginning on fol. 45r, is George Lily, *Virorum aliquot in Britannia, qui nostro seculo eruditione et doctrina clari memorabilesque fuerunt, Elogia*. In his *elogium* of Grocyn (fol. 48r–v, at 48v), Lily writes: "Aristotelis vero, una cum Linacro et Latemerio communicato labore interpretandi provinciam est aggressus, quam tamen paulo post, oblato sibi sacerdotii honore, mutato consilio deseruit." ("But along with Linacre and Latimer, he took up the task of collaboratively translating Aristotle, which however he soon abandoned once a priesthood was offered him.") How Lily's text, which he dedicated to Giovio, came to be published along with the latter's *Descriptio* remains unclear. See Zimmermann (1995), 216; and Thomas F. Mayer, "Reginald Pole in Paolo Giovio's *Descriptio*: A Strategy for Reconversion," *Sixteenth Century Journal* 16 (1985): 431–50, who writes (at 450) that determining what if any role Lily played in its composition "may be impossible, and we will never have more than plausible conjecture." In the second edition of his *Summarium* (first published 1548), John Bale added (with attribution) a portion from Giovio's *Descriptio* including, at 18, the anecdote about the project for a joint translation of Aristotle: see Bale, *Scriptorum illustrium maioris Brytanniae, quam nunc Angliam et Scotiam vocant: Catalogus* (Basel, [1557–59]), 2:18. The editors of *Essays on the Life and Work of Thomas Linacre*, at xl n43, suggest that the anecdote (retold in Lily) may refer to Grocyn's appointment in 1506 as Master of All Hallows, Maidstone, Kent. With respect to the collaboration,

they write that "in so far as this enterprise was ever seriously embarked upon, it appears that one of Linacre's tasks was to translate the *Meteorologica*."

470. In 1518 Linacre had founded the College of Physicians (later, Royal College of Physicians), over which he presided until his death.

471. The poem is in elegiac couplets.

472. Perhaps the Cevennes mountain range in south-central France. The editors of *Linacre Studies*, xliv, gloss "Gebenna" as "Sc. at the mouth of a mountain pass, leading to Geneva (Gebenna), probably the Little St. Bernard." As a cross-reference for "Gebenna," *Orbis Latinus* gives "Cebanum," i.e., Geneva, Switzerland.

473. On Elio Antonio de Nebrija (baptized Antonio Martínez de Cala), see *EH*, 320; *CE*, 3:9–10; Ottavio di Camillo, "Humanism in Spain," in Rabil, 2:55–108, at 91–93; Byron Ellsworth Hamann, *The Translations of Nebrija: Language, Culture, and Circulation in the Early Modern World* (Amherst: University of Massachusetts Press, 2015), 11–42. On his stay in Italy, see A. Caro Bellido and J. M. Tomassetti Guerra, *Antonio de Nebrija y la Betica (sobre arqueologia y paleografia del Bajo Guadalquivir)* (Cádiz: Servicio de Publicaciones, Universidad de Cádiz, 1997), 78–87. Giraldi, 135–37, speaks well of him in passing.

474. Better known as Lebrija, the city (on the site of the ancient city Nebrissa Veneria) is on the left bank of the Guadalquivir River, in Andalusia.

475. His early grammatical works include *Institutiones grammaticae* (Seville, 1481); *Introductiones latinae* (Salamanca, 1481); *Lexicon hoc est dictionarium ex sermone latino in hispaniensem* (Salamanca, 1492); and *Gramática . . . sobre la lengua castellana* (Salamanca, 1492). Among other notable works are *Quinquagenae* of critical notes on the Scriptures (1514–16) and *De litteris graecis et hebraicis cum quibusdam annotationibus in scripturam sacram* (1563). *CE*, 3:10.

476. Perhaps this dictionary is the unpublished, lost work itemized as "Vocabulario de las palabras extrañas que muchos creen latinas o griegas" in Antonio Odriozola, "La Caracola del Bibliófilo Nebrisense; o La casa a cuestas indispensable al amigo de Nebrija para navegar por el proceloso

de sus obras," *Revista de bibliografía nacional* 7 (1946): 3–114, at 109, no. 3. According to Hamann, *Translations*, 25, "When their father [i.e., Antonio] died in 1522, Sebastián and Sancho de Nebrija promptly sought a royal decree granting them monopoly privileges for the printing of his works. This would effectively block any further publications by Arnao Guillén de Brocar (legal publications, that is; piracy was always an option). They were initially successful in their suit, but were immediately defeated by a counterclaim: in July 1523, the crown extended Guillén de Brocar's permission to print the writings of Nebrija. But he did not enjoy this privilege for long: he died before the end of the year. Nevertheless . . . Guillén de Brocar's son-in-law continued to print Nebrija's works for the next decade." In 1534 Nebrija's sons did in fact begin publishing his texts in Granada (ibid., 24). The history of the War of Granada first appeared in a collection of histories and chronologies assembled by Nebrija's son Sancho: *Habes in hoc volumine Amice Lector . . .* (Granada: Sancho de Nebrija, 1545). For a recent bilingual edition based on the *editio princeps*, see Elio Antonio de Nebrija, *Guerra de Granada (De bello Granatensi)*, ed. and trans. María Luisa Arribas (Madrid: Universidad Nacional de Educacion a Distancia, 1990).

477. This uprising is the Revolt of the Comuneros (1520–22), which began while Cardinal Adrian Florensz of Utrecht (soon to be elevated as Pope Adrian VI) was ruling in Castile as Charles V's regent. The rebels took Valladolid, Tordesillas, and Toledo, but suffered a crushing defeat at the Battle of Villalar (April 23, 1521), following which several of their leaders, including Juan de Padilla, were executed. From May 1521 to February 1522 Padilla's widow, María Pacheco y Mendoza, led the final, unsuccessful resistance of Toledo against royal forces. See Giovio's praise of her leadership and valor in the third Ischian dialogue, *NMW*, 371–73. The mention of the Flemish governing *avare* (stingily, avariciously) may well allude to Adrian of Utrecht himself, who as pontiff gained infamy for his tightfisted approach to patronage.

478. The poem is in dactylic hexameter alternating with iambic dimeter.

479. An echo of Ennius (quoted by Cicero in *Tusculan Disputations* 1.15.34): "Nemo me lacrumis decoret neque funera fletu faxit. Cur? volito vivos per ora virum."

480. Giorgio Patrizi, "Dovizi, Bernardo, detto il Bibbiena," *DBI* 41 (1992); Giraldi, 91, 107, 201, 263; Carlo Dionisotti, "Ricordo del Bibbiena," in his *Machiavellerie* (Turin: Einaudi, 1980), 155–72; G. L. Moncallero, *Il cardinale Bernardo Dovizi da Bibbiena umanista e diplomatico (1470–1520)* (Florence, 1953); *Epistolario di Bernardo Dovizi da Bibbiena*, ed. G. L. Moncallero, 2 vols. (Florence: Olschki, 1955–65); Pastor, 8:110–13 and *passim*.

481. After Piero de' Medici fled Florence in autumn 1494, Bibbiena and his brother Piero were among the Medici partisans also declared exiles. They rejoined their patron in Bologna, whence they would go to Venice. Within weeks after Piero de' Medici's demise (December 28, 1503), Bibbiena went to Rome to serve as secretary to Piero's brother, Cardinal Giovanni (subsequently Pope Leo X, 1513–21). There, he quickly developed a reputation for diplomatic skill and for advocacy on behalf of his patron.

482. In 1513, the year of his election, Leo elevated to the cardinalate not only Bibbiena but also two of his own kinsmen: Innocenzo Cibò, his sister Maddalena's son; and Giulio di Giuliano de' Medici, his cousin. Four years later he elevated another cousin, Luigi de' Rossi, whose mother was Maria de' Medici. Cardinals Luigi and Giulio are included in Raphael's *Portrait of Leo X* (1518), which, according to John Shearman, "was painted to hang in Palazzo Medici in Florence as a memorial for posterity to the extraordinary fact of this family's ascendancy in the Church" (Shearman, *Only Connect . . . Art and the Spectator in the Italian Renaissance* [Washington, DC: The National Gallery of Art, and Princeton: Princeton University Press, 1992], 129).

483. See the detailed account in G. L. Moncallero, *Il cardinale Bernardo Dovizi da Bibbiena*, 259–358 (= pt. 3, chap. 1: "L'elezione di Giovanni de' Medici al Pontificato, opera del Bibbiena").

484. Giovio describes the performance similarly in his *Life of Leo X* (*IO*, 6:94). Although the performance has often been dated to the autumn of 1514 (e.g., by Pastor, 8:171), Giovio explicitly says that the work was performed before Isabella d'Este during Carnival (*ludis Lupercalibus*), and February 1515 is now firmly established as the time of that performance:

see G. L. Moncallero, "Precisazioni sulle rappresentazioni della 'Calandria' nel 'Cinquecento,'" *Convivium* 6 (1952): 819–51, at 836–42.

485. In Giovio's dialogue *Notable Men and Women*, women are likened to the uneducated (*idiotis*) on account of sharing their preference for translations of Greek and Latin histories over the originals. His interlocutor Muscettola observes that the Tuscan dialect is "dear to the elderly, pleasant and convenient to the young, and desirable and delightful to the dispositions of women." Vernacular dramas, says Giovio, delight "women and the illiterate multitude": *NMW*, 259, 285. This position sits in unresolved tension alongside the survey of outstanding noblewomen later in the dialogue, where many are recognized explicitly for their superb Latinity. See Jessica Goethals, "The Flowers of Italian Literature: Language, Imitation and Gender Debates in Paolo Giovio's *Dialogus de viris et foeminis aetate nostra florentibus*," *Renaissance Studies* 29 (2014): 749–71, who notes (at 768) how Giovio attempts to square such criticisms with his lavish praise of the woman who commissioned the dialogue, herself notable as a vernacular poet: "Giovio is generally a critic of the vernacular and its audiences but is also a client of [Vittoria] Colonna's; to reduce the dissonance between these positions he largely lifts her outside of the language debate, distances her from her female peers, and imbues her with the virtue he associates with fine Latin composition."

486. As a physician, Giovio had taken part in a trial that showed how an antidote for poisoning could work in one man but not in his brother. Thus he could see that Bibbiena's failure to recover when under expert medical care was not of probative value. See Minonzio's comments in *Elogi*, 192n5.

487. The poem is in elegiac couplets.

488. Flavio Santi, "Maino, Giasone del," *DBI* 67 (2006). As Giovio writes in his *Dialogo dell'imprese militari et amorose* (*IO*, 9:377), Maino had chosen *Virtuti Fortuna comes* (Fortune is the Companion of Virtue) as his personal motto but did not settle on a suitable image to combine with it for an *impresa* (personal device). The motto was inscribed above the entry to Maino's house.

489. Maino studied civil law, first in Pavia in the early 1450s, then in Bologna under Alessandro Tartagna in 1456–57. After further study in Pavia, he returned to Bologna to work under Tartagna once more, probably from 1461 to 1466. See also *NMW*, 139, where Giovio rails against the damage that excessive gambling does both to military commanders and to common soldiers.

490. At Pavia he held the *lectura ordinaria* of the *Institutiones*. In 1482 his salary, 1,250 florins, was the highest in the university: Grendler (2002), 86. In 1485 the Venetian Senate approved his appointment to the *cattedra* (chair) in civil law at the University of Padua.

491. In 1488 he left Padua to teach at the University of Pisa. At Ludovico "il Moro" Sforza's urging, he returned to Pavia in November 1489.

492. *Sic.* According to Santi, "Maino," he is entombed in the Church of San Giacomo (not San Paolo) Fuori le Mura, and his funerary inscription appears above a bas-relief of him "nel cortile Volta dell'Università pavese."

493. The poem is in elegiac couplets. Sixteen of Bernardino Dardano's poems are included in the *Corcyciana*, and Arsilli celebrates him in *De poetis Urbanis*. See *Coryciana*, 134–41, and 356–57 (lines 313–26).

494. That is, the golden fleece from the ram that Phrixus had sacrificed to Zeus.

495. Th. Simar, *Christophe de Longueil, humaniste (1488–1522)* (Paris: A. Picard et Fils, 1911); *EH*, 276; *CE*, 2:342–45; *DLI*, 28–30, 175–77, 302–3, and *passim*; *NMW*, 315; Giraldi, 95–97. His father, Antoine de Longueil, was bishop of Saint-Pol-de-Léon in Brittany.

496. He arrived in Paris no later than 1497, studying at the Collège de Plessis until 1500. After being in the service of Louis XII and Philippe le Beau (d. 1506), he studied law in Bologna (1507) and Poitiers (1508–10), and probably went to Rome in 1516.

497. In fact, Longueil's initial host in Rome was not Flaminio Tomarozzi but his father, Giulio, a wealthy merchant living in the neighborhood of Sant' Eustachio. The Tomarozzi palazzo, which boasted a collection of marbles and classical inscriptions, served as a gathering spot for

Roman humanists: Simar, *Christophe de Longueil*, 52. After a year there
tutoring Flaminio, with whom he became close, Longueil went to live in
Mario Castellani's house in Trastevere, on the via Longarina near Ponte
Rotto. Simar, *Christophe de Longueil*, 52n2, writing in 1911, describes it as
extant. Following his composition of five speeches in honor of Rome
(August 1518), the city council proposed ( January 31, 1519) to grant him
the title *civis Romanus*, a distinction rich in symbolic significance albeit
not in actual privileges, that had previously been accorded only to Italians. On the significance of the controversy that ensued, see ibid., 62–74;
Domenico Gnoli, "Un giudizio di Lesa Romanità sotto Leone X," *Nuova
antologia* 115 (1891): 251–76 and 691–716.

498. Longueil, *Oratio de laudibus divi Ludovici atque Francorum* (Paris: H.
Estienne, 1512), which praised the Franks as the true heirs of classical Roman culture.

499. On Celso Mellini, see *DLI*, 309. His oration is preserved in BAV
MS Vat. Lat. 3370. On the event see, e.g., *DLI*, 28–30; Gnoli, "Un giudizio."

500. Roman humanists were divided on the issue. Longueil's supporters
included Pietro Bembo, Jacopo Sadoleto, Lelio Massimo, Francesco Maria Molza, and Girolamo Negri. His declared enemies included Celso
Mellini and his brother Pietro, Tommaso Pighinuzzi da Pietrasanta, and
Lorenzo Grana. Other prominent literati present at the "trial" on June 16,
1519, included Castiglione, Colocci, and Goritz. See Simar, *Christophe de
Longueil*, 66–70 and *passim*.

501. *Orationes duae pro defensione sua*, published in August 1519. Longueil's
request that they be read *in absentia* at his trial had been denied.

502. Initially Bembo's guest at the Villa Noniana, Longueil subsequently
stayed with the Sauli family. By July 1521 he was a protégé of Pole, in
whose house he died the following year (in *NMW*, 315, the cause of death
is specified as a stomach disorder). An oration of his against Luther appeared in a collection published in 1524, and again, separately, in 1529: *Ad
Luterianos iam damnatos oratio, omnibus numeris absoluta*. In his *Ciceronianus*
(1528), Erasmus criticized Longueil for a slavish imitation of Cicero that
rendered his advocacy of the faith less effective. He also asserted that in

Longueil's writings *persuasio* replaced *fides,* and he alleged that the word "Christian" appeared therein only by an oversight. See Erasmus, *Ciceronianus,* 692–98; idem, *Ciceronian,* 430–36.

503. The poem is in dactylic hexameter.

504. See Roberto Weiss, "Augurelli, Giovanni Aurelio," *DBI* 4 (1962); Giraldi, 71, 258. In *NMW* (at 231), Giovio puts Augurelli in the category of those who write at length rather than with skill. Giraldi, 71, writes somewhat more positively about the *Chrysopeia,* "for which he undoubtedly merits far from middling praise, for he has produced an outstanding poem despite the difficult and dry nature of his topic." Giulio Cesare Scaligero, by contrast, viewed his verse as metrically flawed and lifeless.

505. After sojourns in Rome and Florence, from 1476 to 1485 he studied law in Padua, where he also pursued classical studies and poetry while teaching privately.

506. Many of his Latin poems are collected in Augurelli, *Carmina* (Verona, 1491); idem, *Carmina* (Venice, 1501). The elegies he wrote in Florence are published in his *Carmina nondum vulgata,* ed. C. Zollio (Rimini: Marsoner et Grandi, 1818).

507. Augurelli, *Chrysopoeiae libri III et Geronticon liber primus* (Venice, 1515). See Zweder von Martels, "Augurello's 'Chrysopoeia' (1515) — A Turning Point in the Literary Tradition of Alchemical Texts," *Early Science and Medicine* 5 (2000): 178–95; and Minonzio (2002), 2:334–38.

508. In 1517, at age thirteen, Lippomano was named bishop of Bergamo. In 1544 he succeeded Giberti (d. 1543) as bishop of Verona. See Giuseppe Gullino, "Lippomano, Pietro," *DBI* 65 (2005).

509. In 1515 Augurelli became a canon of the cathedral in Treviso, and at least in 1518 he was its librarian.

510. The poem is in iambic trimeter.

511. He received the moniker "Postumo" because he was born after his father's death. See Guido Arbizzoni, "Silvestri, Guido Postumo," *DBI* 92 (2018); Berni, 330–31; William Roscoe, *The Life and Pontificate of Leo the Tenth,* 6th ed., revised by Thomas Roscoe, 2 vols. (London: Henry G.

Bohn, 1853), 2:173–76. Giraldi, 73–75, wrote dismissively of his abilities and character: "Guido Postumus from Pesaro shows some ability in his elegiac verse. He ventured into Phalaecians and hexameters as well, but neither attempt was successful. In his philosophical and medical studies he accomplished no more than he did with his poetry, because of his addiction to parties and royal banquets, an addiction that has ruined his health." The interlocutor Sanga in Berni's *Dialogue Against Poets* (Berni, 211) remarks that "Postumus, warned for ages by malarial fever that he was doing the wrong thing writing poetry, in the end was killed by it as an unbeliever." He did, however, appear as an interlocutor in early drafts of Castiglione's *Courtier* and was lauded briefly by both Ariosto (*Orlando furioso* 42.89) and Arsilli (*De Poetis Urbanis*, lines 297–300).

512. After having taught in Ferrara, in late 1517 Postumo went to Leo X's court in Rome, perhaps having been sent for by his erstwhile Maecenas, Ercole Rangoni, created cardinal (along with thirty others) on July 1 of that year. While serving as Leo's doctor, Postumo composed the elegies, for which he is best known today, which describe the pope's court and include a detailed account of a hunting expedition in Palo. See Guido Postumo Silvestri, *Elegiarum libri II*, ed. Ludovico Siderostomo (Bologna: Girolamo Benedetti, 1524).

513. See Catullus 81.3: "moribunda ab sede Pisauri."

514. Capranica looks out over the Sutri valley to the south of Lago di Vico in Latium.

515. The poem is in elegiac couplets.

516. The poem is an elegiac couplet.

517. Paolo Pellegrini, "Niccolò da Lonigo (Niccolò Leoniceno)," *DBI* 78 (2013); *EH*, 269; *CE*, 2:323; M. Jellinek, "Giovio, Leoniceno, Dosso: un ritratto dimenticato," in *Il camerino delle pitture di Alfonso I*, vol. 6 (Cittadella: Bertoncello artigrafiche, 2007), 129–58; Minonzio (2002), 2:507–12; Daniela Mugnai Carrara, *La biblioteca di Niccolò Leoniceno. Tra Aristotele e Galeno: cultura e libri di un medico umanista* (Florence: Olschki, 1991). On his role in the movement called "medical humanism," see Grendler (2002), 324–28.

518. A number of these seminal translations of Galen appeared first in manuscript, then appeared in print in the early Cinquecento. These include *Ars medicinalis* (Venice: Giacomo Pincio, 1508); *Ars parva* (Ferrara: Mazzocchi, 1509); and *De differentiis morborum, De inaequali intemperatura, De arte curativa ad Glauconem,* and *De crisibus,* published in *Galeni opera* (Paris: Henri Estienne, 1514). Leoniceno also produced influential commentaries, including *In libros Galeni e Graeca in Latinam linguam a se translatos praefatio communis* (printed along with Galen's *Ars parva* by Mazzocchi in 1509).

519. *Medici Romani Nicolai Leoniceni discipuli Antisophista* ([Bologna: H. de Benedictis, 1519]) (evidently, Giovio errs by taking "Medicus Romanus" as part of the work's title rather than as an honorific); *De tribus doctrinis ordinatis secundum Galeni sententiam praefatio,* bound in with the *Ars parva* (Ferrara: Mazzocchi, 1509); *De virtute formativa, liber unus* (n.p.: Boneto Locatelli, 1506).

520. Cassius Dio, *Dione historico delle guerre e fatti de romani* ([Venice: Zoppino], 1533). See R. Gualdo, "Sul volgarizzamento della Storia Romana di Dione Cassio di N. Leoniceno," *Studi linguistici italiani* 16 (1990): 223–46. Lucian, *I dilettevoli dialogi: le vere narrationi: le facete epistole di Luciano philosopho,* trans. Niccolò Leoniceno (Venice: Zoppino, 1525).

521. The name and the location of the church are omitted in the Latin, but present in Orio's translation. The *MS,* in scribal hand, specifies that space is left on the page for added material.

522. The poem is in elegiac couplets.

523. Vittoria Perrone Compagni, "Pomponazzi, Pietro," *DBI* 84 (2015); *EH,* 354; *CE,* 3:109–10; *ER,* 5:16–18.

524. Pomponazzi, *Traité de l'immortalité de l'âme = Tractatus de immortalitate animae,* ed. and trans. Thierry Gontier (Paris: Les Belles Lettres, 2012).

525. See Eckehart Stöve, "De Vio, Tommaso (Tommaso Gaetano, Caetano)," *DBI* 39 (1991); *EH,* 144; *CE,* 1:239–42. John W. O'Malley, *Trent: What Happened at the Council* (Cambridge, MA: Harvard University Press, 2013), 42, describes De Vio (better known as Cajetan) as "probably the greatest commentator on Aquinas in history." Pomponazzi specifi-

cally defended the doctrine of the soul's mortality in 1516 but "was moving towards that position as early as 1504, and was aware of its derivation from Alexander. If we restrict the term Alexandrism to this specific meaning, it will apply to a rather small group of thinkers which includes, oddly enough, besides Pomponazzi the leading Thomist of his time, Cardinal Caietanus": Paul Oskar Kristeller, *Renaissance Thought and the Arts: Collected Essays* (Princeton: Princeton University Press, 1965), 116–17. For the wider context of the invocation of Cajetan in this *Elogium*, see *Elogi*, 209n5.

526. Both *De fato* and *De naturalium effectuum admirandorum causis seu de incantationibus liber* are included in his *Opera* (Basel: Sebastian Heinrich Petri, 1567).

527. The poem is in elegiac couplets.

528. This *elogium* draws heavily and in places verbatim upon the description of Marone in *NMW*, 227. The sketch complements Valeriano's account of Marone's gift for extemporaneous versification, in *DLI*, 184–87 (= bk. 2, §25). See also Floriana Calitti, "Marone, Andrea," *DBI* 70 (2008); Giraldi, 81–83, 309. For the tradition of performing extemporaneous Latin verse, see F. Alberto Gallo, *Music in the Castle: Troubadours, Books and Orators in Italian Courts of the Thirteenth, Fourteenth and Fifteenth Centuries* (Chicago: University of Chicago Press, 1995), chap. 3.

529. Cf. L&S, s.v. "bajulus" II.A, in support of the rendering "pallbearer."

530. The Mamluk sultan ("soldan") of Egypt, al-Ashraf Kansuh al-Ghuri, was killed in the Battle of Marj Dabiq, north of Aleppo, on August 24, 1516. In October, Tumanbey was chosen to succeed him. Selim won a decisive victory at Raidaniyah and entered Cairo near the end of January 1517. Subsequently, Tumanbey was betrayed to him; he was hanged in Cairo on April 14. See Setton, 3:165–66; and for a contemporary's description of the death of al-Ghuri, see Muhammed Ibn Ahmed Ibyn Iyas, *An Account of the Ottoman Conquest of Egypt in the Year A.H. 922 (A.D. 1516)*, trans. W. H. Salmon (Westport, CT: Hyperion Press, 1981; orig. pub. 1921), 41–44.

531. The sculpted image of a *scrofa* (sow) had long adorned a wall of the Augustinian convent facing the eponymous Via della Scrofa. At least by 1518, there was an inn nearby on the Vicolo della Campagna, which joins Via della Scrofa to Piazza Nicosia. See Umberto Gnoli, *Topografia e toponomastica di Roma medioevale e moderna* (Rome: Staderni, [1939]), 48; Alessandro Rufini, *Dizionario etimologico-storico delle strade, piazze, borghi e vicoli della città di Roma* (Rome: Tipografia della R. C. A., 1847), 36.

532. The situation described by Giovio would date Marone's death to the summer of 1527. Within a few weeks after the Sack, plague had begun to ravage Rome, and on July 10 the Imperial army (excepting two thousand troops guarding the pope and Castel Sant'Angelo) departed to spend the summer outside the city, returning in the autumn. More probably, however, he died on March 24, 1528, as recorded by an anonymous papal scriptor. See Calitti, "Marone"; *DLI*, 305.

533. The poem consists of two stanzas in which the first line is a choliamb, the second and third being in iambic trimeter.

534. S.n., "Acquaviva d'Aragona, Andrea Matteo," *DBI* 1 (1960); Francesco Tateo, *Chierici e feudatari del Mezzogiorno* (Rome and Bari: Laterza, 1984), 69–96.

535. Plutarch, *De virtute morali. Libellus graecus cum latina versione et commentariis Andrea Matthei Aquivivi Hadrianorum ducis* (Naples: Antonio Frezza da Corinaldo, 1526). Searches for the *Encyclopedia* Giovio here mentions have been fruitless.

536. S.n., "Acquaviva d'Aragona, Belisario," *DBI* 1 (1960). He died of plague in 1528. The books are *De venatione et de aucupio* (1519) and *De re militari et singulari certamine* (1519).

537. The poem is in elegiac couplets. Palonio wrote a poem (no. 219) included in *Coryciana*, 159–60, and is mentioned in Arsilli's *De Poetis Urbanis* (ibid., 356, lines 311–12).

538. Palonio puns on Atri (*Hadria*) and Adriatic.

539. The Adriatic Sea and Tuscan Sea were termed, with respect to each other, *mare superum* and *mare inferum*.

540. Monica Cerroni, "Gravina, Pietro," *DBI* 58 (2002); *DLI*, III, 296; Giraldi, 41, 298–99; *NMW*, 243.

541. Gonsalvo "the Great" is Gonzalo Fernández de Córdoba (1453–1515), duke of Terranova and Santángelo, known as "El Gran Capitán." See Mary Purcell, *The Great Captain: Gonzalo Fernández de Córdoba* (London: Alvin Redman, 1963). A critical edition of Giovio's *Vita* of Gonsalvo, edited by M. Cataudella, is forthcoming in volume seven of *IO*. For a modern edition of a sixteenth-century translation, see Giovio, *Le vite del Gran Capitano e del Marchese di Pescara*, trans. Lodovico Domenichi, ed. Costantino Panigada (Bari: Laterza, 1931). Gravina never finished the *Consalvia*, his epic poem celebrating the captain's exploits.

542. Gonsalvo had left for Spain in June 1507. The king in question is Ferdinando III of Naples (r. 1504–16). Probably after Prospero Colonna's death in 1523, Gravina moved into the service of Giovanni Francesco Di Capua.

543. The elegy *De Surrenti amoenitate* (also known as *Lucubratio Surrentina*); see Cerroni, "Gravina, Pietro."

544. Many of his poems, epigrams, elegies, his *Sylvae*, and the unfinished *Consalvia* (under the name *Epicum carmen*) are included in *Neapolitani poematum libri ad illustrem Ioannem Franciscum de Capua Palenensium comitum* (Naples: Sulzbach, 1532).

545. Conca della Campania.

546. Valeriano, *DLI*, III, gives an entirely different account of Gravina's demise: "when he was overwhelmed by the pestilence that the Spanish sackers of Rome brought to Naples, he succumbed in that wretchedness, abandoned by all his friends."

547. The poem is in elegiac couplets.

548. This Fano, in the area where Pliny the Elder (*Natural History* 2.70) located the Temple of the Argive Juno, is in Campania (not to be confused with the town Fano in the Marches). On Gaurico see Franco Bacchelli, "Gaurico, Pomponio," *DBI* 52 (1999); *EH*, 200; Minonzio (2002), 2:523–29; Erasmo Pèrcopo, "Pomponio Gaurico umanista napoletano," *Atti della R. Accademia di archeologia, lettere e belle arti* 16 (1891–93): 145–261.

On his brother see Franco Bacchelli, "Gaurico, Luca," *DBI* 52 (1999); *EH*, 200. In *NMW*, 243, Giovio wrote that Pomponio "gave himself so devotedly to Greek letters that in the opinion of some he is considered to have forsaken Latin completely." At ibid., 245, he is included among those who "Hellenize on every occasion as if we were native Athenians, appearing to seek from it personal glory." By his delivery of "a half-Greek eulogy at the funeral of a girl of the Requesens family," Pomponio "wrested from us mourners laughter instead of tears." Giraldi, 101, notes his range of publications, though faults his epigrams: they "seem rather lascivious and effete, but they are thought to display some talent and charm."

549. Giovio refers to Gaurico's *De physiognomia* and *De perspectiva*, both parts of his *De sculptura* (Florence: [Giunta], 1504). According to Minonzio in *Elogi*, 220n4, there is no foundation for the claim that Gaurico was seeking to rival Crinito, but he did provide a brief series of *vitae* of Greek authors in comments in his edition of Horace, *De arte poetica ad Franciscum Puccium Florentinum* (Rome: Silber, 1509).

550. At *Elogi*, 220n7, Minonzio speculates that the work described here may be the chapter entitled *De chimica* in the volume *De sculptura* (see preceding note).

551. Antonio Sebastiani (ca. 1500–1574), better known as Minturno, in *De poeta ad Hectorem Pignatellum Vibonensium ducem libri sex* (Venice: Rampazetus, 1559), 435, would provide an alternate account of Gaurico's demise: after being taken prisoner by the French during their siege of Naples in the first half of 1528, he was freed when the occupation ended, but the Spanish governor accused him of having colluded with the French, and he died while on his way into exile from Naples. On Minturno see Gennaro Tallini, "Sebastiani Minturno, Antonio," *DBI* 91 (2018).

552. The poem is in phalaecean hendecasyllables.

553. See Gianni Ballistreri, "Casanova, Marco Antonio," *DBI* 21 (1978); *DLI*, 276–77; Giraldi, 85; and *NMW*, 231–37, including two of his poems.

554. His prominence is attested by the fact that in the festivities for Leo X's coronation in 1513, one of his distichs appeared on a triumphal arch financed by the banker Agostino Chigi: see Ballistreri, "Casanova."

555. In fact, the *Heroica* includes poems not only on classical Romans (e.g., Julius Caesar, Cicero) but also on other ancients (e.g., Demosthenes, Hannibal) and on many on his contemporaries, including Popes Julius II and Leo X, Ludovico Sforza, and Antonio Tebaldeo. See Casanova, *Heroica*, ed. Filippo Volpicella (n.p., 1867).

556. A slightly different version of this anecdote appeared in *NMW*, 235: "With admirable leniency, Clement recently protected him when he was thrown in jail and convicted, since it was from foolishness rather than spite that he had insulted the majesty of His Holiness in a scandalous poem. For he had thought, misled by frivolity, that it would ingratiate him with his patron, Pompeo Colonna, who, with his armies advancing, was then engaged in a vehement feud with the pope." Casanova himself wrote about the episode, which occurred in 1526–27, in an elegy, *Ad divum Pompeium* (BAV MS. Vat lat. 5227, vol. 1, fol. 11v).

557. See, e.g., Catullus 29, 54, 57, 93.

558. Valeriano's account of Casanova's demise (*DLI*, 219) differs substantially: "After the fall and abominable sack of Rome, even though he was a keen partisan of the Colonna faction and had incurred the hostility of powerful princes thereby, he still could find no way to escape unharmed from robbery and captivity in the disastrous period when that faction allied itself with Spaniards and Germans and exercised its cruel domination over all the goods of the Romans. In fact, he fell into such poverty that he had to beg in vain for bread, and finding none he died afflicted with hunger, disease, and general misfortune." Ultimately Pompeo Colonna had expelled him from the household, seemingly in part because of his association with a woman of ill repute. See Gaisser's analysis in *DLI*, 276, including a translation of a letter Casanova sent to Colonna's chamberlain in a final, futile attempt to regain the cardinal's favor (the letter is preserved in Vatican Library MS. Vat lat. 5227, vol. 1, fol. 10v).

559. On May 6, 1527, as the Imperial army was sacking Rome, Pope Clement (accompanied by Giovio) had fled along the *Passetto di Borgo* from the Vatican to the papal fortress, the Castel Sant'Angelo. By nightfall the invading troops had conquered the city, but Clement, trapped in the fortress, did not capitulate until a month later, after which he was

held under guard of an Imperial garrison until early December. On Colonna's audience with the pope at the start of June, at which both were in tears, see Pastor, 9:421; Judith Hook, *The Sack of Rome, 1527* (London: Macmillan, 1972), 209.

560. The church is the minor basilica of San Lorenzo in Lucina, in the Rione Colonna in Rome. Seemingly, Giovio was unaware that the "Lucina" in the church's name is owed not to Juno Lucina, but to the fourth-century CE Roman matron who allowed it to be built on that site. The *naumachia* (artificial lake for a Roman sea battle) may be that of Domitian, as Orio specified in his translation, Giovio (1552), 143. See *OCD*, 1029; *Elogi*, 223n.

561. The poem is in phalaecean hendecasyllables.

562. Claudio Mutini, "Castiglione, Baldassare," *DBI* 22 (1979); *CE*, 1:279–80; Giraldi, 69.

563. *Poesie volgari, e latine del conto Baldessar Castiglione, corrette, illustrate, ed accresciute di varie cose inediti* (Rome: Niccolò and Marco Pagliarini, 1760). See the discussion of the elegies in Mutini, "Castiglione." For a modern edition of *Cleopatra*, see *RLV*, 193–95; and for a translation and an analysis, see Brian A. Curran, "Love, Triumph, Tragedy: Cleopatra and Egypt in High Renaissance Rome," in *Cleopatra: A Sphinx Revisited*, ed. Margaret M. Miles (Berkeley and Los Angeles: University of California Press, 2011), 93–131, at 116–17. The poem celebrates an ancient statue of Ariadne purchased by Julius II that was thought to have been of the Egyptian queen (now called *Sleeping Ariadne*, but still on occasion referred to as the "Belevedere *Cleopatra*"). The poem first appeared in print in 1530 and circulated widely thereafter.

564. The truce made with the pope by the Imperial viceroy of Naples, Charles de Lannoy, in mid-March 1527 was supposed to have stopped Bourbon's troops from advancing on Rome; it did not. See Hook, *Sack*, 131–46, especially 134. The see of Ávila became available on the death of Francisco Ruiz on October 23, 1528, eight months after the Imperial army had left Rome. The following January, Pope Clement granted approval to the emperor's request that Castiglione be assigned the see. Just days after his investiture as bishop of Ávila, however, Castiglione fell mortally ill

with plague. See Vittorio Cian, *Un illustre nunzio pontificio del Rinascimento: Baldassar Castiglione* (Vatican City: Biblioteca Apostolica Vaticana, 1951), 123–24.

565. The prophecy turned out (as so often) to be ambiguous, since an alternative Latin name for Madrid is "Mantua Carpetanorum." Giovio errs twice: Castiglione died at age fifty (on February 8, 1529), and not in Madrid but in Tolédo.

566. The poem is in elegiac couplets.

567. These are Scipio Africanus and Scipio Aemilianus, both of whom carried out campaigns in Spain.

568. The poem is in elegiac couplets.

569. The first couplet of the Latin poem plays on the similarity of *Castellio*, the Latinized form of "Castiglione," to *castellum* (a fortified settlement or garrison). The second couplet juxtaposes *Castellio* with *Castalia*, the nereid of the spring at Delphi, who is frequently invoked in references to refined poetry.

570. The poem is in elegiac couplets.

571. The vocabulary of the first couplet (*horrida, terribilis, arma*) alludes to the *Aeneid*, that of the second couplet (*molli, vacuus, requiescis, umbra*), to the *Eclogues*.

572. See Igor Melani, "Navagero, Andrea," *DBI* 78 (2013); *EH*, 319; *CE*, 1:8–9. Among contemporary accounts, see *NMW*, 247–49 (including translations of two of his epigrams), 279; Giraldi, 67; *DLI*, 161.

573. On d'Alviano (1455–1515) see note 403 above. Leonardo Loredan (1436–1521) was doge of Venice, 1501–21. For the orations see Navagero, *Orationes duae, carminaque nonnulla* ([Venice]: Tacuino, 1530); and Navagero, *Opera omnia*, ed. G. A. and C. Volpi (Venice: ex Typographia Remondiniana, 1754).

574. A reference to disputes regarding the relative merit of the imitation of just one author (Cicero in prose, Vergil in poetry) as opposed to eclectic imitation. See *Ciceronian Controversies*, ed. JoAnn DellaNeva and trans. Brian Duvick, ITRL 26 (Cambridge, MA: Harvard University Press, 2007).

575. That is, he burned them.

576. Only eighteen of his vernacular poems have survived. In contrast, his *Lusus* contains forty-four Latin poems: *Lusus*, ed. and trans. Alice E. Wilson (Nieuwkoop: B. de Graaf, 1973). He was in d'Alviano's service from 1508 to 1515, and a member (along with Fracastoro and Cotta) of the general's Accademia Alviana. See Melani, "Navagero." For another military leader's maintenance of a literary circle while on campaign, see the account of Francesco Sperulo's service to Cesare Borgia in Paul Gwynne, *Patterns of Patronage in Renaissance Rome: Francesco Sperulo: Poet, Prelate, Soldier, Spy*, 2 vols. (Oxford: Peter Lang, 2015), 1:8–13, 285–312. On soldier-poets see, in addition to Gwynne, Giovio's *elogium* of Marullo Tarcaniota (no. 28) and the accompanying notes.

577. Navagero, *Historia veneta ab origine urbis usque ad annum 1498*, in *Rerum italicarum scriptores*, ed. L. I. Muratori, vol. 23 (Milan: ex tipographia Societatis Palatinae, 1733), cols. 923–1216.

578. The poem is in elegiac couplets.

579. Gianni Ballistreri, "Cattaneo, Giovanni Maria," *DBI* 22 (1979); *EH*, 81; *CE*, 1:286–87; *DLI*, 52–53 (Valeriano named an interlocutor after him). See also Giraldi, 81; *NMW*, 229.

580. Pliny the Younger, *Epistolarum libri IX. Eiusdem Plinii libellus epistolarum ad Traianum cum rescriptis eiusdem principis. Eiusdem Panegyricus Traiano Caeari dictus cum enarrationibus Io. Mar. Catanei* (Milan: apud Alexandrum Minutianum, 1506). Cattaneo studied under Demetrius Chalcondyles from 1491 to 1494, and subsequently under Giorgio Merula. In 1504 Cattaneo and Giovio may have met in Milan, where Giovio too attended Chalcondyles's lectures.

581. Sebastiano del Piombo's group portrait of Bendinello Sauli (1516), in which Giovio figures prominently, also includes a figure usually identified as Cattaneo. See Zimmermann (1995), 14; Josephine Jungic, "Prophecies of the Angelic Pastor in Sebastiano del Piombo's Portrait of Cardinal Bandinello Sauli and Three Companions," in *Prophetic Rome in the High Renaissance Period*, ed. Marjorie Reeves (Oxford: Clarendon Press, 1992), 345–70.

582. Lucian, *Convivium seu Lapithae omnium eius dialogorum urbanissimus et suavissimus*, ed. Giovanni Maria Cattaneo (Rome: Étienne Guillery, no later than 1524); Lucian, *De componenda historia nuper a Ioanne Maria Cataneo Latinitate donata* (Bologna: Caligula Bacilerius, 1507). Zimmermann (1995), 24: "Although Cattaneo evidently changed his mind in respect to the dedication, Giovio became a disciple of Lucian and began adopting the methods of Greek eyewitness historiography."

583. The Greek name assumed by Scipione Forteguerri (1466–1515), who worked with Aldo Manuzio in Venice from 1495 to 1504 and collaborated in founding the "Neakademia" devoted to the diffusion of Greek culture. See Francesco Piovan, "Forteguerri, Scipione," *DBI* 49 (1997); *DLI*, 291; Manutius, *The Greek Classics*, 87, 157–59, 289–91, 296–99.

584. Cattaneo, *Genua* ([Rome: Jacobus Mazochius, 1514]).

585. On the *Solymidos*, a hexameter Latin poem that is no longer extant, see the comments of Ballistreri, "Cattaneo."

586. Johannes Franciscus Philomusus was the pen name of Gianfrancesco Superchi of Pesaro, who studied under Guido Postumo (on whom see *elogium* 69). His *Exultatio in creatione Pont. Max. Leonis decimi* is reproduced in William Roscoe, *The Life and Pontificate of Leo X*, 4 vols. (Liverpool, 1805), 2: Appendix LXIX, pp. 33–38. See L. B. T. Houghton, "*Salve, Magna Parens*: Virgil's *Laudes Italiae* in Renaissance Italy and Beyond," *International Journal of the Classical Tradition* 22 (2015): 180–208, at 188; and Giraldi, 75, 337.

587. The coronation took place on February 24, 1530, the emperor's birthday (and fifth anniversary of his victory in the Battle of Pavia), but the festivities began in late 1529.

588. That is, they wished to have first shot at petitioning Clement for Cattaneo's benefices, an opportunity that could be lost should the pontiff learn of the death while in Bologna and at once assign them to others.

589. Perhaps a reference to the hot springs near Viterbo. On Vetulonia, see *A Dictionary of Greek and Roman Geography*, ed. William Smith, 2 vols. (London: John Murray, 1872–73), 2:1285–86.

590. The poem is in choliambic verse.

591. Carlo Vecce, "Sannazaro, Iacopo," *DBI* 90 (2017); *CE*, 3:193–94; *ER*, 5:394–96; Kidwell (1993). Through his father, Nicola (Cola), he was descended from nobility in Lombardy; his mother, Masella di Santomango, was of a prominent noble family in Salerno.

592. The Ticino is a major tributary of the Po, which it joins downstream from Pavia.

593. Frederick (r. 1496–1501) succeeded his nephew, Ferdinand II (Ferrandino; r. 1495–96), as king of Naples.

594. When Charles VIII of France (r. 1483–98) led his army into Naples on February 22, 1495, King Alfonso II was expelled, and Charles became (albeit briefly) king of Naples. Pontano's reputation has suffered from Francesco Guicciardini's unsympathetic account, in his *History of Italy*, of Pontano's delivery of the oration for Charles: Guicciardini (1971), 1:169–70. Kidwell (1991), 12–14, reviews the limited contemporary evidence. In a letter to Francesco Caracciolo (ca. July 1495), Pontano defended himself against others' charge that he had shown ingratitude to the House of Aragon by praising the French king: "For in those confused and most dangerous times, when the Aragonese cause was absolutely desperate and had been abandoned, necessity compelled me, for my own safety and that of my friends and of the city, to praise and approve all things which it was both useless and risky to attack and oppose. . . . I certainly did not do this of my own free will but unwillingly, in answer to the prayers of the citizens. And I was not a member of the French party and I never manoeuvred for honours and wealth from them nor can anyone in his right mind doubt my gratitude and devotion towards the Aragonese kings" (ibid., 13).

595. In 1501, Louis XII of France and Ferdinand of Aragon, acting together, ousted King Frederick from power, giving him the consolation prize of the duchy of Anjou and a pension. Sannazaro accompanied Frederick to France, but upon the latter's death in 1504 he returned to Naples to live in his villa at Mergellina, which Frederick had bestowed upon him.

596. Although *On the Birth of the Virgin* was received enthusiastically by many, including Bembo, Egidio da Viterbo, and Clement VII, it came under fire from Erasmus in the *Ciceronianus* for its excessive classicizing. Kidwell (1993), 154–56; Erasmus, *Ciceronianus*, 700–701; Erasmus, *Ciceronian*, 437–38.

597. In July 1527 Philibert de Châlon, prince of Orange (1502–30), had been named lieutenant general of the Imperial forces in Italy. On his destruction of the tower of the villa in April 1528, see Benedetto Croce, "La chiesetta di Iacopo Sannazaro," in his *Storie e leggende napoletane*, ed. G. Galasso (Milan: Adelphi, 2001; orig. pub. 1919), 208–29; Kidwell (1993), 168. Some speculate that the tower's destruction was not capricious but instead a strategic precaution (ibid., 241n39).

598. This is the Church of Santa Maria del Parto, built no later than 1524. Kidwell (1993), 161; Croce, "La chiesetta." Bembo's poem is in elegiac couplets.

599. The poem is in elegiac couplets.

600. On this *elogium* see Minonzio (2002), 2:529–40. See also Daniela Mugnai Carrara, "Mainardi, Giovanni," *DBI* 67 (2006); *EH*, 286; *CE*, 2:372; Franco Minonzio, "'Fra Leandro, dolce cosmografo e brusco inquisitore, leccardo del arrosto di carne umana'. I rapporti tra Leandro Alberti e Paolo Giovio e l'ombra inquieta della memoria (tra Giovanfrancesco Pico e Giovanni Mainardi)," in *L'Italia dell'Inquisitore: Storia e geografia dell'Italia del Cinquecento nella* Descrittione di Leandro Alberti (Atti del Convegno Internazionale di Studi, Bologna, 27–29 May 2004), ed. Massimo Donattini (Bologna: Bononia University Press, 2007), 51–79.

601. According to Carrara, "Mainardi," at the end of 1513 he left Ferrara to become personal physician to Ladislaus (Władysław) II Jagiello, king of Bohemia (r. 1471–1516) and of Hungary (r. 1490–1516). Following Ladislaus's death, Mainardi served his successor, Louis II (r. 1516–26), in the same capacity for two years, then returned to Ferrara. With the expression "healing arts" (*medendi artem*), Giovio may refer to Mainardi's advocacy for medicine as *ars* rather than *scientia*, and for Galen's *Methodus medendi*. See D. M. Carrara, "The *Epistolarum medicinalium* libri XX by Giovanni Mainardi," *Medicina nei secoli* 17.2 (January 2005): 363–81.

602. The *Epistolae medicinales* were first published in six books (Ferrara: B. de Odonino, 1521), then expanded to eighteen (Basel: J. Bebel, 1535), and a final revised edition, comprising twenty books, appeared posthumously (Basel: M. Isengrin, 1540). It was frequently reprinted. For this work Carrara credits him with having inaugurated a new genre of scientific literature. The letters treated both the theory and the practice of medicine, detailing medicinals and botanicals, clarifying textual problems in earlier works, and glossing terminology. *CE*, 2:372 (s.n. Manardo), describes Mainardi as "[o]ne of the most important physicians of the first half of the sixteenth century," noting his collaboration in restoring ancient medical texts, his publication of a popular edition of Galen's *Ars medicinalis* (Rome: Calvo, 1525), and his development of new methods for analyzing and classifying diseases. Given Mainardi's contributions to medical thought and practice, it is striking that Giovio gives such short shrift to him. Particularly odd, given Giovio's attention elsewhere in the *Elogia* to the practices of astrology and divining, is his failure to mention Mainardi's collaboration with Gianfrancesco Pico in editing the works of the latter's uncle, Giovanni Pico della Mirandola, notably the *Disputationes adversus astrologiam divinatricem* (Bologna: B. Hector, 1496).

603. Although Mainardo remained active, his health was precarious for the last decade and a half of his life. When he married his second wife, Giulia Sassoli of Bergamo, he was seventy-three years old; she bore him a daughter, named Marietta (*CE*, 2:372). Giulia was not in fact so young as Giovio implies and had previously been widowed. On this and other misrepresentations in the *elogium*, and hypotheses regarding why Giovio presented Mainardi less than sympathetically, see Minonzio (2002), 2:536–40.

604. The poem is in elegiac couplets. On the poet see Petrucci, "Corsi, Pietro," *DBI* 29 (1983); *CE*, 1:344; *DLI*, 59–61 and *passim*; Gouwens, 73–102; *Coryciana*, poems 12, 13, 52, 278; Arsilli, lines 361–70. A participant in the Roman academies of Colocci and Goritz, Corsi is best known for his poem *Romae urbis excidium*, a lament on the Sack of Rome, which he personally experienced. Several of his poems appear in the *Coryciana*, and Valeriano made him an interlocutor in his dialogue *De litteratorum infelicitate*.

605. In legend, Coronis was the mother of the great physician Aesculapius.

606. A legendary physician, the son of Aesculapius.

607. On Querno see Grant's summary in Giraldi, 271; Domenico Gnoli, *La Roma di Leone X* (Milan: Ulrico Hoepli, 1938), 121–24. Among primary sources see Sannazaro's negative assessment of his talents, cited by Giovio in his famous letter to Girolamo Scannapeco (1534–35), *IO*, 1:174–79, at 177; Giraldi, 105, 107; and Arsilli, lines 351–60. Although renowned for improvisational poetry, he did also publish substantial works: Querno, *De bello neapolitano libri duo carmine heroico compositi* (Naples: Sulzbach and Cancer, 1529), now in a modern edition: *La guerra di Napoli*, ed. Debora D'Alessandro (Naples: Loffredo, 2004); and *Victoria inclyti Francisci Sforciae invictissimi Mediolanensium ducis de expulsis gallis triumphantis* (Rome: Silber, 1522). One of his poems appears in *Coryciana*: 318A (pp. 216–17).

608. See *OCD*, 28, s.n. Aesculapius: "The miraculous transferral of the god of healing Asclepius from Epidaurus to Rome and the origin of the important healing-cult of the Tiber island there in 292 BC constituted significant moments in Roman narratives of the history of their religion."

609. See Pliny the Elder, *Natural History* 20.34: "As cabbage is the enemy of the vine, they [i.e., the Greeks] say that it opposes wine; that if taken in food beforehand it prevents drunkenness, taken after drinking it dispels its unpleasant effects" (LCL). Earlier sources on the remedy include [pseudo] Aristotle, *Problemata* 873a–b; and Cato the Elder, *De agricultura*, 156.1: "If you wish to drink deep at a banquet and to enjoy your dinner, eat as much raw cabbage as you wish, seasoned with vinegar, before dinner, and likewise after dinner eat some half a dozen leaves; it will make you feel as if you had not dined, and you can drink as much as you please" (LCL).

610. The meter of the Latin is phalaecean hendecasyllables.

611. By September 1519 he would be assigned a stipend of nine ducats a month. See Gnoli, *Roma*, 122.

612. Giraldi, 105, attributes both lines to Leo, and writes: "If I were to adduce such men who are more truly gourmandizers than poets, I would

think I would be causing you vexation rather than giving pleasure. Don't you know that Gazoldo has often had a lashing from Leo for his dreadful, limping verses and has become a byword to everyone, while Archipoeta guzzles down vast goblets of wine from the debauchee Alessandro and his ears and nose have been disfigured[?] This is why he rarely sits at the pope's table."

613. A pun on Querno's gout-ridden extremities and his weak poetic meters, playing on Vergil, *Georgics* 2.93–94, where Lagean vines are said to yield wine "sure some day to trouble the feet and tie the tongue" (*tempatura pedes olim vincturaque linguam* [LCL]), followed in line 96 by: "Yet even so, seek not to rival Falernian Cellars!" (*nec cellis ideo contende Falernis* [LCL]). As noted in *Elogi*, 242–43n4, Leo's verse here may also echo *Aeneid* 9.611 ("nec tarda senectus / debilitat viris animi mutatque vigorem" = "and sluggish age does not weaken our hearts' strength or change our vigour" [LCL]).

614. Evidently a generalized reference to Spanish possessions in southern Italy, not exclusively the city of Naples. In 1504 the Kingdom of Naples, over which France and Spain had been fighting, came decisively under Spanish rule, where it remained for over two centuries. Querno's home town of Monopoli, on the Adriatic coast of Italy, had been a Venetian possession at the time of his birth, but in 1509, during the War of the League of Cambrai, it had passed into Spanish hands, where it too remained.

615. The poem is in phalaecean hendecasyllables.

616. Fabio Forner, "Pio, Alberto," *DBI* 84 (2015); *CE*, 3:86–88; Forner, "L'ultimo principe," in *Storia di Carpi*, vol. 2, ed. M. Cattini (Modena: A. M. Ori, 2009), 69–85; *Società, politica e cultura a Carpi ai tempi di Alberto III Pio*, Atti del Convegno internazionale, Carpi, 19–21 maggio 1978, 2 vols. (Padua: Antenore, 1981).

617. An invocation of Giovio's motto, FATO PRVDENTIA MINOR (prudence is unequal to fate), which reverses an epigram from Vergil (*Georgics* 1.416). See Zimmermann (1995), 267 and 281–82.

618. In placing Carpi in the Nacrian Fields, Giovio here follows Raffaele Maffei, but Leandro Alberti placed them in a different locale: see *Elogi*, 246n3.

619. That is, Castel Sant'Angelo.

620. Rodolfo Pio was created cardinal in 1536.

621. Pio's criticisms of Luther became subsumed into his vitriolic exchanges with Erasmus, whom he viewed as having sympathized with Luther and even supported him. See Erasmus, *Controversies with Alberto Pio*, ed. Nelson H. Minnich and trans. Daniel Sheerin, vol. 84 (2005) in *Collected Works of Erasmus* (Toronto: University of Toronto Press, 1974–).

622. The poem is in elegiac couplets.

623. The poem is in elegiac couplets.

624. In late December 1524, Pio's wife, Cecilia (a daughter of Cardinal Franciotto Orsini), had given birth to a son and potential heir, possibly named Francesco, who died the following June.

625. Natalino Sapegno, "Ariosto, Ludovico," *DBI* 4 (1962); *CE*, 1:71; Albert Russell Ascoli, *Ariosto's Bitter Harmony: Crisis and Evasion in the Italian Renaissance* (Princeton: Princeton University Press, 1987); *Lettura dell' Orlando furioso*, vol. 1, ed. Guido Baldassarri, Marco Praloran, et al. (Florence: Edizioni del Galluzzo per la Fondazione Ezio Franceschini, 2016); *"Dreaming Again on Things Already Dreamed": 500 years of Orlando Furioso (1516–2016)*, ed. Marco Dorigatti and Maria Pavlova (Oxford: Peter Lang, 2019). In fact, although Ariosto grew up in Ferrara, he was born in Reggio Emilia.

626. Ariosto had been in the service of Cardinal Ippolito since October 1503. Their falling out regarding a trip to Hungary occurred in 1517. Evidence of Ariosto having gone on an earlier mission of the cardinal to Hungary is lacking. Caruso, in Giovio (1999), 242–43n1, thinks it improbable. Minonzio, in *Elogi*, 249n2, suggests reading *Adhaesit comes Hippolyto Atestino Cardinali in Pannoniam profecto* as "Entrò nel seguito del cardinale Ippolito d'Este, che già in precedenza si era recato in Ungheria."

627. The first redaction of the *Satires* was published in 1517.

628. *I suppositi* (*The Pretenders*) was first performed in 1509.

629. *Orlando furioso* (*Mad Roland*) was published in three different redactions (Ferrara: Giovanni Mazocco del Bondeno, 1516; Ferrara: G. B. da la Pigna, 1521; and Ferrara: Francesco Rosso da Valenza, 1532).

630. Matteo Maria Boiardo (1441–94) and Luigi Pulci (1452–1501). Boiardo, who preceded Ariosto in the ducal court in Ferrara, was famed for his narrative poem *Orlando innamorato* (*Roland in Love*), published in its final form in 1495. Pulci wrote his *Morgante* at the urging of Lucrezia Tornabuoni de' Medici (wife of Piero di Cosimo, "the Gouty"). Its definitive edition first appeared in print in 1482.

631. Giovio errs: Ariosto died aged fifty-eight, not at fifty-six or sixty-three. See *OLD*, s.v. climacter.

632. The poem is in phalaecean hendecasyllables. For a comparative analysis of versions of this epitaph, see Claudio Mutini, "Nota sull' 'Epitaphium Ludovici Areosti'" [sic], *Bibliothèque d'humanisme et Renaissance* 25 (1963): 198–206.

633. Egidio Antonini (1469–1532). For a close reading of this *elogium*, see Zimmermann (1995), 206–7. See also Germana Ernst and Simona Foà, "Egidio da Viterbo," *DBI* 42 (1993); *CE*, 1:64–65; John W. O'Malley, *Giles of Viterbo on Church and Reform: A Study in Renaissance Thought* (Leiden: Brill, 1968); Ingrid D. Rowland, *The Culture of the High Renaissance: Ancients and Moderns in Sixteenth-Century Rome* (New York: Cambridge University Press, 1998), *passim*; Giraldi, 189. He is the namesake and main subject of Pontano's *Aegidius*; see Pontano, *Dialogues*, 3:2–115.

634. Probably a reference to the *Book on Hebrew Letters* (*Libellus de litteris hebraicis*) of 1517, presented to Cardinal Giulio de' Medici (the future Clement VII), printed along with his *Shekhinah* (begun in 1530) in Egidio da Viterbo, *Schechina e Libellus de litteris Hebraicis*, ed. François Secret, 2 vols. (Rome: Centro internazionale di studi umanistici, 1959). The *Libellus*, written in hopes of persuading Leo X to reform the Roman alphabet, drew extensively upon the Kabbalah and analyzed what he believed to be the sexual anatomy of Hebrew letters. With reference to the "sacred numbers signified in the letters passed down by God to Moses," Egidio writes that Cardinal Giulio had wanted "their forms and parts to be summarized as briefly as possible . . . wrapping them all in holy silence": Brian Copenhaver and Daniel Stein Kokin, "Egidio da Viterbo's *Book on Hebrew Letters*: Christian Kabbalah in Papal Rome," *Renaissance Quarterly* 67 (2014): 1–42, at 9. On the manuscript's limited circulation and possible

reasons for its not being printed in the sixteenth century, see ibid., 36–37, 37n101. In his *History of Twenty Ages* (*Historia XX Saeculorum*), which explicitly treated God's special revelations to Moses, Egidio wrote of the need to guard the wisdom of the esoteric tradition: "That Law, which was given to Moses by God, Greatest and Best in words of plain meaning, was exhibited to all the people, and that which was given in the secrets of letters and certain divine names [i.e., the Kabbalah] was handed down to the understanding of Moses alone, and of certain holy men who were truly wise, for them to examine and ponder deep within. The meaning of the former is common knowledge, of the latter recondite" (Rowland, *Culture*, 215).

635. *Aegidius*, in Pontano, *Dialogues*, 3:23. The meter is sapphic strophe. An Augustinian hermit noted for his eloquence, Mariano Pomicelli da Genazzano (1412–98) was prior general of the Augustinian order and a bitter adversary of Savonarola. In Florence he benefited from the patronage of Lorenzo de' Medici. See Daniela Gionta, "Pomicelli, Mariano," *DBI* 84 (2015). Pontano praises him at length in the *Aegidius*: Pontano, *Dialogues*, 3:11–13, 21–23. For Poliziano's missive of March 22, 1489, to Tristano Calco, in which he praises Mariano at length, see Poliziano, *Letters*, ed. and trans. Shane Butler, ITRL 21 (Cambridge, MA: Harvard University Press, 2006), 257–61 (vol. 4, lett. 6).

636. In June 1506, following the death of the Prior General of the Order of Augustinian Hermits, Julius appointed Egidio as its interim head. The following spring, the order elected Egidio its Prior General. Giraldi, 189 (2.137), praises Egidio's skill at composing Latin verse.

637. The "Umbrian war" is the War of Urbino. See Cecil H. Clough, "Clement VII and Francesco Maria Della Rovere, Duke of Urbino," in *Pontificate of Clement*, 75–108, at 90–92. Among those implicated as having conspired to poison the pope in 1517 were Cardinals Alfonso Petrucci, Francesco Soderini, and Bendinello Sauli. See Giovio's account of Petrucci's demise in the *Life* of Leo X, IO, 4:85–86. For recent reconstructions of the conspiracy, see Helen Hyde, *Cardinal Bendinello Sauli and Church Patronage in Sixteenth-Century Italy* (Woodbridge, Suffolk: Boydell and Brewer, 2009), 131–72; Marcello Simonetta, *Volpi e leoni: i Medici, Machiavelli, e la rovina d'Italia* (Milan: Bompiani, 2014), 159–201. Leo re-

sponded with his "Great Promotion" on July 1, 1517, in which he asserted dominance over the Sacred College by creating an unprecedented thirty-one cardinals (their candidacy was confirmed on July 3). The "Umbrian war" here refers to renewed fighting between Francesco Maria della Rovere, hereditary duke of Urbino, and papal forces under the command of the pope's nephew, Lorenzo di Piero de' Medici, whom Leo had installed as the new duke. See Pastor, 7:166–69, 208–11; and Clough, "Clement VII and Francesco Maria Della Rovere," 90–93.

638. Selim I (the Grim) conquered the Savafids (then ruled by Ismail I) in the Battle of Chaldiran (August 23, 1514). The two Egyptian rulers are Sultan Al-Ashraf Qansuh al-Ghawri, killed on August 24, 1516, in the Battle of Marj Dabiq, and his successor, Al-Ashraf Abu Al-Nasr Tuman bay (or, "Tuman bay II"), captured in battle at Giza and hanged at the city gate of Constantinople on April 15, 1517. In June of 1518, in Barcelona, Egidio met with Charles V on behalf of Pope Leo.

639. Actually, Egidio died the night of November 11–12, 1532, several weeks before Clement and Charles would reconvene in Bologna. Three years earlier, the pope and sovereign had met there for the discussions and festivities that culminated in Charles V's coronation as Holy Roman Emperor (February 24, 1530).

640. The poem is in elegiac couplets.

641. Beyond his deep knowledge of Latin, Greek, and Hebrew, Egidio also studied Arabic and Aramaic. For around a decade (ca. 1517?–27), he studied under the Jewish grammarian and Masorete Elijah Levita, providing housing for Levita and his family in exchange for advanced lessons in Aramaic and Hebrew. While a legate in Spain in 1518–19, he had a Latin translation made of the Koran, which appears in manuscript facing the Arabic text. See O'Malley, *Giles*, 12, 61, 78.

642. *EH*, 348; *CE*, 3:81; Charles B. Schmitt, *Gianfrancesco Pico della Mirandola (1469–1533) and His Critique of Aristotle* (The Hague: Springer, 1967); and Franco Minonzio, "Sesto Empirico versus gli 'Academica' di Cicerone: Gianfrancesco Pico, Paolo Giovio e alcuni riflessi epistemologici del conflitto tra dissenso religioso e ortodossia nella prima metà del '500," forthcoming in *Raccolta storica della Società Storica Comense* 23 (2019, but delayed).

643. G. F. Pico, *Hymni heroici tres ad Sanctissimam Trinitatem, ad Christum, et ad Virginem Mariam* (Milan: Alessandro Minuziano, 1507), which includes an *argumentum hymnorum carmine elegiaco; Examen vanitatis doctrinae gentium* (Mirandola: G. Mazzocchi, 1520). See Schmitt, *Gianfrancesco Pico*, especially 43–53; and Minonzio, "Sesto Empirico."

644. G. F. Pico, *De imitatione libellus* (dated September 19, 1512), and a second letter, a rejoinder to Bembo's response to the *libellus* (1513). For critical editions and translations, see *Ciceronian Controversies*, 16–43, 91–125.

645. The poem is in phalaecean hendecasyllables.

646. See Giorgio Inglese, "Machiavelli, Niccolò," *DBI* 67 (2006); *EH*, 282; *CE*, 2:364–65; *ER*, 4:1–15; Cochrane, 265–70; *NMW*, 269.

647. These works are, respectively, *The Prince, The Art of War*, and *Discourses on the First Ten Books of Livy*.

648. *Mandragola* ("The Mandrake Root") was performed in Florence in March 1518 and revived at the papal court probably on September 27, 1520.

649. These are Iacopo Cattani da Diacceto and Luigi di Tommaso Alamanni, who were executed on June 7, 1522. See Patricia J. Osmond, "The Conspiracy of 1522 against Cardinal Giulio de' Medici: Machiavelli and '*gli esempli delli antiqui*,'" in *Pontificate of Clement*, 55–72. According to J. N. Stephens, *The Fall of the Florentine Republic 1512–1530* (Oxford: Clarendon Press, 1983), 121, Luigi di Tommaso Alamanni stood out from the other suspected conspirators because "he was a soldier, not a cultured youth, and a hot-headed and violent man, who had been arrested on at least two different occasions since 1512, once for brawling and causing trouble in the streets." At the time of the conspiracy, Alamanni was stationed in the Florentine garrison in the city of Arezzo: see Iacopo Nardi, *Istorie della città di Firenze*, 2 vols., ed. Lelio Arbib (Florence: Società editrice delle Storie del Nardi e del Varchi, 1842), 2:87. While *turma praetoria* is accurate for Alamanni's assignment — the Florentine captain, or *podestà*, in a subject town was termed *praetor* in Latin — it might also conceivably invoke the Praetorian Guard of ancient Rome, whose loyalty to its master could on occasion be as suspect as that of the "men like Brutus and Cas-

sius" invoked earlier in the sentence (cf. the *locus classicus* for praises of Brutus and Cassius: Tacitus, *Annals* 4.34). Perhaps the superlative *levissimus* (here rendered "paltry") implies a derogatory comparison of this Luigi (di Tommaso) Alamanni to his famous kinsman, the poet Luigi Alamanni, who was also implicated in the conspiracy.

650. On meanings of the term "atheist" in the Renaissance, see James Hankins, "Monstrous Melancholy: Ficino and the Physiological Causes of Atheism," in *Laus Platonici Philosophi: Marsilio Ficino and his Influence*, ed. Stephen Clucas, Peter J. Forshaw, and Valery Rees (Leiden: Brill, 2011), 25–43.

651. Machiavelli died on June 22, 1527; Florence capitulated to the Imperial army on August 12, 1530.

652. The poem is in elegiac couplets.

653. Aldo Mazzacane, "Decio, Filippo," *DBI* 33 (1987); *EH*, 145; *CE*, 1:379–80.

654. Already at the University of Pisa, he had come to have a salary higher than that of any other professor (*CE*, 1:380). Giovio omits Decio's four-year stint at the University of Padua.

655. This council was in fact jointly convened, by Louis XII of France and Holy Roman Emperor Maximilian, in May 1511 (Pastor, 6:352), over half a decade after Decio's arrival in Pavia.

656. In a bull of July 18, 1511, posted on the doors of St. Peter's on July 18, Julius II summoned a general council to meet at the Church of San Giovanni in Laterano on April 19, 1512. This would be the Fifth Lateran Council. Pastor, 6:364–65.

657. According to Pastor, 6:386, Decio and Zaccaria Ferreri were the only writers in Italy "who advocated the schismatic Council and the oligarchical revolution in the constitution of the Church at which it aimed." On Decio see also Guicciardini (1971), 2:1021 and note 24, where Seidel Menchi describes him as "Milanese, già maestro del Guicciardini."

658. Matthaeus Schinner, bishop of Sion, was famous for his "blameless life and his strictness in all ecclesiastical matters": Pastor, 6:324. A long-time enemy of the French, he had argued that the Swiss should "stand by

the Emperor in defending the Roman Church against France, whose predominance in Italy was a permanent danger to the freedom and independence of the Holy See." Julius II named him a cardinal on September 10, 1508 (his proclamation, however, was deferred until March 10, 1511). Ibid. 6:325, 344; Eubel, 3:12. It was Schinner who first informed Julius II (June 1512) that Swiss troops had taken Pavia for the pontiff (Pastor, 6:413–16). For a detailed account of the city's capture, see Sanuto, 14: cols. 388–410. On Schinner's role, see Percy Alvin Martin, "The Biography of Matthew Schinner, Cardinal of Sion, with Special Reference to his Activity in Italy in the Years 1510–1516" (PhD diss., Harvard University, 1912), 170–74.

659. The tomb is in the Camposanto Monumentale. For an image that includes the inscription, see https://commons.wikimedia.org/wiki/File:Monumento_funebre_del_giureconsulto_Filippo_Decio_(m._1535)_di_Stagio_Stagi.JPG. The inscription, in which he boasts of the premium his services commanded, reads as follows:

PHILIPPVS DECIVS SIVE DE DEXIO MEDIOLANENSIS IV / RIS-CONSVLTVS CELEBRI FAMA NOTISSIMVS CVM PRIMVM / LOCVM STVDII IN IVRE CANONICO VEL CIVILI TENV / ISSET PISIS SENIS FLORENTIE PADVE PAPIE ET DEMVM / VLTRA MONTES IN GALLIA REVOCATVS IN ITALIAM AB / EXCELSA FLORENTINORVM REPVBLICA POSTEA QVAM / STIPENDIVM MILLE QVINGENTORVM AVREORVM IN AVRO / PRO LECTVRA CONSECVTVS FVISSET DE MORTE CO / GITANS HOC SEPVLCRVM SIBI FABRICARI CVRAVIT NE / POSTERIS SVIS CREDERET.

The jurist Filippo Decio (or, "di Desio") of Milan, renowned for his distinguished reputation while holding the top post in canon and civil law in Pisa, Siena, Florence, Padua, Pavia, and afterward beyond the mountains in France, having been recalled to Italy by the glorious Republic of Florence, having gained for himself by his teaching the salary of 1,500 gold ducats, being mindful of death, had this tomb built for himself so as not to entrust the task to his heirs.

In 1516 his salary to teach civil law at the University of Pisa was 1,400 florins. It rose steadily, and by 1525 reached 2,625 florins (the next highest paid civil law professor that year received 1,400). See Angelo Fabroni, *Historiae Academiae Pisanae*, 3 vols. (Pisa: Gaetano Mugnaini, 1791–95; repr., Bologna: Forni Editore, 1971), 1:383, 389. On Decio's teaching posts and the salaries he commanded, see Grendler (2002), 73.

660. The poem is in phalaecean hendecasyllables.

661. Phalaris (sixth century BCE), the tyrant of Akragas, was infamous for his cruelty.

662. More's famous dialogue *Utopia* (1516) does not, however, explicitly criticize Henry VIII.

663. The poem is in elegiac couplets.

664. The poem is in elegiac couplets. On Jaime Exerich (d. 1552), archpriest of Zaragoza and professor at its university, see Félix de Latassa y Ortin, *Bibliotecas antigua y nueva de escritores aragoneses*, revised and enlarged by Miguel Gomez Uriel (Zaragoza: Impr. De C. Ariño, 1884–86), 460–62.

665. The poem is in elegiac couplets.

666. See Persius *Satirae* 5.48: "Parca tenax veri"; cf. Horace, *Odes*, II.39: "Parca non mendax" ("the Thrifty One that does not belie her name").

667. See Richard Rex, "Fisher, John [St John Fisher]," *ODNB*, s.v.; *CE*, 2:36–39.

668. Evidently a reference to Henry's dissolution of the monasteries and destruction of shrines, both actions providing revenue for the king.

669. Fisher, *Assertionis Lutheranae confutatio* (Antwerp: Michiel Hillen van Hoochstraten, 1523), which "was one of the most frequently reprinted and widely quoted Catholic polemics against Luther, and many of the bishops and even theologians at the Council of Trent knew whatever they knew of Luther largely from Fisher's refutation" (Rex, "Fisher"). See also Jedin, 1:399–400. Fisher, *Sacri sacerdotii defensio*, published together with his *Defensio regiae assertionis* (Cologne: Peter Quentel, 1525); and *De veritate corporis et sanguinis Christi in Eucharistia* (Cologne: Peter Quentel,

1527). On Johannes Oecolampadius (1482–1531), leader of the Reformation movement in Basel, see Giovio's description of him below in the *Peroratio*.

670. Fisher, *Brevis apologia*, which responded to the *Gravissimae censurae* of 1531, in which the case for Henry's divorce was promoted. The *Brevis apologia* "was smuggled out of the country in sections by Eustace Chapuys, and no longer seems to survive in its entirety" (Rex, "Fisher").

671. Rex, "Fisher," describes this work as "the so-called 'king's psalms' (a dozen or so Latin meditations in the style of psalms, perhaps best described as devout pastiche or sacred parody)."

672. The poem is in elegiac couplets.

673. Emilio Russo, "Leonico Tomeo, Niccolò," *DBI* 64 (2005); *EH*, 269–70; *CE*, 2:323–24; Grendler (2002), 151, 273–74, 297–98; and on this *elogium* in particular, Minonzio (2002), 2:540–45.

674. That is, Demetrius Chalcondyles. Leonico Tomeo may have followed his courses in Greek in Padua beforehand but most certainly did so in Florence (starting in 1485) and in Milan. See Russo, "Leonico Tomeo."

675. For a similar sentiment, see the *elogium* of Duns Scotus above.

676. His edition, with Latin translation and commentary, would prove highly influential: Aristotle, *Parva quae vocant Naturalia* (Venice: B. Vitali, 1523). He dedicated the work to Richard Pace.

677. The three works are included in Leonico Tomeo's *Dialogi nunc primum in lucem editi quorum nomina proxima pagina habentur* (Venice: Gregorio de' Gregori, 1524). Their titles are, respectively, *Bembus, sive de animorum immortalitate*; *Bonominus, sive de alica*; and *Samnutus, sive de ludo talario*. The last, a game, was initially played with *astragali*, anklebones, and is also known as "knucklebones" or "jacks."

678. Leonico Tomeo, *De varia historia libri tres* (Venice: Lucantonio Giunta, 1531).

679. According to Russo, "Leonico Tomeo," after initially inclining to Averroës, in his teaching in Padua and then in Venice he sought to reconcile Platonism and Aristotelianism.

680. The poem is an elegiac couplet.

681. Margherita Palumbo, "Nifo, Agostino," *DBI* 78 (2013); *EH*, 323; *ER*, 4:320–21. See also Nifo, *De intellectu*, ed. Leen Spruit (Leiden: Brill, 2011), with a substantial introduction (1–34) and an analytic summary (35–107). See also Paul J. J. M. Bakker, "Natural Philosophy, Metaphysics, or Something in Between? Agostino Nifo, Pietro Pomponazzi, and Marcantonio Genua on the Nature and Place of the Science of the Soul," in *Mind, Cognition and Representation: The Tradition of Commentaries on Aristotle's De anima*, ed. Bakker and Johannes M. M. H. Thijssen (Aldershot: Ashgate, 2007), 151–77.

682. Palumbo, "Nifo," notes that in 1440 Agostino's grandfather Domizio, baron of Joppolo (or, "Tropea"), had moved to Sessa along with his brother Giovanni, in the entourage of Marino Marzano I, fourth duke of Sessa.

683. At various points Nifo held teaching positions in Padua, Naples, Salerno, Rome, and Pisa.

684. Agostino Nifo, *In librum Destructio destructionum Averrois commentarii* (Lyon: Scipion de Gabiano, 1529). It was first published in Venice in 1497. On Al-Ghazali (ca. 1056–1111), see Frank Griffel, "al-Ghazali," *SEP* (Summer 2020 Edition), ed. Edward N. Zalta.

685. Seemingly his *Super tres libros de anima* (Venice: Pietro Quarengi, 1503), although perhaps Giovio refers generically to that and other writings of Nifo on the soul, e.g., the *De immortalitate animae libellum* (1518).

686. Nifo, *De falsa diluvii prognosticatione: quae ex conventu omnium planetarum qui in piscibus contiget anno 1524 divulgata est* (Naples: for Jean Pasquet, 1519; Florence: Giunta, 1520), dedicated to Emperor Charles V, and translated into Italian the following year. In *NMW*, 45, Giovio mentions Nifo in the course of ridiculing the predictions of that supposed great flood: "To be sure, a good many philosophers, especially Agostino Nifo of Sessa Aurunca, were not remiss in their opposition to the astrologers: by debating and writing they freed ignorant peoples from this foolish and womanly anxiety." Perhaps by "pamphlets on morals" (*morales libellos*) Giovio refers to the *De pulchro et amore* (Rome: A. Blado, 1529), written in praise of Giovanna d'Aragona, or perhaps instead the *De re aulica ad Phausinam libri duo* (Naples: G. A. da Caneto, 1534), an etiquette book on

courtly decorum. *On the King and the Tyrant* is *De rege et tyranno* (Naples: E. Presenzani, 1526): his earlier, related work, *De regnandi peritia* (Naples: Caterina Mayr, 1523), was substantially lifted from Machiavelli's *Prince* (as yet unpublished). The work on divination is *De auguriis libri II* (Bologna: heirs of Girolamo Benedetti, 1531).

687. Palumbo, "Nifo," attributes his death to pulmonary angina.

688. On Alessandro's assassination by his cousin, Lorenzo ("Lorenzino") di Pierfrancesco de' Medici, on January 6, 1537, see Najemy (2006), 466.

689. On Florimonte (1484–1565), like Nifo a native of Sessa Aurunca, see Franco Pignatti, "Florimonte, Galeazzo," *DBI* 48 (1997); *EH*, 187.

690. The poem is in elegiac couplets.

691. The poem is in elegiac couplets.

692. *CE*, 1:415; Minonzio (2002), 2:558–60; *NMW*, 331.

693. Starting in 1509, Du Ruel served as personal physician to Francis I. Following his wife's death he took minor orders, and on December 12, 1526, he became a canon to the cathedral chapter of Notre Dame thanks to the patronage of François Poncher (d. 1532), who had become bishop of Paris in 1519, succeeding his father, Etienne, in that position. *CE*, 2:112.

694. Dioscorides, *De medicinali materia libri sex*, trans. Jean Ruel (Lyon: Balthazar Arnoullet, 1552).

695. *Veterinariae medicinae libri II*, trans. Jean Ruel (Paris: Simon de Colines, 1530). The text includes translations from a range of ancient authors, including several from Hippocrates and Theomnestus, which mostly concern equine medicine (hence Giovio's use of the term *mulomedicina*).

696. Giovio errs: Ruel translated not this work (which circulated widely in Ambrogio Leone's Latin translation) but instead another by the same author: Iohannes Actuarius, *De medicamentorum compositione* (Basel: Robert Winter, 1540).

697. *De natura stirpium* (Paris: S. de Colines, 1536).

698. This is Constantinus Africanus, an eleventh-century physician who had left Africa for Salerno and finally became a monk in the Benedictine

abbey at Monte Cassino. See Vera von Falkenhausen, "Costantino Africano," *DBI* 30 (1984). However, Giovio errs: Ruel did not translate this work.

699. Dionysius Coronius (Coroné, Corron, Charron) of Chartres: see *EH*, 132; *CE*, 1:343. He held the royal chair of Greek at Paris from about 1543 to 1551 and published or re-edited posthumously his friend Ruel's translations of Dioscorides and Actuarius. Giovio correctly identifies the translator of the books on agriculture as Janus Cornarius (ca. 1500–1558), originally Johann Hainpol (see *CE*, 1:339–40): *Constantini Caesaris Selectarum praeceptionum de agricultura libri viginti*, trans. Johann Hainpol (Venice: Jacopo da Borgofranco, 1538).

700. Francis I returned to Italy in the autumn of 1537, and the truce was signed on November 27. See Michael Mallett and Christine Shaw, *The Italian Wars, 1494–1559* (London: Routledge, 2014), 236–38.

701. The poem is in elegiac couplets. For its author see above, note 699.

702. On Tebaldeo see Matteo Largaiolli, "Tebaldi, Antonio," *DBI* 95 (2019); Giraldi, 17, 41, 57, 75, 337. Originally from Ferrara, Tebaldeo served as tutor to Isabella d'Este in Mantua and as secretary to Lucrezia Borgia. He went to Rome in 1513. For a critical edition of his works, see Tebaldeo, *Rime*, ed. Tania Basile and Jean-Jacques Marchand, 3 vols. in 5 (Modena: Panini, 1989–92). Largaiolli, "Tebaldi," corrects the birth year traditionally assigned to him from 1463 to 1462.

703. On Serafino Ciminelli (or, "Aquilano"), see Magda Vigilante, "Ciminelli, Serafino," *DBI* 25 (1981); Rowland, *Culture*, 92–105 and *passim*. On possible reasons for the inclusion here of Aldo Manuzio, see Minonzio's conjectures in *Elogi*, 278n2.

704. *Sic*. In fact, he died three days short of his seventy-fifth birthday.

705. A reference to Lannoy's truce of March 1527. See note 564 above.

706. Charles de Bourbon, commander of the army that sacked Rome, died in the initial assault, on May 6, 1527. Juan de Urbina, who had served as campmaster to Giovio's friend Alfonso d'Avalos, marquis of Vasto, died as he was reconnoitering the walls of Florence during the Imperial siege of the city in 1529. Philibert de Chalon, the prince of Or-

ange, died while leading the Imperial troops in that siege, in the Battle of Gavinana on August 30, 1530. Hugo de Moncada, a Spanish captain, died in the Battle of Capo d'Orso against Filippino Doria: Giovio described Moncada's ignominious end in a famous letter to Clement VII (May 1, 1528), *IO*, 1:118–23, at 121.

707. See M. Mutini, "Bruno, Cola," *DBI* 14 (1972). The poem is in dactylic hexameter.

708. For a brief introduction to Erasmus, see *ER*, 2:284–90. New editions of his works in Latin and in English are at present being published in two series, respectively: *Opera Omnia* (Amsterdam: North-Holland Publishing Co., 1969–); and *Collected Works of Erasmus* (Toronto: University of Toronto Press, 1974–).

709. Erasmus had joined the Augustinian canons. Although he did not renounce his vows, a papal dispensation enabled him to live outside the monastery. In 1495 he went to Paris to study theology, living in the Collège de Montaigu.

710. An advocate of eclectic imitation, Erasmus railed against Italian scholars, whom he viewed as mere apes of Cicero, stigmatizing them (particularly in *The Ciceronian*, 1528) not only as uncreative but also as paganizing. See Kenneth Gouwens, "Erasmus, Apes of Cicero, and Conceptual Blending," *Journal of the History of Ideas* 71 (2010): 523–45.

711. The phrase "Friburgo in pago sive, ut aliqui afferunt" was omitted in the 1577 edition, presumably because Erasmus is known to have died in Basel (see *ER*, 2:285).

712. Erasmus died on July 12, 1536. On July 25 an army of Emperor Charles V entered Provence, and it subsequently attacked Picardy. See Pastor, 11:258.

713. The poem is in elegiac couplets.

714. The poem is an elegiac couplet.

715. Giuliano Marchetto, "Rutilio, Bernardino," *DBI* 89 (2017); *EH*, 374.

716. Vicenza came under Venetian rule in the year of Rutilio's birth.

717. *Iurisconsultorum vitae* (Rome: Antonio Blado, 1536), dedicated to Cardinal Ridolfi. Pirated editions soon appeared in Lyon (1538), Strassburg

(1538), and Basel (1539). The work comprises seventy-seven brief biographies that appear in chronological order, from Papirius Maius (during the reign of Tarquinius Superbus) to the Byzantine jurist Tribonian (d. 542). Probably in April 1536 Rutilio delivered three orations to Emperor Charles V: *Pro pontifice romano ad quintum Carolum imperatorem orationes tres* (Rome: Antonio Blado, 1536).

718. The poem is an elegiac couplet.

719. On Bartolomeo Crotti of Reggio Emilia, see *NMW*, 245, 669n68. The poem is an elegiac couplet.

720. The poem is in elegiac couplets.

721. Cf. Horace, *Odes* 3.30.

722. The goddess of funerals.

723. On Budé see *CE*, 1:212–17; *ER*, 1:313–14; *FH*, 1:41–96; Marie-Madeleine de La Garanderie and Luigi-Alberto Sanchi, *Guillaume Budé, philosophe de la culture* (Paris: Classiques Garnier, 2010).

724. Budé, *De asse et partibus eius* (Paris: Josse Bade, 1514); idem, *Summaire et épitome du livre* De asse, ed. Marie-Madeleine de La Garanderie and Luigi-Alberto Sanchi (Paris: Belles Lettres, 2008). See John M. Headley, "The Problem of Counsel Revisited Once More: Budé's *De asse* (1515) and *Utopia I* (1516) in Defining a Political Moment," in *Humanism & Creativity*, 141–68. Budé, *Annotationes . . . in quatuor et viginti Pandectarum libros* (Paris: Josse Bade, 1508); and evidently the *Commentarii linguae graecae* (Paris: Josse Bade, 1529), reprinted in Cologne in 1530; an enlarged edition appeared in 1548.

725. In 1522 Francis I made Budé *maître des requêtes* in the royal household, a post he held for the rest of his life.

726. On the emperor's reception in major cities on his trip across France, see Karl Brandi, *The Emperor Charles V: The Growth and Destiny of a Man and of a World-Empire*, trans. C. V. Wedgwood (Atlantic Highlands, NJ: Humanities Press, 1980), 424–25.

727. The poem is in phalaecean hendecasyllables.

728. Jean Salmon of Loudun (1490–1557), called "Macrin" (Maigret, Macrinus). See *CE*, 3:189. The poem is in elegiac couplets.

729. Giuseppe Alberigo, "Aleandro, Girolamo," *DBI* 2 (1960); *EH*, 29; *CE*, 1:28–32. In *NMW*, 257, Giovio praised his voluminous reading and exceptional memory but faulted him for lack of productivity: "I've been unable to wrest anything from him; and Giberti himself, even with daily reproaches, has never gotten even so much as incidental notations out of him, even though he'd conferred on him personally and with inexhaustible generosity the post of Vatican librarian, riches, diplomatic missions, and most recently the archbishopric of Brindisi."

730. The sexual overtone is intended: Giovio was wont to refer to unproductive scholars as "eunuchs." See Kenneth Gouwens, "Meanings of Masculinity in Paolo Giovio's 'Ischian' Dialogues," *I Tatti Studies in the Italian Renaissance* 17 (2014): 79–102.

731. When he became rector in 1513, Aleandro was the first Italian to hold that position since Marsilio of Padua two centuries before.

732. Aleandro went to Rome in March 1516 as emissary to the papal curia of Erard de la Marck, bishop of Liège. On December 2, 1517, through the intervention of Alberto Pio, he moved to the service of Cardinal Giulio de' Medici. He was dispatched to Germany in the summer of 1520 to implement the papal bull that excommunicated Luther (*Exsurge Domine*), and in 1521 he helped formulate the Edict of Worms.

733. Clement made Aleandro archbishop of Brindisi in 1524. Paul III created him cardinal *in pectore* in 1536; the promotion was published in 1538.

734. That is, before his sixty-third year. See *OLD*, s.v. climacter.

735. The poem is an elegiac couplet.

736. The poem is in elegiac couplets.

737. The Greek lyric poet Stesichorus (ca. seventh–sixth century BCE).

738. Stefano Benedetti, "Lampridio, Giovanni Benedetto," *DBI* 63 (2004); Giraldi, 87. Lampridio was in Rome by 1515. Pope Leo founded the Greek College in 1516, and Lampridio taught there alongside Musurus and Lascaris. While in Rome he was active in the literary gatherings in Colocci's gardens and at the villa of Pietro and Celso Mellini on Monte Mario.

739. He had entered the service of the abbot Lorenzo Bartolini, and by late 1526 they had settled in Padua.

740. Among positions he declined was the chair in Greek and Latin at the University of Padua, for which Bembo and Leonico Tomeo nominated him around 1530.

741. Perhaps because of Bartolini's death, he left Padua in early 1536, and by March 27 was ensconced in Mantua, where Federico II Gonzaga employed him as tutor to his son Francesco.

742. *Carmina*, ed. Ludovico Dolce (Venice: Giolito, 1550), includes twenty-four of Lampridio's odes in the meter of Pindar. On his imitation of Pindar in odes to political leaders including Francesco Sforza, Henry VIII of England, and Pope Leo X, see Stella P. Revard, *Politics, Poetics, and the Pindaric Ode: 1450–1700* (Tempe: Arizona Center for Medieval and Renaissance Studies, 2009), 24–29.

743. Horace, *Sermones* 1.10.31–35. Cf. Giraldi, 87, who notes that Lampridio "wrote Greek verse, and certainly deserves to be commended for this daring enterprise, which Horace warns us against undertaking."

744. The poem is in dactylic hexameter.

745. See Vergil, *Eclogues* 9.28.

746. The poem is in dactylic hexameter. According to Benedetti, "Lampridio," it is inscribed on his tomb in the Church of Sant' Andrea in Mantua.

747. The poem is in elegiac couplets.

748. L. Varius Rufus, an Augustan tragedian and epic poet.

749. Gigliola Fragnito, "Contarini, Gasparo," *DBI* 28 (1983); *DLI*, 57–58; *CE*, 1:334–35; *ER*, 2:77–79; Fragnito, *Gasparo Contarini: Un magistrato veneziano al servizio della cristianità* (Florence: L. S. Olschki, 1988); Elisabeth G. Gleason, *Gasparo Contarini: Venice, Rome, and Reform* (Berkeley and Los Angeles: University of California Press, 1993).

750. Contarini's first such position was as ambassador to Charles V in 1521. On his career as a Venetian diplomat, see Gleason, *Gasparo Contarini*, 29–62.

751. Contarini's *Tractatus de immortalitate animae* first appeared anonymously, published with Pomponazzi's *Apologia* (Bologna: Giustiniano da Rubiera, 1518), which followed upon the latter's controversial *De immortalitate animae* (1516). Subsequently, the *Tractatus* would comprise Book One of Contarini's self-standing publication, *De immortalitate animae libri duo*. See Gleason, *Gasparo Contarini*, 76–82.

752. Contarini, *The Office of a Bishop* = *De officio viri boni et probi episcopi*, ed. and trans. John Patrick Donnelly (Milwaukee: Marquette University Press, 2002); the work was originally published in 1517.

753. *The Republic of Venice: De magistratibus et Republica Venetorum*, ed. Filippo Sabetti, trans. Giuseppe Pezzini with Amanda Murphy (Toronto: University of Toronto Press, 2020); the work was originally published in 1543.

754. A reference to Contarini's service as papal legate at the Colloquy of Regensburg in 1541. See Gleason, *Gasparo Contarini*, 186–256.

755. Paul appointed Contarini legate to Bologna on January 27, 1542.

756. He died in Bologna on August 24, 1542.

757. A Benedictine church in Bologna (ca. 304 CE, under Diocletian, St. Proculus was martyred in the city). In 1563 his body was moved to the family chapel in the Church of the Madonna dell'Orto in Venice.

758. The poem is in elegiac couplets.

759. The poem is in iambic trimeter.

760. The poem is in dactylic hexameter.

761. On Henricus Cornelius Agrippa of Nettesheim, see *EH*, 24; *CE*, 1:17–19; *ER*, 1:24–26; Charles G. Nauert, *Agrippa and the Crisis of Renaissance Thought* (Urbana: University of Illinois Press, 1965); Michael H. Keefer, "Agrippa's Dilemma: Hermetic 'Rebirth' and the Ambivalences of *De vanitate* and *De occulta philosophia*," *Renaissance Quarterly* 41 (1988): 614–53; and Chris Miles, "Occult Retraction: Cornelius Agrippa and the Paradox of Magical Language," *Rhetoric Society Quarterly* 38 (2008): 433–56. On this *elogium* in particular, see Minonzio (2002), 2:560–68, who situates it with respect to both the occult tradition and the thought of Erasmus.

762. The first of these is Agrippa, *De incertitudine et vanitate scientiarum atque artium declamatio* (Antwerp: Joannes Grapheus, 1530), written in 1526. According to Nauert, *ER*, 1:25, "Here Agrippa denounces every human art and science as useless, even harmful, attacking not only the scholastic theologians and worldly clergy but also the learned fields of law, medicine, grammar, and natural philosophy, the practical and mechanical arts, and even the occult sciences, to which he had devoted his scholarly career. Although the work has often been classed as a social satire or a mere literary exercise, it does show some familiarity with ancient skepticism; and at the end he adopts a vaguely 'evangelical' (Protestant) tone, declaring that there is no secure knowledge except for simple faith in scripture." The second is Agrippa, *De occulta philosophia libri tres*, ed. Vittoria Perrone Compagni (Leiden: Brill, 1992). Its initial book appeared in print in 1531; the entirety, in 1533. On its relationship to *De vanitate*, see Minonzio (2002), 2:565–66. Nauert, *Agrippa and the Crisis*, 112, provides details on the brief suppression of *De occulta philosophia*: "The work of printing was under way before the middle of November, 1532; but shortly before Christmas, the Dominican inquisitor, Conrad Colyn of Ulm, denounced Agrippa's book as suspect of heresy and unfit to be printed. The senate or council of the city of Cologne forced the printer, Soter, to suspend work; and it impounded the quaternions already completed." By the following summer, however, Agrippa's "efforts to have the Archbishop permit publication were successful" (ibid., 112–13). Ibid., 209–10, details Agrippa's substantial recantation, which appeared as an appendix to an edition of *De occulta philosophia* printed in 1533. Hermann von Wied, the archbishop who intervened on Agrippa's behalf, would subsequently convert to Protestantism. See also *CE*, 3:444–46. *De occulta philosophia* was put on the index in Leuven in 1546, the year that the *editio princeps* of the *Elogia* appeared, and so probably too late for Giovio to intend it here (the passage regarding censorship was already present in the surviving manuscript draft). The *De vanitate* had already made it onto the index that was promulgated in Leuven in 1544. For official condemnations of Agrippa's works, see J. M. De Bujanda, with the assistance of René Davignon, Ela Stanek, and Marcella Richter, *Thesaurus de littérature interdite au XVI* siècle: Auteurs, ouvrages, éditions avec addenda*

*et corrigenda; Index des Livres Interdits* 10 (Sherbrooke, Canada: Centre d'Etudes de la Renaissance; and Geneva: Librairie Droz, 1996), 53–54.

763. See Paola Zambelli, "Magical and Radical Reformation in Agrippa of Nettesheim," *Journal of the Warburg and Courtauld Institutes* 39 (1976): 69–103.

764. Seemingly a reference to animals serving as witches' "familiars."

765. At *ER*, 1:25–26, Nauert writes: "the diabolical black poodle that comes to claim Faust's soul [in the literary tales of Dr. Faustus] is certainly Agrippan; and Agrippa's pupil Johannes Wier explained in vain that the origin of this ridiculous legend was Agrippa's ownership of two poodles, one black and one white, whom he named Monsieur and Mademoiselle." See also Nauert, *Agrippa and the Crisis*, 113–14, for a measured account of the humanist's waning years.

766. See Pietro Giulio Riga, "Possevino, Giovan Battista," *DBI* 85 (2016). The poem is in elegiac couplets.

767. Giovan Battista (or, Giambattista) Pio of Bologna. See Daniele Conti, "Pio, Giovanni Battista," *DBI* 84 (2015). The sharp criticisms of Pio in *NMW*, 327–29, anticipate those in this *elogium*.

768. Filippo Beroaldo the Elder's commentary on Apuleius was the first produced in the Renaissance. On the "Apuleianism" of Beroaldo and Pio, see John F. D'Amico, "The Progress of Renaissance Latin Prose: The Case of Apuleianism," *RQ* (1984): 361–63, 365–68, and *passim*. The writers mentioned are the grammarian Fabius Panciades Fulgentius (fifth–sixth century CE) and Sidonius Apollinaris (ca. 430–489).

769. Pre-Roman peoples on the Italian peninsula.

770. Tommaso "Fedra" Inghirami.

771. On the ceremony in which Giuliano de' Medici was given Roman citizenship, see Anthony M. Cummings, *The Politicized Muse: Music for Medici Festivals, 1512–1537* (Princeton: Princeton University Press, 1992), 53–66.

772. The public office he held was an appointment to the University of Rome (by Paul III, in 1534).

773. Probo, who had taught school in Rieti, became tutor to the children (notably, Angelo) of the wealthy and influential Roman nobleman Domenico de' Massimi. Known for his distinctive attire, Probo was also said to have attempted unsuccessfully to "cure" himself of being left-handed. See Pio Pecchiai, *Roma nel Cinquecento* (Bologna: Cappelli, 1948), 332, 463.

774. The poem is an elegiac couplet.

775. The poem is in elegiac couplets.

776. José Ruysschaert, "Arsilli, Francesco," *DBI* 4 (1962); *NMW,* 249; and Giraldi, 165, whose appraisal of him dovetails with Giovio's: "At Rome I also knew Francesco Arsilli of Sinigaglia, who taught at the same time medicine and poetry. His elegy on the poets of Rome of his time is still read, as are his Hippocratic propositions [*proloquia*], written in very appropriate verse. He was an honest man and had no time for the atmosphere of the court; consequently he was not at all held in high regard."

777. Perhaps invoking Horace, *Epodes* 2.7–8: "forumque vitat et superba civium potentiorum limina" (he avoids the forum and the proud portals of powerful citizens).

778. According to Ruysschaert, "Arsilli," the poet's two books of medical *Praedictiones* were a rather free reworking of the first nineteen *Pronostica* of Hippocrates. The book on Roman humanists, *De poetis Urbanis,* was first published as an appendix to the gathering of poems named *Coryciana* (in Goritz's honor), ed. Blosio Palladio (1524). See *Coryciana,* 344–64. He and Giovio were colleagues (*sodales*) in the informal Roman academies of Angelo Colocci and Johannes Goritz.

779. Goritz held the post of *receptor supplicationum* in the papal curia.

780. This is the sculpture of St. Anne with the Virgin Mary and the Christ Child, by Andrea Sansovino, commissioned by Goritz (St. Anne was his patron saint). See Virginia Anne Bonito, "The Saint Anne Altar in Sant' Agostino: A New Discovery," *The Burlington Magazine* 122 (1980): 805–12; Bonito, "The Saint Anne Altar in Sant' Agostino: Restoration and Interpretation," *The Burlington Magazine* 124 (1982): 268–76; Julia Haig Gaisser, "The Rise and Fall of Goritz's Feasts," *Renaissance Quarterly*

48 (1995): 41–57; and *eadem*, "Poets at the St. Anne Altar: Self-reflection in the Coryciana" (forthcoming). Each year on July 26, the Feast of St. Anne, Goritz and his sodality gathered at this altar, to which they affixed poems celebrating the occasion. The festivities extended to Goritz's *vigna*, where humanists read poems aloud and posted them on trees.

781. The poem is in elegiac couplets.

782. A certain Pirmilla of Senigallia figures as his beloved in two unpublished poetry collections: *Pirmilleidos libri III* and *Amorum libri III*.

783. The poem's odd lines are in iambic trimeter; the even, in iambic dimeter.

784. Franco Pignatti, "Molza, Francesco Maria," *DBI* 75 (2011); *idem*, "Francesco Maria Molza e la scrittura epistolare," in *Scrivere lettere nel Cinquecento: Corrispondenze in prosa e in versi*, ed. Laura Fortini, Giuseppe Izzi, and Concetta Ranieri (Rome: Edizioni di Storia e Letteratura, 2016), 127–53; Jean Balsamo, with Franco Tomasi, *Poètes italiens de la Renaissance dans la bibliothèque de la Fondation Barbier-Mueller: de Dante à Chiabrera: catalogue*, 2 vols. (Geneva: Droz, 2007), 1:503–5; Berni, *ad indicem*. In *NMW*, 227, Giovio wrote: "Francesco Maria Molza of Modena, a poet of learning, sophistication, and gentleness, excels in the most charming Latin elegies, and especially in Tuscan rhymes; the gentler, most obliging Muses have taken him to their bosom as one whom cruel passion has often reduced to ruin and exile. He celebrates his beloved Furnia's hair in Latin verses so tender, in his Tuscan love poetry displays so much distinction, and in his humorous tales, delightfully composed after the manner of Boccaccio, provokes so much laughter, that in his utterly gentle nature you don't feel the need of the seriousness characteristic of a supreme poet." From an old noble family in Modena, Molza studied in Bologna before going to Rome, initially at the court of Julius II. He spent three decades in the city supported by a variety of patrons, and in the late 1530s he and Giovio would both take part in the Accademia della Virtù that Claudio Tolomei established there in 1535. See A. Moroncini, "The Accademia della Virtù and Religious Dissent," in *The Italian Academies 1525–1700: Networks of Culture, Innovation, and Dissent*, ed. Jane E. Everson, Denis V. Reidy, and Lisa Sampson (Cambridge: Le-

genda, 2016), 88–101. Giraldi, 95, writes of him with expectation of his future success: "For after his work in the vernacular, in which he has given sure proof of his erudition, to his knowledge of Latin Francesco is adding Greek and Hebrew; although he seems to be too much enthralled with love of women, he should be counted among the finest of talents."

785. Pignatti, "Molza," dates to summer 1534 the Latin oration against Lorenzino de' Medici (1513–48). Lorenzino's motivations for mutilating statues on the Arch of Constantine and elsewhere in Rome remain unclear, but by doing so he elicited a public outcry and Pope Clement's wrath.

786. It was Lorenzino who plotted the murder of Alessandro de' Medici, in the bed of one of his mistresses, on January 6, 1537.

787. The poem, by Molza's good friend Trifone Benci, is an elegiac couplet.

788. The poem is an elegiac couplet. On Franchino di Cosenza, see note 76 above.

789. The poem is in elegiac couplets.

790. CE, 3:84–85. Antonie Vos, "Pigge and Calvin on the Will of God," in *The Doctrine of Election in Reformed Perspective: Historical and Theological Investigations of the Synod of Dordt 1618–1619*, ed. Frank van der Pol (Göttingen: Vanderhoeck et Ruprecht, 2019), 65–94.

791. Pigge, *Hierarchiae ecclesiasticae assertio* (Cologne: Melchior of Neuss, 1538).

792. The poem is in phalaecean hendecasyllables.

793. Simona Foà, "Giovio, Benedetto," *DBI* 56 (2001); Zimmermann (1995), 4 and *passim*.

794. The first of these is Benedetto Giovio, *Historiae patriae libri duo: Storia di Como dalle origini al 1532* (Como: New Press, 1982; anastatic repr. of 1887 ed.). Cochrane, 260–61, notes its exquisitely narrow focus on the local, to the near exclusion even of major events not bearing directly on Como. Thus the French invasion of Italy in 1494 by Charles VIII is "mentioned only as background for the siege of nearby Novara." The second is evidently the *Balci descriptio Helvetiae*, published under the title

*De antiquitate, de moribus et terra Svitensium* . . . *opusculum perbreve* in *Quellen zur schweizer Geschichte*, ed. August Bernoulli (Basel: F. Schneider, 1884), vol. 6. On its attribution to Benedetto, see *Elogi*, 311n3.

795. The poem is in elegiac couplets.

796. The poem is in phalaecean hendecasyllables. The author is presumably the poet Giovanni Antonio Serone, several of whose letters survive in Milan, Biblioteca Ambrosiana, MS H 175 inf., fols. 8r–9v, 22r–26v.

797. On Maffeo Vegio see *EH*, 419; Giraldi, 43, 341–42; Vegio, *Short Epics*, trans. Michael C. J. Putnam, ITRL 15 (Cambridge, MA: Harvard University Press, 2004); Luigi Raffaele, *Maffeo Vegio: Elenco delle opere; scritti inediti* (Bologna: N. Zanichelli, 1909); and, on his *Palinurus*, see Elizabeth McCahill, *Reviving the Eternal City: Rome and the Papal Court, 1420–1447* (Cambridge, MA: Harvard University Press, 2013), 63–65. Vegio composed his Book 13 as an appendix to the *Aeneid* when he was twenty-one. It was often included in early printed editions of Vergil. Having studied law and literature in Pavia, Vegio taught there for around a decade before moving to Rome.

798. Vegio joined the papal Curia, not under Martin V (pope, 1417–31), as Giovio supposes, but under Eugenius IV (pope, 1431–47) in 1436, serving initially as an abbreviator and later as *datarius* (apostolic datary), the head of the chief institution controlling the selling of ecclesiastical offices.

799. Vegio, *Disceptio inter terram, solem et aurum* (Milan: Guillerme Le Signerre, 1497).

800. The poem is in phalaecean hendecasyllables. Jacopo Guidi (1514–88) of Volterra served as a secretary in the court of Duke Cosimo I de' Medici. In a letter to Cosimo's majordomo Pier Francesco Riccio (September 16, 1549), Guidi praised Giovio's skills as a conversationalist: see Zimmermann (1995), 229.

801. On this elogium see Minonzio (2002), 2:571–73. See also *Giovanni Tortelli, primo bibliotecario della Vaticana: miscellanea di studi*, ed. Antonio Manfredi, Clementina Marsico, and Mariangela Regoliosi (Vatican City: Biblioteca Apostolica Vaticana, 2016); and Mariangela Regoliosi, "Grego-

rio Tifernate tra Lorenzo Valla e Giovanni Tortelli," in *Gregorio e Lilio: Due Tifernati protagonisti dell'Umanesimo italiano*, ed. John Butcher, Andrea Czortek, and Matteo Martelli (Sansepolcro: Centro Studi "Mario Pancrazi," 2017), 159–70. After studying under Vittorino da Feltre, Tortelli obtained a degree in medicine at Bologna in 1433.

802. Seemingly a reference to his service as the pope's librarian. See Girolamo Mancini, "Giovanni Tortelli, cooperatore di Niccolò V nel fondare la Biblioteca Vaticana," *Archivio Storico Italiano* 78 (1920): 161–282.

803. Tortelli, *De orthographia* (Rome: Ulrich Han and Simon Nicolai Chardella, 1471; Venice: Nicholas Jenson, 1471). The manuscript had been presented to Nicholas V around 1450. See Paola Tomè, "Metodo compilativo e stratificazione delle fonti nell'*Orthographia* di Giovanni Tortelli," *Humanistica Lovaniensia* 63 (2014): 27–75; and Gemma Donati, *L'Orthographia di Giovanni Tortelli* (Messina: Centro interdipartimentale di studi umanistici, 2006).

804. See Athanasius of Alexandria, *Omnia opera*, ed. Giovanni Tortelli, Ambrogio Traversari, Angelo Poliziano, Johann Reuchlin, and Desiderius Erasmus (Cologne: Eucharius Cervicornus, 1532).

805. Twenty letters between them appear in Lorenzo Valla, *Correspondence*, ed. and trans. Brendan Cook, ITRL 60 (Cambridge, MA: Harvard University Press, 2013). On their close relationship and Valla's influence upon Tortelli's *De orthographia*, see Mariangela Regoliosi, "Ritratto di Giovanni Tortelli Aretino," in *Giovanni Tortelli, primo bibliotecario*, 17–57, at 36–41; and for Valla's influence on the *De orthographia*, see ibid., 41–54.

806. Paolo Viti, "Facio, Bartolomeo," *DBI* 44 (1994); *EH*, 178.

807. Facio, *De bello Veneto Clodiano liber* (Lyon: Gaspard à Portonariis, 1568). Dedicated to Gian Giacomo Spinola, a humanistically inclined Genoese merchant who had been his student, this poem of over five thousand verses treats the war between Genoa and Venice from 1377 to June 1380. On the relationship between Facio and Spinola, see David Rundle, "Humanism Across Europe: The Structures of Contacts," in *Humanism in Fifteenth-Century Europe*, ed. Stephen J. Milner et al., rev. ed. (Oxford: Society for the Study of Medieval Languages and Literature, 2016), 307–36, especially 328–29.

808. Facio, *De rebus gestis Alphonsi Aragonii regis libri VII, ad Caesarem Gonzagam* (Mantua: Filoterpse and Clidano Filoponi, 1536). The book was presented to Alfonso at the start of June 1457, the king being so delighted that he provided its author with a generous stipend.

809. The tensions between them had begun earlier: Valla had recommended against the publication of Facio's *De bello Veneto Clodiano*. Evidently at the urging of Panormita, Facio obtained the manuscript of Valla's history of the deeds of Alfonso's predecessor, King Ferdinand, which Valla had intended to follow with a life of Alfonso. With Panormita's assistance, Facio wrote his *Invective in Laurentium Vallam*. Beyond its attacks on Valla's Latin diction, stylistic choices, uses of history, and personal character, it includes Facio's defense against Valla's criticisms of his own *De vitae felicitate* (written in the second half of 1445). In 1447 Valla responded with *Antidotum in Facium*, ed. M. Regoliosi (Padua: Antenore, 1981).

810. Arrian, *De rebus gestis Alexandri regis*, trans. Bartolomeo Facio (Pisa: Gershom Soncino, 1508). He began this work in 1454 at the request of King Alfonso.

811. The poem is an elegiac couplet.

812. See Gino Pistilli, "Guarini, Guarino," *DBI* 60 (2003); *EH*, 223; *ER*, 3:97–99; and Grafton and Jardine, *From Humanism*, 1–28.

813. On the translations of Strabo's *Geography* and of Plutarch's *Lives*, see Pistilli, "Guarini." He did the former at the behest of Pope Nicholas V, sharing the responsibility of translation with Tifernate, and dedicating the completed text in 1458 to his new patron, the Venetian patrician Giacomo Antonio Marcello. Guarino's translations from Plutarch first appeared together with translations by other humanists in Plutarch, *Vitae parallelae* (1470?), cited in full in note 89 above.

814. On Vergerio see *EH*, 421; *ER*, 6:242–44; John M. McManamon, *Pierpaolo Vergerio the Elder (ca. 1369–1444): The Humanist as Orator* (Tempe: MRTS, 1996). See also idem, *Pierpaolo Vergerio the Elder and Saint Jerome: An Edition and Translation of* Sermones pro Sancto Hieronymo (Tempe: MRTS, 1999). Capodistria, a small town on the Gulf of Trieste, was under Venetian rule (the city that grew from it is now in Slovenia).

815. Vergerio, *De ingenuis moribus et liberalibus adulescentiae studiis liber*, in *Humanist Educational Treatises*, ed. and trans. Craig W. Kallendorf, ITRL 29 (Cambridge, MA: Harvard University Press, 2002), 2–91. The work was written in 1402–3 and dedicated to Ubertino da Carrara, son of Francesco "il Novello" da Carrara, *signore* of Padua. According to Zimmermann (1995), 5–6, "Traces of Vergerio's influence can be found throughout Giovio's life and works — in his insistence that learning should not merely inform but civilize; in his preference for comeliness of manners, morals, and persons; in his Ciceronian conception of history; in his admiration of *virtù*; in his lifelong cult of fame and glory, and his strong sense of the interdependence of heroes and historians; and, finally, in his hard work and somewhat old-fashioned morality. . . ." On Vergerio's approach to history, see also Cochrane, 71–72 and *passim*.

816. See Cecil Grayson, "Bracelli, Giacomo," *DBI* 13 (1971).

817. On the Ligurians see Cicero, *De lege agraria* 2.95.

818. This is *On the Spanish War* (*De bello hispaniensi libri V*), published posthumously. In composing it Bracelli drew upon both his own diplomatic experience and documents to which he had access in the chancellery. The work includes a celebration of the Genoese victory in the Battle of Ponza (1435), in which they captured King Alfonso the Magnanimous (Alfonso V of Aragon, Sicily, and Sardinia, 1416–58; Alfonso I of Naples, 1442–58).

819. On Giorgio Valla see *EH*, 416; *DLI*, 123, 328–29. An avid collector of Greek manuscripts, he translated Greek philosophical and scientific texts into Latin. After teaching rhetoric in several northern Italian cities, thanks to the support of Ermolao Barbaro in 1485 he obtained a post at the Scuola di San Marco in Venice. In 1496, suspecting him of involvement with Gian Giacomo Trivulzio's opposition to Ludovico "il Moro" Sforza in Milan, the Venetians imprisoned him for several months. Thereafter, he returned to teaching.

820. This is his encyclopedic miscellany, *De expetendis et fugiendis rebus opus*, ed. Giovanni Pietro Valla (Venice: Aldo Manuzio, 1501).

821. See Maria Nadia Covini, "Simonetta, Giovanni," *DBI* 92 (2018); Simonetta (2004), especially 90–93, 120–25.

822. *Rerum gestarum Francisci Sfortiae commentarii*, ed. G. Soranzo in *Rerum italicarum scriptores*, ed. L. I. Muratori, vol. 21 (Milan: ex tipographia Societatis Palatinae, 1732), cols. 167–782. See Cochrane, 113–17; Ianziti, 211–31; Simonetta (2004), 90–93, 120–25.

823. Giovanni Simonetta, *Commentarii rerum gestarum Francisci Sfortiae*, trans. Cristoforo Landino (Milan: Antonio Zarotto, 1490).

824. Cicco (properly, "Francesco") Simonetta (1410–80) was born in Calabria. In 1444 he became chancellor of Milan under Francesco Sforza (duke, 1450–66), and he later served as a secretary to Galeazzo Maria Sforza (duke, 1466–76). On his career see Maria Nadia Covini, "Simonetta, Cicco," *DBI* 92 (2018); and Simonetta (2004), especially 127–70, 223.

825. That is, Galeazzo Maria Sforza.

826. The assassinated father is Galeazzo Maria Sforza; the son, Giangaleazzo Sforza (1469–94). Although technically the latter was duke of Milan from 1476 to 1494, the duchy was effectively under the control first of his mother, Bona of Savoy (1449–1503), and then of his uncle, Ludovico "the Moor" (*il Moro*) Sforza (1452–1508), who officially became duke upon Giangaleazzo's death. See *ER*, 4:137–40.

827. That is, Francesco Sforza.

828. Gino Pistilli, "Giustinian, Bernardo," *DBI* 57 (2001); *EH*, 209; Cochrane, 80–81; King, 381–83 and *passim*; and Patricia H. Labalme, *Bernardo Giustiniani: A Venetian of the Quattrocento* (Rome: Edizioni di Storia e Letteratura, 1969). Bernardo Giustinian entered the Great Council of Venice in 1427. Among his teachers were Francesco Filelfo, Guarino Guarini, and George of Trebizond.

829. This history was published posthumously: *De origine urbis Venetiarum rebusque eius ab ipsa ad quadringentesimum usque annum gestis historia, libri XV* (Venice: B. Benali, [1492]). Its terminus ad quem is the dogeship of Agnello Particiaco (810/11–827).

830. Leonardo Giustinian (ca. 1389–1446), Bernardo's father, served on the Venetian Council of the Ten. In 1443 he became its head, and also a procurator of San Marco. He translated Plutarch into Latin, in which

language he wrote extensively in a range of genres, including funeral oratory, letters, and poetry. See *EH*, 209; King, 383–85 and *passim*; Cochrane, 80.

831. Carla Frova, "Persona, Cristoforo," *DBI* 82 (2015); *EH*, 343–44.

832. Giovio here refers to the dedicatory letter included in Leonardo Bruni, *De bello Italico adversus Gothos* (Venice: Nicholas Jenson, 1471). See Alfred A. Strnad and Katherine Walsh, "Cesarini, Giuliano," *DBI* 24 (1980). This Cardinal Giuliano Cesarini (1398–1444), who played a prominent role in the Council of Basel, was killed by the Ottoman sultan Murad II at the Battle of Varna in 1444. By providing this detail, Giovio distinguishes him from his eponymous grand-nephew, also a cardinal (Giuliano Cesarini, 1466–1510). For an account of the whole episode that is more sympathetic to Bruni's claim of authorship than either Persona or Giovio, see Gary Ianziti, *Writing History in Renaissance Italy: Leonardo Bruni and the Uses of the Past* (Cambridge, MA: Harvard University Press, 2012), 278–300.

833. On Tifernate see *EH*, 404; *CE*, 3:326 (s.n. Tiphernas, Gregorius); *Gregorio e Lilio: Due Tifernati*; Girolamo Mancini, "Gregorio Tifernate," *Archivio storico italiano* 81 (1923): 65–112; King, *passim*; and on this *elogium*, Minonzio (2002), 2:575–78. Tifernate was also known as Gregorio da Città di Castello. A student of George Gemistus Pletho, he taught Greek and medicine in Italy and France. In the *editio princeps* of the *Elogia* (1546), the title of the *elogium* incorrectly reads "Georgii Tiphernatis" rather than "Gregorii Tiphernatis." Giovio refers here to his Latin translation of Books 11 to 17 of Strabo's *Geography*, printed along with Guarino's translation of the first ten books, in Strabo, *De situ orbis* (Venice: Filippo Pincio, 1510).

834. This is the prominent Roman humanist Raffaele Maffei. See Stefano Benedetti, "Maffei, Raffaele," *DBI* 67 (2006); *EH*, 283; *CE*, 2:366–67; and D'Amico, especially 189–211. Giovio here refers to Maffei's encyclopedic *Commentariorum Urbanorum libri octo et triginta* (1506), which he dedicated to Julius II. He claimed that in writing it he drew upon a thousand books in Greek and Latin. See Cochrane, 49–50; D'Amico, 84 and *passim*.

835. Evidently a reference to Maffei's *Brief History of Julius II and Leo X*, analyzed in John F. D'Amico, "Papal History and Curial Reform in the Renaissance: Raffaele Maffei's *Brevis Historia* of Julius II and Leo X," article VI in his *Roman and German Humanism, 1450–1550* (Aldershot: Ashgate, 1993), VI: 157–210, with edition of the text at 191–210. D'Amico notes that since Leo was alive at the time of its composition, Maffei "was necessarily tentative in his final evaluation of the pontificate" (ibid., 178). For example, in a section that he subsequently deleted, Maffei had criticized Leo for having spent in one year what it had taken Julius II a decade to accumulate: ibid., 179. Overall, D'Amico's judgment of Maffei's skills as a historian is far more positive than that of Giovio.

836. This is Antonio De Ferrariis, a member of Pontano's academy. See Angelo Romano, "De Ferrariis, Antonio," *DBI* 33 (1987); Kidwell (1991), 252–54, 286–87, 300–301, 310, 394n57, 403n179; and specifically on this *elogium*, Minonzio (2002), 2:578–82. De Ferariis got the name "Galateo" from his home town of Galatone, in Salento, in the southeastern Italian province of Lecce.

837. That is, Ermolao Barbaro the Younger (1453/54–92).

838. *Liber de situ Iapygiae* (Basel: Perna, 1558). "Iapygia" refers to the region of the heel of Italy inhabited by the ancient Iapygians. In a letter to Alberto Pio, Giovio wrote (echoing Polybius) that chorography is "the mirror necessary for whoever wishes to see and clarify the where, how, and when of events" (Zimmermann [1995], 66). On the distinction between chorography and chronicle, see Richard Helgerson, *Forms of Nationhood: The Elizabethan Writing of England* (Chicago: University of Chicago Press, 1992), 132.

839. On the commonalities of Galateo's *Della gotta* and Giovio's *De optima victus ratione*, see *Elogi*, 334n5. In *On Speech* (*De sermone*), Pontano uses De Ferrariis to exemplify *humanitas*, saying that "he brings the maximum pleasantness and charm to an encounter": Kidwell (1991), 287.

840. Franco Pignatti, "Ricchieri, Lodovico Maria," *DBI* 87 (2016); *EH*, 366; *CE*, 3:155. Born at Rovigo, Ricchieri (who Latinized his name as "Caelius Rhodiginus") studied philosophy under Niccolò Leoniceno in Ferrara, where he also met Celio Calcagnini. He taught Latin and Greek

initially in Rovigo and then in other locales, including Bologna, Vicenza, Ferrara, and Padua.

841. This is the *Antiquarum collectionum libri* (Venice: Aldo Manuzio, 1516), reprinted by Froben in Basel the following year.

842. Among the harsh critics of Ricchieri's book were Beatus Rhenanus and Erasmus, the latter of whom believed that the Rovigan humanist had lifted material from the *Adagia* without giving credit, and had botched some of it in the process. See *CE*, 3:155.

843. In 1515 Francis I of France, then in control of Milan, appointed him to the chair of Greek there. He returned to Rovigo in 1523.

844. On Lefèvre see *EH*, 268; *CE*, 2:315–18; *ER*, 3:396–97; *Elogi*, 336–37nn1–6. Giovio had praised his scholarship in passing in *NMW*, at 333.

845. Lefèvre taught for many years at the Collège du Cardinal Lemoine in Paris. By the early 1500s he was at the center of a circle of scholars, including Josse Clichtove, his future collaborator in editing and publishing ancient texts. Thanks to the patronage of Guillaume Briçonnet, abbot of Saint-Germain-des-Prés, by 1508 he was able to leave his college post to reside in that abbey. Thereafter, Lefèvre's writings focused increasingly on the need for scholarly contributions to religious and ecclesiastical reform. *CE*, 2:316–17.

846. *Faber ingeniorum* puns on the Latinization of "Lefèvre" as *Faber* (builder, artisan).

847. By "foreigners," Giovio evidently means non-Italians or transalpines.

848. For example, *Artificialis introductio per modum epitomatis in decem libros Ethicorum Aristotelis* . . . (Paris: Henri Estienne [the Elder], 1517).

849. As Henry Heller notes (*CE*, 2:318), by 1525 "Lefèvre was prepared to question the intrinsic spiritual authority of the priesthood, the efficacy of the sacraments apart from faith, the sacrificial character of the Eucharist, and the doctrine of the real presence. He rejected the practice of invoking the saints and the veneration of images. The contemporary forms of confession and extreme unction he held to be suspect on the basis of the Gospel." Starting with the *Quincuplex Psalterium* (Paris: Henri Estienne [the Elder], 1509), Lefèvre wrote extensively on Scripture, including com-

mentaries on the Pauline Epistles. The Paris theologian Noël Béda, one of Erasmus's fiercest critics, also wrote against Lefèvre repeatedly: see *CE*, 1:116–18. In October 1525 Lefèvre fled for safety to Strasbourg, but the following year he returned at the invitation of Francis I, whose children he tutored. He spent his final years (1530–36) in the court of Marguerite de Navarre.

850. Luca Addante, "Telesio, Antonio," *DBI* 95 (2019); Antonio Pagano, *Antonio Telesio: Memoria premiata dall'Accademia Pontaniana di Napoli nella tornata del 5 giugno 1921* (Naples: P. Federico and G. Ardia, 1922). For brief biographical sketches, see *RLV*, 224–26; Antonio Altamura, *L'Umanesimo nel mezzogiorno d'Italia: Storia, bibliografie e testi inediti* (Florence: Bibliopolis, 1941), 183–85; *EH*, 402.

851. These are, respectively, the *Lucerna*, the *Reticulum*, and the *Cicindela*. The first two are included in Telesio's *Poemata* (Rome: Calvo, 1524); the last is printed in with a posthumous edition of the *Libellus de coloribus*. Giovio had praised Telesio in passing in *NMW*, noting the beauty of his poem *On Crowns* and saying that he "composes verses so elegant and sweet that now and then I would rather read his *Mesh Purse* and *Crafted Pottery Oil-Lamp* and *Night-Flying Firefly* than the entire *Venetiad* of our [Publio Francesco] Modesti": *NMW*, 229. In *Modern Poets*, Lilio Gregorio Giraldi offered a less flattering assessment of Telesio's poetry: "It's compressed in its expression, but it's learned and not without grace; the style, to be sure, is rather crude and labored" (Giraldi, 93). Three quatrains by Telesio appear in *Coryciana*, 224–25.

852. Telesio, *Imber aureus tragoedia* (Venice: Bernardino Vitali, 1529); *De coronis libellus* (Rome: Calvo, 1525), which Giovio encouraged him to publish (see Zimmermann 1995, 310n27); and *Libellus de coloribus* (Paris: Wechel, 1529).

853. Related to these lectures is his book, *In odas Horatii Flacci auspicia ad iuventutem Romanam* (Rome: [Calvo], ca. 1527). Initially called the Studium Urbis, the University of Rome would subsequently become known as *La Sapienza*.

854. Gragg's rendering of this passage, "he obtained a benefice from Giberti, thus escaping the ruin of the capital" (Giovio [1935], 152), is also

consistent with the Latin, but Pagano (*Antonio Telesio*, 10–11) makes a compelling circumstantial case that Telesio left Rome only after the city was at least under attack if not occupied.

855. *Hybridam*, here rendered as "of mixed parentage," evidently refers to Alcionio being an unhappy product of marriage between residents of two different cities. It also establishes a parallel between the man and the "hybrid" quality of his prose (see below). Girolamo Negri corroborates that Alcionio kept his origins closely guarded: in a letter of June 22, 1525, he wrote to Marcantonio Michiel that Alcionio "is accustomed now and then to talk about his homeland in various ways, perhaps with this hope, that all the most famous cities of Italy might someday fight among themselves over him" (Kenneth Gouwens, "Ciceronianism and Collective Identity: Defining the Boundaries of the Roman Academy, 1525," in *Journal of Medieval and Renaissance Studies* 23:2 [Spring 1993]: 173–95, at 195; Latin at 192).

856. On Alcionio (1490s?–1528), see Gouwens, 31–72, 177–212; George Hugo Tucker, Homo Viator: *Itineraries of Exile, Displacement and Writing in Renaissance Europe* (Geneva, 2003), 153–94 (= pt. 3, chap. 1: "Writing on Exile: Petrus Alcyonius (1487–1528?), an Exile in the Republic of Letters"). For useful brief summaries (all of which, however, misdate his death to 1527), see Mario Rosa, "Alcionio, Pietro," *DBI* 2 (1960); *EH*, 28; and *CE*, 1:26–27. Giovio discussed Alcionio briefly, and unfavorably, in *NMW*, 327; and in his tract *On Fish*, published in 1526, he called him a "most-learned man" (*vir doctissimus*): *IO*, 9:50. For contemporaries' scathing appraisals of Alcionio's character, see Giraldi, 89; *DLI*, 179–81; and Berni, 183, 193.

857. A reference to Juvenal 5.2. Sixteenth-century literati debated the exact meaning of *quadra* in this passage. Cf. Erasmus's adage *Quadra propria* (v.i.59; no. 4060), which, according to John Grant and Betty I. Knott (*Collected Works of Erasmus* [Toronto: University of Toronto Press, 1974–], 36:576n), may be the Dutch humanist's own coinage based on Juvenal 5.2.

858. Alcionio had studied medicine. Giovio's "at the very edge of his bed" (*in lecti limine . . . ipso*) is a sarcastic allusion to Lucretius 2.960: "leti . . . limine ab ipso" (from the very threshold of death).

859. On Juan Ginés de Sepúlveda (ca. 1490–1573), see *EH*, 377–78; *CE*, 3:240–42. From humble origins in a town near Córdoba, he studied at the University of Alcalá (1510–13) and at Bologna (1515–23), where he worked with Pietro Pomponazzi. In the 1520s his patrons included Alberto Pio, prince of Carpi, and Giulio de' Medici (both when a cardinal and then as Pope Clement VII). In 1536 he became official chronicler and chaplain to Emperor Charles V. He is best known today neither for his histories nor for his extensive translations of Aristotle into Latin, but instead for his defense of the Spaniards' enslavement of the Indians of the New World, a position he justified on Aristotelian grounds in his *Democrates alter seu de justis belli causis* (1544). Only one copy of Sepúlveda's *Errata P. Alcyonii in interpretatione Aristotelis* (Bologna, 1522) is known to have survived. For analysis of its contents and of the ensuing feud, see Kenneth Gouwens and Christopher S. Celenza, "Humanist Culture and its Malcontents: Alcionio, Sepúlveda, and the Consequences of Translating Aristotle," in *Humanism & Creativity*, 347–80.

860. Both Christophe de Longueil and Girolamo Negri related versions of this anecdote. See Gouwens and Celenza, "Humanist Culture," 350–51.

861. Pietro Alcionio, *Medices legatus: de exsilio* (Venice: Aldus and Andrea Asolano, 1522). See Tucker, *Homo Viator*, 153–94. In the year following publication of the *Elogia*, Paolo Manuzio more explicitly made the accusation of plagiarism from Cicero, noting the disappearance of the *De gloria* from a monastic library to which (he says) Alcionio, in his capacity as a doctor, had enjoyed privileged access: Paolo Manuzio, *In epistolas Ciceronis ad Atticum Pauli Manutii commentarius* (Venice, 1547), fol. 446r–v. Although Giovio presents the theft as a fact, no modern commentator has found the story credible. It may be noteworthy, however, that according to Valeriano (*DLI*, 203), while in Castel Sant' Angelo during the Sack of Rome, Alcionio made off with four of Pietro Martelli's books on mathematics.

862. The orations to which Giovio refers are *A Declamation against Caesar's Letter* (*Declamatio in literas Caesaris*) and *On the Deliverance of the City* (*De Urbe servata*), a panegyric to Pompeo Colonna for having "saved" Rome. Before these, he had already penned at least two other orations on

the Sack of Rome. See Gouwens, 31–72, 179–212. Giovio's diction and phrasing imply that Alcionio's orations on the Sack of Rome, like his dialogue *On exile*, betrayed excessive borrowing from Cicero, only that here his thievery was perceived as less odious because it served a good cause. The locution *vehementissime invectus* continues the motif of excessive Ciceronianism, with Alcionio here imitating Cicero's *Philippics* against Mark Antony; and the phrase *summa perfecti oratoris eloquentia* invokes Cicero's *On the Orator*, e.g., 1.128: "among humankind, there is nothing harder to find than a perfect orator" (*nihil in hominum genere rarius perfecto oratore inveniri potest*).

863. Roberto Almagià, "Anghiera, Pietro Martire d'," *DBI* 3 (1961); Cochrane, 339–40.

864. Anghiera, *De orbe novo Petri Martyris ab Angleria Mediolanensis . . . decades* (Alcalá de Henares: Miguel d'Eguia, 1530). Anghiera went to Spain in 1486 in the retinue of Iñigo Lopez de Mendoza, count of Tendilla, who had served as Spanish ambassador in Rome. Subsequently, he was at times in the service of King Ferdinand II of Aragon.

865. This mission to al-Ashraf Kansu al Ghuri, the penultimate Mamluk sultan (r. 1501–16), took place near the start of his reign. Anghiera's account of the Mamluk dynasty is the so-called *Babylonian Legation*, printed in Anghiera, *De rebus oceanicis et novo orbe: decades tres; Item eiusdem De babylonica legatione libri III* (Cologne: Quentel and Calenius, 1574).

866. On the Mamluk knights, see David Ayalon, *The Mamluk Military Society* (London: Variorum Reprints, 1979); James Waterson, *The Knights of Islam: The Wars of the Mamluks* (London: Greenhill, 2007).

867. See Fausto Nicolini, "Altilio, Gabriele," *DBI* 2 (1960); and Pontano, *Actius*, in Pontano, *Dialogues*, 2:351.

868. Altilio's pupil is King Alfonso II of Naples's son Ferdinando d'Aragona (1469–96), who would be King Ferdinando II (or, "Ferrante II") in 1495–96. Altilio wrote the epithalamium for the wedding in 1488 of Isabella d'Aragona (the daughter of Alfonso II of Naples) to Gian Galeazzo Sforza (duke of Milan). Giraldi, 41, praised the eloquence and "marvelous and outstanding erudition" that Altilio displayed in the poem. Isabella is the sole woman Giovio featured in his portrait gallery: see *elo-*

*gium* 14 in Book 5 of *Elogia virorum bellica virtute illustrium*. The poem appeared posthumously, in an appendix to a 1528 edition of Sannazaro's *The Birth of the Virgin* (*De partu Virginis*).

869. Gragg and Minonzio read *in sacrata sacerdotii sede* as meaning that he died in his epicopal palace, but were that the case one would expect *palatio* or *episcopio* rather than *sede*. Pontano laments Altilio's death in *Tumuli* 1.18 and in *Aegidius*.

870. Giovanni Miccoli, "Adriani, Marcello Virgilio detto il Dioscoride," *DBI* 1 (1960); *EH*, 23; and Peter Godman, *From Poliziano to Machiavelli: Florentine Humanism in the High Renaissance* (Princeton: Princeton University Press, 1998), 180–234. Valeriano describes an equestrian accident that resulted in Virgilio having his tongue crushed, rendering him mute: *DLI*, 194–95.

871. This is *On Medical Material*, an encyclopedic pharmacopeia, written in Greek in the mid-first century CE: Dioscorides, *De medica materia libri sex*, trans. Marcello Virgilio (Florence: heirs of Filippo Giunta, 1523).

872. These are Dioscorides, *In Dioscoridem ab Hermolao Barbaro tralatum* . . . (Venice: Barberi, 1516; see Giovio's *elogium* of Barbaro, no. 36); and Dioscorides, *De medicinali materia libri quinque*, trans. Jean Ruel (Paris: Henri Etienne, 1516; see the *elogium* of Ruel, no. 93).

873. This is his *Oration on the Glories of the Military*, delivered at the ceremony where Lorenzo received the *bastone* (marshal's baton) that symbolized command of Florence's military: Virgilio, *De militiae laudibus oratio Florentiae dicta* (Basel: Froben, 1518). For analysis of this oration, using the text in the Biblioteca Riccardiana in Florence, see Godman, *From Poliziano to Machiavelli*, 242–44.

874. On Giano Parrasio (= Giovan Paolo Parisi, Aulo Giano Parrasio), see Fablo Stok, "Parisio, Giovan Paolo," *DBI* 81 (2014); *EH*, 335–36; Francesco D'Episcopo, *Aulo Giano Parrasio, fondatore dell'Accademia Cosentina* (Cosenza: Pellegrini, 1982).

875. During his sojourn in Milan at some point between 1501 and 1506, Giovio frequented the lectures of Parrasio on Latin and those of Chalcondyles on Greek. See Zimmermann (1995), 6. Parrasio married Chalcondyles's daughter Theodora in 1504.

876. This is Gian Giacomo Trivulzio (1441–1518), called "The Great." Giovio devotes an *elogium* to him in the volume on men of arms (bk. 4, no. 17). See also *NMW, ad indicem*.

877. Parrasio, *De rebus per epistolam quaesitis sylloge* (Geneva: Henri Etienne, 1567), is a collection of philological annotations presented in epistolary form.

878. In 1515 Parrasio began teaching at the Studium Urbis, an appointment that Leo X made upon the recommendation of Tommaso Fedra Inghirami and Janus Lascaris. On Basil Chalcondyles, see Peter Schreiner, "Calcondila, Basilio," *DBI* 16 (1973). On his sudden death in Rome in 1514, see the *elogium* of Demetrius Chalcondyles above (no. 29), and Valeriano's account in *DLI*, 172–73.

879. Valeriano provides a similar account of Parrasio's illness in *DLI*, 188–89.

880. On Georg Sauermann see *CE*, 3:197–98; *DLI*, 323–24. Originally from Silesia, he studied at the universities of Wittenberg and Leipzig before moving to Bologna, where, in 1514, he was promoted to doctor of civil and canon law.

881. The orations are Sauermann, *Ad Carolum Hispaniarum regem et Ferdinandum archiducem Austriae post obitum avi oratio* (1519); and *Hispaniae consolatio* (ca. 1520). The locution "totius academiae," which could be rendered in a general sense as "all the learned," seemingly refers to the humanist sodality (academy) of Johannes Goritz in Rome. Sauermann appears in an informal list of its members probably written by Giovio: see Federico Ubaldini, *Vita di Mons. Angelo Colocci*, ed. Vittorio Fanelli (Vatican City: BAV, 1969), 114–15. On Christophe de Longueil, see *elogium* 67 above.

882. In 1520 Charles V appointed Sauermann as his procurator at the papal curia.

883. In Valeriano's account of Sauermann's wretched demise, he was captured not by the Spaniards but by German troops: see *DLI*, 218–21.

884. Valerio Marchetti, "Calcagnini, Celio," *DBI* 16 (1973); *EH*, 92; *CE*, 1:242–43; *RLV*, 203–6; Giraldi, 77. *NMW*, 311, mentioned him favorably in passing. Marchetti identifies Celio's father as an apostolic protonotary

from a wealthy and distinguished family, and his mother as a certain Lucrezia Costantini.

885. In fact, Calcagnini served in the armies of the Este dukes and of Emperor Maximilian for around a decade (1496–1506) before being appointed to the chair in Greek and Latin at the University of Ferrara. In 1510 he became chancellor for the newly elevated Cardinal Ippolito d'Este (a son of Duke Ercole I). Giovio makes no mention of Calcagnini's distinction as a diplomat or of his having polemicized against Luther.

886. Giraldi, for his part, viewed Calcagnini's verse as affected: "For although he wishes to be thought of everywhere as quite learned, as indeed he is, he is actually to be criticized on account of this. The flowery adornments of all disciplines, inserted in their appropriate places, give sparkle to poems like shining jewels, but when they are crammed in everywhere, as in his verse, they somehow serve to cheapen the poems" (Giraldi, 77).

887. Calcagnini, *Epistolicarum quaestionum et epistolarum familiarium libri XVI*, in *Opera aliquot . . .* (Basel: Froben, 1544); Calcagnini, *Disquisitiones aliquot in libros Officiorum Ciceronis* (Basel: Robert Winter, 1538).

888. Marcantonio Maioragio, *Decisiones XXV. quibus M. Tullium Ciceronem ab omnibus Caelii Calcagnini criminationibus liberat* (Lyon: Sebastian Gryphius, 1544). On Maioragio's polemics against the arch-Ciceronian Mario Nizzoli, in which Calcagnini intervened, see Paolo Rossi, "La celebrazione della rettorica e la polemica antimetafisica nel *De principiis* di Mario Nizolio," in *La crisi dell'uso dogmatico della ragione*, ed. Antonio Banfi (Rome and Milan: Fratelli Bocca, 1953), 99–121, especially 103–8. On invocations and echoes of Cicero in Giovio's works, see "Paolo Giovio volgarizzatore del *De officiis* di Cicerone?" in Minonzio (2002), 1:185–212.

889. See Aurelio Cevolotto, "Giustiniani, Agostino," *DBI* 57 (2001); *EH*, 208; *CE*, 2:102–3.

890. Giustiniani's *Psalterium octuplex* (1516) presented the Psalms in parallel in the Hebrew, Septuagint, Aramaic, Targum, and Arabic, along with Latin translations of the first three. His subsequent publications included editions of Hebrew grammars and a translation into Latin of

Maimonides's *Guide for the Perplexed* (1520). In *NMW*, 291, Giovio briefly praises Giustiniani's linguistic achievements.

891. The diocese of Nebbio, on Corsica, was a suffragan of Genoa. Giustiniani became its bishop on September 22, 1514, thanks to the support of his kinsman Cardinal Bendinello Sauli. His book on Genoa is *Castigatissimi annali con la loro copiosa tavola della eccelsa et illustrissima repubblica di Genova, de fideli et approvati scrittori* (Genoa: Antonio Bellono Taurinense, 1537; anastatic reprint: Forni Editore: Sala Bolognese, 1981).

892. For his biography see Aldo Francesco Massèra, *Roberto Valturio "Omnium Scientiarum Doctor et Monarcha" (1405–1475)* (Faenza: Lega, 1958).

893. Valturio, *De re militari* (Verona: Giovanni di Niccolò, 1472), composed around 1450. Frequently reprinted, it was translated into Italian in 1483 and into French in 1532. A modern scholar describes it as "essentially an encyclopedia of ancient military and naval science with a nod to modern weapons": Guy Wilson, "Military Science, History, and Art," in *Artful Armies, Beautiful Battles: Art and Warfare in Early Modern Europe*, ed. Pia Cuneo (Leiden: Brill, 2002), 13–33, at 15. See also Anthony F. D'Elia, *Pagan Virtue in a Christian World: Sigismondo Malatesta and the Italian Renaissance* (Cambridge, MA: Harvard University Press, 2016), which includes close readings of Valturio's works.

894. Eighty-two woodcuts accompany the text.

895. Elena Valeri, "Palmieri, Matteo," *DBI* 80 (2014); *EH*, 333; *ER*, 4:376–77; Alessandra Mita Ferraro, *Matteo Palmieri: Una biografia intellettuale* (Genoa: Name, 2005). Giovio here refers to Palmieri's *Book Concerning the Times* (*Liber de temporibus*), written 1445–48. It extends to the present the chronological record of historical events that the ancient historian Eusebius had begun in his *Universal History* (*Chronicon*) and which Jerome had continued in his *Book of Times* (*Chronicon*, or *Temporum liber*). Along with his teacher, Sozomeno da Pistoia, Palmieri covered the years from 1294 (where an earlier writer had stopped) to 1448. His pupil, Mattia Palmieri of Pisa (not a relative), would continue the *De temporibus* down to 1483. See Cochrane, 23–24; Valeri, "Palmieri."

896. The *De captivitate Pisarum liber* in fact celebrates not Pisa's liberation, but instead its reconquest by Florence in 1406. For its ideology see

Mikael Hörnqvist, "The Two Myths of Renaissance Humanism," in *Renaissance Civic Humanism: Reappraisals and Reflections*, ed. James Hankins (Cambridge: Cambridge University Press, 2000), 105–42. For a recent edition of the work, see *La presa di Pisa*, ed. Alessandra Mita Ferraro (Bologna: Mulino, 1995). The work modeled on the *Divine Comedy* is *The City of Life* (*Città di vita*), a one hundred–canto poem in *terza rima*, edited only in the twentieth century: *Libro del poema chiamato Città di vita*, ed. Margaret Rooke, 2 vols., Smith College Studies, vol. 8, nos. 1–2 (Northampton: Department of Modern Languages, Smith College, 1927–28). Like Dante's *Commedia*, Palmieri's poem centers on a pilgrim who has otherworldly visions and revelations. See Claudio Finzi, *Matteo Palmieri dalla 'Vita Civile' alla 'Città di vita* (Rome: Giuffrè, 1984); Fabrizio Crasta, "'Intentio Auctoris' e 'causa operis' nella *Città di vita* di Matteo Palmieri: Il MS. Laur. Plut. XL 53," *Camenulae* 11 (October 2014): 1–11; Ferraro, *Matteo Palmieri*, 353–478 ("Palmieri poeta teologo"); idem, *Senza aver penne non si può volare: un sommario della Città di vita di Matteo Palmieri* (Florence: Le Lettere, 2012).

897. The initial reception of the *Città di vita* remains obscure. A polished copy of the manuscript survives in the Biblioteca Medicea Laurenziana in Florence: MS Laur. Plut. XL 53. Paralleling the poem throughout that manuscript is the Latin commentary by Palmieri's friend Leonardo Dati (1408–82), which provides theological justification for its content. See Renzo Ristori, "Dati, Leonardo," *DBI* 33 (1987). The most controversial element of the *Città di vita* is its description of the neutral angels being reincarnated as humans so as to have a second chance to decide, exercising free will. Although the work appears not to have circulated widely and was not printed until centuries later, Giovio's claim that it was condemned and burned remains unsubstantiated. Its theology more resembles that of Origen than of Arius.

898. Paolo Farzone, "Iacopo di Angelo da Scarperia," *DBI* 62 (2004). Angeli studied Greek under Manuel Chrysoloras and was a protégé of the Florentine chancellor Coluccio Salutati.

899. Chrysoloras had begun this translation, working from a manuscript of Ptolemy's *Geographike Hyphegesis* (ca. 150 CE) that he had brought to Florence in 1397. Around 1405 Leonardo Bruni began translating the text

but left it unfinished. Around 1406/9, Angeli revised and completed Chrysoloras's version, presenting it to Alexander V (elevated to the papacy by the schismatic Council of Pisa in 1409). See James Hankins, "Ptolemy's *Geography* in the Renaissance," in his *Humanism and Platonism in the Italian Renaissance*, vol. 1: *Humanism* (Rome: Edizioni di Storia e letteratura, 2003), 457–68. Angeli's dedicatory letter to Pope Alexander V tells the pontiff, "A kind of divine presentiment of your soon-to-be-realized empire impelled you to desire the work, so that you could learn clearly from it how ample would be the power you would soon hold over the entire world" (ibid., 459); and for a critical edition of the preface, ibid., 465–68. See also Katharina N. Piechocki, "Erroneous Mappings: Ptolemy and the Visualization of Europe's East," in *Early Modern Cultures of Translation*, ed. Jane Tylus and Karen Newman (Philadelphia: University of Pennsylvania Press, 2015), 76–96, with notes at 283–91. The maps, which did not appear in Jacopo's original version, were added "during the 1410s, through the combined efforts of Francesco di Lapacino and Domenico di Lionardo Boninsegni, both members of the circle around the bibliophile Niccolò Niccoli" (Hankins, "Ptolemy's *Geography*," 458). On the transmission of maps accompanying manuscripts of this work from antiquity to the time of the Byzantine scholar Maximus Planudes (d. 1305), see Florian Mittenhuber, "The Tradition of Texts and Maps in Ptolemy's *Geography*," in *Ptolemy in Perspective: Use and Criticism of His Work from Antiquity to the Nineteenth Century*, ed. Alexander Jones (Dordrecht: Springer, 2010), 95–119.

900. In his preface Angeli faulted the ancient Romans, especially Pliny the Elder, for their inaccuracies in depicting scale and in calculating longitude and latitude. Moreover, "none of our Latin writers explains how our globe, which is spherical, can be described on a two-dimensional surface" (ibid., 459). See also Piechocki ("Erroneous Mappings," 81), who writes that Ptolemy was "the first to theorize and elaborate a system of digital cartographic translatability and the conversion of iconic into numeric data. While his maps are not extant—or never existed, as some scholars claim—his *Geography* offered, for the first time, a method for producing and reproducing visual images by transposing alphanumeric data onto a gridded and uniformly scaled surface."

901. On Boece (or, "Boethius") see *CE*, 1:158, and the entry on him by Nicola Royan in *ODNB*. Born in Dundee, Scotland, he studied at the Collège de Montaigu at the University of Paris. He returned to Scotland, probably in 1496, where he assisted in the founding of the University of Aberdeen. His *Scotorum historiae a prima gentis origine, cum aliarum et rerum et gentium illustratione non vulgari* (Paris: Josse Bade, 1527) covers the period from the purported foundation of the Scottish realm in 330 BCE to the death of James I in 1437 and the punishment of his assassins the following year.

902. Polidoro Virgilio (better known as Polydore Vergil) was born in Urbino and educated at the University of Padua (and probably also at Bologna). See *EH*, 421; *CE*, 3:397–99; the entry by William J. Connell, "Polydore Vergil," in *ODNB*; and Giovio's brief description of him in *NMW*, 279. He is best known for *De inventoribus rerum*, written while he was in Urbino: Polydore Vergil, *On Discovery*, ed. and trans. Brian P. Copenhaver, ITRL 6 (Cambridge, MA: Harvard University Press, 2002). In 1502 Virgilio went to England as subcollector of the Church tax known as "Peter's Pence," working under Adriano Castellesi, its collector since 1489.

903. Polidoro Virgilio, *Proverbiorum libellus* (Venice: Cristoforo Pensi, 1499), dedicated to Duke Guidobaldo da Montefeltro. The first edition of Erasmus's *Adages* appeared the following year. Whereas Giovio portrays Erasmus as having drawn extensively upon Polydore's book, Erasmus himself denied any indebtedness. Polydore's initial patron in England was Henry VII (r. 1485–1509). He later wrote in his *English History* that upon his arrival he was received by Henry and "ever after was entertained by him kindly": Connell, "Polydore," *ODNB*. Both Gragg, at Giovio (1935), 158, and Minonzio, in *Elogi*, 361, read *flamenque Londinii creatus* as meaning that Virgilio was made Bishop of London, a position he never held. The phrase may refer to his obtaining the prebend of Oxgate in St. Paul's in London (1513). Already under Henry VII he had gained preferments, including the prebends of Lincoln and Hereford cathedrals (1507) and the archdiaconate of Wells (1508). See *CE*, 3:397; *ODNB*.

904. Polydore Vergil, *Anglica historia* (Basel: Johann Bebel, 1534); revised and expanded in 1546 and again in 1555. He probably began research for

the book in 1506–7, encouraged by Henry VII, and completed the first manuscript of it in 1512–13.

905. Robert Gaguin, of Colline-Beaumont in Pas-de-Calais, was elected general of the Trinitarian Order in 1473. See *EH*, 195; *CE*, 2:69–70; Suzanne Moreau-Rendu, *Les Captifs libérés: Les Trinitaires et Saint-Mathurin de Paris* (Paris: Nouvelles éditions latines, 1974), 105–35. Cochrane, 346, describes Gaguin as "the first French historian to adopt at least the externals of ancient historiographical models."

906. Evidently a reference to Gaguin's treatment of Italy in his *Compendium de origine et gestis Francorum* (Paris: D. Gerlier, 1497), which he subsequently revised repeatedly. The work circulated widely. See *CE*, 2:70.

907. Giovio incorrectly identifies this humanist as "Marinus Becichemus" (1468–1526), on whom see Cecil H. Clough, "Becichemo, Marino," *DBI* 7 (1970); *EH*, 58–59. The *elogium*, however, describes Becichemo's contemporary Marino Barlezio (Barletius), who also was born in Scutari. See Franz Babinger, "Barlezio, Marino," *DBI* 6 (1964). Scutari (Scodra, Shkodër), in Albania, was under Venetian rule when both humanists were born. It would come under the control of the Ottoman Turks in 1479. See Setton, 2:327–28.

908. Marino Barlezio, *Historia de vita et gestis Scanderbegi Epirotarum principis* (Rome: Bernardino Vitali, ca. 1509).

909. Setton, 2:72–73n119, passes a similar judgment on the work: "Quite apart from his constant exaggerations and chronological errors, Barletius . . . invented the correspondence between Scanderbeg and Ladislas the Jagiellonian in 1443. . . . He also invented a correspondence between Scanderbeg and Sultan Mehmed II to fit his interpretation of events in 1461–1463."

910. See *EH*, 435; *CE*, 3:474–76. Ziegler was born in Landau, in Bavaria.

911. Ziegler, *Holmiae civitatis regie Suetiae deplorabilis excidii per Christiernum Datiae Cimbricae regem historia*, published in Strasbourg in a volume with others of his works in 1532 by Oporinus. Christian II (1481–1559) of the royal house of Oldenburg was king of Denmark and Norway from 1513 to 1523, when he was deposed by his uncle, Frederick I. In 1520 Christian conquered Sweden, but only a few days after being anointed king, he

presided over a purge of enemies known as the "Stockholm Bloodbath," in which over eighty Swedes were declared heretics and executed. Rebellion ensued, and in 1523 Gustav Vasa became king of Sweden.

912. The Cimmerians had flourished in Asia Minor in the seventh century BCE. See L&S, OLD s.vv. Cimmerii, Cimmerius.

913. Raffaella Zaccaria, "Emili, Paolo," DBI 42 (1993); CE, 1:429; Cochrane, 345 and passim. Emili studied theology in Paris and by 1489 had become the official historian of the monarchy of France. Contemporaries called him the "French Livy." In NMW, 279, Giovio emphasized the patronage that provided him leisure to write: "Paolo Emili, whom we see has attained this undisturbed state of life through royal generosity, in his old age is the prolific practitioner of an exuberant style. Living in Paris, he is tracing the history of France from the initial recovery of liberty all the way up to the present, correcting the sequence of events."

914. The first four books of his History of the Franks were printed in 1516/17, two more appeared in 1519, and two decades later the entire ten-book history appeared (Daniele Zavarizzi of Verona completed the last of its books): De rebus gestis Francorum (Paris: Michel de Vascosan, 1539).

915. "medium iter . . . tenuisse"; cf. Vergil, Aeneid 5.12. Giovio appears to refer to the account of the First Crusade in Book 4 of the History of the Franks, which treats the reign of Philip I (r. 1059–1108).

916. See EH, 83; CE, 1:200–202.

917. Germain de Brie, Chordigerae navis conflagratio (Paris: Jossé Bade, 1513). The poem valorizes the captain of the Marie de la Cordelière, the Breton Hervé de Portzmoguer (known as "Primauguet"), who died in the fire. This took place in the Battle of Saint-Mathieu (August 10, 1512) near Brest, France. For a detailed account of the battle, see Angus Konstam, Sovereigns of the Seas: The Quest to Build the Perfect Renaissance Battleship (Hoboken: John Wiley and Sons, 2008), 50–54. The Cordelière was inded massive, weighing at least seven hundred tons, but the English ship that grappled it and ultimately burned and sank along with it, the Regent, weighed one thousand tons. (The other ship that had assailed the Cordelière was the three hundred–ton Mary James.) De Brie's poem may

have "won poetic laurels" from some, but in a letter to the author, Thomas More ruthlessly pilloried him for its inaccuracies and infelicities. To give but two examples: (1) "When you described this sea battle in verse, you set out not only to combine truth with falsehood but to fabricate practically the whole of your story from out-and-out lies, tailoring new facts according to your personal whim"; and (2) "By a lapse of memory (a trap liars often slip into) you made Hervé, whom you had left in the *Regent*, turn up suddenly on the burning *Cordelière*, as if he had two bodies, to deliver himself, there in the flames, of a long-winded sermon. You chose to put off his death for no other reason, I suspect, than to have him sing, in the meantime, of your future election as a nursling of Phoebus to sing of Hervé's own demise." The letter is printed and translated, along with de Brie's *Chordigera* and some broadsides the humanists subsequently fired at each other, in *The Complete Works of St. Thomas More*, vol. 3, pt. 2, ed. Clarence H. Miller, Leicester Bradner, et al. (New Haven: Yale University Press, 1984), Appendix A (the above quotations from More's *Letter to Brixius*, trans. Daniel Kinney, appear at pp. 601 and 603, respectively).

918. Chrysostom, *Liber contra gentiles, Babylae Antiocheni episcopi ac martyris vitam continens* (Paris: Simon de Colines, 1528); *Dialogus D. Ioannis Chrysostomi de episcopatu et sacerdotio* (Marburg: Eucharius Cervicornus, 1537). On de Brie's Greek scholarship more generally, see *FH*, 1:11–40.

919. On Tegrimi see Cochrane, 267, and Minonzio's comments in *Elogi*, 369–70nn1–3.

920. Tegrimi, *Vita Castruccii* (Modena: Rococciola, 1496). See also Giovio's *elogium* of Castruccio Castracane (1281–1328), in *Elogia virorum bellica virtute illustrium*, bk. 1, no. 20: *IO*, 8:277–82.

921. On Machiavelli's use of Tegrimi's text, see Louis Green, "Machiavelli's *Vita di Castruccio Castracani* and Its Lucchese Model," *Italian Studies* 42 (1987): 37–55.

922. Camillo Ghilini appears in the *Enciclopedia italiana* (at treccani.it) entry on "Ghilini" as an ambassador of Sforza Milan to the court of Emperor Charles V, and as the father of Gian Giacomo Ghilini (d. 1532), who wrote a history of the last days of Ludovico "il Moro" Sforza.

923. On Fregoso (1452–1504), see Giampiero Brunelli, "Fregoso, Battista," *DBI* 50 (1998).

924. Battista Fregoso, *De dictis factisque memorabilibus collectanea a Camillo Gilino*, Latin trans. Camillo Ghilini (Milan: J. Ferrario, 1509).

925. Ghilini was a legate for Francesco II Sforza, duke of Milan (r. 1521–35). After Charles V defeated Barbarossa in Tunis, he sailed to Sicily, arriving at Trapani on August 22, 1535. For a description of his triumphal entry into Messina, see Brandi, *Emperor Charles V*, 368.

926. On Reuchlin see *EH*, 364; *CE*, 3:145–51; Spitz, 61–80; Erika Rummel, *The Humanist-Scholastic Debate in the Renaissance and Reformation* (Cambridge, MA: Harvard University Press, 1995), 85, 87–89; Jan-Hendryk de Boer, *Unerwartete Absichten: Genealogie des Reuchlinkonflikts* (Tübingen: Mohr Siebeck, 2016); Giraldi, 145. "Fumeus" = "Smokey," a play on the resemblance of his surname to the German prefix *Räucher-* (= "tasting or smelling of smoke").

927. *De verbo mirifico* (Basel: Johann Amerbach, 1494); *De arte cabalistica libri tres Leoni X. dicati* (Haguenau: Thomas Anshelm, 1517).

928. *Epistolae obscurorum virorum ad . . . Ortuinum Gratium* (1515–17); English version, *Letters of Obscure Men*, trans. Francis Griffin Stokes (Philadelphia: University of Pennsylvania Press, 1972). Although the collection's principal authors were Johannes Crotus Rubianus and Ulrich von Hutten, it was frequently attributed to Reuchlin. The title plays upon Reuchlin's *Latin, Greek, and Hebrew Letters of Famous Men* (*Clarorum virorum epistolae Latinae, Graecae et Hebraicae* [Tübingen: Thomas Anshelm, 1514; enlarged, 1519]), in which he promulgated a selection of letters to him vouching for his scholarly expertise.

929. Perhaps a comic erasure of the distinction Paul makes in Romans 2:28–29 (GNC): "To be a Jew is not to be a Jew outwardly; to be circumcised is not to be circumcised outwardly, with a mark made in the flesh. He is a Jew who is one inwardly. And true circumcision is a matter of the heart — spiritual, not literal" (*circumcisio cordis in spiritu non littera* — Vulg.).

930. In 1510, the Dominican friar Jacob of Hoogstraten was appointed inquisitor of the archdioceses of Cologne, Mainz, and Trier. A conserva-

tive theologian, he supported Johann Pfefferkorn (a Jewish convert to Christianity who advocated the confiscation of all Jewish books opposed to Christianity) and opposed Reuchlin. In 1514–17 he went to Rome to advocate for Pfefferkorn. Far from dying of embarrassment, as Giovio claims, Hoogstraten continued his campaign against Reuchlin for years thereafter; he died in 1527. See the entries on Hoogstraten and Pfefferkorn in *CE*, 2:200–202 and 3:76–77, respectively.

931. Johann Reuchlin, *Epistolae obscurorum virorum* (Speyer: Jakob Schmidt, 1517). The frontispiece whimsically claims that the book was published at the Roman *Curia* (*Impressum Romanae Curiae*). For a reconstruction of the controversy set in theological context, see Alfredo Serrai, *Storia della bibliografia. I: Bibliografia e Cabala: Le Enciclopedie rinascimentali 1*, ed. Maria Cochetti (Rome: Bulzoni, 1988), 76–78.

932. The poem here presented, in elegiac couplets, draws upon two different epitaphs that appear in a letter jokingly attributed to Hoogstraten in the appendix to part one of *Epistolae obscurorum virorum*. See Caruso's remarks in Giovio (1999), 246–47n4.

933. *EH*, 363; *CE*, 3:134. Regiomontanus (Johann Müller, or Molitor, of Königsberg) studied under Georg von Peuerbach at the University of Vienna and subsequently taught there. In 1461 he followed Cardinal Bessarion to Italy.

934. These are the pre-Socratic philosopher Thales of Miletus (ca. 624–ca. 546 BCE), the ancient Greek astronomer Eudoxus of Cnidus (ca. 390–385 to ca. 342–337 BCE), the ancient Greek mathematician and astronomer Calippus of Cyzicus (ca. 370–ca. 300 BCE), and Claudius Ptolemy (ca. 100–ca. 170 CE). While careful to identify Ptolemy as the greatest ancient astronomer, here he proceeds in chronological order and so comes only in the end to "Alfraganus," the Latin name used for the famous Muslim astronomer Ahmad ibn Muhammad ibn Kathir al-Farghani (800/805–870 CE).

935. Regiomontanus, [*Epithome in Almagestum Ptholomei*] ([Rome]: [ca. 1460]). A new edition appeared just three years before publication of the *Elogia*: J. Regiomontanus and G. Peuerbach, *Epitome in Cl. Ptolemaei magnam compositionem* (Basel: Henrich Petri, 1543). Regiomontanus, *De trian-*

*gulis omnimodis libri quinque* (Nuremberg: Petreius, 1533); *On Triangles*, ed. and trans. Barnabas Hughes (Madison: University of Wisconsin Press, 1967).

936. Sixtus IV may have invited Regiomontanus to Rome in 1475, but there is no evidence that the latter ever occupied the episcopal see of Regensburg.

937. *Kalendarius cum vero motu solis et duplici modo inveniendi verum motum lune* ([Zwolle?]: [Peter van Os?], 1502).

938. See *EH*, 426; *CE*, 3:409–13. In his native Catalan, Juan Luis Vives's name is written "Joan Lluis Vives."

939. Upon leaving Paris in 1512, he had taken up residence in Bruges in the home of Bernardo Valdaura. He married Bernardo's daughter, Margarita, in April 1524. For the commentary, see Augustine, *De civitate Dei*, ed. Juan Luis Vives (Basel: Johann Froben, 1522). On the pressure Vives felt from Erasmus to complete the project expeditiously, see *CE*, 3:411.

940. Gessoriacum, on the northwest coast of ancient Gallia, was mentioned by Pliny the Elder, *Natural History* (4.16, 4.23).

941. Vanna Arrighi, "Pazzi, Cosimo de'," *DBI* 82 (2015); *EH*, 338. His mother was Bianca de' Medici, daughter of Piero "the Gouty" and sister of Lorenzo "the Magnificent," who had married Guglielmo di Antonio de' Pazzi in 1459.

942. Cosimo de' Pazzi became archbishop of Florence on July 5, 1508. Maximus of Tyre, *Sermones e Graeca in Latinam linguam versi Cosmo Paccio interprete* (Basel: Johann Froben, 1519). Cosimo's teacher, Janus Lascaris, had brought a copy of the Greek text with him from Constantinople. For an English version, see Maximus Tyrius, *The Dissertations of Maximus Tyrius*, trans. Thomas Taylor, 2 vols. (London: C. Whittingham, 1804).

943. *Sic.* In fact, Leo (Giovanni de' Medici) was his cousin on his mother's side (*sobrinus*), not his uncle (*avunculus*).

944. Alessandro Pazzi de' Medici (1483–1530). See Paola Cosentino, "Pazzi de' Medici, Alessandro," *DBI* 82 (2015); *EH*, 338.

945. Alessandro completed his translation of Aristotle's *Poetics* in 1524 and in 1527 dedicated it to Niccolò Leonico Tomeo. It was published posthumously (1536).

## PERORATION

1. On Oecolampadius (1482–1531), see *EH*, 326; *CE*, 3:24–27.

2. See Theophylact of Ohrid, *In quatuor Evangelia enarrationes denuo recognitae*, trans. Johannes Oecolampadius (Basel: Andreas Cratander, 1525). Oecolampadius argued against the Real Presence of Christ in the Eucharist (thus aligning himself on this issue with Zwingli, and against Luther). See *De genuina verborum Dei: 'hoc est corpus meum' etc. expositione* (Strasbourg: [Johann Knobloch], 1525); and *Antisyngramma*, which appeared in his *Apologetica* (Zürich: C. Froschauer, 1526). John Fisher, later cardinal of Rochester, attacked the *De genuina verborum Dei* in his *De veritate corporis et sanguinis Christi in Eucharistia . . . adversus J. Oecolampadium* (Cologne: Peter Quentel, 1527). Although Oecolampadius expressed his intention of writing against Fisher (as well as against Josse Clichtove), he appears not to have done so. See Thérèse Marie Dougherty, "John Fisher and the Sixteenth-Century Eucharistic Controversy," *Moreana* 6, no. 21 (1969): 31–38.

3. Ulrich Zwingli (1484–1531). See *EH*, 350; *CE*, 481–86.

4. Willibald Pirckheimer (1470–1530). See *EH*, 350; *CE*, 3:90–94.

5. Gregory of Nazianzus, *Orationes Sex*, trans. Willibald Pirckheimer (Nuremberg: Friedrich Peypus, 1521); and, with additional texts and more substantial commentary, idem, *Orationes XXX*, trans. Willibald Pirckheimer (Basel: Froben, 1531); Ptolemy, *Geographicae enarrationis libri octo*, trans. Willibald Pirckheimer (Strasbourg: Johannes Grüninger, 1525); and Pirckheimer, *Germaniae ex variis scriptoribus perbrevis explicatio* (Nuremberg: Johann Petreius, 1530). Curiously, Giovio omits mention of Pirckheimer's response to Oecolampadius's criticisms of his views on the Eucharist: *De vera Christi carne et vero eius sanguine ad J. Oecolampadium responsio* (Nuremberg: Johann Petreius, 1526).

6. Joachim Vadianus (1484–1551). See *EH*, 414; *CE*, 3:364–65.

7. Pomponius Mela, *De orbis situ libri tres, accuratissime emendati, una cum commentariis Joachimi Vadiani Helvetii castigatioribus et multis in locis auctioribus factis* (Basel: Andreas Cratander, 1522). In 1518 Vadian had published a translation of this text with less extensive commentary.

8. On Johannes Cuspinian (1473–1529), see *EH*, 141.

9. Cuspinian, *De Caesaribus atque imperatoribus Romanis opus insigne* (Strasbourg: Crato Mylius, 1540); and *Austria . . . cum eiusdem omnibus marchionibus, ducibus, archiducibus ac rebus praeclare gestis ab iisdem ad haec usque tempora* (Frankfurt, 1601). See Albert Schirrmeister, "Authority through Antiquity — Humanist Historiography and Regional Descriptions: The Cases of Erasmus Stella, Johannes Cuspinian and Robert Gaguin," in *Authority in European Book Culture 1400–1600*, ed. Pollie Bromilow (London: Routledge, 2013), 67–84.

10. Guillaume Cop (ca. 1450–1532) had become one of Francis I's royal physicians at least by 1523. See *EH*, 126; *CE*, 1:336–37. In *NMW*, 331–33, Giovio expressed admiration for him "as an outstanding healer and as a translator from Greek into Latin. He is as renowned for his wealth and charm as for his diligence and intelligence."

11. On Conrad Goclenius (ca. 1489–1539) see *EH*, 210; *CE*, 2:109–11. From Mengeringhausen in Westphalia, Goclenius (né Conrad Wackers) was educated at Cologne and then Leuven, where he became famous as a humanist pedagogue.

12. On Ulrich Zasius (1461–1535), see *EH*, 434–35; *CE*, 3:469–73; Steven W. Rowan, *Ulrich Zasius: A Jurist in the German Renaissance, 1461–1535* (Frankfurt am Main: V. Klostermann, 1987).

13. *Harudum*, used here for Konstanz, refers to the Harudes (or "Arudes"), an ancient Germanic people whose army, commanded by Ariovistus, made war on Julius Caesar's troops (Caesar, *Gallic War* 1.31, 37, 51).

14. On Beatus Rhenanus (1485–1547), see *EH*, 365; *CE*, 1:104–9; John F. D'Amico, *Theory and Practice in Renaissance Textual Criticism: Beatus Rhenanus Between Conjecture and History* (Berkeley and Los Angeles: University of California Press, 1988); D'Amico, *Roman and German Humanism, 1450–1550*, ed. Paul F. Grendler (Brookfield, VT: Variorum, 1993), essays X–XII.

15. Joachim Camerarius (1500–1574); see *CE*, 1:247–48; *ER*, 1:335–36.

16. The astronomer Nicolaus Copernicus (1473–1543); see *CE*, 2:82–86.

17. On Krantz, see Donald R. Kelley, "Humanism and History," in Rabil, 3:236–70, at 246–47. Krantz wrote two books on the problem of Germanic origins: *Saxonia* (Cologne: n.p., 1520) and *Wandalia* (Cologne: Johannes Soter alias Heil ex Bentzheim, et socii, 1519).

18. Albert Krantz, *Chronica regnorum aquilonarium; Daniae, Suetiae, Norvagiae* (Strasbourg: I. Schottus, 1546).

19. On Caspar Ursinus Velius (d. 1539), see *CE*, 3:356–57; *Coryciana*, ad indicem. In 1509 Ursinus entered the service of Matthäus Lang. The following year he went to Italy, initially studying Greek under Scipione Forteguerri at the University of Bologna. He was in Rome from 1512 to 1514, and again in 1522 to 1523. It was said that, beset by despondence, Ursinus drowned himself in the Danube.

20. Horace, *Odes* 1.22.1: "integer vitae scelerisque purus."

21. These are Holy Roman Emperors Maximilian II (r. 1564–76); his father, Ferdinand I (r. 1556–64); and Ferdinand's brother, Charles V.

22. Although the use of guns in Italy is documented as early as 1326, humanist historians, following Flavio Biondo in his *Roma triumphans*, routinely attributed the invention of firearms to a mid-fourteenth-century German. See J. R. Hale, "Gunpowder and the Renaissance: An Essay in the History of Ideas," in idem, *Renaissance War Studies* (London: The Hambledon Press, 1983), 389–420, at 391; and *NMW*, 55–57, where Giovio calls the printing press and firearms "perhaps the most famous of all" inventions.

23. Jacopo Sadoleto (1477–1547) studied under Niccolò Leoniceno in Ferrara before going to Rome around 1499. He served as domestic secretary to Leo X and to Clement VII. In 1527 he went to his diocese (Carpentras, in France), then returned to Rome the year of his elevation to the cardinalate by Paul III. Thereafter, he played a leading role in efforts of Catholic Reform. See Francesco Lucioli, "Sadoleto, Iacopo," *DBI* 89 (2017); *EH*, 375; *CE*, 3:183–87; *ER*, 5:383–84; *NMW*, 277–79.

24. Cf. Pliny the Younger, *Letters* 2.1.2: "posteritati suae interfuit."

25. On Bembo, see The Portraits, note 266, above.

26. Giambattista Cipelli, called "Egnazio" (1478–1553), whom the Venetian government appointed to to a public lectureship in Latin in 1520. See Elpidio Mioni, "Cipelli, Giovanni Battista," DBI 25 (1981); EH, 118; CE, 1:424–25; NMW, 293.

27. On Sadoleto, see above, note 23.

28. Gian Giorgio Trissino (1478–1550) of Vicenza studied Greek in Milan (ca. 1507–8) under Chalcondyles. After spending time in Venice and Florence, in 1514 he moved to Rome, where he would serve as a diplomat for Popes Leo X, Clement VII, and Paul III. Trissino is noted for his efforts to reform the vernacular by blending Italian dialects into a shared "courtly" language, and especially for his proposal that letters from the Greek alphabet be introduced into Italian. See EH, 411; ER, 6:171–72; Giraldi, 91–93; and NMW, 267.

29. Girolamo Fracastoro (ca. 1478–1553) of Verona studied astronomy, philosophy, medicine, and anatomy at the University of Padua, the last subject under Marcantonio della Torre, with whom Giovio also worked. In 1505 he joined the college of physicians in Verona. His most famous work, the poem Syphilis sive morbus gallicus (1530), is edited with an English translation in Fracastoro, Latin Poetry, trans. James Gardner, ITRL 57 (Cambridge, MA: Harvard University Press, 2013). See Enrico Peruzzi, "Fracastoro, Girolamo," DBI 49 (1997); CE, 2:49; Balsamo, Poètes italiens, 1:353–55; Giraldi, 99–101; NMW, 231.

30. Marco Girolamo Vida (ca. 1485–1566), from Cremona, went to Rome in 1510. There he enjoyed the patronage of Gian Matteo Giberti, Leo X, and Clement VII. He was created bishop of Alba in 1533 and attended the Council of Trent in 1546 and 1547. On the strength of his epic poem on the life of Christ, the Christiad (1535), he came to be called "the Christian Vergil": Vida, Christiad, ed. and trans. James Gardner, ITRL 39 (Cambridge, MA: Harvard University Press, 2009). See also CE, 3:391–92; Giraldi, 67–69; NMW, 223–25, 233.

31. The best brief account of the life of Pierio Valeriano (1477–1558) is that of Julia Haig Gaisser in the introduction to her edition and transla-

tion of his *De litteratorum infelicitate: DLI*, 2–23. See also Vera Lettere, "Dalle Fosse, Giovanni Pietro," *DBI* 32 (1986); *EH*, 415–16; Giraldi, 87–89, 179; and *NMW*, 225. He is best known for *Hieroglyphica* (Basel: Palma Ising, 1556), a fifty-eight-book compendium that took several decades to complete.

32. Romolo Quirino Amaseo (1489–1552), from Udine, moved in 1509 to Bologna, where his friends included Achille Bocchi and Giambattista Pio. He spent most of his career at the University of Bologna, where he lectured in Latin and Greek (1513–20 and 1524–44). He published translations of Xenophon's *Anabasis* (Bologna: Baptista Phaellus, 1533) and Pausanias's *Graeciae descriptio* (Florence: Lorenzo Torrentino, 1551). His son Pompilio edited and published his *Orationum volumen* (Bologna: Giovanni Rossi, 1564). See Rino Avesani, "Amaseo, Romolo Quirino," *DBI* 2 (1960); *EH*, 34; *CE*, 1:39; Giraldi, 181; *NMW*, 311.

33. Andrea Alciato (1492–1550), born either in Milan or in Alzata (near Como), was a correspondent and longtime friend of Giovio. Famous and influential as a jurisconsult, Alciato is most widely known for his *Emblematum liber*. Completed in 1522 and first published in 1531, it initiated a new genre and inspired Giovio's influential dialogue on *imprese* (devices): i.e., emblems (each combining an epigram, a motto, and a visual image) that were particular to the individual for whom they were invented (*IO*, 9:351–425). See Roberto Abbondanza, "Alciato, Andrea," *DBI* 2 (1960); *EH*, 28; *CE*, 1:23–26; Giraldi, 155, 177, 205.

34. Marcantonio Flaminio (1498–1550), from the Veneto, studied in Rome, Naples, Bologna, and Padua. In 1524 he met Gian Matteo Giberti, who would be his patron in Rome and, from 1528 on, in Verona. See Alessandro Pastore, "Flaminio, Marcantonio," *DBI* 48 (1997); Carol Maddison, *Marcantonio Flaminio: Poet, Humanist and Reformer* (Chapel Hill: University of North Carolina Press, 1965); Thomas F. Mayer, *Reginald Pole: Prince and Prophet* (Cambridge: Cambridge University Press, 2000), *passim*. See also Arsilli, lines 177–78; Balsamo, *Poètes italiens*, 1:346–48; Giraldi, 95; *NMW*, 225.

35. On Luther's protégé Philipp Melanchthon (1497–1560), see *EH*, 300–301; *CE*, 2:425–29; *ER*, 4:109–11.

36. On Vitale (1485–1559), see The Portraits, note 3, above.

37. Reginald Pole (1500–1558), of the Plantagenet line, was a cousin of King Henry VIII of England. He studied at Oxford under Thomas Linacre and William Latimer. From 1521 to 1526/27, with King Henry's financial support, Pole attended the University of Padua, where he studied under Niccolò Leonico Tomeo and befriended Christophe de Longueil and Pietro Bembo. By the 1530s his advocacy of Church unity set him against Henry VIII. A close friend of Vittoria Colonna, he was active as a religious reformer and in 1549 would come close to being elected pope. See CE, 3:103–5; ER, 5:105–7; T. F. Mayer, "Pole, Reginald," in ODNB (revised January 3, 2008); Mayer, *Reginald Pole*.

38. On Daniele Barbaro (1514–70), see Giuseppe Alberigo, "Barbaro, Daniele Matteo Alvise," DBI 6 (1964); EH, 53. He taught moral philosophy at the University of Padua beginning in 1537 and remained connected with the university until 1546, when he began service in a series of posts for the Republic of Venice.

39. Antonio Bernardi (1502–65) of Mirandola. See Paola Zambelli, "Bernardi, Antonio," DBI 9 (1967); and Minonzio's synopsis in *Elogi*, 412n16.

40. Guillaume Philandrier (1505–65), an architect and diplomat, who published editions of Quintilian and Vitruvius. Other publications include his *Castigationes atque annotationes pauculae in XII libros Institutionum Marci Fabii Quintiliani* (Lyon: Gryphius, 1535), and *In decem libros Marci Vitruvii de architectura annotationes* (Rome: Andrea Dossena, 1544). See EH, 346.

41. On Fascitelli (1502–64), see Liminal Poem, note 1, above.

42. On Basilio Zanchi (ca. 1501–58) of Bergamo, see Luigi Ferrari, *Onomasticon* (Milan: Hoepli, 1947), 701; *Elogi*, 414n19.

43. Jan Dantyszek of Gdansk (1485–1548). He became bishop of Warmia (Ermland) in 1537. See CE, 1:377; Eubel, 3:327; Segel, *Renaissance Culture*, 161–90 and *passim*.

44. Filip Padniewski (d. 1572), identified by Segel, *Renaissance Culture*, 256, as vice-chancellor of the Polish Crown. In 1560 he became bishop of Cracow (Eubel, 3:180).

45. Marcin Kromer (1512–89). See *EH*, 138; Segel, *Renaissance Culture*, 13, 120. His *De origine et rebus gestis Polonorum libri XXX* (Basel: Oporinus, 1555) covers Polish history up to 1506. In 1570 he became bishop of Warmia (Eubel, 3:327).

46. Otto Truchsess von Waldburg (1514–73) became bishop of Augsburg in 1543 and was elevated to the cardinalate the following year. See Thomas Groll with Walter Ansbacher, *Kardinal Otto Truchseß von Waldburg (1514–1573)* (Lindenberg: Kunstverlag Josef Fink, 2015); Noes M. Overbeeke, "Cardinal Otto Truchsess von Waldburg and His Role as Art Dealer for Albrecht V of Bavaria (1568–73)," *Journal of the History of Collections* 6 (1994): 173–80; Pastor, vol. 9 *passim*; Eubel, 3:29, 123.

47. Seemingly a reference to Cardinal Truchsess's role at a diet that opened not in Worms but in Nuremberg in August 1542, to which Pope Paul III had sent him to convey the papal bull instituting the Council of Trent. See Pastor, 9:145–46; Jedin, 1:460 and *passim*.

48. The Silesian nobleman Georg von Logau (1485–1553) spent many years in Italy, including a visit to Rome from 1533 to 1534 that prompted him to polemicize against Erasmus's *Ciceronianus*. See *EH*, 275; *CE*, 2:338–39; Peter Schaeffer, "Humanism on Display: The Epistles Dedicatory of Georg von Logau," *Sixteenth Century Journal* 17 (1986): 215–23.

49. Baron Tamás Nádasdy (1498–1562), Hungarian statesman and soldier, was educated at Graz, Bologna, and Rome. Emperor Charles V's brother Ferdinand, following his coronation as King of Hungary in 1527, made Nádasdy commandant of Buda. After the city's capture by Suleiman, Nádasdy went over to the protection of John Zápolya. In 1533, however, he returned to the service of Ferdinand, and "from 1537 onwards became Ferdinand's secret but most influential counsellor." A promoter of education, he founded a school and established a printing press at Új-Sziget. See *EB* 11, online; Setton, 4:565, 568, 572.

50. Perhaps Janus Pannonius (1434–72), who in 1458 joined the retinue of King Matthias Corvinus in Hungary and in 1460 was created bishop of Pécs. See *EH*, 246–47; *CE*, 2:233–34; *ER*, 4:377–78. His *Epigrammata* are published in Pannonius, *The Epigrams*, ed. and trans. Anthony A.

Barrett (Budapest: Corvina Kiadó, 1985). Giovio may have juxtaposed the long-deceased Pannonius with Filip More (whose name immediately follows) because they were both bishops of Pécs. Cf. Minonzio, however, who conjectures that Giovio here is referring to Janos Vértesy, a student of Marcus Musurus (*Elogi*, 416n26).

51. Filip More of Ciula (1470?–1526) was bishop of Pécs from 1524. He served in the entourage of George Szatmáry (1457–1524), who was archbishop of Esztergom, 1522–24. More died in the Battle of Mohács. See Răzvan Mihai Neagu, "Considerations Regarding the Intellectual Background of the Bishops of Oradea in the Middle Ages up to the Year 1526," *Anuarul Institutului de Istorie "G. Bariţiu" din Cluj-Napoca, Series Historica*, Suppl. 1 (2015): 207–19, at 216; Alexandru Madgearu, *The Romanians in the Anonymous* Gesta Hungarorum: *Truth and Fiction* (Cluj-Napoca: Center for Transylvanian Studies, Romanian Cultural Institute, 2005), 102, 177n74.

52. István Brodarics (Stjepan Brodarić) (ca. 1471–1539) became Bishop of Syrmia (Szerém) in 1526 and then of Vác in 1539 (dying a few months after his appointment). He is best known for his eyewitness account of the Battle of Mohács: *De conflictu Hungarorum cum Turcis ad Mohatz verissima descriptio* (Cracow: H. Wietor, 1527). See *CE*, 1:203–4; Eubel, 3:301, 335; Rabil, 2:284–85.

53. Ferencz Frangepán (d. 1543), archbishop of Kalocsa-Bacs, 1530–43. On behalf of the Hungarian crown, he delivered an oration at the Diet of Regensburg: *Oratio ad Caesarem, electores et principes Germaniae* (Wittenberg, 1541). See Simeone Gliubich, *Dizionario biografico degli uomini illustri della Dalmazia* (Vienna: Rod. Lechner, 1856), 136–37.

54. John Statilius, bishop of Alba Iulia (now in Romania), 1539–54. See Setton, 3:318–19, 321–22, 436–37, 444n; Eubel, 3:100–101.

55. Matthias Corvinus (1443–90), king of Hungary and Bohemia. See *CE*, 2:408–9; *ER*, 2:91–93.

56. Tranquillus Andronicus Parthenius (Fran Trankvil Andreis) of Trogir (1490–1571). After a storied diplomatic career, in 1544 he retired and concentrated on his writing. Already in 1518 he had published an oration

against the Turks, and in 1566 his poetic exhortation for a crusade appeared in print. See CE, 1:56–57.

57. This is Antoine Perrenot de Granvelle (1517–86), who became bishop of Arras in 1538 and would be created cardinal in 1561. Starting in 1530, he was a highly trusted advisor of Emperor Charles V, active in diplomacy in Germany, and on January 9, 1543, addressed the Council of Trent in the name of the emperor. See EB 11, s.n. Granvella; *Catholic Encyclopedia* (New York: Robert Appleton Company, 1913), available online at www.newadvent.org/cathen; Setton, *ad indicem*.

58. Nicholas Perrenot, lord of Granvelle, and imperial minister (1486–1550). See Setton, *passim*.

59. Pieter Nanninck (1500–1557), canon of the cathedral of Arras, and professor of Latin at Leuven. See EH, 317–18.

60. Cornelis de Schepper (ca. 1502/3–55) of Flanders studied in Leuven. After several years in the service of King Christian II of Denmark and his chancellor, Godschalk Ericksen, in 1526 Schepper entered the service of Charles V, for whom he went on numerous important embassies, and he became a regular member of Charles's privy council in 1538. Giovio mentions him in a letter to Duke Cosimo I de' Medici (October 14, 1540), in IO, 1:254–56, at 255.

61. Jean du Bellay (1498–1560), made bishop of Bayonne in 1524 and then of Paris in 1532, was created cardinal by Paul III in 1535. A book of his Latin poems was published with Jean Salmon's *Odarum libri tres* (Paris: Robert Estienne, 1546). See CE, 1:407.

62. Joachim Périon (1499–1559), a Benedictine who taught at the University of Paris, most famous for his humanistic translation of Aristotle's works. See EH, 343; FH, 1:349–479; and *Elogi*, 417n36.

63. Jacques Louis Strébée (or, d'Estrebay) (Jacobus Ludovicus Strebaeus; 1481–ca. 1550?). See EH, 396; FH, 1:121–62; and especially *Elogi*, 417–18n37. Strébée devoted a tract to describing how his own approach to translating Aristotle differed from Périon's: *Quid inter Lodoicum Strebaeum et Ioachimum Perionium non conveniat in Politicon Aristotelis interpreta-*

*tione* (Paris: Michel de Vascosan, 1543). Périon returned fire in his *Oratio in Iacobum Lodoicum Strebaeum, qua eius calumniis et convitiis respondet* (Paris: Thomas Richard, 1551).

64. Pierre Danès (1497–1577), who had produced a new edition of Pliny the Elder's *Natural History* in 1532. On July 8, 1546, as a French envoy to the Council of Trent, Danès held forth for an hour about the services rendered the Church and papacy by kings of France from Clovis to Francis I. See *EH*, 142; *FH*, 1:97–120; *Elogi*, 418n38; and Jedin, 1:183.

65. Lazare de Baïf (ca. 1496–1547) went to Rome around 1516 with Christophe de Longueil. By 1521 he had returned to France, where he would enter the service of Cardinal Jean de Lorraine in 1525. *EH*, 49; *CE*, 1:87–88.

66. Baïf, *De re vestiaria* (Basel: Johann Bebel, 1526); *De re navali* (Paris: R. Estienne, 1536).

67. Guillaume Pellicier (ca. 1490–1568), created bishop of Maguelonne in 1529 and then transferred to the see of Montpellier in 1536, served Francis I on important missions, including the arrangement of the marriage of the Duc d'Orléans to Catherine de' Medici in 1533, and later as ambassador to Venice. See *Elogi*, 418n40; *EB* 11.

68. Pierre du Chastel (d. 1552), active in the court of Francis I, would be appointed grand almoner of France by Henry II in 1548. See *CE*, 1:409–10.

69. Jacques Toussain (d. 1547) studied under Budé and became his lifelong friend and correspondent. See *CE*, 3:336–37.

70. Jean Salmon (1490–1557), called "Macrin" or "Maigret." In Paris he studied under Jacques Lefèvre d'Etaples and Girolamo Aleandro. By 1530 he was a client of Guillaume and Jean Du Bellay. See *EH*, 378; *CE*, 3:189.

71. Nicolas Bourbon (ca. 1503–ca. 1550), who studied Greek under Jacques Toussain, published a collection of poetry entitled *Nugae* (Paris: Michel de Vascosan, 1533), expanded for a second edition (Lyon: S. Gryphius, 1538). See *CE*, 1:179–80.

72. Louis Le Roy (1510–77). A prolific translator from Greek into French of works by Plato, Aristotle, Xenophon, Isocrates, and Demosthenes, he also wrote political and historical treatises, most famously *De la vicissitude ou variété des choses en l'univers* (Paris: Pierre L'Huillier, 1575). See *EH*, 266–67; *ER*, 3:415.

73. François Vatable (ca. 1493–1547) was educated in Paris and Avignon, where he learned Greek and Hebrew, respectively, and between 1516 and 1521 he served as Lefèvre d'Etaples's assistant at St. Germain-des-Prés. In 1530 he was named royal professor of Hebrew. See *EH*, 418; *CE*, 3:379.

74. Perhaps "Hebraica" here invokes Vatable's appointment in 1530 as royal professor of Hebrew.

75. Garcilaso de la Vega (ca. 1501–36); see *ER*, 3:16–17.

76. Garcilaso sustained this injury in the village of Le Muy, approximately sixty-five miles east of Aix en Provence. When a group of over a dozen locals who had hidden in the tower near the entrance to Le Muy refused to leave, Charles V ordered his troops to lay siege to it. While Garcilaso and another of the emperor's men were climbing into the breach, the resisters dropped a heavy stone that broke the ladder, causing them both to fall. Garcilaso would die within a few days from the head wound he sustained. On contemporary accounts of the incident, see Hayward Keniston, *Garcilaso de la Vega: A Critical Study of His Life and Works* (New York: Hispanic Society of America, 1922), 153–59.

77. On Juan Ginés de Sepúlveda (ca. 1490–1573), see The Portraits, note 859, above.

78. Juan Martínez Siliceo (1486–1557) taught logic in Salamanca. He became bishop of Cartagena in 1540, then was translated to the see of Toledo in 1546. See *EH*, 295; Eubel, 3:154, 314.

79. Francisco de Mendoza y Bobadilla (1508–56) was created cardinal in December 1544, at the request of Emperor Charles V. See *CE*, 2:431–32.

80. Miguel da Silva (1475–1556) was dispatched by King Manuel I of Portugal in 1514 to serve as ambassador to the papal court, a position he maintained for a decade. He was elevated to the cardinalate *in pectore* in

1539, the promotion being announced only in 1541. Castiglione dedicated to him the *editio princeps* of *The Courtier*. See *Elogi*, 420n51; and Sylvie Deswarte-Rosa, *Il 'Perfetto Cortegiano": D. Miguel da Silva* (Rome: Bulzoni, 1989).

### ANONYMOUS LIMINAL POEM

1. The poem alternates between iambic dimeter and iambic trimeter.

# Bibliography

❧§❧

## EDITIONS

*Elogia veris clarorum virorum imaginibus apposita quae in musaeo Ioviano Comi spectantur, addita in calce operis Adriani pontificis vita.* Venice: Michele Tramezzino, 1546.

*Le iscrittioni poste sotto le vere imagini de gli huomini famosi: le quali à Como nel museo del Giovio si veggiono.* Translated by Hippolito Orio. Florence: Lorenzo Torrentino, 1552. [actually published December 1551]

*Elogia doctorum virorum ab avorum memoria publicatis ingenii monumentis illustrium.* Basel: Pietro Perna, 1556.

*Elogia doctorum virorum ab avorum memoria publicatis ingenii monumentis illustrium.* Antwerp: Jean Bellère, 1557.

*Le iscrittioni poste sotto le vere imagini de gli huomini famosi in lettere.* Translated by Hippolito Orio. Venice: Francesco Bindoni, 1558.

*Le iscrittioni poste sotto le vere imagini de gli huomini famosi in lettere.* Translated by Hippolito Orio. Venice: Giovanni de' Rossi, 1558.

*Elogia doctorum virorum ab avorum memoria publicatis ingenii monumentis illustrium.* Basel: Pietro Perna, [1561].

*Elogia virorum bellica virtute illustrium: veris imaginibus supposita, quae apud Musaeum spectantur, in libros septem digesta; Doctorum item virorum ingenii monumentis illustrium ab avorum memoria publicatis, altera tomo comprehensa.* Basel: Pietro Perna, 1561.

*Elogia doctorum virorum ab avorum memoria publicatis ingenii monumentis illustrium. Praeter nova Ioannis Latomi Bergani in singulos epigrammata adiecimus ad priora Italicae editionis illustrium aliquot poetarum alia.* Basel: Pietro Perna, 1571.

*Elogia virorum literis illustrium quotquot vel nostra vel avorum memoria vixere, ex eiusdem Musaeo (cuius descriptionem una exhibemus) ad vivum expressis imaginibus exornata.* Basel: Pietro Perna, 1577.

*Opera quotquot extant omnia. Vitae illustrium virorum, rerum turcicarum commentarius, elogia virorum bellico virtute illustrium, elogia virorum literis illustrium.* Basel: Perna, 1596.

*An Italian Portrait Gallery; Being Brief Biographies of Scholars Illustrious within the Memory of Our Grandfathers for the Published Monuments of Their Genius.* Translated by Florence Alden Gragg. Boston: Chapman & Grimes, 1935.

*Elogia veris clarorum virorum imaginibus apposita quae in musaeo [Ioviano] Comi spectantur.* In *Gli elogi degli uomini illustri (Letterati – Artisti – Uomini d'arme)*, edited by Renzo Meregazzi, vol. 8 in *Pauli Iovii opera*, 31–225. Rome: Istituto Poligrafico dello Stato, 1972.

*Ritratti degli uomini illustri.* Edited and translated by Carlo Caruso. Palermo: Sellerio editore, 1999. [significantly abridged]

*Elogi degli uomini illustri.* Edited by Franco Minonzio. Translated by Andrea Guasparri and Franco Minonzio. Turin: Einaudi, 2006.


MODERN LITERATURE

Agosti, Barbara. *Paolo Giovio: uno storico lombardo nella cultura artistica del Cinquecento.* Florence: L. S. Olschki, 2008.

Aleci, Linda Klinger. "Images of Identity. Italian Portrait Collections of the Fifteenth and Sixteenth Centuries." In *The Image of the Individual. Portraits in the Renaissance*, edited by Nicholas Mann and Luke Syson, 67–79. London: British Museum Press, 1998.

———. "Portraits and Historians." In *Coming About . . . : A Festschrift for John Shearman*, edited by Lars R. Jones and Louisa Chevalier Matthew, 359–65. Cambridge, MA: Harvard University Art Museums, 2001.

Baker, Patrick. *Italian Renaissance Humanism in the Mirror.* Cambridge: Cambridge University Press, 2015.

Cannata, Nadia. "Giorgio Vasari, Paolo Giovio, Portrait Collections and the Rhetoric of Images." In *Giorgio Vasari and the Birth of the Museum*, edited by Maia Wellington Gahtan, 67–79. Aldershot: Ashgate, 2014.

Cochrane, Eric. *Historians and Historiography in the Italian Renaissance.* Chicago: University of Chicago Press, 1981.

*Collezioni Giovio: Le immagini e la storia.* Catalogue of the Exhibition, "Paolo Giovio," edited by Rosanna Pavoni. Como: Musei Civici, 1983.

Costamagna, Philippe. "La constitution de la collection de portraits d'hommes illustres de Paolo Giovio et l'invention de la galerie historique." In *Primitifs italiens: le vrai, le faux, la fortune critique*, edited by Esther Moensch-Scherer, 167–90. Milan: Silvana Editoriale, 2012.

Della Torre, Stefano. "Le vedute del museo gioviano." *Quaderni erbesi* 7 (1985): 39–48.

Gaisser, Julia Haig. *Pierio Valeriano on the Ill Fortune of Learned Men: A Renaissance Humanist and His World.* Ann Arbor: University of Michigan Press, 1999.

Gianoncelli, Matteo. *L'antico museo di Paolo Giovio in Borgovico.* Como: New Press, 1977.

Klinger, Linda Susan. "The Portrait Collection of Paolo Giovio." 2 vols. PhD diss., Princeton University, 1991.

Maffei, Sonia. "Il Museo: Commento." In Paolo Giovio, *Scritti d'arte: Lessico ed ecfrasi*, edited by Sonia Maffei, 129–70. Pisa: Scuola Normale Superiore, 1999.

———. "Lo spazio delle parole. Gli Elogia e il Museo di Paolo Giovio tra innovazione e tradizione." *Raccolta Storica della Società Storica Comense* 24 (2007): 9–29; = *Atti del Convegno. Sperimentalismo e dimensione europea della cultura di Paolo Giovio* (Como, December 20, 2002), edited by Sonia Maffei, Franco Minonzio, and Carla Sodini.

Michelacci, Lara. *Giovio in Parnaso: tra collezione di forme e storia universale.* Bologna: Il Mulino, 2004.

Minonzio, Franco. "Cinque brevi biografie inedite di Paolo Giovio: *disiecta membra* delle perdute *Vite de' filosofi del nostro tempo.*" *Filologia e critica* 37 (2012): 235–63.

———. "*Con l'appendice di molti eccellenti poeti.*" Gli epitaffi degli Elogia degli uomini d'arme di Paolo Giovio. Cologno Monzese: Lampi di stampa, 2012.

———. "Il Museo di Giovio e la galleria degli uomini illustri." In *Testi, immagini e filologia nel XVI secolo*, edited by Eliana Carrara and Silvia Ginzburg, 77–146. Pisa: Edizioni della Normale, 2007.

———. *Studi gioviani: scienza, filosofia e letteratura nell'opera di Paolo Giovio.* 2 vols. Como: Società Storica Comense, 2002 [= *Raccolta storica della Società Storica Comense* 21 (2002) and 22 (2002)].

Reynolds, Anne. *Renaissance Humanism at the Court of Clement VII: Francesco Berni's* Dialogue Against Poets *in Context. Studies, with an edition and translation.* New York: Garland, 1997.

Tarallo, Claudia. *Anatomie letterarie. Ritratti di intellettuali negli* Elogia *di Paolo Giovio.* Rome: Aracne editore, 2021.

Wilson, N. G. *From Byzantium to Italy: Greek Studies in the Italian Renaissance.* 2nd ed. London: Bloomsbury Academic, 2017.

Zimmermann, T. C. Price. "Giovio, Paolo." In *Dizionario Biografico degli Italiani* 56 (2001).

——. "Guicciardini, Giovio, and the Character of Clement VII." In *The Pontificate of Clement VII: History, Politics, Culture*, edited by Kenneth Gouwens and Sheryl E. Reiss, 19–27. Aldershot: Ashgate, 2005.

——. "Paolo Giovio and the Evolution of Renaissance Art Criticism." In *Cultural Aspects of the Italian Renaissance: Essays in Honour of Paul Oskar Kristeller*, edited by Cecil H. Clough, 406–24. Manchester: Manchester University Press, 1976.

——. "Paolo Giovio and the Rhetoric of Individuality." In *The Rhetorics of Life-writing in Early Modern Europe: Forms of Biography from Cassandra Fedele to Louis XIV*, edited by Thomas F. Mayer and Daniel R. Woolf, 39–62. Ann Arbor: University of Michigan Press, 1995.

——. *Paolo Giovio: The Historian and the Crisis of Sixteenth-Century Italy.* Princeton: Princeton University Press, 1995.

——. *Paolo Giovio. Uno storico e la crisi italiana del XVI secolo.* Translated by Franco Minonzio. Cologno Monzese: Lampi di Stampa, 2012.

# Index

Abano, Pietro d', 181
Aberdeen, University of, 602n901
Aborigines (pre-Roman peoples on Italian peninsula), 357, 580n769
Abu Al-Nasr Tuman bay, Al-Ashraf (Tuman bay II), 565n638
Academicians, 321
academy: of Bessarion, 95, 486n111, 491n147; of Colocci, ix, 167, 559n604, 576n738, 581n778; of d'Alviano, 195, 526n404; of Ficino, 491n147; of Goritz, ix, 361, 559n604, 581n778, 581–82n780, 597n881; of Pomponio Leto, xiii, 149, 175–77, 486n111, 497n197, 508n281, 509n283, 509–10n292; of Pontano, 535n542, 590n836
Acciaiuoli, Donato, 69–71, 484n89; "Life of Charlemagne," 484n90
Acciaiuoli, Giovanni, 528n416
Acciaiuoli, Niccolò, 484n92
Acciaiuoli family, 71
Achillini, Alessandro, 191, 203–5, 247, 323, 525n396, 529n423; On Intelligences, 205; On Spheres, 205; On the Elements, 205
Acquaviva d'Aragona, Andrea Matteo, 253–57

Acquaviva d'Aragona, Belisario (ruler of Nardò), 255, 549n536
Acqui (place), 137
Actius Syncerus (Jacopo Sannazaro). See Sannazaro, Jacopo
Actuarius, Iohannes, 573n699; On Urine, 327
Adda (river), 195
Adige (river), 195, 526n401
Adrian VI (pope), 367, 401, 540n477
Adriani, Marcello Virgilio, 309, 397, 596n870, 596n873
Adriatic Sea (Mare Superum), 255–57, 351, 449, 549nn538–39, 561n614
Aegean Sea, 17
Aeneas, 375
Aesculapius/Asclepius, 285, 359, 560n605, 560n608
Aesop, 127
Africa/African, 331, 572n698; North, 403
Agricola, Rudolf (Roelof Huisman), 123–25, 499–500nn215–18
Agrippa, Heinrich Cornelius, 353–55, 580n765; "Monsieur" and "Mademoiselle" (pet poodles), 580n765; On Occult Philosophy, 353, 579n762; On the Vanity of the Sciences, 353, 579n762
Aix-en-Provence, 335, 445, 619n76

Alamanni, Luigi (poet), 567n649
Alamanni, Luigi di Tommaso, 309, 566n649
Albania, 494n177, 603n907
Albergati, Cardinal Niccolò, 485n99
Alberti, Leandro, 56n618
Alberti, Leon Battista, 125–27, 501n224; *Apologues*, 127; *Momus*, 127; *On Painting*, 501n223
Alberti family, 125
Albertus Magnus, xii, 29–31
Alcalá, University of, 594n859
alchemy, 239–41, 545n507
Alciati, Andrea, 435, 613n33
Alcionio, Pietro, xiii, 391–93, 593nn855–56, 593n858, 594nn861–62
Aleandro, Girolamo, 341–45, 576n729, 576nn731–33, 618n70
Aleppo, 548n530
Alessandria, 137
Alexander I (king of Poland), 510n294, 510–11n297
Alexander V (pope), 405, 601n899
Alexander VI (pope), 151, 157, 173, 513n307, 519n345, 520n354
Alexander of Aphrodisias, 201, 249, 528n421, 548n525; *On the Intellect*, 201
Alfonso I (king of Naples/Alfonso V; king of Aragon), 59, 63, 67, 73, 171, 377, 381, 481nn61–62, 483n83, 519n348, 586n808, 586n810, 587n818
Alfonso II (king of Naples), 557n594, 595n868

Alfraganus (Ahmad ibn Muhammad ibn Kathir al-Farghani), 419, 607n934
Al-Ghazali, 325, 571n684
All Hallows (Maidstone, Kent, England), 538n469
Alpheus (river), 299
Alps, 7, 21, 161, 329; Carnic, 177
Altilio, Gabriele, 167, 395–97, 595–96nn868–69
Alviano, Bartolomeo d', 195–97, 271, 273, 496n195, 503n237, 526nn403–4, 527n406, 556n576
Alviano, Bernardino d', 526n403
Alzata (place), 613n33
Amaseno (river), 31
Amaseo, Pompilio, 613n32
Amaseo, Romolo Quirino, 435, 613n32
Ambrogini, Angelo (Poliziano). *See* Poliziano
Ambrose, Saint, 481n56
Amiterno, Antonio d', 117
Ammannati-Piccolomini, Cardinal Jacopo, 81–83, 487nn119,–20, 488n131; *Commentaries*, 81
Ammirato, Scipione, 530n430
Anacharsis, 33
Andalusia, 539n474
Andes: villa, 215, 535n453; Andean spring, 217
Andronicus Parthenius, Tranquillus (Fran Trankvil Andreis), 439, 616n56
Anfratta (place), 167, 517n336
Angeli, Jacopo (Iacopo di Angelo

da Scarperia), 405, 600–
601nn898–900
Anghiera, Roberto, 595n864
Aniene (river), 175
Anjou, duchy of, 557n595
*Annals of France*, 35
Anne, Saint, 361; Feast of, 582n780
Anselmi, Giorgio, 219, 537n461
Antipodes, 147
Antonini, Egidio (Egidio da Vi-
terbo). *See* Egidio da Viterbo
Antonio da Rho, 53, 63, 479n43,
482n73
Antonio De Ferrariis (Antonio
Galateo), 387
Aonia/Aonian, 111, 495n184
Apennines, 55
Apollo (deity), 19, 21, 85, 111, 175,
243, 359, 361, 451, 495n181,
495n184; Phoebus, 195, 253,
605n917
Apostoli, Arsenio, 528n420
*Appendix Vergiliana*, 476n15
Appian, 67, 77, 483n83
"Apuleianism," 580n768
Apuleius, 477n22; *Golden Ass*, 185,
355
Apulia/Apulian, 167, 255, 285, 289
Aquila (city), 489n133
Aquileia, patriarchate of, 135, 177,
503n246, 537n466
Aquinas, Thomas, Saint, xii–xiii,
31–33, 475n5, 547n525
Arab/Arabic, 131, 223, 303, 321,
502n231
Arabic language, 565n641,
598n890

Aragon/Aragonese, 167, 257, 279,
557n594
Aramaic language, 303, 565n641,
598n890
Arcella, Laura, 59, 482n65
Archpoet, the (Camillo Querno).
*See* Querno, Camillo
Arco, Nicolò d', 211
Arezzo/Aretine, 49, 51, 227, 375,
566n649
Argyropoulos, John, 95, 105–9,
159, 494n174
Ariadne, statue of (*Sleeping Ariadne*; Belvedere *Cleopatra*),
553n563
Arianism, 405
Ariosto, Ludovico, 295–97,
562n626, 563nn630–31; *Orlando
furioso*, 295–97, 546n511; *Pretenders*, 295; *Satires*, 295
Ariovistus, 610n13
Aristides of Miletus, *Milisiaka*,
477n22
Aristophanes, 307
Aristotle/Aristotelian, 49, 99, 135,
159, 205, 223, 247, 249, 321,
323, 325, 349, 393, 443,
492n155, 493n165, 494n174,
525n396, 538n469, 570n679,
594n859, 617nn62–63, 619n72;
*Ethics*, 69, 107; *Meteorology*,
539n469; *Nicomachean Ethics*,
484n88; *On Animals*, 103,
494n169; *On the Soul*, 325,
528n421; *Physics*, 107; *Poetics*,
423, 609n945; *Prior Analytics*,
325; [*Problems*], 103, 492n158,

Aristotle/Aristotelian (*continued*)
493n167, 560n609; *Short Trea-
tises on Nature,* 321
Arius, 600n897
Arno (river), 55, 133; deity of, 111,
496n187
Arquà (village), 41
Arras, 617n59
Arrian, *Anabasis of Alexander,* 379
Arsilli, Francesco, xvi n8, 359–63,
543n493, 546n511, 549n537,
581n776; *On Roman Poets,* 361,
581n778
Artemisia (sister and wife of
Mausolus), 525n393
Arthur, Prince of Wales, 221,
537n467
Ascra, 151
Asia, 119
Asia Minor, 497n202, 604n912
Aspasia, 347
astrology, 131–33, 145–47, 191–95,
261, 325, 506–7n272, 515n314,
559n602, 571n686
Athanasius of Alexandria, Saint,
377, 585n804
atheism, 309, 567n650
Athena/Minerva (deity), 21, 293,
303, 365, 431, 437; Pallas, 223,
285
Athens/Athenian, 71, 123, 223,
551n548; a Roman, 97
Atilius Crescens, 21, 474n19
Atlantic (ocean), 447
Atri (Hadria), 253–55, 549n538
Attic, 57, 93, 115, 163, 309

Augsburg, 512n300, 615n46
Augurelli, Giovanni Aurelio, 239–
41, 545n504, 545n506, 545n509;
*Chrysopoeia,* 241; *Elegies,* 239;
*Geronticon,* 241; *Odes,* 239
Augustine, Saint, *On the City of
God,* 421
Augustinian Order (Order of
Hermits of St. Augustine), xiii,
301, 564nn635–36, 574n709,
609n939
Aurispa, Giovanni, 51, 479n41
Ausonia/Ausonian, 145
Auxerre, 411
Avalos, Alfonso d', Marchese del
Vasto, 13, 31, 249, 251, 473n6,
475n4, 573n706
Avalos family, 173
Averroës, 119, 203, 205, 223, 247,
325, 498n205, 570n679
Avignon, 475n5, 619n73
Avila, 269, 553n564

Baflo (place), 499n215
Baïf, Lazare de, 443, 618n65
Balami, Ferdinando, 29, 293,
475n2
Baldus (Baldo degli Ubaldi), 47–
49
Bale, John, 538n469
Balsamo, Ferdinando (the Sicil-
ian), 171
Bandini dei Baroncelli, Bernardo,
119, 498n205
Baptista of Mantua. *See* Spagnolo,
Baptista

Barbarigo, Agostino, 510n297

Barbaro, Daniele, xvii n12, 435, 614n38

Barbaro, Ermolao, the Elder, 123–25, 135–37, 161, 221, 271, 500n220, 503n242, 503n244, 503–4nn246–47

Barbaro, Ermolao, the Younger, 387, 397, 503n241, 515n317, 537nn465–66, 587n819, 590n837

Barbaro, Francesco, 91

Barbarossa (Barbaros Hayreddin), 606n925

Barcelona, 565n638

Bari (place), 255

Barigioni, Filippo, 492n156

Barlezio, Marino (Barletius), 409, 603n907, 603n909

Bartolini, Lorenzo, 577n739, 577n741

Bartolus (Bartolo da Sassoferrato), 45–47, 75

Basel, 335, 427, 570n669, 574n711; Council of, 589n832

Basilicata (place), 508n279

battles: of Agnadello, 496n195, 527n405, 529n426; of Ankara, 490n140; of Capo d'Orso, 574n706; of Chaldiran, 565n638; of Garigliano, 503n237; of Gavinana, 574n706; of Marj Dabiq, 548n530, 565n638; of Mohács, 439, 616nn51–52; of Parabiago, 504n251; of Pavia, 556n587; of Ponza, 481n61, 587n818; of Ravenna, 211, 532n442; of Saint-Mathieu, 604n917; of Varna, 153, 385, 511n300, 589n832; of Villalar, 540n477

Bavaria/Bavarian, xii, 475n1, 603n910

Bayezid II (sultan), 91, 119, 490n140, 498nn204–5, 511n297

Bayonne, bishopric of, 617n61

Beatus Rhenanus, 427, 591n842

Beccadelli, Antonio. See Panormita

Beccadelli, Filippa, 482n65

Beccadelli family, 57

Becichemo, Marino, 603n907

Béda, Noël, 592n849

Belgrade, 493n164

Bembo, Bernardo, 39, 476n17

Bembo, Pietro, 39, 143–45, 189, 237–39, 277, 281–83, 305, 323, 331, 431, 435, 506n266, 544n500, 544n502, 558n596, 566n644, 577n740, 614n37

Benci, Trifone, 365, 583n787

Benedictine order, 471n1, 499n215, 572n698, 578n757, 617n62

Bentivoglio, Ercole, 525n389

Bentivoglio, Ermete, 193

Bentivoglio, Giovanni II, 183, 185, 193, 522nn374–75, 524n383

Bentivoglio, Sante, 525n389

Bentivoglio, Violante, 522n374

Bentivoglio family, 529n423

Bergamo, bishopric of, 545n508, 614n42

Bernardi, Andrea, 522n373

Bernardi, Antonio, of Mirandola, 435, 614n39
Berni, Francesco, xvi n8, 546n511
Beroaldo, Filippo, the Elder, 185–87, 355; commentary on Apuleius, 580n768
Beroaldo, Filippo, the Younger, 185, 524n384
Berry (French province), 313
Bessarion, Cardinal (the Nicene), 75, 79, 85, 93–97, 99, 103, 485n104, 486nn111–12, 490n145, 491nn148–49, 492n155, 510n292, 607n933. See also academy: of Bessarion
Bibbiena (town), 227
Bibbiena, Cardinal (Bernardo Dovizi), 227–31, 528n416, 541nn481–82, 542n486
Bible: Gospel, 591n849; Holy Scripture, 500n217; Old and New Testaments, 299, 403; Sacred Book, 533n450; Scripture, 147, 353, 367, 591n849; Septuagint, 598n890; Targum, 598n890
biblical books: 1 Corinthians, 529n428; 2 Corinthians, 476n21; Pauline Epistles, 592n849; Psalms, 319, 598n890; Romans, 606n929
Bilhorod (Akkerman), 511n297
Biondo, Flavio, xiii, 63–65, 95, 611n22; Decades, 65, 483n78
Biondo, Gasparo, 65
Biondo, Margania, 65

Black Sea, 99, 153, 495n177, 511n297
Blois (French city), 273
Boccaccio, Giovanni, 41–43, 309, 582n784; Decameron, 43; Genealogy of the Pagan Gods, 43; On Springs, 43; On the Variability of Fortune, 43
Boccaccio (Boccaccino) of Chellino, 43, 477n24
Boccarino of Arezzo, 231
Bocchi, Achille, 613n32
Boece, Hector (Boethius), 407, 602n901; Scottish History, 602n901
Boeotia, 488n128, 495n184
Bohemia, kings of, 45
Boiardo, Matteo Maria, 297; Orlando innamorato, 563n630
Bologna/Bolognese, 57, 73, 185, 187, 191, 203, 247, 249, 277, 301, 351, 357, 359, 369, 481n58, 485n100, 517n328, 522n375, 525n389, 529n423, 529n426, 541n481, 543n489, 543n496, 556n588, 565n639, 578nn755–57, 580n767, 582n784, 585n801, 591n840, 594n859, 597n880, 613n32, 613n34, 615n49; Church of San Martino, 205; Church of San Procolo, 351; University, 529n423, 529n426, 602n902, 611n19, 613n32
Bolsena (lake), 83, 487n121; San Lorenzo alle Grotte, 83, 487n121

Bona of Savoy, 588n826
Boninsegni, Domenico di Lionardo, 601n899
Bonsi, Domenico, 513n307
Borgia, Cesare, 519n345, 556n576
Borgia, Girolamo, 195
Borgia, Lucrezia, 524n388, 573n702
Bosnia (Bossina), 209, 531n436
Bourbon, Charles de, 331, 553n564, 573n706
Bourbon, Nicolas, Fancies (Nugae), 618n71
Braccio Fortebraccio da Montone, 489n133
Bracciolini, Iacopo, 53, 480n48
Bracciolini, Poggio. See Poggio
Bracelli, Giacomo, 381, 587n818
Brescia, 251, 534n450
Briçonnet, Guillaume, 591n845
Brie, Germain de, 411–12, 604n917
Brindisi, archbishopric of, 343, 576n733
Britannia, 33
British Isles/Britain/Britons/British, 57, 319, 447, 481n59. See also England/English
Brittany/Breton, 341, 481n59, 543n495, 604n917
Brodarics, István (Stjepan Brodarić), 439, 616n52
Bruges, 421
Brunelleschi, Filippo, 501n224
Bruni, Leonardo, 49–51, 91, 95, 397, 477–78nn33–34, 480n48, 484n90, 490n141, 589n832,

600n899; History of the Florentine People, 49, 51; History of the Gothic War, 385
Bruno, Cola, 331–33
Brutus (Marcus Junius Brutus), 5, 309, 566n649
Buda (city), 615n49
Budé, Guillaume, 327, 339–41, 441, 443, 575n725, 618n69; Commentaries, 339; On Coinage, 339; On the Pandects, 339
Buonaccorsi, Filippo (Callimachus). See Callimachus Experiens
Burchard, Joannes, 502n236
Burckhardt, Jacob, x
Burgundian court, 472n3
Busseto (place), 7, 472n4
Byzantium/Byzantine, 71, 91, 105, 119, 427, 490n140, 491n154, 498n206, 575n717

Caecilius (of Como), 21
Caecuban wine, 363
Cairo, 548n530
Cajetan, Cardinal. See De Vio, Tommaso
Calabria/Calabrian, 103, 323, 493n168, 508n278, 588n824
Calandrini, Cardinal Filippo, 488n131
Calcagnini, Celio, 401–3, 590n840, 597–98nn884–86; Investigations into Letter-Writing, 401
Calco, Tristano, 530n430, 564n635

Calderia (place), 85
Calderini, Domizio, 85–87, 95, 137, 487n124, 491n148
Caledonian Forest, 33, 475n8
Calenzio, Elisio (Luigi Gallucci), 59, 167–69; *Battle of the Frogs with the Mice*, 167; *Elegies*, 167
Calippus of Cyzicus, 419, 607n934
Callimachus, *Hymns*, 499n209
Callimachus Experiens (Filippo Buonaccorsi), 149, 151–55, 509–10nn291–92, 510–11nn297–98, 511n300
Callixtus III (pope), 79
Calpurnius Fabatus, 474n19
Camaldoli (place), 480n51
Camaldulensian Order, 55, 480n51
Cambi, Giovanni, 512n306
Camerarius, Joachim, 427
Campania/Campanian, 323, 395, 550n548
Campano, Giovanni Antonio, 87–89, 95, 488–89nn130–32; *Life of Braccio*, 89
Caninius Rufus, 21, 473n7, 474n19
Cantalice (place), 534n451
Cantalicio (Giovanni Battista Valentini), 215, 534n451
Capece, Scipione, 259
Capilupi, Camillo, 535n453
Capilupi, Ippolito, 217, 535n453
Capilupi, Lelio, 217, 535n453
Capodistria (place), 379, 586n814
Caponi (Coponi), Antonio, 193, 526n399
Capranica (place), 243, 546n514; Church of San Francesco, 243

Capua, 257
Caracciolo, Francesco, 557n594
Carbone, Girolamo, 535n452
Careggi, villa near, 133, 161, 502n235, 515n315
Caria, 525n393
Carinthia, 531n436
Carmelite Order, 215–17, 533n450
Carnival, 229, 541n484
Caro, Annibale, 471n1
Carpentras (French city), 611n23
Carpi (place), 289, 525n398, 561n618
Carteromachus, Scipio (Scipione Forteguerri), 275, 556n583, 611n19
Casanova, Marco Antonio, 265–67, 552n555, 552n558
Casimir IV Jagiellon (king of Poland), 153, 510nn293–94, 510n297, 511–12n300
Cassian of Imola, Saint, 35, 475n10
Cassius (Gaius Cassius Longinus), 309, 566n649
Cassius Dio, 547n520
Castalia (Nereid), 271, 554n569
Castellammare di Stabia (place), 263
Castellani, Mario, 237, 544n497
Castellesi, Adriano, 602n902
Castiglione, Baldassare, 267–71, 544n500, 553–54nn564–65, 620n80; *Cleopatra*, 267; *Courtier*, 546n511
Castile/Castilian, 227, 540n477
Castracane, Castruccio, 413

Catalan language, 608n938
Catania (place), 257
Catherine of Aragon (queen of England; first wife of Henry VIII), 319
Catholic Church. *See* Church, Roman Catholic
Cato the Elder, 5; "of our times," 289; *On Agriculture,* 560n609
Cattaneo, Giovanni Maria, 275–79, 556nn580–82, 556n588; *On the Festivals of the Romans,* 277; *On the Influence and Course of the Sun and Moon,* 277; *Suleiman,* 275–77
Cattani da Diacceto, Iacopo, 309, 566n649
Catullus (Gaius Valerius Catullus), 85, 197, 265, 526n402, 546n513, 552n557; "a new," 197
Cavaniglia family, 195
Cecina (river), 111, 496n187
Cerreto (place), 171
Certaldo (place), 41, 43
Cesarini, Cardinal Giuliano (elder), 385, 589n832
Cesarini, Cardinal Giuliano (younger), 589n832
Cesena (city), 181, 521n369
Cevennes (mountains), 539n472
Chalcondyles, Basilius, 115, 399, 597n878
Chalcondyles, Demetrius, 113–15, 141, 221, 275, 321, 371, 399, 496n190, 498n203, 502n236, 556n580, 570n674, 596n875, 612n28

Chalcondyles, Seleucus, 115
Chalcondyles, Theodora (daughter of Demetrius), 596n875
Chalcondyles, Theophilus, 115
Chaldean, 299, 403
Chapuys, Eustace, 570n670
Charlemagne, 69
Charles IV (Holy Roman Emperor), 45
Charles V (Holy Roman Emperor), x, 21, 269, 273, 277, 291, 301, 331, 335, 369, 401, 415, 445, 471n1, 472n4, 540n477, 565nn638–39, 571n686, 574n712, 575n717, 577n750, 594n859, 597n882, 605n922, 606n925, 611n21, 615n49, 617n57, 617n60, 619n76, 619n79
Charles VIII (king of France), 147, 157, 279, 498n206, 557n594, 583n794
Charles the Bold (duke of Burgundy), 472n3
Chartres (town), 413, 573n699
Chigi, Agostino, 551n554
Chios, 510n293
Christian II (king of Denmark and Norway), 411, 603n911, 617n60
Christianity/Christian, xii, 29, 33, 55, 63, 81, 93, 99, 157, 249, 291, 303, 353, 371, 375, 417, 514n311, 607n930. *See also* Church, Roman Catholic; Lutheran sect; popes; Protestantism
Christians, 55, 299, 301, 367, 514n311

Chrysoloras, Manuel, 71, 91–93, 379, 489–90nn138–41, 490n143, 600nn898–99

Church, Roman Catholic, 69, 95, 317, 490n145, 567–68nn657–58, 569n669, 614n37, 618n64; Eucharist, 425, 591n849, 609n2, 609n5; "Peter's Pence," 602n902; Reform, 611n23

Church councils (or conciliarism), 91, 93, 311, 478n34, 490n143, 490n145, 547n525, 567nn655–57, 569n669, 589n832, 615n47, 617n57, 618n64

Church Fathers, 317

Cibò, Innocenzo, 541n482

Cicero/Ciceronian (Marcus Tullius Cicero), 107, 237, 271, 337, 357, 427, 439, 443, 491n154, 506n266, 544n502, 552n555, 554n574, 574n710, 587n815, 594–95nn861–62, 598n888; On Duties, 403; On Glory, 393; On Laws, 53; On Old Age, 103, 477n27; On the Agrarian Law, 587n817; On the Ends of Good and Evil, 53; On the Orator, 595n862; Philippics, 595n862; Tusculan Disputations, 540n479

Ciminello, Serafino (Aquilano), 329

Cimmeria/Cimmerian, 411, 604n912

Cipelli, Giambattista (Egnazio), 16, 435, 503, 612n26

Cipolla, Bartolomeo, 518n342

Città di Castello (city), 489n132

Claudian, 399

Clement VII (pope; Giulio de' Medici), ix, xvi n2, 265, 269, 277, 291, 301, 343, 369, 401, 497n197, 497n200, 528n416, 541n482, 552n556, 552n559, 553n564, 556n588, 558n596, 563n634, 565n639, 574n706, 576nn732–33, 583n785, 594n859, 611n23, 612n28, 612n30

Clement XI (pope), 492n156

Clichtove, Josse, 591n845, 609n2

Clovis, 618n64

Coccio. See Sabellico, Marcantonio Coccio

Cocles, Bartolomeo, 191–95; Chiromancy, 525n396

Codrus, 61, 482n69

Collenuccio, Pandolfo, 169–71, 518n342, 518n345; Head and Cap, 169; history of the kings of Naples, 169–71; On the Viper, 169

Colline-Beaumont (place), 603n905

Colocci, Angelo, ix, xvi n8, 167, 518n339, 544n500, 559n604, 576n738, 581n778

Cologna Veneta (place), 337

Cologne, 579n762, 606n930, 610n11

Colonna, Pompeo, 552n556, 552–53nn558–59, 594n862

Colonna, Prospero, 259, 550n542

Colonna, Vittoria, 471n1, 542n485, 614n37

Colonna family, 265, 552n558

Colyn, Conrad (of Ulm), 579n762

Commynes, Philippe de, 5, 7, 472n3

Como (city), ix, xiv, xvii n10, 21, 135, 265, 267, 369, 373, 472–73nn4–5, 613n33

Como (lake), xi, 7, 13, 21, 23, 451, 473n5; Kenchreai, 17; Larius, 473n5; Lechaion, 17

Conca della Campania (place), 261, 550n545

Conselice (place), 311

Constance, Council of, 91, 478n34, 490n143

Constantinople, 73, 119, 490n140, 490n145, 498n205, 510n293, 565n638, 608n942

Constantinus Africanus, 329, 572n698

Contarini, Gasparo, 349–53, 577–78nn750–51, 578nn754–56; *On the Venetian Republic*, 349

Contarini, Girolamo, 531n437

Contarini family, 508n282

Contarini di Valsanzibio, Pietro, 529n421

Conversano (place), 255

Cop, Guillaume, 427, 610n10

Copernicus, Nicolaus, 427, 611n16

Córdoba, 445, 594n859

Coriano (place), 522n376

Corinna (of Ovid), 111, 496n186

Corinth, 17, 488n128

Corio, Bernardino, 205–7, 530n430

Cornarius, Janus (Johann Hainpol), 329, 573n699

Cornelius Sisenna, Lucius, 477n22

Coronis (mother of Aesculapius), 285, 560n605

Coronius, Dionysius (Denis Corone, Coroné, Corron, Charron), 329, 573n699

Corsi, Pietro, 285, 337, 559n604

Corsica, 403, 599n891

Cortés, Hernán, 395

Corvo, Andrea, 525n398

Corvo di Mirandola, Andrea, 191

Cosenza (place), 391, 399

Cossa, Baldassare. *See* John XXIII

Costantini, Lucrezia, 598n884

Cotta, Giovanni, 195–97, 526n401, 556n576; *Chorographies*, 197

Cracow, 511n298, 614n44; Church of the Holy Trinity, 153

Crassi, the, 61

Cremona/Cremonese, 79, 215, 345, 347, 349, 612n30

Crete/Cretan, 99, 115, 203, 271, 289, 497n197, 529n421

Crinito, Pietro (Pietro del Riccio Baldi; Petrus Crinitus), 35, 143, 197–99, 261, 475n10, 502n236, 527n412, 551n549; *On Honorable Learning*, 199; *On Latin Poets*, 199

Crotone, bishopric of, 489n131

Crotti, Bartolomeo, 337

Crotus Rubianus, Johannes, *Letters of Obscure Men*, 417, 606n928, 607n931

Cupid (deity), 43, 89, 187

Curti, Lancino, 139, 211–15; *Epigrams*, 213; *Woods*, 213

Cuspinian, Johannes, 427
Cynthia (of Propertius), iii,
    496n186
Cyprus, 510n293

Dalmatia/Dalmatian, 409, 439
Danaë, 391
Danès, Pierre, 443, 618n64
Dante Alighieri, xi, xii, 35–39,
    476n13; Divine Comedy, 37, 41,
    405, 600n896
Dantyszek, Jan, 437, 614n43
Danube (river), 475n1, 495n177,
    611n19
Dardano, Bernardino, 235,
    543n493
Dati, Leonardo, 600n897
David, King (biblical), 319
death, 47, 51, 57, 143, 145, 231, 337,
    449
Decembrio, Angelo, 474n20
Decembrio, Pier Candido, 67–69;
    Life of Filippo Maria Visconti, 67
Decio, Filippo, 311–13, 567nn654–
    55, 567n657, 568n659
De Ferrariis, Antonio, 590n836,
    590n839
de la Marck, Erard (bishop of
    Liège), 576n732
de la Vega, Garcilaso, 445, 619n76
Delia (of Tibullus), iii, 496n186
della Rovere, Francesco Maria
    (duke of Urbino), 565n637
della Torre, Filippo, 531n439
della Torre, Girolamo, 532n440
della Torre, Marcantonio, 207–11,
    612n29
della Torre, Napoleone (Napo),
    531n439
della Torre family, 209, 531n439
del Maino, Giasone, 231–35, 542–
    43nn488–89
del Nero, Bernardo, 512n306
Delphi, 554n569; Oracle, 520n355
del Piombo, Sebastiano, 556n581
del Riccio Baldi, Pietro. See
    Crinito, Pietro
del Vasto, Alfonso, x
del Vasto, Ludovico II (marquis of
    Saluzzo), 503n237
Demosthenes, 552n555, 619n72
Denmark/Danes, 429
De Vio, Tommaso, Cardinal (Ca-
    jetan, Caietanus, Gaetano,
    Caetano), 249, 547n525
Diano (Teggiano; place),
    508n278
Di Capua, Giovanni Francesco,
    550n542
Dio Cassius, 139, 245, 504n251
Diocletian (Roman emperor),
    578n757
Diodorus Siculus, 53, 77
Diogenes Laertius, 55, 515n314
Diogenes of Sinope, 149
Dionysius the Areopagite
    (pseudo), On the Celestial Hierar-
    chy, 55, 480n54
Dionysus (deity), 363
Dioscorides, 135, 327, 397,
    573n699; On Medical Material,
    596n871
Dirce (spring), 495n185
Dnieper (river), 155

Dolcino, Stefano, 215
Domenichi, Lodovico, 473n5
Dominican Order, 155, 403, 417–
    19, 513n308, 514n312, 579n762,
    606n930
Domitian (Roman emperor),
    553n560
Donà, Girolamo, 201–3,
    528nn416–18, 528nn420–21
Donati, Niccolò, 504n247
Doni, Anton Francesco, 11, 472n5
Doria, Filippino, 574n706
"Doric Echo, The," 15
Dovizi, Bernardo. See Bibbiena,
    Cardinal
Dovizi, Piero, 541n481
drama, xiii, 229, 295, 307–9, 357,
    423, 542n485
Du Bellay, Guillaume, 618n70
Du Bellay, Jean (bishop of Paris),
    441, 617n61, 618n70
Du Chastel, Pierre, 443, 618n68
Dundee, Scotland, 602n901

Earth, 135, 359, 375
Easter, dating of, 419–21
East-West Schism of 1054,
    490n145
East wind, 261
Egidio da Viterbo (Egidio Anto-
    nini), xiii, 299–303, 558n596,
    563–64nn633–34, 564n636,
    565nn638–39, 565n641
Egnazio. See Cipelli, Giambattista
Egypt/Egyptian, x, 301, 395,
    514n312, 553n563, 565n638; obe-
    lisk (called "Macuteo," in Pi-
    azza San Macuto, Rome),
    492n156
elocution, 149–51, 203, 247, 251,
    265, 399
Eloquence (personified), 51
eloquence, 37, 39, 41, 45, 51, 55,
    67, 69, 71, 73, 77, 81, 99, 103,
    113, 123, 131, 145, 163, 167, 169,
    171, 185, 195, 205, 217, 233, 267,
    275, 291, 293, 301, 303, 305, 307,
    329, 337, 343, 353, 381, 385, 393,
    399, 401, 411, 417, 427, 431, 439,
    441, 443, 445, 497n200,
    500n217, 509n287, 564n635,
    595n868
Elysium/Elysian, 205; fields, 253,
    333, 361, 379; grove, 111
Emili, Paolo, 411, 604nn913–15
Encyclopedia (unknown), 255,
    549n535
England/English, xii, 221, 223, 237,
    313, 317, 407, 411, 490n140,
    537n464, 602nn902–3, 604n917
Ennius, 540n479
Epidaurus, 560n608
Epirot, 321, 409
Erasmus, Desiderius, 293, 333–35,
    341, 407, 441, 534n450,
    544n502, 562n621, 574n709,
    574nn711–12, 578n761, 592n849,
    593n857; Adages, 591n842,
    602n903; Ciceronian, 335,
    558n596, 574n710, 615n48;
    Praise of Folly, 333
Erembus (deity), 303
Erfurt, University of, 499n216
Ericksen, Godschalk, 617n60

Este (place), 165
Este, Alfonso I d', 245, 291, 295, 525n389
Este, Beatrice d', 533n449
Este, Cardinal Ippolito d', 295, 562n626, 598n885
Este, Ercole I d' (duke of Ferrara), 171, 245, 518–19nn344–45, 598n885
Este, Isabella d', 229, 519n345, 541n484, 573n702
Este, Niccolò III d', 479n41
Este family, 187, 401, 598n885
Esztergom, archbishopric of, 616n51
Etruscans, 508n278
Eudoxus of Cnidus, 419, 607n934
Euganian Hills, 209, 251, 531n436
Eugenius IV (pope), 51, 55, 73, 93, 95, 375, 377, 480n52, 490n145, 584n798
Euripides, Iphigenia, 423
Europe, x, xi, 91, 253, 333, 339, 439, 441, 490n140
Eusebius of Caesarea, 99; Universal History, 405, 599n895
Eustratius of Nicaea, 69, 484n88
Exerich, Jaime (archpriest of Zaragoza), 315, 569n664

Fabatus (Calpurnius Fabatus), 21
Fabro, Antonio (Antonius Faber Amiterninus), 497n200
Facio, Bartolomeo, 53, 63, 377–79, 482n73, 585–86nn807–9
Falernian wine, 287, 289, 561n613
Fano (place in Campania), 261, 550n548; Temple of the Argive Juno, 550n548
Fano (town in the Marches), 550n548
Farnese, Cardinal Alessandro, ix, 23, 471n1, 472n4
Farnese, Orazio, 471n1
Farnese, Ottavio (duke of Parma), 5–9, 25, 471nn1–2
Fascitelli, Onorato, 3, 361–63, 435, 471n1
Fate/Fates, 33, 37, 47, 49, 81, 83, 111, 123–25, 131, 133, 143, 145, 161, 183, 189, 197, 209, 215, 231, 239, 243, 249, 253, 261, 263, 289, 317, 359, 379, 433, 493n161, 561n617; Cruel, 359
Faustus, Dr. (literary character), 580n765
Federico da Montefeltro, xi
Ferdinand I (Holy Roman Emperor), 429, 611n21, 615n49
Ferdinando I (Ferrante I; king of Naples), 171, 225, 227, 255, 519nn349–50
Ferdinando II (Ferrandino; king of Aragon/Naples), 279, 395, 557n593, 557n595, 586n809, 595n864, 595n868
Ferdinando III (king of Naples), 259, 550n542
Fernández de Córdoba, Gonzalo (Gonsalvo the Great, El Gran Capitán; duke of Terranova and Santangelo), 215, 255, 259, 503n237, 534nn451–52, 550nn541–42

Ferrara, 155, 187, 283, 295, 401, 490n145, 516n324, 518n344, 532n442, 546n512, 558n601, 563n630, 573n702, 590–91n840, 611n23; Church of San Domenico, 245; University, 283, 499n216, 598n885

Ferreri, Zaccaria, 567n657

Ficino, Marsilio, 159–63, 515nn314–15, 515n317, 516n319, 516nn321–22, 533n450; *The Triple Life*, 161, 515n316

Fiera, Battista, 535n455

Filelfo, Francesco, 63, 71–75, 91, 95, 504n249, 588n828

Filelfo, Mario, 73

Fisher, John (cardinal of Rochester), 317–21, 425, 569–70nn669–70, 609n2; *On the Real Presence of the Body and Blood of Christ*, 319

Flaminio, Marcantonio, 159, 175, 197, 271, 275, 283, 327, 349, 351, 367, 435, 471n1, 613n34

Flanders/Flemish, 5, 9, 227, 235, 341, 421, 427, 439, 472n3, 540n477, 617n60

Florence/Florentine, ix, x, xii, xiii, 35–39, 51, 53, 55, 69, 71, 91, 93, 107, 109, 113, 125, 127, 129, 131, 133, 137, 143, 147, 155, 157, 161, 179, 221, 307, 309, 321, 397, 405, 413, 421, 478n34, 478n38, 478–79nn40–41, 479n44, 480n48, 485n100, 490nn140–41, 490n145, 494n174, 495nn177–78, 498n203, 501n224, 507n275, 510n293, 513n307, 514n312, 515n315, 515–16nn317–18, 521n367, 527n412, 528n416, 537n464, 541n481, 545nn505–6, 564n635, 566n649, 567n651, 568n659, 570n674, 573n706, 596n873, 599n896, 600nn898–99, 608n942, 612n28; Bargello, 53, 498n205; Certosa di Val d'Ema (Carthusian church), 71, 484n92; Church of Santa Croce, 51; Convent of San Marco, 513nn308–9; Duomo, 141, 505n259, 516n322; Great Council, 512n306; as "Mother Florence," 53–55; *Ottimati*, 512n305; Palazzo Medici, 541n482; Santa Maria degli Angeli, 55, 57, 480n52; Signoria, 37, 475n12, 512n304, 513n307; Studio (university), 485n100, 505n260

Florensz, Cardinal Adrian. *See* Adrian VI

Florimonte, Galeazzo, 325–27

Foligno (town), 489n132

Forlì (town), 63

Forteguerri, Scipione (Scipio Carteromachus). *See* Carteromachus, Scipio

Fortune, 9, 19, 39, 41, 43, 53, 83, 167, 171, 191–93, 231, 255, 265, 269, 279, 287, 289, 291, 293, 313, 317, 339, 383, 431, 433, 439, 542n488

Fracastoro, Girolamo, 195, 435, 556n576, 612n29

France/French, xiv, 5, 69, 71, 97,
115, 119, 133, 143, 155, 181, 195,
197, 201, 207, 211, 213, 217, 231,
255, 259, 273, 279, 287, 291, 311,
313, 329, 339, 341, 389, 397, 407,
409, 411, 427, 435, 441, 449,
472n3, 481n61, 484n91,
490n140, 496n195, 498n206,
503n237, 504n252, 507n275,
516n319, 522n373, 528n417,
530n432, 532n442, 536n458,
539n472, 551n551, 557nn594–95,
561n614, 567–68nn658–59,
583n794, 589n833, 603n905,
604n913, 611n23, 618nn64–65,
618n68; Gallic, 341. *See also*
French language
Francesco di Lapacino, 601n899
Francesco "il Novello" da Carrara
(lord of Padua), 587n815
Franchino (Francesco) da
Cosenza, 63, 365
Franciscan Order, 49, 513n308
Francis I (king of France), 231,
329, 335, 339–41, 427, 572n693,
573n700, 575n725, 591n843,
592n849, 610n10, 618n64,
618nn67–68
Franco, Zorzi (Giorgio),
523n376
Frangepán, Ferencz (of Eger), 439,
616n53
Franks (people), 544n498
Fratte (Ausonia), 517n336
Frederick (king of Naples), 279,
557n593, 557n595

Frederick I (king of Denmark and
Norway), 603n911
Fregoso, Battista, 415
French language, 5, 518n344,
599n893, 619n72
French pox (syphilis), 177
Fribourg, 335
Frisia/Frisian, 123, 500n217
Friuli, 251, 520n359, 531n436
Friuli-Venezia Giulia (region),
503n239
Frosinone (province), 517n336
Fulgentius (Fabius Panciades Ful-
gentius), 355, 580n768
Furnia (Molza), 582n784

Gaguin, Robert, 409, 475n10,
603nn905–6
Galatone (place), 590n836
Galen, 131, 179, 209, 243, 359,
502n231, 521n366, 531n438,
537n464, 538n468, 547n518,
558–59nn601–2; *On the Need to
Preserve One's Health*, 221
Gallia, 608n940
Gallucci, Lucio, 167, 169, 518n338
Gallucci, Luigi (Elisio Calenzio).
*See* Calenzio, Elisio
gambling, 233, 543n489
Ganges (river), 147
Garda (lake), 87, 211
Garigliano (river), 133
Gaurico, Luca, 193, 261, 263
Gaurico, Pompeo, 471n1
Gaurico, Pomponio, 261–63,
551nn548–49, 551n551; *On Archi-*

tecture, 261; *On Metals*, 261–63;
*On Physiognomy*, 261
Gazoldo (Giovanni Francesco Ippoliti), 561n612
Gdansk, 614n43
Gebenna, 223
Geldenhouwer, Gerald, 500n217
Gellius, Aulus, *Attic Nights*, 485n105
Geminus, 537n467
Genoa/Genoese, 233, 275, 377, 403, 415, 585n807, 587n818, 599n891
George of Trebizond, 53, 95, 99–101, 159, 479n44, 491–92nn154–55, 492nn158–59, 588n828. *See also* Trebizond
Germany/German, xiv, 7, 21, 29, 123, 125, 329, 343, 351, 401, 417, 425, 427, 429–31, 437, 533n450, 552n558, 597n883, 611n22, 617n57
Gessoriac coast, 421
Gessoriacum, 608n940
Ghilini, Camillo, 415, 605n922, 606n925
Ghilini, Giacomo, 415
Ghilini, Gian Giacomo, 605n922
Giberti, Gian Matteo, 391, 545n508, 576n729, 612n30, 613n34
Giovanna d'Aragona, 571n686
Giovio, Benedetto (brother of Paolo), xiv, 369–73, 473n7, 583n794
Giovio, Paolo, ix, xvii n10, 275,

361, 373, 449, 472n4, 475n3, 483n83, 496n190, 497n197, 498n205, 502n231, 506n272, 511n298, 512n306, 529n423, 537n464, 552n559, 556nn580–82, 571n686, 576n730, 581n778, 582n784, 584n800, 587n815, 590n838, 592n851, 596n875, 597n881, 604n913, 610n10, 612n29, 617n60; motto, 561n617
Giovio, Paolo, museum of, 373, 425, 431–47; Doric columns, 21; Doric portico, 17, 19; Farnesian courtyand, 15
Giovio, Paolo, works: *Descriptio Britanniae*, 538n469; *Dialogo dell'imprese militari et amorose*, 542n488; *Elogia* (2 vols.), ix–xv; *Histories of Our Times*, ix–x, xiv–xv; *Life of Leo X*, xiv, xvi n7, 541n484; *Notable Men and Women*, x, 542n485; *On Fish*, 593n856; *Scotia*, 475n8
Giovio family, 371
Giustinian, Bernardo, 383, 588n828
Giustinian, Leonardo, 588n830
Giustiniani, Agostino, 403, 598–99nn890–91
Giza (place), 565n638
Goclenius, Conrad (Conrad Wackers), 427, 610n11
God, 43, 69, 95, 97, 281, 321, 331, 425, 563n634; Almighty, 323; Father on High, 235; Great Father, 59; Lord, 135, 157, 183, 191,

God (*continued*)
245, 387, 393, 395, 419, 423,
437, 443, 445; Maker, 37; mind
of, 163; Most-High, 369; will
of, 365, 513n307
Godfrey of Bouillon, 275, 411
Gonsalvo the Great. *See* Fernán-
dez de Córdoba, Gonzalo
Gonzaga, Cardinal Ercole, 249
Gonzaga, Cardinal Francesco,
486nn111–13
Gonzaga, Federico, 217, 535n455,
577n741
Gonzaga, Federico II, 347
Gonzaga, Ferrante, 474n13
Gonzaga, Francesco (son of Fe-
derico II), 577n741
Gonzaga, Francesco II, 535n455
Gonzaga, Giulio, 293
Goritz, Johannes, ix, 361, 544n500,
559n604, 581nn778–80
Goths/Gothic, 41, 51, 61, 407, 409
Graces, 21, 89, 231
Grana, Lorenzo, 544n500
Granada, 225, 227, 540n476
Grapaldo, Francesco Mario, 217–
19, 536nn458–59, 537n462; *On
the Parts of Houses*, 219
Gravina, Pietro, 167, 215, 257–61,
535n452, 550nn541–42,
550n546; *De Surrenti amoenitate*,
259, 550n543
Graz (place), 615n49
"Great Promotion," 497n198,
565n637
Greece/Greeks, 61, 73, 75, 91, 93,
95, 97, 99, 101, 103, 105, 107,

109, 111, 113, 115, 117, 119, 121, 125,
141, 195, 201, 209, 299, 345, 429,
423, 494n169, 500n217,
551n549, 556nn582–83; ancient,
xiii, 67, 69, 131, 403, 576n737,
607n934
Greek: Church, 490n145; lan-
guage/literature, xiii, xiv, 49, 51,
53, 61, 63, 67, 69, 71, 73, 75, 77,
91, 95, 97, 99, 101–3, 107, 109,
111, 113, 115, 117, 119, 121, 123, 137,
141, 159, 209, 211, 221, 225, 239,
243, 261, 267, 271, 275, 277, 309,
321, 327, 329, 333, 339, 343, 345,
347, 371, 377, 379, 385, 399, 403,
405, 413, 417, 421, 423, 425,
427, 437, 441, 445, 479n41,
483n83, 485n100, 491n154,
496n194, 497n196, 499nn207–
10, 499–500nn216–17, 518n342,
528n420, 537n464, 538n468,
542n485, 551n548, 556n583,
565n641, 570n674, 573n699,
576n738, 577nn740, 577n743,
583n784, 587n819, 589nn833–34,
590n840, 591n843, 596n871,
596n875, 598n885, 598n890,
600n898, 608n942, 610n10,
611n19, 612n28, 613n32, 618–
19nn71–73; names, adopted by
humanists, 151, 509n292,
556n583
*Greek Anthology*, 499n209
Gregory of Nazianzus, Saint, 427,
609n5
Gregory of Sanok, 510n293
Gregory XII (antipope), 490n143

Grocyn, William, 221–23, 538n469
Groningen, 123, 499n215
Grosseteste, Robert, 477n33
Guadalquivir (river), 225, 539n474
Guarini, Guarino (of Verona), 91, 379, 516n324, 588n828
Guazzelli, Demetrio, 79
Guicciardini, Francesco, 502n236, 528n418, 557n594
Guidi, Jacopo, 375, 584n800
Guidobaldo da Montefeltro, 602n903
Guido da Bagno (Guerra), 181, 183, 521n373
Guillén de Brocar, Arnao, 540n476
Gurk, bishopric of, 536n459
Gustav Vasa (king of Sweden), 604n911

Hades, 471n1
Hannibal, 552n555
Harudes (Arudes; ancient Germanic people), 610n13
Heaven, 367
Hebraic, 445
Hebrew language/literature, xiv, 123, 215, 225, 343, 403, 417, 425, 500n217, 563n634, 565n641, 583n784, 598n890, 619n73–74
Hebrides (islands), 407
Heidelberg, 500n219
Helicon, Mount, 111, 485n96, 495n184, 525n391
Heliopolis, Temple of Ra, 492n156
Hell, 37
Hellenizing, 551n548

Henry II (king of France,) 618n68
Henry VII (king of England), 407, 537n467, 602–3nn903–4
Henry VIII (king of England), 223, 313, 315, 319, 569n662, 569n668, 570n670, 577n742, 614n37
Hereford, Cathedral of, 602n903
heresy, 343, 389, 425, 486n113, 508n282, 514n311, 579n762, 604n911
Hermogenes of Tarsus, 99, 491n154
Herodian, 141, 505n261; Histories, 385
Herodotus, 61
Herronesou, bishopric of, 497n197
Hervé de Portzmoguer (Primauguet), 604n917
Hesperides, Gardens of, 175
Hierapetra, bishopric of, 497n197
Hippocrates/Hippocratic, 73, 103, 179, 303, 361, 485n99, 493n167, 521n366, 572n695, 581n776, 581n778
Hippocrene, the, 71, 485n96
History (personified), 51
Holland/Dutch, 333, 341, 367, 369, 593n857
Holophernes (character in Love's Labor's Lost), 534n450
Holy Faith, 317
Holy League, 528n417, 532n442
Homer/Homeric, 115, 167; Batrachomyomachia (attrib.), 518n338
Horace/Horatian, 347, 391, 445;

Horace/Horatian (*continued*)
   *Epodes*, 581n777; *Odes*, 569n666,
   611n20; *Satires*, 577n743
Hungary/Hungarian, xiv, 283, 295,
   437, 516n324, 562n626,
   615nn49–50, 616n53
Hutten, Ulrich von, and *Letters of
   Obscure Men*, 417, 606n928,
   607n931
Hylas, 496n187

Iamblichus, 159
Iapygia/Iapygian, 387, 590n838
Illyria, xii
immortality of the soul, 247–49,
   349–53, 547–48n523, 570n677,
   571n685, 578n751
Imperia (courtesan), 475n3
Imperial: army, 249, 259, 309, 329,
   549n532, 552n559, 558n597,
   567n651, 573–74n706; viceroy,
   553n564
Indians, New World, 594n859
Inghirami, Tommaso (called Fe-
   dra), 357, 524n384, 580n770,
   597n878
Ingolstadt (place), 123
Innocent VII (pope), 49
Innocent VIII (pope), 135, 149,
   503nn246–47, 507n273,
   537n466
*Institutiones*, 233
Insubrians/Insubrian (Milanese),
   213, 399
Ionian Sea, 17
Isaac, Heinrich, 506n267

Isabella d'Aragona, 395, 595n868
Ischia, 249
Isernia (place), 471n1
Isidore of Kiev, 93, 490n146
Islam, 514n311
Ismail I, 565n638
Isocrates, 619n72
Isonzo (river), 531n436
Istria, 503n246, 520n359
Italian language/literature, 5, 41,
   75, 472n6, 501n223, 518n344,
   571n686, 599n893, 612n28. *See
   also* Tuscan language/literature
Italy/Italian, x, xi, xii, xiv, 9, 35,
   37, 45, 49, 71, 91, 93, 101, 103,
   109, 115, 119, 127, 131, 147, 155,
   161, 169, 181, 201, 221, 223, 225,
   273, 293, 311, 313, 323, 383, 387,
   401, 407, 409, 413, 415, 429,
   433, 449, 484n91, 489n139,
   493n164, 494n177, 502n236,
   527n405, 533n450, 536n458,
   537n464, 558n597, 561n614,
   567–68nn657–59, 573n700,
   574n710, 576n731, 583n794,
   589n833, 590n838, 593n855,
   603n906, 607n933, 611n19,
   611n22, 615n48; east-central,
   507n278; northern, 181, 395,
   587n819; northwestern, 111;
   southern, 103, 471n1, 481n61,
   508n279, 561n614

Jacob of Hoogstraten, 417–19,
   606–7nn930–31
James I of Scotland, 602n901

Jason, 235, 508n278
Jean de Lorraine, Cardinal,
618n65
Jerome, Saint, *Book of Times*,
599n895
Jerusalem, 123, 411
Jesus Christ, 349, 361, 609n2,
612n30
Jews/Jewish/Judaism, 417, 514n311,
565n641, 606–7nn929–30
John (Byzantine emperor), 91
John I Albert (Jan Olbracht; king
of Poland), 153, 510n294, 510–
11nn296–97
John XXII (pope), 31, 475n5
John XXIII (antipope; Baldassare
Cossa), 91, 478n34, 478n40,
490n143
John Chrysostom, Saint: *Life of St.
Babylas*, 413; *On the Priesthood*,
413
John Duns Scotus, xiii, 33–35
John Scottus Eriugena, 35,
475n10
Jove/Zeus/Jupiter (deity), 129,
329, 449, 543n494; Thunderer,
299
Juan de Urbina, 331, 573n706
Julian vines, 17
Julio-Claudian principate, 471n2
Julius Caesar, 5, 265, 383, 552n555;
*Gallic War*, 610n13
Julius II (pope), 115, 197, 201, 211,
217, 219, 233, 301, 311, 524n383,
528n416, 529n423, 536nn458–
59, 552n555, 553n563, 567n656,

568n658, 582n784, 589–
90nn834–35
Juno (deity): Argive, 261, 550n548;
Lucina, 267, 553n560
Justice, Divine, 317
Justinian (Roman emperor), 177
Juvenal (Decimus Junius Juvena-
lis), 482n69, 593n857

Kabbalah, 417, 507n273, 563–
64n634
Kalocsa-Bacs, archbishopric of,
616n53
Kampen, 367
Kansuh al-Ghuri (Qansuh al-
Ghawri), al-Ashraf (sultan of
Egypt), 253, 395, 548n530,
565n638, 595n865
Kilia (Chilia, Kilya), 511n297
Königsberg, 607n933
Konstanz, 427, 610n13
Koran, 565n641
Krantz, Albert, 427, 611n17
Kromer, Marcin, 437, 511n298,
512n300, 615n45

Lactantius (Lucius Caecilius
Firmianus), 471n1
Ladislaus II Jagiellon (king of Bo-
hemia and Hungary), 283,
510n294, 510n297, 558n601,
603n909
Ladislaus III (king of Poland and
Hungary), 153, 511n300
Lagean vines, 561n613
Lago di Vico (place), 546n514

Lampridio, Giovanni Benedetto, 345–49, 576n738, 577nn742–43

Landau (place), 603n910

Landi, Agostini, 473n5

Landino, Cristoforo, 161, 383, 515n317

Lang, Mattias (bishop of Gurk), 536n459, 611n119

Lannoy, Charles de, 553n564, 573n705

Lascaris, Janus, 107–9, 119–21, 345, 413, 491n150, 498nn203–4, 498–99nn206–7, 576n738, 597n878, 608n942

La Spezia (town), 377

Lateran Council, Fifth, 567n656

Latimer, William, 221–23, 538n469, 614n37

Latin language/literature, xi, xii, xiv, 41, 43, 45, 53, 55, 67, 69, 71, 73, 75, 77, 87, 95, 97, 99, 101, 103, 107, 109, 111, 113, 121, 123, 135, 137, 139, 141, 157, 159, 167, 169, 171, 177, 185, 211, 223, 225, 239, 243, 251, 261, 267, 271, 275, 277, 281, 295, 305, 307, 309, 321, 325, 327, 329, 331, 335, 339, 343, 347, 363, 367, 377, 379, 381, 383, 385, 387, 389, 399, 405, 407, 409, 411, 415, 417, 421, 423, 425, 427, 437, 439, 441, 445, 477n22, 480n48, 491n154, 494n169, 500n218, 508n280, 518n344, 521n366, 535n453, 537n464, 537–38nn467–68, 542n485, 545n506, 551n548, 554n565,

564n636, 565n641, 566n649, 570n671, 572n696, 582–83nn784–85, 586n809, 587n819, 588n830, 589n834, 590n840, 594n859, 596n875, 598n885, 598n890, 601n900, 610n10, 612n26, 613n32, 617n59

Latium/Latins, 31, 61, 69, 89, 93, 111, 113, 121, 125, 129, 137, 163, 221, 494n169, 500n217, 546n514

Lauingen, 29, 475n1

Lautrec (Odet de Foix, Vicomte de Lautrec), 255

Law, Mosaic, 564n634

law, study, teaching and practice of, 45–49, 53, 61, 169, 231–35, 311–13, 337–39, 413, 427, 518n342, 543nn489–90, 543n496, 568n659, 574–75n717, 579n762, 597n880, 584n797, 610n12, 613n33

Lazzaro of Piacenza, 133

Lecce (province), 590n836

Lefèvre d'Etaples, Jacques, 389, 591nn844–46, 591n849, 618n70, 619n73

Legnago (place), 195, 526n401

Leipzig, University of, 597n880

Lelio, Antonio, 524n384

Le Muy (place), 619n76

Leonardo da Vinci, 498n205

Leone, Ambrogio, 572n696

Leoni, Piero, 131–33, 502n236

Leoniceno, Niccolò (Niccolò da Lonigo), 169, 243–47, 547n518, 590n840, 611n23; *The Antisophist Roman Doctor*, 245; *On the Gen-*

erative Force, 245; *On the Three Orders of Learning*, 245

Leonico Tomeo, Niccolò, 321–23, 570n674, 570n679, 577n740, 609n945, 614n37; *On Groat Porridge*, 321; *On Jacks*, 321; *On the Intellect*, 321; *On Various Kinds of History*, 321

Leo X (pope; Giovanni de' Medici), ix, xvi n2, 101, 115, 117, 119, 127, 129, 141, 185, 227, 229, 231, 235, 241, 253, 285, 287, 301, 309, 343, 345, 357, 361, 399, 401, 417, 421–23, 496n195, 497nn197–98, 497n200, 506n266, 524n384, 541nn481–82, 546n512, 551–52nn554–55, 560–61nn612–13, 563n634, 564–65nn637–38, 576n738, 577n742, 590n835, 597n878, 608n943, 611n23, 612n28, 612n30

Leo XIII (pope), 533n450

Le Roy, Louis, 443, 619n72

Lesbia (of Catullus), 111, 496n186

Lethe, 3

*Letters of Obscure Men* (Johannes Crotus Rubianus and Ulrich von Hutten), 417, 606n928, 607n931

Leuven, 579n762, 610n11, 617nn59–60; University, 441, 499n216

Levita, Elijah, 565n641

Libethron (Libethros, Libethra), fountain of Sisyphus, 87, 488n128

Libitina (deity), 339

Liguria/Ligurian, 63, 69, 233, 377, 381

Lily, George, 538n469

Linacre, Thomas, 221–23, 537n464, 537–39nn466–70, 614n37

Lincoln, Cathedral of, 602n903

Lippomano, Pietro, 241, 545n508

Lithuania, 510n293, 510n297

Liuzzi, Mondino de, 209

Livy (Titus Livius), 207, 472n1; "French," 604n913

Lodi (place), 195, 375

Logau, Georg von, 437, 615n48

Loire (river), 273, 413

Lombardy/Lombard, 205, 207, 209, 490n141, 557n591

London, England, 602n903; College of Physicians, 223, 539n470; Royal Society, 507n272; St. Paul's, Oxgate, 602n903

Longueil, Antoine de, 543n495

Longueil, Christophe de, 235–39, 401, 544nn500–501, 594n860, 614n37, 618n65

Lopez de Mendoza, Iñigo (count of Tendilla), 595n864

Loredan, Leonardo (doge of Venice), 271, 554n573

Lorenziani, Lorenzo, 179–81

Loudon (place), 575n728

Louis II (king of Bohemia and Hungary), 558n601

Louis XI (king of France), 472n3, 484n91

Louis XII (king of France), 119,

Louis XII (*continued*)
161, 233, 311, 411, 498n206,
516n319, 527n405, 532n442,
543n496, 557n595, 567n655
Low Countries, xiv. *See also* Holland/Dutch
Lucan (Marcus Annaeus Lucanus), 223
Lucania, 508n278
Lucca, 83, 357, 413
Lucian of Samosata, 333, 556n582;
*Dialogues*, 245; *Lapithae*, 275;
*Loves*, 275; *Rules for Writing History*, 275
Lucina (Roman matron), 553n560
Lucretius (Titus Lucretius Carus), 355, 593n858
Luni, harbor of, 377
Luther, Martin, 237, 293, 319, 367,
369, 389, 544n502, 562n621,
569n669, 576n732, 598n885,
609n2
Lutheran sect, 343, 351
Lyon, 353
lyre, 105

Macedonia, 488n128, 495n185
Machiavelli, Niccolò, 307–11, 413,
567n651; *Mandragola*, 566n648;
*Nicia*, 309; *Prince*, 572n686
Maddaleni, Fausto, 101
Madrid (Mantua Carpetanorum),
269, 554n565
Maeander (river), 299
Maecenas/Maecenases, xiv, 23, 75,
363, 546n512; "a foreign," 259
Maffei, Raffaele, xvi n8, 385–87,

492n159, 561n618, 589–
90nn834–35
Maggiore (lake), 395
Magii, Costanza de, 534n450
Magna Graecia, 103
Maguelonne, bishopric of, 618n67
Maimonides, *Guide for the Perplexed*, 599n890
Mainardi, Arlotto, 49, 478n35,
558–59nn601–3; *Book of Jests*,
49, 478n35
Mainardi, Giovanni, 283–85; *Letters*, 283
Mainardi, Marietta, 559n603
Maino, Giasone, 311
Mainz, archdiocese of, 606n930
Maioragio, Marcantonio, 403
Maiorano of Salento, 97, 107–9,
121, 491n150
Malatesta, Pandolfo (Pandolfaccio; tyrant of Rimini), 181, 183,
521–22nn373–74, 522n376,
523nn378–79
Malatesta, Roberto "the Magnificent," 522n374
Malatesta, Sigismondo (lord of
Rimini), 403, 523n379
Malcantone a San Gervasio (villa),
502n235
Mamluks, 395, 548n530, 595n865
Manetti, Giannozzo, 476n16
Manfredonia, archbishopric of, 77,
95, 486n106, 491n148
Mantua/Mantuan, 215, 217, 229,
247, 249, 267, 269, 347, 373,
486n111, 533–34n450, 573n702,
577n741; Church of

Sant'Andrea, 347, 577n746; Convent of San Francesco, 535n455; Museo della Città at Palazzo San Sebastiano, 536n455; Porta Nuova, 535n455

Mantuanus (Mantuan). *See* Spagnolo, Baptista

Manuel I (king of Portugal), 619n80

Manuel II Palaeologus (Byzantine emperor), 489–90nn138–40

Manuzio, Aldo, 329, 556n583, 573n703

Manuzio, Paolo, 471n1, 594n861

Marcello, Giacomo Antonio, 586n813

Marches, the, 507n278, 550n548

Margaret of Parma, 471n1

Marguerite de Navarre, 592n849

*Marie de la Cordelière* (ship), 411, 604n917

Mark Antony, 5, 595n862

Marone, Andrea, 249–53, 549n532

Mars (deity), 109, 165, 189, 271, 281, 437

Marsi, Pietro (Petrus Marsus Cesensis), 151, 509n289

Marsi da Pescina, Paolo, 509n289

Marsilio of Padua, 576n731

Marso, Leonardo, 359

Marsuppini, Carlo, 51, 61, 478n38

Martelli, Pietro, 199, 594n861

Martial (Marcus Valerius Martialis), 77, 223, 265, 273, 474n22

Martínez Siliceo, Juan (bishop of Cartagena), 447, 619n78

Martin V (pope), 375, 584n798

Marullo Tarcaniota, Michele, 109–11, 494n177, 495n181, 496n187, 534n450

Mary, Virgin Mother, 41, 281, 361, 535n454

*Mary James* (ship), 604n917

Marzano (Marino I; duke of Sessa), 571n682

Marzio, Galeotto, 137, 163–65, 516n324, 517n328, 517n331; *On Humankind*, 163–65

Masella di Santomango, 557n591

Masorete, 565n641

Massimi, Angelo de', 581n773

Massimi, Domenico de', 581n773

Massimo, Lelio, 544n500

Matthaeus of Sion, Cardinal, 311

Matthias Corvinus (Mátyás Hunyadi; king of Hungary), 153, 163, 439, 510n295, 516n324, 517n328, 615n50, 616n55

Mausolus, 189, 525n393

Maximilian (Holy Roman Emperor), 201, 529n421, 529n426, 536n459, 567n655, 598n885

Maximilian II (Holy Roman Emperor), 429, 611n21

Maximus of Tyre, 421, 608n942

Mazè, Paola de, 534n450

Mechelen (place), 235

Medici, Alessandro de', 325, 583n786

Medici, Bianca de', 608n941

Medici, Catherine de', 618n67

Medici, Cosimo I de', ix, 55, 105–7, 127, 129, 161, 163, 472n5,

Medici, Cosimo I de' (*continued*)
480n48, 480n52, 481n54,
515n315, 584n800, 617n60
Medici, Giovanni de'. *See* Leo X
Medici, Giuliano de', 141, 357,
505n257, 505n259, 580n771
Medici, Giulio de'. *See* Clement
VII
Medici, Lorenzo di Piero de' (il
Magnifico), 69–71, 107, 113, 119,
127–29, 131, 141, 143, 145, 161,
163, 221, 485n100, 498nn203–4,
502n236, 506n267, 507n273,
515n317, 564n635, 565n637,
608n941
Medici, Lorenzo (Lorenzino) di
Pierfrancesco de', 365, 397,
572n688, 583nn785–86, 596n873
Medici, Lucrezia Tornabuoni de'
(wife of Piero di Cosimo),
563n630
Medici, Maria de', 541n482
Medici, Piero di Cosimo de' (the
Gouty), 107, 133, 161, 502–
3nn236–37, 507n275, 512n306,
541n481, 563n630, 608n941
Medici family, 107, 143, 155, 227,
309, 397, 495n177, 507n275,
516n318, 521n367
medicine, practice of, ix, 83, 131–
33, 179, 209–211, 221–23, 231,
243, 283, 327–29, 343, 387, 427,
502n231, 502n233, 529n423,
532n440, 539n470, 542n486,
546n512, 558–59n601–2,
560nn605–6, 572nn693–98,

579n762, 581n776, 585n801,
589n833, 593n858, 594n861,
610n10, 612n29
Mehmed II (sultan), 498n205,
603n909
Melanchthon, Philipp, 435
Mellini, Celso, 237, 544n500,
576n738
Mellini, Pietro, 544n500, 576n738
Melozzo da Forlì, 487n114
Mendoza y Bobadilla, Cardinal
Francisco de, 447, 619n79
Mengeringhausen (place), 610n11
Mercury (deity), 21, 89
Mergellina, villa at, 281, 557n595;
Church of Santa Maria del
Parto, 558n598
Merlani, Giorgio. *See* Merula,
Giorgio
Merlo, Enrico, 526n401
Merula, Giorgio (Giorgio Mer-
lani), 137–39, 163, 211, 275,
504nn249–51, 505n253,
530n430, 533n450, 556n580
Messina (city), 331
Michael Scot, 525n396
Michiel, Marcantonio, 593n855
Michiel family, 508n282
Miguel da Silva, Cardinal, 447,
619n80
Milan/Milanese, ix, x, 67, 69, 113,
115, 137, 205, 207, 211, 231, 357,
371, 389, 399, 415, 471n1,
474n19, 479n43, 481n62,
482n73, 490n140, 496n190,
504n249, 504nn251–52, 516n319,

522n373, 527n406, 530n430,
531n436, 531n439, 568n659,
570n674, 587n819, 588n824,
591n843, 596n875, 605n922,
612n28, 613n33; Basilica of
Sant'Ambrogio, 67; Basilica of
Sant'Eustorgio, 139; Beatrice
Gate, 213, 533n449; Cam-
posanto Monumentale,
568n659; Church of San
Marco, 213
Milesian tales, 43
Mirandola (place), 305, 525n398
Mirteo, Pietro, 43, 47, 53–55, 57,
73–75, 77, 129, 175, 179–81, 187,
199, 203, 217, 227, 247, 253, 263,
279, 307, 347, 369
Modena, 289, 363, 518n344,
582n784
Modesti, Publio Francesco,
592n851
Moldavia/Moldavian, 153,
511nn297–98
Molza, Francesco Maria,
544n500, 582–83nn784–85
Molza, Mario, 363–67
Momus, 89
Moncada, Hugh de, 331, 574n706
Mondragone (place), 325
Monemvasia, archbishopric of, 117,
497n197
Monopoli (town), 285, 561n614
Montagnana (place), 165, 517n328,
517n331
Monte Cassino, abbey, 573n698
Monte Mario, villa at, 576n738

Montepulciano, 505n256
Montpellier, 618n67
Moors, 223, 225, 227
More, Filip (of Ciula), 439,
616nn50–51
More, Thomas, 313–17, 605n917;
Utopia, 315, 569n662
Moses, 299, 563n634
Müller, Johann. See Regiomontanus
Murad II (Sultan), 101, 153, 385,
493n164, 512n300, 589n832
Muscovy, x
Muse/Muses, xi, xvii n10, 5, 11, 21,
23, 39, 51, 53, 59, 61, 85, 87, 97,
105, 109, 111, 129, 143, 149, 165,
173, 195, 197, 215, 217, 219, 227,
243, 251, 253, 255, 259, 263, 273,
275, 277, 281, 347, 361, 363, 367,
381, 391, 395, 425, 431, 435, 437,
441, 451, 485n96, 488n128,
495n184, 520n353, 582n784;
Calliope, 243; Urania, 175,
520n353
Musurus, Marcus, 115–17, 271,
496nn194–95, 497n197,
497n199, 518n342, 576n738,
616n50

Nacrian Fields, 289, 561n618
Nádasdy, Tamás (Thomas Ná-
dasty), 437, 615n49
Nanninck, Pieter, 441, 617n59
Naples, Peace of (1455), 480n48,
550n546
Naples/Neapolitan, x, 59, 87, 143,

Naples/Neapolitan (*continued*)
167, 171, 195, 255, 259, 279, 287,
481n61, 482n65, 495n177,
498n206, 518n344, 519n348,
519n350, 526n402, 535n452,
551n551, 553n564, 557nn594–95,
561n614, 571n683, 613n34
Nature, 13, 17, 29, 31, 89, 165, 167,
239, 257, 303, 317, 321, 323, 367,
525n396
Navagero, Andrea, 195, 271–75,
554n573, 555n576
Neakademia (of Aldus), 556n583
Nebbio, bishopric of, 403, 599n891
Nebrija (Lebrija; Nebrissa Veneria), 225, 539n474
Nebrija, Elio Antonio de (Antonio Martínez de Cala), 223–27,
445, 539n473, 539–40nn475–76
Nebrija, Sancho de, 540n476
Nebrija, Sebastián de, 540n476
Negri, Girolamo, 544n500,
593n855, 594n860
Neptune (deity), 15, 111, 449
Nero (Roman emperor), 21, 171
Newton, Isaac, 507n272
Niccoli, Niccolò, 601n899
Nicholas V (pope), 51, 55, 95, 375,
480n52, 482n72, 483n83,
493n165, 493n167, 585n803,
586n813
Nifo, Agostino, 323–27, 571n682,
571n686; *On Divination*, 325; *On
the King and the Tyrant*, 325
Nifo, Domizio (baron of
Joppolo; Tropea), 571n682

Nifo, Giovanni, 571n682
Nile (river), 514n312
Niobe, 121
Nizzoli, Mario, 598n888
Nocera Umbra, bishopric of,
518n339
Noniana, Villa, 544n502
North Sea, 429
Novara (town), 275, 583n794
Nuremberg, 427, 615n47
nymphs, 17

Octavian (Augustus), 5
Odi da Montopoli, Pietro,
508n280
Oecolampadius, Johannes, 319,
425, 570n669, 609n2
Ogygius/Ogyges, spring of, 111,
495n185
Oldenburg, House of, 603n911
Olesnicki, Zbigniew, 510n293
Orcus, 3
Oreads, 17
Origen, 600n897
Orkney (islands), 407
Orláns, Duc d', 618n67
Orpheus, 145
Orsini, Cardinal Franciotto,
562n624
Oscans, 357
Ottoman Empire/Ottomans, x,
91, 119, 493n164, 497n197,
498n204, 511n297, 589n832,
603n907. *See also* Turks/Turk-
ish
Ovid (Publius Ovidius Naso),

471n1; *Ibis*, 399, 488n124; *Loves*, 495n181; *Metamorphoses*, 499n213

Oxford (city), 537n464, 614n37

Pace, Richard, 570n676

Pacheco y Mendoza, María, 540n477

Padilla, Juan de, 540n477

Padniewski, Filip, 437, 614n44

Padua/Paduan, 41, 131, 203, 209, 233, 237–39, 271, 301, 321, 323, 345, 389, 496nn194–95, 498n203, 504n250, 529n423, 529n426, 531n436, 543n491, 545n505, 568n659, 570n674, 570n679, 571n683, 577n739, 577n741, 591n840, 613n34; University, 115, 205, 518n342, 529n426, 532n440, 543n490, 567n654, 577n740, 602n902, 612n29, 614nn37–38

Paleologus, House of, 71

Palermo, 61, 475n3, 481n58

Palladio, Blosio, 267

Palmieri, Matteo, 405, 599–600nn895–97

Palo (place), 546n512

Palonio, Marcello, 255, 549n537

Pannonius, Janus (János Csezmicze), 439, 516n324, 615n50

Panormita (Antonio Beccadelli), 53, 57–61, 63, 171, 481n58, 481n60, 481n62, 482n64, 519n349, 586n809; as "Father of Elegance," 57

Papal States, 536n458. *See also* Church, Roman Catholic

Papirius Maius, 575n717

Paris, France, 181, 235, 291, 327, 339, 343, 543n496, 574n709, 592n849, 604n913, 608n939, 618n70, 619n73; bishopric of, 572n693; Cathedral of Notre Dame, 327, 411, 572n693; Collège de Montaigu, 574n709, 602n901; Collège du Cardinal Lemoine, 591n845; Collège du Plessis, 543n496; University, 343, 573n699, 602n901, 617n62

Parma, 217, 235, 536n458; Monastery of San Giovanni Evangelista, 537n462

Parnassus, Mount, 71, 89, 151

Parrasio, Aulo Giano, 399, 496n190, 596n875, 597nn877–79

Particiaco, Agnello, 588n829

Pas-de-Calais, 223

Paul, Saint (apostle), 476n21, 606n929

Paul II (pope), 79, 87, 95, 149, 151, 293, 486n113, 489n131, 508nn281–82

Paul III (pope), ix, 261, 319, 343, 349, 357, 369, 472n4, 506n266, 576n733, 578n755, 580n772, 612n28, 615n47, 617n61

Pausanias, 613n32

Pavia, ix, 67, 81, 91, 115, 133, 209, 231, 233, 311, 490n140, 543nn489–90, 557n592,

Pavia (*continued*)
567n655, 568nn658–59,
584n797; bishopric of, 83,
487n120; Church of San Gia-
como Fuori le Mura, 543n492;
Church of San Paolo Fuori le
Mura, 235; University, 49, 211,
490n141, 499n216, 502n234
Pazzi, Cosimo de', xiii, 421–23,
608n942
Pazzi, Guglielmo di Antonio de',
608n941
Pazzi Conspiracy, 53, 69, 141,
505n257
Pazzi de' Medici, Alessandro de',
xiii, 423, 608–9nn944–45
Pécs, bishopric of, 516n324, 615–
16nn50–51
Pegasus, 485n96
Pellicier, Guillaume, 443, 618n67
Peloponnese, 495n177, 497n197
Pena (river), 495n185
Peneian caves, 111
Périon, Joachim, 443, 617n62
Peripatetics, 99, 247, 321, 349
Permessus (river), 87, 189, 488n128
Perotti, Niccolò, 75–77, 95–97,
485n103, 486n106, 491n148;
*Cornucopiae*, 77, 485n105
Perrenot, Nicholas (lord of Gran-
velle), 441, 617n58
Perrenot de Granvelle, Antoine
(bishop of Arras), 439, 617n57
Persia/Persian, 51, 301
Persius, *Satires*, 569n666
Persona, Cristoforo, 51, 385
Perugia/Perugian, 47, 49, 77, 87,

486n106, 488n130, 519n348;
Chiesa di San Francesco al
Prato, 47, 477n28; University,
45
Pesaro, 169, 241, 277, 518–19n345,
525n389, 546n511
Peter Martyr d'Anghiera, 395;
*Babylonian Legation*, 395,
595n865; *Decades of the New
World*, 395
Petrarch, Francesco, xi, xii, 39–41,
43, 329, 367, 375, 476n18,
535n453; *Africa*, 39
Petronius (Gaius Petronius Arbi-
ter), 477n22, 524n387
Petrucci, Cardinal Alfonso, 301,
564n637
Peuerbach, Georg von, 607n933
Pfefferkorn, Johann, 607n930
Phalaecian meter, 546n511
Phalaris (tyrant of Akragas), 315,
569n661
Philandrier, Guillaume, 435,
614n40
Philibert de Châlon (prince of
Orange), 281, 331, 558n597,
573n706
Philip I (king of France), 604n915
Philip II (king of Spain), 447
Philippe le Beau, 543n496
philology, 61, 137–39, 185, 377,
483n75, 496n195, 597n877
Philomusus, Johannes Franciscus
(Gianfrancesco Superchi), 277,
556n586
Phlegethon, 37
Phoenix, 145

Phrixus's ram, 235, 543n494

Piacenza, 235, 381, 536n458

Picardy, 574n712

Piccinino, Niccolò, 481n62

Piccolomini, Cardinal Jacopo. *See* Ammannati-Piccolomini, Cardinal Jacopo

Piccolomini family, 81

Picentia/Picentine, 147, 261, 507–8n278

Picenum, 508n278

Pico della Mirandola, Alberto, 305

Pico della Mirandola, Galeotto, 305

Pico della Mirandola, Gianfrancesco, 303–7, 559n602; *On the Best Kind of Imitation*, 305

Pico della Mirandola, Giovanni, 137, 145–47, 161, 303, 495n177, 507nn273–74, 515n317, 533n450, 559n602; *Apology*, 147, 507n273; *Heptaplus*, 147, 507n273

Piety (personified), 351

piety, religious, 31–37, 55–57, 63, 79–81, 97–99, 119, 149, 155–59, 237, 315, 317–19, 333, 349-55, 367–69, 397, 417, 421, 425–27, 439, 443, 514n312, 614n37

Pigge, Albert, xiv, 367–69; *On the Hierarchy*, 367

Pighinuzzi da Pietrasanta, Tommaso, 544n500

Pimpinella, Vicenzo, 536n459

Pindar/Pindaric, 347, 349, 577n742

Pio, Alberto (prince of Carpi), 289–93, 562n624, 576n732, 590n838, 594n859

Pio, Battista, 355–59

Pio, Cardinal Rodolfo, 293, 562n620

Pio, Cecilia (wife of Alberto), 562n624

Pio, Francesco? (son of Alberto), 562n624

Pio, Giovan Battista (Giambattista), 580n767, 613n32

Pirckheimer, Willibald, 427, 609nn4–5

Pirmilla of Senigallia, 361, 582n782

Pisa, 157, 179, 311, 313, 405, 413, 516n318, 568n659, 571n683, 599nn895–96; Conciliabulum of, 532n442; Council of, 601n899; University, 543n491, 567n654, 569n659

Pistoia, 413

Pius II (pope), 59, 79, 81, 83, 87, 89, 95, 486n106, 488n131

Plantagenet, House of, 614n37

Planudes, Maximus, 601n899

Platina (Bartolomeo Sacchi), 79–81, 89, 95, 149, 486n111, 486–87nn113–14; *History*, 79; *On the Best Citizen*, 79; *On the True Good*, 79; *On True Nobility*, 79

Plato/Platonic/Platonism, 37, 97, 99, 101, 117, 159, 163, 221, 345, 351, 359, 421, 515n314, 516n321, 570n679, 619n72; *Phaedrus*, 221

Plautus, 295, 355, 359; *Poenulus*, 357

Pletho, George Gemistus, 95, 491n148, 589n833

Pliny the Elder, xvi n9, 21, 135, 169, 197, 327, 475n8, 601n900; *Natural History*, 618n64; *Natural History Pref.*, 472n4; *Natural History 2*, 550n548; *Natural History 3*, 508n278, 531n436; *Natural History 4*, 488n128, 608n940; *Natural History 8*, 514n312; *Natural History 20*, 560n609

Pliny the Younger, xvi n9, 13, 15, 21, 205, 473n7, 473n10, 556n580; *Letters*, 275, 474n19, 530n431, 535n454, 611n24

Plotinus, 159

Plutarch, 69, 77, 484n89, 588n830; *Lives*, 73, 379, 485n99, 586n813; *On Moral Virtue*, 255

Po (river), 67, 189, 279, 293, 331, 557n592

Podalirius (son of Aesculapius), 285, 560n606

Poggio (Poggio Bracciolini), 51–55, 63, 91–93, 95, 397, 478n40, 479n42, 479n44; *Facetiae*, 53, 479n42, 479n46; *History of the Florentine People*, 53, 480n48; *On Avarice*, 53; *On the Ill Fortune of Princes*, 53; *On the Variability of Fortune*, 53

Poitiers, 543n496

Poland/Poles/Polish, xii, 153, 437, 510n293, 510–11n297, 512n300, 614–15nn44–45

Pole, Reginald, 237, 435, 544n502, 614n37

Policastro (Bussentino, Buxentum; place), 395, 493n168

Poliziano (Angelo Ambrogini), 71, 85, 89, 105, 109, 113, 125, 137, 141–45, 161, 199, 221, 271, 299, 385, 484n93, 495n177, 500n217, 505nn256–57, 506n263, 506nn267–68, 515n317; *Letters*, 299; *Miscellanea*, 139, 141, 505n253

Polybius, 77, 499n208, 590n838; *Military Tactics*, 121

Polydore Vergil (Polidoro Virgilio), 407, 602nn902–3; *English History*, 407, 602nn903–4

Pomicelli da Genazzano, Mariano, 299, 564n635

Pompeo, Cardinal, 265

Pomponazzi, Pietro, 203, 247–49, 323, 349, 529n423, 529n426, 547n525; *On Fate*, 249; *On the Hidden Power of Incantations*, 249

Pomponio Leto, Giulio, xiii, 79, 147–51, 175, 486n111, 497n197, 508n278, 508nn280–82, 509n292, 551n548; *Academy*, 85, 95, 101, 151, 275, 285, 486n111, 486n113, 497n197, 508–9nn281–82

Pomponio Mela, 427, 503n244

Poncher, François, 327, 572n693

Pontano, Giovanni, 57, 105, 111, 151, 167, 171–75, 195, 215, 257, 279, 299, 387, 395, 496n187, 519nn348–50, 520nn353–54, 526n402, 535n452, 557n594, 590n836, 590n839, 596n869;

*Charon*, 173; *Egidio* (dialogue), 299; *Gardens of the Hesperides*, 173; *Tumuli*, 397, 509n290, 596n869
popes: Pala Index, 579n762; Roman pontiff, 201, 317, 369; Roman see, 369; supreme pontiff, 69. *See also names of popes*; Vatican
Pordenone (place), 195, 526n404
Portugal, xiv, 447
Posillipo (place), 281
Possevino, Giovanni Battista, 355, 373
Postumo, Guido (Silvestri), 193–95, 241–43, 545–46nn511–12, 556n586; *Elegies*, 241
Pot, Jan, 510n297
Praetorian Guard, 566n649
pre-Socratics, 607n934
Priscian (Priscianus Caesariensis), 357
Probo da Piperno, 359, 581n773
Procopius, 385, 387; *Gothic History*, 51
Proculus, Saint, 578n757
Propertius, 496n187
Protestantism/Protestants, xviii n12, 579n762
Provence, 335, 574n712
Psellos, Michael, 159
ps.-Proclus, *Sphere*, 221, 537n464, 537n467
Ptolemy (Claudius Ptolemaeus), 419, 600n899, 607n934; *Almagest*, 419; *Cosmography*, 427; *Geography*, 405, 601n900

Pucci, Giannozzo, 512n306
Pulci, Luca, 141, 297, 505n258
Pulci, Luigi, 505n258; *Morgante*, 563n630
Pyrene, 488n128
Pyrrhic victory, 532n442

Querno, Camillo (the Archpoet), 285–89, 561n612; *Alexiad*, 285
Quintilian (Marcus Fabius Quintilianus), 53, 614n40; *Institutes of Oratory*, 480n47

Ragusa, 531n437
Raidaniyah, 548n530
Raince, Nicolas, 5, 472n3, 472n6
Rallo, Manilio Cabacio, 117, 497n197
Rangoni, Cardinal Ercole, 243, 546n512
Raphael (Raffaello Sanzio da Urbino), *Portrait of Leo X*, 541n482
Ravenna/Ravennan, 37, 97, 476n17
Reason (personified), 31
Reformation, 570n669
Regensburg: bishopric of, 419, 608n936; Colloquy of, 578n754; Diet of, 616n53
*Regent* (ship), 604n917
Reggio, 518n344
Regiomontanus (Johann Müller, Molitor), 419–21, 607n933, 608n936; *On Triangles*, 419
René of Anjou, 481n61
Requesens family, 551n548
Reuchlin, Johann (Capnion), 417–

Reuchlin, Johann (*continued*)
19, 606n928, 607nn930–31; *On the Marvelous Word,* 417; *On the Tenets of Kabbalistic Knowledge,* 417
Revolt of the Comuneros, 227, 540n477
Rhabanus Maurus, 533n448
Rhallis, Nicola, 109, 495n177
Rhine (river), 293
Rhyndacus (place), 497n202
Riario, Pietro, Cardinal, 487n114
Ricchieri, Lodovico Maria (Lodovico Celio; Caelius Rhodiginus), 389, 590n840, 591n842
Riccio, Pier Francesco, 584n800
Ridolfi, Cardinal Niccolò, 337, 512n306, 574n717
Ridolfi, Vincenzo, 513n309
Rieti (town), 581n773
Rimini (town), 183, 239, 522nn373–74, 522n376, 523nn378–79
roads: Emilian Road, 63; Valerian Way, 175; Via Cassia, 487n121
Romagna, 481n62
Roman Empire/Roman emperors, 149, 337
Romania, 616n54
Roman language/literature, xiii, 55, 61, 63, 73, 77, 103, 109, 123, 560n608, 563n634. *See also* Latin language/literature
Roman/Romans, ix, xiii, 5, 61, 63, 65, 87, 101, 137, 167, 195, 221, 229, 235, 237, 255, 357, 365, 393, 443, 544nn497–98, 544n500,

552n558, 580n771, 581n773, 581n776, 581n778, 589n834; ancient, 265, 403, 429, 492n156, 496n186, 552n555, 601n900
Rome/Roman, ix, x, xii, xiii, xiv, 23, 51, 75, 79, 85, 89, 91, 97, 99, 101, 107, 109, 117, 135, 137, 147, 149, 151, 175, 177, 193, 201, 207, 231, 235, 237, 249, 265, 269, 275, 277, 285, 301, 309, 331, 343, 351, 359, 361, 363, 375, 399, 401, 409, 419, 421, 431, 471n1, 486n111, 488n131, 490n143, 494n168, 495n177, 497nn196–97, 500n217, 503n246, 504nn249–50, 507n273, 508n280, 513n307, 517n331, 537n466, 541n481, 543n496, 545n505, 546n512, 553n564, 559n604, 560n608, 573n702, 576n732, 576n738, 582n784, 584n797, 593n854, 595n864, 607n930, 608n936, 611n19, 611n23, 612n28, 612n30, 613n34, 615nn48–49, 618n65; Academy (Pomponio Leto), 85, 95, 101, 151, 275, 285, 486n111, 486n113, 497n197, 508–9nn281–82; Accademia della Virtù, 582n784; ancient, 65, 149, 445, 566n649; Arch of Constantine, 583n785; Argive, 97; Augustinian convent facing Via della Scrofa, 549n531; Aventine Hill, 385; Basilica of San Lorenzo in Lucina, in Rione Colonna, 553n560; Basilica of Santa Maria Maggiore, 79; Campido-

glio, 65; Campo Marzio, 137, 253, 267; Capitoline Hill, 39, 237, 357, 476n18; Castel Sant'Angelo, 486n113, 508n282, 510n292, 549n532, 552n559, 562n619, 594n861; Church of San Crisogono, 345; Church of San Giovanni in Laterano, 63, 567n656; Church of San Lorenzo, 267; Church of Sant'Agata dei Goti, 121; Church of Sant'Agostino, 361; Church of Santa Maria della Pace, 117; Church of Santa Maria sopra Minerva, 99, 492n156; Church of Sant'Eustachio, 359, 489n131; Church of Santi Apostoli, 95, 97; Church of the Virgin Mother of God (Basilica of Santa Maria in Aracoeli), 65, 483n80; Egyptian obelisk called "Macuteo," in Piazza San Macuto, 492n156; Esquiline Hill, 79; Eternal City, 221, 251; Flumentine Gate, 137; Monastery of Santa Balbina, 385; Palace of the Senate, 476n18; Palazzo della Cancelleria, 479n44; Piazza della Rotonda, 492n156; Piazza of San Macuto, 99, 492n156; Pincian Hill, 137; Ponte Rotto, 544n497; Quirinal Hill, 79, 95, 121, 149, 175, 345; Sack of, 101, 265, 291, 391, 393, 401, 523n379, 549n532, 550n546, 552nn558–59, 559n604, 573n706, 594–

95nn861–62; Sant'Eustachio neighborhood, 543n497; Studium Urbis (University of Rome; *La Sapienza*), 115, 391, 488n124, 497n200, 508n280, 524n384, 571n683, 580n772, 592n853, 597n878; Suburra, 121; Temple of Juno Moneta, 483n80; Temple of Thundering Jupiter, 65; Theater of Pompey, 53, 479n44; Trastevere neighborhood, 345, 544n497; Via Lata, 331; via Longarina, 544n497; Vicolo della Campagna, 549n531. *See also* Vatican

Romuald, Saint, 480n51

Romulus and Remus, 65

Rossi, Luigi de', 541n482

Rotterdam, 293, 333

Roverella, Bartolomeo (cardinal of Ravenna), 510n292

Rovigo (place), 590n840

Rucellai, Palla, 125, 501n224

Ruel, Etienne, 572n693, 572n696

Ruel, Jean, 327–29, 397, 572n693, 573n699; *On Agriculture*, 329; *On the Nature of Plants*, 327–29; *On Veterinary Medicine*, 327

Ruiz, Francisco, 553n564

Russia, patriarchate of, 490n146

Rutilio, Bernardino, 337–39, 574n716

Sabellico, Marcantonio Coccio, 175–79, 271, 506n266, 518n344, 520nn360–61, 530n430; *Enneads*, 177

Sabini, Florido, 183
Sacchi, Bartolomeo (Platina). *See* Platina
Sadoleto, Jacopo, xvi n8, 431, 435, 544n500, 611n23
Saint Gall, 427, 480n47
Saint-Germain-des-Prés, 591n845, 619n73
Saint-Pol-de-Léon, bishopric of, 543n495
Salamanca, 619n78
Salento (place), 387, 590n836
Salerno (province), 147, 508n278, 557n591, 571n683, 572n698
Sallust (Gaius Sallustius Crispus), 155, 512n302
Salmon, Jean (Macrin, Maigret, Macrinus), 341, 443, 575n728, 618n70
Salutati, Coluccio, 478n34, 600n898
San Gimignano (place), 151
San Giovanni a Piro (monastery), 493–94n168
San Nazzaro (place), 279
Sannazaro, Jacopo (Actius Syncerus), 133, 167, 197, 215, 259, 279–83, 331, 395, 518n337, 527n408, 535n452, 557n595; *On the Birth of the Virgin*, 281; *Piscatorial Eclogues*, 281
Sannazaro, Nicola (Cola), 557n591
Sanseverino, Giovanni (count of Marsico), 508n279
Sanseverino, Laura, 475n4
Sanseverino, Roberto (prince of Salerno), 508n279

Sanseverino family, 147, 195
Sansovino, Andrea, *Saint Anne with Virgin Mary and Christ Child* (sculpture), 581n780
Saône (river), 293, 355
Sarajevo, 531n436
Sarmatian, 155
Sassoferrato (Sentinum; town), 45, 75, 77
Sassoli, Giulia (of Bergamo), 559n603
Sassone, Adriana (Arianna, Ariadne; wife of Pontano), 173, 519n350
Sauermann, Georg, 401, 597n880, 597nn882–83
Sauli, Cardinal Bendinello, ix, xvi n2, 275, 555n581, 564n637, 599n891
Sauli family, 544n502
Savafids, 565n638
Savonarola, Girolamo, 155–59, 161, 512–13nn306–7, 514nn311–12, 515n317, 564n635; *Triumph of the Cross*, 157
Scala, Alessandra, 109
Scala, Bartolomeo, 109, 495n178
Scaligero, Giulio Cesare, 545n504
Scanderbeg, Giorgio Castriota, 409, 603n909
Scandiano (place), 199
Scannabecchi, Bernardo Canaccio, 476n14
Scannapeco, Girolamo, 560n607
Schepper, Cornelis de, 441, 617n60

Schinner, Matthaeus (bishop of Sion), 567n658

Scipios, the (Africanus and Aemilianus), 269, 554n567

Scotland/Scots, 407, 602n901

Scutari (place), 409, 603n907

Scythia/Scythian, 367, 437

Sebastiani, Antonio (Minturno), 551n551

Selim I (the Grim), 253, 301, 548n530, 565n638

Selward (Siloë), Benedictine convent of, 499n215

Senecas, the, 223

Senigallia (Sinigaglia; place), 359, 581n776

Sepúlveda, Juan Ginés de, 393, 445, 594n859

Serone, Giovanni Antonio, 373, 584n796

Sessa Aurunca (place), 323, 325, 571n682, 571n686, 572n689

Sforza, Camilla, 518n345

Sforza, Cardinal Ascanio, 207, 530n432

Sforza, Costanzo, 518n345

Sforza, Francesco (duke of Milan), 67, 73, 383, 577n742, 588n824, 588n827

Sforza, Francesco II (duke of Milan), 415, 606n925

Sforza, Galeazzo Maria (duke of Milan), 383, 525n389, 588nn824–26

Sforza, Giangaleazzo Maria (duke of Milan), 383, 588n826, 595n868

Sforza, Giovanni (tyrant of Pesaro), 171, 519n345

Sforza, Ludovico "il Moro" (duke of Milan), 111, 113, 133, 139, 207, 233, 383, 495n182, 505n254, 530n432, 533n449, 543n491, 552n555, 587n819, 588n826, 605n922

Sforza family, 485n94, 605n922

Sforza Castle, 485n94

Shakespeare, William, Love's Labor's Lost IV.ii, 534n450

Sibyls, 253

Sicily/Sicilian, 57, 63, 257, 415, 606n925

Sidonius Apollinaris, 355, 580n768

Siena/Sienese, 83, 89, 313, 568n659

Sigismund I the Old (king of Poland), 510n294

Silaro (river), 508n278

Silesia/Silesian, 429, 597n880, 615n48

Silius Italicus, 223

Simonetta, Francesco (Cicco), 383, 588n824

Simonetta, Giovanni, 383

Sirens, 21

Sirius (star), 19

Sisyphus, fountain of (Libethron), 87, 488n128

Sixtus IV (pope), 69, 79, 83, 89, 97, 103, 149, 165, 419, 486n106, 489n132, 492n157, 493n165, 494n169, 517n329, 608n936

Skander Bey (Iskender Pasha, Sanjakbey of Bosnia), 209, 531nn436–37

Slovenia, 586n814
Soca (river), 177
Socrates/Socratic, 97, 199
Soderini, Cardinal Francesco, 564n637
Soderini, Piero, 179, 309, 521n367
Soissons, 327
Sophoclean tragedy, 349
Sorrento, 257, 259, 263, 508n278; Temple of Argive Juno, 508n278
Soter, Johann (printer), 579n762
Sotion of Alexandria, 485n105
South wind, 261
Sozomeno da Pistoia, 599n895
Spagnolo, Baptista (Mantuan, Mantuanus), 215–17
Spagnolo, Pietro, 534n450
Spagnolo, Tolomeo, 534n450
Spain/Spanish, xii, xiv, 63, 215, 223, 225, 255, 259, 269, 301, 315, 341, 393, 401, 421, 445, 532n442, 550n542, 550n546, 551n551, 552n558, 554n567, 561n614, 565n641, 574n706, 594n859, 595n864, 597n883
Spanish language, 518n344
Sparta/Spartan, 109, 411
Sperulo, Francesco, 556n576
Spinelli (unknown individual), 57
Spinola, Gian Giacomo, 585n807
Spiriteo, Prospero, 81, 487n114
spirituali, 471n1
Spoleto, 131; Church of San Niccolò, 502n236
Stabiae, 263

Statilius, John (bishop of Alba Iulia), 439, 616n54
Statius, Caecilius, 474n19, 488n124, 495n184
Stella, Mount, 91
Stephen III (the Great, of Moldavia), 511n297
Stesichorus, 345, 576n737
Steuco, Agostina, 483n75
Stimmer, Tobias, xviii n12
Stockholm Bloodbath, the, 604n911
Stoic, 245
Strabo, 379, 385, 586n813, 589n833
Strasbourg, 592n849
Strébée (d'Estrebay), Jacques Louis (Jacobus Ludovicus Strebaeus), 443, 617n63
Strozzi, Ercole, 187–89, 507n276, 525n389
Strozzi, Tito Vespasiano, 187, 524n386
Styx/Stygian, 289, 337, 355, 363
Suetonius (Gaius Suetonius Tranquillus), 67
Suleiman I (sultan), 291, 615n49
Superchi, Gianfrancesco. See Philomusus, Johannes Franciscus
Sutri (place), 243, 546n514
Swabia/Swabian, 29
Sweden/Swedish, 429, 603n911
Switzerland/Swiss, 111, 335, 371, 425, 427, 567–68n658
Synesius, 159
syphilis. See French pox

Syrmia (Szerém), bishopric of, 616n52

Szatmáry, George, 616n51

Tacitus (Publius Cornelius Tacitus), 65, 155, 524n387; *Annals*, 471n2, 474n19, 475n6, 567n649

Tagliamenta (river), 531n436

Tagus (river), 147

Tamerlane, 91, 490n140

Tarquinius Superbus, 575n717

Tartagna, Alessandro, 543n489

Tartarus, 355

Teano (place), 261

Tebaldeo, Antonio, 329–33, 552n555, 573n702

Tebaldi, Ippolita di Sebastiano, 523n379

Tebaldi, Lazzaro (Tebaldeo), 111, 121, 147, 189, 243, 502n234

Tebaldi family, 510n293

Tegrimi, Niccolò, 413; *Life of Castruccio Castracane*, 413

Telesio, Antonio, 391, 592n851, 593n854; *On Crowns*, 391; *On Grammatical Shadings*, 391; *Shower of Gold*, 391

Temple of Virtue, 11, 472n1

Teramo (place), 253–55; bishopric of, 87, 489n131

Terence (Publius Terentius Afer), 229; *Phormio*, 474n12

Terranova (place), 51

Teutonic, 335. *See also* Germany/German

Thales of Miletus, 419, 607n934

Thebes, 495n185

Themistius, 135, 503n243

Theodore of Gaza, 95, 99–105, 107, 109, 113, 159, 179, 492n158, 493nn164–65

Theodore I of Mistra, 489n138

Theomnestus, 572n695

Theophrastus, 327; *On Plants*, 103

Theophylact of Ohrid, 425

Thespian caves, 151

Thessalonica, 101, 493n164

Thessaly, 495n185

Thrasyllus, 515n314

Thucydides, 61, 77, 482n72

Tiber (river), 97, 293, 333, 494n169

Tiber Island, 285, 560n608

Tiberius (Roman emperor), 515n314

Tiberti, Antioco, 181–83, 191, 522n376, 523n378, 525n395; *On Palmistry*, 181; *On Physiognomy and Pyromancy*, 181

Tiberti family, 521n369

Tibullus (Albius Tibullus), 367

Ticino (river), 279, 557n592

Tifernate, Gregorio (Gregorio da Città di Castello), 141, 385, 533n450, 586n813, 589n833

Timavo (river), 133, 503n239

Timothy (a Greek), 73, 75

Tintoretto, Jacopo, 473n5

Tivoli (place), 175, 253

Todeschini-Piccolomini, Cardinal Francesco, 489n131

Todi (place), 489n132

Toledo, 540n477, 554n565; bishopric of, 619n78
Tolentines, 71
Tolomei, Claudio, 582n784
Tomarozzi, Flaminio, 237, 543n497
Tomarozzi, Giulio, 543n497
Tomarozzi palazzo, 543n497
Tordesillas, 540n477
Torelli, Barbara, 189, 525n389
Torelli, Marsilio (count of Montechiarugolo), 525n389
Torelli family, 189
Tornabuoni, Lorenzo, 512n306
Tornabuoni, Simone, 513n309
Tortelli, Giovanni, 375–77, 585nn801–2, 585n805; *On the Power of Letters*, 377
Toussain, Jacques, 443, 618n69, 618n71
Transylvania, 439
Trapani (place), 606n925
Traversari, Ambrogio (The Monk), 55–57, 480n50
Trebizond (place), 490n145
Trebizond, Andreas (son of George of Trebizond), 99, 492nn157–58, 493n160
Trebizond, Faustina (daughter of Andreas, granddaughter of George of Trebizond), 101, 493n160
Trent, Council of, 569n669, 612n30, 615n47, 617n57, 618n64
Treviso/Trevisan, 195, 241; cathedral, 545n509
Triballi (people), 531n436

Tribonian, 575n717
Trier, 361, 606n930
Trieste (province), 503n239
Trieste, Gulf of, 586n814
Trinitarian Order, 603n905
Trissino, Gian Giorgio, 435, 612n28
Trivulzio, Gian Giacomo "The Great," 399, 587n819, 597n876
Trogir (place), 616n56
Tropea (place), 323
Truchsess von Waldburg, Otto, 437, 615nn46–47
Tumanbey (sultan of Egypt), 253, 548n530
Tunis, 415, 606n925
Turks/Turkish, 73, 95, 105, 253, 439, 490n140, 495n177, 498nn204–6, 511n298, 520n359, 531n436, 603n907, 617n56
Tuscan language/literature, xiii, 37, 39, 53, 133, 171, 251, 267, 269, 273, 281, 295, 309, 311, 329, 331, 363, 387, 405, 413, 423, 506n266, 535n453, 542n485, 582n784
Tuscan river, 111
Tuscan Sea (Mare Inferum), 549n539
Tuscany/Tuscan, 11, 37, 43, 51, 107, 127, 151, 155, 197, 307, 325, 423, 480n51, 519n348
Tyrrhenian Sea, 263, 449

Ubaldi, Baldo degli. *See* Baldus
Ubaldi family, 47
Ubertino da Carrara, 587n815

Udine (place), 177, 613n32
Új-Sziget, 615n49
Ulm, 579n762
Umbria/Umbrian, 45, 75, 77, 131,
    171, 301, 564n637
Urbino, xi, 407, 602n902
Ursinus Velius, Caspar, 429,
    611n19
Utrecht, 540n477

Vác, bishopric of, 616n52
Vacca, Antonio, 311, 359
Vadian ( Joachim Vadianus), 427,
    609–10nn6–7
Valdaura, Bernardo, 608n939
Valdaura, Margarita, 608n939
Valencia, 421
Valentini, Giovanni Battista (Can-
    talicio). See Cantalicio
Valeriano, Pierio (Giovanni Pie-
    rio), 435, 494n169, 495nn180–
    81, 497n199, 502n236, 559n604,
    612–13n31; On the Ill Fortune of
    Learned Men, x
Valerius Flaccus (Gaius Valerius
    Flaccus), 355
Valerius Maximus, 415
Valla, Catarina, 63
Valla, Giorgio, 381, 520n360,
    587n819
Valla, Lorenzo, xiii, 53, 55, 59, 61–
    63, 67, 95, 147, 377–79, 479n42,
    482n64, 508n280, 533n450,
    585n805, 586n809; Concerning
    the False Donation of Constantine,
    63; Elegances, 61, 482n71
Valladolid, 540n477

Valori, Francesco, 157, 513n309
Valturio, Roberto, 403–5, 599n893
Vandals, 51, 223
Vangadizza (place), 526n401
Vardar (river), 495n185
Varius Rufus, Lucius, 349,
    577n748
Varro (Marcus Terentius Varro),
    335
Vasari, Giorgio, 501n224; Lives of
    the Artists, ix
Vatable, François, 443, 619n73
Vatican, 95, 219, 229, 361; College
    of Abbreviators, 486nn112–13;
    College of Cardinals, xvi n2,
    157, 229, 319, 343, 349, 437,
    480n53, 515n317, 565n637; Cu-
    ria, 53, 492n157, 581n779,
    584n798, 607n931; Exsurge Do-
    mine (papal bull), 576n732;
    Gardens of the Belvedere,
    536n458; Greek College,
    576n738; Holy See, 568n658;
    Library, 79, 185, 221, 483n75,
    524n384, 576n729, 585n802;
    Passetto di Borgo, 552n559; St.
    Peter's Basilica, 375, 567n656
Vegio, Maffeo, 51, 375, 584n797
Veneto, the, 247, 613n34
Venice/Venetian, xii, 7, 91, 115, 117,
    119, 131, 137, 149, 165, 195, 201,
    239, 271, 321, 349, 377, 383,
    476n17, 481n62, 493n167, 494–
    95n177, 496–97nn195–96,
    498n206, 503nn246–47,
    506n266, 508n282, 517n331,
    518n344, 520n360, 522n373,

Venice/Venetian (*continued*)
526–27nn403–6, 528n416,
529n421, 529n426, 530n430,
531nn436–37, 541n481, 554n573,
556n583, 561n614, 570n679,
574n716, 585n807, 586nn813–14,
587n819, 603n907, 612n26,
612n28; Basilica of San Marco,
588n830; Church of the Madonna dell'Orto, 578n757;
Council of Ten, 588n830; Great
Council, 588n828; Piazza (Piazzetta) San Marco, 165,
517n330, 520n359; Scuola di
San Marco, 520n360, 587n819;
Senate, 135, 177, 273, 510n297,
520n360, 527n406, 543n490
Venus (deity), 43, 89, 189, 263,
285, 365
Vergerio, Pier Paolo (elder), 379–
81, 490n141, 587n815
Vergil (Publius Vergilius Maro),
217, 267, 283, 287, 375, 534n450,
535n453, 535n455, 554n574; *Aeneid*, 375, 472nn2–3, 502n232,
554n571, 561n613, 604n915; "another," 500n217; "Christian,"
612n30; *Eclogues*, 488n128,
554n571, 577n745; *Georgics*,
529n428, 561n613, 561n617;
Maro, 217, 271, 347; "new
Maro," 251; "second Maro," 253
vernacular (*volgare*), Giovio's views
on, xiii, 37, 39, 41, 169–71, 205,
229, 245, 267, 295, 307–9, 329–
31, 383, 423, 530n430, 542n485
Verona/Veronese, 85, 197, 207, 211,

411, 516n324, 526n401, 604n914,
612n29, 613n34; bishopric of,
241, 545n508; College of Physi-
cians, 612n29
Vértesy, Janos, 616n50
Vesuvius, wines of, 257
Vetulonia, hot springs at, 277
Vicenza/Vicenzan, 177, 243, 337,
574n716, 591n840, 612n28
Vicovaro (place), 175
Vida, Marco Girolamo (bishop of
Alba), 435, 612n30; as "Chris-
tian Vergil," 612n30
Vienna, 291, 427, 510n297; Univer-
sity, 607n933
Vigevano (town), 67
Villa Fugicura (Niccolò Perotti),
77
Virgilio, Polidoro. *See* Polydore
Vergil
Visconti, Azzone, 504n251
Visconti, Filippo Maria (duke of
Milan), 57–59, 481n61, 485n99
Visconti, Giangaleazzo (duke of
Milan), 49, 91, 490n141
Visconti, Ottone, 531n439
Visconti family, 139
Vitale, Giano, 31, 35, 61, 65, 97,
127, 129, 133, 155, 165, 205, 219,
223, 243, 249, 261, 269, 289,
303, 313, 315, 335, 337–39, 341,
345, 351, 361, 435, 475n3,
503n240
Vitelli, Nicolò, 489n132
Vitelli, Paolo, 161, 516n318
Viterbo, 197, 299, 556n589
Vitéz, János, 516n324

Vitruvius, 125, 614n40
Vittorino da Feltre, 101, 491n154, 585n801
Vives, Juan Luis, 421, 608n938
Volterra (place), 111, 375, 385, 584n800
Vries, Hendrik, 499n215
Vulcan (deity), 189, 273

Warmia, bishopric of, 437, 614n43, 615n45
wars: of the Barons (first), 520n352; of Granada, 225, 540n476; of the League of Cambrai, 529n426, 561n614; Persian, 387; of Urbino, 564n637; Vandal, 387
Wells, archdiaconate of, 602n903
Westphalia, 610n11
Wied, Archbishop Hermann von, 579n762
Wier, Johannes, 580n765
Wimpfeling, Jakob, 533–34n450

wine. *See* Caecuban; Falernian; wines of Vesuvius
Wittenberg, University of, 597n880
Worms: Diet of, 437, 615n47; Edict of, 576n732

Xenophon, 613n32, 619n72; *Cyropaedia*, 73

Zanchi, Basilio, 435, 614n42
Zápolya, John, 615n49
Zaragoza, 569n664
Zasius, Ulrich, 427
Zavarizzi, Daniele, 604n914
Zerbi, Gabriele, 209, 531nn436–38
Ziegler, Jakob, 409–11, 603n910
Zimmermann, Price, xi
Zoanno Batista da Monte Colombo, 522n376
Zwingli, Ulrich, 425–27, 609nn2–3

Publication of this volume has been made possible by

The Myron and Sheila Gilmore Publication Fund at I Tatti
The Robert Lehman Endowment Fund
The Jean-François Malle Scholarly Programs and Publications Fund
The Andrew W. Mellon Scholarly Publications Fund
The Craig and Barbara Smyth Fund
for Scholarly Programs and Publications
The Lila Wallace–Reader's Digest Endowment Fund
The Malcolm Wiener Fund for Scholarly Programs and Publications